THE COMPLETE
HARROWSMITH
COOKBOOK

CLASSIC AND CREATIVE CUISINE

THE COMPLETE
HARROWSMITH
COOKBOOK

All Three Harrowsmith Cookbooks
in One Volume

CLASSIC AND CREATIVE CUISINE

By the Editors and Readers of Harrowsmith Magazine

Compiled from the private recipe collections of the Editors,
Readers, Contributors and Staff of *Harrowsmith* magazine.

FIREFLY BOOKS

A FIREFLY BOOK

First published in three volumes as *The Harrowsmith Cookbook Volume Number One*, *The Harrowsmith Cookbook Volume Two* and *The Harrowsmith Cookbook Volume Three* in 1981, 1984, and 1987 respectively by Camden House Publishing (a division of Telemedia Communications Inc.)

Second Printing, 2009.

Cataloguing in Publication Data

Main entry under title:
    The complete Harrowsmith cookbook
Includes index.
ISBN-13: 978-1-55209-072-5
ISBN-10: 1-55209-072-8
1. Cookery.
TX714.C65 1996   641.5   C96-930938-4

Published in the United States by
Firefly Books (U.S.) Inc.
P.O. Box 1338, Ellicott Station
Buffalo, New York 14205

Published in Canada by
Firefly Books Ltd.
66 Leek Crescent
Richmond Hill, Ontario L4B 1H1

Editor: Pamela Cross
Illustrations: Marta Scythes, page 1, 22, 60, 110, 193, 228, 265, 340, 413, 437, 521, 574; Joanne T. L. Fitzgerald, page 564
Cover Illustration: Roger Hill
Photography: Ernie Sparks
Food Design: Mariella Morrin

Book Design: Fortunato Aglialoro,Falcom Design & Communications Inc

Printed in Canada

The publisher gratefully acknowledges the financial support for our publishing program by the Government of Canada through the Book Publishing Industry Development Program.

Contents

Breakfast & Snacks

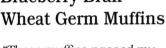

Virginia Corn Muffins

"My grandmother from Tennessee taught me this recipe — why she called it 'Virginia' Corn Muffins, I don't know."

1 cup white cornmeal
½ cup flour
¼ cup sugar
5 tsp. baking powder
¾ tsp. salt
1 egg
½ cup milk
2 tsp. oil

Mix together cornmeal, flour, sugar, baking powder and salt. Beat together egg, milk and oil. Quickly stir liquid into dry ingredients. Place in 12 greased muffin cups and bake at 375° F for 25 minutes.

Makes 12 muffins.

—Ruth Ellis Haworth

Blueberry-Bran-Wheat Germ Muffins

"These muffins passed my daughter's test — and she does not care for bran or wheat germ." We thought they were great — really moist and flavourful.

3 eggs
1 cup brown sugar
½ cup oil
2 cups buttermilk
1 tsp. vanilla
1 cup wheat germ
1 cup bran
2 cups flour
2 tsp. baking powder
2 tsp. baking soda
½ tsp. salt
1½ cups blueberries

Beat eggs well, add sugar and beat, then add oil, buttermilk and vanilla and mix well. Stir in wheat germ and bran.

In smaller bowl, combine flour, baking powder, baking soda and salt, then stir in blueberries. Pour into liquid ingredients and stir until just mixed. Spoon into greased muffin cups and bake at 400° F for 20 to 25 minutes.

Makes 24 muffins.

—Sandy MacLennan

Banana Muffins

1 cup white sugar
½ cup butter
1 egg, beaten
1 cup mashed bananas
1½ cups flour
1 tsp. baking soda
½ tsp. nutmeg
½ tsp. vanilla
salt

Cream sugar and butter, then add egg and mix well. Add bananas and flour. Dissolve baking soda in 1 Tbsp. hot water, then add to creamed mixture along with nutmeg, vanilla and salt. Spoon into greased muffin cups and bake at 350° F for 20 minutes.

Makes 12 muffins.

—Ann Coyle

Oat Muffins

"I first made these when I was 10, and I make and enjoy them to this day." They are light muffins with an even, spongy texture.

1 cup rolled oats
1 cup buttermilk
1 cup flour
1 tsp. baking powder
½ tsp. baking soda
1½ tsp. salt
½ cup brown sugar
1 egg, beaten
¼ cup oil or melted butter

Soak oats in buttermilk for 1 hour. Combine flour, baking powder, baking soda, salt and sugar and mix well. Stir egg and oil into oat mixture. Make a well in dry ingredients, pour in liquid and stir quickly until just mixed. Pour into greased muffin cups and bake at 400° F for 20 minutes.

Makes 12 muffins.

—Faye Cassia

Aunt Nell's Hush Puppies

Light and flavourful, crispy outside and moist inside, these hush puppies are quick and easy to make.

1 cup cornmeal
1 tsp. baking soda
1 cup flour
2 Tbsp. sugar
1 clove garlic, crushed
1 egg
1 large onion, chopped
1 cup buttermilk
fat for frying

Combine all ingredients. Let rise for 30 minutes. Drop by tablespoonful into deep hot fat and fry until golden brown.

Makes approximately 18 hush puppies.

—Carolee Gosda

Grandma's Scottish Potato Scones

"On all of her visits, Grandma would take leftover potatoes from the day before and make us potato scones to have hot, slathered with butter, as a bedtime snack." Our tasters thought these scones good enough to warrant purposely cooking extra potatoes.

Mash cold potatoes well on well-floured surface. Knead in as much flour as potatoes will absorb. Add salt to taste. Roll out to ¼-inch thickness and cut into large circles. Quarter circles and cook on slow griddle, turning when lightly flecked with brown.

Eat hot with butter or honey.

—Lesley-Anne Paveling

Upside-Down Rhubarb Muffins

Our Vermont tester says, "These muffins are terrific — not too sweet, with a good combination of tastes and textures."

1 cup finely chopped
    rhubarb
¼ cup melted butter
½ cup packed brown sugar
⅓ cup soft butter
⅓ cup sugar
1 egg
1½ cups flour
2 tsp. baking powder
½ tsp. salt
½ tsp. nutmeg
½ cup milk

Combine rhubarb, melted butter and brown sugar in small bowl and mix well. Place in 12 greased muffin cups.

Beat together butter, sugar and egg until fluffy. Combine flour, baking powder, salt and nutmeg and add to creamed mixture alternately with milk. Stir just to moisten, then spoon on top of rhubarb mixture.

Bake at 350° F for 20 to 25 minutes. Invert on cooling rack and leave pan over muffins for a few minutes so all rhubarb moisture runs out. Serve warm.

Makes 12 muffins.

—Joan Airey

Orange Pecan Muffins

1 cup buttermilk
¼ cup melted butter
1 egg
½ tsp. vanilla
juice & grated rind
    of 1 orange
1 cup rolled oats
1⅓ cups flour
⅓ cup demerara sugar
1½ tsp. baking powder
½ tsp. baking soda
½ tsp. salt
⅔ cup coarsely chopped
    pecans

Combine buttermilk, butter, egg, vanilla, orange juice, orange rind and rolled oats and let stand for 15 minutes. Combine remaining ingredients and add to liquid mixture. Mix lightly. Fill greased muffin cups ⅔ full. Bake at 375° F for 15 to 20 minutes.

Makes 12 muffins.

—Beth Caldwell

German Bread Griddle Cakes

Our Camden East tester declared these to be "Delicious! Especially light. Just excellent." We agreed and thought they made a tasty, light alternative to pancakes.

1½ cups milk
2 Tbsp. butter
1½ cups stale bread crumbs
2 eggs, well beaten
½ cup flour
4 tsp. baking powder
½ tsp. salt
oil for cooking

Scald milk, then add butter and stir until butter has melted. Pour over bread crumbs and let soak for 30 minutes. Beat in remaining ingredients. Cook in hot oil over medium heat until golden brown.

Serves 2 to 3.

—Jean Perkins

Puff Ball Doughnuts

Also known as Beaver Tails and Elephant Ears in other parts of Canada, these are a real treat. Roll in sugar, roll up with grated cheese as a filling, or brush with garlic butter.

3 eggs
1 cup sugar
2 cups milk
lemon extract
3 cups flour
3 tsp. baking powder
½ tsp. salt
oil for deep-frying

Beat eggs, add sugar and beat well. Add milk and lemon extract. Sift together flour, baking powder and salt and fold into egg mixture. Using two spoons, drop into oil heated to 375 degrees F. Fry until golden brown. Dough should turn by itself. If not, turn with a fork making certain not to pierce dough.

Serves 4 to 6.

—Myrna Smith

Thistle-Down Place Scones

½ cup raisins
2 cups flour
3 Tbsp. sugar
2 tsp. baking powder
½ tsp. salt
½ tsp. baking soda
5 Tbsp. butter
1 cup sour cream
1 egg, separated
1 tsp. sugar
½ tsp. cinnamon

Cover raisins with warm water and let stand for 5 minutes. Drain well and set aside.

Combine flour, sugar, baking powder, salt and baking soda. Cut in butter to make a coarse crumb texture. Stir in raisins.

In another bowl, combine sour cream and egg yolk. Make well in centre of dry ingredients and pour in egg-cream mixture. Stir just until dough clings together.

Turn out onto floured surface and knead gently 10 or 12 times. Pat into ½-inch-thick circle and cut into 4-inch rounds. Place on ungreased baking sheet, brush with egg white and sprinkle with sugar and cinnamon. Cut each round into quarters but do not separate. Bake at 425° F for 15 minutes, or until golden.

Makes 16 scones.

—Irene Louden

Finnish Oven Pancake

"This pancake puffs up, then collapses. It is good hot or cold. I serve it with syrup and sliced fresh fruit."

3 eggs
1 cup milk
½ cup flour
2 Tbsp. sugar
¼ tsp. salt
1 tsp. vanilla (optional)
¼ cup butter

Beat eggs until fluffy. Add remaining ingredients, except for butter, beating continuously. Melt butter in ovenproof skillet, then pour in batter. Bake at 400° F for 20 to 25 minutes, or until knife inserted in middle comes out clean.

Serves 2.

—*Jeanne Reitz*

Buckwheat Pancakes

One cup of blueberries can be added to this recipe. The pancakes are tender, moist and delicate.

½ cup buckwheat flour
½ cup flour
2 tsp. baking powder
1 Tbsp. sugar
3 eggs
2 Tbsp. oil
1 cup milk
oil for cooking

Combine flours, baking powder and sugar. Beat together eggs, oil and milk, then beat into dry ingredients. Heat oil in skillet, and cook pancakes over medium heat, turning when bubbles form on uncooked side.

Serves 2 to 3.

—*Lorna Palmer*

Gingerbread Waffles

A flavourful winter breakfast, these waffles are also cakey enough to be served (perhaps dusted with confectioners' sugar) as part of an afternoon tea.

2 cups flour
½ tsp. salt
1 tsp. baking powder
2 tsp. ginger
1 tsp. cinnamon
¼ tsp. cloves
1 cup molasses
¾ cup milk (approximately)
1 egg, beaten
½ cup oil

Combine flour, salt, baking powder, ginger, cinnamon and cloves. Mix together molasses, milk, egg and oil and stir into dry ingredients, adding additional milk if necessary. Bake in hot waffle iron until golden brown. Serve with sweetened whipped cream.

Serves 4.

—*Sybil D. Hendricks*

Orange Waffles

Use unpeeled oranges for this recipe — but wash them well and remove seeds first. If your oranges are not very juicy, you may need to add a bit more liquid.

1½ cups flour
½ tsp. salt
1½ tsp. baking powder
2 eggs, separated
1 cup milk
¼ cup oil
2 oranges, quartered

Sift dry ingredients together. Blend egg yolks, milk and oil well in blender or food processor. Add orange quarters one at a time and blend well. Beat egg whites until stiff. Add orange mixture to dry ingredients and stir well. Gently fold in egg whites. Bake in waffle iron until golden brown.

Serves 4.

—*George Driscoll*

Apple Pancakes

"These pancakes freeze well. The recipe is of Polish origin and has been handed down through my family for three generations."

2 Tbsp. yeast
2 cups warm water
½ cup honey
2 cups milk
¼ cup butter
4 eggs, beaten
6 cups flour
½ tsp. salt
6 apples, peeled & thinly
   sliced
oil for cooking

Proof yeast in water and honey for 10 minutes. Add remaining ingredients and mix well. Knead briefly, then let rise for at least 1 hour. Fry in hot oil over medium heat until golden brown.

Makes 2 dozen large pancakes.

—*Karen Havelock*

Banana Bran Bread

Vary this recipe by substituting dark rum for the orange juice or walnuts for the raisins. This is a delicious bread with a wonderful texture.

¾ cup butter
1½ cups brown sugar
3 eggs
2 cups bran
3 cups mashed banana
¼ cup orange juice
3 cups flour
4 tsp. baking powder
1 tsp. salt
1 tsp. baking soda
1½ cups raisins

Cream butter and sugar, then add eggs and beat until light. Stir in bran. Mix bananas with orange juice. Sift together dry ingredients. Add dry ingredients alternately with bananas to creamed mixture, beating after each addition. Fold in raisins. Pour into greased and floured loaf pans and bake at 350° F for 1 hour.

Makes 2 loaves.

—*Donna Jubb*

Fruit Pancake

"This is our favourite leisurely morning breakfast. I use apples, plums or peaches — fresh or frozen." Add a brandy sauce, and this pancake becomes a tasty dessert.

¼ cup butter
¼ cup brown sugar
1 tsp. cinnamon
4 apples, plums **or** peaches
4 eggs, separated
⅓ cup sugar
⅓ cup flour
½ tsp. baking powder
⅓ cup milk

Heat oven to 400° F and melt butter in 10"-round baking dish. Remove from oven and sprinkle with brown sugar and cinnamon. Slice fruit and arrange in dish, then return to oven for 8 to 10 minutes.

Meanwhile, beat egg whites until foamy and gradually beat in sugar until stiff. In another bowl, combine flour and baking powder, beat in milk and yolks, then fold in egg white mixture. Spread evenly over fruit.

Bake for 20 minutes. Loosen edges and invert onto serving plate.

Serves 2 to 3.

—*Adele Dueck*

Ten-Year Granola

"The title refers to the 10 years during which this recipe evolved, each batch being appraised and modified by my husband."

6 cups oatmeal
1 cup wheat flakes
1 cup rye flakes
1 cup almonds **or** cashews
1 cup sunflower seeds
½ cup sesame seeds
¼-½ cup whole wheat flour
1 cup brown sugar
salt
½ cup oil
½ cup honey
3 tsp. vanilla

Combine dry and wet ingredients separately and then mix together, stirring well to moisten. Lightly grease large roasting pan, then scoop in granola. Bake at 300° F for 40 minutes, stirring frequently.

Makes approximately 10 cups.

—Susanna Barnett

John's Bread

Our Vermont tester says, "I'll definitely make this again. It's a hearty, chewy brown bread. Just great!" Serve warm with cream cheese.

5¼ cups graham flour
3 cups flour
¾ cup sugar
1½ tsp. salt
1 Tbsp. baking soda
1 Tbsp. baking powder
1 cup molasses
3 cups sour milk

Combine all ingredients and mix thoroughly. Place in 2 greased loaf pans and bake at 350° F for 1 hour.

Makes 2 loaves.

—Susan Holec

Lemon Bread

This is a sweet cakelike bread, rich with lemon flavour.

1 cup butter
2 cups sugar
4 eggs
½ tsp. salt
½ tsp. baking soda
3 cups flour
1 cup buttermilk
grated rind of 1 lemon
1 cup chopped pecans
GLAZE:
1 cup sugar
juice of 3 lemons

Cream butter and sugar, then add eggs one at a time and mix well. Sift together salt, baking soda and flour and add to creamed mixture alternately with buttermilk. Add lemon rind and nuts and pour into 2 large greased and floured loaf pans. Bake at 350° F for 1 hour.

Meanwhile, prepare glaze. Heat sugar and lemon juice slowly to dissolve sugar. Pour over loaves while cooling in pans.

Makes 2 loaves.

—Susan Robinson

French Honey Bread

1 cup honey
1 cup milk
½ cup sugar
2 egg yolks, beaten
2½ cups flour
1 tsp. baking soda
½ tsp. salt
¾ cup currants **or** chopped nuts

Combine honey, milk and sugar in heavy pot and heat slowly until well blended. Cool slightly, then add egg yolks. Combine flour, baking soda and salt, then stir slowly into honey mixture. Stir in currants or nuts. Pour into greased loaf pan and bake at 325° F for 1 to 1½ hours.

Makes 1 loaf.

—Giedre Abromaitis

Banana-Oatmeal Coffeecake

¾ cup flour
¾ cup whole wheat flour
¾ cup oats
1 tsp. baking powder
¾ tsp. baking soda
½ tsp. salt
½ cup butter, softened
½ cup brown sugar
½ cup white sugar
2 eggs
1 tsp. vanilla
2 ripe bananas, mashed
⅓ cup sour milk
TOPPING:
⅓ cup brown sugar
¼ cup chopped pecans
3 Tbsp. flour
2 Tbsp. butter

Combine flours, oats, baking powder, baking soda and salt and mix well. Cream together butter and sugars, then add eggs and vanilla. Beat in bananas, then milk. Fold wet ingredients into dry.

Make topping by combining ingredients and mixing until crumbly. Pour batter into greased and floured 9" x 13" pan, sprinkle with topping and bake at 375° F for 20 to 25 minutes.

—Ann Lutz

Honey Sour Cream Coffeecake

"I found this coffeecake and the recipe for it on my doorstep shortly after my daughter's birth. What a treat!" The recipe is very versatile — add fruit or cocoa for a different taste.

¼ cup butter
½ cup honey
2 eggs, lightly beaten
1 tsp. baking soda
1 cup sour cream or yogurt
1½ cups flour
1½ tsp. baking powder
1 Tbsp. vanilla
TOPPING:
¼ cup chopped nuts
½ tsp. cinnamon
2 Tbsp. butter
1 Tbsp. honey

Cream together butter, honey and eggs. Stir baking soda into sour cream, then add to butter mixture. Combine flour and baking powder, then stir into liquid ingredients. Add vanilla. Pour into greased and floured tube pan.

Combine topping ingredients and sprinkle over cake. Bake at 350° F for 45 minutes, open oven door and let cool in oven.

—Leslie Pierpont

Cheddar Dill Loaf

"We serve this loaf, a family favourite, very thinly sliced and lightly buttered with smoked turkey and ham as a pre-dinner snack."

2 cups flour
2 Tbsp. sugar
3 tsp. baking powder
1½ Tbsp. dill seed
2 Tbsp. minced onion
1 cup grated sharp Cheddar cheese
1 cup milk
1 egg
3 Tbsp. melted butter

Combine flour, sugar, baking powder and dill in large bowl. Add onion and cheese and mix well.

Combine milk, egg and butter in small bowl. Add all at once to dry ingredients and stir to moisten. Bake in greased loaf pan at 350° F for 50 to 55 minutes.

Makes 1 loaf.

—Jim & Penny Wright

Christine's Cornbread

¾ cup sugar
½ cup butter
2 eggs, beaten
½ tsp. salt
2 tsp. baking powder
1½ cups flour
1 cup cornmeal
1½ cups milk

Cream together sugar, butter and eggs. Sift together salt, baking powder, flour and cornmeal, then add to creamed mixture alternately with milk. Bake in greased 9" x 13" pan at 375° F for 25 to 30 minutes.

—Laine Roddick

German Fruit Crumb Coffeecake

"I grew up with this recipe. Whenever we would go to visit my grandmother, she had one of these coffeecakes in her pantry waiting to be sliced and enjoyed by her children and grandchildren. More recently, I have made this for our local natural-food market, where it was extremely popular." Use plain water if you do not have just-boiled potatoes.

CAKE:
2 cups hot potato water
¼ cup honey
1 tsp. salt
2 pkgs yeast
1 egg, beaten
½ cup melted unsalted
   butter
7 cups flour
TOPPING:
4 cups flour
2 cups sugar
¼ tsp. salt
1 tsp. cinnamon
1 cup melted unsalted butter
milk
6-8 cups sliced fruit

For cake: Combine water, honey and salt and stir until honey is dissolved. When lukewarm, add yeast and let dissolve. Stir in egg, then add butter and 3½ cups flour. Beat well, then gradually add remaining flour.

Turn out on lightly floured surface and let rest for 10 minutes. Knead until smooth and elastic. Place in greased bowl, turning once to grease all sides of dough. Let rise until doubled in size — about 1 hour.

While dough is rising, make topping. Combine flour, sugar, salt and cinnamon, then stir in butter until mixture forms crumbs.

Punch down dough. (It can be covered with a damp cloth and kept refrigerated for up to 5 days, if desired, at this point.) Divide in half and pat each half out onto a greased cookie sheet. Prick with fork and brush with milk. Spread fruit out evenly over dough, then cover with crumb mixture. Let rise for 30 minutes more, then bake at 350° F until lightly brown — 30 to 45 minutes.

Makes 2 cakes.

—Nancy Wellborn

Cranberry Coffeecake

"My husband and I run a small seasonal marina and waterfront café. This coffeecake is a favourite among our clientele."

8 oz. cream cheese, softened
1 cup butter
1½ cups sugar
1½ tsp. vanilla
4 eggs
2¼ cups flour
1½ tsp. baking powder
2 cups fresh cranberries
½ cup chopped nuts
confectioners' sugar

Thoroughly cream together cream cheese, butter, sugar and vanilla. Add eggs one at a time, mixing well after each addition.

Gradually add 2 cups flour and baking powder. Combine remaining ¼ cup flour with cranberries and nuts and fold into batter.

Pour into greased and floured tube pan and bake at 350° F for 1 hour and 15 minutes. Let stand for 5 minutes before removing from pan. Dust with confectioners' sugar.

—Mrs. Robert Uttech

Apricot-Prune Coffeecake

¾ cup prunes
¾ cup dried apricots
2 cups flour
2 tsp. baking powder
½ tsp. salt
¾ cup butter
¾ cup sugar
2 eggs
¾ cup milk
1 tsp. vanilla
FILLING:
⅔ cup brown sugar
1 Tbsp. flour
1 Tbsp. cinnamon
4 Tbsp. melted butter

Soak prunes and apricots in boiling water to cover for 5 minutes. Drain and set aside.

Combine flour, baking powder and salt. Cream together butter and sugar, then beat in eggs. Combine milk and vanilla. Add milk and dry ingredients alternately to butter mixture, mixing well after each addition. Stir in fruit.

Pour ⅓ of the batter into greased and floured tube pan. Combine filling ingredients and pour half of this onto batter. Repeat, ending with layer of batter. Bake at 350° F for 55 minutes.

—Maureen Marcotte

Tarragon Cheese Bread

Use Swiss, mozzarella or Monterey Jack cheese for this recipe. This makes a fragrant, hearty bread that is delicious warm or cold.

bread dough for 1 loaf
1½ lbs. white cheese
3 eggs, beaten
1 Tbsp. tarragon

Roll bread dough into a 22- to 24-inch circle. Grate cheese, then mix with 2 eggs and tarragon. Grease a 9"-round cake pan and line with dough, leaving a large overhang. Fill with cheese then bring dough up and over filling, folding into pleats. Grab pleats 3 inches from end and twist to seal. Set to rise in warm place until doubled in bulk — about 1 hour.

Bake at 375° F for 45 minutes. Brush with remaining egg, then bake for 15 minutes more. Let cool slightly, then cut into wedges to serve.

—*Debi Larson*

Tarragon Tea Wafers

"Sesame seed is the symbol of immortality, and tarragon is an ingredient of the drink of kings. The two herbs are brought together in these tea wafers."

½ cup butter
1 cup firmly packed brown
 sugar
1 tsp. vanilla
1 egg
½ cup toasted sesame seeds
½ cup crushed pecans
1½ tsp. crushed tarragon
¾ cup flour
¼ tsp. baking powder
¼ tsp. salt

Cream butter and sugar, then mix in vanilla and egg. Beat in sesame seeds, pecans and tarragon. Add dry ingredients and mix well. Drop in small mounds, about 3 inches apart, on greased baking sheet. Bake at 375° F for 8 to 10 minutes. (Watch them: they burn easily.) Let cool for a minute before removing from pan.

Makes about 4 dozen wafers.

—*Cary Elizabeth Marshall*

Cheesy Curry Biscuits

2 cups flour
3 tsp. baking powder
½ tsp. salt
½ tsp. curry powder
4 Tbsp. butter
⅔ cup grated sharp Cheddar
 cheese
⅞ cup milk

Sift together flour, baking powder, salt and curry powder. Cut in butter until mixture is mealy. Add cheese, then make well in centre. Gradually add milk, stirring, until soft dough is formed.

Turn onto floured board and knead briefly. Roll out to ¾-inch thickness. Cut into 2-inch biscuits. Bake on ungreased cookie sheet at 450° F for 12 to 15 minutes.

Makes 16 biscuits.

—*Carol Swann-Jacob*

Honey-Pecan Butterballs

1 cup butter
¼ cup honey
2 cups flour
½ tsp. salt
2 tsp. vanilla
2 cups finely chopped
 pecans

Cream butter and honey, then stir in flour, salt and vanilla. Fold in nuts. Form into small balls and place on greased cookie sheets. Bake at 300° F for 40 to 45 minutes or until lightly browned.

Makes 3 to 4 dozen cookies.

—*Teresa Caret*

Honey-Pecan Rolls

"We keep bees, so this recipe helps us use up our plentiful supply of honey."

1 Tbsp. yeast
2 tsp. honey
½ cup warm water
1 tsp. salt
¼ cup honey
2 eggs, lightly beaten
½ cup butter, melted
3-3½ cups flour
1 cup coarsely chopped
  pecans
GLAZE:
¾ cup honey
¾ cup brown sugar
6 Tbsp. butter
FILLING:
melted butter
½ cup brown sugar
2 tsp. cinnamon

Combine yeast, 2 tsp. honey and water and let sit for 10 minutes. Add salt, ¼ cup honey, eggs and ½ cup melted butter and mix well. Add flour to make thick dough.

Turn out onto floured board and knead for 5 minutes. Place in greased bowl, turning once. Cover and let rise until double — 1 hour.

Place pecans in bottom of 9" x 13" pan. For glaze, combine honey, ¾ cup sugar and butter in heavy saucepan. Bring to a boil, remove from heat and cool slightly.

Roll dough into 15-by-13-inch rectangle. Brush with melted butter and sprinkle with ½ cup brown sugar and cinnamon. Roll up and cut into 1-inch slices. Place over pecans, pour glaze over and let rise for 1 hour. Bake at 350° F for 30 minutes.

Makes 15 rolls.

—*Mary Ellen Hoar*

Cinnamon Buns

Make up the dough the night before and let the buns rise for the final time in the refrigerator overnight. This then becomes a quick but very special breakfast.

½ cup warm water
½ tsp. white sugar
1 pkg. yeast
2 cups milk
½ cup butter, softened
1 cup white sugar
1 tsp. salt
1 tsp. vanilla
5 cups flour
melted butter
¼ cup brown sugar
1 Tbsp. cinnamon

Combine water and ½ tsp. white sugar, then add yeast. Let sit for 10 minutes, then add milk, butter, 1 cup white sugar, salt, vanilla and flour (only enough so dough can still be mixed with a wooden spoon). Mix well, then let rise for 2 to 3 hours.

Turn out onto well-floured work surface. Punch down, then flatten into rectangular shape. Brush with melted butter, then sprinkle with brown sugar and cinnamon. Roll up and cut into 1 ¼-inch slices. Place in greased muffin tins and let rise until doubled in size. Bake at 375° F for 30 minutes.

Makes approximately 24 buns.

—*Rose Strocen*

Cinnamon-Sour Cream Twists

There are few people who will turn down this breakfast delicacy. Served hot from the oven and dripping with butter, they are irresistible. Make this dough the day before and then bake up the twists for a special breakfast.

1 pkg. yeast
¼ cup warm water
4 cups flour
1 cup butter, melted
1 cup sour cream
2 eggs, beaten
1 tsp. salt
1 tsp. vanilla
1 cup sugar
1 tsp. cinnamon

Sprinkle yeast into water and stir until dissolved. Combine flour, butter, sour cream, eggs, salt and vanilla. Stir in yeast and work until smooth. Cover with damp cloth and refrigerate for at least 2 hours or up to 2 days.

Combine sugar and cinnamon. Roll dough into 15-by-18-inch rectangle, then coat both sides with sugar-cinnamon mixture. Fold over in thirds, then roll into ¼-inch-thick rectangle. Cut into 1-inch-wide strips, twist and place on greased baking sheet. Bake at 375° F for 15 minutes.

Makes approximately 18 twists.

—*Marklyn A. Hallett*

Caramel Rolls

There can be few things better at tempting people out of bed in the morning than the smell of sticky buns baking and coffee brewing. These are attractive, delicious and easy to make. Eat them right away, though, as they do not keep well.

2 cups flour
4 tsp. baking powder
½ tsp. salt
½ cup butter
¾ cup milk
2 Tbsp. soft butter
1 cup brown sugar
1 Tbsp. cinnamon

Combine flour, baking powder and salt. Cut in ¼ cup butter until butter is size of peas, then stir in milk. Mix this to a soft dough.

Turn onto floured board and pat into a ⅜-inch-thick rectangle. Spread dough with 2 Tbsp. soft butter and sprinkle with ½ cup brown sugar mixed with cinnamon. Roll up and cut into 1-inch slices.

Place remaining ¼ cup butter in two 9"-round pans and melt. Sprinkle with remaining ½ cup sugar. Arrange rolls on this, and bake at 450° F for 15 to 20 minutes, moving to top oven shelf after 12 minutes. Turn out onto serving dish at once, scraping out any caramel that remains in pan.

Makes 12 rolls.

—*Janeen Clynick*

Potato Sticky Buns

"These sticky buns are a favourite with my family. Whenever we travel to our son's or daughter's house for a visit, I am asked to bring along a package of sticky buns. Luckily, they can be made ahead of time and frozen."

1 cup hot mashed potatoes
½ cup sugar
1½ tsp. salt
½ cup butter
1 pkg. yeast
2 eggs
1½ cups warm potato water
7 cups flour
brown sugar
chopped nuts
melted butter
cinnamon

Combine potatoes, sugar, salt and butter. When lukewarm, add yeast, eggs and potato water. Stir in flour to make a stiff dough. Knead until smooth, then let rise until doubled in size — 1 hour. Punch down, refrigerate and chill thoroughly.

Butter four 9"-round pans. Cover with ⅓-inch brown sugar, then sprinkle with nuts. Roll dough to ½-inch thickness. Brush with butter and sprinkle with brown sugar and cinnamon. Roll dough up and cut into ½-inch circles. Place in pans and let rise again until doubled — 30 minutes. Bake at 350° F for 25 to 35 minutes.

Makes 2 dozen buns.

—*Marilyn Vincent*

Sticky Buns

As with the other yeast recipes in this section, work on these buns can be started the evening before they are to be eaten. Breakfast-eaters will be most appreciative and will think you rose before the sun to make them.

1 Tbsp. yeast
¼ cup lukewarm water
1 cup scalded milk
¾ cup sugar
2 Tbsp. shortening
1 tsp. salt
4 cups flour
1 egg
¼ cup melted butter
2 tsp. cinnamon
¼ cup raisins
light corn syrup
½ cup chopped pecans

Soften yeast in water and let stand for 10 minutes. Combine scalded milk, ¼ cup sugar, shortening and salt and cool to lukewarm. Stir in 1½ cups flour and egg. Stir in the yeast then add remaining flour. Mix well, let rest for 10 minutes, then knead until smooth.

Let rise until doubled — 1 hour. Punch down and roll out to ¼-inch-thick rectangle. Brush on melted butter, then sprinkle with remaining ½ cup sugar, cinnamon and raisins. Roll dough up.

Butter a 9" x 13" baking pan. Drizzle thin layer of corn syrup in bottom of pan, and sprinkle with nuts. Cut dough into 12 slices, and place in pan. Bake at 350° F for 20 to 30 minutes.

Makes 12 buns.

—*Anne Morrell*

Chocolate-Peanut Butter Squares

A rich, tasty combination of chocolate and peanut butter, these squares ranked high with the Camden East staff who tasted them.

1½ cups graham cracker
   crumbs
1 cup icing sugar
½ cup butter
¾ cup peanut butter
6 oz. chocolate chips

Combine cracker crumbs and icing sugar. Melt butter and peanut butter, then pour into crumbs, mix well and pat into bottom of greased 8" x 8" pan. Melt chocolate chips and pour over crust. Chill for 30 minutes, then cut into squares.

Makes 16 squares.
—Barbara Littlejohn

Tante Vivien's Butterscotch Brownies

Not too sweet, these brownies are very quick and easy to make.

½ cup melted butter
1 cup brown sugar
1 egg, beaten
1 tsp. vanilla
¾ cup flour
1 tsp. baking powder
½ cup walnuts
½ cup coconut
½ cup currants

Combine all ingredients and mix well. Bake in greased 9" x 9" pan at 350° F for 30 minutes. Cut into squares while still warm.

Makes 12 to 16 squares.
—Olga Zuyderhoff

White Chocolate Mocha Java Bars

Cut these bars before the white chocolate hardens completely. They are a deliciously decadent variation of Nanaimo Bars.

¾ cup butter
½ cup sugar
1 tsp. vanilla
1 egg
2 cups graham cracker
   crumbs
1 cup desiccated coconut
½ cup finely chopped
   toasted hazelnuts
2 tsp. instant coffee crystals
2 Tbsp. hot coffee
2½ cups icing sugar
¼ cup cocoa
2 Tbsp. milk
6 oz. white chocolate

Combine ½ cup butter, sugar, vanilla and egg in top of double boiler. Cook, stirring, over boiling water until slightly thickened. Blend in cracker crumbs, coconut and hazelnuts and spread evenly in greased 9" x 9" baking pan. Let stand 15 minutes.

Meanwhile, dissolve instant coffee crystals in hot coffee. Blend well with icing sugar, cocoa, remaining ¼ cup butter and milk. Spread over crust and chill for 10 minutes. Melt chocolate and spread over filling. Chill well.

Makes 16 to 18 squares.
—Denise Atkinson

Fergosa

½ cup chopped onion
3 Tbsp. butter
1 cup flour
1½ tsp. baking powder
salt
1½ cups grated cheese
⅓ cup milk
1 egg, lightly beaten
poppy seeds

Sauté onion in 1 Tbsp. butter until transparent, then set aside. Combine flour, baking powder, salt, 2 Tbsp. butter, ½ cup cheese and milk and beat until smooth. The dough will be sticky. Knead 10 times on floured board, working in a bit of flour if necessary.

Grease an 8-inch pie plate and your hands, then spread dough evenly in pan. Combine remaining 1 cup cheese and egg. Spread on dough. Sprinkle with onion and poppy seeds. Bake at 425° F for 20 minutes.

Serves 4 to 6.
—Rosande Bellaar-Spruyt

Chris Warkentin's Apricot Bars

Probably just about any dried fruit could be substituted for interesting variations. These are quite sweet, sticky and sinful.

⅔ cup dried apricots
½ cup butter
1¼ cups brown sugar
1⅓ cups flour
2 eggs
½ tsp. baking powder
½ cup chopped walnuts
1 tsp. almond extract

Cover apricots with water and simmer for 10 minutes. Drain, cool and chop.

Mix butter, ¼ cup sugar and 1 cup flour with fork and then fingers until crumbly. Press into 8" x 8" pan and bake at 350° F for 20 minutes, or until lightly browned.

Meanwhile, beat eggs well. Beat in remaining 1 cup sugar, then add ⅓ cup flour and baking powder. Stir in apricots, nuts and almond extract and spread over baked crust. Bake for 20 to 30 minutes more.

Makes 12 to 16 squares.
—*Andrea Stuart*

Carrot-Zucchini Squares

Moist and tasty, these squares are a good way to get children to eat the often unpopular zucchini.

⅔ cup firmly packed light brown sugar
½ cup butter
1 egg
1 tsp. vanilla
1½ cups flour
1 tsp. baking powder
salt
⅔ cup coarsely grated carrot
⅔ cup coarsely grated zucchini, drained
½ cup raisins

Beat sugar and butter together. Add egg and vanilla and beat thoroughly. Add remaining ingredients and stir together. Spoon into greased 9" x 9" pan. Bake at 350° F for 30 minutes, or until a toothpick inserted in the centre comes out clean.

Makes 12 to 16 squares.
—*Rosalind Mechefske*

Poppy Seed Squares

Poppy seeds, coconut and honey are a winning combination. The squares are chewy and delicious.

1¾ cups flour
1 tsp. baking powder
¼ tsp. baking soda
1¼ cups sugar
½ tsp. salt
½ cup butter, melted
⅓ cup honey
2 eggs
2 Tbsp. milk
1 tsp. vanilla
1 cup coconut
½ cup poppy seeds
icing sugar

Sift flour, baking powder, baking soda, sugar and salt into mixing bowl. Add butter, honey, eggs, milk and vanilla. Beat with electric mixer until well blended, then stir in coconut and poppy seeds. Spread evenly in greased 9" x 13" pan. Bake at 350° F for 25 to 30 minutes. Remove to wire rack and cool, then sprinkle top with icing sugar.

Makes approximately 24 squares.
—*Tracy Willemsen*

Swedish Ginger Cookies

"I love to make these cookies with my children, not only because they are delicious to eat, but also because the children enjoy watching the baking soda reaction in the saucepan." An enticing winter bedtime snack is ginger cookies accompanied by hot chocolate or warm milk. Ginger is the underground stem of a plant that grows in Asia, the West Indies, South America, Africa and Australia. It is equally at home in cakes, cookies and desserts as well as in curries and other savoury dishes.

⅔ cup unsulfured molasses
⅔ cup honey
1 Tbsp. ginger
1 Tbsp. cinnamon
2 tsp. baking soda
⅔ cup butter, cut into 1"
   chunks
1 egg, lightly beaten
2 cups whole wheat flour
2 cups white flour

In heavy 2-quart saucepan over moderate heat, bring molasses, honey, ginger and cinnamon just to a low boil, stirring occasionally. Add baking soda and stir until mixture foams to top of pan. Remove from heat, add butter and stir until melted. Mix in egg and gradually stir into flours in bowl.

Turn dough out of bowl and knead lightly until well blended. Divide dough into 2 balls. Roll out on lightly floured board to ⅛-inch thickness. Cut cookies with cutters, or freehand with sharp knife, and place on foil-lined cookie sheet. Bake at 325° F for about 13 minutes.

Makes approximately 8 dozen 2½-inch cookies.

—Leslie Pierpont

Welsh Currant Cakes

"These cookies take some practice to make perfectly. They should look like English muffins and be as light and flaky as biscuits." Well-cleaned empty tuna cans can be kept and used as cutters for these and similar biscuits.

3 cups flour
1 cup sugar
1½ tsp. baking powder
1¼ tsp. salt
½ tsp. baking soda
2 tsp. nutmeg
1 cup shortening
1 cup currants
2 eggs
6 Tbsp. milk

Sift together flour, sugar, baking powder, salt, baking soda and nutmeg. Cut in shortening, then add currants. Beat eggs and milk together. Add to flour mixture and mix to make a stiff dough. Chill for 1 to 2 hours.

Divide dough into thirds, then roll out to ¼-inch thickness on lightly floured board. Cut into round biscuits.

Heat griddle until water drops bounce off it. Lightly grease, then cook biscuits until tops puff and turn shiny. Flip and bake until golden.

Makes 24 biscuits.

—Mary Bacon

Lace Cookies

"Thin, crisp and almost transparent, these splendid cookies are easy to make." Bake the cookies on parchment paper — it is available in cooking supply stores, can be used over and over, and the cookies will lift off easily, thus eliminating the frustration of having a perfect cookie glued forever to the cookie sheet.

1½ cups oatmeal
1½ cups light brown sugar
2 Tbsp. flour
½ tsp. salt
⅔ cup melted butter
1 egg, lightly beaten
½ tsp. vanilla

Combine oatmeal, sugar, flour and salt and mix well. Stir in melted butter, then egg and vanilla. Line cookie sheets with parchment paper. Drop batter by half-teaspoonful, 2 inches apart. Flatten cookies with fork dipped in water.

Bake at 350° F until lightly browned — approximately 5 minutes. Cool cookies on parchment paper, just slide off cookie sheet, then lift off with spatula.

Makes approximately 40 cookies.

—Sharon McKay

Grandma Marion's Coconut-Oatmeal Cookies

"The taste and texture of these cookies vary depending on their thickness. If pressed very thin, they are crisp, caramel-like and quick-cooking. If thicker, they are a softer, heartier cookie."

¾ cup brown sugar
¼ cup white sugar
1 cup butter
1 egg
1½ cups flour
1 tsp. baking powder
1 tsp. baking soda
1½ cups rolled oats
¾ cup coconut
¼ tsp. vanilla

Cream sugars and butter, then add egg. Sift in flour, baking powder and baking soda, then mix in rolled oats and coconut. Stir in vanilla. Shape into balls, place on greased cookie sheet and flatten with fork dipped in cold water. Bake at 375° F for 5 to 10 minutes.

Makes 3 dozen cookies.

—Isabel Bradley

Cinnamon Crunchies

"This recipe was given to me by my mother-in-law. It reminds me of the 'Cinnamon Pie' we made out of leftover pie crust as children."

1 cup flour
¼ tsp. salt
½ tsp. cinnamon
⅓ cup butter
½ cup sugar
1 egg yolk
2 tbsp. milk
¼ tsp. vanilla
TOPPING:
1 egg white
3 tbsp. sugar
½ tsp. cinnamon
¼ cup chopped walnuts

Sift together flour, salt and cinnamon. Add remaining ingredients and mix well. Spread in an ungreased 8" x 8" baking pan.

To make topping: Beat egg white until frothy and spread over dough. Mix sugar, cinnamon and walnuts and sprinkle over top. Bake at 350° F for 30 minutes.

Makes 12 to 16 squares.

—Marla J. Davis

Kipfel

Kipfel, or butterhorns, are a traditional German cookie, often served with afternoon tea or coffee. These are also delicious dipped in hot chocolate as a bedtime snack. For a real treat, add a dash of chocolate or almond liqueur to the hot chocolate and top with sweetened whipped cream.

2 Tbsp. warm water
¼ tsp. sugar
1 Tbsp. yeast
2 cups flour
½ cup butter
2 egg yolks
½ cup sour cream
confectioners' sugar
FILLING:
1 cup finely chopped
   walnuts
½ cup sugar
1 tsp. vanilla
2 egg whites
pinch cream of tartar

Combine water and sugar, then stir in yeast and set aside for 10 minutes. Place flour in bowl, cut in butter, then add yeast, egg yolks and sour cream. Mix well, form into a ball and knead. Divide into 3 parts and chill for at least 1 hour.

Sprinkle pastry board with confectioners' sugar, roll dough out into circle and cut into 12 wedges.

Make filling by combining nuts, sugar and vanilla. Beat egg whites with cream of tartar until stiff, then fold into nut mixture. Fill wide end of dough with 1 tsp. filling and spread toward narrow end. Roll up from wide end to narrow. Bake at 350° F for 15 minutes.

Makes 36 butterhorns.

—Gladys Sykes

Rigo Jancsi

These Hungarian squares are made for chocolate fanatics. They take a lot of time to prepare so are definitely for special occasions.

CAKE:
3 oz. unsweetened chocolate
4 eggs, separated
½ cup sugar
¾ cup butter
⅔ cup flour
¼ tsp. salt
1 tsp. vanilla
FILLING:
10 oz. semisweet chocolate
2 cups heavy cream
2 Tbsp. coffee liqueur
FROSTING:
1 cup superfine sugar
½ cup hot coffee
6 oz. semisweet chocolate
2 Tbsp. light corn syrup
2 Tbsp. butter
2 Tbsp. coffee liqueur

To make cake: Melt chocolate in top of double boiler over hot water, then cool to lukewarm. Grease 15" x 10" baking pan, line with waxed paper and grease the paper.

Beat egg whites until foamy and double in volume in medium-sized bowl. Beat in 1¼ cup sugar, 1 Tbsp. at a time, until meringue stands in soft peaks.

Beat butter in large bowl. Gradually add remaining ¼ cup sugar and continue beating until mixture is well blended. Beat in egg yolks until smooth, then cooled chocolate. Sift flour and salt into chocolate mixture. Stir to blend, then add vanilla.

Stir ⅓ of the meringue mixture into chocolate mixture, then fold in remaining meringue mixture until well blended. Spread batter evenly into prepared pan.

Bake at 350° F for 15 minutes, or until top springs back when lightly touched. Cool in pan on wire rack for 5 minutes, then loosen cake around edges with sharp knife and invert onto a large cookie sheet. Peel off waxed paper, invert cake onto a large cake rack and cool completely.

Meanwhile, make filling. Cut chocolate into small pieces. Combine with cream in saucepan and heat slowly, stirring constantly, until chocolate melts. Remove from heat and stir in coffee liqueur. Pour into bowl and chill for 1½ hours, or until mixture is completely cold. Beat chilled chocolate-cream mixture until stiff and thick.

Cut cooled cake in half crosswise. Place half on small cookie sheet. Top with whipped chocolate cream, spreading to make a layer about 1½ inches thick. Top with second half of cake. Chill for at least 1 hour, or until filling is firm.

To make frosting: Heat sugar and coffee until sugar dissolves. Cut chocolate into small pieces and add to saucepan along with corn syrup. Heat to boiling, stirring constantly, then cook at a slow boil, still stirring constantly, for 5 minutes. Remove from heat and add butter and coffee liqueur. Beat for 5 minutes, or until mixture thickens. Quickly spread over cake layer about ¼-inch thick. Chill for at least 1 hour.

Makes 12 squares.

—*Kristine Mattila*

Wonderful Oatmeal-Raisin Cookies

No exaggeration—these are truly wonderful, chewy and crisp at the same time.

1 cup shortening
1 cup brown sugar
½ cup white sugar
1 egg
1 tsp. vanilla
½ tsp. cinnamon
½ tsp. ginger
¼ tsp. nutmeg
1 tsp. salt
1 tsp. baking soda
2 cups rolled oats
1 cup flour
½ cup whole wheat flour
1 cup raisins

Cream shortening and sugars. Add egg, vanilla, cinnamon, ginger, nutmeg, salt and baking soda, then stir in oats, flours and raisins. Roll into small balls and place on greased cookie sheet. Flatten with floured fork. Bake at 350° F for 8 to 10 minutes.

Makes 4½ dozen.

—*Mary Burbidge*

Oatmeal Cookies

1 cup raisins
2½ tsp. baking soda
3 eggs
1 tsp. vanilla
1 cup butter
1 cup brown sugar
1 cup white sugar
2½ cups flour
1 tsp. salt
1 tsp. cinnamon
2 cups oatmeal

Place raisins and 2 cups water in saucepan and boil for 5 minutes. Add 1 tsp. baking soda, stir, then remove raisins and drain, discarding water and baking soda. Beat eggs well, add raisins and vanilla and let stand, covered, for at least 1 hour.

Cream butter and sugars. Add flour, salt, cinnamon and remaining 1½ tsp. baking soda. Mix well, then blend in egg-raisin mixture and oatmeal. Drop by large teaspoonful on ungreased cookie sheet and bake at 350° F for 10 to 12 minutes.

Makes 5 to 6 dozen cookies.

—*Laurabel Miller*

Old-Fashioned Chocolate Chip-Oatmeal Cookies

"These cookies have a light, crunchy texture when finished. They have been filling our cookie jar for many years — a longtime family favourite!"

1 cup butter
1 cup brown sugar
¾ cup white sugar
1 egg, lightly beaten
1 tsp. vanilla
2 cups flour
1 tsp. salt
1 tsp. baking soda
1 cup rolled oats
12 oz. chocolate chips
½ cup chopped walnuts

Cream butter and sugars until creamy. Add egg, 1 Tbsp. water and vanilla and continue to beat until fluffy. Sift flour, salt and baking soda. Blend into creamed mixture. Stir in remaining ingredients. Drop by teaspoonful onto greased cookie sheets. Bake at 350° F for 8 to 10 minutes, or until lightly browned.

Makes 3 dozen cookies.

—*Susan Varga*

Old-Fashioned Coconut Macaroons

1 egg
¼ cup sugar
2 cups shredded coconut

Beat egg, then beat in sugar and stir in coconut. Drop onto greased cookie sheet to form small mounds. Bake at 350° F for 12 minutes, or until golden. Cool on pan for a few minutes before transferring to cooling rack.

Makes 2 dozen macaroons.

—*I. Atkins*

Pumpkin Cookies

Even non-pumpkin fans will enjoy this moist, spicy cookie. Pumpkin can be baked, puréed and frozen in the fall and then thawed for use during the winter and spring.

½ cup shortening
1 cup brown sugar
1 cup mashed pumpkin
1 cup raisins
½ cup nuts
1 tsp. vanilla
2 cups flour
1 tsp. baking soda
1 tsp. cinnamon
1 tsp. baking powder
icing sugar (optional)

Cream shortening and sugar, then add pumpkin, raisins, nuts and vanilla and mix well. Sift together flour, baking soda, cinnamon and baking powder and add to creamed ingredients. Mix well, then drop by teaspoonful onto greased cookie sheet. Bake at 350° F for 8 to 10 minutes. When cool, dust with icing sugar if desired.

Makes 3 dozen cookies.

—*Leslie Ann Gray*

Linzer Cookies

"This recipe has been passed through five generations of my family. The book containing it is close to disintegration from so many years of use."

¾ cup lard
¾ cup butter
¾ cup sugar
2 eggs
rind & juice of 1 lemon
4 cups flour
jam
icing sugar

Cream lard and butter, then add sugar, eggs and lemon rind and juice. Mix in flour. Roll out to ¼-inch thickness and cut into 2-inch rounds. Bake at 350° F for 20 minutes, or until golden. Cool on rack. Spread half the rounds with jam, then cover with remaining cookies. Dust with icing sugar.

Makes 2 dozen sandwich cookies.

—*Margaret Smit*

Prize Mincemeat Cookies

1 cup butter
1½ cups sugar
3 eggs
3 cups flour
1 tsp. baking soda
½ tsp. salt
1⅓ cups mincemeat

Cream butter and sugar, then beat in eggs, one at a time, until smooth. Set aside. Combine flour, baking soda and salt. Gradually add to creamed mixture, then stir in mincemeat. Drop by rounded teaspoonsful onto greased cookie sheet, spacing cookies 2 inches apart. Bake at 375° F for 8 to 10 minutes.

Makes 6½ dozen cookies.

—*Fran Bakke*

Apricot Pinwheel Cookies

1 cup chopped dried apricots
¼ cup sugar
1 cup butter, softened
1 cup icing sugar
1 egg
1 tsp. almond extract
3 cups flour
¼ tsp. salt

Combine apricots with ½ cup boiling water in small bowl, set aside until water is absorbed, then stir in sugar. Chop in blender or food processor until consistency of thick, spreadable purée. Set aside. Cream together butter and icing sugar until fluffy. Beat in egg and almond extract. Stir together flour and salt and add, mixing until well blended and dough forms a ball. Chill dough for 30 minutes.

Roll half of dough into a 9-by-12-inch rectangle; spread with half apricot mixture. Roll up from widest side. Wrap in plastic wrap. Repeat with remaining ingredients. Refrigerate rolls for 3 hours or overnight.

Cut into ½-inch slices, then place on greased cookie sheets. Bake at 350° F for 15 minutes, flip cookies over and bake for another 5 minutes.

Makes 5 dozen cookies.

—*Lynn Tobin*

Perfect Peanut Butter Cookies

A lofty claim, perhaps, but one that our testers assure us is valid. Use either smooth or crunchy peanut butter.

½ cup butter
½ cup peanut butter
½ cup white sugar
½ cup packed brown sugar
1 egg
¾ tsp. vanilla
1¼ cups flour
¾ tsp. baking soda
¼ tsp. salt

Beat butter, peanut butter, white sugar and ¼ cup brown sugar until light and fluffy. Beat in egg and vanilla. Combine flour, baking soda and salt, then beat into butter mixture until blended. Sprinkle remaining ¼ cup brown sugar on top of dough and gently fold so sugar granules are still visible.

Roll dough into teaspoonful-sized balls and place 2 inches apart on ungreased cookie sheets. Press into ¼-inch-thick circles. Bake at 375° F for 8 to 10 minutes.

Makes 3 dozen cookies.

—*Carlene T. Blankenship*

Cookie Jar Gingersnaps

These are light and gingery — they won't last long in your cookie jar.

³/₄ cup shortening
1 cup sugar
1 egg
¹/₄ cup molasses
2 cups flour
1 Tbsp. ginger
2 tsp. baking soda
1 tsp. cinnamon
¹/₂ tsp. salt
granulated sugar

Cream shortening, then add sugar, egg and molasses. Mix in flour, ginger, baking soda, cinnamon and salt. Form teaspoonsful of dough into round balls, roll in granulated sugar and place 2 inches apart on ungreased cookie sheets. Bake at 350° F for 10 to 15 minutes.

Makes 3 dozen cookies.

—Hazel Schwartz

Molasses Sugar Cookies

Increase the baking time if you prefer a crisp cookie. The time given here will result in a soft, chewy cookie.

³/₄ cup shortening
1 cup sugar
¹/₄ cup molasses
1 egg
2 cups flour
2 tsp. baking soda
¹/₂ tsp. cloves
¹/₂ tsp. ginger
1 tsp. cinnamon
¹/₂ tsp. salt

Melt shortening in heavy pan, remove from heat and let cool. Combine sugar, molasses and egg, beat well, then add shortening. Sift together flour, baking soda, cloves, ginger, cinnamon and salt. Add to sugar mixture and mix well. Chill, then form into 1-inch balls. Roll in granulated sugar and place on greased cookie sheets 2 inches apart. Bake at 375° F for 8 minutes.

Makes 3 dozen cookies.

—Mrs. John Schobelock

Chocolate-Dipped Raspberry-Almond Crisps

These make an elegant treat for an afternoon tea party or a special dessert.

1 cup flour
1 cup finely chopped, blanched almonds
¹/₂ cup butter, softened
6 Tbsp. sugar
1¹/₂ tsp. vanilla
¹/₄ cup raspberry jam
2 oz. semisweet chocolate, melted

Combine flour and almonds. Cream butter, sugar and vanilla, then stir in flour mixture, using hands to work mixture into smooth dough. Shape into roll 2 inches in diameter. Wrap and chill for at least 3 hours. Cut into ¹/₄-inch slices. Bake on ungreased cookie sheet at 350 degrees for 10 to 12 minutes. Cool.

Spread half the cookies with jam and top with remaining cookies. Dip half of each cookie into melted chocolate, then place on waxed paper until chocolate is set. Store refrigerated.

Makes 18 sandwich cookies.

—Alice M. Gibson

Crunchy Maple Cookies

"This is my husband's favourite cookie to take on fishing or hunting trips."

1 cup shortening
1 cup brown sugar
1 egg
1 cup maple syrup
1 tsp. vanilla
4 cups flour
½ tsp. salt
2 tsp. baking soda
granulated sugar

Cream shortening and brown sugar, then blend in egg, syrup and vanilla. Add flour, salt and soda, and beat until blended. Shape into 1-inch balls, and coat with granulated sugar. Bake on greased cookie sheets at 350° F for about 10 minutes.

Makes about 5 dozen cookies.
—*Helen Potts*

Chocolate Shortbread Cookies With Chocolate Chips

1 lb. butter, softened
1 cup icing sugar
1¾ cups flour
1 cup cornstarch
¼ cup cocoa
¼ tsp. vanilla
⅓ cup mini chocolate chips

Cream butter and sugar together. Sift together flour, cornstarch and cocoa. Stir into butter mixture, then fold in vanilla and chocolate chips. Drop by teaspoonful onto ungreased cookie sheet. Bake at 275° F for 30 to 35 minutes.

Makes 4 dozen cookies.
—*Patricia Forrest*

Brown Sugar-Jam Cookies

"This recipe came from my grandmother, through my mother, with very indefinite quantities. It has required a certain amount of experimentation to pin down. We've all eaten a lot of these cookies over the years." Use a tart jam rather than an overly sweet one.

1 cup butter
1 cup white sugar
1 cup brown sugar
2 eggs
2 tsp. vanilla
2½ cups flour
¾ tsp. baking powder
jam

Cream butter and sugars, then add eggs and vanilla and beat well. Add dry ingredients, beating thoroughly. Roll three-quarters of the dough into balls, about 1 inch in diameter, place on greased cookie sheets, and flatten with fork. Place ¼ tsp. jam on each cookie, and top with a very small "hat" of cookie dough. Bake at 400° F for 8 to 10 minutes.

Makes 3 dozen cookies.
—*Muriel Doris*

Almond-Orange Cookies

2 eggs
2 Tbsp. orange juice
½ tsp. almond extract
⅔ cup honey
6-7 cups ground almonds
1 cup whole wheat flour
2 tsp. dry orange peel
semisweet chocolate

Beat eggs and orange juice together until frothy. Beat in almond extract and honey, then stir in almonds, flour and peel. Knead lightly, adding more flour until dough does not stick to work surface. Roll dough into 2 cylinders, 1 inch wide. Chill for 1 to 2 hours, then cut into slices ¼ inch thick with a serrated knife.

Bake on foil-covered cookie sheets at 350° F for 12 to 15 minutes. Frost each cookie with melted semisweet chocolate when cooled. When chocolate is solid, store cookies in airtight containers.

Makes 5 to 6 dozen cookies.
—*Susan O'Neill*

Eggs & Cheese

Tofu Millet Quiche

1 cup millet
2½ cups boiling water
1 tsp. salt
1 tsp. butter
1½ cakes tofu
1 Tbsp. oil
1 onion, finely chopped
2 cloves garlic, minced
3 cups raw spinach, cleaned
    & stemmed
2 Tbsp. tamari sauce
2 Tbsp. arrowroot
Basil, thyme & paprika
½ tsp. nutmeg
Handful sliced mushrooms
¼ lb. medium Cheddar
    cheese, grated

Add millet to boiling water and add salt. Simmer for 25 to 30 minutes. Butter a 10-inch pie plate and pat in the cooked millet while still warm. Bake at 425° F for 5 to 7 minutes.

Place tofu in colander, weight it and let sit 30 minutes to drain.

Sauté onion and garlic in oil until tender but not browned. Remove from heat.

Steam spinach until limp, chop coarsely and add to onion and garlic.

In 2 batches, using a blender, mix until smooth the tofu, tamari, seasonings (except paprika) and arrowroot. If mixture is too thick, add a little water. Add this to onion-spinach mixture.

Pour into crust and arrange sliced mushrooms on top. Sprinkle cheese and paprika over all.

Bake at 425° F for 10 minutes, reduce heat to 325° F and bake 20 minutes longer.

Serves 6.

—Francine Watanabe

Quiche Lorraine

This quiche can also be made into individual pies in muffin tins and served as hors d'oeuvres. Variations are almost endless — asparagus, shrimp, leeks, ham and mushrooms all make delicious additions.

Pastry for 9-inch pie shell
8 slices bacon
1 cup grated Swiss cheese
4 eggs
1½ cups milk or light cream
½ tsp. salt
⅛ tsp. pepper
⅛ tsp. nutmeg

Bake pie shell at 400° F for 10 minutes. Remove from oven and reduce temperature to 350° F.

Chop bacon and fry until crisp. Drain and place in pie shell. Top with grated cheese. Beat eggs, milk and seasonings together. Pour into shell and bake 25 to 35 minutes or until firm and lightly browned.

—Mary Lou Ross

Cheese and Onion Pie

This egg pie is very dense, and with only a green salad is a meal in itself. Chopped cooked bacon or ham may be added for variety.

Pastry for 9-inch pie shell
3 medium onions
1 cup water
4 eggs
½ cup milk
1-1½ cups grated Cheddar
    cheese

Line pie plate with pastry, prick with a fork and bake at 350° F for 10 minutes.

Peel and slice onions, place in saucepan and cover with 1 cup boiling water and boil, covered, for 5 to 10 minutes. Cool. Beat together eggs and milk. Alternate layers of onions and grated cheese in the pastry shell. Pour custard over all. Bake at 350° F for 20 minutes or until set.

—Rae Anne Huth

Tomato & Basil Tart

This fragrant tart can be served hot or cold, for breakfast, lunch or as an opening course with dinner.

Pastry for 9-inch pie shell
3 Tbsp. sweet butter
2 medium onions, finely
  chopped
2 lbs. tomatoes, peeled,
  seeded & chopped
1 cup whipping cream
3 large eggs
1½ tsp. salt
½ tsp. pepper
2 tsp. dried basil
1½ tsp. finely sliced green
  peppers

Melt the butter in a frying pan. Add onions and cook until transparent. Strain the tomatoes and add to the onions. Cook over low heat until the tomatoes are reduced to a pulp. Remove from the heat and cool.

Beat together cream and eggs. Add cooled tomato mixture and season with salt, pepper, basil and green onions.

Line tart pan with pastry and bake at 350° F for 5 minutes. Add filling and bake 30 to 35 minutes longer.

—Auberge du Petit Prince

Salmon-Leek Quiche

With winter-stored leeks and fresh parsley from an indoor herb garden, this makes a pleasant midwinter dinner.

Pastry for 9-inch pie shell
2 large leeks
1 Tbsp. butter
16-oz. can salmon
1 cup grated old Cheddar
  cheese
3 eggs
¾ cup milk
½ tsp. salt
Freshly ground pepper
Fresh parsley, chopped

Bake pie shell at 400° F for 5 minutes. Remove from oven and lower heat to 375° F.

Slice leeks in half lengthwise, wash carefully, slice thinly and sauté in 1 Tbsp. butter. Drain salmon, flake and distribute over the bottom of the pie shell. Sprinkle with leeks and grated cheese.

Beat eggs with milk, salt and pepper and pour over mixture in shell. Top with a handful of fresh chopped parsley. Bake at 375° F for 25 to 35 minutes.

—Beth Hopkins

Spinach Quiche

Spinach, Swiss chard or beet greens—whatever your garden provides—are good in this quiche.

1 cup flour
½ tsp. salt
¼ cup oil
2 Tbsp. milk
1 lb. fresh spinach
1 small onion, chopped
2 Tbsp. oil
2 eggs
1 cup yogurt
½ cup dried milk
½ tsp. salt
⅓ cup grated Parmesan
  cheese

To prepare crust, combine flour and salt. Add oil and milk and mix with a fork. Roll out to fit a 9-inch pie plate, or simply spread dough in plate with your fingers.

Wash and cook spinach until just limp. Drain and chop well. Heat oil in a frying pan and add onion and spinach, cooking a few minutes until liquid has evaporated.

In a bowl, beat eggs and stir in yogurt, milk and salt. Add spinach and onions. Stir together and pour into the unbaked pie crust. Sprinkle with cheese and bake at 375° F for 25 minutes or until firm and starting to brown.

—Mikell Billoki

Asparagus & Chicken Soufflé

6 oz. fresh asparagus, cut
   into ¼-inch pieces
¼ cup butter
¼ cup flour
¼ tsp. thyme
¼ tsp. dry mustard
½ tsp. Tabasco sauce
¼ tsp. salt
1¼ cups milk
4 eggs, separated
½ cup cooked, shredded
   chicken
¾ cup grated Parmesan
   cheese
¼ tsp. cream of tartar

Prepare a 1½-quart straight-sided soufflé dish with collar. To do this, fold a 26-inch sheet of aluminum foil in half lengthwise; wrap it around the dish with a 3-inch rim extending above the top edge. Tape or tie in place.

In a medium saucepan, steam asparagus in 1 inch of boiling water for 6 minutes or until tender. Drain and set aside.

In the same pan, melt butter and blend in flour, thyme, mustard, Tabasco sauce and salt. Cook for 1 minute. Gradually stir in milk. Cook over medium heat, stirring constantly, until sauce thickens and boils. Reduce heat and simmer for 1 more minute.

In a medium-sized bowl, beat egg yolks, then quickly stir in sauce. Add chicken, cheese and asparagus and mix well. Cool slightly.

In large bowl of electric mixer, beat egg whites with cream of tartar until whites are stiff, but not dry. Gently fold in the sauce mixture. Turn into prepared soufflé dish. Bake at 375° F for 45 to 50 minutes or until golden brown. Remove collar and serve immediately.

Serves 4.

—Gregg A. Collis

Corn Meal Quiche

The addition of corn meal to the crust and kernel corn to the filling gives this quiche an unusual but pleasant texture and flavour.

½ cup corn meal
¾ cup flour
½ tsp. salt pepper
⅓ cup shortening
3 tbsp. cold water
1 cup shredded cheese
1 small onion, chopped
2 cups whole kernel corn,
   drained
⅓ cup milk
6 eggs
1 tsp. salt
¼ tsp. cayenne

For crust, mix corn meal, flour, salt and pepper in a bowl. Cut in shortening. Sprinkle water over while stirring with a fork. Roll out and fit loosely into a 9-inch pie plate. Flute edges.

Spread cheese in bottom of unbaked pie shell. Sauté onion, then add it and the corn to the cheese. Mix milk, eggs and seasonings together and pour into pie shell.

Bake at 400° F until firm and slightly browned on top — 20 to 30 minutes.

—Mikell Billoki

Nettle Pie

½ paper grocery bag of
   young nettles
3 Tbsp. butter
2 Tbsp. chopped onion
2 cloves garlic, chopped
2 Tbsp. flour
1 cup milk
Bay leaf
1 cup grated Cheddar cheese
2 eggs
⅔ cup flour
⅓ cup milk
⅓ cup water
¼ tsp. salt
½ cup Parmesan cheese

Wearing rubber gloves, remove central stem from nettles. Steam until tender, then place in a large greased casserole dish.

In a frying pan, melt butter, add onion and garlic and cook until limp. Mix in flour. Add milk and bay leaf and cook, stirring, until thickened. Pour this mixture over the nettles. Spread grated cheese over nettles and sauce. Beat remaining ingredients together for 2 minutes and pour over the cheese. Sprinkle with Parmesan cheese. Bake at 400° F for 20 minutes.

Serves 6.

—Dianne Radcliffe

Cheese Soufflé

This is a basic soufflé recipe. Once mastered, almost endless variations are possible.

¼ cup butter
¼ cup flour
½ tsp. salt
1½ cups hot milk
½ lb. Cheddar cheese, grated
4 eggs, separated

Blend butter, flour and salt together in a saucepan. Add hot milk and cook, stirring, until the mixture thickens. Remove from heat and blend in cheese.

Stir a little of the cheese mixture into the egg yolks, then pour into the saucepan and mix thoroughly.

Beat egg whites until stiff and fold gently into the egg and cheese mixture.

Turn into a buttered soufflé dish and bake at 375° F for 35 minutes. Serve immediately.

Serves 4.

—Shirley Thomlinson

Overnight Soufflé

12 slices bread, trimmed & cubed
½ lb. sharp Cheddar cheese, grated
3¼ cups milk
7 eggs, beaten
¾ tsp. salt
1 tsp. Worcestershire sauce
¼ cup grated Parmesan cheese

In a buttered 9" x 13" casserole dish, layer the bread and cheese: first spread out half the bread, cover with half the cheese, then the rest of the bread and the rest of the cheese.

Mix milk, eggs and seasonings, and pour over bread and cheese. Cover and refrigerate overnight.

Sprinkle with Parmesan cheese and bake uncovered at 325° F for 45 to 55 minutes, or until set. Serve immediately.

Serves 6.

—Joan Panaro

Broccoli Cheese Soufflé

An interesting and attractive dish, this soufflé is good served with rolls and a green salad.

1 tsp. butter
1 Tbsp. Parmesan cheese
3 Tbsp. butter
3 Tbsp. flour
⅓ cup powdered milk
¾ cup boiling water
½ tsp. salt
⅛ tsp. pepper
Cayenne & nutmeg
4 egg yolks
⅔ cup grated Swiss, Parmesan or Cheddar cheese
⅔ cup cooked chopped broccoli
1 egg white
Salt

Preheat oven to 400° F. Butter a 6-cup soufflé dish with 1 tsp. butter and sprinkle with 1 Tbsp. Parmesan cheese.

Melt the 3 Tbsp. of butter in a saucepan and stir in the flour. Cook for about 2 minutes without letting it brown. Remove from heat and add powdered milk mixed with boiling water. Beat with a wire whisk until well blended. Add seasonings and return to moderate heat. Remove from heat after 1 minute.

Add egg yolks to mixture, one at a time, beating well after each one. Correct the seasoning. Add cheese and broccoli.

Beat egg white with a pinch of salt until stiff. Blend one-quarter of the egg white into the cheese mixture, then carefully fold in the remaining egg whites.

Turn the mixture into the soufflé dish and smooth the top. Place on middle rack of oven and reduce heat to 375° F. Do not open the oven door for at least 20 minutes. Bake 25-30 minutes (4-5 minutes longer if you like it quite firm). Serve immediately.

Serves 4 to 6.

—Olga Harrison

Spinach Pie

Spinach, eggs and feta cheese combined in layers with filo pastry give this dish a delectably rich flavour.

¼ cup olive oil
½ cup finely chopped onions
¼ cup finely chopped scallions
2 lbs. fresh spinach, washed, drained & finely chopped
¼ cup finely cut fresh dill leaves (2 Tbsp. dried)
¼ cup finely chopped parsley
½ tsp. salt
Freshly ground black pepper
⅓ cup milk
½ lb. feta cheese, finely crumbled
4 eggs, lightly beaten
½ lb. butter, melted
16 sheets filo pastry

Heat olive oil in a heavy skillet. Add onions and scallions and cook, stirring frequently, until soft but not brown. Stir in spinach, cover tightly and cook for 5 minutes. Add dill, parsley, salt and a few grindings of pepper while stirring and shaking pan. Cook uncovered for about 10 minutes — until most of the liquid has evaporated and spinach sticks slightly to the pan.

Transfer to a bowl, add milk and cool to room temperature. Add cheese and slowly beat in eggs. Taste for seasoning.

With a pastry brush, coat the bottom and sides of a 7" x 12" dish with melted butter. Line the dish with a sheet of filo, pressing the edges into the corners of the dish. Brush the surface of the pastry with 2 or 3 tsp. of butter. Lay another sheet on top. Again, spread with 2 to 3 tsp. of butter. Continue until there are 8 layers of filo in the pan.

Spread the spinach mixture on top of the filo. Place another layer of filo on top, coat with butter, and repeat, as before, until there are 8 layers. With scissors, trim the excess filo from around the edges of the dish. Brush top with remaining butter.

Bake at 300° F for 1 hour or until pastry is golden brown. Cut into squares and serve hot or at room temperature.

—*Carol Gasken*

Salmon Soufflé

A light yet filling supper dish, salmon soufflé is nicely complemented with hot biscuits and a tossed salad.

3 Tbsp. butter
3 Tbsp. flour
1 cup milk
1 tsp. salt
Pepper
6-oz. can salmon
3 eggs, separated

Melt the butter, add flour, milk, salt and pepper. Boil until thick, then remove from heat. Add salmon and slightly beaten yolks. Beat egg whites and fold in. Pour into well greased soufflé dish or other deep baking dish. Bake at 350° F for 20 to 25 minutes, or until golden brown.

Serves 2 to 3.

—*Lynda Howson*

Spinach Cream Cheese Pie

Although this pie has no crust, the wheat germ bakes to a crispy texture, resulting in a quiche-like dish.

10 oz. spinach
8 oz. cream cheese
1 Tbsp. minced onion
Dash nutmeg
6 eggs
Wheat germ
¼ lb. Cheddar cheese, sliced
Paprika
1 Tbsp. flour
1 tsp. water

Cook spinach, drain and press out excess water. Soften cream cheese and add spinach, onion and nutmeg. Beat 5 of the eggs and stir into the spinach mixture. Grease sides and bottom of a pie plate, sprinkle it with wheat germ and pour in spinach mixture. Cover with cheese slices and sprinkle with paprika. Beat remaining egg with flour and water and pour over the cheese. Bake at 350° F for 35 to 45 minutes, until top is lightly browned.

Serves 4.

—*Laura Poitras*

Egg and Cheese Puffs

Light, satisfying and tasty, these make an interesting addition to a brunch menu.

4 eggs
1 Tbsp. chopped onion
⅓ cup flour
½ tsp. salt
1 tsp. baking powder
⅓ cup sharp Cheddar
    cheese, cut into ¼-inch
    cubes
⅓ cup shortening

Beat eggs and combine with onion, flour, salt and baking powder. Add cheese.

Heat shortening in a frying pan. Drop batter into pan using a tablespoon and fry the puffs, turning them over until golden brown on both sides.

Serves 2.

—*Lew Harpelle*

Summer Omelette

An omelette can contain almost any filling, including cooked meats and seafood. The two presented here make use of summer vegetables. Variations could include tomatoes, green pepper or other vegetables.

6 eggs
⅓ cup milk
Salt & pepper
¼-½ cup chopped celery
2-3 Tbsp. chopped onion
¼ cup sliced mushrooms
¼-½ cup grated Cheddar or
    Swiss cheese

Beat together eggs, milk, salt and pepper. Lightly sauté celery, onion and mushrooms. Add to egg mixture along with the cheese. Mix well and pour into greased 8-inch square cake pan. Bake at 350° F for approximately 30 minutes or until knife comes out clean. Serves 4.

Zucchini Omelette

Zucchini recipes are always welcome. This one, an Italian standard, is a boon for those overburdened with both zucchini and eggs.

2 small zucchini
2 Tbsp. cooking oil
2 eggs
Salt & pepper
½ tsp. dried oregano
½ cup grated Romano or
    Parmesan cheese

Cut zucchini into ⅛-inch slices. Sauté in hot oil in a small cast-iron frying pan, stirring constantly, until golden brown. Reduce heat to medium low. Beat eggs with wire whisk until well blended but not frothy, and add to zucchini in pan. Sprinkle with remaining ingredients.

Cook, covered, until egg is set. Fold omelette in half, allow to cook a few seconds longer, then remove to warmed plate and cut into wedges.

Serves 2.

—*Dorothy Farniloe*

Crêpes

The variety of fillings for crêpes is almost unlimited. A few suggestions follow the crêpe batter recipe. Crêpes may be served hot or cold, as a main course or as a dessert.

¾ cup flour
Salt
1 egg yolk
1 egg
1¼ cups milk
1 Tbsp. melted butter or
    light oil

Sift the flour into blender or mixing bowl. Add salt, egg yolk, whole egg and half the milk. Blend for 1 minute or stir with a wire whisk until smooth. Add the rest of the milk and the melted butter or oil.

Let rest, refrigerated, for 1 hour.

To cook, heat 1 Tbsp. butter in small, heavy frying pan. When bubbling, pour in a very small amount of batter and immediately swirl pan to coat. The thinner the crêpe the better.

Cook over high heat for approximately 1 minute, or until crêpe is lightly browned and firm enough to flip with a spatula. Brown other side and remove to a warmed plate. Continue cooking and stacking crêpes until batter is used up. No additional greasing should be necessary. The crêpes will not stick together when stacked. If the first few crêpes do not turn out, do not become discouraged — it often takes a little time to season the pan and to refine the swirling technique.

Makes 12 crêpes.

Cooked crêpes may be kept refrigerated for several days or frozen for several months. Crêpe batter may be refrigerated overnight, but it may need to be thinned with 1-2 Tbsp. milk when used.

—*Jeanne Nugent*

Crêpe Filling Ideas

Meat
    Chicken in Cream Sauce
    Beef Stroganoff
    Boeuf Bourguignon
    Ham and Cheese
    Chicken Divan
Seafood
    Coquilles Saint Jacques
    Shrimp Curry
    Sole Amandine
    Lobster Newburg
    Seafood Creole
Vegetable
    Broccoli in Cheese Sauce
    Creamed Spinach
    Green Beans Amandine
    Stir-Fried Snow Peas
Dessert
    Any fresh fruit topped with
      whipped cream or yogurt
    Vanilla ice cream topped
      with hot chocolate sauce
    Cottage cheese with fruit
      or nuts

To serve, place a crêpe flat on a plate, put filling in centre and fold 2 sides over it.

Pancake Mix

This homemade pancake mix, as well as being convenient, has the additional charm of flexibility — it can be tailor-made to suit individual tastes by using, for example, whole wheat flour, wheat germ or buttermilk flour.

12 cups flour
4 cups milk powder
¾ cup baking powder
¾ cup sugar
2 Tbsp. salt

Mix well and store in airtight containers.

Makes 16 cups mix.

To use: Combine 1½ cups mix, 1 cup water, 1 egg and 2 Tbsp. oil.

Makes 8 pancakes.

—*Dawn Livingstone*

Bran Pancakes

1 cup bran
1 cup whole wheat flour
1 cup unbleached white flour
½ cup raisins (optional)
¼ cup brown sugar
1 Tbsp. baking powder
½ tsp. salt
2½ cups milk
2 eggs
¼ cup oil

In a large mixing bowl, combine flour, bran, raisins, sugar, baking powder and salt, and mix well.

In a small bowl, beat milk, eggs and oil until blended. Add to flour mixture and mix well.

Pour batter, using about ⅓ cup for each pancake, into a hot, greased frying pan. Cook, turning once, until both sides are golden brown.

Serves 5 to 6.

—*Marnie Horton*

A Quick Pancake

A cross between a pancake and an omelette, this has a light texture and a pleasant, nutty flavour. Fresh fruit, chopped, sautéed in butter and brown sugar and placed in the bottom of the pan, can provide a delicious variation.

2 eggs, separated
1 cup yogurt
1 cup quick cooking oats
1 Tbsp. sugar
¼ tsp. baking soda
¼ tsp. baking powder
¼ tsp. salt
1 Tbsp. butter

Beat egg yolks well and stir in yogurt. Add dry ingredients and mix well. Beat egg whites until stiff, then gently fold into batter.

Melt butter in a large frying pan which can be used in the oven. Spoon batter into pan and bake for 20 minutes at 350° F.

Serve with honey or jam.

—*Carol Frost*

Egg Casserole

A hearty, substantial casserole of particular interest to garlic lovers, this dish makes a good brunch when you have a lot of visitors.

12 eggs
½ lb. bacon
¼ cup butter
¼ cup flour
1 cup light cream
1 cup milk
1 lb. sharp Cheddar cheese, grated
2 small cloves garlic, crushed
¼ tsp. thyme
¼ tsp. marjoram
¼ tsp. basil
¼ tsp. chopped parsley
¾ cup bread crumbs

Hard boil the eggs, peel and slice them. Broil the bacon until crisp, drain and crumble. Melt butter, stir in flour and gradually mix in cream and milk. Heat, stirring constantly, until sauce thickens. Add cheese and seasonings. Pour half the sauce into a well-greased casserole dish. Add the eggs as the next layer, then the bacon. Top with the rest of the sauce and sprinkle bread crumbs over it. Bake at 350° F for 30 minutes.

Serves 8 to 10.

—*Jody Schwindt*

Potato Pancakes

4 medium raw potatoes, shredded
Salt & pepper
3 Tbsp. flour
1 egg, beaten
¼ cup grated onion
½ cup grated Cheddar cheese
Heavy cream
Butter

Mix shredded potatoes with flour, egg, onion, cheese, salt and pepper. Add enough cream to make a moist but not wet batter.

Heat butter in a heavy skillet and drop batter by spoonfuls into the hot fat. Fry until both sides of pancakes are golden brown, then slide onto a cookie sheet. Bake at 400° F for 4 minutes.

Serve hot with butter and maple syrup.

Serves 4 to 6.

—*Pearl Lentz*

Curried Eggs

Good for brunch, lunch or dinner, this attractive and easy-to-prepare dish hints at the exotic.

2 Tbsp. butter
2 Tbsp. flour
1 cup milk
1 tsp. curry powder
½ cup peas
4 hard-boiled eggs, chopped into bite-sized pieces

Melt butter and stir in flour. Add milk gradually, stirring constantly. Add curry powder and peas. Cook over low heat, still stirring, until peas are soft. Gently fold in eggs. Serve on toast points.

Serves 4.

—*Mrs. L.H. Lowther*

Eggs Kariel

Tasty, nutritious and quick to prepare, this serve-it-anytime dish can be easily adjusted to suit the number of hungry people present.

1 lb. fresh spinach
8 eggs
1 cup Cheddar cheese

Clean and rinse spinach. Place in a wide saucepan containing enough water to cover bottom of the pan, cover and steam briefly — until spinach is wilted.

Make hollows in spinach and break eggs into them. Replace cover and continue to steam until eggs are poached. Sprinkle cheese over top, recover, and cook until cheese is melted.

Serves 4 for lunch, 8 for breakfast.

—*N. Kariel*

Baked Eggs

A hearty, tasty breakfast or brunch dish, this can be prepared the night before, ready to pop into the oven in the morning.

1 lb. ground sausage meat or ham
6 eggs
2 cups milk
2 slices bread, trimmed & cubed
1 tsp. dry mustard
1 cup grated mild cheese

Brown sausage meat or ham and drain on towels. Beat eggs and combine all ingredients in a 9" x 13" baking dish. Bake at 350° F for 45 minutes or until lightly browned.

Serves 6.

—*Mrs. J. Hall-Armstrong*

Egg McRivers

2 English muffins split, toasted & buttered
4 slices cooked ham
4 poached eggs
½ cup Cheddar cheese, grated

Place English muffins on a cookie sheet. On each, place a slice of ham and a poached egg, and sprinkle Cheddar cheese on top. Broil until cheese is bubbly.

Serves 4.

—*Deborah Rivers*

Eggs Mayonnaise

4 eggs
Lettuce
½ cup mayonnaise
1 egg yolk
1 Tbsp. oil
Parsley
Grated carrot
Dash cayenne pepper

Boil eggs until they are semi-hard (5 minutes). Shell and slice them in half lengthwise and place them yolk side down on crisp lettuce leaves.

Combine mayonnaise, egg yolk and oil. Mix well and spoon over the eggs. Sprinkle with parsley, carrot and cayenne pepper.

Serves 4.

—*Sandra James-Mitchell*

Devilled Tofu

It's not just healthy, it looks pretty and tastes good. Try this spread on open-faced sandwiches with alfalfa sprouts, cucumber and tomato.

18 oz. (3 cakes) tofu
2 stalks celery, finely chopped
3-4 green onions, finely chopped
1 cup mayonnaise
3 Tbsp. vinegar
1 tsp. celery seed
¾ tsp. salt
1 tsp. garlic powder
½ tsp. dry mustard
1¼ tsp. turmeric

Slice tofu lengthwise and press with paper towels to remove water. Chop finely and mix with celery and onions.

Combine mayonnaise, vinegar and remaining ingredients, then stir into the tofu and vegetable mixture. Chill.

Makes 3 cups.

—*Sass'frass Saloon*

Scotch Eggs

Hot or cold, these eggs are delicious as hors d'oeuvres, snacks or accompaniments to salads.

12 hard-boiled eggs, peeled
½ cup flour
2 lbs. skinless sausage meat
1 egg
1 Tbsp. water
Fine bread crumbs or quick
   cooking rolled oats

Roll cooked eggs in flour. With floured hands, coat each egg with sausage meat.

Combine raw egg and water and beat together. Dip sausage-covered eggs into egg mixture, then roll in bread crumbs.

Fry in deep fat until golden brown. If preferred, eggs can be cooked in shallow fat or baked at 350° F until the bread crumbs are crisp and the meat is thoroughly cooked.

—*Sherri McMillan*

Eggs Florentine

Another brunch, lunch or dinner favourite, this is a delicious and attractive dish.

2 Tbsp. butter
1 Tbsp. minced onion
1½ tsp. flour
¼ tsp. salt
Pepper & nutmeg
1 cup milk
¼ cup Parmesan cheese
1 pkg. spinach
4 eggs
Parmesan cheese

Sauté onion in melted butter. Add flour, salt, pepper and nutmeg and stir until smooth. Blend in milk, bring to a boil, then reduce heat and simmer, stirring constantly, for 3 minutes. Add ¼ cup Parmesan cheese.

Cook and drain spinach and combine with milk mixture. Turn into a shallow baking dish.

Poach the eggs and arrange them on top of the spinach mixture. Sprinkle with Parmesan cheese and place under the broiler just long enough to melt the cheese.

Serves 4.

—*Brenda Eckstein*

Ticini

The sardines give this dish a decidedly sharp and salty flavour, but blend well with the eggs to make a tasty spread.

4 hard-boiled eggs
4-oz. tin sardines, drained
1½ Tbsp. mayonnaise
2 Tbsp. lemon juice
2 tsp. Worcestershire sauce
Salt & pepper

Chop eggs and sardines coarsely. Combine and add remaining ingredients. Chill. Garnish with paprika and fresh parsley and serve with crackers or rye bread.

Makes 2 cups.

—*Nita Hunton*

Egg Salad

This cool, refreshing spread is good served on whole wheat bread, pita bread, sesame crackers, or wrapped in spinach or lettuce leaves.

5 hard-boiled eggs
⅓ cup finely chopped carrot
⅓ cup finely chopped celery
⅓ cup finely chopped onion
½ cup toasted sunflower
   seeds
½ cup toasted sesame seeds,
   ground
½ cup ricotta cheese
¼ cup yogurt
¼ cup mayonnaise
Salt
Paprika

Mash the eggs in a bowl. Add other ingredients and mix well. Refrigerate for several hours before serving.

Serves 4 to 6.

—*N. Burk*

Eggs Molière

4 eggs
4 tomatoes
2 Tbsp. oil
½ lb. mushrooms, thinly
sliced
2 scallions, chopped
2 Tbsp. flour
1½ cups hot chicken stock
Salt & pepper

Boil eggs until they can be peeled but are not hard cooked, about 5 minutes. Peel and set aside.

Cut off the tops of the tomatoes and hollow them out with a spoon. Season with salt and pepper and place in an ovenproof baking dish. Bake for 10 minutes at 375° F and set aside.

Heat the oil in a saucepan. Add the mushrooms and the scallions, season to taste and cook over medium heat for 3 to 4 minutes. Stir in the flour and continue to cook for 2 to 3 minutes. Add the hot chicken stock and correct seasoning. Cook over low heat for another 15 minutes.

Place 1 peeled egg inside each cooked tomato shell. Cover with the sauce and bake for 7 to 8 minutes. Garnish with parsley.

Serves 4.

—Brenda Eckstein

Tofu Parmesan

2 two-inch cubes tofu, thinly
sliced
2 Tbsp. butter
2-4 Tbsp. tamari sauce
2 Tbsp. oil
2 cloves garlic
1 medium zucchini, sliced
½ lb. mushrooms, sliced
1 cup tomato sauce
½ lb. mozzarella cheese,
thinly sliced
Parmesan cheese

Brown tofu slices in butter and tamari sauce. When crisp, line the bottom of a buttered shallow casserole dish.

Sauté garlic in oil, then discard garlic. Add zucchini and mushrooms to oil and lightly brown. Remove with a slotted spoon and spread over tofu.

Cover with tomato sauce and then Mozzarella cheese. Sprinkle with Parmesan cheese and bake, covered, at 350° F until bubbly — 10 to 15 minutes.

Serves 4.

—Jane Pugh

Rarebit Fondue on Toast

An adaptation of a traditional fondue recipe, this rarebit has a very satisfying and pleasantly garlicky flavour.

8 thick slices whole wheat
bread
Butter
½ lb. mushrooms, sliced
½ cup finely chopped onion
2 cups dry white wine
½ clove garlic, chopped
½ lb. Gruyère cheese, grated
2 Tbsp. or more whole wheat
flour
Freshly ground pepper

Butter bread on both sides and bake at 400° F for 5 to 8 minutes — until golden brown on both sides.

Sauté mushrooms and onion in butter until the onion is soft. Add garlic and wine. Mix flour and cheese and add to the hot wine mixture, 1 handful at a time, stirring until each addition of cheese melts. Cook, stirring, over low heat until the sauce bubbles and thickens. Season with pepper.

Place the toast on individual serving plates and top with sauce.

Serves 4.

—Janet Flewelling

Zucchini Egg Foo Yung

4 medium unpeeled
  zucchini, grated
3 eggs, beaten
¼ cup flour or ½ cup wheat
  germ
¼ tsp. garlic powder
1 tsp. salt
1 onion, grated
1 cup vegetable stock
2 Tbsp. soya sauce
1 Tbsp. cornstarch

Mix together zucchini, egg, flour or wheat germ, garlic powder, salt and onion. Drop by tablespoonfuls into hot oiled skillet and fry, turning once, until golden brown on both sides. Combine remaining ingredients in a saucepan and cook, stirring, until thickened. Arrange zucchini patties on a platter and top with sauce. Serves 4 to 6.

—*Chris Nofziger*

Kafkades

These traditional Greek patties are delicious as well as wholesome.

2 cups cottage cheese
2 egg yolks
1 cup flour
2 cups loosely packed
  bite-sized spinach
Olive oil
Salt & pepper

Combine cottage cheese, egg yolks and flour. Mix well, if necessary, adding more flour, until mixture becomes a thick paste. Add spinach.

In a large skillet, heat oil to cover the bottom of the pan to a medium high temperature. For each patty, drop batter from a large spoon onto the pan. Cook until golden brown on one side, then turn carefully and cook until the other side is done. Season with salt and pepper.

Makes 10 to 12 patties.

—*Susan Gammon*

Baked Fondue

⅔ cup butter
2 cloves garlic
1 tsp. dry mustard
1 loaf French or Italian bread
3 cups grated Swiss cheese
3 Tbsp. grated onion
1½ tsp. salt
1 tsp. paprika
¼ cup flour
3 cups milk
1 cup dry white wine
3 eggs, beaten

In small bowl, cream ⅓ cup butter with garlic and ½ tsp. mustard until blended.

Remove ends of bread and cut loaf into ¼-inch slices. Spread with butter mixture and place, buttered side down, in bottom and along sides of heavy casserole dish.

In large bowl, combine cheese, onion, salt, paprika and remaining mustard. Toss until well blended.

Melt remaining butter in heavy saucepan. Remove from heat, stir in flour and return to heat. Gradually stir in milk and bring to a boil. Reduce heat and stir in wine. Add a little hot mixture to the eggs, stir and pour back into hot milk.

Arrange alternate layers of cheese mixture, egg mixture and remaining bread slices, ending with bread, buttered side up.

Refrigerate, covered, overnight or all day. Bake at 350° F for 35 to 45 minutes, until puffy and golden brown.

—*Dorothy Hurst*

Cheese Snacks

These tasty instant canapes can be prepared ahead of time, frozen, brought out and baked as the need or the inclination arises.

1 loaf unsliced whole wheat bread
¾ cup butter, softened
2 egg whites
½ lb. old Cheddar cheese, grated
Salt
½ tsp. dry mustard

Cut bread into bite-sized pieces.

Beat butter, egg whites, cheese, salt and mustard together until creamy and smooth — about 5 minutes. Spread cheese mixture on bread.

Freeze on a cookie sheet, then pack into plastic bags to store.

To serve, bake at 350° F for 8 to 10 minutes, until bubbly. Serve warm.

—Marie Blundell

Apple 'n' Cheese Nibbles

This is an unusual snack, tangy and flavourful, which can be prepared ahead of time and simply heated when ready to serve.

2 McIntosh apples
2 Tbsp. sweet butter
1 tsp. lemon juice
1 cup grated Cheddar cheese
Freshly ground pepper
16 slices whole wheat bread

Peel, core and slice apples. Add, with lemon juice, to melted butter in a saucepan and simmer over medium heat until apples are soft — do not let them brown. Add cheese and pepper and stir just to mix. Cook until cheese melts.

Cut a 3- to 3½-inch round from each slice of bread and toast. Place on a cookie sheet and top with the apple and cheese mixture. Cover and keep cool until serving time.

To serve, run under broiler, 3 inches away from heat, until brown.

Makes 16 rounds.

—Shirley Hill

Onion Cheese Squares

Delicious as a main course for lunch or dinner, these squares are inexpensive and simple to make.

¾ cup chopped onion
2 Tbsp. butter
¾ cup scalded milk
2 eggs, beaten
1 cup grated Cheddar cheese
Salt & pepper
¼ cup pimento, diced *or* 1 tomato, chopped
2 Tbsp. chopped fresh parsley
2 Tbsp. wheat germ
2 Tbsp. (or more) bread crumbs
Sesame seeds

Sauté onion in butter until soft and golden. Remove from heat. Combine milk and eggs and add to onion. Add all remaining ingredients except sesame seeds. If mixture seems very runny, add extra bread crumbs. Pour into greased 8-inch pie plate. Sprinkle with sesame seeds. Bake at 325° F for 45 minutes, or until knife inserted into centre comes out clean.

—Pam Collacott

Cheese & Tomato Bake

5 slices bacon
4 Tbsp. flour
3 cups tomato juice
1 tsp. salt
½ small onion, minced
1 cup grated Cheddar cheese
3 cups cooked whole wheat
¼ cup buttered bread
    crumbs

Fry bacon until lightly browned. Cut into ½-inch pieces and set aside. Reserve 1 Tbsp. of the fat.

Stir flour into reserved bacon fat. Add tomato juice, salt and onion and cook, stirring, until thickened. Remove from heat and add the bacon and three-quarters of the cheese.

Place wheat in a greased baking dish and pour the tomato mixture over it. Sprinkle with bread crumbs and remaining cheese. Bake at 350° F for 45 minutes.

Serves 4 to 6.

—*Joanne Ramsy*

Corn, Cheese & Chili Pie

2 tsp. shortening
3 large eggs
8½-oz. can creamed corn
1½ cups corn kernels
½ cup butter, melted
½ cup corn meal
1 cup sour cream
¼ lb. Monterey Jack cheese,
    cut in ½-inch cubes
¼ lb. sharp Cheddar cheese,
    cut in ½-inch cubes
Diced green chilies to taste
½ tsp. salt
¼ tsp. Worcestershire sauce

Grease 9-inch pie plate with shortening. In a large bowl, beat eggs. Add remaining ingredients and mix well. Pour into pie plate and bake at 350° F for 1 hour, until pie is firm in centre.

Serves 6.

—*Veronica Green*

Potato Cheese Casserole

½ cup milk
2 large eggs, beaten
2 cups mashed potatoes
1-2 onions, chopped
½-¾ cup grated Parmesan
    cheese
4 Tbsp. wheat germ

Combine milk, eggs, potatoes and onions. Pour into a 9-inch square buttered pan and sprinkle with Parmesan cheese and wheat germ. Bake at 350° F for 30 minutes, until top is golden brown.

Serves 4 to 6.

—*Richard & Elaine Domsy*

Sunflower Special

This childhood invention of John Travers, the owner of The Sunflower Restaurant, is the restaurant's most popular sandwich.

Coat one slice of lightly buttered whole wheat toast with mayonnaise. Layer, in order listed, all or any of chopped green onions, alfalfa sprouts, tomato slices, sliced old Cheddar cheese and a sprinkling of sunflower seeds.

Broil until cheese is melted and seeds are browned.

Serves 1.

—*The Sunflower Restaurant*

Almond Cheese Spread

½ cup almonds, with skins
8 oz. cream cheese, softened
½ cup mayonnaise
5 slices bacon
1 Tbsp. chopped green onion
1 Tbsp. chopped celery
1 Tbsp. green pepper
½ tsp. dill weed
⅛ tsp. pepper

Place almonds on cookie sheet and bake at 350° F for 20 to 25 minutes. Fry bacon until crisp; crumble.

Beat cream cheese, then gradually stir in mayonnaise. Add bacon, vegetables and seasonings. Mix well, cover and chill overnight.

When chilled, cover top surface with almonds. Serve with crackers and raw vegetables.

Makes about 1¼ cups.

—*Genie & Peter Suffel*

Potted Cheese

This cheese spread has a delicious blue cheese flavour, and is best served with crackers or as a dip for raw vegetables.

8 oz. cream cheese
½ cup soft margarine
1 tsp. Worcestershire sauce
2 cups finely shredded
    Gouda, Gruyère or
    Cheddar cheese
¼ tsp. garlic powder
¼ lb. crumbled blue cheese
¼ cup grated Parmesan
    cheese
Chopped pecans

Beat first 5 ingredients together until well blended. Work in remaining cheeses. Press into attractive serving dish and sprinkle with pecans. Cover well and keep chilled. Will keep refrigerated for up to 3 weeks.

—*Pamela England*

Cheddar Cheese Ball

½ lb. old Cheddar cheese,
    grated
½ cup ground pecans
½ small green pepper, finely
    chopped
1 stalk celery, finely chopped
2 green onions, finely
    chopped
4 oz. cream cheese, at room
    temperature

Combine Cheddar cheese, pecans and vegetables. Mix in cream cheese. If too dry to work with, add a small amount of milk, yogurt or beer. Form into a ball and sprinkle with chopped nuts or parsley.

Chill well before serving.

Makes 2 cups.

—*Joan Hoepner*

Gouda Sesame Log

3 cups coarsely grated
    Gouda cheese
1 cup coarsely grated
    ice-cold butter
1 tsp. hot mustard
2 Tbsp. whiskey
¾ cup toasted sesame seeds

Cream cheese and butter together until well blended. Mix in mustard and whiskey. Shape into log and roll in sesame seeds. Refrigerate for 24 hours before serving.

Makes 3 to 4 cups.

—*Kumari Campbell*

Mrs. Shaver's Cheese Ball

3 cups grated Cheddar
    cheese
8 oz. cream cheese
¼ cup sour cream
¼ cup chopped green onion
Dash Tabasco &
    Worcestershire sauce
Caraway seeds

Soften cream cheese and thoroughly blend in the rest of the ingredients except the caraway seeds. Shape into a ball, place on a serving dish and sprinkle with caraway seeds. Refrigerate.

Makes 4 to 5 cups.

—*Laurie Shaver*

Hot Cheese Dip

2 cups light cream
2 tsp. dry mustard
1 Tbsp. Worcestershire
    sauce
1 clove garlic, cut in half
3 Tbsp. flour
6 cups coarsely grated sharp
    Cheddar cheese
¼ tsp. salt
2 Tbsp. sherry

In a glass or enamel saucepan, heat cream, mustard, Worcestershire sauce and garlic. Mix cheese with flour, and drop, a handful at a time, into the hot cream. Cook over low heat, stirring with a wooden spoon, until cheese is melted and mixture is smooth. Add salt and sherry. If only a mild hint of garlic is desired, remove it now from the dip.

Pour dip into a chafing dish or heavy fondue pot and serve with such dunking delights as raw vegetables, chunks of good fresh bread or cooked shrimp.

Makes 4 to 6 cups.

—*Dorothy Hurst*

Party Cheese Ball

½ lb. mild Cheddar cheese,
   grated
½ lb. Jack cheese, grated
8 oz. cream cheese
Salt & pepper
Nutmeg & paprika
¼ tsp. parsley
½ tsp. Worcestershire sauce
2 oz. chopped walnuts

Allow cheeses to reach room
temperature. Blend together
cream cheese, Cheddar cheese
and Jack cheese. Add
seasonings and blend well.

Form cheese into a ball on a
serving dish and cover with
walnuts. Refrigerate until 2
hours before serving.

Makes 3 cups.

—*Johanna Vanderheyden*

Cheese Spread

*Devised as a substitute for the
commercial varieties, this
versatile spread can be used for
anything from sandwiches to
canapés. For variety, virtually
any flavouring you like with
cheese may be added: onion,
garlic, parsley, oregano or curry
to mention a few.*

½ lb. sharp Cheddar cheese,
   grated
1 tsp. dry mustard
4 tsp. cornstarch
½ tsp. salt
1 cup water
⅓ cup powdered milk
1 tsp. Worcestershire sauce

Melt cheese in the top of a
double boiler. Combine mustard,
cornstarch and salt. Add a little
water and mix into a paste.
Gradually stir in the rest of the
water, then add milk powder and
Worcestershire sauce. Stir this
mixture into the cheese and
cook until thick. Pour into jars
and refrigerate.

Makes 2 cups.

—*Janet Caldwell*

Boursin

*A homemade recipe for this
delicate cheese spread is a
boon to addicts, since it is easy
to make and considerably less
expensive than the
commercially produced
versions.*

16 oz. cream cheese
¼ cup mayonnaise
2 tsp. Dijon mustard
2 Tbsp. finely chopped
   chives
2 Tbsp. finely chopped dill
1 clove garlic, minced

Soften cheese, then, using an
electric mixer, thoroughly blend
in mayonnaise, mustard, chives,
dill and garlic. Spoon into a
small serving bowl, cover and
refrigerate for 24 hours.

Serve with bagels, crackers,
Melba toast, rye bread,
pumpernickel bread, celery,
mushrooms or other raw
vegetables.

Makes 2½ cups.

—*Shirley Hill*

Herbed Cheese Dip

8 oz. cream cheese, softened
½ cup butter, softened
2 cloves garlic, minced
½ tsp. salt
¼ tsp. pepper
¼ cup chopped fresh parsley

Beat cream cheese and butter
with electric mixer until well
mixed and airy. Beat in
remaining ingredients. Spoon
into a mould lined with plastic
wrap and chill for several hours.
Unmould and serve with raw
vegetables or crackers.

Makes 1½ to 2 cups.

Val's Onion Cheese Pie

CRUST:
¾ cup flour
½ tsp. salt
½ tsp. dry mustard
1 cup grated sharp Cheddar
  cheese
½-1 cup melted butter
FILLING:
2 cups thinly sliced onions
2 Tbsp. butter
1 cup cooked thin egg
  noodles
2 eggs
1 cup hot milk
1 cup grated Cheddar cheese
Salt & pepper

To make crust, mix together flour, salt, mustard and cheese. Slowly pour in melted butter until a workable dough results. Press into a deep 9-inch pie plate.

For filling, sauté onions in butter and add noodles. Place in pie shell. Beat eggs, then add hot milk and cheese while continuing to beat. Add salt and pepper to taste. Pour over onion and noodle mixture. Bake at 350° F for 40 minutes.

Serves 6 to 8.

—Kirsten McDougall

Tomato Cheese Pie

FILLING:
2 Tbsp. butter
¼ cup chopped green onions
1 cup bread crumbs
¼ cup chopped parsley
1 tsp. basil
⅛ tsp. salt
Pepper
10 firm red tomatoes, peeled
TOPPING:
1 cup flour
1½ tsp. baking powder
½ tsp. salt
2 Tbsp. butter
¼ cup milk
½ cup grated Cheddar
  cheese

Melt butter in skillet. Add onions and cook for 3 or 4 minutes. Stir in bread crumbs and cook until golden. Remove from heat; stir in parsley, basil, salt and pepper.

Cut tomatoes into slices ½-inch thick. Place half the slices in greased pie plate. Sprinkle with half the bread crumb mixture. Repeat.

To make the topping, sift together flour, baking powder and salt. Cut in butter to make fine crumbs. Add milk to make a soft dough, then work in cheese. Knead until smooth, wrap and refrigerate for 1 hour. On lightly floured surface, roll dough to a 9-by-12-inch rectangle, ½-inch thick. Cut into 12 strips ½-inch wide. Make lattice top for pie, crimping edges to pan. Bake at 350° F for 30 to 35 minutes, or until crust is golden.

Serves 6 to 8.

—Jill Leary

Cauliflower Cheese Pie

2 cups packed, grated
  potatoes
1 tsp. salt
3 eggs
¼ cup grated onion
1 cup chopped onion
1 clove garlic, minced
3 Tbsp. butter
Thyme
Pepper
Paprika
½ tsp. basil
1 cauliflower, broken into
  florets
1 heaping cup grated
  Cheddar cheese
¼ cup milk

Salt the grated potatoes with ½ tsp. salt. Let stand for 10 minutes, then squeeze out excess water. Beat 1 egg and add along with grated onion. Pat into well-oiled pie plate and bake at 375° F for 30 minutes or until golden brown.

Sauté chopped onion and garlic in butter. Add herbs (including ½ tsp. salt) and cauliflower and cook for 10 minutes. Spread half the cheese in pie plate, then cauliflower mixture, then remaining cheese. Beat together 2 remaining eggs and milk and pour over all.

Bake at 375°F for 30 to 40 minutes, or until set.

Serves 4.

—Nancy Beltgens

Spinach Feta Cheese Quiche

Pastry for 9-inch pie shell
2 Tbsp. olive oil
½ cup finely chopped
   mushrooms
1 shallot, chopped
¼ cup pine nuts
2 cups finely chopped
   spinach
2 eggs, beaten
¼ lb. feta cheese, crumbled
¼ cup milk
Parmesan cheese
Nutmeg

Heat oil and sauté mushrooms, shallot and pine nuts. Steam spinach until limp but still bright green. Beat together eggs, feta cheese and milk. Add vegetables and spoon into pastry-lined pie plate. Top with Parmesan cheese and nutmeg. Bake at 350° F for 40 to 45 minutes.

Serves 4 to 6.

—P.S. Reynolds

Spinach Quiche

Pastry for 9-inch pie shell
2 Tbsp. finely chopped onion
1 cup grated cheese
2 eggs
1 cup yogurt
1 Tbsp. flour
½ tsp. salt
¼ tsp. pepper
Dash nutmeg
1 cup chopped cooked
   spinach

Bake crust at 450° F for 10 minutes. Let cool and sprinkle onion and cheese over crust.

Beat eggs, then add yogurt, flour and seasonings. Stir well. Add and stir in spinach. Pour this mixture into the baked pie shell.

Bake at 450° F for 15 minutes. Reduce heat to 350° F and bake for 30 minutes longer.

Serves 4 to 6.

—Susan Lord

Cheese Pie

1 egg
Salt & pepper
1 cup grated cheese
1 cup milk
¾ cup flour

Butter a 9-inch pie plate. Blend milk, flour, egg, salt and pepper. Stir in half of cheese. Pour into pie plate and bake at 350° F until puffed and golden, about 25 minutes. Sprinkle remaining cheese over top. Continue baking until cheese melts — 3 to 4 minutes. Serve immediately.

Serves 2.

—Barb Alguire

Delicious Onion Quiche

Pastry for 9-inch pie shell
4-6 onions
4 Tbsp. butter
1 tsp. salt
1 tsp. pepper
1 cup grated Gruyère cheese
¾ cup milk
¾ cup whipping cream
6 eggs

Line pie plate with pastry and bake at 400° F for 5 minutes. Set aside. Thinly slice onions and cook in butter over medium heat until transparent. Add salt and pepper; mix and drain. Spread over bottom of pie shell. Add cheese. Mix together milk, cream and eggs and pour over onions. Bake at 350° F for 30 minutes, or until custard is set.

Serves 6 to 8.

—Jane Cardona

Carrot Quiche

Pastry for 9-inch pie shell
4 cups sliced carrots,
    cooked
4 eggs
¼ cup whipping cream
1 tsp. salt
¼ tsp. pepper
¼ tsp. nutmeg
1 cup grated Swiss cheese

Line pie plate with pastry and arrange carrots in shell. Beat together eggs and cream. Mix in salt, pepper, nutmeg and cheese and pour over carrots.

Bake at 425° F for 10 minutes. Reduce heat to 350° F and bake for another 30 to 35 minutes. Let stand for 10 minutes before serving.

Serves 6.

—Elizabeth Clayton Paul

Potato Pie

Pastry for 10-inch pie shell
1 lb. cottage cheese
2 cups mashed potatoes
½ cup sour cream
2 eggs
2 tsp. salt
⅛ tsp. cayenne
½ cup scallions, sliced
3 Tbsp. grated Parmesan
    cheese

Line pie plate with pastry. Process cottage cheese in blender until smooth, then beat in mashed potatoes. Beat in sour cream, eggs, salt and cayenne. Stir in scallions. Spoon into pastry shell and sprinkle with cheese.

Bake at 450° F for 50 minutes or until golden brown.

Serves 4 to 6.

—Marsha Plewes

Vegetable Cheese Pie

Pastry for 9-inch pie shell
1½ cups broccoli, cut into
    bite-sized pieces
1½ cups cauliflower, cut into
    bite-sized pieces
1 cup sliced carrots
1½ cups sliced mushrooms
1 Tbsp. butter
1 Tbsp. vegetable oil
3 Tbsp. whole wheat flour
1 cup milk
Salt & pepper
Thyme
1 cup shredded Swiss or
    Cheddar cheese

Steam broccoli, cauliflower and carrots until tender but crisp; drain and arrange in pie shell. Sauté mushrooms in butter and oil. Stir in flour and cook for about 1 minute. Add milk slowly and bring to a boil, stirring constantly. Cook for about 2 minutes.

Remove from heat; add seasonings and half the cheese, stirring until smooth. Pour sauce over vegetables. Sprinkle with remaining cheese.

Bake at 425° F until sauce is bubbly and cheese is golden brown — about 20 minutes.

Serves 4.

—Lise Gall

Eggplant Tomato Quiche

Pastry for 9-inch pie shell
1 cup chopped tomatoes
1 Tbsp. chopped parsley
½ tsp. oregano
½ tsp. basil
1 Tbsp. butter
½ cup chopped mushrooms
1 clove garlic, minced
1 shallot, chopped
1 small eggplant, unpeeled
3 eggs
1 cup grated Cheddar cheese
Bread crumbs

Simmer tomatoes, parsley, oregano and basil for 20 minutes. Heat butter and sauté mushrooms, garlic and shallot. Add to tomato mixture and let cool.

Thinly slice unpeeled eggplant and bake at 350° F for 10 minutes. Line pie plate with pastry and cover with eggplant slices.

Beat eggs and mix with tomatoes. Spoon half of this over eggplant, then add ½ cup cheese. Repeat layers and top with bread crumbs. Bake at 375° F for 40 to 45 minutes.

Serves 6 to 8.

—P.S. Reynolds

Chicken Quiche

Pastry for 9-inch pie shell
3 eggs
3 Tbsp. cornstarch
½ tsp. salt
⅛ tsp. pepper
½ tsp. thyme
¼ tsp. sage
1½ cups chicken stock
1 cup grated Cheddar cheese
½ cup chopped green pepper
1-2 cups minced cooked
 chicken

In large bowl, beat eggs until creamy. Mix cornstarch, salt, pepper, thyme and sage and slowly stir in chicken stock until smooth. Slowly beat into eggs. Add remaining ingredients and mix. Pour into pastry shell.

Bake at 425° F for 15 minutes; lower temperature to 325° F and bake 30 to 45 minutes longer or until filling is set. Cool for 5 to 10 minutes before serving.

Serves 4 to 6.

—Janice Chammartin

Mushroom Beef Quiche

Pastry for 9-inch pie shell
½ lb. ground beef
1 cup thinly sliced onions
2 Tbsp. butter
¾ cup grated Cheddar
cheese
2 eggs
1½ tsp. prepared mustard
2½ cups cream of
 mushroom sauce (page 132)

Line pie plate with pastry. Brown ground beef and set aside. Sauté onions in butter until tender. Spread beef on pie shell, then spread onions over meat and sprinkle with cheese.

Blend together eggs, mustard and mushroom sauce. Pour over ingredients in pie plate.

Bake at 350° F for 45 to 60 minutes or until firm. Let stand for 5 minutes before cutting.

Serves 4 to 6.

—Kathy Labelle

White Fish Soufflé

1 lb. white fish
3 Tbsp. butter
3 Tbsp. flour
½ cup milk
3 eggs, separated
½ cup peas
½ tsp. salt

Cook fish gently in lightly salted boiling water until it flakes. Melt butter, blend in flour and gradually add milk. Cook, stirring constantly, until smooth and thickened. Add yolks and beat well. Stir in fish, peas and salt. Beat egg whites until stiff, then fold into fish mixture. Pour into greased soufflé dish and place in pan of hot water. Bake at 350° F for 45 minutes, or until soufflé is firm and well browned.

Serves 4.

—Janice Graham

Zucchini Custard Soufflé

This soufflé is also delicious served cold.

4 cups sliced zucchini
1 medium onion, finely
 chopped
3 large eggs, well beaten
2 Tbsp. flour
⅓ cup cream
1 cup cubed Cheddar cheese
Salt & pepper

Steam zucchini briefly and drain well. Gently combine with onion, eggs and flour. Stir in cream and cheese and pour into a buttered soufflé dish. Bake at 325° F for 75 minutes, or until set and golden. Let stand for a few minutes before serving.

Serves 4.

—Kathleen Gray

Leek Soufflé

This soufflé can be made using leeks that have been sliced and frozen for a pleasant midwinter taste of spring.

½ cup & 2 Tbsp. Parmesan
  cheese
2 leeks, sliced
6 Tbsp. butter
3 Tbsp. water
½ tsp. salt
¼ tsp. pepper
3 Tbsp. flour
1 cup milk
4 egg yolks, slightly beaten
Salt & pepper
6 egg whites

Coat inside of greased, 2-quart soufflé dish with 2 Tbsp. Parmesan cheese. Simmer leeks in 3 Tbsp. butter and water with salt and pepper, covered, until water evaporates — about 5 minutes.

Melt remaining 3 Tbsp. butter, then stir in flour. Cook over low heat, stirring constantly, for 2 minutes. Gradually stir in milk. Heat to boiling, stirring. Add leeks and ½ cup Parmesan cheese. Cook over medium heat, stirring constantly, until mixture boils. Remove from heat.

Stir ¼ cup of leek mixture into egg yolks, then gradually stir this back into leek mixture. Season with salt and pepper and cool to lukewarm.

Beat egg whites until stiff but not dry and fold into leek mixture. Pour into prepared soufflé dish. Bake at 400° F for 35 minutes, or until golden and firm.

Serves 6.

—*Pam Collacott*

Fettuccine Soufflé

Served with a green salad and garlic bread, this soufflé makes a complete meal — especially for real pasta lovers.

½ lb. fettuccine noodles
1⅓ cups milk
1 clove garlic, minced
½ cup & 3 Tbsp. Parmesan
  cheese
¼ lb. Fontina cheese, grated
¼ lb. unsalted butter, cut
  into small pieces
Salt & pepper
1-2 tsp. chopped parsley
½ cup peas, steamed
6 large eggs, separated
1 Tbsp. milk

Cook fettuccine until just tender — about 5 minutes. Bring milk to a boil. Mix drained fettuccine with hot milk, garlic, ½ cup Parmesan cheese, Fontina cheese and butter. Season with salt and pepper to taste, then add parsley and cool. Add peas and egg yolks to cooled noodles and mix. Beat egg whites until stiff, then fold carefully into noodle mixture.

Butter soufflé dish and dust with remaining 3 Tbsp. of Parmesan cheese. Pour soufflé into dish. Bake at 350° F for 45 minutes, then increase heat to 425° F and cook for 5 more minutes.

Serves 6.

—*Robyn Pashley*

Bulgur Mushroom Omelette

1½ Tbsp. butter
3 green onions, sliced
Large handful mushrooms,
  sliced
¾ cup cooked bulgur
2 large eggs
2 Tbsp. milk
Salt
Basil
Curry
Grated Cheddar cheese

Melt butter and sauté onions and mushrooms. Add bulgur and heat through. Combine eggs, milk, salt, basil and curry and pour over bulgur-mushroom mixture. Cook, shaking pan, until custard is nearly set, then sprinkle with grated cheese. Cover pan and cook over low heat until cheese is melted.

Serves 1.

—*Rosande Bellaar Spruyt*

German Omelette

1 lb. sausage meat
1 medium onion, chopped
Salt & pepper
1 tsp. dry mustard
2 Tbsp. parsley
6 eggs
2 cups milk
3 slices bread, cubed
1 cup grated Cheddar cheese
1 cup grated mozzarella
   cheese

Brown sausage meat and drain off excess fat. Add onion, salt, pepper, mustard and parsley and cook until onion is tender.

Mix together eggs, milk, bread and cheeses. Add meat mixture and stir. Pour into a 9" x 13" baking dish and chill overnight. Bake at 350° F for 45 minutes, or until knife inserted in centre comes out clean.

Serves 6 to 8.

—Lynda Watson

Potato Omelette

1 medium potato
Butter
2 eggs
Milk
Salt & pepper
Sliced mushrooms

Slice the potato ⅛- to ¼-inch thick and lay on a lightly oiled cookie sheet. Dot with butter and bake at 350° F until golden brown, turning once. Meanwhile, beat eggs with a little milk and season with salt and pepper. Sauté mushrooms.

Layer potato slices in an oiled frying pan. Add mushroom-egg mixture. Cover and cook slowly on both sides.

Serves 1.

—Veronica Clarke-Hanik

Basque Omelette

½ lb. bacon, cut into
   ¼-inch pieces
1 cup thinly sliced potatoes
1 medium onion, sliced
½ cup chopped celery
½ cup sliced green pepper
¼ cup sliced zucchini
1 clove garlic, minced
1 cup stewed tomatoes,
   drained
5-6 drops Tabasco sauce
Salt & pepper
8 eggs
¼ cup milk or cream
¼ tsp. salt
⅛ tsp. paprika
4 Tbsp. butter

Fry bacon to medium crispness and drain off all but 2 Tbsp. fat. Add potatoes, onion and celery and cook until tender. Add green pepper, zucchini, garlic, tomatoes, Tabasco sauce and salt and pepper and cook until vegetables are tender. Keep warm.

Combine eggs, milk, salt and paprika. Divide mixture into quarters. Melt 1 Tbsp. butter and cook first omelette by frying gently until firm and lightly browned on bottom. Slide onto plate and heap with one-quarter of hot vegetables. Repeat 3 times with remaining mixture.

Serves 4.

—Charlene Skidmore

Buckwheat Crêpes with Maple Orange Sauce

CRÊPES:
1½ cups buckwheat flour
½ tsp. salt
3 eggs & milk to make 4 cups
Oil
MAPLE ORANGE SAUCE:
1 cup maple syrup
½ cup butter
¼ cup grated orange peel
Cottage cheese

Combine flour and salt in large bowl. Add 1 cup of egg-milk mixture at a time, whisking well. Continue adding liquid until mixture is consistency of heavy cream. Reserve extra liquid.

Pour ⅓ cup batter into hot pan and roll around to coat bottom evenly. Cook on medium-high until crêpe is golden brown on bottom and sturdy enough to flip — 30 to 45 seconds per side. If batter thickens as cooking continues, add some of reserved liquid.

To make sauce, place maple syrup, butter and orange peel in saucepan. Bring to a boil, lower heat and simmer for 5 minutes.

To serve, fill crêpes with cottage cheese and pour sauce over top.

Makes approximately 15 crêpes.

—Marilyn Rootham

Neptune Omelette

2 eggs
1 Tbsp. water
¾ tsp. parsley
Salt & pepper
2 Tbsp. mayonnaise
2 Tbsp. Parmesan cheese
2 Tbsp. crabmeat
6 asparagus tips, steamed until tender
Grated Cheddar cheese

Combine eggs, water, parsley and salt and pepper. Set aside. Mix together mayonnaise, Parmesan cheese and crabmeat and set aside.

Pour egg mixture into buttered skillet and cook over medium heat until nearly set. Lay asparagus spears on one side of omelette, spread with mayonnaise mixture and fold over. Cover pan and finish cooking. Sprinkle grated Cheddar cheese over top and allow to melt.

Serves 1.

—Bonnie Lawson

Cream Cheese & Walnut Omelette

3 eggs
3 drops Tabasco sauce
1 Tbsp. water
Salt
4 Tbsp. chopped walnuts
3½ Tbsp. butter
2 Tbsp. tamari sauce
2 oz. cream cheese, softened

Beat eggs, Tabasco sauce, water and salt and set aside. Brown walnuts in 2 Tbsp. butter add tamari sauce and set aside.

Heat remaining 1½ Tbsp. butter in omelette pan until foamy. Pour in egg mixture and cook until almost set. Top with cream cheese and all but a few walnuts. Fold omelette over filling and cook for half a minute longer. Slide out of pan and top with walnuts.

Serves 1.

—Gillian Barber-Gifford

Poppy Seed Pancakes

The most flavourful poppy seeds are grown in Holland. The seed is best when steamed or roasted, then crushed to release its full flavour. For those who really enjoy poppy seeds, it is possible to buy a hand mill to grind the seeds at home.

1 cup whole wheat flour
1 Tbsp. sugar
½ tsp. salt
1 Tbsp. baking powder
1 egg, beaten
1 cup milk
2 Tbsp. oil
2 Tbsp. poppy seeds

Mix together flour, sugar, salt and baking powder. Beat egg and add milk, then oil. Add to dry ingredients. Add poppy seeds and stir until seeds are just moistened.

Pour batter by scant quarter cupfuls onto hot greased griddle. Cook until bubbly. Turn with pancake turner and cook until underside is golden. Place on platter and keep warm.

Makes about 15 three-inch pancakes.

—Suzanne Moore

Cheese Corn Pancakes

2 cups flour
3 tsp. baking powder
1 tsp. salt
2 Tbsp. brown sugar
2 cups milk
2 eggs, slightly beaten
¼ cup oil or melted butter
2 cups corn
Small cubes Cheddar cheese

Combine flour, baking powder, salt and sugar. In another bowl, combine milk, eggs, oil and corn. Pour liquid ingredients over flour mixture and combine with a few strokes — batter should be lumpy.

Pour ¼ cup of batter onto greased griddle. While first side is cooking, top with 5 or 6 cheese cubes. Flip to cheese side and cook until golden brown.

Makes 8 to 10 pancakes.

—Rae Anne Huth

Buckwheat Pancakes

2 eggs
1¼ cups buttermilk
2 Tbsp. oil
½ cup buckwheat flour
½ cup whole wheat flour
¼ cup wheat germ
½ tsp. baking soda
1 tsp. baking powder
½ tsp. salt
1 cup diced fruit (optional)

Beat together eggs, buttermilk and oil. Gradually mix in flours, wheat germ, baking soda, baking powder, salt and diced fruit. Fry on hot greased griddle.

Makes approximately 16 pancakes.

—Marjorie Moore

Corn Meal Pancakes

¼ cup flour
1 tsp. sugar
2 tsp. baking powder
¾ tsp. salt
½ tsp. baking soda
1 cup corn meal
3 eggs, beaten
1½ cups buttermilk
2 Tbsp. melted butter

Combine and mix flour, sugar, baking powder, salt and baking soda. Stir in corn meal. Add eggs, buttermilk and butter and stir until dry mixture is moistened. Pour ¼ cup batter onto hot griddle. Brown one side, turn and brown on other. Repeat with remaining batter.

Makes 12 pancakes.

—Judy Cushman

Oatmeal Pancakes

1½ cups oatmeal
2½ cups milk
1 cup flour
1 Tbsp. brown sugar
½ tsp. salt
1 tsp. cinnamon
1 Tbsp. baking powder
1 egg, beaten
¼ cup oil

Pour milk over oatmeal and let sit for 10 minutes. Sift flour, sugar, salt, cinnamon and baking powder together, then add to oatmeal mixture. Add egg and oil and mix well. Cook on hot griddle.

Makes 10 to 12 pancakes.

—Judy Wuest

Banana Pancakes

2 eggs
2 cups buttermilk
1 Tbsp. baking soda
1 Tbsp. baking powder
2 cups flour
5 Tbsp. oil
1 cup mashed ripe bananas

Mix together eggs, buttermilk, baking soda and baking powder. Add flour and then oil, stirring only until blended. Fold in bananas. Spoon onto hot griddle or frying pan.

Makes approximately 12 pancakes.

—Marilynn Janzen

Aland Pancake

This recipe was received when the contributor visited the Aland Islands, Finland, one summer. After giving the Alanders a feast of Canadian pancakes and maple syrup, they reciprocated with their own pancake.

4 cups milk
½ cup wheatlets
½ cup sugar
1 tsp. salt
1 cup butter
4 eggs
1 tsp. cardamom
2 Tbsp. wheat meal

Boil 2 cups milk. Mix in wheatlets and bring to a boil for 2 minutes. Add sugar, salt and butter. Mix together eggs, cardamom and wheat meal in a bowl and add rest of milk. Mix everything with wheatlets.

Pour into a large, flat greased pan. Cook at 325° F for 30 minutes. While it is baking, break the hills that will form. Cut into sections and serve with a topping of any berry jam and whipped cream.

Serves 4.

—Lorne Davis

Zucchini Egg Casserole

This dish has the consistency of creamy scrambled eggs. Freeze zucchini in the summer for making this dish in winter. A 1-quart bag will hold the 2 pounds required for this recipe.

Oil
2 lbs. zucchini, thawed if frozen
1 medium onion, chopped
Salt
Basil
Oregano
Cornstarch
6 eggs, separated
½-¾ cup milk
6 Tbsp. flour
½ cup grated Parmesan cheese

Heat oil in skillet and sauté zucchini, onion, salt, basil and oregano until onion is translucent — about 15 minutes. Thicken with cornstarch if necessary.

Combine egg yolks, milk, flour and Parmesan cheese. Beat egg whites until stiff, then fold into egg mixture.

Pour zucchini mixture into greased baking dish, then spoon egg mixture over top. Stir together and bake at 350° F for 30 to 45 minutes, or until firm.

Serves 6.

—Winn Horne

Huevos Rancheros

2 medium onions, finely
    chopped
1 clove garlic, finely chopped
3 Tbsp. oil
1 large green or red pepper,
    sliced
1 cup stewed tomatoes,
    chopped
Salt & pepper
2 tsp. chili powder
¼ tsp. oregano
¼ tsp. cumin
6-8 eggs
Grated Cheddar cheese

Sauté onion and garlic in oil.
Stir in pepper, tomatoes, salt,
pepper, chili powder, oregano
and cumin, and simmer until
sauce is thick but not pasty.
Poach or fry the eggs in butter
without breaking the yolks.
Spoon the simmered sauce into
a shallow baking dish and nest
the eggs in the sauce. Sprinkle
with cheese. Bake at 250° F until
the cheese melts — about 15
minutes.

Serves 6 to 8.

—Carroll MacDonald

French Creamed Scrambled Eggs with Leek

5 Tbsp. butter
4 medium leeks, white part
    only, thinly sliced
20 eggs, beaten just to blend
8 oz. cream cheese, softened
    or chopped
1 Tbsp. minced fresh mint
Salt & pepper
Fresh mint sprigs to garnish

Melt 3 Tbsp. butter in heavy
pan over low heat. Add leeks,
cover and cook, stirring
occasionally, until soft — about
20 minutes. Uncover and
continue to cook, allowing liquid
to evaporate. Remove leeks from
pan.

Melt remaining 2 Tbsp. butter
in same pan over low heat. Add
eggs, cream cheese, mint and
salt and pepper and cook,
stirring, until eggs begin to set.
Stir in leeks and cook until
mixture forms soft curds. Adjust
seasoning. Turn out onto heated
platter and garnish with mint
sprigs.

Serves 10.

—Lisa Calzonetti

Poached Eggs Italia

4 Tbsp. oil
1 clove garlic, minced
⅓ cup chopped green onions
3 cups chopped tomatoes
1 Tbsp. chopped parsley
Cayenne
¼ tsp. salt
6 eggs

Heat oil in heavy pan. Add
garlic and onions and sauté for 2
minutes. Add tomatoes, parsley,
cayenne and salt. Simmer over
low heat for about 25 minutes.
Replace lid if too much liquid is
evaporating. Carefully drop the
eggs into sauce, one at a time.
Cover and return to boil. Simmer
for 3 minutes, or until eggs are
desired firmness. Serve on
noodles or on toast with a salad.

Serves 6.

—Lisa Calzonetti

Devilled Eggs

6 eggs, hard cooked
½ cup mayonnaise
Salt & pepper
Curry
12 capers

Shell eggs and cut in half
lengthwise. Scoop out yolks and
place them in a small bowl. Mash
lightly. Add mayonnaise, salt and
pepper and curry, and mix well.
Spoon carefully into egg whites
and garnish with capers.

Refrigerate until well chilled,
then remove from refrigerator for
30 minutes before serving.

Makes 12.

Shrimp Stuffed Eggs

8 hard-boiled eggs, shelled
½ cup mayonnaise
1 Tbsp. chopped dill
¼ tsp. salt
1½ cups small shrimp,
    cooked

Halve eggs lengthwise, scoop out yolks and mash them thoroughly with a fork. Beat in mayonnaise, dill and salt.

Reserve 16 whole shrimp. Chop remaining shrimp finely and fold into yolk mixture.

Refill egg whites, garnish with reserved shrimp and fresh dill sprigs and refrigerate until thoroughly chilled.

Makes 16 appetizers.

— *Claudette Spies*

Debby's Quick Vreniki

4 cups cottage cheese
4 eggs, beaten
½ cup melted butter
½ pkg. bow-tie macaroni,
    cooked
1 tsp. baking powder
1-1½ cups grated Cheddar
    cheese

Mix cottage cheese, eggs, butter, macaroni, baking powder and half of cheese. Place in baking dish and spread remaining cheese on top. Bake, uncovered, at 350° F for 40 to 60 minutes, or until firm.

Serves 6.

—*Mary Giesz*

Herbed Cheese

The contributor of this recipe uses fresh goat's milk cream cheese, which adds flavour. This, of course, is not imperative, but fresh herbs must be used.

1½ lbs. creamed cottage
    cheese, drained
1 lb. cream cheese
3 tsp. sour cream
3 cloves garlic, finely minced
½ tsp. salt
½ tsp. white pepper
1 tsp. minced basil
1 tsp. minced tarragon
½ tsp. minced thyme
½ tsp. minced sage
2 Tbsp. minced chives
2 Tbsp. minced parsley

Beat cheeses and sour cream until smooth, then beat in herbs. Cover and refrigerate for 24 hours to cure.

Place in a 3-cup mould lined with plastic wrap, refrigerate until set and remove from mould. Garnish with fresh herbs.

Makes 3 cups.

—*Janet Ueberschlag*

Knedlyky

This recipe for cottage cheese dumplings is a simplified version of a traditional Czechoslovakian dish prepared the way they used to be made during the harvest, when there was not much time to fuss in the kitchen. It is usually served as a side dish in place of noodles or potatoes.

1 cup cottage or ricotta
    cheese
1 egg
2 cups fine semolina

Mix cheese well with egg. If cheese curds are very large, break first with a pastry cutter or fork. Add semolina to make a workable dough — the exact amount will depend upon how moist the cheese is.

Form dough into walnut-sized balls, moistening hands with water to prevent sticking. Drop into a large pot of boiling salted water and cook for 7 minutes. Drain and serve.

Serves 6.

—*Moira Abboud*

Olive Ball Snacks

Both this recipe and the one that follows can be made up in quantity and frozen. A quick reheating provides an almost instant party snack or hors d'oeuvres.

2 cups grated old Cheddar
   cheese
½ cup soft butter
1 cup flour
½ tsp. salt
½ tsp. paprika
48 green, pimento-stuffed
   olives

Combine cheese, butter, flour, salt and paprika and mix well. Wrap 1 tsp. of mixture around each olive. Place on cookie sheets and freeze. (Once frozen, the balls may be transferred to a covered container if they are to be stored for any length of time.)

Bake at 400° F for 20 minutes.

Makes 48 balls.

—*Jane Cardona*

Hot Cheese Balls

½ lb. grated Cheddar cheese
¼ lb. butter
1 cup flour
Cayenne pepper

Mix cheese and butter, then flour and cayenne. Mix well and form into small balls. Bake on cookie sheet at 400° F for 15 to 20 minutes. Serve hot.

Makes 24 balls.

—*Mary Kelley*

Potted Cheese

1 lb. medium Cheddar
   cheese, grated
3 Tbsp. chopped scallions
3 Tbsp. chopped parsley
1 clove garlic, minced
1 tsp. Dijon mustard
2 Tbsp. softened butter
2 Tbsp. dry sherry
Tabasco sauce
Worcestershire sauce

Mix cheese, scallions, parsley, garlic and mustard in a bowl. Beat in butter, sherry and Tabasco and Worcestershire sauces. Stir the mixture until it becomes creamy, then pack it into a wide-mouthed jar or crock and refrigerate until ready to use.

Serve at room temperature with crusty bread.

—*Valery Martinelli*

Tiopetes

This Greek recipe for cheese puffs makes delicious hors d'oeuvres — it can even be reheated successfully.

3 eggs
½ tsp. salt
¼ tsp. pepper
1 lb. feta cheese
½ cup finely chopped
   parsley
½ lb. butter
½ lb. filo pastry

Beat eggs briefly in bowl. Sprinkle in salt and pepper. Crumble feta into small pieces and add to beaten eggs. Mix in parsley.

Melt butter in small pan over low heat. Cut filo into 3 equal strips about 3 to 4 inches wide. Cover two sections of the filo with a slightly dampened towel to prevent drying out and set aside until ready to use.

Working with the remaining one-third of the pastry, take one sheet, place on working area and butter with pastry brush. Place 1 Tbsp. of cheese mixture in bottom right hand corner of the buttered strip of filo, about an inch from the bottom of the strip. Fold left bottom corner over the cheese mixture to begin triangle. Then continue folding up, maintaining triangle shape. Lightly butter the finished triangle to seal the edge and place on an ungreased cookie sheet. Repeat process until all strips of filo are used. Cook in hot oil until golden brown — about 10 to 15 minutes.

Makes 3 to 4 dozen triangles.

—*Zoe Mavridis Farber*

Frittata Fairbanks

This frittata was the top prizewinner in the egg, brunch and party categories at the 1986 Tanana Valley State Fair in Alaska, as well as being declared "Grand Champion Purple Rosette in Culinary Capers." As its creator says, "This is not only the most delectable omelette I have ever eaten, it is one of the most beautiful dishes imaginable."

½ cup butter
1 Tbsp. soy sauce
1 clove garlic, diced
¼ cup sunflower seeds
3 small onions, diced
1 zucchini, sliced
1 head broccoli, sliced
12 eggs
3 Tbsp. plain yogurt
3 Tbsp. bran
1 sprig dill
3 cups grated Cheddar
　cheese
1 cup sour cream
1 avocado, sliced
2 cups alfalfa sprouts
½ cup salsa
nasturtiums & fuchsia to
　garnish

Melt butter in large, heavy, ovenproof skillet. Add soy sauce, then sauté garlic, sunflower seeds, onions, zucchini and broccoli until onions are transparent. Mix together eggs, yogurt, bran and dill. Pour over vegetables in skillet. Bake, uncovered, at 350° F for 30 to 45 minutes or until cooked through. Cover with cheese, then bake for 10 minutes longer, or until cheese is melted.

Remove from oven. Cover with sour cream. Place avocado slices around omelette in spokelike fashion. Spread sprouts in centre of omelette and spoon salsa between sprouts and avocado. Garnish with nasturtiums and fuchsia.

Serves 6 to 8.

—Mark Boberick

Baked Vegetable Frittata

A frittata is little more than an omelette, the difference being that the filling is usually mixed into the eggs before they are cooked. Frittatas may be baked or cooked, covered, on top of the stove.

2 Tbsp. butter
1 onion, finely chopped
1 clove garlic, minced
1 green pepper, diced
¼ cup chopped parsley
19-oz. can tomatoes, drained
　& chopped
4-5 eggs
½ cup bread crumbs
1 tsp. salt
¼ tsp. pepper
1 tsp. Worcestershire sauce
2 cups grated Swiss cheese
1 green pepper, cut in rings

In skillet, melt butter over medium heat and cook onion and garlic until tender. Add green pepper and parsley and cook for 1 minute longer. Remove from heat and add tomatoes.

In large bowl, beat eggs well. Stir in bread crumbs, salt, pepper, Worcestershire sauce and cheese. Gently stir in vegetables. Pour mixture into buttered 9"-round baking dish. Bake, uncovered, at 350° F for 30 to 35 minutes, or until top is golden brown. Let stand for 5 minutes before serving. Garnish with green pepper rings.

Serves 4.

—Grace Neumann

Simple Potato Omelette

Omelettes require delicate handling, but with a little practice can be mastered by anyone. They come in 2 basic varieties — plain, in which the eggs are beaten whole, and soufflé, in which the yolks and whites are beaten separately. Plain omelettes are generally savoury (like those here) while soufflé omelettes are commonly sweet and served as dessert. This is a simple, tasty omelette. Serve with spicy tomato salsa for added colour and flavour.

4 potatoes, diced
2 onions, finely chopped
¼ cup oil
salt & pepper
6 eggs
2 Tbsp. milk

Sauté potatoes and onions in oil until tender. Add salt and pepper to taste. Beat eggs and milk together. Pour over potatoes and mix evenly. Cover and cook gently until mixture is set. Cut in wedges and serve hot or cold.

Serves 4 to 6.

—Dorothy Cage

Pizza Omelette

Special omelette pans are available for those who are regular omelette-makers. They should be kept for omelettes only. Any heavy-bottomed skillet can be used successfully, though, especially the non-stick variety. The following makes a great pizza flavoured meal without the heaviness of pizza.

3 Tbsp. butter
3 eggs
1 Tbsp. milk
½ cup thick tomato sauce
½ cup sliced cooked sausage
½ cup sliced mushrooms
½ cup grated mozzarella
      cheese

Melt butter in skillet. Beat eggs with milk, then pour into skillet and cook until firm, lifting edges to prevent sticking. Spread tomato sauce over half the omelette, then add sausage, mushrooms and cheese. Fold omelette in half, cover skillet, reduce heat and cook for 3 to 4 minutes, or until cheese melts.

Serves 1.

—*Wendy Moore-MacQueen*

Vegetable Omelette

10 eggs
4 mushrooms, sliced
2 green onions, sliced
1 Tbsp. finely chopped green
    pepper
1 Tbsp. cooked squash
1 Tbsp. finely chopped sweet
    red pepper
1 Tbsp. finely chopped celery
⅔ cup grated Cheddar
    cheese
salt & pepper

Beat eggs until frothy. Add remaining ingredients and mix well. Pour into ungreased casserole dish and bake, uncovered, at 350° F for 25 to 30 minutes.

Serves 4 to 6.

—*Kelvin Mayes*

Egg Curry

Serve this curry over rice or toast for a mild but flavourful lunch dish.

6 eggs
¼ cup oil
1 large onion, chopped
3 slices gingerroot, minced
  or 1 tsp. ground ginger
2 Tbsp. minced parsley
1 tsp. turmeric
2 tsp. curry powder
3 tomatoes, peeled, seeded &
    chopped
1 cup plain yogurt
¼ lb. mushrooms, sliced
2 Tbsp. lemon juice

Hard-boil eggs, drain, peel, halve and set aside. Heat oil in wok, then stir in onion and ginger. Stir-fry until onion is golden — 3 to 4 minutes — over medium heat. Add parsley, turmeric and curry powder, lower heat and simmer for 4 minutes, stirring occasionally. Add tomatoes and simmer for another 8 minutes. Add yogurt and mushrooms, mix well and cook for 10 minutes longer. Add eggs, then simmer for 3 minutes. Stir in lemon juice just before serving.

Serves 2 to 4.

—*Diane & David Ladouceur*

Spinach Squares

2-3 eggs
6 Tbsp. whole wheat flour
1 lb. fresh spinach
1 lb. cottage cheese
½ lb. grated Cheddar cheese
½ tsp. salt
3 Tbsp. wheat germ

Beat eggs and flour in large bowl. Tear up spinach and add. Mix in cottage cheese, Cheddar cheese and salt. Combine well. Pour into a well-greased 9" x 13" baking pan and sprinkle with wheat germ. Bake, uncovered, at 350° F for approximately 45 minutes. Cut into squares for serving.

Serves 6 to 8.
—*Barbara Zikman*

Indian Eggs

This makes a great brunch for corn lovers.

8 slices bacon
1 onion, chopped
1½ cups corn
1 Tbsp. Worcestershire
   sauce
salt & pepper
8 eggs, lightly beaten

Fry bacon, drain, then crumble and set aside. Pour off half the bacon fat and add onion. Sauté until onion is soft. Add corn and seasonings. Heat through, then add eggs. Cook, stirring, until set. Serve with bacon sprinkled over the top.

Serves 3 to 4.
—*Ann Kostendt*

New Zealand-Style Eggs

This is a quick and easy egg dish for a late breakfast or a lunch. Served with a salad it makes a satisfying light meal.

4 Tbsp. butter
¼ cup minced onion
1 cup cold diced cooked
   potatoes
5 eggs
½ cup milk
salt & pepper
2 Tbsp. snipped parsley
4 tomatoes, quartered

In 3 Tbsp. butter, sauté onion and potatoes until golden. Beat eggs with milk, ¾ tsp. salt, pepper and parsley, until just blended, then pour over potatoes. Cook over medium heat, gently scraping the mixture from the bottom as it cooks, until it is set but still moist.

Meanwhile, sprinkle tomatoes with salt and pepper. Sauté until tender in 1 Tbsp. butter in another skillet. Arrange tomatoes around potatoes.

Serves 4.
—*Alyson Service*

Chilies Relleños Casserole

This casserole is delicious—the flavour of the chilies permeates the cheesy custard for a dish that is smooth in texture but has a bite to its taste. Use jalapeño peppers if your taste buds would like a real treat. Serve as a brunch, lunch or supper dish with refried beans and salad.

16-oz. can green chilies,
   rinsed, split & laid flat
1 lb. Monterey Jack cheese,
   grated
1 lb. sharp Cheddar cheese,
   grated
4 Tbsp. flour
2 13-oz. cans evaporated
   milk
4 large eggs

Grease bottom of 9" x 13" glass pan. Layer chilies and cheeses, topping with layer of chilies. Mix flour with some evaporated milk to make a paste, then mix in remaining milk. Beat in eggs. Pour over chilies and bake at 350° F for 45 to 50 minutes, or until mixture is somewhat firm. Remove from oven and let stand for 10 minutes before serving.

Serves 10.
—*Sandra Senchuk-Crandall*

Golden Eggs Mayonnaise

4 Tbsp. butter
1 Tbsp. oil
2 Tbsp. curry powder
8 eggs, hard-cooked &
  peeled
1 cup mayonnaise
3 Tbsp. chopped chutney
1 head lettuce
½ cup chopped olives

Heat butter and oil in saucepan over medium heat. Stir in curry powder until well blended. Add eggs and cook, turning constantly, over low heat for 10 minutes. Remove to plate with slotted spoon, cover and cool, but do not refrigerate.

To serve, mix mayonnaise with chutney. Cut eggs in half. Make a nest of lettuce in salad bowl, add eggs, then pour mayonnaise over them. Sprinkle chopped olives around the mayonnaise.

Serves 4 to 6.

—Donna Jubb

Crab & Asparagus Tart

A delicious appetizer, this tart is also suitable for a lunch or supper main dish and can be frozen successfully.

Pastry for single 9-inch pie
  shell
1 Tbsp. butter
1 Tbsp. flour
½ cup milk
nutmeg
½ cup whipping cream
2 Tbsp. sherry
12 oz. crabmeat
salt & pepper
2 egg yolks
12 stalks asparagus, lightly
  steamed
¼ cup grated Gruyère cheese

Line pie plate with pastry and bake at 350° F for 10 minutes.

Melt butter, stir in flour until smooth, then stir in milk and cook until thickened. Add a grating of nutmeg. Remove from heat, stir in cream and sherry. Add crab and salt and pepper. Lightly beat egg yolks, then add to crab mixture and stir gently. Pour into pastry shell. Lay asparagus decoratively on top, then sprinkle with cheese.

Bake at 350° F for 20 minutes.
Serves 6.

—Sandy Campisano

Snails

So named because they look like snails when cooked. These hors d'oeuvres can be made using any variety of fillings — we provide two here.

Pastry for a double 9-inch
  pie shell
WALNUT MUSHROOM
  FILLING:
4 Tbsp. butter
3 cups finely diced
  mushrooms
¼ cup finely diced onion
1 cup finely chopped
  walnuts
¼ cup grated sharp Cheddar
  cheese
½ clove garlic, crushed
pepper
2 tsp. caraway seeds
BACON CHEESE FILLING:
5 slices bacon
1½ cups grated Monterey
  Jack cheese
1½ cups grated sharp
  Cheddar cheese
4 Tbsp. chopped chives

Roll dough into 2 large, thin rectangles.

For Walnut Mushroom Filling: Melt butter and briefly sauté mushrooms and onion. Remove from heat and add remaining ingredients. Mix well. Spread on 1 dough rectangle and roll up like a jelly roll. Wrap well and chill for 1 hour. Cut into ½-inch-thick slices and bake at 425° F for 25 to 30 minutes, or until golden brown.

For Bacon Cheese Filling: Cook bacon until very crisp. Crumble. Mix with cheeses, then add chives. Spread on remaining dough and proceed as above.

Makes approximately 40.

—Diane Milan

Shirred Eggs Deluxe

Served with a fruit salad and warm muffins, these eggs make a delicious and attractive brunch.

2 Tbsp. butter
12 eggs
salt & pepper
6 slices bacon
¾ cup sliced mushrooms
⅓ cup Parmesan cheese

Butter 6 individual custard dishes. Break 2 eggs into each dish and add a dash of salt and pepper. Bake at 325° F for 15 minutes.

Meanwhile, cook bacon until crisp, then crumble. Sauté mushrooms in bacon drippings until golden brown. Top eggs with bacon, mushrooms and cheese. Return to oven for 5 more minutes, or until whites are set but yolks are still soft.

Serves 6.

—*Jayne Simms-Dalmotas*

Egg & Cheese Puffs

Less tricky to make than a soufflé, these individual egg puffs still rise beautifully.

6 eggs
½ cup light cream
3 Tbsp. flour
1½ tsp. dry mustard
¼ tsp. salt
⅛ tsp. white pepper
1½ cups grated Cheddar cheese

Combine all ingredients but cheese and beat well. Grease 4 10-oz. soufflé dishes or custard cups well, then sprinkle cheese in them. Pour in egg mixture.

Bake at 350° F for 30 to 35 minutes, or until puffy and golden.

Serves 4.

—*Elaine Darbyshire*

Italian Cheese Loaf

This loaf can be served hot or cold, or it can be cut into 2-inch squares, fried in butter and served with bacon. We served this with Tomato Curry (see page 180) with delicious results.

1 cup dry rice
4 eggs
6 Tbsp. oil
½ tsp. basil
¼ cup minced parsley
1 cup grated sharp Cheddar cheese
salt & pepper

Cook rice. Beat 3 eggs, add oil and beat well. Add remaining ingredients (except last egg) and cooked rice.

Grease loaf pan. Pour in mixture, spreading it evenly and spread with remaining egg, well beaten. Bake at 350° F for 1 hour.

Serves 6.

—*Donna Jubb*

Summer Cheese Soufflé

This soufflé can be assembled up to two days before cooking and serving. It puffs up beautifully while baking and is a very attractive dish, equally delicious for brunch or lunch, or served with ham for dinner.

5 slices crusty Italian bread
butter, softened
¾ lb. sharp Cheddar cheese, grated
4 eggs, beaten
2 cups milk
1 tsp. dry mustard
1 tsp. Worcestershire sauce
½ tsp. curry powder
½ tsp. salt

Butter each slice of bread lightly on both sides and cut into cubes. Layer bread and cheese in ungreased 1-quart casserole dish. Combine remaining ingredients and pour over bread and cheese. Cover and refrigerate for up to 2 days.

Bake, uncovered, at 350° F for 50 minutes.

Serves 6.

—*Donna Jubb*

Egg Casserole

3 cups cubed, cooked ham
½ lb. sharp Cheddar cheese,
   grated
3 cups cubed rye bread
3 Tbsp. melted butter
3 Tbsp. flour
1 tsp. dry mustard
4 eggs
3 cups milk

Layer ham, cheese and bread in greased 9" x 13" pan. Drizzle with butter. Combine flour and mustard and sprinkle over mixture in pan. Beat eggs, add milk and mix well. Pour over pan mixture. Refrigerate for 4 to 24 hours.

Bake, uncovered, at 350° F for 1 hour.

Serves 8 to 10.

—*Jackie Dysart*

Eggs in Nests

Simpler to make than its appearance would lead you to believe, this is a delicious brunch dish.

2 Tbsp. butter
2 Tbsp. flour
½ tsp. salt
pepper
1 cup milk
½ cup grated sharp Cheddar
   cheese
4 slices toast
4 eggs
cream of tartar
16-20 asparagus spears,
   steamed

Melt butter, then stir in flour and cook over low heat for 1 minute. Stir in salt, pepper and milk. Bring to a boil, stirring, and cook until thickened. Stir in cheese. Set aside, keeping warm.

Place toast on cookie sheet. Separate eggs, keeping yolks whole and separate from one another. Beat whites with a pinch of cream of tartar until stiff.

Place 4 or 5 asparagus spears on each slice of toast. Pile egg whites over asparagus, then make a dent in each pile. Drop 1 yolk into each dent.

Bake at 350° F for 8 to 10 minutes, or until meringue edges are golden and yolks are still runny. Serve with cheese sauce.

Serves 4.

—*Cary Elizabeth Marshall*

Chili Egg Puff

Served with salad and fresh whole-grain bread, this makes a complete supper; with fruit bread or muffins and fruit salad, it functions as a delicious brunch.

10 eggs
½ cup flour
2 cups cottage cheese
1 lb. Monterey Jack cheese,
   grated
½ cup melted butter
2 4-oz. cans California green
   chilies, diced

Beat eggs until light and lemon-coloured. Add flour, cottage cheese, Monterey Jack cheese and melted butter. Blend until smooth, then stir in chilies. Pour into greased 9" x 13" dish. Bake, uncovered, at 350° F for 35 minutes. Let stand for a few minutes, then serve.

Serves 6 to 8.

—*Nancy R. Franklin*

Bacon & Egg Pie

Pastry for single 9-inch pie
   shell
½ lb. bacon
1 tomato
6 eggs
6 Tbsp. milk
salt & pepper
1 cup grated Cheddar cheese

Line pie plate with pastry. Fry bacon, drain well and place on pastry. Slice tomato over bacon. Beat eggs and milk together. Pour over tomato and bacon. Season with salt and pepper to taste. Top with grated cheese. Bake at 450° F for 45 minutes.

Serves 4.

—*Sheelagh Stone*

Ross's Betterave Pie

Using star anise seed clusters rather than ground anise results in a fresher taste. The clusters really do look like stars and have a musty licorice smell. Betterave is another word for beet.

2 star anise seed clusters
1 tsp. fenugreek
3 dried chili peppers
1 Tbsp. brandy
¾ lb. side bacon, chopped
1 onion, chopped
6 large eggs
⅛ tsp. white pepper
juice of 1 lemon
¼ cup chopped parsley
1 tsp. soy sauce
1 tsp. Worcestershire sauce
olive oil
filo pastry
1 lb. beet greens, washed & stems removed
1 lb. brick cheese, thinly sliced
1 cup sliced pitted black olives

Grind star anise, fenugreek and chili peppers to a powder with mortar and pestle. Add to brandy and let sit for 1 hour. Force through cheesecloth; keep the liquid and discard the rest.

Meanwhile, fry bacon until almost crisp. Drain off fat. Add onion to bacon and sauté for 5 minutes, or until onion is transparent. Combine eggs, pepper, lemon juice, parsley, soy sauce and Worcestershire sauce. Mix well, then stir in bacon and onion.

Brush 9" x 13" dish with olive oil. Place 4 layers of filo pastry in dish, brushing each layer with olive oil. Smooth on ½ the beet greens, then the egg mixture. Place cheese over this, then the olives. Add remaining beet greens, then top with 4 layers of filo brushed with oil. Bake at 350° F for ½ hour, or until golden brown.

Serves 4 to 6.

—*Steve D. Ross*

Broccoli & Cheese Pie

CRUST:
1 cup grated Cheddar cheese
¾ cup flour
¼ tsp. salt
¼ tsp. dry mustard
¼ cup butter, softened
FILLING:
1½ cups broccoli florets, steamed
1 cup evaporated milk
1 cup chopped onion
1 cup sliced mushrooms
½ tsp. salt
¼ tsp. nutmeg
pepper
3 eggs, lightly beaten

Combine crust ingredients and press into 9-inch pie plate. Place broccoli in pie plate. Combine milk, onion, mushrooms, salt, nutmeg and pepper in saucepan and simmer for a few minutes. Stir a bit of this into the eggs, then stir eggs into remaining hot mixture. Pour over broccoli.

Bake at 400° F for 15 minutes, reduce heat to 375° F and bake for another 30 to 35 minutes, or until firm. Let stand for 5 minutes before serving.

Serves 4 to 6.

—*Ingrid Magnuson*

Chilies Relleños Quiche

Pastry for single 9-inch pie shell
2 cups grated Monterey Jack cheese
4-oz. can whole green chilies
4 eggs
1 cup light cream
¼ tsp. pepper
2 eggs, separated
taco sauce

Bake crust at 425° F for 5 minutes. Sprinkle 1 cup cheese on crust, then layer with ½ the chilies. Repeat. Beat together 4 whole eggs, cream and pepper and pour over cheese and chilies. Bake at 375° F for 30 minutes.

In a small bowl, beat egg whites until stiff. Fold in lightly beaten yolks carefully. Spoon mixture over hot filling to edge of crust. Return to oven and bake for 5 minutes longer, or until golden brown. Serve with taco sauce.

Serves 6 to 8.

—*Linda Stanier*

French Canadian Onion Cheese Quiche

CRUST:
¾ cup flour
½ tsp. salt
¼ tsp. dry mustard
1 cup grated Cheddar cheese
¼ cup melted butter
FILLING:
2 cups finely chopped onion
2 Tbsp. butter
1 cup cooked noodles
2 eggs
1 cup hot milk
½ tsp. salt
pepper
1 cup grated Cheddar cheese

For crust: Combine flour, salt, mustard and cheese. Add melted butter and mix well. Pat into bottom and sides of 9-inch pie plate.

For filling: Cook onions in butter until transparent, then add noodles. Mix, then pour into pie plate. Beat together eggs, hot milk, salt, pepper and cheese. Pour over noodles.

Bake at 325° F for 35 to 40 minutes.

Serves 6.

—Jeannine Bélanger

Tamale Pie

This appealing dish, together with a green salad, makes a satisfying vegetarian meal.

2 onions, chopped
3 cloves garlic, crushed
¼ cup oil
1 green pepper, chopped
2 cups tomatoes, chopped
1½ cups corn
1 cup pitted black olives
½ Tbsp. chopped thyme
½ Tbsp. chopped oregano
½ Tbsp. chopped basil
1 tsp. chili powder
¾ cup yellow cornmeal
2 cups milk
3 eggs
2 cups shredded Cheddar cheese

Fry onions and garlic in oil until transparent. Add green pepper and cook 5 minutes longer. Add tomatoes, corn and olives. Cook, stirring, until heated through. Add herbs and chili powder, then set aside.

Cook cornmeal in milk over medium heat until thickened — about 8 to 10 minutes — stirring frequently. Remove from heat, beat in eggs, then add to vegetable mixture. Stir well. Place in greased casserole dish and bake, uncovered, at 350° F for 30 minutes. Sprinkle with cheese and bake for 20 minutes longer.

Serves 6.

—Terri d'Aoust

Liptauer Cheese Spread

Prepare in advance to allow the flavours to blend thoroughly. The paprika gives this Viennese cheese spread its beautiful colour. All ingredients should be at room temperature.

8 oz. cream cheese
½ cup butter
1 Tbsp. finely minced onion
1 Tbsp. dry mustard
2 anchovies
1 tsp. capers
1 Tbsp. caraway seeds
¼ tsp. paprika
1 clove garlic, crushed

Combine all ingredients and blend until smooth.

Makes approximately 1½ cups.

—Lillian Steinfeld

Herb Garden Cheese Ball

The herbs can be varied in this recipe—use whatever your garden produces.

1 cup ricotta cheese
¼ cup chopped basil
1 Tbsp. chopped chives
2 cloves garlic, crushed
1 Tbsp. Parmesan cheese
1 tsp. kelp powder
3 Tbsp. minced parsley

Combine all ingredients except parsley, blend well and form into a ball. Roll in parsley. Chill.

Makes approximately 1½ cups.

—Helen Shepherd

Parmesan Cheese Ball

Every cook has his or her own favourite cheese ball recipes. They are good for a nutritious, relatively unfattening accompaniment to raw vegetables, crackers or potato chips, and make ideal potluck fare. They can also be made well ahead of time, wrapped carefully, and kept refrigerated until needed. The following recipe makes a very mild cheese ball that is well complemented by raw vegetables.

8 oz. cream cheese, softened
⅓ cup Parmesan cheese
1 small onion, finely
   chopped
1 clove garlic, crushed
2 tsp. soy sauce
1 Tbsp. finely chopped
   parsley
¼ tsp. white pepper
½ cup finely chopped dill *or*
   parsley

   Combine cream cheese, Parmesan cheese, onion, garlic, soy sauce, 1 Tbsp. parsley and white pepper. Blend well and form into ball. Roll in chopped dill or parsley. Chill.

   Makes approximately 2 cups.
                 —Trudi Keillor

Blue-Cheese Spread

This cheese spread has a delicate blue-cheese flavour and a creamy consistency. It is equally delicious served with crackers or vegetables.

12 oz. cream cheese, softened
4 oz. blue cheese
juice of ½ lemon
½ tsp. Worcestershire sauce

   Combine all ingredients and blend until smooth. Chill.

   Makes approximately 2 cups.
         —Kathryn MacDonald

Potted Cheddar

This is a New Year's tradition with the contributor's family. It makes a flavourful addition to a holiday feast and, pressed into small crockery pots, is a wonderful gift. Serve at room temperature to appreciate the full cheese flavour.

1 lb. sharp Cheddar cheese,
   grated
1 onion, chopped
¼ cup chopped parsley
¼ tsp. salt
¾ tsp. dry mustard
⅛ tsp. Tabasco sauce
½ tsp. Worcestershire sauce
¼ cup tomato sauce
⅓ cup sherry

   Combine all ingredients and blend well. Chill.

   Makes approximately 4 cups.
        —Kathryn MacDonald

Spicy Cheddar Beer Dip

As well as making a tangy dip for vegetables or crackers, this makes a fine topping for soyburgers and hamburgers.

2½ cups grated sharp
   Cheddar cheese
½ cup beer
¼ cup mayonnaise
1 tsp. caraway seeds
1 tsp. Worcestershire sauce
¼ tsp. salt
¼ tsp. cayenne

   In a blender, at medium speed, combine all ingredients until smooth. Cover and refrigerate for at least 20 minutes.

   Makes approximately 3 cups.
        —Kristine Mattila

Dilly Cheese Ball

The combination of the dill and the cheeses creates a very pleasant taste. Garnish with (or roll in) fresh dill when it is in season for added dill flavour.

8 oz. cream cheese, softened
1½ cups grated sharp
   Cheddar cheese
½ cup chopped dill pickles
¼ cup finely chopped green
   onion
2 Tbsp. mayonnaise
1 tsp. Worcestershire sauce
½ cup finely chopped
   walnuts
2 Tbsp. finely chopped
   parsley

   Combine cream cheese, Cheddar cheese, dill pickles, green onion, mayonnaise and Worcestershire sauce. Beat until smooth. Cover and chill until firm. Shape into a ball and roll in mixture of nuts and parsley.

   Makes approximately 3 cups.
           —Virginia Grant

Soups & Chowders

Beef Stock

2 - 3 lbs. beef bones
8 cups water
1 onion, unpeeled
1 carrot, scrubbed & sliced
Celery leaves
2 - 3 sprigs parsley
5 - 6 whole peppercorns
3 whole cloves
Several basil leaves (1 tsp.
   crushed)
1 clove garlic
2 Tbsp. vinegar
2 tsp. salt

Brown bones slowly in a heavy pot. Add remaining ingredients and simmer, covered, for several hours. Strain broth and cool. Skim fat from top of stock.

—Jan Gilbert

Turkey Stock

1 turkey carcass
1 onion, halved
1 carrot, halved
1 - 2 celery stalks
2 - 3 sprigs parsley
5 - 6 peppercorns
1 - 2 bay leaves
1 tsp. savory
1 tsp. basil
4 whole cloves
2 tsp. salt
1 Tbsp. vinegar

Place all ingredients in a large pot and cover with cold water. Cover and simmer for several hours.

Strain and chill. Skim fat from top of stock.

—Jan Gilbert

Chicken & Mushroom Soup

¼ cup minced shallots
¼ cup diced celery
¼ cup sliced mushrooms
1½ tsp. butter
6 cups chicken stock
¼ tsp. salt
Pepper
½ cup fine egg noodles
⅓ cup diced chicken
½ tsp. fresh parsley

Sauté vegetables in butter. Add chicken stock, salt and pepper and cook for 20 minutes.

Cook egg noodles separately in salted water. Drain and rinse well under cold water. Add to soup. Add chicken and parsley.

Serves 6.

—Nicole Chartrand

Cock-A-Leekie

This soup originated in Scotland in the days when cock fights were popular. The loser in the fight was unceremoniously thrown into the soup pot.

3 lb. boiling chicken
1 bunch leeks, chopped
12 prunes
2 sprigs parsley
Salt & pepper

Simmer the chicken, covered with water, in a covered pot for 2 or 3 hours. Remove, separate meat from bones and return meat to pot.

Add the leeks along with the prunes, parsley and salt and pepper.

Simmer for another 45 minutes.

Serves 6.

—Cary Elizabeth Marshall

Potato Peel Broth

To make a vegetable broth or stock, use any leftover or over-ripe vegetables, no matter how unusable they appear, in addition to the ingredients listed below. Strongly flavoured vegetables, such as cabbage or broccoli, will impart their own flavour to the stock.

Peel from 6 to 7 large
   brown-skinned potatoes
1 large onion, peeled
2 carrots, scrubbed but
   unpeeled
1 stalk celery
2 qts. water
1 large sprig parsley
1½ Tbsp. olive oil
Small bay leaf
¼ tsp. thyme
Pinch sage
1 clove garlic
Tabasco sauce
1 tsp. lemon juice

Combine all ingredients except Tabasco sauce and lemon juice in a large pot and simmer for 1½ to 2 hours.

Strain out the vegetables for a clear broth, sieve or purée in blender for a thicker broth, removing the garlic and bay leaf first.

Add a few drops of Tabasco sauce and lemon juice before serving to bring out the flavours.

Makes 6 cups.

—Cary Elizabeth Marshall

Chicken Velvet Soup

The cream and milk impart a rich, smooth, velvety texture to this soup.

6 Tbsp. butter
⅓ cup flour
½ cup milk
½ cup light cream
3 cups chicken broth
1 cup finely chopped cooked
  chicken
Pepper to taste
Parsley & pimento to
  garnish

Melt butter in saucepan and blend in flour. Add milk, cream and broth and cook, stirring, until mixture thickens and comes to a boil. Reduce heat.

Stir in chicken and pepper. Heat again to boiling. Serve at once, garnished with parsley and pimento.

Serves 4.

—*Pam Collacott*

Turkey Noodle Soup

1 turkey carcass
1 onion, finely chopped
Small handful celery leaves,
  finely chopped
¼ tsp. each of savory,
  marjoram, thyme, sage &
  curry powder
Salt & pepper
2 tsp. soya sauce
2 cups fine egg noodles
Chopped parsley

Cover turkey carcass with cold water. Bring to a boil and simmer for several hours. Remove bones and meat from broth and chop meat. Return meat to the broth and chill. Skim off fat.

Reheat broth to boiling, add onion, celery leaves, seasonings and soya sauce. Simmer gently for 3 hours. Add egg noodles half an hour before serving. Top with chopped parsley.

Serves 6 to 8.

—*Ruth Anne Laverty*

Snapping Turtle Soup

4 cups turtle meat
Cold water
½ stalk celery
4 onions
1 carrot
4 cups peas
2 cups corn
4 hard-boiled eggs
4 potatoes
1 handful pickling spice in
  cheesecloth
Juice from 3 or 4 lemons
½ cup ketchup
Salt & pepper
½ cup flour

Cover turtle meat on bone with water and cook until meat falls off bone. Strain through cloth, reserving broth, and leave meat to cool.

Grind meat, celery, onions, carrot, peas, corn, eggs and potatoes.

Combine broth, spice bag, ground ingredients, lemon juice, ketchup and salt and pepper. Cook 1½ to 2 hours over medium heat, stirring often. Remove spice bag.

Brown flour in skillet and stir into soup to thicken.

Serves 8 to 10.

—*Mrs. H. G. Fetzer*

Beef Lentil Soup

1½ cups raw lentils
2-3 lbs. beef soup bones
2 onions, chopped
3 stalks celery, chopped
¼ lb. spinach, torn into
    bite-sized pieces
3 large tomatoes, chopped
Salt & pepper
Oregano & basil
2 cloves garlic, minced
2-3 bratwurst sausages,
    chopped

Soak lentils in water for 2 hours. Brown soup bones, then cover with water and pressure cook for 1 hour. Remove bones and skim fat. Sauté onions, celery, spinach and tomatoes and add to beef and stock. Add lentils, seasoning, garlic and sausages. Simmer for several hours, adding water if necessary.

Serves 6 to 8.

—D. Parsons

Beef & Barley Soup

2 cups stewing beef, browned
9 cups cold water
1 cup tomato juice
1 cup raw barley
½ cup finely chopped onion
½ cup carrots, cut in very
    thin strips
3 beef bouillon cubes
    (optional)
1 tsp. salt
⅓ cup finely chopped celery

Combine all ingredients in large pot and simmer, covered, for 3 hours or until barley is tender. Taste for salt and adjust if necessary.

—Wendy Neelin

Hearty Winter Soup

3 lbs. meaty soup bones
10 cups water
2 tsp. salt
3 slices onion
3 peppercorns
¾ lb. ground beef
1 egg
½ cup dry bread crumbs
¼ cup tomato juice
¾ tsp. salt
¼ cup chopped onion
¼ tsp. garlic powder
1 cup egg noodles
15-oz. can tomatoes
2 cups mixed chopped
    vegetables

Cover bones with water and add salt, onion and peppercorns. Simmer, covered, for 3 hours. Remove bones and boil to reduce stock to 6 cups.

Meanwhile, combine ground beef, egg, bread crumbs, tomato juice, salt, onion and garlic powder. Shape into small balls and fry until a rich brown colour. Drain and set aside.

Cook noodles in salted water and drain.

Add vegetables and tomatoes to stock and cook until just tender. Add noodles and meatballs and boil gently for 15 minutes.

Serves 8.

—Shirley Hill

Habitant Pea Soup

Considered a national dish, This soup originated in Quebec and is simple, substantial and delicious.

1 lb. split yellow peas
2 qts. water
1 small carrot, grated
1 medium onion, diced
2 tsp. salt
2 sprigs parsley, minced
1 bay leaf
2 thick slices heavily
    smoked bacon
Pepper

Soak the peas in water overnight. In the morning, bring to a boil in a large saucepan and add carrot, onion and salt. Reduce heat to simmer.

Add parsley, bay leaf and chopped bacon to the soup and simmer for 3 to 4 hours, until thick, adding additional water as needed.

Remove bay leaf, adjust seasonings and serve.

Serves 6 to 8.

—Cary Elizabeth Marshall

Vegetable Beef Soup

This soup can be stored in the refrigerator and reheated, with additional leftover vegetables, for several days running.

Beef bones
2 cups canned tomatoes or tomato juice
2 onions, chopped
Small handful celery leaves, chopped
3 large potatoes, peeled & diced
6 carrots, diced
2 cups leftover cooked vegetables & gravy
½ cup rice or barley
¼ tsp. each of savory, marjoram, thyme & cumin
1 bay leaf
Salt & pepper
1 tsp. Worcestershire sauce or soya sauce

Cover bones with cold water and bring to a boil. Simmer for several hours. Remove bones, cut off meat and return meat to stock. Chill and skim off fat. Reheat stock to boiling and add vegetables and seasonings. Simmer until vegetables are tender.

Serves 6 to 8.

—*Ruth Anne Laverty*

Minestrone

1 clove garlic, minced
1 medium onion, chopped
½ cup chopped celery
1 Tbsp. oil
1 cup diced carrots
1 cup shredded cabbage
19-oz. can tomatoes
5 cups beef stock
½ cup chopped parsley
½ tsp. pepper
Salt
1 cup broken spaghetti noodles
1 cup thinly sliced zucchini
2-3 cups cooked kidney beans, undrained
2 cups cooked beef, finely chopped
Grated Parmesan cheese to garnish

In a heavy pot, sauté garlic, onion and celery in oil. Add carrots, cabbage, tomatoes, stock, parsley, pepper and salt. Cover and simmer for 20 minutes.

Add noodles, zucchini, beans and meat. Simmer 10 minutes longer or until spaghetti and vegetables are cooked. Add more salt if necessary.

Serve topped with freshly grated Parmesan cheese and accompanied by hot crusty bread.

Serves 6.

—*Jan Gilbert*

Beef Soup

2 Tbsp. butter
Beef bones
1½ cups chopped beef scraps
1 large onion, chopped
½ tsp. celery seed
6 cups water
Salt & pepper
Chopped vegetables

Melt butter in heavy pot. Add bones, chopped beef, onion and celery seed. Fry, stirring, until browned. Add water and salt and pepper.

Simmer, covered, for 2 to 3 hours. Remove bones. Add chopped vegetables.

Serves 4 to 6.

—*Velma Hughes*

Pork Hock & Lima Bean Soup

1 lb. dry baby lima beans
2 pig's feet or pork hocks
2 bay leaves
1 Tbsp. salt
4 onions, coarsely chopped
Several stalks celery, chopped

Soak beans overnight in water to cover. Drain and combine with remaining ingredients, add water and cook until the beans are tender and meat falls away from the bones.

Serves 6.

—*V. Alice Hughes*

Bean & Ham Soup

1½ cups dried lima beans
2 lbs. ham, with bone
1 large onion, quartered
1 large clove garlic, crushed
8¾ cups water
1 bouquet garni, consisting
  of 4 parsley sprigs, 1 spray
  thyme & 1 bay leaf
½ tsp. white pepper
20 large black olives, cut in
  half
3 Tbsp. chopped parsley to
  garnish

Put the beans in a bowl, cover with water and let soak overnight. Drain and place in a large saucepan with the ham, onion and garlic. Add water, place the pot on high heat and bring to a boil.

Add the bouquet garni and pepper to the pot and stir well. Lower the heat and simmer the soup for 1½ to 2 hours, or until the beans are cooked.

Remove the meat and cut into pieces. Remove the bouquet garni and discard. Purée some of the beans and return to soup to thicken. Stir in the ham pieces and the olives. Taste and add more salt and pepper if necessary. Pour the soup into bowls and garnish with parsley.

Serves 6 to 8.

—Dolores de Rosario

Pea Soup

1 ham bone
1 large onion, chopped
1 rib celery, chopped
1 cup chopped celery leaves
1 carrot, finely diced
1 bay leaf
1 lb. split peas
Salt & pepper
2 sprigs fresh parsley
1 cup sour cream

Place all ingredients except sour cream in large, heavy pot and cover with cold water. Bring to a boil, lower heat and simmer for several hours, until peas are very soft.

Remove bone and chop meat. Put soup through blender, 2 cups at a time, and return to pot with chopped ham. Add sour cream, stir and heat through.

Serves 12.

—Virginia Mitchell

Green Pea Purée

1 large potato
2 large carrots
2 large onions
2 stalks celery, diced
4 stalks asparagus (optional)
2 qts. fresh peas
4 cups chicken stock
1 Tbsp. tarragon

Peel potato, carrots and onions and slice thinly. Combine with celery and asparagus and cover with water in a saucepan. Boil until soft — 10 to 15 minutes. Drain. Meanwhile, cook peas until tender in chicken stock with tarragon. Place 3 large spoonfuls of vegetables in blender and add 1½ cups of stock. Liquify. Continue until all the vegetables and stock are blended. Makes 10 cups. This purée may be frozen and stored until needed for soup. To make soup: to 1 cup of purée, add 2 cups of milk and heat gently, adding salt and pepper to taste.

—John D. Perkins

Borscht

6 medium beets
1 medium onion
1 medium potato
1 medium apple
2 carrots
½-1 lb. beef, tenderized &
   thinly sliced
2 Tbsp. butter
6-8 cups boiling water
½ small cabbage
Salt & pepper
1 tsp. dill weed
½ cup lemon juice
Sour cream to garnish

Peel vegetables and apple and grate coarsely. Brown meat in oil in large soup pot.

Melt butter, add vegetables except cabbage, and cook, covered, for 1 hour, stirring occasionally.

Add boiling water, cabbage, salt, pepper, dill weed and lemon juice. Cook 15 minutes longer. Adjust seasonings if necessary. Serve with sour cream.

Serves 8.

—Lois Pope

French Onion Soup

2 medium onions, thinly
   sliced
1 Tbsp. butter
2 cups beef stock
2 Tbsp. lemon juice
¼ tsp. nutmeg
Worcestershire sauce
Salt & pepper
4-6 Tbsp. Parmesan cheese
¾ cup grated Swiss cheese
2 cups toasted croutons

Cook onions in butter over medium heat for 3 minutes. Add stock, lemon juice, nutmeg and a few drops of Worcestershire sauce. Cook gently until onions are tender. Season with salt, pepper and 2 Tbsp. Parmesan cheese.

To serve, place the Swiss cheese in 2 soup bowls. Ladle soup into bowls and top with croutons. Sprinkle with remaining Parmesan cheese.

Broil until cheese is lightly browned.

Serves 2.

—Christine Collis

Navy Bean Soup

2 cups navy beans
6 cups water
1 large onion
1 large stalk celery
2 carrots
Bay leaf
Salt

Cook beans in water until tender — 45 minutes to 1 hour. Add remaining ingredients and cook until vegetables are tender — 1 to 2 hours.

Serves 6.

—Nel vanGeest

Fresh Tomato Soup

½ cup chopped onion
¼ cup butter
¼ cup flour
1 cup water
6 medium tomatoes, peeled,
   seeded & diced
1 Tbsp. minced parsley
1¼ tsp. salt
½ tsp. thyme leaves
¼ tsp. pepper
1 bay leaf
Lemon slices to garnish

In a 3-quart saucepan over medium heat cook onion in butter until tender. Stir in flour until blended. Gradually stir in water.

Add tomatoes and remaining ingredients, except lemon slices, and heat mixture until boiling. Reduce heat to low, cover and simmer for 30 minutes, stirring frequently. Add more water if needed. Discard bay leaf. Serve with lemon slices.

Serves 3 to 4.

—Margaret Godbeer Houle

Freezer Cream of Tomato Soup

2 onions, chopped
2 carrots, diced
6 Tbsp. butter
½ cup flour
6 cups water
2 lbs. chicken backs or
  necks
6 cups ripe tomatoes
¼ tsp. thyme
Salt & pepper
Celery leaves
Parsley & basil

In a deep pot, sauté onions and carrots in butter. Slowly stir in flour, then gradually add water. Cook, stirring constantly, until thickened.

Add remaining ingredients, cover and simmer for 1 hour. Discard bones. Purée soup in blender. Freeze.

To serve, combine equal amounts of milk and tomato purée and heat thoroughly.

Makes 12 cups of purée.

—Mrs. L.H. Lowther

Curried Pea Soup

1 lb. garden peas
3 Tbsp. butter
3 Tbsp. flour
4 Tbsp. curry powder
4 cups vegetable stock
1 cup milk

Blend peas. Melt butter and stir in flour. Add peas, curry powder, milk and stock and mix well. Cook until slightly thickened.

Serves 4 to 6.

—Mrs. A.E. Nehua-Cafe

Tomato Wine Soup

1 cup dry white wine
½ cup dry sherry
3 cups beef stock
4 cups tomato juice
½ cup sliced onion
2 sprigs parsley
2 stalks celery, chopped
1 Tbsp. honey
½ tsp. pepper
2 cloves
1 lemon, sliced

Combine all the ingredients in a saucepan and bring to a boil. Reduce the heat, cover and cook slowly for 20 minutes.

Strain the soup and return it to the saucepan. Adjust seasoning. Heat thoroughly and serve.

Serves 8 to 10.

—Janet Flewelling

Tomato & Cheddar Cheese Soup

4 cups finely chopped onions
½ lb. butter
12 cups crushed tomatoes
12 cups water
18 cups grated Cheddar
  cheese
12 cups sour cream

Sauté onions in butter until soft. Add tomatoes, water and cheese and cook, stirring, until cheese is mostly melted.

Stir in sour cream.

Serves 50 to 70.

—Terry Shoffner

Mushroom Barley Soup

½ cup raw barley
4 cups vegetable or chicken
  stock
½ cup chopped celery
½ cup diced carrots
3 Tbsp. butter
1 clove garlic
1 cup chopped mushrooms
½ cup chopped onion
Salt

Cook barley in stock over low heat for 45 minutes or until barley is tender.

Meanwhile, sauté celery and carrots in butter with garlic. After 10 minutes add mushrooms and onion. Cook until onion is soft. Remove garlic.

Add vegetables to barley and stock and cook for 5 minutes.

Serves 4.

—Debbi Walsh

Spinach Soup

4 cups chicken stock
¾ lb. spinach
Hard-boiled eggs & sour
  cream to garnish

Bring stock to a boil. Wash spinach and tear into bite-sized pieces. Add to boiling stock and simmer briefly.

Place in individual bowls and garnish with sour cream and hard-boiled eggs.

Serves 4.

—Carole Peterson

Artichoke Soup

6 medium artichokes
2 Tbsp. oil
4 cloves garlic, crushed
Salt
3 eggs
½-¾ cup grated Parmesan
　　cheese
½-¾ cup bread crumbs
1 tsp. paprika
2 cups water

Wash artichokes and trim outer leaves. Cut into quarters, place in a pot and cover with water. Add oil, garlic and salt to taste. Cook over medium heat for 45 minutes.

Meanwhile, combine 1 egg with enough cheese and bread crumbs to make a moist paste. Stir in salt and paprika. Roll into tiny balls.

Add cheese balls to the soup and simmer gently for 15 minutes. Add water and salt to taste. Beat together remaining 2 eggs and slowly pour into soup, stirring gently. Simmer for 10 minutes.

Serves 4.

—Mary Andrasi

Cream of Shrimp Soup

¼ cup butter
2 tsp. chopped onion
¼ cup flour
1 Tbsp. chicken stock
1 cup light cream
2 cups milk
1 tin small shrimp,
　　undrained
2 Tbsp. sherry
Parsley to garnish

Melt butter in top of double boiler, add onion and flour and blend well. Add stock, cream and 1 cup milk and cook, stirring constantly, until slightly thickened.

Stir in undrained shrimp and cook, covered, over boiling water for 10 minutes. Add sherry and remaining cup of milk. Heat through.

Serve garnished with parsley.

Serves 3.

—Shirley Hill

Cream of Fiddlehead Soup

3 cups fiddleheads
3 cups cream
2 Tbsp. butter
⅛ tsp. pepper
Marjoram
Chicken stock to thin

Cook fiddleheads in salted water for 15 to 20 minutes. Drain and chop.

To chopped fiddleheads, add cream, butter, pepper and marjoram to taste. Heat gently and add chicken stock, if desired, to thin soup. Simmer for 10 to 20 minutes.

Serves 4.

—Trudy Mason

Sherried Wild Rice Soup

2 Tbsp. butter
1 Tbsp.-½ cup minced onion
¼ cup flour
4-5 cups chicken stock
1-2 cups cooked wild rice
½ tsp. salt
1 cup light cream
¼ cup dry sherry
Parsley or chives, minced

Melt butter in saucepan, add onion and cook until onion is golden. Blend in flour and stock, stirring constantly until thickened. Stir in rice and salt and simmer 5 minutes.

Blend in cream and sherry and simmer until well heated. Garnish with minced parsley or chives.

Makes 6 cups.

—Anne Ulmer

Miso Soup

2 carrots
2 onions
Oil for frying
4 cups water
1 strip kombu (seaweed),
　　chopped & soaked until
　　soft
4 Tbsp. miso

Chop carrots and onions and fry in oil. Bring water to a boil, add vegetables and seaweed and simmer for 20 to 30 minutes.

Remove from heat and add miso. Stir.

Serves 4.

—Terry Bethune

Maritime Clam Chowder

4 large onions, chopped
¼ cup butter
8 medium potatoes, peeled &
  cubed
1 Tbsp. salt
½ tsp. pepper
4 cups milk
2 cups grated Cheddar
  cheese
2 cans clams
3 Tbsp. parsley

Sauté onions in butter in large, heavy saucepan until tender. Add potatoes, salt and pepper and cover with boiling water. Simmer, covered, for 20 minutes or until potatoes are tender.

Add milk and cheese, stirring until cheese is melted. Add clams. Heat through, but do not boil. Stir in parsley.

Serves 8.

—Debbie Walker

Manhattan Clam Chowder

¼ cup chopped onion
2 Tbsp. butter
1 cup diced potato
¼ cup chopped celery
2 cups boiling water
1 cup canned tomatoes
1 tsp. salt
Pepper
¼ tsp. thyme
1 cup chopped clams
1 cup clam liquor

Brown onion in butter. Add potato, celery and boiling water and cook for 10 minutes or until potato is tender.

Add remaining ingredients and simmer for 20 minutes.

Serves 4 to 6.

—Delia Schlesinger

Fish Chowder

2 slices bacon
1 medium onion, chopped
¼ green pepper, chopped
1 medium potato, peeled &
  sliced
½ pkg. frozen cod fillets,
  thawed
1 cup water
1 tsp. salt
1 bay leaf
⅛ tsp. basil, thyme **or** fennel
3 Tbsp. flour
1 cup milk
1 cup table cream

Fry bacon in large heavy saucepan until crisp. Lift out and crumble. Turn heat to low and fry onion and green pepper for 2 minutes. Drain and reserve bacon fat. Put potato, fish, water and seasonings in pot, bring to a boil and simmer gently, covered, for 10 minutes.

Remove fish, separate into large chunks and return to the pot. Blend together 3 Tbsp. reserved bacon fat, flour and milk. Add to pot, discarding bay leaf. Add cream and bacon bits. Reheat, without boiling, and stir gently as it thickens.

Serves 4 to 6.

—Joan Graham

Oyster chowder

6 slices bacon, diced
1 cup chopped onion
1 pint fresh oysters
2 cups diced potatoes
¾ cup diced carrots
4 cups light cream
2 tsp. salt
Pepper
½ cup dry white wine
¼ cup chopped parsley

In a large frying pan, cook bacon until crisp. Remove, then sauté onion in fat until golden brown. Simmer oysters in their liquor for 3 minutes. Drain and reserve liquid. Add water to reserved oyster liquor to make 1 cup. Add vegetables and liquid to onion, cover and simmer until vegetables are tender — about 15 minutes. Stir in cream, salt and pepper and bring soup to a boil. Reduce heat, add oysters and wine and heat through.

Serves 8.

—Carol Frost

Cream of Cauliflower Soup

½ cup butter
1 onion, finely chopped
2 stalks celery, finely chopped
1 apple, peeled & finely chopped
1 tsp. curry powder
¼ cup flour
4 cups chicken stock
1 small head cauliflower, cut into small flowerettes
1 egg yolk, lightly beaten
1 cup light cream
Salt & pepper
2 Tbsp. parsley, to garnish

Melt butter and sauté onions, celery and apple. Sprinkle with curry powder and flour. Cook, stirring, for 2 more minutes.

Gradually stir in stock. Bring to a boil and add the cauliflower. Cook, covered, for 10 minutes. Combine egg yolk and cream and gradually stir into mixture. Heat but do not boil.

Sprinkle each serving with parsley.

Serves 4.

—Olga Harrison

Potato Soup

5 medium potatoes
Garlic salt
½ small onion, chopped
Celery salt
2 Tbsp. butter
¼ cup flour
3 cups milk

Peel and wash potatoes and cut into 1-inch pieces. Cover with water and bring to a boil. Add garlic salt, onion and celery salt and cook until potatoes are tender.

Remove from heat; do not drain. Mash well. Cover with a lid and set aside.

Melt butter in a small saucepan and slowly add flour to make a fine paste. Remove from heat.

Return potatoes to heat and add flour paste a little at a time. Bring to a boil, stirring constantly. Add milk slowly, stirring to avoid scorching, and cook until thoroughly heated.

Serves 4.

—Deborah Exner

Cream of Swiss Chard Soup

⅓ cup chopped onion
¼ cup melted butter
⅓ cup flour
2 tsp. salt
¼ tsp. pepper
⅛ tsp. nutmeg
6 cups milk
2 cups chopped, cooked Swiss chard

Sauté onion in butter until tender. Blend in flour, salt, pepper and nutmeg. Cook slowly until mixture is smooth and bubbly. Gradually stir in milk and Swiss chard. Bring to a boil, stirring constantly, and cook for 1 minute.

Serves 6 to 8.

—Florence Graham

Leek & Potato Soup

This is a hearty variation of the cold soup, vichyssoise. It can be blended immediately before serving for a smoother texture.

1 slice bacon
1 oz. butter
1 lb. potatoes
2 large leeks
1½ cups chicken stock
Salt & pepper
½ cup milk
½ cup grated cheese
Parsley

Cut up the bacon and fry in butter. Peel and cut potatoes, and clean and cut up leeks. Add to the saucepan and fry for 5 minutes. Stir in stock, add salt and pepper to taste. Cover and simmer for 30 minutes until the vegetables are tender. Add milk and reheat but do not boil. If desired, blend for a few seconds. Serve with grated cheese and parsley.

Serves 4.

—Mary Rogers

Cheesy Onion & Potato Soup

3 medium onions, chopped
2 Tbsp. butter
4 medium potatoes, peeled & cubed
2 cups chicken stock
¼ tsp. salt
Pepper
3 cups milk
1 cup shredded Cheddar cheese

Cook onions in butter until soft but not brown. Add potatoes, stock, salt and pepper. Cover, bring to a boil, then simmer until potatoes are tender, about 15 minutes.

Remove from heat and blend in parts in blender or food processor. Return to saucepan, add milk and cheese and reheat slowly until cheese melts. Do not boil.

Makes 6 servings.

—Christine Steele

Turnip Soup

1 medium turnip
1 onion
2 cups chicken stock
Pinch garlic salt
Pinch curry powder
1½ cups cream
Salt
Sour cream

Chop turnip and onion and boil with stock, garlic salt and curry powder until tender. Place in blender and purée. Cool and add cream.

Heat soup, adding salt to taste. Garnish generously with sour cream.

Serves 2 to 4.

—Michael Bruce-Lockhart

Chunky Corn Chowder

This soup takes only minutes to put together—with ingredients which are usually on hand.

4 slices bacon, diced
1 small onion, chopped
1 cup chopped celery
2 large potatoes, peeled & cubed
1 qt. milk
¾ lb. kernel corn
1 tsp. salt
½ tsp. dried dill
Freshly ground pepper
¼ tsp. Tabasco sauce

Cook the bacon in a large saucepan just until it begins to brown. Add onion, celery and potatoes. Cook over medium heat, stirring occasionally, until the onion is soft — about 5 minutes.

Add the remaining ingredients. Cover and heat, but do not boil. Reduce heat and simmer 20 to 30 minutes or until potatoes are tender. Stir often.

Serves 6.

—Shirley Hill

Cheese Soup

½ cup grated carrot
2 onions, chopped
4 Tbsp. oil
½ cup flour
4 cups vegetable stock
4 cups milk
2 Tbsp. soya sauce
1 tsp. dry mustard
1 tsp. paprika
1 lb. sharp Cheddar cheese, grated
¼-½ lb. Swiss cheese, grated
1 green pepper, chopped
4 stalks celery, chopped

Sauté grated carrot and one of the onions in oil in a frying pan. Gradually add the flour, then some of the vegetable stock, stirring and keeping the mixture consistently smooth. Pour into a large soup pot over low heat. Gradually add remaining stock, milk and seasonings. Add cheese slowly and stir constantly as it melts. Add remaining onion, green pepper and celery.

For variety, add any other chopped green vegetables and simmer until cooked.

Serves 8.

—Sandra Wozniak

Wild Country Cream Soup

1 cup fiddlehead ferns
½ cup butter
¾ cup finely chopped wild leeks
¼ cup finely chopped green onions
1 cup sliced mushrooms
1 tsp. salt
Cayenne
¼ cup flour
1 cup chicken stock
3 cups milk
1 tsp. salt
1 tsp. lemon juice

Clean fiddleheads thoroughly. In a saucepan, cook ¼ cup of the butter, the leeks, onions, fiddleheads and mushrooms until tender but not browned. Add salt and cayenne.

Gradually add remaining butter, flour and chicken stock, stirring constantly, and bring to a boil. Add milk and cook on low heat for 1 hour. Allow to cool, then reheat to serve.

Serves 6.

—Janet Mayhew

Parsnip Chowder

¼ lb. pork belly
2 slices lean bacon, cut into strips
1 large onion, diced
1 large leek, diced
4 parsnips, diced
3 potatoes, diced
2 cups chicken stock
Juice of ½ lemon
1 cup whipping cream
Salt & pepper
Chopped parsley or chives to garnish

Dice pork and fry slowly in heavy saucepan until well browned. Remove with slotted spoon and set aside.

In remaining fat, fry bacon, onion and leek until golden brown. Remove. Fry parsnips and potatoes until golden, adding butter if necessary.

Return onion and bacon to pan, add stock, bring to a boil and simmer until tender but not mushy — about 10 to 12 minutes. Add lemon juice.

Stir in cream, salt and pepper, and bring chowder back to a boil. Serve garnished with pork and chopped parsley or chives.

Serves 6.

—Sheila Bear

Fresh Vegetable Soup

2 cups diced unpeeled potatoes
1 cup diced carrots
1 cup diced kohlrabi
1 cup peas
1 cup sliced green beans
2-3 small onions
Parsley
Salt & pepper
2 cups milk
2 cups cream
2 Tbsp. butter

Cook potatoes, carrots and kohlrabi in 2 cups of water. Add remaining vegetables after 5 minutes and cook a further 7 minutes.

Add remaining ingredients, bring just to the boiling point and serve.

Serves 4 to 6.

—Jean Stewart

Springtime Soup

This soup is a wonderful way to serve fresh, young vegetables — their delicate flavours are preserved by the short cooking time. Vegetables may be varied according to season.

1 cup chopped green onions
1 cup chopped baby beets & tops
1 cup chopped new carrots & tops
1 cup chopped new potatoes
1 cup edible podded peas
1 cup sliced green beans
6 cups goat's milk (light cream may be substituted)
Salt

Cook vegetables until tender in just enough water to prevent scorching. Add milk or cream and salt to taste. Heat to serving temperature, but do not boil.

—Harvey Lyons

Won Ton Soup

2 water chestnuts, finely
  chopped
½ lb. ground pork
1 lb. won ton wrappers
6 cups chicken stock
1 small head chard or
  spinach, chopped
Chopped green onion to
  garnish

Mix water chestnuts with ground pork.

Place a small amount of the meat on one corner of each won ton wrapper. Fold up meat and roll toward the centre. Shape into a crescent. Boil the won ton in batches in boiling water and drain. Combine chicken stock and chard or spinach. Add won ton and heat thoroughly.

Serve sprinkled with green onion.

Serves 6.

—Bryanna Clark

Heavenly
Egg Drop Soup

6 cups chicken stock
½ cup matchstick-cut
  bamboo shoots
4 dried forest mushrooms,
  soaked to soften & cut in
  matchsticks
2 eggs, beaten
2 Tbsp. chopped green
  onions or chives
½ tsp. Oriental sesame oil

Heat stock and add bamboo shoots and mushrooms. Simmer for 15 minutes, then bring to a boil. Reduce to a simmer and gradually add beaten eggs in a thin stream. Stir constantly.

Remove from heat, add onion or chives and sesame oil.

Serves 6.

—Lois Pope

Mushroom Soup

½ cup butter
¼ cup chopped onion
½ lb. mushrooms, chopped
¼ cup flour
1 tsp. salt
Pepper
1 cup chicken broth
3 cups milk
1 Tbsp. lemon juice
Parsley

Sauté onions in butter until tender. Remove and set aside. Sauté mushrooms until soft — about 10 minutes. Blend in flour, salt and pepper and gradually stir in broth and milk. Cook until mixture thickens and comes to a boil.

Add onions, lemon juice, salt and pepper and simmer 10 minutes. Serve with sprinkle of parsley.

Serves 6.

—Mary VanderSchaaf

Carrot Purée

3 cups diced carrots
½ cup chopped onion
1 stalk celery, diced
4 cups chicken stock
1 bay leaf
Nutmeg
⅔ cup milk or light cream

Combine carrots, onion, celery, chicken stock and bay leaf in a 1 ½-quart saucepan. Cover and simmer for 30 minutes or until carrots are soft. Remove bay leaf.

Process in a blender until smooth. Return to saucepan, add nutmeg and bring to a boil. Remove from heat and stir in milk. Reheat but do not boil.

Serves 6.

—E.A. Desfossés

Squash Blossom Soup

This soup provides a tasty way to thin out the garden in late July when the squash looks as though it is going to overrun everything else.

3 Tbsp. butter
⅔ cup minced onion
36 squash blossoms, stems
  discarded & coarsely
  chopped
3 cups chicken stock
1 cup light cream
1 egg yolk
Salt, pepper & nutmeg

Melt butter in heavy saucepan over medium heat. Add onion and sauté until soft. Stir in blossoms and soften.

Add stock and bring to a boil, reduce heat, cover and simmer for 10 minutes.

Beat cream with egg yolk, then stir in a small amount of hot stock. Slowly add this mixture to the rest of the soup, stirring constantly. Heat through and season to taste.

Serves 3 to 4.

—Ingrid Birker

Pesto soup

6-8 cups stock or water
1 onion, chopped
1 cup chopped potato
2 tsp. salt
4 Tbsp. olive oil
4 cups canned tomatoes
1 cup green beans, cut into
   1-inch pieces
1 cup zucchini, finely
   chopped
Pepper
4 cloves garlic
¼ cup fresh or 1 Tbsp.
   dried basil
¼ cup grated Parmesan
   cheese

Combine in a large pot the stock or water, onion, potato, salt and l Tbsp. of olive oil. Boil gently until potatoes are tender — 15 to 20 minutes.

Add drained tomatoes, green beans, zucchini and pepper to taste. Cook until vegetables are tender.

Meanwhile, crush garlic in a small wooden bowl. Pound in basil and, when well blended, work in Parmesan cheese and remaining 3 Tbsp. of oil.

Blend a few tablespoons of hot soup into pesto sauce, then add sauce to soup. Blend well and heat through.

Serves 8 to 10.

—Jan Post

Soupe au Pistou

A favourite in this London restaurant, Soupe au Pistou takes some time to cook, but is well worth the effort.

3 cups water
¾ cup dry navy beans
4 Tbsp. olive oil
1 cup diced onions
1 lb. tomatoes, peeled,
   seeded & finely chopped
3 qts. water
1½ cups diced carrots
1½ cups finely diced
   potatoes
1 cup chopped leeks
1 Tbsp. salt
Pepper
1½ cups sliced green beans
1½ cups diced zucchini
½ cup broken pasta
2 pinches saffron
3 cloves garlic
½ cup fresh or 3 Tbsp. dried
   basil
1 Tbsp. tomato paste
¼ cup Parmesan cheese
3 Tbsp. olive oil

Bring the 3 cups of water to a boil in a 1-quart saucepan. Drop in the dry beans and boil them for 2 minutes. Remove from heat and let the beans soak for 1 hour. Return to a low heat and simmer, uncovered, for 1 to 1½ hours, adding water if necessary, or until the beans are tender. Drain the beans and reserve cooking liquid.

Meanwhile, heat olive oil in a heavy soup pot. Stir in diced onions and cook over a moderate heat until transparent. Add the tomatoes and cook for 3 to 4 minutes. Pour in the 3 quarts of water and bring to a boil over high heat, stirring occasionally. Add the carrots, potatoes, leeks, salt and pepper. Reduce the heat and simmer, uncovered, for 15 minutes. Stir in the white beans and their liquid, the green beans, zucchini, pasta and

saffron. Simmer for another 15 minutes.

To make the pistou, mince the garlic and basil into a paste, using a mortar, food processor or blender. Work in the tomato paste and the cheese. Finally, beat in the olive oil one tablespoon at a time.

Add the pistou to the soup, or serve the soup accompanied with bowls of pistou.

Serves 12 to 15.

—Auberge du Petit Prince

Norwegian Sweet Soup

More common in other cultures than in our own, fruit soups, with their delicate, light flavours, are ideal first courses for heavy meals.

1 lb. dried fruits
½ cup tapioca
2 cups fruit juice
1 cup sugar
1 stick cinnamon
1 lemon, sliced

Cover fruit with water and bring to a boil. Stir in the tapioca and add the rest of the ingredients.

Cook over low heat for about 1 hour, stirring frequently. Serve hot.

Serves 4.

—Cary Elizabeth Marshall

Avoglimono

This Greek lemon soup has a smooth texture and is simple to assemble.

2 eggs
1 lemon
6 cups chicken stock
Salt
4 slices lemon to garnish

Beat eggs until frothy. Squeeze juice from lemon into the eggs, drop by drop, beating the whole time.

Heat chicken stock and stir in the lemon and eggs, adding salt to taste. Beat while heating for 1 minute.

Serve each bowl with a thin slice of lemon floating on top.

Serves 4.

—*Cary Elizabeth Marshall*

Apple Curry Soup

1 tart apple, unpeeled & quartered
1 onion, peeled & halved
2 cups beef or miso stock
1 tsp. honey
1 tsp. curry powder
Salt
1 cup light cream

Combine apple, onion and stock in a heavy saucepan. Add honey and bring to a boil. Reduce heat and simmer until the apple and onion are soft.

Blend in a blender, return to saucepan and add spices. Stir in cream and slowly heat through.

Serves 4.

—*Suezan Aikins*

Fruit Moos

Frozen or dried fruits are as good in this soup as fresh ones. If you are using dried fruit, soften it first in water or juice.

1 cup plums
1 cup peaches
1 cup rhubarb
1 cup cherries, pitted
Water
1 cup sugar
3 Tbsp. flour

Slice plums and peaches and chop rhubarb into 1-inch pieces. Place in saucepan with cherries and water to cover. Cook until tender. Remove fruit.

Combine sugar and flour and blend with enough water to make a thick paste. Stir into the water in saucepan and cook, stirring, over low heat until the mixture resembles a white sauce.

Add fruit and heat through. Taste and add sugar if a sweeter soup is desired.

Serve with heavy sweet cream.

Serves 4 to 6.

—*Valerie Lanctôt*

Chunky Gazpacho Summer Soup

2 large tomatoes, peeled & coarsely chopped
1 small cucumber, chopped
3 green onions, finely chopped
1 small green pepper, chopped
1 cup tomato juice
4 Tbsp. olive oil
1 Tbsp. cider vinegar
½ tsp. salt
⅛ tsp. pepper
Tabasco sauce
1 clove garlic, crushed

Mix all ingredients well. If a smooth soup is desired, it may be blended. Cover and refrigerate for at least 2 hours until icy cold.

Serves 4.

—*Margaret Silverthorn*

Hungarian Soup

3-4 medium potatoes
3 Tbsp. butter
2 Tbsp. flour
1 large tsp. Hungarian
  paprika
1-2 carrots, chopped
½ onion, chopped
1 small tomato, minced
1½ cups cubed turnip
Salt
8 cups water
1 cup spaghetti, broken into
  1-inch lengths

Peel potatoes, cut into small cubes and reserve in cold water. Melt butter in large pot and add flour, stirring until golden brown. Add paprika, potatoes, carrots, onion, tomato, turnip and salt. Add water.

Simmer, covered, until vegetables are partially done. Add spaghetti and cook until tender.

Serves 6.

—Darlene Abraham

Cold Yogurt Cucumber Soup

2 medium-sized cucumbers
Olive oil
½ tsp. salt
1 tsp. minced garlic
2 Tbsp. chopped fresh dill
Pepper
2 cups yogurt
1 cup iced water
⅓ cup chopped walnuts or
  almonds

Peel cucumbers if necessary. Cut in quarters lengthwise, then slice. Toss with a little olive oil to glaze them lightly. Add salt, garlic, dill and pepper to taste.

Chill for 1 to 3 hours. Drain and combine with yogurt, iced water and nuts. Check seasoning and serve very cold.

Serves 4.

—N. Burk

Cold Avocado Soup

3 avocados, peeled
1½ cucumbers, peeled &
  sliced
3 cups chicken stock
¾ cup sour cream
3 Tbsp. lemon juice
1½ tsp. salt
Tabasco sauce
Parsley to garnish

Chop avocados and cucumbers coarsely and purée in blender. Add stock, sour cream, lemon juice, salt and Tabasco sauce and mix well.

Chill thoroughly. Garnish with parsley and serve.

Serves 6 to 8.

—Joan Stevens

Cold Cucumber Soup

2 Tbsp. butter
¼ cup chopped onion
2 cups diced, peeled
  cucumber
½ cup chopped celery leaves
1½ cups basic white sauce,
  page 132
1 large potato, cooked,
  peeled & finely diced
Salt & pepper
¼ tsp. dry mustard
¾ cup water
Parsley to garnish

Melt butter, add onion and cook until transparent. Add cucumber, celery leaves, white sauce, potato, salt, pepper, mustard and water. Bring to a boil, reduce heat and cook for 10 minutes.

Blend in a blender for 40 seconds. Chill for several hours. Serve garnished with parsley.

Serves 4 to 6.

—Shirley Hill

Chilled Zucchini Soup

3 Tbsp. butter
2 cups sliced zucchini
1 slice onion
⅛ tsp. curry powder
2 cups chicken stock
½ cup light cream
Salt & pepper

Combine butter, zucchini, onion and curry powder in a heavy saucepan. Cook, stirring occasionally, until vegetables are tender. Add chicken stock and bring to a boil. Reduce heat and simmer for 15 minutes. Process in blender until smooth. Add cream and seasonings.

Chill for at least 1 hour before serving.

Serves 2 to 4.

—Carol Frost

Dill Cabbage Soup

This hearty soup takes only 30 minutes to prepare. For an even more substantial soup, sauté a half-pound of sausage pieces and add them to the soup after the first 5 minutes of simmering.

½ small head cabbage
2 small onions, chopped
1 tsp. dill seeds
½ tsp. caraway seeds
2 Tbsp. butter
3 garlic cloves, minced
1 Tbsp. mild vinegar
1 Tbsp. red or white grape
 juice
1½ cups tomato juice
2 tsp. tamari sauce
3 cups stock
1 large potato, diced
Pepper
6 Tbsp. plain yogurt
2 Tbsp. minced parsley or
 dill

Cut the cabbage into small pieces. In a 3-quart saucepan, sauté the cabbage, onion, dill seeds and caraway seeds in butter, stirring occasionally, until cabbage is translucent and wilted — about 10 minutes. Add garlic, vinegar and grape juice. Cook for 1 minute. Add tomato juice, tamari sauce, stock and potato.

Cover and simmer until potato is tender, about 15 to 20 minutes. Add pepper to taste.

Serve topped with a spoonful of yogurt and some minced parsley or dill.

Serves 6.

—*Irene Louden*

Mushroom Potato Soup

½ lb. mushrooms, chopped
1 medium onion, minced
1 Tbsp. butter
5 cups water
2 potatoes, peeled & cubed
2 tsp. soya sauce
Worcestershire sauce
1 Tbsp. lemon juice
1 tsp. salt
Pepper
1½ Tbsp. cornstarch
⅛ tsp. nutmeg
Chopped chives

In a Dutch oven, cook mushrooms and onion in butter for about 5 minutes. Stir in water and bring to boil. Add potatoes, soya sauce, Worcestershire sauce, lemon juice, salt and pepper. Cover and simmer for about 45 minutes. Add cornstarch (in a paste made by adding a small amount of cold water) and stir until mixture thickens slightly. Top with nutmeg and chopped chives.

Serves 8.

—*Anne Ulmer*

Scotch Soup

6 cups cold water
½ cup rolled oats
1 cup diced potatoes
2 cups diced turnips
¼ cup sliced carrot
¼ cup sliced celery
Bay leaf
2 Tbsp. butter
¼ cup chopped onion
2 cups tomatoes
½ tsp. salt

Combine water and oats in soup pot, bring to a boil and simmer for 30 minutes. Add vegetables and bay leaf and cook until vegetables are tender.

Meanwhile, in frying pan, melt butter and sauté onion. Add tomatoes and salt and cook for 15 minutes. Add to soup pot.

Serves 6.

—*Rose Strocen*

Mulligatawny Soup

This soup, also known as Mulligatawny Hotpot, is traditionally served accompanied by rice à la créole. This is prepared by covering the raw rice with water, cooking it and then setting the covered pan at the side of the stove for an hour to allow it to dry out.

1 onion, sliced
¼ cup butter
1 carrot, diced
1 stalk celery, sliced
1 green pepper, chopped
1 apple, sliced
1 cup diced cooked chicken
⅓ cup flour
1 tsp. curry
⅛ tsp. mace
2 whole cloves
Minced parsley
Pepper
2 cups chicken stock
1 cup stewed tomatoes

Sauté onion in butter in large, thick pot. Add vegetables, apple and chicken. Stir in flour and spices and gradually add chicken stock. Add tomatoes and simmer, covered, for half an hour or more.

—Cheryl Peters

Mushroom Leek Soup

2 bunches leeks
½ cup butter
½ lb. mushrooms, chopped
  or sliced
¼ cup flour
1 tsp. salt
Cayenne
1 cup chicken stock
3 cups milk
1 Tbsp. dry sherry
Salt & pepper

Wash leeks well; slice and use white part only. In ¼ cup butter, sauté leeks until tender but not browned. Remove and set aside. In remaining butter, sauté mushrooms until soft — about 10 minutes. Blend in flour, salt and cayenne. Gradually stir in stock and milk. Cook, stirring, until mixture thickens and comes to a boil. Add leeks, sherry and salt and pepper to taste. Simmer for 10 minutes.

Serves 4.

—Vanessa Lewington

Cabbage Soup

1 lb. ground beef
1 onion, chopped
½ cup chopped celery
2 Tbsp. oil
1½ tsp. salt
¼ tsp. pepper
½ tsp. paprika
28-oz. can tomatoes
10-oz. can tomato paste
4 cups beef stock
3 Tbsp. chopped parsley
2 cups diced carrots
1 small cabbage, shredded

Sauté ground beef, onion and celery in oil. Drain off excess fat. Add remaining ingredients except cabbage, and simmer, uncovered, for 1 hour. Add cabbage and simmer for l hour longer.

Serves 8 to 10.

—Patricia E. Wilson

Noel's Soup

1 cup finely chopped
  zucchini
1 cup finely chopped celery
¼ cup finely chopped green
  pepper
48-oz. can tomato juice
2 cups chicken or beef stock
1 small onion, chopped
Oregano
Salt & pepper

In a large pot, lightly sauté the zucchini, celery and green pepper. Add juice, stock and onion. Season with oregano, salt and pepper and simmer for 20 minutes.

Serves 4 to 6.

—Patricia Daine

Mushroom Rice Soup

1 clove garlic
1 large onion
1 Tbsp. oil
1 lb. mushrooms
1½ cups chicken stock
1 cup milk
1 cup cooked rice
Salt & pepper
Juice of ½ lemon
Parsley to garnish

Crush garlic, chop onion and sauté both in oil. Set aside.

Slice mushrooms into stock, bring to a boil and cook for 10 minutes. Pour half of the mushrooms and liquid together with the garlic and onion into the blender. Add milk and blend until creamy. Pour back into soup pot, mixing with the unblended mushrooms and liquid and the rice. Season and heat through. Remove from heat and add lemon juice.

Serves 4.

—Lorraine Murphy

Onion Soup

4-6 large onions
3-4 Tbsp. butter
4-5 cups chicken stock
¼ tsp. thyme
2 egg yolks, beaten with a
little water

Halve onions and slice thinly. Sauté in butter until golden. Add stock and thyme, bring to a boil and cook for 15 minutes.

Blend about three-quarters of the soup in blender and return it to soup pot. Bring back to a boil and stir in egg yolks. Serve.

Serves 4.

—Gabriele Klein

Vegetable Basil Soup

3 Tbsp. butter
1 onion, chopped
½ cup chopped celery
1 carrot, sliced
1 potato, peeled & cubed
2 ripe tomatoes, diced
4 cups chicken stock
½ tsp. salt
⅛ tsp. pepper
1 tsp. dry basil
1 tsp. oregano
¾ tsp. thyme
½ small head cauliflower,
chopped
¼ lb. fresh green beans,
sliced
2 small zucchini, sliced
½ lb. fresh green peas
Parmesan cheese

Melt butter in large soup pot over medium heat. Add onion, celery and carrot, and cook until limp. Add potato, tomatoes, stock, salt, pepper, basil, oregano and thyme to the pot. Partly cover and simmer for 20 minutes. Add cauliflower, green beans and zucchini and simmer for 10 minutes. Add peas and simmer for 5 minutes. Sprinkle Parmesan cheese over each serving.

Serves 4 to 6.

—Linda Stanier

Zucchini Soup

There can never be too many zucchini recipes for those who garden. This soup can be made from either freshly harvested or frozen zucchini. The addition of cream cheese makes the flavour irresistible.

1 large onion, sliced
1 clove garlic, crushed
4 Tbsp. butter
4 medium zucchini, chopped
1 tsp. basil
½ tsp. oregano
4 cups chicken stock
4 oz. cream cheese
Salt & pepper

Sauté onion and garlic in butter for 5 minutes. Add zucchini and herbs and cook over low heat for 5 minutes. Stir in chicken stock and heat through. Blend with cream cheese until smooth. Return to pot, add salt and pepper and heat.

Serves 4.

—Sharon Sims

Parsley Soup

4 cups chicken stock
2 cups firmly packed,
    chopped parsley
½ cup chopped onion
½ tsp. salt
Pepper
1 cup milk
2 cups peeled & diced
    potatoes
2 Tbsp. butter
¼ cup flour
1 Tbsp. dry sherry
Parsley

Place chicken stock, parsley, onion, salt and pepper in heavy saucepan. Bring to a boil, reduce heat and simmer, covered, for 30 minutes. Strain and reserve stock.

Place milk and potatoes in small saucepan, cover and cook over medium heat until potatoes are tender — about 15 minutes. Set aside.

Melt butter, stir in flour and cook over low heat, stirring constantly, until smooth and bubbly. Slowly stir in stock, heat to boiling and cook, continuing to stir, until slightly thickened — about 2 minutes. Reduce heat. Add potato mixture and sherry and heat through. Garnish with parsley.

Serves 4.

—Pam Collacott

Fruit & Vegetable Soup

This recipe was created for the adventurous soup quaffers of the Sunflower Restaurant.

Oil
6 large onions, finely
    chopped
3 large leeks, finely chopped
1 bunch celery, finely
    chopped
6 cups chopped assorted
    root crops (yams, potatoes,
    turnips, carrots)
4 cups chopped sweet & hot
    peppers
4 quarts vegetable stock
2 cups apple cider
2 cinnamon sticks
6 cloves
1 cup chopped parsley
Several sprigs thyme
4-6 cups coarsely chopped
    assorted dried & fresh
    fruits (apricots, apples,
    plums, dates, figs, grapes)
Salt & pepper
Orange slices

In hot oil, sauté onions, leeks and celery. Add chopped vegetables and stock. Bring to a boil, cover, lower heat and simmer until vegetables are tender.

Add apple cider, cinnamon sticks, cloves, parsley and thyme. Stir in fruit and salt and pepper to taste. Cook until flavours are well blended. Garnish with orange slices.

Serves 10 to 12.

—Deborah Washington

Rhubarb Soup

In Finland, as in other Scandinavian countries, fruit soup is popular and may be served either as a dessert or at the beginning of a meal.

2 lbs. red rhubarb
8 cups water
1 stick cinnamon
2 slices lemon
1½ cups sugar
2 Tbsp. cornstarch
⅓ cup cold water
1 egg yolk, beaten
½ cup heavy cream, whipped

Cut rhubarb in l-inch pieces and cook in 8 cups water until tender. Drain liquid through sieve, discarding pulp. Return juice to saucepan and cook with cinnamon and lemon for 5 minutes. Add sugar.

Mix cornstarch with ⅓ cup water and stir into hot juice. Cook, stirring constantly, for 5 minutes. Remove cinnamon and lemon.

Just before serving, combine beaten egg yolk with whipped cream and stir into hot soup.

Serves 8 to 10.

—Ingrid Birker

Strawberry Soup

2 pints strawberries
2 cups yogurt
½ cup orange juice
½ cup sugar
½ cup water
⅛ tsp. cardamom

Combine all ingredients and mix well in blender. Chill and serve.

Serves 4 to 6.

—M. Cummings

Portuguese Chicken with Lemon & Mint

12 cups water
½ cup chicken stock
¼ cup butter
3 large onions, chopped
3 large carrots, sliced
1 chicken
3-4 Tbsp. raw rice
6 Tbsp. lemon juice
Mint

Bring water to boil, add chicken stock and reduce heat to low. In another pan, sauté onions in butter until soft. Add to stock along with carrots, chicken and rice.

Cook until meat is tender — 2 to 3 hours. Remove chicken, discard bones and skin, chop meat and return to soup. Add lemon juice.

Sprinkle with chopped mint when serving.

Serves 8 to 10.

—Cindy McMillan

Chicken Corn Soup

1 quart chicken stock
2 cups corn
1 medium onion, chopped
1 green pepper, diced
1 cup cooked chicken
⅓ cup chopped parsley
Salt & pepper
2 Tbsp. cornstarch,
    dissolved in water
1 Tbsp. soya sauce

Bring stock to a boil and add corn, onion, green pepper, chicken and seasonings. Simmer for 5 minutes.

Thicken with cornstarch-water mixture and add soya sauce. Heat through.

Serves 4.

—Andrew Camm

Chicken Curry Soup

3 lbs. chicken
10 cups water
½ cup butter
1 onion, chopped
1 Tbsp. flour
1 Tbsp. curry powder
26-oz. can tomatoes
1 green pepper, diced
1 lb. carrots, diced
2 apples, diced
2 stalks celery, diced
1 tsp. mace
½ tsp. pepper
¼ cup rice

Cook chicken in water until tender — about 2 hours. Remove chicken from stock and set stock aside. Debone chicken, fry in butter and return to stock. Brown onion in remaining butter.

Combine flour and curry powder, adding a little water to form a paste. Add to onion and mix well.

Stir remaining ingredients into onion mixture, then add stock and chicken. Bring to a boil, reduce heat and simmer until vegetables are tender and rice is cooked.

Serves 8.

—Kathryn MacDonald

Hearty Meatball Soup

2 Tbsp. oil
1 medium onion, chopped
1 stalk celery with top,
    chopped
28-oz. can tomatoes
2 cups beef stock
1 lb. ground beef
1 egg
Grated Parmesan cheese
Salt & pepper
½ cup elbow macaroni
Chopped fresh parsley

Heat oil in large saucepan and sauté onion and celery for 5 minutes, or until tender. Add tomatoes and stock and cook over medium heat until mixture comes to a boil. Reduce heat and simmer.

Meanwhile, combine beef, egg, 1 Tbsp. Parmesan cheese, 1 tsp. salt, and pepper to taste. Shape into small (about 1-inch) meatballs and fry until browned. Drain off fat and drop into soup. Cover and simmer for about half an hour. Add macaroni, cover and simmer for 20 minutes longer, or until macaroni is tender.

To serve, sprinkle with Parmesan cheese and chopped parsley.

Serves 6.

—Judith Asbil

Oxtail Soup

3 oxtails, cut up
1½ Tbsp. salt
⅛ tsp. pepper
½ cup barley
2 cups diced onions
2 cups sliced carrots
1½ cups diced turnip
1 cup diced celery with tops
2 cups shredded cabbage
2 cups canned tomatoes
1 tsp. parsley

Wash oxtails well in cold water. Cover with fresh, cold water, bring to a boil and simmer for 1½ hours. Add salt and pepper and simmer for another 2½ to 3 hours, or until oxtails are barely tender. Remove from heat, add barley and let stand, covered, in a cool place overnight.

In the morning, remove layer of fat from stock. Remove oxtails, discard bones, chop meat and return to stock. Put stock on medium heat.

As stock heats up, add onions, carrots, turnip, celery, cabbage and tomatoes. Bring to a boil and add parsley. Lower heat and simmer for 1 hour.

Serves 8 to 10.

—Brian Lawrence

Meal in a Soup

1 lb. ground beef
2 medium onions, sliced
3 stalks celery, sliced
2 large carrots, sliced
1 medium potato, diced
1 parsnip, diced
1½ cups cauliflower florets
19-oz. can tomatoes
1½ tsp. salt
⅛ tsp. pepper
½ tsp. basil
¼ tsp. rosemary
½ tsp. thyme
½ tsp. sage
6 cups water
1 cup macaroni

Brown ground beef and drain well. Add remaining ingredients except macaroni. Cover and bring to a boil. Reduce heat and simmer for 30 minutes.

Add macaroni about 7 to 10 minutes before end of cooking time.

Serves 4 to 6.

—Susan Ching

Chinese Hot & Sour Soup

The variations of this recipe are almost endless. Chicken and chicken stock may be used in place of the beef and beef stock. Any crunchy vegetables may be added to, or replace, those mentioned below. If an egg-drop effect is desired, simply pour in a well-beaten egg after the soup has been removed from the heat and stir it in lightly. The two constants in the recipe are the hot pepper sauce and the vinegar to provide the hot and sour taste.

2 cloves garlic, halved
3 oz. beef flank, diced
2 Tbsp. oil
4 cups beef stock
2 tsp. dark soya sauce
½ tsp. Worcestershire sauce
¼ cup red wine
1 tsp. hot pepper sauce
Vinegar
2 oz. tofu
4 oz. fresh Chinese noodles
12 Chinese mushrooms
1 carrot, sliced
2 slices large onion
3 leaves Chinese cabbage
12 snow peas

Sauté garlic and beef in oil until garlic is golden. Add stock, soya sauce and Worcestershire sauce. Bring to a boil and cook for 10 minutes. Add wine, pepper sauce, vinegar to taste and tofu. Bring back to a boil. Add remaining ingredients except snow peas and cook briefly. Add snow peas and serve immediately.

—Lawrence Gellar

Legume Grain Soup

2 cups split peas
¼ cup brown rice
¼ cup pot barley
4 Tbsp. oil
1 medium onion, chopped
3-5 cloves garlic, crushed
2 stalks celery, chopped
½ green pepper, chopped
2 pork hocks
1 Tbsp. dried parsley
1 Tbsp. tamari sauce
1½ tsp. salt
⅛ tsp. pepper
Few drops Worcestershire
    sauce

Bring 4 cups water to a boil. Add split peas, rice and barley; cover and simmer.

Meanwhile, in a large soup pot, heat oil. Sauté onion, garlic, celery, green pepper and pork hocks for 10 minutes. Add 10 cups hot water, split pea mixture and remaining ingredients. Simmer, covered, for 1½ to 2 hours, stirring occasionally.

Remove meat and bones from soup, discard bones, chop meat and return to pot.

Serves 12.

—John Osborne

Beef Lentil Soup

1 lb. ground beef
1 medium onion, chopped
1 clove garlic, finely chopped
1 cup chopped mushrooms
28-oz. can tomatoes
1 medium stalk celery, sliced
1 large carrot, sliced
1 cup dried green lentils
3 cups beef stock
¼ cup red wine
1 bay leaf
2 Tbsp. snipped parsley
2 tsp. sea salt
¼ tsp. pepper

Cook and stir ground beef, onion and garlic in large pot until beef is light brown; drain. Stir in remaining ingredients. Heat to boiling, then reduce heat. Cover and simmer, stirring occasionally until lentils are tender — about 40 minutes.

Serves 4 to 6.

—Lois Verfaillie

Indian Lentil Soup

This soup makes an excellent accompaniment to a curry, and is delicious topped with a spoonful of yogurt. For a hearty lunch, serve this soup with warmed pita bread.

2 cups lentils
8 cups chicken or vegetable
    stock
1 onion, chopped
1 stalk celery, chopped
1 carrot, shredded
1 tsp. salt
¼ tsp. pepper
1 tsp. curry
½ tsp. cumin
½ tsp. coriander
¼ tsp. turmeric
¼ tsp. garlic powder

Put lentils in soup pot, cover with stock and bring to a boil. Add vegetables. Lower heat to simmer and add all spices. Simmer until lentils are soft, and soup is thickened with dissolved lentils — about 1 hour.

Serves 8.

—Marcy Goldman-Posluns

Leek & Lentil Soup

2 Tbsp. butter
2 Tbsp. oil
2 large leeks, chopped
1 medium onion, chopped
1 clove garlic, minced
1 cup lentils, washed
¼ cup pot barley
6 cups chicken stock
1 large carrot, sliced
1 large potato, chopped
1 stalk celery, chopped
2 cups canned tomatoes,
    chopped
Thyme
1 bay leaf, crumbled
Salt & pepper
Chopped parsley

In a big, heavy soup pot, melt the butter and oil. Add leeks, onion and garlic. Cook for a few minutes to soften.

Add lentils, barley and stock. Bring to a boil, then cover and simmer for about half an hour.

Add vegetables and seasonings. Cover and simmer about an hour longer, or until the vegetables are tender. Add parsley during last few minutes. Season to taste.

Serves 12.

—Sylvia Petz

Lamb & Lentil Soup

1 cup dried lentils
1½ lbs. lamb shoulder,
    trimmed of fat & diced
2 Tbsp. vegetable oil
1 large onion, chopped
1 small turnip, peeled &
    diced
2 carrots, peeled & diced
6 cups beef broth
Salt & pepper

Rinse lentils in cold water, place in bowl and cover with fresh, cold water. Soak for 2 hours, then drain.

In a pot, cook the lamb in oil over medium heat until evenly browned. Add the onion and cook until soft. Stir in the drained lentils, turnip, carrots, broth and salt and pepper.

Simmer, stirring frequently, for 3 hours, or until the lamb is fork-tender. Adjust seasonings.

Serves 6.

—Janet Ueberschlag

Bean Soup

3 cups dry white pea beans
10 slices bacon
3 cups chopped onion
1½ cups diced celery
10 cups liquid (use bean
    stock, adding water if
    necessary)
1 Tbsp. salt
1 tsp. pepper
2½ quarts milk
¼ cup chopped parsley
1½ cups grated carrot or
    other vegetable

Soak beans. For each cup of beans, add 2½ to 3 cups of water. Let stand for 12 hours, or overnight. Or, for a quick soak, slowly bring to a boil and cook gently for 2 minutes. Remove from heat and let stand 1 hour. Drain beans, reserving liquid.

Fry bacon until crisp, then drain. Sauté onion and celery in bacon fat until onion is transparent. Add bean liquid, beans and seasonings. Cover and cook until beans are tender and water is almost absorbed, about 2 hours. Add milk, parsley and carrot and bring to a boil. Sprinkle with crumbled bacon and serve.

Serves 16.

—Nancy Willard

Austrian Cream Cheese Soup

6 Tbsp. butter
6 medium leeks, finely
  chopped
4 celery stalks, finely
  chopped
6 Tbsp. flour
8 cups chicken stock
1 tsp. salt
1 lb. cream cheese, at room
  temperature
2 cups yogurt, at room
  temperature
4 egg yolks, beaten
White pepper
Parsley, chopped

Melt butter in heavy soup pot and sauté leeks and celery until limp. Stir in flour and cook, stirring, for 2 to 3 minutes. Add stock and salt, bring to a boil and simmer for 15 minutes.

Whisk cream cheese, yogurt and egg yolks until smooth. Add 2 cups of soup to cheese mixture, blend thoroughly and return to the pot. Stir until smooth and heat through, but do not boil. Sprinkle with pepper and parsley.

Serves 10.

—Charlene Skidmore

Souppa Fakki

This thick Greek bean soup served with fresh baked rolls and a salad can take the chill out of a cold winter's day.

1 lb. brown lentils
1 medium onion, coarsely
  chopped
2 stalks celery with tops,
  chopped
2 cloves garlic, minced
½ cup olive oil
3 Tbsp. tomato paste
1 Tbsp. wine vinegar
Salt & pepper

Put lentils in a 2-quart saucepan and cover with water 2 inches above lentils. Add onion, celery, garlic, olive oil, tomato paste and pepper. Cover, bring to boil, reduce heat and cook slowly over medium heat for 30 minutes.

Check occasionally and add more water if needed. Soup should be thick. Just before serving, add vinegar and salt to taste.

Serves 4.

—Jan Post

Cheddar Onion Soup

3 cups hot water
2 tsp. salt
8 potatoes, peeled & sliced
¼ cup butter
8 onions, sliced
5 cups milk
Parsley & celery leaves
¼ tsp. pepper
½-2 cups grated Cheddar
  cheese

Combine water, salt and potatoes and cook until potatoes are tender. Meanwhile, melt butter and cook onions until tender.

Combine onions, potatoes, 2 cups milk, parsley, celery leaves and pepper and blend until smooth. Return to pot and add remaining 3 cups milk. Heat to scalding but do not boil. Reduce heat, stir in cheese and cook until cheese is melted.

Serves 6.

—Marion Destorenis

Broccoli Garbanzo Soup

¼ cup butter
¼ cup flour
1 tsp. salt
⅛ tsp. pepper
2 tsp. turmeric
4 cups milk
1 cup cream
2 cups broccoli, steamed &
    cut into ½-inch pieces
1½ cups cooked garbanzo
    beans, drained

Melt butter in 3-quart
saucepan. Stir in flour, salt,
pepper and turmeric. Cook
slowly until mixture is smooth
and bubbly. Using a wire whisk,
gradually stir in the milk. Bring
to a boil, stirring constantly, and
cook for 1 minute. Add the
cream, broccoli and garbanzo
beans and heat through gently.

Serves 4.

—Kristine Reid

Cheese & Vegetable Chowder

4 Tbsp. butter
¼ cup finely chopped onion
1 cup chopped green pepper
1 cup pared, sliced carrots
1 cup pared, diced potatoes
1 cup peas
5 Tbsp. flour
3 cups chicken stock
3 cups grated, sharp cheese
2 cups milk
Salt & pepper
Chopped parsley

In a large saucepan, melt the
butter and cook the vegetables,
covered, stirring occasionally, for
20 to 25 minutes or until tender.
Remove from heat and stir in
flour mixing well. Cook 1
minute, stirring occasionally.

Add chicken stock to vegetable
mixture and bring to a boil,
again stirring to prevent any
sticking. Gradually add grated
cheese and cook over medium
heat until cheese has melted.
Add milk and seasonings. Bring
just to boiling point but do not
boil. Sprinkle with parsley.

Serves 6 to 8.

—Rebecca Gibson Spink

Creamy Cauliflower Soup

*The addition of Worcestershire
sauce to this recipe gives the
soup a pleasant bite. For those
wishing a milder flavour, it
could be omitted.*

1 head cauliflower, cut into
    bite-sized pieces
¼ cup butter
1 medium onion, chopped
2 Tbsp. flour
2 cups chicken stock
2 cups milk or cream
½ tsp. Worcestershire sauce
¾ tsp. salt
1 cup grated Cheddar cheese

Cook cauliflower in about 1
cup water. Drain and reserve
liquid. Set cauliflower aside. Melt
butter, add onion and cook until
soft.

Blend in flour, add stock and
bring to a boil, stirring well. Stir
in 1 cup cauliflower liquid, milk,
Worcestershire sauce and salt.
Add cauliflower and cheese and
heat through.

Serves 6.

—Ann Kostendt

Cream of Leek Soup

The leek is considered by many to be king of the soup onions. Because of their growing method, it is essential to wash leeks extremely carefully to rid them of all the trapped dirt.

5 large leeks
¼ cup butter
Salt & pepper
3 cups milk
1 Tbsp. flour
2-3 egg yolks, beaten

Wash and cut up leeks and cook in butter in heavy pan until soft but not browned. Add water to cover and salt and pepper. Simmer for 15 minutes. Blend well. Add milk and flour and bring to a boil. Just before serving, add egg yolks, beating the soup well as you add the yolks.

Serves 4.

—*Annick Hardie*

Mushroom Bisque

4 cups chicken stock
½ lb. mushrooms, chopped
1 onion, minced
¼ cup butter
¼ cup flour
1 cup milk
1 tsp. thyme
Salt & pepper

Combine stock, mushrooms and onion and simmer for 20 minutes.

In another pot, melt butter and stir in flour. When smooth, gradually add milk, stirring constantly, and cook until thick. Gradually stir into soup. Add seasonings.

Serves 4.

—*Billie Sheffield*

Green Meadow Soup

¼ cup minced green onions
   with tops
1½ Tbsp. unsalted butter
1½ Tbsp. flour
2 cups fresh peas
½ head Boston lettuce,
   shredded
½ cup spinach leaves
3 cups chicken stock
¼ tsp. salt
½ cup whipping cream
2 egg yolks
White pepper

Sauté onions in butter until soft, about 5 minutes. Stir in flour and cook, stirring constantly, for 2 minutes. Add 1½ cups peas, lettuce, spinach and salt. Stir in stock and heat to boiling. Reduce heat and simmer, covered, for 45 minutes. Cool slightly. Purée vegetable mixture in blender or food processor until smooth.

Beat cream, egg yolks and pepper in small bowl until smooth. Combine with puréed mixture in pot. Cook over low heat, stirring constantly, until soup is hot. Do not boil. Stir in remaining ½ cup peas.

Serves 4.

—*Pam Collacott*

Cream of Almond Soup

Especially delicious served cold in the summer, this unusual soup is also tasty served hot and can be quickly and easily prepared.

2 cups blanched almonds
3 Tbsp. butter
1 small onion or 1 stalk
   celery, sliced
3 Tbsp. flour
12 cups hot chicken stock
1 tsp. salt
½ tsp. pepper
2 cups thin cream, heated
1 tsp. almond extract

Sliver 30 almonds and toast at 225° F until brown. Grind remaining almonds. Melt butter in large saucepan, add onion or celery and cook until soft. Stir in flour. Add chicken stock, ground almonds and seasonings and cook, stirring, until mixture boils. Simmer for 1 hour, stirring occasionally, strain and add hot cream, toasted almonds and extract. Serve hot, or chill and serve cold.

Serves 8.

—*Hazel Baker*

Dilled Tomato Soup

This soup can be made equally successfully with canned or frozen tomatoes as with fresh. The dill, however, must be fresh — this is what gives the soup its delicious, definitive flavour.

10 large ripe tomatoes
1 large onion
2 cloves garlic, minced
3 Tbsp. butter
5 Tbsp. flour
2 tsp. tomato paste
5 cups chicken stock
1 cup whipping cream
4 Tbsp. dill weed
Salt & pepper

Coarsely chop 8 tomatoes without removing skins. Chop onion and sauté with garlic and 4 of the tomatoes in butter for 3 minutes. Remove from heat. Blend in flour, tomato paste and stock and bring to a boil. Lower heat, add 4 tomatoes and simmer for 15 minutes. Add cream.

Peel and chop remaining 2 tomatoes and add to soup with dill, salt and pepper. Heat through, stirring well so cream does not curdle.

Serves 8.

—Ingrid Birker

Vegetable Chowder

3 slices bacon, diced
½ cup chopped onion
1 cup creamed corn
1 cup chopped green beans
1 cup tomatoes
½ tsp. salt
¼ tsp. pepper
4 cups hot milk

Fry bacon in a large saucepan, add onion and sauté until tender. Add remaining ingredients and heat to almost boiling, stirring constantly.

Serves 4.

—Vicki deBoer

Ham & Potato Chowder

1 large onion, chopped
3 Tbsp. butter
½ cup water
6 medium potatoes, cut in ½-inch cubes
4 Tbsp. flour blended with ½ cup milk
3½ cups milk
2 cups cubed, cooked ham
1 tsp. salt
½ tsp. thyme
¼ tsp. pepper

Sauté onion in butter until tender. Stir in water and potatoes, cover and cook for 10 to 15 minutes. Stir in flour-milk mixture. Add milk, ham, salt, thyme and pepper and stir well.

Cover and cook for 5 to 10 minutes, or until potatoes are tender and soup is hot.

Serves 6.

—Janice Chammartin

Ol' Magic Tomato Soup

28-oz. can tomatoes
1 onion
1 bay leaf
2 cloves
¼ tsp. baking soda
½ tsp. sugar
2 Tbsp. butter
2 Tbsp. flour
1 quart milk, heated
½ tsp. salt
¼ tsp. paprika

Put tomatoes, onion, bay leaf and cloves in saucepan and cook for 10 minutes. Purée and strain. Add soda and sugar.

Melt butter and add flour. Cook for 2 minutes. Add hot milk. Season with salt and paprika. Mix this cream sauce into the tomato mixture and serve immediately.

Serves 6.

—Vera Fader

Corn Tomato Chowder

¼ lb. bacon
1 small onion
2 cups corn
2 cups tomatoes
2 cups diced potatoes
2 tsp. salt
½ tsp. paprika
⅛ tsp. pepper
1 tsp. basil
3 cups boiling water
1 cup cream

Fry bacon until crisp, then crumble. Sauté onion in drippings and add the rest of the ingredients except cream. Simmer until potatoes are tender. Add cream and warm over low heat.

Serves 6 to 8.

—Sally Ireland

Fish Chowder

2 Tbsp. butter
2 medium onions, coarsely
    chopped
28-oz. can tomatoes, with
    juice
2 cups chicken stock
1 tsp. fresh basil
Pepper
2 cloves garlic
Worcestershire sauce
1 lb. frozen fish fillets, cut
    into 1-inch pieces
½ cup long grain rice

Melt butter in large saucepan,
add onions and cook until soft -
about 5 minutes. Add tomatoes
with their juice, stock,
seasonings and fish. Add rice
and bring to a boil. Reduce heat,
cover and simmer over low heat
for 20 to 25 minutes, or until
fish flakes easily with a fork.

Serves 6.

—Janet Ueberschlag

Tuna Chowder

2 stalks celery, sliced
2 large potatoes, cubed
3 large carrots, sliced
1 large onion, diced
2 cups corn
1 cup cooked, flaked tuna
3 cups cream of mushroom
    sauce (see page 132)

Boil celery, potatoes, carrots,
onion and corn in a small
amount of water until tender.
Add tuna and mushroom sauce.
Cook over medium-low heat
until hot.

Serves 6.

—Carrie Osburn

Seafood Chowder

½ lb. fresh halibut or cod
½ lb. fresh salmon
½ lb. fresh crabmeat
Lobster meat
Clams
2-3 Tbsp. butter
1 onion, finely chopped
2-3 stalks celery, chopped
Celery leaves, finely chopped
1 small clove garlic, minced
3-4 potatoes, peeled & diced
2 large carrots, sliced
1 bay leaf
2 cups milk or cream
2 Tbsp. cornstarch
1 tsp. salt
¼ cup butter

Chop and combine halibut,
salmon and crabmeat, adding
lobster and clams to taste. Set
aside.

Melt butter in large, heavy pot
and sauté onion, celery, celery
leaves and garlic until tender.
Add potatoes, carrots and bay
leaf and cover with water. Cover
and simmer until vegetables are
tender but crisp — 15 to 20
minutes.

Add fish mixture and continue
to simmer until fish is flaky.
Combine milk and cornstarch
and stir into soup. Add salt and
butter. Simmer until thoroughly
heated.

Serves 4.

—Donna Parker

Pickerel Cheek Chowder

*Pickerel cheeks are so small
that they are usually discarded.
The true fish connoisseur,
however, knows that they
constitute the tastiest part of
the fish.*

2 cups diced potatoes
½ tsp. vinegar
1½ tsp. salt
¼ cup butter
1½ cups pickerel cheeks
1 cup chopped celery
1 cup chopped onions
¼ cup diced back bacon
¼ cup flour
2 cups milk
2 cups light cream
¼ cup chopped chives

Place potatoes in pot and cover
with water. Add vinegar and salt
and cook until tender.

Melt butter and sauté pickerel
cheeks for 2 to 3 minutes.
Remove and set aside. Sauté
celery, onions and back bacon.
Add flour and stir. Add milk and
cream gradually, stirring
constantly. Add potatoes,
undrained, and mix thoroughly,
then add pickerel cheeks.
Garnish with chives.

Serves 4.

—Robert Currier

Creole Bouillabaisse

¼ cup oil
2 onions, chopped
3-4 cloves garlic, crushed
1 stalk celery, diced
2 green peppers, cut in chunks
2 Tbsp. parsley
2 tsp. oregano
2 tsp. marjoram
1 bay leaf
4 Tbsp. flour
28-oz. can tomatoes
3 cups chicken stock
1 lb. cod, cut in bite-sized pieces
Salt & pepper

Heat oil. Add onions, garlic, celery, green peppers, parsley and spices. Sauté for a few minutes, then add flour. Cook slightly, stirring well. Add tomatoes and chicken stock. Stir and heat until bubbly. Add fish, cover and cook gently for 15 minutes. Season with salt and pepper to taste.

Serves 6.

—Beth Hopkins

Haddington Reef Bouillabaisse

2 Tbsp. salad oil
2 cloves garlic, minced
1 onion, sliced
1 green pepper, diced
28-oz. can tomatoes
½ cup white wine
2 carrots, sliced
2 Tbsp. minced fresh parsley
1 tsp. salt
½ tsp. basil
⅛ tsp. fresh ground pepper
1 lb. cod fillets
½ cup water
4 tsp. cornstarch

In a 5-quart pan, heat oil and garlic, add onion and green pepper and cook until tender. Stir in tomatoes, wine, carrots, parsley, salt, basil and pepper, heat to boiling point and simmer for 15 minutes.

Cut cod into bite-sized chunks and add to mixture, bringing it to a boil. Reduce heat, cover and simmer for 10 minutes. Blend water with cornstarch, and slowly stir into stew to thicken.

Serves 6.

—Paula Compton

Italian Fish Soup

1 lb. fish fillets
3 Tbsp. lemon juice
2-3 stalks celery, sliced
1 medium onion, thinly sliced
3-4 medium carrots, sliced
1½ Tbsp. butter
19-oz. can tomatoes
4 cups water
1 tsp. pepper
½-2 tsp. oregano
½ tsp. basil
Bay, thyme, rosemary
1 tsp. garlic powder
¼-½ cup uncooked egg noodles

Cut fish into serving-sized pieces and sprinkle with lemon juice.

In a large pot, sauté celery, onion and carrots in butter, stirring until coated. Add tomatoes, water and spices and simmer for 20 minutes. Add noodles and simmer for another 10 to 15 minutes. Add fish and simmer for 20 minutes longer.

—Marjorie Maund

Salmon-Leek Quiche, page 24

Chunky Gazpacho Summer Soup, page 75

Shrimp and Avocado Salad, page 125

September Garden Zucchini, page 121

Manitoba Wild Rice Casserole, page 205

Coquilles St. Jacques, page 237

Sweet and Sour Orange Chicken, page 269

Rabbit Pâté Camille, page 283

Bergen Fish Soup

FISH STOCK:
½ cup coarsely chopped turnip
½ cup coarsely chopped carrots
1 large yellow onion, coarsely chopped
1 potato, peeled & chopped
1 tsp. salt
6 whole black peppercorns
1 Tbsp. chopped parsley stems
1 bay leaf
3 stalks celery with leaves
2 lbs. fish trimmings (heads, bones, etc.), washed
4 quarts cold water
SOUP:
4 Tbsp. butter
4 Tbsp. flour
Fish stock
½ cup finely chopped carrots
¼ cup finely chopped parsnips
1 lb. boneless halibut, cod or haddock, in one piece
½ cup finely sliced leeks, white parts only
2 egg yolks
Salt & pepper
3 Tbsp. finely chopped parsley
6 Tbsp. sour cream

To prepare the fish stock, combine turnip, carrots, onion, potato, salt, peppercorns, parsley, bay leaf, celery and fish trimmings in a large, heavy saucepan. Add water and bring to a boil. Cover the pan, lower heat and simmer for 30 to 40 minutes.

Strain the stock, discarding the vegetables and fish trimmings. Wash the saucepan and return the stock to it. Boil rapidly for 20 minutes to reduce stock to 6 cups. Strain again and set aside.

To make the soup, melt butter in large, heavy saucepan. Add flour and stir until mixed. Gradually add stock, stirring constantly as stock thickens.

Add carrots, parsnips and fish. As soon as soup reaches a boil, lower heat and simmer, uncovered, for 10 minutes. Add leeks and simmer for 3 to 4 minutes longer. Remove from heat, lift out fish and set aside on a platter.

In a small bowl, beat egg yolks with wire whisk. Beat in ½ cup of hot soup, one tablespoon at a time. Pour this back into the soup in a thin stream, beating continuously with a whisk.

With a fork, separate fish into flakes and add to soup. Season with salt and pepper and reheat, but do not boil. To serve, garnish with parsley and sour cream.

Serves 6.

—Louise Oglaend

Salmon Soup

Quickly and easily assembled from ingredients usually in the pantry, this soup is handy to serve to unexpected guests. Add a salad and hot biscuits for a complete meal.

1 small onion, minced
2 Tbsp. butter
2 Tbsp. flour
4 cups milk
2 cups cooked, flaked salmon
Salt & pepper
½ cup cream

Cook onion in butter until soft. Add flour and stir well. Gradually add milk, stirring constantly, and cook for 1 minute. Add salmon, salt and pepper and cook until heated through and thickened. Stir in cream and heat.

Serves 4.

—Judy Bachelder

Spicy Halibut Soup

The use of a whole, dried cayenne pepper gives this dish its distinctive hot flavour. The amount of pepper used can be varied to suit individual tastes.

1 cup diced onion
Butter
6 cups chicken stock
1 dried red cayenne pepper, broken into pieces
½ lb. halibut, cut in small chunks
2 Tbsp. flour
½ tsp. basil
½ tsp. chervil
Thyme

Sauté onion in butter until transparent. Add chicken stock and cayenne and bring to a boil. Add halibut, lower heat and simmer for 10 minutes.

Mix the flour with a small amount of the soup stock and then gradually stir the flour mixture into the soup. Add spices.

Serves 4.

—Nancy Newsom

George's Aphrodisiac Oyster Soup

The contributor is so confident of the results of this soup that he strongly recommends that it be eaten only after the children are asleep in bed.

1 cup sliced mushrooms
3 Tbsp. butter
1 Tbsp. oil
1 pint fresh oysters
4 cups milk
½ tsp. salt
Pepper
⅛ tsp. oregano
Cayenne

Brown mushrooms in butter and oil. Drain oysters, reserving liquid, and add to mushrooms. Sauté briefly and set aside.

Heat milk to scalding, then add the oyster-mushroom mixture and the oyster liquid. Slowly heat to boiling point, adding salt, pepper, oregano and cayenne.

Serves 4.

—George Belcher

Lebanese Soup

This is a tasty cold soup to serve on hot summer days, when mint is plentiful in most Canadian gardens.

½ English cucumber, seeds removed, cut into small pieces
3 cups plain yogurt
6 cups chicken stock
4 cloves garlic, minced
4 Tbsp. finely chopped mint leaves
Salt & pepper
1 ripe avocado

Salt the cucumber pieces lightly and let stand, refrigerated, for a few hours. Rinse and drain.

Combine yogurt with the stock; add cucumber, garlic and mint. Add salt and pepper to taste. Refrigerate until thoroughly chilled.

Immediately before serving, peel an avocado, cut it into small pieces and add to the soup. Serve cold.

Serves 6.

—Ulla Sterm Troughton

Cape House Inn Iced Buttermilk with Shrimp Soup

The contributor of this recipe discovered this soup while on holiday in Nova Scotia last summer. The owner of the Cape House Inn in Mahone Bay generously shared his recipe.

3 cups shrimp
3 quarts buttermilk
1½ English cucumbers, coarsely chopped
3 Tbsp. fresh dill weed
2 Tbsp. dry mustard
3 Tbsp. chopped dill pickle
1 Tbsp. salt
1 tsp. pepper
Cayenne

Cook shrimp in boiling water until tender. Peel and chop into 1-inch pieces. Combine all ingredients, adding cayenne to taste. Mix well and chill. Serve garnished with thin cucumber slices.

Serves 12.

—Billie Sheffield

Beet Vegetable Soup

"An exceptionally pretty soup—pink with lots of colourful vegetables. Garnish with fresh dill," says our Vermont tester.

1 cup cubed potatoes
1 cup cubed carrots
1 cup cubed beets
¼ tsp. salt
Pepper
1 cup sour cream

Cook potatoes, carrots and beets in 1 cup water until just done. Add salt and pepper, remove from heat and stir in sour cream.

Serves 4.

—Deborah Elmer

Cold Buttermilk Soup

2½ cups buttermilk
¼ green pepper, sliced
½ cucumber or zucchini,
   sliced
Salt & white pepper
Parsley

Place ½ cup buttermilk and remaining ingredients in blender and purée at high speed. Add remaining buttermilk and blend briefly. Chill thoroughly.

Serves 2.

—Mrs. M.H. Moloney

Fresh Tomato & Cabbage Soup

2 Tbsp. butter
1 clove garlic, crushed
2 cups coarsely chopped
   cabbage
1 tsp. salt
2 Tbsp. flour
4 tomatoes, peeled, seeded &
   chopped
2 Tbsp. parsley
½ tsp. basil
⅛ tsp. celery seed
⅛ tsp. pepper
2 cups milk

Melt butter and sauté garlic and cabbage for 3 to 4 minutes. Add 2 cups water and salt, bring to a boil, reduce heat and simmer for 5 minutes. Dissolve flour in ¼ cup water, then stir into soup, cooking until thickened. Add tomatoes, parsley, basil, celery seed and pepper. Simmer for 5 to 10 minutes, stirring often. Stir in milk and heat through.

Serves 4 to 6.

—Norma Somers

Fresh Pea Soup

4 cups peas
5 Tbsp. oil
1 tsp. salt
1 cup chopped celery heart
1 bunch parsley
2 Tbsp. flour
1 Tbsp. sweet paprika
1 tsp. pepper
SOFT NOODLES:
1 egg
1 cup flour

Braise peas in 3 Tbsp. oil, stirring gently, for 5 minutes. Add salt, celery heart, parsley and 4 cups water. Cover and cook over low heat for 20 minutes, or until peas are tender.

Meanwhile, in small pot, heat remaining 2 Tbsp. oil. Stir in flour, paprika and pepper and cook gently for 2 minutes. Slowly add 1 cup water. When thickened, stir into soup and boil for 5 minutes.

Prepare noodles: Mix egg and ¼ cup cold water, adding enough flour to make a very soft dough.

Remove cover from soup, and drizzle dough into soup with a fork. Cook for 5 to 10 minutes.

Serves 4 to 6.

—Julie Herr

Creamy Celery Soup

Our Vermont tester reports, "Lovely green colour—especially appropriate for spring. The cream stock and crunchy celery make for a very pleasant combination of textures."

4 stalks celery with leaves,
   chopped
¼ tsp. crushed garlic
⅛ tsp. thyme
3 leaves parsley, minced
2 Tbsp. butter
¼ cup flour
2 cups milk
½ cup chicken stock
Salt & pepper

Cover celery with water in heavy pot. Bring to a boil and cook until celery is just tender. Reduce heat to simmer and add garlic, thyme and parsley. Continue cooking until most of juice is absorbed. Remove from heat, cover and set aside.

Melt 1 Tbsp. butter and stir in flour. Remove from heat and slowly stir in milk, then stock, then remaining 1 Tbsp. butter. Return to heat and cook, stirring, until almost boiling. Remove from heat.

Return celery to heat. Slowly add cream sauce, stirring constantly. Cook for 5 minutes over low heat. Season with salt and pepper.

Serves 2.

—Deborah Elmer

Cauliflower Soup

The parsley roots and greens in this recipe aid digestion. The soup has a delicate flavour and makes a very attractive beginning to a meal.

1 cauliflower, broken into
    florets
1 tsp. salt
3 Tbsp. oil
1 clove garlic, chopped
2 parsley roots, sliced
1 bunch parsley, chopped
2 Tbsp. flour
1 Tbsp. sweet paprika
1 cup cooked rice or small
    noodles
½ cup sour cream

Cook cauliflower in 5 cups water with salt until tender - 20 minutes. Meanwhile, heat oil in skillet and sauté garlic, parsley roots and parsley for 5 minutes. Stir in flour and paprika, then add 1 cup water. Cook, stirring, until thickened, then stir into cauliflower and water. Boil for 5 minutes, then add rice or noodles and sour cream.

Serves 4.

—*Julie Herr*

Creamed Artichoke Soup

A rich and mild-tasting cream soup that is best made with homemade chicken broth.

4 cups chicken stock
20 oz. frozen or canned
    artichoke hearts, defrosted
    & drained
3 Tbsp. butter
3 Tbsp. flour
1½ cups light cream
¼ tsp. ground thyme
¼ tsp. white pepper
salt
½ cup dry long-grain rice,
    cooked (optional)

Bring stock to a boil in a saucepan; add artichoke hearts, cover and simmer over low heat for 10 minutes. Purée the artichokes with some of the stock in a blender or food processor. Return to saucepan with remaining stock.

Melt butter in a small saucepan, add flour, stir to blend well; stir in cream and thyme. Add pepper and salt to taste. Simmer over low heat for 5 minutes, stirring constantly. Pour cream mixture into the saucepan with stock and artichokes; stir and simmer for 5 minutes. If you add rice, simmer for 10 minutes.

Serves 6 to 8.

—*Nancy R. Franklin*

Egg Lemon Soup

3-4 cups chicken stock
½ cup white wine
¾ cup cooked rice or fine
    egg noodles
3 eggs
3 Tbsp. lemon juice
pepper

Heat stock and wine to rolling boil. Add rice or pasta. Whisk eggs and lemon juice together until frothy, then quickly whisk into boiling stock. Pepper generously and serve immediately.

Serves 4 to 6.

—*Elizabeth Templeman*

Cream of Tomato Soup

Serve this soup topped with grated cheese and garlic croutons for a dressier dish.

4 cups canned tomatoes
1 bay leaf
2 carrots, chopped
2 onions, chopped
2 stalks celery, chopped
5 Tbsp. butter
5 Tbsp. flour
3 cups milk
salt & pepper

Cook tomatoes, bay leaf, carrots, onions and celery until tender — 35 to 40 minutes. Discard bay leaf. Purée soup.

Melt butter and stir in flour. Stir in milk and cook, stirring, until thickened. Slowly add puréed mixture. Add salt and pepper to taste.

Serves 4.

—*Caren Barry*

Sharon's Cream of Eggplant Soup

1 cup butter
1½ cups chopped onion
1½ cups chopped celery
1½ cups chopped potato
2 eggplants, peeled & chopped
½ tsp. curry
¼ tsp. thyme
¼ tsp. basil
4 cups chicken stock
2 cups heavy cream
parsley

Melt butter in heavy skillet. Sauté onion, celery, potato, eggplants, curry, thyme and basil for 15 minutes, stirring constantly. Add stock and bring to a boil. Reduce heat, cover and simmer for 25 to 30 minutes. Remove from heat, stir in cream and garnish with parsley.

Serves 4 to 6.

—Mary Matear

Spinach & Dandelion Soup

If dandelion greens are not available, this soup can be made with all spinach or with spinach and escarole. The nutmeg adds a different taste.

6 cups chicken stock
3 cups chopped dandelion
  greens
3 cups chopped spinach
3 green onions, chopped
1 clove garlic, crushed
salt & pepper
nutmeg
2 hardcooked eggs, chopped

Heat chicken stock and add dandelion greens. Cook for 3 minutes, then add spinach, onions, garlic and salt and pepper. Cook until greens are tender — 5 minutes. Serve with nutmeg and eggs.

Serves 6.

—Cary Elizabeth Marshall

Cream of Mushroom & Wild Rice Soup

½ cup dry wild rice
⅓ cup butter
3 stalks celery, finely
  chopped
1 bunch green onions,
  including tops, chopped
1½ lbs. mushrooms, sliced
¼ cup chopped fresh parsley
⅓ cup flour
3 cups chicken broth
2 13-oz. cans evaporated
  milk
salt & pepper

Rinse wild rice thoroughly. Cook, covered, in 1¼ cups water until tender — about 40 minutes. Melt butter in soup pot and add celery and onions. Sauté for a few minutes. Add mushrooms and parsley. Cook over high heat, stirring, until juices start to evaporate. Stir in flour and cook at least one more minute. Gradually stir in broth until smooth. Add evaporated milk, wild rice and salt and pepper to taste.

Serves 4.

—Sandy Lance

Mushroom & Leek Soup

Whether garnished and served formally or eaten from mugs by the fireplace, this soup is sure to satisfy.

6 leeks
½ cup butter
½ lb. mushrooms, sliced
¼ cup flour
1 tsp. salt
1 tsp. pepper
1 cup chicken stock
3 cups milk
1 Tbsp. sherry
lemon slices & fresh parsley

Wash white part of leeks thoroughly and slice thinly. Sauté leeks in ¼ cup butter until soft but not brown. Remove leeks. In remaining butter, sauté mushrooms until soft. Blend in flour, salt and pepper. Gradually add stock and milk and stir until mixture is thick and creamy. Add leeks and simmer for 10 minutes. Stir in sherry just before serving. Garnish with thin slices of lemon and chopped fresh parsley.

Serves 6.

—Denise Ford

Cilantro Soup

You may substitute watercress for the cilantro, but the taste will be less spicy. This soup has a lovely, delicate "green" taste.

4½ Tbsp. butter
1½ cups chopped onions
4½ cups sliced leeks
¾ cup chopped celery
3 cups peeled, sliced
    potatoes
5½ cups chicken stock
1½ tsp. salt
½ tsp. white pepper
3 cups cilantro or
    watercress, leaves & fine
    stems only
1½ cups light cream
sour cream & chopped
    cilantro for garnish

Melt butter and sauté onions, leeks and celery until tender but not brown. Cover and cook over low heat for 15 minutes. Add potatoes, stock, salt, pepper and cilantro. Simmer, covered, for 15 to 20 minutes. Purée until smooth in blender or food processor.

Return mixture to clean pot, add cream and heat but do not boil. Serve, hot or cold, garnished with a dollop of sour cream and some chopped cilantro.

Serves 8 to 10.

—*Louise Routledge*

Swiss Potato Soup

"This recipe has been in my family for years—it's a favourite with us after a winter day spent hiking in the woods. Creamy, but not too rich, this is a homey soup with surprising sophistication."

4 medium potatoes, pared
2 slices bacon, diced
¼ cup minced onion
2 Tbsp. butter
1 Tbsp. snipped parsley
2 tsp. salt
½ tsp. nutmeg
cayenne
¼ tsp. dry mustard
1 tsp. Worcestershire sauce
3 cups milk
½ cup grated Swiss cheese

Cook potatoes in boiling water until tender; drain. Meanwhile, sauté bacon and onion over low heat, stirring, until brown and tender. Mash potatoes; add bacon, onion, butter, parsley, salt, nutmeg, cayenne, mustard and Worcestershire sauce. Stir in milk. Cook over low heat, stirring. Sprinkle with cheese and serve at once.

Serves 4.

—*Alyson Service*

Almond Soup

"A sweetish, summer soup, this would make a simple but tasty way to begin a meal. It can be served hot or cold."

3 Tbsp. almond paste
⅔ cup finely chopped
    blanched almonds
5 cups chicken stock
3 egg yolks, beaten
2 cups light cream
½ tsp. sugar
½ tsp. salt
¼ tsp. almond extract

Combine almond paste, almonds and chicken stock in saucepan. Cover and bring to a gentle boil. Reduce heat and simmer for 30 minutes.

In bowl, combine egg yolks, cream, sugar and salt. Beat ½ cup hot stock into egg mixture, then beat back into stock. Cook until slightly thickened. Stir in almond extract.

Serves 6 to 8.

—*Sandra K. Bennett*

Blue Cheese Soup

1½ Tbsp. butter
½ cup chopped onion
3 Tbsp. flour
3 cups chicken stock
1 cup milk
⅛ lb. blue cheese
¼ lb. spinach, chopped
¼ cup heavy cream

Melt butter and sauté onion for 3 minutes. Stir in flour, then slowly add chicken stock and milk. Cook, stirring, for 5 minutes. Crumble blue cheese and add. Cook until melted, then add spinach and cream and heat through.

Serves 2 to 4.

—*Rhonda Barnes*

Latin Soup with Garnishes

SOUP:
3½-lb. chicken
2 stalks celery with leaves, halved
2 onions, peeled & quartered
3 bay leaves
2 sprigs parsley
¼ tsp. coriander
3½ tsp. salt
¼ tsp. pepper
2 carrots, peeled & sliced
8 potatoes, peeled & quartered
2 Tbsp. dry rice
7 ears corn
AJI SAUCE:
6 Tbsp. chopped coriander
½ cup olive oil
3 Tbsp. minced onion
1 Tbsp. lemon juice
2 tsp. parsley
1 Tbsp. wine vinegar
¾ tsp. crushed hot red pepper
½ tsp. salt
¼ tsp. pepper
GARNISHES:
1 cup heavy cream
3 avocados, diced
½ cup capers
5 hard-cooked eggs, chopped

Bring chicken and water to cover to boil in large heavy pot. Simmer for 5 minutes, drain liquid and rinse chicken. Return chicken to pot with 8 cups water, celery, onions, bay leaves, parsley, coriander, salt, pepper, carrots and 5 potatoes. Cover, bring to a boil, then simmer for 1 hour, or until chicken is tender.

Remove chicken and potatoes from stock. Strain stock and return to pot. Mash potatoes and stir into stock. Add 3 uncooked potatoes and rice and cook until just tender — about 15 minutes. Skin and bone chicken, then cut into large chunks. Cut kernels from 3 ears of corn and cut remaining ears into 2-inch pieces. Add chicken and corn to stock and cook until corn is tender — about 7 minutes.

Meanwhile, prepare sauce: Combine all sauce ingredients and mix well. Serve soup with pitcher of cream, platter of garnishes and sauce.

Serves 10.

—Kristine Mattila

Potato Soup

"A perfect Idaho soup where we have plenty of spuds and cold weather. We serve it with bread, hot and fresh out of the oven."

¼ cup oil
1 cup chopped onion
1 cup diced carrots
1 cup chopped celery
5 potatoes, diced
1 tsp. oregano
1 tsp. salt
1½ tsp. dill weed
½ tsp. paprika
6 cups chicken or vegetable stock
½ cup beer
½ cup evaporated milk

Heat oil in large heavy pot and sauté onion, carrots, celery and potatoes until onions are transparent. Add oregano, salt, dill weed, paprika, stock and beer and bring to a boil. Reduce heat and simmer for 30 minutes, or until potatoes are tender. Add milk and heat for 2 minutes.

Serves 4.

—Christine Leazer

Wild Rice Soup

"This soup has a subtle savoury flavour and it is an innovative way to serve wild rice to a crowd without going broke!"

1½ Tbsp. cornstarch
10 cups beef stock
3 Tbsp. butter
2 cups diced celery
½ cups diced carrot
½ cups diced onion
½ lb. mushrooms, sliced
1¼ cups wild rice
1 Tbsp. chopped thyme
1 bay leaf
pepper
parsley sprigs

Mix cornstarch with 1 cup stock and set aside. Melt butter in large heavy pot and sauté celery, carrot and onion until soft. Add mushrooms and sauté for 5 minutes more. Add remaining 9 cups stock, rice, thyme and bay leaf and bring to a boil. Reduce heat, cover and simmer for 45 minutes, or until rice is tender. Stir in cornstarch mixture and cook until slightly thickened. Add pepper to taste. Remove bay leaf and garnish with parsley.

Serves 12.

—Pam Collacott

Mexican Bean Soup

Our Vermont tester says, "I wholeheartedly recommend this recipe. It has just the right amount of spice, is very well balanced and is the right consistency for a soup."

7 oz. dry pinto beans, soaked overnight & drained
½ lb. ham, cubed (optional)
2½ cups water
1½ cups tomato juice
2½ cups chicken stock
2 onions, chopped
½-2 cloves garlic, minced
1½ Tbsp. chopped parsley
2 Tbsp. chopped green pepper
2 Tbsp. dark brown sugar
2 tsp. chili powder
½ tsp. salt
1 bay leaf
½ tsp. oregano
¼ tsp. cumin
¼ tsp. rosemary
¼ tsp. celery seed
¼ tsp. thyme
¼ tsp. basil
⅛ tsp. marjoram
⅛ tsp. curry
⅛ tsp. cloves
½ cup dry sherry
chopped scallions

Combine all ingredients except sherry and scallions in large heavy pot. Simmer, partially covered, for 3 hours, or until beans are tender. Remove bay leaf.

Add sherry just before serving, then sprinkle with scallions.

Serves 6.

—Beazie Larned

Sambar

"This is a South Indian dhal-based soup usually served with plain boiled rice. It is hot and delicious." If you can't find tamarind in an Oriental grocery store, substitute lemon juice.

2 Tbsp. tamarind
¾ cup yellow split peas
½ tsp. turmeric
¼ tsp. salt
4 tomatoes, chopped
½ tsp. cumin seed
5 dried hot red peppers
½ tsp. peppercorns
¼ tsp. fenugreek seeds
1 tsp. ground coriander
2 Tbsp. dry-roasted coconut
6 Tbsp. butter
1 small eggplant, cubed
1 potato, peeled & cubed
1 onion, sliced
½ tsp. sugar (optional)
salt
½ tsp. mustard seed
½ cup coriander
asafoetida

Soak tamarind in ½ cup water. Bring 5 cups water to boil in large pot. Add peas, turmeric and salt. Boil for a few minutes, then cook over low heat until most of the liquid evaporates — 30 minutes. Mash. Add 5 cups water and bring to a boil. Reduce heat, add tomatoes, then simmer.

Roast cumin seed, peppers, peppercorns and fenugreek separately. Cool, then grind together along with coriander and coconut. Add to soup. Melt 2 Tbsp. butter in skillet and sauté eggplant for 2 to 3 minutes. Add potato and cook for 2 minutes, then add eggplant and potato to soup.

Melt another 2 Tbsp. butter in skillet. Sauté onion until translucent, then add to soup along with sugar and salt to taste and simmer for 15 to 20 minutes. Strain tamarind juice and discard pulp. Add juice to soup and simmer for 5 minutes.

Melt remaining 2 Tbsp. butter and add mustard seed and coriander. When mustard seeds stop crackling, add a pinch of asafoetida. Stir into dhal.

Serves 8 to 10.

—Ingrid Birker

Creamy Cheddar Cheese Soup

"This makes a rich and delicious soup. The flavours blend well, and it is quick and easy to make. Add fresh-baked bread and butter, and you have a hearty winter meal that will delight everyone."

½ cup butter
½ cup diced carrot
¾ cup diced onion
½ cup diced celery
½ cup flour
2 Tbsp. cornstarch
4 cups rich chicken stock
4 cups milk
⅛ tsp. baking soda
1½ cups grated sharp Cheddar cheese
½ tsp. salt
pepper
finely chopped parsley

Melt butter in large heavy pot. Add carrot, onion and celery and sauté until they are soft. Add flour and cornstarch and mix well, then add chicken stock and milk, mixing well. Cook, stirring constantly, until mixture has a smooth texture and thickens. Add baking soda and cheese and stir until smooth and blended. Season with salt and pepper. Sprinkle with parsley just before serving.

Serves 8 to 10.

—James Mottern

World's Best French Onion Soup

'This recipe, generously shared by a local French restaurant, has ingredients that are deceptively simple and inexpensive.'

2 large sweet onions
  (Spanish or Bermuda)
½ cup butter
1 clove garlic, crushed
3 Tbsp. flour
1 tsp. salt
seasoned croutons (large,
  garlicky, homemade ones
  are best)
1 lb. Swiss Emmentaler
  cheese, shredded

Peel and thinly slice onions. Separate slices into rings. In large saucepan or 4-quart Dutch oven, melt ¼ cup butter. Add onions. Over high heat, stirring frequently, sauté onions until they appear almost burnt: quite brown with the odd black bit.

Reduce heat to low and add garlic. Sauté until garlic is soft. Do not allow garlic to brown. Add 10 cups hot water and return to boil, then simmer slowly, uncovered, until liquid is reduced by half — 5 to 7 hours.

In a small skillet, melt remaining butter and stir in flour. Stir constantly over low heat to produce a caramel-coloured roux. Add a couple of tablespoonsful of the hot stock, stirring constantly. Then add this to stock in pot, stirring constantly. Allow to boil for about 5 minutes to thicken slightly and eliminate any raw flour taste. Add salt.

In 4 ramekins or onion-soup bowls, place a couple of tablespoonsful of shredded cheese. Then ladle in the soup to within a half inch of the top of each bowl. Cover soup with seasoned croutons, then carefully divide the cheese over each bowl, taking care that the croutons and cheese don't sink. Place under broiler, or in a 450 degree F oven, until cheese is melted and begins to brown.

Serves 4.

—Sandy Robertson

Carrot Soup

"A favourite Saturday supper in our household is a large bowl of this soup with a slice of homemade bread." If you like a really thick soup, thicken with a paste of 3 Tbsp. flour and ¼ cup milk just before serving.

2 Tbsp. butter
1 onion, chopped
5 cups chicken stock
1 lb. carrots, grated
3 potatoes, grated
½ tsp. thyme
¼ tsp. Tabasco sauce
1 tsp. Worcestershire sauce
1½ cups milk
2 cups grated Cheddar
  cheese
salt

Melt butter and sauté onion until tender. Add chicken stock and bring to a boil. Add carrots, potatoes, thyme, Tabasco sauce and Worcestershire sauce and simmer until vegetables are tender — 30 to 40 minutes. Add milk and cheese and cook until cheese is melted. Salt to taste.

Serves 6 to 8.

—Lois B. Demerich

Crème Senegalese Soup

4 Tbsp. butter
6 leeks, chopped
1 large green apple, peeled,
  cored & chopped
¾ cup chopped onion
1 clove garlic, minced
2 Tbsp. curry
1 lb. potatoes, peeled &
  diced
6 cups chicken stock
salt & pepper
1 cup heavy cream
Tabasco sauce
½ cup diced cooked chicken

Melt butter, then add leeks, apple, onion and garlic. Cook until leeks are limp — 10 to 15 minutes. Sprinkle with curry and cook for 5 minutes more. Add potatoes, cook for 3 minutes, then add stock. Simmer for 45 minutes. Add salt and pepper to taste.

Blend soup in batches. Add cream, Tabasco sauce to taste and chicken just before serving. Serve hot or cold.

Serves 8.

Wine & Cheese Mushroom Soup

2 Tbsp. olive oil
1 cup chopped onion
1 clove garlic, chopped
1 lb. mushrooms, sliced
2 Tbsp. tomato paste
4 cups chicken stock
5 egg yolks
⅓ cup Parmesan cheese
2 Tbsp. chopped parsley
¼ cup port
4 slices French bread,
    toasted & buttered

Heat oil in heavy pot and cook onion and garlic for 6 minutes over moderate heat. Add mushrooms and cook, stirring, for 10 minutes. Stir in tomato paste, then stock, and bring to a boil. Reduce heat and simmer for 15 minutes.

In a small bowl, combine egg yolks, cheese and parsley. Add 1 cup hot stock in a stream, beating well, then stir this back into pot. Add port and simmer for 15 minutes. Place bread in 4 bowls and ladle soup over.

Serves 4.

—John W. Houston

Cabbage Soup

A zesty, spicy soup with an Italian flavour, this would be great for a hearty after-ski repast. Add crusty bread and bowls of marinated olives to round out the meal.

4 hot Italian sausages
3 Tbsp. olive oil
2-3 cloves garlic, crushed
1 onion, chopped
1 carrot, sliced
2 stalks celery, chopped
2 28-oz. cans crushed
    tomatoes
2 potatoes, peeled & cubed
2 cups cooked navy beans
2 cups coarsely chopped
    cabbage
½ cup white wine
½ tsp. pepper
1 Tbsp. oregano
2 tsp. basil
salt
Parmesan cheese

Cook sausages in large heavy pot. Discard fat and slice sausages; set aside. Heat oil and sauté garlic and onion until transparent. Add carrot and celery and sauté briefly. Stir in tomatoes and raise heat. Add potatoes, beans, cabbage, wine, pepper, oregano, basil, salt and sausages. Boil for 10 to 15 minutes, reduce heat, cover and simmer until potato and cabbage are tender. Sprinkle with Parmesan cheese and serve.

Serves 6 to 8.

—Elizabeth Templeman

Golden Squash Soup

Cook and freeze squash in the fall, then use it to make this soup in the winter. If you prefer a completely smooth soup, the potatoes can be puréed as well.

4 Tbsp. butter
⅛ cup diced onions
1 large potato, finely diced
1 cup chicken stock
2 cups cooked squash
¼ tsp. salt
¾ tsp. curry
white pepper
¾ cup milk
paprika

Melt butter and sauté onions until softened. Add potato, stock, squash, salt, curry and pepper. Heat through over medium heat, then simmer for 10 minutes, or until potatoes are tender. Stir in milk. Sprinkle with paprika.

Serves 4.

—Linda Russell

Broccoli Soup

Made with fresh-from-the-garden broccoli, this soup is a lovely early summer lunch dish. Serve with sliced tomatoes and garlic mayonnaise.

6 cups chicken stock
1 head broccoli, cut into
    florets
1 cup chopped onion
1 Tbsp. chopped tarragon
salt & pepper
nutmeg
1 cup sour cream or yogurt

Bring stock to a boil. Add broccoli and onion and cook for 6 to 8 minutes, or until broccoli is tender. Purée soup. Reheat, then add tarragon, salt and pepper and nutmeg. Add sour cream or yogurt, whisking thoroughly. Do not allow soup to boil.

Serves 4 to 6.

Harvest-Time Pumpkin Soup

1 small pie pumpkin,
   cleaned out
2 potatoes
2 carrots
1 onion, finely chopped
2 cloves garlic, crushed
olive oil
fresh parsley, basil & thyme,
   chopped
salt & pepper
4 Tbsp. cream
2 Tbsp. butter
2 Tbsp. soy sauce (optional)
sour cream
chopped chives

Cut pumpkin, potatoes and carrots into pieces and steam until tender. Remove peel from pumpkin. Save steaming water. Sauté onion and garlic in a little olive oil until transparent. Purée onion, garlic and vegetables in a food processor, adding reserved water. Return the purée to a saucepan and add spices, salt and pepper, cream, butter and soy sauce. If soup is too thick, thin with a little water, milk or chicken stock. Heat but do not boil. Garnish with a dollop of sour cream and chopped chives.

Serves 4 to 6.

—Robin Mello

Mussel Chowder with Corn

"This recipe was created a few summers ago while my husband and I were vacationing on a remote island in Maine. Mussels were free for the picking; other ingredients depended on the limited supplies of the island's general store."

4 slices bacon, diced
2 onions, diced
2 potatoes, diced
strained stock from
   steaming mussels
3 cups mussel meat
2 cups milk
12-oz. can evaporated milk
1½ cups corn
salt & pepper

Fry bacon until crisp, then drain. Sauté onions until translucent in bacon fat, then place in large pot with potatoes. Add stock and water to cover. Simmer until potatoes are tender. Add remaining ingredients, including bacon, and heat through.

Serves 2 to 4.

—Wendy Gwathmey

Carrot, Cashew & Curry Soup

"I tasted a soup like this in a little place called The Soup Kitchen *in Calgary, Alberta. I liked it so much that I developed this version of it for my own use."*

¼ cup butter
5-6 carrots, sliced
1 onion, halved & sliced
1 green pepper, chopped
4 cloves garlic, crushed
1 cup cashews
4 cups soup stock
2 tsp. curry
1 bay leaf
salt & pepper

Melt butter and sauté carrots, onion, green pepper, garlic and cashews until onion is transparent. Add remaining ingredients and simmer until carrots are tender but not mushy — 30 minutes. Remove bay leaf before serving.

Serves 4.

—Bonnie Lawson

Oxtail Soup

"This is a rich and hearty soup for a mean February day. Start early to make the stock so it can cool and the fat can be removed. My grandmother's secret was to add whatever root vegetables were available."

2 Tbsp. butter or oil
2-3 lbs. disjointed oxtails
½ cup chopped onion
3 cloves garlic, chopped
1 bay leaf
8 cups water
1½-2 cups chopped
    tomatoes
1½ tsp. salt
4-6 peppercorns
2 cups diced potatoes
1 cup sliced carrots
1 cup sliced celery
1 turnip or parsnip or
    celeriac or combination,
    chopped
¼ cup chopped parsley
1 tsp. basil
½ tsp. thyme
⅓-½ cup dry barley

Heat butter or oil and brown oxtails. Add onion and garlic and sauté for 2 to 3 minutes. Add bay leaf, water, tomatoes, salt and peppercorns. Bring to a boil, reduce heat, cover and simmer for 2 to 4 hours.

Strain stock and chill to remove fat. Set oxtails aside. When cool, remove meat from bones and chop. Bring defatted stock to a boil and add chopped meat and remaining ingredients. Simmer for 30 to 40 minutes, or until vegetables are tender.

Serves 8 to 10.

—*Lynne Roe*

Lamb Soup

1 leftover meaty lamb leg
2 cups chopped spinach
2 tomatoes, cubed
½ cup peas
½ cup corn
3 potatoes, cubed
¾ cup sliced mushrooms
salt & pepper
Worcestershire sauce
1 onion, diced
¼ cup dry barley

Simmer lamb leg in 6 to 8 cups water for 4 hours. Strain, reserving liquid. Chop meat.

Combine meat, reserved stock and remaining ingredients in large heavy pot. Simmer for 1 hour, or until vegetables are tender, adding liquid if necessary.

Serves 6.

—*Patricia E. Wilson*

Borscht

8 whole fresh beets
1 small onion, diced
2 Tbsp. butter
4 cups chicken stock
2 medium-sized potatoes
1½ cups sour cream
salt & pepper

Boil unpeeled beets for 30 minutes, or until tender. Peel and set aside. In large pot, sauté onion in butter for 5 minutes or until transparent. Add chicken stock, potatoes and beets and simmer for 20 minutes, or until potatoes are soft. Purée and chill for at least 3 hours. Whisk sour cream into soup just before serving and season to taste with salt and pepper. Garnish each bowl with a dollop of sour cream.

Serves 6.

Landlubber's Gumbo

Buy filé powder at a specialty food store—be sure not to let the soup boil after it has been added.

3-4-lb. chicken
1 Tbsp. salt
1 stalk celery
1 carrot
1 onion
2 Tbsp. butter
2 cups diced smoked pork
    shoulder, bone reserved
2 lbs. okra, stems removed
1 green pepper, diced
4 onions, sliced
2 cloves garlic, crushed
28-oz. can plum tomatoes
4 cups fish stock
⅓ cup chopped parsley
4 dashes Tabasco sauce
4 Tbsp. Worcestershire
    sauce
juice of ½ lemon
2 bay leaves
½ tsp. thyme
12 oz. crabmeat
2 lbs. shrimp, shelled
1 tsp. filé powder

Cook chicken, salt, celery, carrot and onion in 4 cups water (or to cover) for 30 minutes. Cool, then remove chicken and vegetables, skim fat from stock, and reserve stock. Discard vegetables. Chop chicken.

Melt butter in large pot. Sauté chicken and pork for 2 minutes. Add okra, green pepper and onions and cook for 5 minutes. Add garlic, tomatoes, chicken and fish stocks, parsley, Tabasco sauce, Worcestershire sauce, lemon juice, bay leaves, thyme, pork bone and crabmeat. Simmer for 2½ to 3½ hours. Add shrimp and cook for 5 minutes. Remove bay leaves and add filé powder just before serving.

Serves 12.

—*Elizabeth Alexander*

Ham-Lentil Soup with Cheese Tortellini

"A richly flavoured, chill-chasing soup—especially favoured by the harvest crew after a cold day of combine repairs. Serve in prewarmed bowls and garnish with chives. Good accompanied by warm garlic toast and a platter of sliced fresh fruits and vegetables."

2 Tbsp. butter
⅓ cup chopped onion
1 clove garlic, minced
1⅓ cups dry lentils, rinsed & drained
1 cup cubed ham
1 stalk celery, sliced
1 cup peeled, seeded & chopped tomatoes
3" sprig thyme
1 tsp. salt
1 large bay leaf
Tabasco sauce
3¼ cups dry cheese-filled tortellini
snipped chives for garnish

Melt butter in large, heavy pot over moderate heat. Add onion and garlic and cook, stirring frequently, until onion is limp. Add lentils, ham and celery. Cook, stirring frequently, until lentils just start to brown. Add 8 cups water, tomatoes, thyme, salt, bay leaf and Tabasco sauce and stir to blend. Cook, covered, for 1 hour. Add tortellini and cook for another 30 minutes. Garnish with chives.

Serves 4.

—Ellen Ross

Asparagus & Crab Soup

Vietnamese in origin, this soup is elegant enough to begin a dinner party, but simple to prepare.

1 Tbsp. oil
1 clove garlic, minced
2 Tbsp. minced shallots
¾ lb. flaked crabmeat
8 cups chicken stock
2 Tbsp. fish sauce or 1 tsp. anchovy paste
3 Tbsp. cornstarch, mixed with 3 Tbsp. water
1 lb. asparagus, steamed & cut in 1" lengths
salt & pepper
toasted croutons for garnish

Heat oil in a large skillet and sauté garlic and shallots until tender, about 6 minutes. Stir in the crabmeat and cook for 4 to 5 minutes, stirring constantly. In the soup pot, heat the chicken stock to a gentle boil. Stir in fish sauce, if available, or anchovy paste. Add the crab mixture and return to simmer. Stir cornstarch mixture into soup. Simmer and stir until thickened, about 5 minutes. Add asparagus. Add salt and pepper to taste. Ladle into heated bowls and garnish with croutons.

Serves 8 to 10.

Meal-in-a Soup

1 Tbsp. butter
¾ lb. ground beef
2 onions, sliced
3 stalks celery, sliced
2 large carrots, sliced
1 potato, diced
1½ cups cauliflower florets
19-oz. can tomatoes
1½ tsp. salt
⅛ tsp. pepper
¾ cup dry macaroni

Melt butter, add ground beef and brown slightly, stirring. Add remaining ingredients, except pasta. Cover and bring to a boil. Reduce heat and simmer for 30 minutes. Add macaroni about 7 to 9 minutes before the end of cooking time.

Serves 4 to 6.

—Eileen Caldwell

Tunisian Sourba

The cook controls the heat produced by the chilies, from mildly flavourful to tongue-searing. Serve with dunkers of crusty bread.

1½ lbs. beef, cut into 1" cubes
3 carrots, cut into discs
1 large onion, chopped
4 Tbsp. olive oil
2 Tbsp. tomato paste
1-3 tsp. finely chopped red
  chilies, seeds removed
6 cups beef stock or
  consomme
salt & pepper
1 cup dry pasta shells
1½ tsp. lemon juice

In a heavy pot, sauté meat, carrots and onion in olive oil, stirring frequently until meat is browned and onions are tender. Add tomato paste, 1 tsp. chilies, stock and salt and pepper. Simmer for 30 minutes. Taste liquid and add more chilies if desired. Simmer until meat is tender. Add pasta and cook until tender. Stir frequently. Just before serving, stir in lemon Juice.

Serves 6 to 8.

Mandarin Hot & Sour Soup

"I developed this recipe after living in China for two years and growing to love hot and sour soup." Hotness and sourness can be adjusted by adding to or subtracting from the amount of vinegar and chili oil.

6-8 cups chicken stock
¼ lb. lean pork, shredded
2-3 dried black mushrooms,
  soaked & shredded
3-4 dried tree ears, soaked &
  shredded (optional)
½-1 square tofu, diced
¼ cup shredded bamboo
  shoots
½ cup sliced mushrooms
2 green onions, chopped
1 slice cooked ham,
  shredded
4 Tbsp. vinegar
1 tsp. chili oil
¼ tsp. white pepper
¾ tsp. salt
½ tsp. sesame oil
½ tsp. sugar
1 Tbsp. soy sauce
3 Tbsp. cornstarch dissolved
  in 3 Tbsp. water
2 eggs, lightly beaten

Bring stock to a boil, add pork, black mushrooms and tree ears. Cook for 2 to 3 minutes. Add remaining ingredients except for cornstarch and eggs, reduce heat, and simmer for 2 minutes more. Slowly stir cornstarch mixture into soup and continue cooking until stock is thickened. Turn off heat. Slowly pour in eggs in a thin stream while stirring.

Serves 6 to 8.

—Barb McDonald

Smoky Potato & Bacon Soup with Cheddar Croutons

This is a meal-in-a-bowl soup, especially good on a cold winter's day. The croutons would be tasty in other soups as well — double or triple the recipe, and freeze the rest for later use.

1 thick strip bacon, with rind
¼ cup butter
1 cup chopped onion
½ cup chopped celery
½ cup chopped leek
5 cups chicken stock
½ tsp. salt
½ tsp. white pepper
2 cups peeled, cubed
  potatoes
½ cup heavy cream
CROUTONS:
 1 cup grated sharp Cheddar
  cheese
1 egg, lightly beaten
½ tsp. Dijon mustard
1 green onion, chopped
cayenne
4 slices bread

Remove rind from bacon and reserve. Chop bacon. Melt butter, then add rind, onion, celery and leek and cook for 10 minutes over medium heat, stirring. Add stock, salt and pepper and bring to a boil. Add potatoes and simmer for 25 minutes. Remove rind and discard. Purée soup, then return to pot and add cream. Fry bacon until crisp and add to soup,

To make croutons: Combine cheese, egg, mustard, onion and cayenne. Spread onto bread. Bake at 375° F for 10 to 15 minutes or until dry. Cool, then cut into cubes. Sprinkle on soup.

Serves 6 to 8.

—Terry Seed

Friday Night Chicken Soup & Matzo Balls

1 stewing hen
4 lbs. chicken necks &
    backs
1 onion, studded with 5-6
    cloves
1 clove garlic, peeled
1 tsp. salt
6 peppercorns
½ tsp. thyme
1 bay leaf
2 leeks
2 carrots
2-3 stalks celery with leaves
1 turnip
1-2 parsley roots
¼ cup chopped parsley
MATZO BALLS:
3 eggs, separated
1 tsp. salt
¾ cup matzo meal
2 Tbsp. oil
¼ tsp. pepper

In large stockpot, combine chicken, necks and backs, onion, garlic, salt, peppercorns, thyme, bay leaf and 12 cups water. Bring to a boil, reduce heat, cover and simmer for 1½ hours. Remove chicken, bones, garlic, onion and bay leaf. Add remaining ingredients and return to boil. Simmer for 1 hour, then strain.

Meanwhile, prepare matzo balls: Beat together egg yolks, salt, matzo meal, oil and pepper. Beat egg whites until stiff and fold into egg yolk mixture. Chill for 1 hour, then form into balls, using 2 Tbsp. per ball. Cook, covered, for 20 minutes in simmering soup.

Serves 8 to 10.

—Lynne Roe

Spinach Soup with Dill & Lemon

Serve this soup hot or chilled—it is delicious either way.

3 Tbsp. butter
2 onions, chopped
1 lb. spinach, washed &
    stems removed
3 Tbsp. dry rice
2 cups peas
2 Tbsp. chopped dill
4 cups chicken stock
salt & pepper
nutmeg
grated peel of ½ lemon
1 cup heavy cream
½ cup sour cream
chopped dill

Melt butter and sauté onions until tender. Add spinach and cook, stirring, until it wilts. Add rice and peas and toss, then add dill and chicken stock. Bring to a boil, stir in salt and pepper, nutmeg and lemon peel. Reduce heat, cover and simmer for 20 minutes, or until rice is tender.

Purée, in batches, in blender or food processor. Stir in cream just before serving. Serve with a dollop of sour cream and chopped dill in each bowl.

Serves 6 to 8.

—G. Rogne & F. Goodwin-Rogne

David's Cream of Crab Soup

A rich, creamy broth underlies the crab flavour of this soup. Taste improves if the soup is made ahead of time, chilled and then reheated over very low heat.

¼ cup butter
¼ cup minced onion
2 Tbsp. flour
¼ tsp. celery seed
1 tsp. salt
⅛ tsp. pepper
Tabasco sauce
1 cup chicken or vegetable
    stock
¼ cup dry sherry
2½ cups milk
2½ cups light cream
1 lb. crabmeat

Melt butter in heavy pot, then sauté onion until tender. Slowly blend in flour, celery seed, salt, pepper and Tabasco sauce to taste, stirring constantly. Add stock, sherry, milk and cream and cook over medium heat, stirring constantly, until thick enough to coat a spoon.

Stir in crabmeat and heat through.

Serves 4 to 6.

—David G. Weifenbach

Avocado Coriander Soup

No vegetable is as creamy as an avocado, and it is shown off at its best in this delicate, pale green soup.

2 ripe avocados, peeled & halved
2 scallions, roughly chopped
2 cups light cream
juice of ½ lime
½ cup chicken stock
¼ tsp. salt
¼ tsp. cayenne
¼ cup fresh coriander leaves
salt & pepper
fresh coriander leaves for garnish

Put all ingredients except garnish in food processor or blender, and process until smooth. Refrigerate for 3 hours until completely chilled. Thin with more chicken stock if necessary, and season to taste with salt and pepper. Garnish with fresh coriander leaves.

Serves 4.

Scallop Chowder

"When I lived in the tropics, my favourite dish was Conch Chowder. This is my West Coast adaptation of that soup."

¼ cup oil
½ cup chopped bacon
½ cup chopped onion
½ cup chopped celery
½ cup chopped carrot
½ cup chopped green pepper
1 cup diced potato
1 bay leaf
1½ tsp. thyme
⅓ cup tomato paste
1 cup scallops, halved
salt
Tabasco sauce

Heat oil and cook bacon until crisp. Add onion, celery, carrot, green pepper, potato, bay leaf and thyme and sauté for 3 minutes. Add tomato paste and cook, stirring, for 6 minutes. Add 4 cups water, bring to a boil, reduce heat and simmer for 1 hour.

Stir in scallops, salt and Tabasco sauce to taste and cook for 5 minutes, or until scallops are cooked.

Serves 4.

—Barbara Brennan

Mary's Pozole (Pah-zó-lay)

"In an effort to reproduce a soup I enjoyed in Mexico, I devised this version of pozole. The basic soup is made, then each person adds the vegetables he likes at the table. The bracing heat provided by the chilies is balanced by the crunch of raw vegetables."

1 stewing hen
2 onions, chopped
2 carrots, chopped
3 stalks celery & leaves, chopped
1 tsp. thyme
1 tsp. sage
1 tsp. rosemary
1 tsp. salt
1 tsp. pepper
2 red chilies
1 cup cooked chickpeas
any combination of radishes, cabbage, zucchini, green onions, tomatoes, Swiss chard, chopped or sliced finely & placed in separate bowls
1 lemon or lime, thinly sliced

Place hen, onions, carrots, celery, thyme, sage, rosemary, salt and pepper in a stockpot. Cover with water and simmer until hen is tender — 1 to 2 hours. Remove chicken, strain stock and reserve 8 cups. Strip meat from bones, removing skin; chop and place in soup pot. Add stock. Simmer chilies in about 1 cup water for 10 minutes. Place chilies and water in blender and purée. Add to soup, a few teaspoonsful at a time, until desired level of spiciness is reached. Add chickpeas and simmer soup for 10 minutes.

To serve: Fill soup bowls about half full of chicken soup. Add desired vegetables and complete with a squeeze of lemon or lime juice. Extra hot sauce can be passed.

Serves 10 to 12.

—Mary McCollam

Grandma Gesine's Clam Chowder

"My great-grandparents came to the United States from Germany in the late 1800s. They settled in New York City, where they opened a bar and restaurant. This chowder was always on the menu, and it has stayed in the family ever since."

18 clams
1 small piece salt pork or ½ lb. bacon, diced
28-oz. can crushed tomatoes
2-4 tsp. thyme
2 bay leaves
¼ tsp. pepper
2 lbs. potatoes, diced
6 carrots, diced
3 stalks celery, diced
2 onions, diced
¼ head cabbage, diced

Steam clams until shells open. Chop clams and set aside, reserving cooking liquid. Fry pork until crisp in large heavy pot. Add 8 cups water, strained clam juice, tomatoes, thyme, bay leaves, pepper and clams. Add vegetables, bring to a boil, reduce heat, cover and simmer for at least 3 hours. Remove bay leaves before serving.

Serves 4 to 6.

—Barbara Tanzosh

Chilled Curried Zucchini Soup

"I served this to a friend who insisted he hated zucchini, onions, curry powder and buttermilk and didn't know what cumin was. He was most enthusiastic about all of them combined in this soup, however!"

2 lbs. zucchini
6 Tbsp. butter
1 cup minced green onions
1 Tbsp. curry
1 Tbsp. cumin
2 cups chicken stock
3 cups buttermilk
salt & pepper

Scrub, trim and chop zucchini. Melt butter and slowly cook zucchini and onions, covered tightly, over medium-low heat, for 15 minutes, or until zucchini is soft. Add curry and cumin and cook for 2 minutes. Stir in stock. Purée soup in blender or food processor in batches. Place puréed soup in large bowl, then stir in buttermilk and salt and pepper. Chill for at least 4 hours.

Serves 6.

—Sandy MacLennan

Green Vichyssoise

A green-flecked cool soup with a hearty texture, this is ideal for a light meal in itself. Serve with a green salad and fresh bread.

2 Tbsp. butter
5 small leeks, white part only
6 cups chicken stock
2 medium baking potatoes, peeled & diced
4 bunches watercress, leaves & tender stems *or* 4 cups fresh spinach leaves
1 cup heavy cream
salt & pepper

Heat butter and gently sauté leeks for 10 minutes, then add chicken stock and potatoes and simmer until potatoes are tender — about 20 minutes. Add watercress or spinach and simmer 5 minutes longer. Purée soup, leaving flecks of green, and chill for at least 3 hours. Add cream and season to taste with salt and pepper. Garnish with sprigs of watercress or parsley, and serve.

Serves 6.

Fish & Wild Rice Chowder

This is a creamy, delicate chowder but with considerable depth. It takes only a short time to prepare, which adds to its freshness of flavour.

½ cup dry wild rice
½ tsp. salt
½ cup butter
1 cup chopped onion
½ cup chopped green pepper
1 cup sliced celery
1 cup sliced mushrooms
¾ cup flour
7 cups chicken stock
1 tsp. salt
½ tsp. white pepper
1 lb. orange roughy or scrod, cubed
1 cup light cream
2 Tbsp. white wine

Cook rice with salt in 2 cups water for 35 minutes. Drain and set aside.

Melt butter and sauté onion, green pepper, celery and mushrooms over low heat for 5 to 7 minutes. Stir in flour and cook for 3 to 4 minutes longer. Add chicken stock and bring to a boil. Add salt, pepper and fish and simmer for 5 to 10 minutes, or until fish is tender. Add rice, cream and wine.

Serves 6 to 8.

—*Jerald G. Riessen*

African Lentil Soup

"I first made this soup with spices my sister brought from Kenya. Now I make my own blend to create a flavourful and spicy meal that is perfect for vegetarians." This is not a soup for the fainthearted — it is hot.

SPICE PASTE:
½ tsp. cayenne
1½ tsp. paprika
½ tsp. ginger
½ tsp. cardamom
1½ tsp. turmeric
¼ tsp. coriander
¼ tsp. cinnamon
2 tsp. red wine vinegar
SOUP:
4 cloves garlic, crushed
3 carrots, sliced
1 onion, chopped
4 green onions, chopped
¼ cup oil
½ cup tomato paste
2 cups dry lentils
1 small chili, chopped

Make a paste of the spices by combining cayenne, paprika, ginger, cardamom, turmeric, coriander and cinnamon. Mix in vinegar and 1 Tbsp. water to make a smooth paste.

Sauté garlic, carrots and onions in oil over medium heat until soft. Stir in tomato paste, spice paste and ½ cup water. Simmer over low heat, stirring, for 5 minutes. Add remaining ingredients and 5 cups water, bring to a boil, reduce heat and simmer for 45 minutes.

Serves 6.

—*Judith Christensen*

Clam Chowder

This is a hearty soup with a velvety-smooth, nicely coloured broth. Real clam aficionados could easily increase the amount of clams. This chowder combines the cream of a New England clam chowder with the tomatoes of a Manhattan chowder.

2 oz. salt pork or bacon, chopped
1 clove garlic, chopped
½ cup chopped onion
3 cups diced potatoes
1½ tsp. thyme
1 bay leaf
4 cloves
2 tsp. salt
½ tsp. pepper
10-oz. can clams
½ cup chopped green pepper
½ carrot, diced
¼ cup chopped celery
3 cups diced tomatoes
2 Tbsp. flour
4 cups scalded milk
2 cups cream
3 Tbsp. butter
¼ cup chopped parsley

In large heavy pot, sauté pork. Add garlic and onion and sauté until onion is golden.

Add 3 cups water, potatoes, thyme, bay leaf, cloves, salt and pepper and simmer for 15 minutes. Add clams and their juice, green pepper, carrot, celery and tomatoes. Simmer for 10 minutes.

Mix flour with ½ cup milk. Stir into soup with remaining milk and cream and simmer for 10 minutes more. Stir in butter and parsley.

Serves 8 to 10.

—*Xenia Von Rosen*

Andalusian Gazpacho

An authentic and simply made version of the zesty Spanish classic. Most North American vegetable gardens will be able to supply all the fresh ingredients.

2½ cups chicken stock
1½ cups cubed white bread, crust removed
4 cups crushed & drained tomatoes strained to remove seeds
1 small white onion, quartered
1 green pepper, quartered
½ large cucumber, peeled, seeded & diced
1 clove garlic
¼ cup red wine vinegar
2 Tbsp. mayonnaise
1 cup light cream
Salt & pepper
GARNISH:
1 cup each diced white onion, diced green pepper, diced cucumber, toasted croutons

Pour ½ cup chicken stock over bread cubes and let soak while you put all other ingredients, except mayonnaise and cream, in a food processor or blender and purée until smooth. Add soaked bread cubes and continue puréeing. Put mixture through food mill to remove remaining tomato seeds and green pepper skins. Chill for at least 3 hours until flavours blend and soup is well chilled. Whisk in mayonnaise and cream. Season to taste with salt and pepper. Serve with garnishes.

Serves 6 to 8.

Avgolemono Soup

Golden yellow and zingy with lemon, this soup is an ideal summer addition to your cold-soup repertoire.

6 cups chicken stock
1 cup uncooked rice
juice of 2 lemons
3 egg yolks
salt & pepper
chopped parsley for garnish

Bring stock to a boil and add rice; half cover pot and cook rice until tender, about 20 minutes. Meanwhile, beat lemon juice and egg yolks together until smooth. Whisk 1 cup of hot broth into yolk mixture, then slowly add this mixture back to stock and rice in the pot. Stir soup gently over low heat for 3 to 5 minutes until the soup thickens slightly. Be careful not to curdle the egg yolks. Chill for 3 hours; stir well to circulate the rice, and season to taste with salt and pepper. Garnish with chopped parsley.

Serves 4.

Consommé Madrilène

The tomato gives this clear, shimmering soup a slightly rosy tinge. It is lightly gelatinous, elegant and refreshing.

3 quarts chicken stock
1½ lbs. lean beef chuck, cut into small chunks
2 carrots, finely diced
1 leek, white part only, finely diced
6 tomatoes, seeded & chopped
1 tsp. coarse salt
chives for garnish

Put everything into stockpot and bring to a gentle boil. Skim scum off surface and lower heat to keep soup at a gentle simmer, uncovered, for 1½ hours. You should have about 3 cups of liquid when finished. Strain through a double thickness of dampened cheesecloth, then chill consommé until lightly set — about 2 hours. Serve garnished with chives.

Serves 2.

Salads & Vegetables

Beet Holuptis

This rich dish wraps a bread-like dough in beet leaves.

2 tsp. yeast
1½ cups warm water
1 Tbsp. honey
1 Tbsp. oil
3 cups whole wheat flour
3 cups white flour
36 beet leaves
4 green onions, chopped
2-3 Tbsp. butter
1 cup whipping cream
¼-½ cup fresh dill, chopped

Dissolve yeast in water and honey and let stand 5 minutes. Add oil. Combine two flours and add to water to form a bread dough. Knead for 10 minutes. Place in a bowl and let rise in warm place until doubled in size — 1 to 1½ hours. Punch down and set aside.

Wash beet leaves and cut out main vein if it is very large. Steam just until limp.

Pinch off pieces of dough large enough to wrap a leaf around. Roll leaves around dough, then place on greased cookie sheets and let rise until doubled in size. Bake at 350° F until golden brown — 20 to 30 minutes.

Before serving, sauté onions briefly in butter. After about a minute, add the holuptis. Pour cream over them and add dill. Stir over low heat until holuptis are warm and have absorbed most of the cream. Serve warm.

Makes 36 holuptis.

—*Kay Chornook*

Stir-Fried Green Beans

1 qt. fresh green beans
2 Tbsp. oil
½ tsp. ground ginger
3 drops Tabasco sauce
½ tsp. sugar
Salt
2 Tbsp. Sesame seeds
2 Tbsp. vinegar
Chopped green onion

Wash beans and remove ends if desired. Heat oil in wok, add beans and cook quickly over high heat, tossing constantly, for 2 to 3 minutes.

Add remaining ingredients, toss and serve.

Serves 4.

—*Billie Sheffield*

Green Bean Casserole

This recipe provides a quick and easy way to dress up an everyday vegetable.

1 lb. green beans, cooked
2 Tbsp. vinegar
2 tsp. honey
2 slices toast, cubed
2-4 Tbsp. Parmesan cheese

Place beans in greased baking dish. Stir in vinegar and drizzle with honey. Toss in toast. Sprinkle cheese on top.

Bake at 450° F for 15 minutes, then broil 2 minutes to brown top.

—*Sharon Steele*

Swiss Green Beans

2 Tbsp. butter
2 Tbsp. flour
1 tsp. salt
¼ tsp. pepper
½ tsp. grated onion
1 cup sour cream
4 cups green beans, cooked
  & drained
¼ lb. Swiss cheese, grated
1 cup bread crumbs
2 Tbsp. melted butter

Melt butter and stir in flour, salt, pepper and onion. Add sour cream gradually. Fold in green beans. Pour into greased casserole dish. Sprinkle cheese over beans. Mix bread crumbs with melted butter and sprinkle over cheese.

Bake at 400° F for 20 minutes.

Serves 6.

—*Jayne Campsall*

Glazed Beets

Beets
Butter
Honey or maple syrup

Cook beets until tender. Drain, peel and, if beets are large, slice. Combine equal quantities of butter and honey or maple syrup in a saucepan. Add the beets and let simmer until the sauce is thickened and beets are shiny with the glaze, usually 10 to 20 minutes.

—*Donna Jubb*

Beets & Greens in Sour Cream

12 small beets
Honey
2 Tbsp. butter
1 small onion, minced
Salt & pepper
½ cup sour cream

Separate beet roots from greens. Cook the roots, drain, skin and slice them.

Rinse and chop the greens. Steam them briefly with a drop of honey, butter and onion. When greens are wilted, add the beet roots, salt and pepper and sour cream.

Serves 2-4.

—Bryanna Clark

Baked Carrots

4 carrots
4 Tbsp. butter
Nutmeg

Grate carrots into a buttered casserole dish. Dot with butter and sprinkle with nutmeg. Bake at 350° F for 20 to 30 minutes.

Serves 4.

—Jenny MacDonald

Broccoli Medley

A pleasant and unusual way to serve either fresh or frozen broccoli, this dish can be made ahead and reheated at serving time.

2 heads fresh broccoli or 2 10-oz. pkgs. frozen broccoli
1 cup chicken stock
¼ lb. bacon, cut in 1-inch pieces
2 cups mushrooms, sliced
1 can water chestnuts, drained & sliced
¼ cup slivered almonds
1 tsp. salt
⅛ tsp. pepper
Pimento strips

Cook broccoli in stock until crisp-tender, about 6 minutes. Drain, reserving ⅓ cup of cooking liquid. Cut broccoli into bite-sized pieces.

Fry bacon until slightly crisp, then add remaining ingredients except pimento, broccoli and cooking liquid. Cook and stir until bacon is crisp and mushrooms are tender, about 5 minutes. Add broccoli and reserved cooking liquid. Continue cooking until hot. Arrange on serving dish and garnish with pimento.

Serves 12.

—Pam Collacott

Broccoli Casserole

2 heads broccoli, chopped
1½ cups cream of mushroom sauce, page 132
½ cup shredded Cheddar cheese
¼ cup milk
¼ cup mayonnaise
1 egg, beaten
¼ cup bread crumbs
1 Tbsp. butter

Cook broccoli and drain. Place in a casserole dish. Mix remaining ingredients together and pour over broccoli. Bake at 350° F for 45 minutes.

Serves 6 to 8.

—Karen Brouwers

Red Cabbage & Apples

2 lbs. red cabbage
¼ cup butter
½ cup chopped onion
1½ tsp. salt
¼ tsp. pepper
3 Tbsp. vinegar
1½ cups peeled & diced apples
Sour cream to garnish

Shred cabbage coarsely. Melt butter, add cabbage, onion, seasonings and vinegar. Cook, covered, for 20 minutes over low heat, stirring occasionally. Add apples, cover and cook a further 20 minutes or until tender, stirring every few minutes.

Serve with sour cream.

Serves 6.

—Florence Graham

Carrot Casserole

8 carrots
1 cup finely chopped celery
1 medium onion, finely
  chopped
1 Tbsp. prepared mustard
½ cup mayonnaise
½ cup buttered bread
  crumbs

Boil carrots until tender. Drain and mash. Combine celery, onion, mustard and mayonnaise and add to carrots. Spoon into buttered casserole dish and top with bread crumbs.

Bake at 300° F for 1 hour.

—*Grace Zomer*

Stir-Fried Cauliflower

An unusual and attractive way to cook cauliflower, this dish is fast and simple to prepare.

2 Tbsp. oil
2 cloves garlic, minced
1 slice fresh ginger, the size
  of a quarter
1 head cauliflower, washed &
  broken into florets
1 red pepper, seeded & cut
  into strips
½ cup chicken stock
½ tsp. oregano
½ tsp. basil
3 tomatoes, peeled, seeded &
  cut into strips
1 cup peas, fresh or frozen

Heat oil in a large skillet. Add garlic, ginger and cauliflower. Stir-fry for 3 minutes. Stir in pepper and cook for 2 minutes. Add stock and herbs, cover and steam for 5 minutes. Remove cover, stir in tomatoes and peas and cook 3 to 4 more minutes or until vegetables are tender-crisp. Remove from heat and serve quickly.

—*Ingrid Birker*

Celery Crunch with Cheese-Nut Pastry

⅔ cup flour
1 tsp. salt
6 Tbsp. butter
1 cup diced almonds, toasted
2¼ cups shredded Cheddar
  cheese
2-3 Tbsp. cold milk
2½ cups diced celery
¼ cup flour
1½ cups milk

Sift together flour and ½ tsp. salt. Cut in 3 Tbsp. butter until mixture is crumbly. Stir in ⅓ cup almonds and ¾ cup cheese. Sprinkle 2-3 Tbsp. milk over mixture, stirring with a fork until dough holds together. Flatten into a ½-inch-thick square. Roll out to fit top of baking dish. Set aside.

Cook diced celery in boiling water until tender, drain and add 3 Tbsp. butter. Stir in ¼ cup flour and ½ tsp. salt. Mix well. Gradually blend in 1½ cups milk. Cook over medium heat, stirring constantly, until thickened. Stir in remaining almonds and cheese.

Place in baking dish and top with pastry. Bake at 425° F for 20 to 25 minutes.

Serves 8.

—*Susan Gillespie*

Creamy Cabbage

2 lbs. cabbage, shredded
½ lb. cooked ham, cubed
Salt
1 Tbsp. dill seeds
4 Tbsp. oil
1 small onion, diced
2 Tbsp. flour
1 Tbsp. paprika
½ cup sour cream

Place shredded cabbage in a heavy saucepan with ½ inch of water. Add cubed ham, salt to taste and dill seed (in a cheese-cloth bag). Simmer for 10 minutes.

Meanwhile, heat oil in a small saucepan. Add onion and cook slowly for 2 minutes. Add flour and paprika and cook over medium heat, stirring constantly, for 2 minutes. Add ½ cup hot water and stir until mixture thickens. Remove from heat.

Add this sauce to cabbage. Cook slowly until cabbage is tender — 10 minutes. Remove from heat and add sour cream.

Serves 6 to 8.

—*Mary Andrasi*

Eggplant Parmesan

1 large eggplant
2 eggs
¼ cup milk
½ cup flour
¼ cup sesame seeds
1¼ cups grated Parmesan
   cheese
2-3 cups spaghetti sauce
2 cups grated mozzarella
   cheese

Slice eggplant into ¼-inch slices. Beat eggs with milk. Mix flour with sesame seeds and ¼ cup Parmesan cheese. Dip eggplant slices in egg mixture and then in flour mixture.

Heat oil in frying pan and fry slices until brown on both sides.

Arrange a layer of fried eggplant slices on the bottom of a greased casserole dish. Spoon some spaghetti sauce over these and then sprinkle with some of the Parmesan and mozzarella cheeses. Repeat layers twice.

Bake at 350° F for 30 to 45 minutes.

Serves 6.

—Mikell Billoki

Eggplant Cream Cheese Cheddar

3 eggplants
1 cup flour
1 tsp. salt
2 eggs
¼ cup milk
2 cups corn meal
½ tsp. oregano
½ tsp. basil
Salt & pepper
1 lb. Cheddar cheese, grated
4 cups tomato sauce, page 414
1 lb. cream cheese

Slice eggplants ¼-inch thick. Mix flour and salt together. Beat together eggs and milk. Sift together corn meal, oregano, basil, salt and pepper.

Dip slices first in flour mixture, then in egg-milk mixture and then in corn meal. Coat both sides.

Lightly grease 2 baking sheets and lay eggplant slices on them. Bake at 350° F for 15 minutes, turn slices over and bake 15 minutes longer.

Place one-third of the eggplant in greased 9" x 13" baking pan. Sprinkle with one-third of the grated cheese and then add one-third of the tomato sauce. Repeat layers two more times. Top with sliced cream cheese. Bake at 350° F for 45 minutes.

Serves 6.

—Donna Blair

Celery with Almonds

½ cup slivered almonds
2 Tbsp. butter
4 cups diced celery
½ cup chopped onion
Pepper
2 Tbsp. dry white wine

In a skillet, cook the almonds in 1 Tbsp. butter, stirring constantly, until they are lightly browned. Drain on paper towels.

Sauté the diced celery and onion in the remaining butter. Season with pepper, if desired. Cook over low heat, stirring occasionally, for about 7 minutes.

Add the wine and cook, covered, for 2 minutes. Transfer to a serving dish and garnish with the almonds.

Serves 4 to 6.

—Janet Flewelling

Corn Fritters

Delicious with maple syrup at breakfast, corn fritters can also be served as a vegetable with dinner.

15-oz. can creamed corn
2 eggs, beaten
2 Tbsp. melted butter
2 cups flour
2 tsp. baking powder
1 tsp. salt
½ tsp. curry powder
4-5 cups oil for deep frying

Combine corn, eggs and butter. Sift dry ingredients together and blend in corn mixture. Drop mixture by spoonfuls into hot oil (375° F). Fry for approximately 4 minutes, turning once to cook evenly. Drain well.

Makes 15-18 fritters.

—Janice Clynick

Eggplant Entrée

1 large eggplant
2 Tbsp. olive oil
4 tomatoes
1 green pepper
½ lb. mushrooms
1 bunch shallots or ½
   medium onion
½ tsp. salt
¼ tsp. pepper
¼ tsp. oregano
¼ tsp. basil
¼ tsp. dry mustard
1 Tbsp. cider vinegar
1 Tbsp. honey

Slice eggplant and sauté in oil. Chop vegetables and add to eggplant with remaining ingredients. Simmer gently for 5 minutes.

Serves 4 to 6.

—*David Slabotsky*

Fiddlehead Harmony

2 cups fresh fiddleheads
1 lb. tofu
1-2 Tbsp. butter
3 large tomatoes, sliced
2 Tbsp. tamari sauce
Salt & pepper
5 wild leeks, chopped, or 1
   Tbsp. garlic powder

Wash the fiddleheads and boil in water for 5 minutes. Change the water and boil another 3 to 4 minutes, until chewy-tender.

Cut the tofu into strips and sauté in butter until lightly browned on both sides. Add fiddleheads, sliced tomatoes, tamari sauce, seasonings and leeks or garlic powder. Heat thoroughly.

Serves 6.

—*Kay Chornook*

Fiddlehead Casserole

1-1½ cups steamed
   fiddleheads
7-oz. can tuna
½ cup mayonnaise, page 132
1 tsp. curry powder
2 cups cream of mushroom
   sauce, page 132
½ cup buttered bread
   crumbs

Combine fiddleheads and tuna in a casserole dish. Mix together mayonnaise, curry powder and mushroom sauce. Add to fiddlehead mixture and mix well. Top with bread crumbs.

Bake at 350° F for 30 minutes.

Serves 4 to 6.

—*Jenny MacDonald*

Greens Chinese Style

This is an interesting way to prepare all kinds of green, leafy vegetables, such as kale, Swiss chard or leaf lettuce.

Wash greens and pat dry. Plunge briefly into a pot of boiling water until wilted. Mix with a dressing of equal parts oil and tamari sauce.

Serve immediately.

—*Brigitte Wolf*

Eggplant Casserole

2 medium-sized eggplants
4 strips bacon
1 onion
1 green pepper
2 cloves garlic
3 slices bread
1 cup milk
2 cups shrimp, minced
   clams or tuna
4 eggs, well beaten
Salt & pepper

Peel eggplants and boil until tender. Drain, mash and set aside. Fry bacon until crispy, remove from pan and crumble. Finely chop onion, pepper and garlic and fry in bacon fat until tender. Soak bread in milk then gently squeeze out excess.

Mix together eggplant, bacon, vegetables, shrimp and bread. Stir well. Add eggs and salt and pepper to taste.

Place in casserole dish and bake at 350° F for 25 to 30 minutes.

Serves 6.

—*James R. Wilson*

Herb Stuffed Mushroom Caps

This dish, excellent as a vegetable side dish or as an appetizer, can be assembled ahead of time, refrigerated and baked before serving.

24 very large fresh
    mushrooms (1½ lbs.)
½ cup butter
3 Tbsp. finely chopped green
    onion
1 cup fresh bread crumbs
½ cup chopped fresh parsley
⅛ tsp. powdered savory
⅛ tsp. pepper

Wipe mushrooms with a damp cloth. Remove stems and chop them finely. Melt ¼ cup butter in a large skillet and toss mushroom caps in this for 1 minute. Remove mushroom caps to a flat baking dish or a cookie sheet.

Melt remaining ¼ cup of butter in the same skillet. Sauté stems and onions briefly. Remove from heat and stir in bread crumbs, parsley, savory and pepper, tossing lightly. Spoon this mixture into caps.

Bake mushrooms at 350° F for 10 minutes.

—Wendy Searcy

Mushroom Loaf

3 Tbsp. butter
1 onion, finely chopped
1 lb. mushrooms, sliced
2 cups bread crumbs
1 egg, beaten
½ cup water or tomato juice
3 Tbsp. butter
Salt & pepper

Melt 3 Tbsp. butter in heavy pan, add onion and sliced mushrooms and cook for 10 minutes. Lift vegetables out with slotted spoon and add to bread crumbs. Mix well.

Add beaten egg, liquid, remaining butter and salt and pepper. Bake in a greased loaf pan at 375° F for 25 to 30 minutes.

Serves 4.

—Jacqueline Dysart

Stuffed Mushrooms

12-20 large mushrooms
6-8 slices of bacon, fried &
    crumbled
Parsley
Salt & pepper
½ cup Cheddar cheese
1 egg
½ cup bread crumbs
¼ cup finely chopped green
    pepper
2 cloves garlic, finely
    chopped
1 onion, finely chopped

Remove mushroom stems and chop. Mix all ingredients except mushroom caps. Place a tablespoon of mixture in each mushroom cap. Bake at 425° F for 30 minutes.

—Diane Adrian

Mushroom Bake

½ lb. mushrooms
½ cup butter
1 lb. tomatoes
1 cup fresh bread crumbs
1 small onion, grated
¾ cup grated Cheddar cheese
Juice & rind of ½ lemon
Cheese sauce, page 132

Wash and slice mushrooms and fry in ¼ cup butter for 5 minutes. Slice tomatoes and set aside.

Blend together the bread crumbs, onion, cheese, remaining butter and lemon rind, and press half the mixture into a casserole dish.

Spread mushrooms on top of crumb layer and follow with sliced tomatoes. Season well and sprinkle with lemon juice. Press on remaining crumb mixture.

Bake at 375° F for 30 minutes. Serve with cheese sauce.

Serves 2.

—Mrs. A.E. Nehua-Cafe

Mushroom Patties

4 eggs
2 cups chopped mushrooms
2-4 green onions, chopped
1½ cups grated Cheddar
    cheese
1 cup bread crumbs
½ tsp. salt
½ tsp. garlic powder
Pepper
¼ tsp. basil
¼ tsp. oregano

Beat eggs together. Add remaining ingredients and mix well. Shape into 6 patties and fry slowly in butter until crispy on both sides.

Makes 6 patties.

—Carol Bomke

Orange Glazed Parsnips

This glaze can quickly turn an everyday vegetable into an attractive side dish.

3 lbs. parsnips
½ tsp. salt
¼ cup butter
½ cup orange marmalade
¼ tsp. ginger
1 large navel orange to
garnish

Wash and peel parsnips and cut into 3-inch pieces. Cook in boiling salted water until tender.

Melt butter in skillet and stir in marmalade, ginger and ¼ cup water. Boil 5 minutes. Add parsnips and stir to glaze well. Place in serving dish. Spoon glaze over parsnips and garnish with orange slices.

Serves 6.

—Brenda Eckstein

Dusty Potatoes

¾ cup dry bread crumbs
1½ tsp. nutmeg
½ tsp. salt
¼ tsp. pepper
4 medium potatoes, pared &
quartered
⅓ cup melted butter

Mix bread crumbs and seasonings. Dip potatoes in melted butter and then roll in crumb mixture. Place on greased baking sheet. Bake at 350° F until crisp and brown about 1 hour.

Serves 4.

—Pam Collacott

Mediterranean Potato Pie

2 small onions, chopped
3 large potatoes, peeled
1 cup flour
½ tsp. pepper
1 tsp. salt
¼ cup olive oil
3 Tbsp. butter
3 Tbsp. flour
3 large ripe tomatoes,
chopped
½ green pepper, chopped
½ bay leaf
2 cloves
1 tsp. oregano
½ lb. mozzarella cheese,
diced
¼ cup grated Parmesan
cheese

Sauté chopped onion in a little oil. Boil the potatoes and mash until smooth. Blend in 1 cup flour, salt and pepper. Press mixture ½-inch thick in the bottom of a shallow baking dish. Spoon olive oil on top.

Melt butter in a skillet and stir in 3 Tbsp. flour. Add tomatoes, remaining onion, green pepper, bay leaf, cloves and oregano. Simmer for 20 minutes. Remove bay leaf and cloves.

Spoon sauce over potato mixture and top with cheeses.

Bake at 350° F for 15 minutes.

Serves 4.

—Brenda Kennedy

Scalloped Onions

A pleasant change from simple baked onions, this casserole can be quickly and easily assembled with ingredients which are usually on hand. The combination of cheese and onion provides a satisfying accompaniment to meat dishes.

6 medium onions
¼ cup butter
¼ cup flour
2 cups milk
½ tsp. salt
2 cups grated Cheddar
cheese

Slice onions and separate into rings. Place in 1½-quart casserole dish. Melt butter and blend in flour. Slowly stir in milk and cook, stirring, until thickened. Stir in salt and grated cheese. Pour over onions. Bake, uncovered, at 375° F for 1 hour.

Serves 6.

—Wendy Fitzgerald

Scalloped Potatoes

3 cups peeled & sliced
  potatoes
1 large onion, thinly sliced
1½ cups cream of
  mushroom sauce, page 132
4 Tbsp. flour
1½ tsp. salt
½ tsp. pepper
4 Tbsp. butter
3 cups milk

Place a layer of potatoes in a
deep casserole dish and add a
layer of sliced onion. Spread half
the mushroom sauce over this,
sprinkle with flour, salt and
pepper and dot with butter.
Repeat layers.

Pour milk around the potatoes
until it reaches the top layer of
potatoes.

Bake, covered, at 375° F for 30
minutes. Uncover and bake
another 30 to 45 minutes —
until top is golden brown.

Serves 4.

—Aurora Sugden

Twice-Baked Potatoes

*Almost any filling can be mixed
with the cooked potatoes. Some
suggestions are cooked bacon,
ham, mushrooms, onions or
other vegetables.*

6 medium potatoes
½ tsp. salt
Pepper
4 Tbsp. butter
¼ cup sour cream
Shredded mozzarella cheese
Parsley

Wash potatoes and bake at
400° F until done, about 1 hour.
Remove from oven, split tops
and scoop out insides. Place this
in a bowl and mash, combining
with all other ingredients except
cheese and parsley.

When well blended, scoop
mixture back into potato shells.
Top with cheese, sprinkle with
parsley. Put back into oven at
300° F. Serve when cheese has
melted.

Serves 6.

—Johanna Vanderheyden

Potato Casserole

6 large potatoes, cooked
  until just tender
1½ cups cream of
  mushroom sauce, page 92
1 cup chopped onion
2 cups sour cream
½ cup butter
½ lb. old Cheddar cheese,
  grated
Salt & pepper
½ cup bread crumbs
4 Tbsp. Parmesan cheese

Pare and grate cooked
potatoes. Combine with all
remaining ingredients except
bread crumbs and Parmesan
cheese. Place in a 9" x 13"
baking dish and top with bread
crumb-Parmesan cheese
mixture.

Bake at 375° F for 1 hour.

Serves 12.

—Mrs. G. Fellows

Potato Puff

*This is an easy and delicious
way to use up leftover potatoes.*

3 cups mashed potatoes
2 Tbsp. butter
1 tsp. chopped parsley
¼ tsp. salt
Few grains cayenne
1 tsp. onion juice
3 eggs, separated

Mix potatoes with butter,
parsley, salt, cayenne and onion
juice. Beat egg yolks, add to
potatoes and mix well. Beat egg
whites until stiff and fold in.
Place in greased baking dish and
bake at 350° F for 40 minutes or
until golden brown.

—Shirley Morrish

Sweet Potato Cashew Bake

½ cup brown sugar
⅓ cup broken cashews
¼ tsp. ground ginger
½ tsp. salt
2 lbs. sweet potatoes, cooked, peeled & sliced
8 peaches, peeled & halved
3 Tbsp. butter

Combine sugar, cashews, ginger and salt. In a shallow baking dish, layer half the potatoes, half the peaches and half the nut mixture. Repeat layers and dot with butter.

Bake, covered, at 350° F for 30 minutes. Uncover and bake 10 minutes longer.

Serves 6 to 8.

—Elizabeth Clayton

Scalloped Tomatoes

3 cups canned tomatoes
¼ cup butter
3 cups bread crumbs
1 tsp. salt
⅛ tsp. pepper
Ground allspice

Heat tomatoes and butter in saucepan until butter melts. Mix in bread crumbs, salt and pepper.

Spoon into buttered 9-inch square baking dish and sprinkle ground allspice lightly over the top. Bake, uncovered, at 375° F until the mixture is set and lightly browned. Serves 4.

—Doris Cober

Dum Arvi

This spicy sweet potato dish of Indian origin may be eaten as a meal in itself or as an accompanying vegetable to a meat meal.

1 lb. sweet potatoes
½ cup ghee (clarified butter)
1 small onion
½ tsp. ground ginger
1 tsp. coriander powder
½ tsp. garam masala (a mixed spice)
½ tsp. paprika
1 tsp. salt
2 green chilies, chopped

Peel sweet potatoes and chop into 1-inch cubes. Fry in ghee, remove and set aside.

Slice onion and fry in remaining ghee. Stir in ginger, coriander, garam masala, paprika, salt and green chilies.

Cover and bake at 375° F for 30 to 45 minutes, until potatoes are tender.

—Sheila Bear

Spaghetti Squash with Tomato Sauce

1 onion, finely chopped
1 clove garlic, minced
Butter or oil
1 lb. tomatoes, peeled seeded & chopped
Fresh parsley & basil
½ tsp. lemon juice
Salt & pepper
1 spaghetti squash

Sauté the onion and garlic in butter or oil. Add the chopped tomatoes and their juices, the herbs, lemon juice and salt and pepper. Simmer briefly.

Place the squash, whole, in a 325° F oven and bake 20 to 30 minutes, until tender. Pierce one end to test for tenderness. Cut the squash in half, gently remove the seeds, then lift out the flesh. Pile on a plate, toss with a bit of oil and pour the hot tomato sauce over it.

Serves 6.

—Kathee Roy

Scalloped Turnips

4 cups cubed turnip
2 Tbsp. butter
2 Tbsp. flour
1 cup milk
½ tsp. salt
¼ tsp. pepper
Nutmeg
⅓ cup bread crumbs
2 Tbsp. melted butter

Cook turnip in salted water for 20 minutes. Mash.

Melt 2 Tbsp. butter, add flour and stir. Add milk slowly, stirring constantly. Stir in salt, pepper and nutmeg to taste. Cook until thick. Add turnip and spoon into buttered casserole dish.

Combine bread crumbs with melted butter and sprinkle on top of the turnip. Bake at 350° F for 20 minutes.

—*Irene MacPhee*

Spinach Provençale

2 lbs. spinach
1 large onion, sliced
1 clove garlic, minced
Olive oil
Butter
2 eggs, beaten
1 cup grated Parmesan
    cheese
Salt & pepper

Wash and tear spinach. Sauté onion and garlic in olive oil until the onion is transparent. Add spinach, cover and cook until spinach is wilted — about 2 minutes. Remove from heat and cool slightly.

In a baking dish, combine spinach mixture, beaten eggs and half the cheese. Season, and sprinkle the remaining cheese on top. Dot with butter and bake at 375° F for 10 to 15 minutes.

Serves 6 to 8.

— *Jean Hally*

Tomatoes Provençales

In the late summer and early fall, when tomatoes are ripening all too quickly, this dish is an appetizing complement to any meal.

4 large tomatoes
3 Tbsp. olive oil
½ tsp. salt
½ tsp. pepper
2 cloves garlic, crushed
1 Tbsp. chopped parsley
1 tsp. basil
½ tsp. oregano
2 Tbsp. coarse bread crumbs
2 Tbsp. Parmesan cheese

Halve tomatoes crosswise and remove seeds by pressing each half in your hand.

Heat the oil in a large frying pan. Place tomatoes in oil, cut side down, and cook over medium heat for 3 minutes. Turn, and sprinkle cut side with salt and pepper. Place crushed garlic in bottom of pan and cook another 2 minutes.

Place tomatoes on a cookie sheet and sprinkle with parsley and basil mixed together. Top with bread crumbs mixed with Parmesan cheese. Broil for 5 to 10 minutes — until tomatoes are golden brown on top but still firm.

Serves 4.

—*Carolyn Hills*

Zucchini Parmesan Loaf

¾ cup flour
2 tsp. salt
⅓ cup milk
2 lbs. zucchini, cut lengthwise into ¼-inch slices
Salad oil
1 cup tomato sauce, page 414
½ cup grated Parmesan cheese
1 cup grated mozzarella cheese

Combine flour and salt on a sheet of wax paper. Pour milk into pie plate. Dip the zucchini in milk, then coat with flour.

In a 12-inch skillet over medium-high heat, cook zucchini in oil, a few slices at a time, until golden. Drain on paper towels.

In a greased loaf pan arrange half the zucchini, spoon on half the tomato sauce and sprinkle with half the mozzarella and Parmesan cheeses. Repeat layers.

Bake at 350° F for 40 minutes, until browned and bubbly.

Serves 4.

—Margaret Orr

Apple & Turnip Bake

2-3 turnips
2 apples, diced
6 Tbsp. butter
4 tsp. sugar
3 tsp. salt
¼ tsp. pepper
2 eggs
1¾ cups fine bread crumbs
2 Tbsp. melted butter

Peel and cut up turnip and cook in boiling salted water until tender. Drain and mash with electric mixer. Add apples, butter, sugar, salt, pepper, eggs and half the bread crumbs. Mix well.

Pour into greased 2-quart casserole dish and top with remaining bread crumbs that have been tossed in the melted butter. Cool, cover and refrigerate.

Remove from refrigerator 1 hour before dinner and heat at 350° F for 30 minutes.

Serves 12.

—William E. Nelson

September Garden Zucchini

This recipe can be easily adapted to barbecue cooking. Wrap layered vegetables in a square of aluminum foil and cook on grill, turning three or four times.

4 Tbsp. oil
1 large onion, cut in rings
1 zucchini, sliced
1 stalk celery, sliced
1 green pepper, sliced
2 tomatoes, quartered

Heat oil in a heavy frying pan and sauté onion, zucchini, celery and green pepper. When onions are transparent, add tomatoes.

Cover and simmer until tomatoes are soft.

—Donna Gordon

Minestra

A rice-vegetable stew, minestra gets its name from the Italian minestrare, *meaning "to serve."*

l large onion, chopped
1-2 Tbsp. butter
1½ cups raw rice
2 carrots, coarsely grated
½ cup sliced mushrooms
½ head cabbage, shredded
Salt & pepper
Marjoram
3 cups chicken stock
Chopped parsley to garnish
Parmesan cheese to garnish

In a large, heavy casserole dish, cook the onion in butter until soft. Add rice and carrots, stirring until rice begins to turn yellow. Add mushrooms, cabbage and seasonings. Cook and stir for 1 minute. Add stock. When it boils, reduce heat, cover, and simmer for 20 to 30 minutes.

When rice is cooked and liquid absorbed, remove from heat. Sprinkle with parsley and cheese.

Serves 4 to 6.

—*Winifred Czerny*

Tempura

BATTER:
1 cup brown rice flour
1 Tbsp. cornstarch
Salt
1 egg, beaten
½ cup cold water
VEGETABLES:
Use almost any vegetable
    that will cook quickly.
    When using long-cooking
    vegetables such as carrots,
    lightly steam first.
DIPPING SAUCE:
1 cup chicken stock
½ cup tamari sauce
⅓ cup honey
2 Tbsp. sherry

Mix flour with cornstarch, salt, egg and cold water to make a thin batter. Chill 15 minutes.

To prepare vegetables, wash and dry thoroughly. Cut into small pieces and chill well. Dredge in flour before dipping into batter.

For sauce, combine all ingredients and mix well.

To cook, heat several inches of oil in a wok. Dip each vegetable piece in batter, shake and fry briefly until golden, turning often. Drain and serve immediately with sauce.

—*Bryanna Clark*

Zucchini Supreme

Small zucchini
Parmesan cheese
Butter

Wash zucchini and slice in half lengthwise. Spread with butter and sprinkle on cheese. Place on cookie sheet on bottom rack of oven. Broil for 10 minutes or until bubbly and brown on top and crisp inside.

—*Beth Hopkins*

Vegetable Pie

Pastry for double 9-inch pie
    crust
½ cup each of 5 or 6
    different cooked vegetables
    (mushrooms, corn, beans,
    celery, carrots, zucchini,
    peas, broccoli, cauliflower,
    etc.)
½ cup diced onion
1 clove garlic, minced
1 Tbsp. butter
5 tsp. flour
1 cup milk
¼ cup grated Cheddar
    cheese
Salt & pepper

Line pie plate with pastry. Sauté onion and garlic in butter until garlic is browned. Add flour. Stir in milk. Cook and stir until thickened. Add cheese, salt and pepper and cook gently until cheese is melted. Mix together vegetables and place in pastry shell. Pour cheese sauce over vegetables and top with remaining pastry. Bake at 375° F for 30 minutes.

Serves 4.

—*Andra Hughes*

Almond Vegetables Mandarin

1 cup thinly sliced carrots
1 cup green beans, cut in
  1-inch slices
2 Tbsp. salad oil
1 cup thinly sliced
  cauliflower
½ cup sliced green onion
1 cup chicken stock
2 tsp. cornstarch
Pinch garlic powder
½ cup unblanched whole
  almonds

Stir carrots and beans in oil over medium heat for 2 minutes. Add cauliflower and onion, and cook 1 minute longer. Add chicken stock, cornstarch and garlic. Cook and stir until thickened and vegetables are crispy tender. Add almonds.

Serves 4 to 6.

—Kathenne Dunster

Zucchini Medley

2 small zucchini
2 slices eggplant, peeled
2 cooking onions
½ sweet red pepper
4 Tbsp. butter
Salt & pepper

Cut zucchini into ¼-inch slices, eggplant into ½-inch squares, onions into rings and pepper into 1-inch strips. Stir-fry in melted butter and season with salt and pepper.

—Eleanor Bell

Zucchini Boats

When large zucchini are in abundance, recipes such as the following provide delightful meals. Almost any combination of vegetables and cheese, with or without meat, can be used in these "boats."

1 large zucchini (approx. 12")
1 green pepper, cut in small
  squares
½ cup dry bread crumbs
½ cup grated Cheddar
  cheese
Butter
Salt & pepper

Cut zucchini in half lengthwise and then crosswise. Remove centre, except for a piece at each end, to form a boat. Fill with green pepper. Dot with butter, add salt and pepper to taste. Sprinkle bread crumbs on top and cover with grated cheese.

Bake in covered baking dish at 350° F for 20 minutes, then remove lid and bake 10 to 15 minutes longer.

—Eleanor Bell

Baked Vegetable Loaf

1½ cups diced raw potatoes
2 cups diced raw carrots
½ cup beef stock
¼ cup finely chopped green
  pepper
¼ cup finely chopped onion
1 cup wheat germ, toasted
¼ cup melted butter
2 eggs, beaten
1 tsp. salt
¼ tsp. pepper
½ tsp. savory Cream of
  mushroom sauce, page 132

Cook potatoes and carrots in a small amount of boiling water until barely tender. Drain.

Combine all ingredients except mushroom sauce and spoon into greased loaf pan. Bake at 350° F for 1 hour or until set. Slice thickly and serve with mushroom sauce.

Serves 4.

—Gerri Bazuin

Vegetable Morsels

An excellent filling for pita, these vegetable balls taste delicious with yogurt and marinated tomatoes, cucumbers and onions.

3 eggs
2 tsp. seasoned salt
1 tsp. ground cumin
¼ tsp. pepper
3 Tbsp. sesame seeds
3 Tbsp. flour
3 Tbsp. wheat germ
2 carrots, shredded
1½ cups cooked, drained &
  chopped spinach
1½ cups chopped green
  beans

Combine all ingredients in order listed. Drop by spoonfuls onto greased cookie sheets and bake at 450° F for 10 minutes.

Serves 6 to 8.

—*Bryanna Clark*

Ratatouille

For a satisfying meal with Italian overtones, this succulent vegetable stew can make a complete meal when served with black olives and warm fresh bread.

½ cup salad oil
2 large onions, thinly sliced
2-3 cloves garlic, minced
1 eggplant, peeled & diced
4 tomatoes, peeled & diced
1 zucchini, peeled & diced
2 green peppers, cleaned &
  diced
3 stalks celery, diced
2 tsp. fresh basil
1 tsp. oregano
Salt & pepper

Heat oil in heavy saucepan and brown onion and garlic. Add eggplant and tomatoes and cook for a few minutes.

Add remaining ingredients, bring to a boil and lower heat. Simmer for at least 1 hour.

Serves 4 to 6.

—*Mrs. E. Imboden*

Vegetable Stew

The special appeal of this dish is that it does not use salt but rather relies upon the subtle flavours of each vegetable for seasoning.

¼ cup butter
4 carrots, cut into ¼-inch
  slices
1 large turnip, cut into strips
1 celeriac root, cut into
  strips
4 potatoes, cubed
2 green peppers, cut into
  rings
4-6 tomatoes, chopped
6 small whole onions
4 tsp. chopped parsley
½ tsp. thyme
3 soya cubes mixed in 3
  cups water or 3 cups
  chicken stock
¼ cup arrowroot
½ cup water

Melt butter in stewing pot. Add carrots and turnip, cover and cook for 10 to 15 minutes.

Add celeriac, potatoes, peppers, tomatoes, onions, seasonings and broth. Simmer for 1 hour.

Mix arrowroot with water and add to stew when vegetables are tender. Simmer for 10 more minutes.

Serves 4.

—*Christine Taylor*

Tossed Vegetable Salad

1 lb. broccoli, cauliflower,
  Brussels sprouts or
  combination
¼ lb. mushrooms
½ cup olive oil
¼ cup wine vinegar
1 clove garlic, minced
½ large red onion, chopped
1 tsp. dry parsley
½ tsp. salt
¼ tsp. basil
¼ tsp. pepper
6 slices bacon, cooked until
  crisp
1 cup croutons

Cut broccoli into bite-sized pieces and steam until cooked but still crunchy. Drain and cool. Slice mushrooms. Mix together oil, vinegar, garlic, onion and herbs. Marinate all together in refrigerator for at least 4 hours. Toss with croutons and crumbled bacon just before serving.

Serves 6.

—*Elizabeth Templeman*

Celery Salad

¼ cup olive oil
Juice of ½ large lemon
1 tsp. dried mustard
Salt
1 bunch celery, washed &
  sliced

Combine olive oil, lemon juice, mustard and salt. Mix well. Pour over celery, toss and marinate for at least 24 hours.

Serves 6 to 8.

—*Dawn Hermann*

Shrimp & Avocado Salad

1 avocado, peeled & chopped
½ cup shrimp, cleaned &
  cooked
½ English cucumber, cubed
½ head Boston lettuce,
  broken
1 cup alfalfa sprouts
¼ cup mayonnaise, page 132
¼ cup sour cream
1-2 Tbsp. lemon juice
Salt & pepper

Combine avocado, shrimp, cucumber, lettuce and sprouts and toss. Mix remaining ingredients. Pour over salad and toss gently.

Serves 2.

—*Jane Pugh*

Marinated Onion Rings

4 medium onions
1 cup vinegar
1 cup water
½ cup sugar
½ tsp. salt
Pepper
1 cup sour cream
Poppy seeds

Slice and separate onions. Cover with boiling water and drain immediately. Combine vinegar, water, sugar, salt and pepper in saucepan. Bring to a boil. Pour over onions and marinate, refrigerated, for 1 hour. Drain. Add sour cream and poppy seeds. Toss gently.

Serves 4.

—*Mary Reid*

Vegetarian Egg Rolls

1 cup bean sprouts
1½ cups shredded cabbage
1 medium broccoli stalk,
  chopped
2 onions, chopped
2 stalks celery, thinly sliced
1 carrot, grated
2 Tbsp. oil
¾ cup cashews, chopped
½ cup tofu, mashed
1½ cups grated Cheddar
  cheese
Salt
Garlic powder
1 pkg. egg roll wrappers

Stir-fry vegetables in oil. Add nuts, tofu, cheese and salt and garlic powder to taste.

Fill egg roll wrappers with approximately ¼ cup of filling each, and wrap, following package directions.

Deep fry for approximately 3 minutes on each side or until lightly browned.

Serves 6.

—*Kristine Reid*

Marinated Cucumber Salad

2 medium cucumbers, pared
   & thinly sliced
1 medium onion, thinly
   sliced
1 tsp. salt
3 Tbsp. vinegar
3 Tbsp. water
½ tsp. sugar
¼ tsp. paprika
¼ tsp. pepper
1-2 cloves garlic, crushed

Combine cucumbers and onion in a bowl and sprinkle with salt. Mix lightly and set aside for 1 hour.

Meanwhile, combine remaining ingredients. Drain cucumbers, pour dressing over them and toss until well mixed.

Chill for 1 to 2 hours, stirring occasionally. Discard garlic before serving and sprinkle with additional paprika.

Serves 6.

—Valerie Gillis

Carrot Salad

1 lb. carrots, sliced
½ Spanish onion, quartered
   & separated
½ green pepper, cut into
   rings
1 cup finely cut celery
¾ cup tomato sauce, page
   414
¼ cup vinegar
½ cup granulated sugar
½ tsp. prepared mustard
½ tsp. dry mustard
½ tsp. salt
½ tsp. pepper
½ Tbsp. Worcestershire
   sauce
¼ cup salad oil

Boil carrots until tender, drain and cool. Add onion, green pepper and celery.

Combine tomato sauce, vinegar, sugar, mustards, salt, pepper and Worcestershire sauce in a blender. When well blended, slowly pour in oil and blend well.

Toss salad with dressing and refrigerate for at least 24 hours.

Serves 6.

—V.A. Charles

Sweet Pepper Salad

The red and green of this salad make it a colourful addition to Christmas dinner.

2 large red peppers, sliced
2 large green peppers, sliced
½ lb. mushrooms, sliced
3 green onions, chopped
½ tsp. salt
½ tsp. pepper
¾ cup olive oil
3 Tbsp. vinegar
½ tsp. dry mustard
1-2 cloves garlic

Place all vegetables in a large bowl. Combine remaining ingredients and whirl in a blender. Pour over vegetables. Refrigerate for at least 3 hours before serving.

Serves 6 to 8.

—Pam Collacott

Broccoli Salad

1 head broccoli, broken into
   bite-sized pieces
1 onion, quartered &
   separated
6-8 slices bacon
⅓ cup vinegar
⅓ cup brown sugar

Fry bacon until crisp. Remove from pan and crumble into serving bowl with broccoli. Sauté onion in bacon fat and add to broccoli. Add vinegar and brown sugar to remaining bacon fat and simmer for a few minutes.

Pour over the broccoli, toss and serve.

Serves 4.

—Margaret Robinson

Curried Potato Salad

2 Tbsp. butter
2 Tbsp. flour
2 tsp. curry powder
1 cup chicken stock
½ cup sour cream
½ cup mayonnaise, page 132
½ tsp. salt
½ cup sliced green onion
½ cup diced celery
½ cup sliced green olives
2 Tbsp. chopped parsley
2 Tbsp. chopped green
  pepper
4 cups diced cooked
  potatoes

Melt butter, stir in flour and curry powder. Add chicken stock and cook until thick and smooth. Stir in sour cream, mayonnaise and salt. Add remaining ingredients and combine gently.

Place in a greased baking dish and sprinkle with paprika. Bake at 375° F until hot — 20 to 30 minutes. Serve hot.

Serves 6 to 8.

—Dorothy Hurst

Eggplant Salad

This traditional Jewish dish is a pleasant and unusual way to serve eggplant.

1 large eggplant
1 green pepper, diced
1 large onion, diced
2 tomatoes, chopped
2 Tbsp. oil
¼ cup vinegar
Salt

Bake eggplant at 375° F until tender. Peel and chop in a bowl. Add remaining ingredients and mix well. Chill and serve.

—Arlene Pervin

Three Bean Salad

½ cup vinegar
¼ cup oil
1 tsp. salt
Dash pepper
Dash garlic powder
2 Tbsp. sugar
2 cups green beans, cooked,
  drained & chopped
2 cups wax beans, cooked,
  drained & chopped
2 cups red kidney beans,
  cooked & drained
¼ cup chopped green onions

Mix together vinegar, oil, salt, pepper, garlic powder and sugar. Add beans and onions. Toss well.

Cover and refrigerate for 3 hours or overnight, tossing occasionally.

—Wanda Gaitan

Potato Salad

3-4 hard-boiled eggs
5 cooked potatoes
2-3 Tbsp. water
1 Tbsp. tarragon vinegar
1 onion, diced
1 tsp. celery seeds
1 tsp. salt
Mayonnaise, page 132

Peel and dice eggs and potatoes. Set aside. Combine 2 to 3 Tbsp. water, vinegar, onion, celery seeds and salt in saucepan. Cook until onion is tender — about 5 minutes. Pour over the potatoes and eggs, add mayonnaise to taste and toss gently.

Serves 4.

—Nancy McAskill

Orange Bean Salad

This pungent salad serves as an excellent accompaniment to pork or lamb.

¾ lb. fresh green beans cut
  in half
½ cup honey
¼ cup cider vinegar
½ cup oil
½ cup water or chicken
  stock
Dash coriander
¼ cup fresh chopped parsley
2 cups cooked red kidney
  beans
½ cup red onion, chopped
3 oranges, peeled &
  sectioned

Cook green beans in boiling water for 4 minutes.

Mix together honey, vinegar, oil, water or stock, coriander and parsley.

Drain beans. Combine with kidney beans, chopped onion and orange sections in large bowl. Pour ⅓ cup dressing over all ingredients and mix well. The rest of the dressing will keep in the refrigerator.

Serves 6 to 8.

—Ingrid Birker

Dandelion Salad

2 slices bacon
½ cup unopened dandelion
   flower buds
2 cups young dandelion
   leaves
2 Tbsp. oil
1 Tbsp. vinegar
Salt & pepper
1 tsp. tarragon

Cook bacon until crisp.
Remove from pan and drain.

Wash dandelion flowers and
leaves and pat dry with paper
towels. Cook flowers in bacon fat
until the buds burst open.
Drain. Crumble bacon into salad
bowl. Add leaves and flowers.

Combine oil, vinegar and
seasonings, pour over salad and
toss.

Serves 4.

—*Shirley Morrish*

Greek Salad

*Less expensive than restaurant
versions, this delicious salad
may be served as a meal with
warm garlic bread, or as a side
dish.*

1 head romaine lettuce,
   shredded
½ Spanish onion, thinly
   sliced & separated into
   rings
1 green pepper, cut in
   ½-inch squares
4 tomatoes, cut in wedges
½ cucumber, cut into 4
   lengthwise, then sliced
12 or more ripe black olives
½ lb. feta cheese, crumbled
2 cloves garlic, peeled &
   crushed
½ cup olive oil
1 Tbsp. wine vinegar
¼ tsp. salt
Dash black pepper

Place salad ingredients in large
salad bowl. When ready to serve,
place oil in a small container
that has a lid. Drop crushed
garlic clove into the oil, add
vinegar, salt and pepper, cover
and shake vigorously.

Pour over salad and serve
immediately.

—*Don & Foley Boyd*

Caesar Salad

1 head romaine lettuce
3 large cloves garlic
2 anchovy fillets
1 tsp. dry mustard
Juice of 1 lemon
1 egg yolk
2 Tbsp. blue cheese
Salt & pepper
¾ cup olive oil
4 Tbsp. Parmesan cheese

Wash, dry and tear up
romaine lettuce. Set aside.

Crush garlic in a large wooden
bowl, add anchovies, mustard,
lemon juice, egg yolk and blue
cheese. Stir, continuing to flatten
cheese and anchovies against
the bowl until a thick paste is
formed. Add salt, pepper and
olive oil, beating fast to make a
thick and creamy dressing.

Toss in lettuce pieces and mix
thoroughly. Sprinkle with
Parmesan cheese.

Serves 4 to 6.

—*Julienne Tardif*

Wilted Lettuce Salad

2-3 strips bacon
2 Tbsp. vinegar
2 Tbsp. water
2 Tbsp. sugar
1 head lettuce

Cook bacon until crisp,
remove from pan, drain and
crumble. Reserve 2 Tbsp. fat.

To bacon fat, add vinegar,
water and sugar. Bring to a boil

Wash and tear lettuce, arrange
on 4 plates and pour dressing
over it. Toss and serve at once.

Serves 4.

—*Mrs. Neil McAskill*

Spring Salad

2 cups watercress
2 cups dandelion leaves
3 wild leeks, chopped
¼ cup sunflower seeds
2-3 fresh basil leaves
¼ cup salad oil
¼ cup cider vinegar
1 Tbsp. lemon juice
2 tsp. sugar
½ tsp. Worcestershire sauce

Combine cleaned watercress and dandelion leaves. Add leeks, sunflower seeds and basil and toss. Combine remaining ingredients, pour over salad and toss well.

Serves 6 to 8.

—Nora Jones

Chick Pea Salad

Tasty and colourful, this is a good winter salad when fresh produce is scarce.

16-oz. can chick peas or 2 cups home-cooked beans
½ cup sesame seeds
1 medium onion, finely chopped
2 carrots, finely chopped
¼ cup vegetable oil
¼ cup cider vinegar
1 Tbsp. brown sugar
½-1 tsp. salt
Ground pepper
¼ cup fresh chopped chives or green onions
1 large tomato

Drain chick peas. Mix together all ingredients except chives and tomato. Cover the bowl and chill for at least 2 hours. Just before serving chop the tomato into small pieces and mix in, along with the chives.

—Wendy Searcy

Russian Salad

1 lb. pickled beets, diced
1 lb. fresh shelled peas
1 lb. mushrooms, diced
2 fillets of herring or anchovy, chopped
3 large potatoes, cooked & diced
2 hard-boiled eggs, diced
1 dill pickle, finely chopped
Mayonnaise

Mix all ingredients well, then stir in enough mayonnaise to coat. Chill well.

Serves 12.

—Chris Dickman

April Salad

1 cup dry chick peas
3 cups water
1 Tbsp. garlic powder
1½ tsp. celery seed
3-4 cups alfalfa sprouts
1-2 cups fenugreek sprouts
½ lb. feta cheese

Soak chick peas in 3 cups water for at least 4 hours. Add garlic powder, celery seed and more water, if necessary. Bring to a boil and simmer until chick peas are chewy tender — about 1½ hours. Drain and cool.

Make a bed of alfalfa and fenugreek sprouts and crumble feta cheese over them. Top with chick peas.

Serves 8 to 10.

—Susan Ellenton

Herbed Cherry Tomatoes

12-15 cherry tomatoes
4 Tbsp. sunflower seed oil
2 tsp. vinegar
1 tsp. sugar
1 tsp. oregano leaves (about ½ tsp. powder)
1 tsp. salt
½ tsp. pepper
¼ tsp. sweet basil

Slice tomatoes in half and put in a serving bowl. Combine remaining ingredients and pour over the tomatoes.

Cover and refrigerate for at least 2 hours before serving.

Serves 6.

—Nicole Chartrand

Tomato Cucumber Toss

This is an ideal salad for late summer, when gardens abound with tomatoes and cucumbers.

3 ripe tomatoes
3 small cucumbers
¼ cup oil
¼ cup cider vinegar
Salt & pepper

Chop tomatoes and unpeeled cucumbers into chunks. Place in a shallow bowl and toss with the oil, vinegar and seasonings.

—Mikell Billoki

Onion & Mushroom Salad

½ cup olive oil
½ cup white wine
⅓ cup white wine vinegar
2 tsp. salt
2 tsp. thyme
1 tsp. pepper
1 small bay leaf
1 clove garlic, minced
1½ lbs. small pickling
   onions
1½ lbs. small mushrooms
1 head romaine lettuce
¼ cup chopped fresh parsley

In a large saucepan, combine oil, wine, vinegar, salt, thyme, pepper, bay leaf, garlic and onions. Simmer for 10 minutes, add mushrooms and continue simmering, covered, for 5 minutes or until onions are tender.

Refrigerate for at least 12 hours, drain and serve on a bed of lettuce garnished with parsley.

Serves 10.

—Jennifer McGuire

Coleslaw

1 large head cabbage
4 carrots
2-4 green onions, chopped
½ cup vinegar
⅔ cup oil
2 Tbsp. salt
3 Tbsp. sugar

Shred cabbage and carrots into a large bowl. Add green onion.

Place remaining ingredients in a saucepan and bring to a boil. Let cool and pour over cabbage and carrots. Toss gently.

Refrigerate for at least 24 hours, stirring occasionally.

—Helen Owen

Cabbage Salad

When fresh greens are scarce, this tangy cabbage salad will brighten up winter meals. It can also be made with red cabbage for more colour.

1 large cabbage
1 green pepper
1 small onion
3-4 stalks celery
¾ cup white sugar
1 cup white vinegar
¾ cup cooking oil
½ tsp. celery seed
1 tsp. curry powder
1 Tbsp. salt

Shred cabbage and dice remaining vegetables. Combine. Mix remaining ingredients together and boil for 2 minutes. Pour over vegetables. Chill well.

—Rose MacLeod

Spinach, Mushroom & Bacon Salad

10 oz. fresh spinach, washed
1 tomato, cut into wedges
1 small red onion, thinly
   sliced & separated into
   rings
½ cup sliced mushrooms
⅓ cup chopped cooked
   bacon
⅓ cup olive oil
2 Tbsp. wine vinegar
¼ tsp. oregano
¼ tsp. pepper

Tear spinach into bite-sized pieces. Place spinach, tomato, onion rings, mushrooms and bacon in salad bowl. Toss gently.

Combine oil, vinegar, oregano and pepper in a jar. Cover and shake well. Pour over salad and toss.

Serves 10.

—Jane Cuthbert

Spinach-Sprout Salad

1 pkg. fresh spinach, washed
2 cups bean sprouts
¼ cup olive oil
2 oz. slivered almonds
2 Tbsp. malt vinegar
2 Tbsp. soya sauce
¼ tsp. ginger
1 Tbsp. brown sugar
Paprika
Salt

Tear spinach into bite-sized pieces and toss with bean sprouts.

Brown almonds in olive oil and combine them, undrained, with remaining ingredients. Pour over salad and toss.

Serves 8 to 10.

—Marilyn Fuller

Mushroom Paté

2 lbs. unsalted butter
2½ lbs. mushrooms, sliced
1 lb. chicken livers
1½ Tbsp. salt
1½ Tbsp. pepper
1½ Tbsp. curry powder

In a skillet, sauté mushrooms and half the salt, pepper and curry powder in ½ lb. butter until mushrooms are limp.

In another skillet, sauté chicken livers and the remaining seasonings in ½ lb. butter until livers are thoroughly cooked.

Mix together livers and mushrooms and chop coarsely. Cream remaining 1 lb. butter and place in blender with chopped mixture and blend until smooth.

Place in 2 medium-sized moulds. Refrigerate for at least 12 hours.

To serve, unmould and leave at room temperature for 30 minutes.

—Liz Eder & Paul Jett

Fruit Salad with Vermouth

Some suitable fresh fruit combinations for this salad are apples and pears, peaches and melon or oranges, grapefruit and grapes. Toasted sesame or sunflower seeds can also make a tasty addition.

½ cup raisins
½ cup grated coconut
½ cup vermouth
Fruit, whatever is in season

Soak raisins and coconut in vermouth overnight. Slice up fruit, add to raisin mixture and toss. Refrigerate until time to serve.

—Kathe Lieber

Bean Sprout Salad

2 cups bean sprouts
1 clove garlic, crushed
¼ cup oil
2 Tbsp. vinegar
2 Tbsp. soya sauce
2 Tbsp. sesame seeds
Salt & pepper

Mix together all ingredients except sprouts. Pour over sprouts and toss gently.

Serves 4.

—Dawn Hermann

Rice & Sprout Salad

Using home-grown sprouts, this crunchy salad satisfies a winter longing for crispy salad greens.

2 cups cooked brown rice
2 cups bean sprouts (lentil or mung)
3 stalks celery, chopped
1 cup peas, briefly steamed
⅓ cup oil
⅓ cup vinegar
1 Tbsp. honey
½ tsp. salt
Dash pepper

Mix together rice, sprouts, celery and peas. Blend together oil, vinegar, honey, salt and pepper and add to salad. Toss well and chill before serving.

—Mikell Billoki

Marinated Mushrooms

This is an addictive appetizer, perfect for scooping on crackers. The lemon gives it an unusual tangy flavour.

½ cup onions, very thinly sliced
Zest of 1 lemon, cut in julienne matchsticks
3 Tbsp. olive oil
⅛ tsp. mustard seed
⅛ tsp. cardamom
¼ tsp. thyme
¼ tsp. pepper
¼ tsp. salt
¼ tsp. coriander seeds
¾ cup water
2 Tbsp. lemon juice
1 Tbsp. minced parsley
½ lb. (3 cups) fresh mushrooms, quartered

Sauté onions and lemon zest in olive oil until translucent. Add remaining ingredients except mushrooms. Simmer for 5 minutes. Add mushrooms, toss to blend, cover and boil for 3 minutes. Strain mushroom mixture and boil down strained liquid until syrupy. Add to mushrooms, then refrigerate before serving.

—Merilyn Mohr

Tutti Fruity Salad

1 small head romaine lettuce
3-4 red onions, thinly sliced
2 ribs celery, sliced
2 navel oranges
1 tsp. celery seed
1 tsp. salt
1 tsp. dry mustard
1 tsp. paprika
⅓ cup lemon juice
½ cup sugar
¾ cup salad oil

Wash, dry and tear up lettuce. Add onion slices, separated into rings, celery and oranges, peeled, sliced crosswise into three and then segmented.

Combine celery seed, salt, dry mustard, paprika, lemon juice and sugar. Slowly add oil, beating with a whisk, until it thickens.

Pour ½ cup dressing over salad and toss. Remaining dressing will keep for several weeks if refrigerated.

Serves 6.

—*Dorothy Malone*

Basic White Sauce

1 cup milk or light cream
Salt & pepper
2 Tbsp. butter
2 Tbsp. flour

Melt butter and stir in flour. Cook over low heat for 3 or 4 minutes, stirring constantly. Slowly stir in milk or cream and salt and pepper. Cook, stirring, until sauce has thickened. Makes 1 cup.

Cheese Sauce

1 cup basic white sauce, above
½ cup grated Cheddar or Swiss cheese
1 tsp. lemon juice
Nutmeg

Warm the white sauce and gradually stir in grated cheese. Cheddar will give a tangy flavour while Swiss gives a milder, thicker sauce. Add lemon juice and nutmeg. Cook and stir until cheese is completely melted.

Makes 1½ cups.

Cream of Mushroom Sauce

1 cup basic white sauce, above
½ cup chopped mushrooms
2 Tbsp. butter
2 tsp. tamari sauce
½ tsp. thyme

Warm white sauce. Cook mushrooms in butter for 2 minutes. Add to white sauce with tamari sauce and thyme. Stir well and heat through.

Makes 1¼ cups.

Basic Mayonnaise

1 egg
1 tsp. salt
½ tsp. dry mustard
2 cloves garlic, peeled
2 Tbsp. vinegar
1 cup vegetable oil

Combine egg, salt, mustard, garlic, vinegar and ¼ cup oil in blender. Cover and whirl until ingredients are blended. Remove lid and slowly pour in remaining oil, in a steady stream, until mixture has thickened. Keep refrigerated. Makes 1¼ cups.

Herb Mayonnaise

To basic mayonnaise add:
2 Tbsp. chopped parsley
1 Tbsp. minced chives
¼ tsp. dried tarragon
1 tsp. chopped dill

Curry Mayonnaise

To basic mayonnaise add:
1 tsp. curry powder
½ clove garlic, chopped
1 tsp. lemon juice

Thousand Island Dressing

To basic mayonnaise add:
3 Tbsp. chili sauce
1 Tbsp. grated onion
2 Tbsp. finely chopped green pepper
2 Tbsp. chopped chives
⅓ hard-boiled egg, finely chopped

—*Mrs. E. Louden*

Bouquet Garni

1 clove garlic
1 Tbsp. dried parsley
1 tsp. dried basil
1 tsp. dried rosemary
1 tsp. oregano
2 bay leaves
6 whole peppercorns

Mix together and tie in 3 thicknesses of cheesecloth.

Makes 1 bag.

—Shirley Hill

French Dressing

12 Tbsp. olive oil
4 Tbsp. lemon juice
Salt & pepper
2 cloves garlic, peeled
½ tsp. dry mustard

Combine 2 Tbsp. of oil, 2 Tbsp. of lemon juice, salt, pepper and mustard and beat well with a whisk. When smooth, add 4 Tbsp. oil and beat well again. Add remaining lemon juice and oil. Place in a jar, add garlic, cover and refrigerate.

Makes 1 cup.

Olga's Salad Dressing

½ cup oil
⅓ cup cider vinegar
2 Tbsp. honey
1 Tbsp. onion, grated
Salt & pepper
½ tsp. mustard

Combine all ingredients in a jar and shake until well blended. Let sit overnight at room temperature for best flavour.

Javanese Salad Dressing

This dressing has an unusual combination of flavours— peanut and very sharp lemon.

¾ cup lemon juice
½ cup crushed peanuts **or**
   3 Tbsp. peanut butter
1 tsp. salt
1 tsp. sugar
1 tsp. dill
¼ tsp. crushed red pepper

Combine all ingredients and mix well. Refrigerate until ready to use.

Makes 1 cup.

—Susan Bates Eddy

Sesame Dressing

¼ cup olive oil
2 cloves garlic, diced
3 Tbsp. tamari sauce
3 Tbsp. lemon juice
1 tsp. honey
½ tsp. ginger
½ tsp. black pepper
3 Tbsp. toasted sesame
   seeds

Combine oil and garlic. Let sit at room temperature for 1 to 2 hours. Add tamari, lemon juice, honey, ginger and black pepper and shake well. At serving time, add sesame seeds.

—Shiela Alexandrovich

Oil & Vinegar Dressing

⅔ cup oil
½ cup red wine vinegar
½ tsp. sugar
1 tsp. salt
¼ tsp. pepper
½ tsp. basil
½ tsp. tarragon
2 Tbsp. Parmesan cheese

Combine all ingredients, shake well and chill. This dressing is particularly tasty with a buttercrunch lettuce and mushroom salad.

—Beth Hopkins

African Lemon Dressing

Grated peel of 2 lemons
¼ cup lemon juice
1½ tsp. salt
⅛ tsp. red pepper **or** Tabasco
   sauce
2 cloves garlic, chopped
⅔-¾ cup olive oil
½ tsp. ground coriander
½ tsp. ground cumin
½ tsp. dry mustard
½ tsp. honey
½ tsp. paprika

Combine all ingredients in a jar, shake well and refrigerate for several hours.

—Carol Gasken

Blue Cheese
Protein Dressing

1 clove garlic, crushed
1 Tbsp. tahini
Crumbled blue cheese, to
  taste
2 Tbsp. lemon juice
Dash of curry powder
1 Tbsp. cottage cheese
1 tsp. yogurt
¼ cup oil

Combine all ingredients and whisk together to blend.

This is especially good on a spinach salad with hard-boiled eggs, or on sliced tomatoes and raw mushrooms.

—Kathe Lieber

Celery Seed Dressing

1 tsp. salt
1 tsp. dry mustard
1 tsp. celery seed
1 tsp. paprika
½ cup sugar
⅓ cup vinegar
1 cup oil

Place all ingredients in the blender. Purée until well combined.

Store in refrigerator. Shake well before using.

Makes 1½ cups.

—Joanne Bombard

Poppy Seed Dressing

4 Tbsp. lemon juice
2 tsp. Dijon mustard
1 tsp. salt
Cayenne pepper
2 Tbsp. honey
6 Tbsp. olive oil
6 Tbsp. vegetable oil
1 Tbsp. poppy seeds

Combine all ingredients in a jar and shake well. Keep in refrigerator. Makes enough dressing for one large salad.

—Sherrie Dick

Parsley Pesto Sauce

This rich sauce is delicious tossed with hot pasta, or mixed with cream cheese as a spread. It can also be added to soups or stews.

2 cups firmly packed parsley
½ cup fresh basil
½ cup olive oil
2 cloves garlic, peeled &
  chopped
Salt & pepper
¼ cup chopped pine nuts or
  almonds
½ cup freshly grated
  Parmesan cheese

Place all ingredients except cheese in blender and blend at high speed until smooth, stopping occasionally to scrape side with a spatula. Mix in cheese.

Makes 2½ cups.

—Shirley Hill

Tomato Herb Dressing

1 cup salad oil
1 cup tomato sauce, page 414
⅓ cup vinegar
¼ cup sugar
2 cloves garlic, crushed
2 tsp. dry mustard
2 tsp. Worcestershire sauce
1 tsp. paprika
½ tsp. pepper
1 Tbsp. parsley

Place all ingredients in a blender and blend for 1 minute, or shake to blend in a large jar. Chill overnight before using.

Makes 2½ to 3 cups.

—Valerie Gillis

Blue Cheese Marinated
Salad Dressing

For those who are fond of blue cheese, this tangy dressing is an ideal way to liven up winter greens.

½ cup salad oil
2 Tbsp. lemon juice
½ tsp. salt
½ tsp. sugar
Dash pepper
Dash paprika
1 cup blue cheese, crumbled
2 medium onions, thinly
  sliced
½ cup sliced mushrooms

Combine oil, lemon juice, salt, sugar, pepper and paprika and whisk together. Add cheese, onions and mushrooms, stirring gently. Cover and refrigerate for several hours.

Makes 2½ to 3 cups.

—L. Anne Mallory

Yogurt & Bacon Dip

10 slices bacon
1 cup plain yogurt
¼ cup mayonnaise, page 132
1 Tbsp. chopped green onion
1 Tbsp. chopped parsley
½ tsp. salt

Chop bacon and cook until crisp. Drain well and set aside, reserving 1 Tbsp. of drippings. Combine drippings with yogurt, mayonnaise, onion, parsley and salt. Add bacon. Mix well, cover and refrigerate for several hours.

Makes 1½ cups.

—*Christine Steele*

Curry Dip

1 cup mayonnaise, page 132
2 tsp. horseradish
2 tsp. diced raw onion
1 tsp. curry powder
1 tsp. salt

Combine all ingredients and mix well. Serve with raw vegetables.

Makes 1½ cups.

—*Karen Moller*

Guacamole

2 ripe avocados
Juice of 1 lemon
2 cloves garlic, minced
2 Tbsp. chili powder

Peel avocados and then mash with a fork or purée in a food processor. Add remaining ingredients and mix well. Keep covered and refrigerated until ready to serve.

Makes 1½ cups.

—*Bryanna Clark*

Tarragon Cream Dressing

This unusual salad dressing has a tangy flavour which complements cool salad greens.

½ tsp. dry mustard
1 tsp. Dijon mustard
¼ tsp. sugar
1 tsp. lemon juice
1-2 tsp. crushed garlic
5 Tbsp. tarragon vinegar
2 Tbsp. olive oil
10 Tbsp. vegetable oil
1 egg, beaten
½ cup light cream
Salt & pepper

Blend all ingredients well and store in refrigerator.

—*Sheila Couture*

Fruit Salad Dressing

1 egg, well beaten
¼ cup honey
Juice of 1 lemon
Juice of 1 orange
Sour cream

Mix together egg, honey, lemon and orange juice. Cook until thickened and let cool. Mix in sour cream until the dressing reaches the desired consistency. Pour over mixed fruits and toss gently.

Makes 1 cup.

—*Pat McCormack*

Raw Vegetable Dip

1½ cups mayonnaise,
  page 132
3 Tbsp. grated onion
3 Tbsp. honey
3 Tbsp. ketchup
1 Tbsp. curry powder
Dash lemon juice

Mix together all ingredients. Refrigerate for a few hours before serving.

—*Elizabeth Templeman*

Sour Cream Vegetable Dip

Delicious with a variety of raw vegetables, fruit or crackers, this is an easy-to-make dip which will keep well.

1 cup sour cream
1 cup mayonnaise, page 132
1 Tbsp. parsley flakes
1 Tbsp. minced onion
Dash lemon pepper

Mix together all ingredients and refrigerate for 2 hours.

—*Martha Brown*

Marinated Broccoli

1 bunch broccoli
½ cup oil
6 Tbsp. vinegar
1 tsp. minced garlic
¾ tsp. salt
¼ tsp. pepper
½ tsp. tarragon
½ tsp. thyme
½ tsp. dry mustard
⅓ cup sliced green onions
½ cup slivered almonds
Pimento strips
Tomato wedges

Cut florets from stems of broccoli. Slice stems on the diagonal about 4-inch thick. Steam 3 to 5 minutes or until tender but crispy.

To make marinade, combine other ingredients, except almonds, pimento, and tomatoes, in large bowl. Add hot broccoli and toss to mix. Cover and chill for at least 4 hours.

Lift broccoli from marinade and arrange on serving dish. Garnish with almonds, pimento and tomato.

Serves 4 to 6.

—Cheryl Peters

Artichoke Salad

The artichoke has been cultivated in France since the beginning of the sixteenth century. There are several types of artichokes, each best suited to a different method of preparation. Both of these recipes make use of canned artichoke hearts readily available in most food stores. Of course, the same results can be had from fresh, whole artichokes that are cooked and stripped down to the heart.

2 14-oz. cans artichoke hearts
4 medium tomatoes, quartered
1 onion, sliced to form rings
5 Tbsp. corn oil
2 Tbsp. lemon juice
1 Tbsp. red wine vinegar
½ tsp. salt
¼ tsp. pepper
1 tsp. basil
1 Tbsp. chopped parsley

Drain artichoke hearts and chop into quarters. Toss in a salad bowl with tomatoes and onions.

Combine remaining ingredients and pour over artichoke mixture. Mix well. Chill to let flavours blend.

Serves 4.

—Linda Droine

Marinated Artichokes

2 Tbsp. lemon juice
2 Tbsp. oil
Garlic salt
1 Tbsp. sugar
¼ tsp. oregano, crushed
¼ tsp. tarragon, crushed
2 Tbsp. water
1 can artichoke hearts, drained

Combine all ingredients and mix well. Cover. Chill several hours or overnight.

To serve, lift artichoke hearts out of marinade and place on beds of lettuce. Sprinkle lightly with paprika.

Serves 2.

—Joan Morrison

Marinated Brussels Sprouts

1 lb. Brussels sprouts
3 Tbsp. salad oil
1½ Tbsp. lemon juice
Salt & pepper
1 clove garlic, crushed
1 tsp. dried tarragon
¼ cup Parmesan cheese

Clean and steam Brussels sprouts. Meanwhile, mix other ingredients together for dressing. Combine dressing and hot, drained Brussels sprouts in a bowl. Cool, then cover and refrigerate.

Serves 6.

—Pamela Morninglight

Tangy Vegetable Salad

1 carrot, grated
2 stalks celery, chopped
1 cup small cauliflower
   florets
1 tomato, chopped
¼ cup vinegar
3 Tbsp. oil

Mix vegetables. Combine
remaining ingredients to make
dressing. Marinate vegetables
overnight, stirring occasionally.

Serves 8 to 10.

—Linda Townsend

Marinated Leeks

10 large leeks
3 Tbsp. apple cider vinegar
½ cup oil
1½ Tbsp. chopped parsley or
   chives
1 tsp. salt
Pepper
1 tsp. liquid honey
½ tsp. dry mustard

Clean leeks well and steam
until tender — 10 to 15 minutes.
Combine vinegar, oil, parsley or
chives, salt, pepper, honey and
mustard. Pour over leeks, chill
and serve.

Serves 4.

—Leslie Dunsmore

Salpicon

*This Mexican marinated
vegetable dish is especially
attractive in the height of
summer, when most garden
vegetables can be added to the
marinade.*

½ cup olive oil
½ cup vegetable oil
½ cup cider vinegar
¼ cup fresh lemon juice
Salt & pepper
1 cup cooked, thinly sliced
   potatoes
1 cup cooked, thinly sliced
   green beans
1 cup cooked, thinly sliced
   carrots
1 cucumber, peeled & thinly
   sliced
1 Bermuda onion, cut into
   thin rings
1 green pepper, cut into thin
   rings
1 red pepper, cut into thin
   rings
1 cup cooked, thinly sliced
   beets

Combine oils, vinegar, lemon
juice and salt and pepper.
Combine cooked and raw
vegetables except beets and chill
for several hours in marinade.
Garnish with beets at serving
time.

Serves 8 to 10.

—Holly Andrews

Ruth's Fall Vegetable Vinaigrette

1 cup small broccoli florets
1 cup small cauliflower
   florets
1 cup thinly sliced carrots
1 cup turnip, cut into 2-inch
   sticks
1 onion, sliced in rings
¼ cup vinegar
½ cup oil
1 clove garlic, minced
1 tsp. salt
⅛ tsp. pepper
¼ tsp. dried tarragon
¼ tsp. dried basil
1 Tbsp. chopped parsley
Dry mustard

Cook vegetables, except onion,
in boiling water. Drain and cover
with cold water until chilled.
Drain again and combine with
onion in large bowl.

Combine remaining
ingredients for marinade. Pour
over vegetables and mix gently.
Cover and chill for several hours.

Serves 8.

—Marlene Spruyt

Vegetables à La Grecque

This colourful dish, which can make use of many different combinations of vegetables, can be served as an appetizer or as a salad.

1½ cups water
¼ cup olive oil
Juice of 4-6 lemons
4 cloves garlic
1 bay leaf
Celery top
1 tsp. thyme
Sprig of fennel
1 tsp. salt
½ tsp. white pepper
Sprig of parsley
Tabasco sauce
1 lb. asparagus, sliced
6 leeks, sliced
6 zucchini, sliced
8 carrots, sliced
12-16 small onions
3 fennel heads, quartered

Combine all ingredients except vegetables and bring to a boil. Boil for 5 minutes, add vegetables and lower heat. Cook until vegetables are tender but crisp.

Cool. Remove garlic and chill salad.

Serves 8.

—Elizabeth Imboden

Special Winter Salad

1 tsp. Dijon mustard
1 tsp. brown sugar
¾ cup vinegar
¾ cup orange juice, or juice from canned mandarin oranges
1½ cups oil
1 tsp. poppy seeds
1 tsp. curry
1 head romaine lettuce
2 ripe avocados
4 fresh (or 1 tin) mandarin oranges

Shake together mustard, sugar, vinegar, juice, oil, poppy seeds and curry. Tear romaine lettuce into bite-sized pieces. Slice avocados and oranges and arrange on lettuce. Pour dressing over top.

Serves 4.

—Kathe Lieber

Copper Pennies Salad

2 lbs. carrots, sliced
1 cup sugar
¾ cup vinegar
1 tsp. mustard
½ cup vegetable oil
1 tsp. Worcestershire sauce
1 green pepper, thinly sliced
1 onion, finely chopped

Boil carrots in salted water until just tender. Cool and then mix with other ingredients.

Serves 6.

—Isabell Lingrell

Carrot Confetti Salad

A simple but deliciously crunchy salad, this is particularly good during the winter, when fresh vegetables are few and far between.

Grated carrot, allow 1 large carrot per person
1 small onion, finely chopped
1 stalk celery, finely chopped
½ green pepper, finely chopped
½ cup cubed Cheddar cheese
Mayonnaise, thinned with milk
Black pepper

Toss all ingredients together, chill well and serve.

Serves 1.

—Nicolle Fournier

Turkish Yogurt & Cucumber Salad

3 medium cucumbers
¼ tsp. salt
1 clove garlic, chopped
1 Tbsp. vinegar
½ tsp. dill
1 pint unflavoured yogurt
2 Tbsp. olive oil
1 Tbsp. chopped fresh mint leaves, or ½ tsp. dried mint

Peel, quarter and slice cucumbers. Sprinkle with salt. Rub serving bowl with garlic and then swish vinegar around bowl. Add yogurt, oil, dill and mint. Stir until thick. Add cucumbers and toss gently until well coated.

Serves 6.

—Fern Acton

Celery & Yogurt Salad

½ cup yogurt
2 tsp. olive oil
2 generous Tbsp. crumbled
  blue cheese
2 Tbsp. grated sharp
  Cheddar cheese
¼ tsp. salt
4 cups chopped celery
1 cup sliced mushrooms
½ sweet red pepper, chopped

Combine yogurt, olive oil, cheeses and salt. Mix with vegetables and serve.

Serves 4.

—Shan Simpson

Cauliflower Spinach Toss

4 cups spinach, torn into
  bite-sized pieces
½ head lettuce, torn into
  bite-sized pieces
1 small head cauliflower, cut
  into small florets
3 carrots, peeled & sliced
  diagonally
⅔ cup vegetable oil
⅓ cup white vinegar
¼ tsp. salt
¼ tsp. paprika
½ tsp. dry mustard
2 cloves garlic, minced

Combine salad ingredients in a bowl. Place dressing ingredients in a jar with a tight-fitting lid. Shake well to combine. Toss salad with sufficient dressing to coat pieces evenly.

Serves 6 to 8.

—Nan & Phil Millette

Cauliflower Pecan Salad

The cauliflower is a vegetable of Oriental origin, which has been cultivated in Europe since the sixteenth century. Although it is the white head that is commonly eaten either hot, or, as in these recipes, cold, the leaves and stalks are also edible. They should be prepared as broccoli would be.

1½ cups cauliflower florets
¾ cup chopped green pepper
1 cup toasted pecan halves
1 cup grated carrots
1 cup chopped celery
HORSERADISH MUSTARD
DRESSING:
¾ cup mayonnaise
4 Tbsp. horseradish
½ cup sour cream or yogurt
½ tsp. prepared mustard
Salt & pepper

Blanch cauliflower in boiling water for 2 minutes. Drain and chill. When ready to serve, combine all ingredients and toss with dressing.

To make dressing, combine all ingredients and mix well.

Serves 4 to 6.

—Lorraine Murphy

Hot Spinach Salad

1 clove garlic, peeled &
  slivered
¼ cup oil
1 lb. spinach, washed,
  drained & torn into bite-
  sized pieces
1 cup sliced raw mushrooms
6 slices bacon
2 green onions, finely
  chopped
¼ cup vinegar
½ tsp. salt
Pepper

Let garlic stand in oil for 1 hour. Discard garlic. Toss spinach and mushrooms in a bowl and refrigerate.

Fry bacon until crisp, remove from pan and crumble. Reserve 1 Tbsp. of fat. Stir in onions and sauté for 2 to 3 minutes. Add oil, vinegar, salt and pepper and bring to a boil.

Toss with spinach and mushrooms. Sprinkle with bacon.

Serves 4 to 6.

—Carol Frost

Spinach and Fruit Salad with Piquant Dressing

4 slices bacon
4 cups torn spinach
1 cup mandarin orange segments, drained & chopped
½ cup sliced onion
1 cup oil
3 Tbsp. lemon juice
1 tsp. salt
2 tsp. paprika
1 small onion, chopped
1 tsp. dry mustard
1 clove garlic, crushed

Fry bacon until crisp, drain and crumble. Combine with spinach, mandarin orange segments and sliced onion.

To make dressing, combine remaining ingredients, refrigerate and shake vigorously before using.

Serves 6 to 8.

—*Janice Graham*

Spinach, Orange & Mango Salad

If one can find the mangoes, this is a deliciously exotic salad, especially in the dead of winter, when it conjures up thoughts of tropical holidays.

1 lb. fresh spinach
2 navel oranges
2 mangoes
6 strips bacon
DRESSING:
3 tsp. onion
½ tsp. salt
Pepper
1 Tbsp. Dijon mustard
2 Tbsp. white wine vinegar
1 tsp. lemon juice
⅔ cup olive oil

Wash, dry and tear up spinach. Peel and section oranges. Peel mangoes, remove pits, and cut into bite-sized strips. Cook bacon until crispy, drain, then crumble.

For the dressing, combine onion, salt, pepper, mustard, vinegar and lemon juice in a small bowl. Mix well, then beat in the olive oil very slowly. Continue beating until dressing thickens. Pour over spinach, oranges, mangoes and bacon, and toss. Let stand for 10 minutes and serve.

Serves 6.

—*Ingrid Birker*

Avocado Salad

1 avocado
1 green pepper
2 stalks celery
10 raw mushrooms
1 cup oil
¼ cup apple cider vinegar
½ tsp. dry mustard
1 tsp. honey
½ tsp. paprika
½ tsp. salt
1 Tbsp. finely chopped onion
2 cloves garlic, finely chopped
Tarragon, thyme, basil, marjoram

Peel and dice avocado. Dice pepper, celery and mushrooms and combine with avocado.

Combine remaining ingredients and mix well. Pour over vegetables and toss lightly.

Serves 2.

—*Denise Hensher*

Salade Mediterranée

½ cup sliced mushrooms
¼ cup sliced almonds
1 cup sliced stuffed olives
1 tsp. tarragon
Juice of ½ lemon
½ tsp. basil
2 Tbsp. tarragon vinegar
6 Tbsp. olive oil

Boil mushrooms for 2 to 3 minutes, add sliced almonds and boil for another minute. Drain. Mix mushrooms and almonds with sliced olives.

Combine remaining ingredients in screw-top jar; shake to mix. Add dressing to olive, almond and mushroom mixture and toss together.

Refrigerate 24 hours before serving.

Serves 8.

—*Gérard Millette*

Watermelon Boat Salad

½ watermelon
1 cantaloupe
1 honeydew melon
1 cup orange or pineapple juice
2 peaches or nectarines
2 apples
2 pears
1 bunch green grapes
6-10 large strawberries
½ cup Kirsch or Cointreau

Clean watermelon out using melon baller. Save juice. Ball cantaloupe and honeydew melons and place fruit in orange juice. Peel and slice peaches, apples and pears and add to above. Wash grapes and strawberries and add. Place fruit in watermelon boat and pour liqueur over top. Cover with plastic wrap and let marinate for 1 to 2 hours.

—Kirsten McDougall

Beyond Coleslaw

3 cups finely grated cabbage
1 cup finely chopped cauliflower
1 red or green pepper, chopped
⅔ cup oil
⅓ cup apple cider vinegar
Salt & pepper
Garlic powder

Toss together cabbage, cauliflower and pepper. Combine oil, vinegar and seasonings to taste. Pour over vegetables and toss.

Serves 4 to 6.

—Dyan Walters

Apple Bacon Salad

⅔ cup garlic oil (oil which has had 2-3 peeled, sliced garlic cloves standing in it overnight)
2 tsp . lemon juice
3 red apples, quartered, cored & thinly sliced
½ lb. bacon, cooked until crisp
1 head lettuce, torn into bite-sized pieces
½ cup grated Parmesan cheese
1 bunch scallions, chopped
½ tsp. pepper
¼ tsp. salt
1 egg

Mix garlic oil and lemon juice, and drop freshly cut apples into mixture. Combine all ingredients in salad bowl and toss until all traces of egg disappear. Serve immediately.

Serves 4.

—Denise Feeley

Delicious Apple Salad

This light salad is delicious with roast duck or turkey.

1 cup whipping cream
3 tsp. sugar
½ cup mayonnaise
8 medium-sized Delicious apples, diced

Whip the cream and add sugar. Add mayonnaise and mix well. Stir in the cut-up apples and mix until well coated.

Serves 5 to 7.

—Pam Stanley

Antipasto

Served with crackers or Italian bread, Swiss cheese and a variety of salamis, antipasto provides a flavourful start to an Italian meal.

8 oz. olive oil
1 large cauliflower, cut into bite-sized pieces
2 cups chopped black olives
2 cups chopped green olives
2 cups diced onion
2¼ cups sliced mushrooms
2 large green peppers, chopped
2 large red peppers, chopped
1 cup pimentos
4 cups tomato paste
4 cups stewed tomatoes, drained & chopped
1 cup chili sauce
3 cups chopped sweet pickles
Pepper
Cayenne
4 7-oz tins water-packed tuna

Mix together oil, cauliflower, olives and onion and stir-fry for 10 minutes, then add mushrooms, peppers, pimentos, tomato paste, tomatoes, chili sauce and pickles. Bring to a boil and simmer for 10 minutes, then add spices and tuna, bring back to a boil and simmer for 10 more minutes. Pack in jars and process in water bath or freeze. Serve, at room temperature, with cheese and whole wheat crackers.

—Charlene Skidmore

Jellied Gazpacho

1 envelope gelatin
1 cup cold beef stock
¼ tsp. salt
2 Tbsp. vinegar
⅛ tsp. dried basil leaves
1 clove garlic, crushed
14-oz. can tomatoes
2 Tbsp. finely sliced green
  onions
¼ cup diced, unpeeled
  cucumber
¼ cup diced green pepper
¼ cup diced celery

Sprinkle gelatin over stock in saucepan. Place over low heat and stir constantly until gelatin has dissolved — about 5 minutes. Remove from heat and stir in salt, vinegar, basil and garlic.

Chop large tomato pieces and add with juice to seasoned gelatin mixture. Chill to consistency of unbeaten egg whites. Stir in green onions, cucumber, green pepper and celery. Cover and chill until set.

Serves 6.

—Nan & Phil Millette

Jellied Beet Salad

1 envelope gelatin
¼ cup cold water
½ tsp. salt
⅓ cup sugar
¼ cup vinegar
¾ cup water or beet liquid
2 cups cooked, diced beets
¾ cup finely diced celery
1 Tbsp. minced onion
1 Tbsp. horseradish Parsley
Pickled beets

Sprinkle gelatin over cold water in saucepan. Place over low heat and stir until gelatin dissolves. Remove from heat and stir in salt, sugar, vinegar and water or beet liquid. Chill to consistency of unbeaten egg white. Stir in beets, celery, onion and horseradish. Turn into 3-cup mould and chill until set. Remove from mould and garnish with fresh parsley and pickled beets.

Serves 6 to 8.

—Lynn Tobin

Blushing Salad

2 cups pickled beets, well
  drained
2 medium-sized apples,
  sliced
¼ cup mayonnaise
¼ cup sour cream

Combine beets and apple slices. Combine mayonnaise and sour cream and gently stir into beets and apples. Chill well.

Serves 4.

—Maggie Christopher

Simple Tomato & Mozzarella Salad

2 Tbsp. olive oil
1 Tbsp. red wine vinegar
1 clove garlic, finely chopped
4-5 basil leaves, chopped
½ tsp. salt
¼ tsp. black pepper
4 tomatoes, sliced
8 thin slices mozzarella
  cheese

Whisk together oil, vinegar, garlic, basil, salt and pepper. Arrange tomato and cheese slices in a bowl. Drizzle with dressing and let marinate, refrigerated, for 1 hour.

Serves 4.

—Francie Goodwin-Rogne

Lithuanian Beet Salad

This salad makes a colourful and flavourful main dish for a winter luncheon.

2 lbs. beets
¾ cup dry navy beans
3-4 medium potatoes
1 quart dill pickles
Salt
1 cup sour cream
Parsley

Cook beets, beans and potatoes separately and cool. Dice beets and potatoes into small pieces and place in large bowl. Add the cooked beans. Finely dice the pickles and add to the bowl. Add salt to taste.

Add the sour cream, as a dressing, no more than ½ hour before serving. Mix thoroughly. Decorate with parsley if you wish.

Serves 10.

—Giedre Abromaitis

Spicy Cucumber Salad

Cucumbers have been cultivated in northwest India for more than 3,000 years. Either regular or English cucumbers can be used with equal success in this recipe.

2 medium cucumbers
1 tsp. soya sauce
1 Tbsp. vinegar
1 Tbsp. sugar
2 tsp. sesame oil
¼ tsp. Tabasco sauce
½ tsp. salt

Peel cucumbers, halve lengthwise and scoop out and discard pulp. Cut crosswise into ¼-inch slices. Mix soya sauce, vinegar, sugar, oil, Tabasco sauce and salt in a small bowl. Add the cucumbers and toss well. Chill before serving.

Serves 4.

—Beth Lavender

Beet & Cabbage Salad

6 beets, cooked & peeled
1 onion, finely chopped
2 cups shredded cabbage
2 tsp. sugar
1 tsp. salt
1 tsp. dry mustard
1 Tbsp. flour
1 egg, beaten
¼ cup vinegar
1 cup sour cream

Chill beets and cut into cubes. Combine with onion and cabbage. For dressing, mix together sugar, salt, mustard and flour and combine with egg and vinegar. Add sour cream and cook over medium heat, stirring constantly until thickened.

Pour hot dressing over combined cold vegetables and toss until well blended.

Serves 8 to 10.

—Ingrid Birker

Herb and Garlic Salad Dressing

⅓ cup vinegar
⅔ cup salad oil
½ tsp. salt
½ tsp. sugar
1 clove garlic, chopped
¼ tsp. pepper
¼ tsp. dry mustard
¼ tsp. basil
¼ tsp. oregano
½ tsp. lemon juice
1 Tbsp. water

Combine all ingredients in a jar with tight-fitting lid. Shake well to combine. Refrigerate. Shake well before each use.

Makes 1 cup.

—Joan Morrison

Garden Salad Dressing

This dressing is particularly tasty tossed with a lettuce and mushroom salad.

½ cup oil
¼ cup vinegar
¼ cup chopped parsley
2 green onions with tops, chopped
1-1½ Tbsp. chopped green pepper
1 tsp. salt
1 tsp. dry mustard
½ tsp. sugar
Paprika
Cayenne

Combine all ingredients, shake well and refrigerate. Shake well before tossing into salad.

—Charlotte DuChene

Maple Syrup Dressing

This simple dressing makes a pleasant topping for a cole slaw of grated cabbage and carrot, raisins and sunflower seeds.

⅓ cup oil
⅓ cup cider vinegar
⅓ cup maple syrup

Mix and store in a covered container in the refrigerator.

—I.F. Robinson

Lemon Mustard Dressing

¼ cup oil
¼ cup lemon juice
1 tsp. basil
1 tsp. oregano
½ tsp. pepper
1 clove garlic, crushed
4 tsp. Dijon mustard
2 cups mayonnaise

Combine all ingredients and blend well. Refrigerate.

Makes 2½ cups.

—Irene Louden

Chili French Dressing

⅓ cup salad oil
2 Tbsp. vinegar
2 Tbsp. ketchup
2 tsp. grated onion
1 tsp. prepared mustard
¾ tsp. chili powder
½ tsp. salt
⅛ tsp. dry mustard
Pepper
Paprika
4 drops Tabasco sauce

Combine all ingredients in jar. Cover, shake and chill. Keep refrigerated and shake before using.

Makes ⅔ cup.

—Nan & Phil Millette

Spinach Salad Dressing

⅓ cup oil
¼ cup vinegar
¼ tsp. Tabasco sauce
¼ tsp. dry mustard
½ tsp. salt
1 clove garlic, crushed

Mix all ingredients well.

—Valerie Cameron

Mother's French Dressing

1 cup oil
⅓ cup vinegar
1½ tsp. dry mustard
¼ tsp. pepper
1½ tsp. salt
1 tsp. paprika
2 cloves garlic, minced

Combine all ingredients together and beat until creamy. Place in glass jar and store in refrigerator for 1 to 2 days.

Strain dressing through sieve to remove garlic and chill.

Makes 1 cup.

—Mary Matear

Curry Vinaigrette

1 Tbsp. curry powder
1 Tbsp. Dijon mustard
1 Tbsp. chopped parsley
1 Tbsp. chopped green onion
9 Tbsp. wine vinegar
1 cup olive oil
Juice of 1 lemon
Salt & pepper

Combine all ingredients and shake to mix well. Store in the refrigerator.

Makes approximately 1½ cups.

—Wendy Neilson

Creamy Cultures Dressing

¾ cup sour cream
¼ cup yogurt
2 cloves garlic
2 Tbsp. olive oil
1 Tbsp. paprika
Salt & pepper

Combine all ingredients and blend well. Keep refrigerated.

Makes 1 cup.

—Georgia White

Creamy Garlic Dressing

This is a salad dressing for real garlic lovers.

1 egg
1 tsp. mustard
1 tsp. salt
1 tsp. celery seeds
1 Tbsp. honey
2 or 3 cloves garlic
3 Tbsp. vinegar
1 cup oil

Put egg, mustard, salt, celery seeds, honey, garlic, vinegar and ½ cup oil in blender. Blend until smooth, then gradually add remaining oil.

Makes 1 cup.

—Crystal Burgess

Green Goddess Dressing

1 cup mayonnaise
½ cup sour cream or yogurt
2 Tbsp. chives, finely
  chopped
¼ cup finely chopped fresh
  parsley
1 tsp. tarragon
1 clove garlic, crushed
1 Tbsp. lemon juice
1 Tbsp. white or tarragon
  vinegar
Salt & pepper

Combine all ingredients and mix well. Keep refrigerated.

Makes 1½ cups.

—Marlene Spruyt

Feta Cheese Dressing

¾ cup oil
Juice of 1 lemon
2 tsp. anchovy paste
½ cup feta cheese
2 cloves garlic, crushed
½ tsp. dry mustard
½ tsp. dill weed
½ tsp. salt
½ tsp. pepper

Combine all ingredients and blend until smooth.

Makes 1 cup.

—P. C. Suche

Avocado Yogurt Salad Dressing

1 very ripe avocado
1 cup unflavoured yogurt
⅓ cup diced onion
⅓ cup diced green pepper
¼ cup mayonnaise
2 tsp. fresh dill weed
½ tsp. lemon juice
2 cloves garlic, minced
Salt & pepper

Blend avocado, yogurt, onion and green pepper for 20 seconds. Add remaining ingredients and blend until smooth.

Makes 1½ to 2 cups.

—Jill Leary

Parmesan Dressing

2 cups mayonnaise
½ cup cider vinegar
½ tsp. basil
½ tsp. oregano
2 cloves garlic, crushed
½ cup Parmesan cheese

Combine all ingredients and mix well with wire whisk. Store, covered, in refrigerator.

Makes 2½ cups.

—Wendy Neilson

Creamy Salad Dressing

½ cup mayonnaise
½ cup sour cream
1½ Tbsp. vinegar
1½ Tbsp. lemon juice
¼ cup chopped chives

Combine all ingredients and mix well. Cover and let stand, refrigerated, for 1 day.

Makes approximately 1 cup.

—Carol A. Smith

Whipped Dressing

2 egg yolks
¼ cup Dijon mustard
½ cup vinegar
Salt & pepper
1½ cups sunflower oil

Beat egg yolks, then add mustard and beat until smooth. Add vinegar and salt and pepper. Very slowly, taking 10 to 12 minutes, add the oil while beating. Refrigerate.

Makes 2½ cups.

—Susan Budge

Tuna Vegetable Dip

6-oz. can white tuna
2 cups sour cream
4 Tbsp. mayonnaise
1 tsp. garlic powder
1 Tbsp. dill weed
1 Tbsp. chopped parsley

Mash tuna, then blend well with sour cream, mayonnaise, garlic, dill and parsley. Refrigerate for a few hours, then serve with raw vegetables.

Makes 3 to 4 cups.

—*Jocelyn Raymond*

Nancy's Dill Dip

1½ cups sour cream
½ cup mayonnaise
2 Tbsp. Dijon mustard
½ cup chopped, fresh dill weed
¼ cup thinly sliced green onion
2 tsp. lemon juice
½ tsp. salt
¼ tsp. pepper

Combine all ingredients, mixing well. Refrigerate, then serve with raw vegetables.

Makes 2 cups.

—*Michèle Raymond*

White Wine Sauce

½ cup white wine
½ cup grated Gruyère cheese
¼ tsp. dry mustard
¼ tsp. parsley
1 tsp. finely minced green onion
Salt & pepper

Heat wine and add cheese slowly, whisking to a smooth consistency. Add mustard, parsley, green onion and salt and pepper. Cover, keep warm and serve over steamed vegetables.

—*Charlene Skidmore*

Peanut Sauce

Any nut butter may be used in place of peanut butter — cashew is a favourite. Serve this sauce over rice, spaghetti, tofu, as a fondue dip or over steamed vegetables.

½ cup peanut butter
1 small onion, grated
1 clove garlic, crushed
¼ cup instant milk powder
½ tsp. honey
2 Tbsp. lemon juice
2 tsp. soya sauce

Blend all ingredients in saucepan over low heat, adding hot water until mixture has consistency of heavy cream. For a smoother sauce, use blender to mix.

Makes 1 cup.

—*Lorna Wollner*

Baba Ghannouj

1 large eggplant
⅓ cup lemon juice
2-3 cloves garlic
3-4 Tbsp. bean stock or water
6 Tbsp. tahini
Paprika

Cut ends off eggplant and bake at 350° F for 20 to 30 minutes, or until soft and partly collapsed. Peel and mash.

Mix together lemon juice, garlic, bean stock or water and tahini until smooth. Add eggplant and continue mixing, adding liquid as needed. Chill for at least 3 hours. Top with paprika and serve with raw vegetables or crackers.

—*Marlene Spruyt*

Cheddar Vegetable Dip

1 cup mayonnaise
1 cup sour cream
1 cup finely grated Cheddar cheese
2 Tbsp. chopped spring onion
1 tsp. lemon juice
Worcestershire sauce
¼ tsp. garlic powder
Salt & pepper

Mix all ingredients and let sit, refrigerated, overnight. Taste and adjust seasonings before serving. Place on a platter and surround with fresh vegetables.

Makes 3 cups.

—*Bonnie Lawson*

Almond & Mushroom Paté

1 Tbsp. finely chopped onion
2 cloves garlic, crushed
½ lb. mushrooms, very finely chopped
2 Tbsp. butter
1 Tbsp. heavy cream
½ cup ground almonds
Salt & pepper
1 Tbsp. dry sherry

Sauté onion, garlic and mushrooms in butter until liquid evaporates, but do not let it brown. Cool. Add cream, almonds, salt and pepper and sherry. Mix well. Form into a ball, cover and chill. Serve with crackers or raw vegetables.

—Louise Olson

Vegetarian Paté

Equally delicious as a cracker spread or a sandwich filling, this paté is quickly and easily prepared.

1 cup sunflower seeds
1 potato, peeled
½ cup whole wheat flour
1½ cups hot water
1 large onion, minced
½ cup butter, melted
1½ tsp. basil
1 tsp. thyme

Chop the sunflower seeds finely by hand or in food processor. Grate the potato. Combine all ingredients and place in greased loaf pan. Bake at 350° F for 1½ hours. Paté will be moist. Serve hot, or chill in refrigerator overnight before serving.

—Suzanne Dignard

Stuffed Artichoke Hearts

8 artichoke hearts, drained
¼ cup mayonnaise
¼ cup grated Parmesan cheese

Place artichoke hearts upright in small baking dish. Combine mayonnaise with Parmesan cheese and spoon into hearts. Broil until stuffing is lightly browned.

Serves 4 as an appetizer.

—Joanne T. Gordon

Stir-Fried Asparagus

2 Tbsp. oil
2 lbs. asparagus, cut into 1½-inch pieces
1 large clove garlic, crushed
1 Tbsp. minced ginger root
Salt
½ cup chicken stock
1 tsp. cornstarch
2 Tbsp. soya sauce
1 tsp. sugar

Place oil in hot wok and heat until hot but not smoking. Stir-fry asparagus, garlic, ginger root and salt for 3 to 4 minutes until slightly tender. Combine stock, cornstarch, soya sauce and sugar and add to wok. Cover and simmer, stirring occasionally, for 2 minutes, or until asparagus is tender but still crisp.

Serves 4.

—Valerie Gillis

Vegetable Dip

1 cup sour cream
¼ cup finely chopped green pepper
¼ cup finely chopped radishes
½ cup grated carrots
2 Tbsp. chopped green onion
2 Tbsp. finely chopped parsley
½ tsp. salt
¼ tsp. pepper
½ tsp. lemon juice

Combine all ingredients and chill well. Serve with raw vegetables or crackers.

Makes 1½ cups.

—Kathy Major

Creamy Liverwurst Dip

8 oz. liverwurst, coarsely chopped
1 cup sour cream
2 Tbsp. minced green onion
1 Tbsp. drained, chopped capers
¼-½ cup chopped water chestnuts
½ tsp. salt
Parsley

Beat liverwurst, then add sour cream and mix until blended. Add onion, capers, water chestnuts and salt, and chill. Garnish with parsley and serve with raw vegetables.

—Mary Howes

Green Bean Casserole

½ cup sliced onion
1 tsp. finely chopped parsley
2 Tbsp. butter
2 Tbsp. flour
½ tsp. grated lemon peel
Squeeze of lemon juice
Salt & pepper
1 cup sour cream
5 cups green beans, partially
    cooked
2 Tbsp. melted butter
½ cup dry bread crumbs
½ cup grated sharp cheese

Cook together onion, parsley, butter, flour, lemon peel, lemon juice and salt and pepper, then add sour cream and green beans. Pour into greased casserole dish and spread evenly, smoothing the top. Combine melted butter and bread crumbs and sprinkle over the top, then distribute the cheese evenly. Bake at 325° F for 30 minutes, or until cheese is melted and browned.

Serves 8 to 10.

—Rebecca Gibson Spink

Greek Beans

3 Tbsp. olive oil
1 small onion, minced
1 small clove garlic, minced
2 Tbsp. minced green pepper
1 lb. green or wax beans, cut
    into 2-inch lengths
¾ cup chopped tomato
1 cup boiling water
2 tsp. wine vinegar
1½ tsp. chopped, fresh mint
    leaves
Salt & pepper

Heat oil in medium saucepan, and sauté onion, garlic and green pepper until soft — about 5 minutes. Add remaining ingredients, cover and cook for 20 to 30 minutes, or until beans are tender. Add salt and pepper to taste.

Serves 4 to 6.

—Valerie Sherriff

Sweet & Sour Green Beans

1 lb. green beans
2 green onions
2 Tbsp. butter
2 Tbsp. chili sauce

Steam beans for about 5 minutes, or until tender but crisp. Sauté chopped green onions in butter over low heat until soft and clear. Add green beans and chili sauce and toss until well blended.

Serves 4 to 6.

—Jennifer Webber

Devilled Green Beans

1 lb. green beans
3 tsp. butter
2 tsp. prepared mustard
½ tsp. Worcestershire sauce
Salt & pepper

Cook beans in boiling water until tender but crisp. Drain. Add remaining ingredients and stir gently until blended.

Serves 4.

—A. Dianne Wilson-Meyer

Baked Green Beans

1½ lbs. green beans
8-oz. can water chestnuts
5 green onions
½ lb. mushrooms, sliced
½ cup butter
½ cup flour
2 cups milk
¾ cup grated Cheddar
    cheese
2 tsp. soya sauce
½ tsp. salt
1 cup slivered almonds

Cut beans diagonally, wash and cook. Slice water chestnuts and add to drained beans. Place in greased casserole dish. Sauté onions and mushrooms in butter, then stir in flour, milk and cheese. Cook over low heat until thickened, stirring occasionally. Stir in soya sauce and salt. Pour sauce over bean mixture and mix gently. Sprinkle almonds on top. Bake at 375° F for 20 minutes.

Serves 6.

—Midge Denault

Zippy Beets

This is a quick and easy way to add some sparkle to frozen beets in the middle of the winter.

3 Tbsp. butter
2 Tbsp. mustard
2-3 Tbsp. honey
1 tsp. Worcestershire sauce
Salt
2 cups hot cooked beets

Combine butter, mustard, honey, Worcestershire sauce and salt in saucepan. Blend well and heat to boiling. Add beets, stir to cover and serve.

Serves 2.

—*Lynn Andersen*

Crunchy Broccoli

This dish can be prepared up to the baking stage early in the day or even the day before and refrigerated, leaving little work for the cook at dinner time.

3 cups chopped broccoli
3 Tbsp. butter
3 Tbsp. grated onion
2 Tbsp. flour
½ tsp. salt
¼ tsp. pepper
1 cup sour cream
¾ cup bread crumbs
¼ cup Parmesan cheese

Cook broccoli for 4 minutes, drain and place in greased casserole dish. Melt 2 Tbsp. butter in pan and sauté onions for 1 minute. Blend in flour, salt and pepper. Stir in sour cream until thick, then pour over broccoli. Melt remaining 1 Tbsp. butter, remove from heat and stir in bread crumbs. Sprinkle on casserole and top with cheese. Bake, uncovered, at 350° F for 20 to 25 minutes.

Serves 4.

—*Kathy Payette*

Green Bean Timbales

The word timbale comes from the Arab thabal, *meaning drum, and describes the traditional round metal dish used in the preparation of this and similar recipes.*

4 cups cut-up green beans
2 Tbsp. butter
1 onion, sliced
1 clove garlic, chopped
½ cup cream
½ tsp. nutmeg
1 tsp. Dijon mustard
1 Tbsp. toasted sesame
  seeds
Salt & pepper
2 eggs

Steam green beans for about 5 minutes, or until tender but crisp. In large frying pan, melt butter and sauté onion, garlic and green beans for 2 minutes. Place mixture in food processor or blender and add cream, nutmeg, mustard, sesame seeds and salt and pepper. Purée thoroughly, then add eggs and blend.

Spoon mixture into 6 well-greased 6-ounce custard cups, cover with foil and place in deep pan filled with water to reach halfway up cups. Bake at 350° F for 30 minutes, or until knife inserted in middle comes out clean. Remove from water and wait 5 minutes before removing foil. Remove from moulds or serve as is.

Serves 6.

—*Megan Sproule*

Broccoli Onion Deluxe

2 cups sliced onion
1 bunch broccoli, chopped
3 Tbsp. butter
3 Tbsp. flour
1¼ cups milk
4 oz. cream cheese
2 Tbsp. melted butter
1 cup soft bread crumbs
Parmesan cheese

Boil onion in salted water until tender. Cook broccoli until tender. Melt butter, stir in flour and milk and cook, stirring, until slightly thickened. Add cream cheese a little at a time, stirring until well mixed.

Place broccoli in greased casserole dish, top with onion and pour sauce over all. Combine butter and bread crumbs and place on top of casserole. Sprinkle Parmesan cheese over top and bake at 350° F until lightly browned — about 30 minutes.

Serves 6.

—*Jill Harvey-Sellwood*

Broccoli with Lemon Butter

16 Brazil nuts, shelled
½ cup butter
¼ cup lemon juice
2 tsp. grated lemon rind
1 lb. broccoli, chopped

Place Brazil nuts in small saucepan and cover with cold water. Bring to a boil, lower heat and simmer for 2 minutes. Drain, then slice nuts thinly. Spread in a single layer on a shallow pan and bake at 350° F for 10 minutes, or until lightly browned, stirring frequently. Cool.

Melt butter, add lemon juice and rind and keep hot. Steam broccoli until tender. Serve broccoli with lemon butter poured over it and sprinkled with Brazil nuts.

Serves 4.

—Barbara Zikman

Cheddar Almond Broccoli Casserole

2 lbs. broccoli florets,
    steamed until barely tender
¼ cup butter
¼ cup flour
1 cup milk
¾ cup vegetable stock
2 Tbsp. lemon juice
2 Tbsp. sherry
Pepper
1 cup shredded Cheddar
¼ cup ground almonds
Parmesan cheese

While broccoli is steaming, melt butter in saucepan and blend in flour. Add milk and stock and cook, stirring, until smooth and thick. Add lemon juice, sherry and pepper. Blend in Cheddar cheese and all but 1 Tbsp. of the almonds. Place broccoli in casserole dish and pour sauce over it. Sprinkle with Parmesan cheese and remaining almonds. Bake, uncovered, at 375° F for 20 minutes.

Serves 4.

—Holly Andrews

Broccoli with Wild Rice

Wild rice makes this an elegant dish which is especially good with seafood. It is also delicious with other vegetable dishes and fresh bread.

¼ cup raw wild rice, cooked
½ cup raw white rice, cooked
1 cup very finely chopped
    onion
1 Tbsp. parsley
⅛ tsp. thyme
¼ tsp. garlic powder
Pepper
1 tsp. paprika
2 cups thick white sauce
    (page 132)
1 cup chopped mushrooms,
    sautéed
1 tsp. salt
2 cups grated Cheddar
    cheese
2 stalks broccoli, cooked &
    chopped

Mix together rices, onion, parsley, thyme, garlic powder, pepper and paprika. Combine white sauce, mushrooms, salt and pepper and 1½ cups cheese. Layer these 2 mixtures, with the broccoli, in casserole dish. Top with remaining ½ cup cheese. Bake at 350° F for 40 minutes.

Serves 4.

—Mary Hague

Country Cabbage Casserole

2 lbs. cabbage, coarsely
   shredded
1 large onion, coarsely
   chopped
¼ lb. mushrooms, sliced
6 Tbsp. butter
¼ cup flour
1½ cups milk
Salt & pepper
½ cup wheat germ, toasted
¼ cup Parmesan cheese

Sauté cabbage, onion and mushrooms in 1 Tbsp. butter until tender — about 15 to 20 minutes.

Meanwhile, prepare white sauce using 3 Tbsp. butter, flour and milk. Cook, stirring, until thickened and season with salt and pepper.

Add white sauce to sautéed vegetables and mix well. Pour the mixture into a greased 9" x 13" baking dish. Melt remaining 2 Tbsp. butter and mix with wheat germ and Parmesan cheese. Sprinkle over cabbage mixture and bake at 350° F until bubbly and heated through — about 20 minutes.

Serves 6.

—Pamela Mason

Indian Cabbage

In Indian cooking, it was traditional to add the salt, dissolved in water, when the dish was about to be served as the blessing was never asked on food that had the salt already in it.

1 Tbsp. clarified butter
1 tsp. black mustard seeds
1 medium onion, chopped
1 medium cabbage, cut into
   ½-inch squares
1 tsp. turmeric
¾ cup water
½ tsp. salt

Place butter and mustard seeds in heavy pot. Cover and cook until all the seeds have popped. Add onion and fry until just turning brown.

Meanwhile, cover cabbage with cold water. When onion is browned, add drained cabbage and cook, stirring frequently, until dry. Dissolve turmeric in ½ cup water and add to pot. Continue cooking, covered, over medium heat until cabbage is tender. Stir in ½ tsp. salt dissolved in ¼ cup water. Serve.

Serves 6 to 8.

—Ethel Hunter

Orange Broccoli Parmigiana

2 heads broccoli, cut into
   bite-sized pieces
2 egg whites
½ cup mayonnaise
6 Tbsp. Parmesan cheese
1 tsp. parsley
1-2 tsp. grated orange peel
1 orange, peeled and sliced
2 Tbsp. butter

Cook broccoli until barely tender. Meanwhile, in a small bowl, beat egg whites until soft peaks form. Fold in mayonnaise, cheese, parsley and orange peel.

Drain broccoli and arrange in an ovenproof serving dish. Arrange orange slices over broccoli and dot with butter. Top with egg white mixture. Bake at 450° F for 5 minutes, or until lightly browned.

Serves 6.

—Marilynn Janzen

Mexican Corn Custard

2 eggs, beaten
3 cups creamed corn
1 cup cooked corn
½ tsp. salt
1 clove garlic, minced
½ tsp. baking powder
⅓ cup melted butter
4 oz. chopped green chilies
½ cup chopped green or red
  pepper
⅓ lb. sharp Cheddar cheese,
  grated

Combine all ingredients in order listed and pour into buttered, 2-quart casserole dish.

Bake at 375° F for 45 minutes; reduce temperature to 325° F and continue to bake for another 30 to 45 minutes, or until set.

Serves 6.

—Joyce Falkowski

California Corn

1 large onion, sliced
1 clove garlic, minced
2 Tbsp. olive oil
½ cup thinly sliced green
  pepper
1 lb. mushrooms, sliced
1 cup minced parsley
½ cup dry bread crumbs
½ tsp. oregano
14-oz. can creamed corn
4 medium tomatoes, peeled
  & sliced
½ lb. sharp Cheddar cheese,
  grated
1 tsp. salt

Sauté onion and garlic in oil until tender. Add green pepper and mushrooms and cook over low heat for 5 minutes. Combine parsley, bread crumbs and oregano in a bowl.

To assemble, place half the creamed corn in a greased casserole dish, then add half the green pepper-mushroom mixture, half the tomatoes, half the cheese, ½ tsp. salt and half the bread crumb mixture. Repeat layers. Cover and bake at 300° F for 45 minutes. Remove cover and bake for 15 minutes more.

Serves 4.

—Enid Campbell

Zesty Carrots

6-8 carrots, cut lengthwise
¼ cup water
2 Tbsp. grated onion
2 Tbsp. horseradish
½ cup mayonnaise
½ tsp. salt
¼ tsp. pepper
¼ cup cracker crumbs
1 Tbsp. melted butter

Cook carrots until tender and place in shallow baking pan. Mix water, onion, horseradish, mayonnaise and salt and pepper and pour over carrots.

Mix crumbs with melted butter and sprinkle on top of casserole. Bake at 375° F for 20 minutes.

Serves 4 to 6.

—Anne Lawrence

Baked Corn

¼ cup chopped onion
2 Tbsp. flour
1 tsp. salt
2 Tbsp. butter
2 tsp. paprika
¼ tsp. dry mustard
Pepper
¾ cup milk
2 cups corn
1 egg

Combine all ingredients and bake at 350° F for 20 to 25 minutes.

Serves 4.

—Kathy Cowbrough

Garbanzo Bean Eggplant Roll-Ups

Eggplants, also called aubergines, are extremely versatile. This recipe for stuffed eggplant is one unusual method of preparation. It is such an attractive vegetable that it is also the perfect vehicle for almost any combination of fillings, with or without the eggplant pulp as one of the ingredients.

1 large eggplant
¼ cup oil
1 cup dry garbanzo beans, cooked
6-oz. can tomato paste
¼ cup sesame seeds
2 tsp. garlic powder
2 tsp. tamari sauce
1 tsp. pepper
1 cup grated mozzarella cheese
3 Tbsp. butter
1 clove garlic, minced
3 Tbsp. flour
1 tsp. garam masala
¼ cup white wine
1¾ cups milk
¼ cup Parmesan cheese
Chopped mint

Peel eggplant and slice ¼-inch-thick lengthwise. Fry in oil until tender.

Mash garbanzo beans until smooth. Add tomato paste, sesame seeds, garlic powder, tamari sauce, pepper and mozzarella cheese and mix together. Place a heaping spoonful of filling on each slice of eggplant and roll up. Place close together in greased casserole dish.

To make sauce, melt butter, add garlic and lightly brown. Stir in flour until smooth, reduce heat to low and add garam masala and wine. As sauce begins to thicken, slowly add milk and heat until slightly thickened, stirring often. Add Parmesan cheese. Pour over rolled eggplant, sprinkle with mint and bake at 350° F for 30 minutes.

Serves 4.

—*Kay Chornook*

Cauliflower Casserole

1 large cauliflower
2 cups sliced mushrooms
⅓ cup finely chopped celery
¼ cup butter
2 Tbsp. flour
½ tsp. salt
½ tsp. dry mustard
1¼ cups milk
1 cup grated Cheddar cheese
½ cup cracker crumbs
2 Tbsp. melted butter

Break cauliflower into florets and cook until tender. Drain. Sauté mushrooms and celery in butter until tender. Blend in flour, salt and mustard. Gradually stir in milk and cook until mixture comes to a boil, stirring constantly. Add cheese and stir until melted. Put cauliflower into buttered, 1½-quart casserole dish and pour sauce over. Combine cracker crumbs with melted butter and sprinkle over casserole. Bake at 350° F for 30 minutes.

Serves 4.

—*Joan Airey*

Dandelions in Batter

Dandelion heads
½ cup flour
¾ tsp. salt
¼ tsp. pepper
½ tsp. baking powder
1 egg, well beaten
½ cup milk
Oil

Gather a few cups of blooms early in the morning, rinse in cold water, then soak in salt water for about 2 hours.

Prepare egg batter by sifting together flour, salt, pepper and baking powder. Blend in egg and milk and mix well. Dip blossoms into batter, then drop, a few at a time, into deep oil heated to 375° F. Fry until golden brown, turning once.

—*Glenda G. Green*

Baigan Subji

This is a thick, rich eggplant curry that is popular in northern India.

5 Tbsp. oil
2 large onions, chopped
1 tsp. minced fresh ginger
1 tsp. turmeric
1 tsp. ground coriander
¼ tsp. cayenne
4 tomatoes, peeled & coarsely chopped
3 large eggplants, cubed
Salt
1 cup water
1 Tbsp. lemon juice
3 Tbsp. chopped coriander leaves

Heat oil and sauté onion and ginger. Add turmeric, coriander, cayenne and tomatoes and cook until tomatoes are liquid and sauce is thick.

Add eggplants, salt and water and cook, covered, until eggplant is soft — about 40 minutes. Add lemon juice and sprinkle with coriander leaves just before serving.

Serves 6 to 8.

—Ingrid Birker

Eggplant Tofu Casserole

Tofu, or bean curd, is a complete-protein product and is therefore a valuable food for those wishing to reduce the amount of meat in their diets. This recipe is but one of many ways to serve tofu. Another recipe is to stir-fry tofu along with a selection of vegetables and rice for a quick and easy complete meal.

1 onion, chopped
5 cloves garlic, chopped
Butter
19-oz. can tomatoes
Salt & pepper
Oregano
1 medium eggplant
¼ cup oil
2 cups cooked rice
14-oz. tofu
1-2 Tbsp. tamari sauce
1 cup grated mozzarella cheese

Fry onion and 3 cloves garlic in butter until onion is limp. Add tomatoes and simmer for 30 minutes, seasoning with salt, pepper and oregano.

Peel eggplant and chop into large cubes. Heat oil and fry eggplant until soft, adding a small amount of water if necessary to keep pan from drying out.

Place rice in bottom of greased 9" x 13" casserole dish. Cover with thin slices of tofu and sprinkle with 2 chopped cloves garlic. Pour tamari sauce over, then top with eggplant. Pour tomato sauce over this and sprinkle cheese over the top. Bake at 350° F for 45 minutes.

Serves 6.

—Lylli Anthon

Eggplant with Ginger Sauce

2 medium eggplants
Oil
1¾ cups chicken stock
2 Tbsp. soya sauce
1 Tbsp. honey
1 Tbsp. cornstarch
1 Tbsp. peeled, minced ginger root
¼ tsp. salt
1 green onion, finely chopped

Cut eggplants lengthwise into ½-inch-thick slices, then cut each slice in half lengthwise.

In skillet over medium-high heat, cook eggplant in ¼ cup oil a few slices at a time until browned on both sides, adding more oil if needed. As they brown, remove slices to paper towels to drain.

In same skillet, mix remaining ingredients and cook over medium heat, stirring constantly, until mixture thickens. Return eggplant to skillet and heat through.

Serves 4.

—Christine Taylor

Braised Leeks

1 bunch leeks
4 Tbsp. butter
½ cup chicken stock

Trim, wash and cut down the middle of white parts of leeks. Melt butter, add chicken stock and bring to a boil. Add leeks, return to boil, cover, reduce heat and simmer for 15 to 20 minutes.

Serves 4.

—Doris Hill

Crab Stuffed Mushrooms

4 oz. cream cheese
2 Tbsp. chopped almonds
1 tsp. chopped chives
8 oz. chopped crabmeat
Salt & pepper
Lemon juice
16 large mushroom caps
10 oz. spinach
2 cloves garlic, minced
4 oz. butter

Mix cream cheese, almonds and chives until smooth. Add crabmeat, salt and pepper and lemon juice.

Drop mushrooms into boiling water for 2 minutes, remove and rinse in cold water. Dry and stuff with cream cheese mixture.

Drop spinach into boiling water for 1 minute, drain and rinse with cold water to stop cooking. Squeeze dry. Sauté briefly in butter, tossing until hot. Place in greased 8" x 8" casserole dish, top with stuffed mushrooms and bake at 500° F for 3 to 5 minutes. Heat garlic with butter until butter is melted. Pour over mushroom caps and serve.

Serves 4 as an appetizer.

—Estelle Lemay

Spinach Stuffed Mushrooms

1 lb. fresh spinach
24 medium to large
   mushrooms, cleaned &
   stemmed, reserving stems
Butter
½ cup grated Parmesan
   cheese
⅔ cup crumbled feta cheese
½ cup finely chopped green
   onion
½ cup chopped fresh parsley

Steam spinach, chop finely, then drain well in sieve, pressing out moisture with wooden spoon. Finely chop mushroom stems and sauté in small amount of butter. Combine all ingredients, except mushroom caps, in bowl and mix well.

Brush outsides of mushroom caps with butter, then fill with spinach mixture, mounding it up in centre. Place on baking sheet and bake at 375° F for 20 minutes, or until mushrooms are soft. Serve warm.

Makes 24.

—Susan Gillespie

Spanish Mushrooms in Garlic Sauce

3 Tbsp. olive oil
2 cloves garlic, minced
1½ Tbsp. flour
1 cup beef stock
½ dried hot red chili pepper,
   seeded & cut into 3 pieces
2 Tbsp. minced parsley
2 tsp. lemon juice
½ lb. mushrooms

Heat 2 Tbsp. oil in skillet over medium-high heat. Add garlic and sauté until golden. Remove from heat, stir in flour and mix until smooth. Return to heat and cook for 2 minutes. Gradually add stock, blend in chili pepper, 1 Tbsp. parsley and lemon juice and stir until smooth and thick. Set aside.

Heat remaining 1 Tbsp. oil in skillet, add mushrooms and stir-fry until lightly browned. Add mushrooms to sauce and simmer for 5 minutes. Sprinkle with remaining 1 Tbsp. parsley and serve.

Serves 4.

—Pam Collacott

Baked Stuffed Onions

4 medium yellow onions
1 cup coarse dry bread
    crumbs
¼ tsp. sage
¼ tsp. savory
¼ tsp. thyme
¼ tsp. paprika
¼ tsp. salt
3 Tbsp. melted butter

Peel onions, cover with boiling water and boil rapidly, uncovered, for 15 minutes. Drain and cool slightly.

Cut onions in half and remove centres, leaving shells of 2 or 3 layers. Chop centres coarsely and combine with bread crumbs and remaining ingredients. Spoon into shells and place in greased, shallow baking dish. Cover and bake at 350° F for 35 to 40 minutes.

Serves 4.

—Mary Rogers

Creamed Mushrooms & Chestnuts

This is an unusual culinary use for chestnuts, which are traditionally roasted and eaten whole or used as an ingredient in stuffings for fowl. Possessing considerable food value (3½ pounds of chestnuts supply the daily caloric needs of the average adult) chestnuts, unfortunately, are so high in starch content as to be indigestible for many people.

1 lb. chestnuts
Cold water
5 Tbsp. butter
1 lb. mushrooms, quartered
2 Tbsp. flour
½ tsp. salt
⅛ tsp. pepper
1½ cups light cream
1 Tbsp. chopped parsley

Prick chestnut shells with sharp knife, cover with cold water and bring to a boil over moderate heat. Boil for 15 minutes, drain and cool. Remove shells and skins and cut into quarters.

Melt butter in skillet, add mushrooms and cook until lightly browned. Add flour and salt and pepper and stir until blended. Gradually add cream and cook over moderate heat, stirring constantly, until thickened. Fold in chestnuts and heat. Garnish with parsley.

Serves 6 to 8.

—Doris McIlroy

Creamed Mushrooms

1 onion, finely chopped
½ lb. mushrooms, finely
    chopped
3 Tbsp. butter
1 Tbsp. sherry
½ cup sour cream
1 tsp. Worcestershire sauce
Tabasco sauce
Salt & pepper
1 tsp. thyme

Fry onion and mushrooms in butter until onion is limp. Add sherry and cook for 1 more minute. Add remaining ingredients and simmer slowly until thick — about 30 minutes.

Serve with crackers.

—Mary Cummings

Roasted Red Onions

6-8 medium red onions,
    peeled
⅔ cup oil
⅓ cup vinegar
Salt & pepper
Rosemary

Boil onions for 5 minutes and drain. Place in lightly greased baking dish, or in roasting pan with meat, and roast at 350° F for 30 minutes, or until onions are browned, adding a little butter if desired.

Meanwhile, combine oil, vinegar, salt and pepper and rosemary. Place cooked onions in serving dish and pour dressing over them.

Serves 6 to 8.

—Linda Valade

Maple Glazed Parsnips

The selection of small, uniformly sized parsnips for this recipe results in a delicious, tender dish.

8 small parsnips, trimmed & pared
⅓ cup maple syrup
1½ Tbsp. unsalted butter
2 tsp. lemon juice
¼ tsp. grated lemon zest

Cook parsnips, covered, in ½ inch of boiling water over medium-high heat until tender but crisp — 3 to 4 minutes. Remove from heat and drain well.

Combine remaining ingredients in same skillet and heat over medium heat until simmering. Return parsnips to skillet and cook, uncovered, turning frequently, until parsnips have absorbed the glaze — about 4 minutes.

Serves 4.

—*Lucia M. Cyre*

Breaded Parsnips

8 small parsnips
1 egg, beaten
2 cups seasoned bread crumbs
Oil

Wash and pare parsnips. Boil until slightly softened, drain and let sit on paper towels to dry. Dip in egg and then bread crumbs. Place in baking dish, which is covered with ¼ inch of oil. Bake at 350° F until golden brown — about 30 minutes turning once.

Serves 4.

—*Evelyn Coleman*

Heavenly Parsnips

12 medium parsnips, peeled
1 cup crushed pineapple, undrained
½ cup orange juice
½ tsp. salt
½ tsp. grated orange peel
2 Tbsp. brown sugar
2 Tbsp. butter

Cook parsnips in boiling water until tender — 25 to 30 minutes. Drain, split lengthwise and place in greased 9" x 13" baking dish. Combine remaining ingredients except butter and pour over parsnips. Dot with butter. Bake at 350° F for 30 to 35 minutes, spooning sauce over parsnips several times.

Serves 6.

—*Midge Denault*

Young Garden Peas with Honey & Mint

1 Tbsp. sesame oil
½ small onion, chopped
1 lb. young peas, shelled
2 sprigs fresh mint
1 tsp. honey
Salt

Heat oil and lightly brown onion. Add peas, mint and honey. Season with salt and cook for 5 to 7 minutes, or until peas are soft, but not mushy, adding 2 Tbsp. water if necessary. Remove the cooked mint and garnish with sprigs of fresh mint.

Serves 2 to 4.

—*Lorraine Murphy*

Potato Casserole

2 cups mashed potatoes
2 cups cottage cheese
½ cup sour cream
1 small onion, minced
1-2 eggs, well beaten
Salt & pepper
Romano or Parmesan cheese

Combine all ingredients and place in greased casserole dish, cover with grated Romano or Parmesan cheese if you wish and bake at 350° F for 1 hour.

Serves 4.

—*Margaret Graham*

Carlos' Potatoes

4 large potatoes
4 cloves garlic, peeled & cut in half
1½ tsp. salt
1 Tbsp. oil

Cut potatoes into quarters, place in saucepan with garlic, salt, oil and water to barely cover. Cover pan, bring to a boil and simmer until tender. Serve potatoes with liquid.

Serves 4.

—*Winifred Czerny*

Potato Lace

½ cup chopped green onion
3 eggs
3 Tbsp. flour
⅓ cup chopped parsley
1 tsp. salt
½ tsp. pepper
3-4 large potatoes
Butter

In stainless steel bowl, combine onion, eggs, flour, parsley, salt and pepper. Grate potatoes onto towel; twist with one hand and press with the other to remove excess starch. Add potatoes to egg mixture.

Heat butter in skillet, drop in 3 Tbsp. batter and spread with back of spoon to make patties very thin. Fry until golden brown — about 2 minutes on each side.

Makes 10 to 12 patties.

—Mrs. James Fuller

Colcannon

6 medium potatoes, peeled & chopped
⅓ cup milk
1 Tbsp. butter
½ tsp. salt
2 cups shredded cabbage
3 slices bacon
½ cup chopped onion
1 cup soft bread crumbs
¼ tsp. paprika
2 Tbsp. melted butter

Cook potatoes in boiling water until tender. Mash with milk, butter and salt.

While potatoes are cooking, steam cabbage until tender but crisp. Fry bacon until crisp, then crumble. Drain off about half the bacon fat. In remaining bacon fat, fry onion until soft.

In greased casserole dish, mix hot mashed potatoes, cooked cabbage, bacon and onion. Mix bread crumbs, paprika and melted butter and sprinkle over casserole. Bake, uncovered, at 400° F until topping is golden — about 10 minutes.

Serves 8.

—Sherran McLennan

Dorothy's Favourite Stuffed Spuds

6 medium-large potatoes
1 lb. mushrooms, sliced
1 onion, finely minced
1-2 cloves garlic, crushed
2 tsp. butter
1 Tbsp. soya sauce
½ cup yogurt
3-4 green onions, sliced
¾ lb. grated old Cheddar cheese
Salt

Scrub potatoes and steam for 35 minutes, or until almost tender. Place on a baking sheet and bake at 350° F until tender.

Sauté mushrooms, onion and garlic in butter with 1 tsp. soya sauce. When potatoes are cool enough to handle, split apart lengthwise and scoop out the insides. Mash with yogurt. If potatoes are very dry, add more liquid, although they should not be as moist as regular mashed potatoes. Mix in mushroom mixture, green onions, the remaining 2 tsp. soya sauce and three-quarters of the cheese. Taste for seasoning and add salt if needed. Place mixture back into the potato shells, top with remaining cheese and bake at 350° F until heated through and cheese is melted.

Serves 6.

—Cindy Panton-Goyert

Potatoes Moussaka

4 potatoes, thinly sliced
Oil
1 medium onion, thinly
   sliced
1 clove garlic, crushed
Parmesan cheese
14-oz. can tomatoes

Fry potatoes in oil until tender, add onion and garlic and cook until onion is limp.

In greased casserole dish, alternate layers of potatoes, cheese and tomatoes, ending with cheese. Bake at 350° F until bubbly — about 30 minutes.

Serves 4.

—Linda Hodgins

Hot German Potato Salad

6 medium potatoes
¼ lb. bacon, chopped
¼ cup sliced green onions
⅓ cup vinegar
⅓ cup beef stock
1 Tbsp. sugar
½ tsp. salt
½ tsp. celery salt
Pepper
Parsley
Paprika

Boil potatoes until tender. Peel, slice and keep warm in serving dish. Cook bacon until crisp, remove, drain and add to potatoes, reserving fat.

In fat, fry green onions. Add vinegar, stock, sugar, salt, celery salt and pepper. Bring to a boil and pour over potatoes. Toss lightly to combine and top with parsley and paprika.

Serves 6.

—Irma Leming

Scalloped Potatoes & Tofu

1 onion, sliced
2 Tbsp. butter
4 oz. tofu, cubed
¼ cup wheat germ
2 large potatoes, thinly
   sliced
Milk
½ tsp. salt
Pepper
½ cup grated cheese

Sauté onion in butter until transparent. Add tofu and sauté for 5 minutes. Stir in wheat germ until well blended. Add potatoes and cook for several minutes longer, stirring carefully so as not to break the slices.

Turn ingredients into a greased casserole dish, adding salt and enough milk to nearly cover — about 1½ cups. Bake, covered, at 325° F for about 45 minutes, or until the potatoes are tender. Uncover during the last 15 minutes and sprinkle with grated cheese if desired.

Serves 3.

—Linda Goddu

Rapure

The name for this dish based on grated potatoes originates with the verb "râper," which means "to grate." This version calls for pork, but chicken or clams can also be used.

½ lb. diced salt pork
1 onion, chopped
12 potatoes, peeled
1 egg
Flour
Salt & pepper

Boil the pork for a few minutes, then discard the water. Sauté the pork for another few minutes, then mix with onion in a greased 9" x 13" baking pan.

Grate potatoes and beat in egg. Add flour, salt and pepper and mix. Pour over pork and mix well. Cook at 250° F for 4 to 5 hours.

Serves 6.

—Rachelle Poirier

Dill & Creamed Spinach

This recipe combines dill and spinach, which often arrive in the garden at the same time, with delicious results.

3 Tbsp. oil
2 Tbsp. flour
1 large clove garlic, minced
2-3 Tbsp. finely chopped dill
2 cups coarsely chopped, steamed spinach
1 Tbsp. brown sugar
1 cup cream
Salt

Heat oil, add flour and stir over high heat until flour browns. Add garlic and cook for 30 seconds. Add dill, remove from heat and let cool slightly. Stir in spinach, brown sugar and cream. Salt to taste, bring to boil and simmer for 2 to 3 minutes.

Serves 4.

—Ann Kostendt

Spinach & Egg Casserole

¼ cup butter
¼ cup flour
½ tsp. salt
¼ tsp. paprika
2 cups milk
1 cup bread crumbs
2 cups chopped, cooked spinach
4 eggs, hard boiled, peeled & sliced
4 slices Cheddar cheese

Melt butter, stir in flour, salt, paprika and milk and cook, stirring constantly, until thickened.

In greased baking dish, assemble casserole as follows: half the bread crumbs, half the spinach, half the eggs, one-third of the sauce, half the cheese, rest of spinach, rest of eggs, one-third of the sauce, rest of cheese, rest of sauce and rest of bread crumbs. Bake at 325° F for 35 to 40 minutes.

Serves 4.

—J. Kristine MacDonald

Savoury Stuffed Pumpkin

1 small pumpkin (approximately 8-10 inches in diameter)
1½ lbs. lean ground beef (enough to stuff both pumpkin halves)
1 cup fine, dry bread crumbs
½ cup diced onion
½ cup diced green pepper
1 cup sliced mushrooms
2 cups canned tomatoes
½ cup catsup
1 Tbsp. Worcestershire sauce
1 Tbsp. brown sugar
1 Tbsp. parsley flakes
½ tsp. basil
½ tsp. oregano
1 tsp. chili powder
½ tsp. cayenne
1 Tbsp. sesame seeds
Garlic powder
Salt & pepper
Parmesan cheese

Slice pumpkin in half vertically, clean out seeds and stringy insides and set aside. Cook ground beef and drain off excess grease. Set aside. Sauté onion, green pepper and mushrooms. Return ground beef to pan and add remaining ingredients except Parmesan cheese. Simmer until most of the liquid has evaporated. Fill pumpkin halves, sprinkle with Parmesan cheese and cover with aluminum foil. Bake at 400° F for about 2 hours, or until pumpkin is cooked.

Serves 6.

—Bonnie Lawson

Spinach Balls

1 lb. spinach, steamed &
   chopped
1 small onion, chopped
3 eggs
1 cup seasoned bread
   crumbs
¼ cup Parmesan cheese
Garlic salt
Thyme
⅓ cup melted butter

Combine all ingredients and mix well. Form into small balls and freeze separately on a cookie sheet. Place in an airtight container and use as required by baking at 350° F for 15 minutes.

Serves 8 to 10 as an appetizer.

—Mrs. J. Wynes

Spinach with Peanut Sauce

2 lbs. fresh spinach
2 Tbsp. butter
1 large onion, chopped
Cayenne
1 Tbsp. whisky
1 tsp. soya sauce
½ cup fresh coconut milk
½ cup unsalted peanuts,
   crushed

Cook spinach, without water, until limp. Cool, then drain to remove all moisture. Melt butter in a pan, and when foam subsides, add onion and cayenne. Cook until onion is soft. Stir in whisky, soya sauce, coconut milk and peanuts. Cook, stirring constantly, for 2 to 3 minutes. Add spinach to frying pan and cook until heated through, about 4 to 5 minutes.

Serves 6 to 8.

—Ingrid Birker

Glazed Squash with Cranberries

This dish is excellent served as part of a traditional Thanksgiving or Christmas dinner.

4 8-oz. pieces Hubbard
   squash
½ cup light maple syrup
2 Tbsp. butter
¼ tsp. salt
½ cup sugar
1 Tbsp. cornstarch
⅓ cup water
1½ cups cranberries

Peel squash, discarding seeds and stringy portion. Rinse and pat dry, then arrange in greased baking dish.

In saucepan over medium heat, combine syrup, butter and salt; heat to boiling, then pour over squash. Cover dish with foil and bake at 350° F for 45 to 55 minutes, or until squash is almost tender.

Meanwhile, prepare cranberries. In saucepan over medium heat, combine sugar, cornstarch and water and heat to boiling, stirring constantly. Add cranberries and cook until they are just tender — about 5 minutes.

Spoon cranberries over squash. Continue to bake squash, covered, for 10 minutes, or until the pieces are tender.

Serves 4.

—Frances Walker

Summer Squash Purée

This purée can be made in the late summer and early fall, when the zucchini are threatening to overrun the garden. Kept in the freezer, it can be thawed out when needed and added to soups or casseroles throughout the winter for a garden-fresh taste.

2 large onions, thinly sliced
6 Tbsp. butter
¼ cup water
3 cloves garlic, minced
2½ tsp. salt
½ tsp. pepper
6 lbs. summer squash
2 green peppers, thinly
   sliced
1 cup chopped parsley

Cook onions in butter until soft. Add water, garlic, salt, pepper, squash and green peppers. Cover and cook for 3 minutes. Lower heat to medium and cook for 12 to 15 minutes, or until squash is tender.

Remove from heat, add parsley and cool. Purée in blender half a cup at a time. Cool. Freeze in 2-cup amounts.

Makes 12 cups.

—Dianne Griffin

Rum Squash

4 cups mashed, cooked
    squash
2 Tbsp. rum
2 Tbsp. maple syrup
½ tsp. salt
1 Tbsp. cream
½ cup well-drained, crushed
    pineapple
5 Tbsp. butter
½ cup brown sugar
½ cup chopped walnuts

Mix squash, rum, syrup, salt, cream, pineapple and 2 Tbsp. butter and pour into a greased, 2-quart casserole dish. Melt remaining 3 Tbsp. butter over low heat and stir in brown sugar and walnuts. Cook, stirring, until creamy and pour over squash. Bake at 350° F for 20 to 30 minutes, or until bubbly.

Serves 4.

—Joan Patricia Cox

Love It Squash

This is an unusual stuffed squash recipe that takes advantage of the celery-like lovage plant. The addition of grapes and sherry gives the dish a slightly sweet taste.

1 large Hubbard squash,
    halved & seeded
5 onions, chopped
6-8 cloves garlic, minced
2 hot peppers, chopped
Fistful lovage, chopped
1 lb. sweet red grapes,
    halved & pitted
½ cup sherry
Olive oil

Bake squash at 375° F for 1½ hours, or until flesh is tender. Scrape out insides without piercing shell. Chop up pulp and combine with onions, garlic, peppers and lovage. Add grapes and sherry and dribble with olive oil. Return to shells and bake at 350° F for 1 hour, or until piping hot, with a pan of water on the rack below the squash to prevent it from drying out.

Serves 4 to 6.

—Deborah Washington

Butternut Squash Medley

3 large onions, sliced
1 large clove garlic, crushed
2-3 Tbsp. butter
2 cups cubed butternut
    squash, steamed until
    tender
1 brick tofu, cubed
½ cup cooked brown lentils
1 cup stewed tomatoes, with
    juice
2 Tbsp. tamari sauce
1 tsp. curry
1 tsp. oregano
Grated mozzarella or
    Cheddar cheese
Parsley

Sauté onions and garlic in butter. Add squash, tofu, lentils, tomatoes, tamari sauce, curry and oregano. Simmer until slightly thickened. Cover with cheese and sprinkle with parsley.

Serves 4 to 5.

—Rosande Bellaar Spruyt

Butternut Squash with Cheese & Walnuts

1 small butternut squash
1 small onion, chopped
1 cup shredded hard cheese
½ cup chopped walnuts

Peel and slice squash and steam until just tender. Oil a casserole dish. Layer squash, onion, cheese and walnuts, ending with a layer of cheese and walnuts on top. Bake, uncovered, at 300° F for 15 minutes.

Serves 4.

—Brenda Thaler

Tofu & Sweet Potato Balls

A native of India, the sweet potato has adapted to grow in all warm countries. Very similar to yams, the two vegetables can be used interchangeably. The leaves of the sweet potato can also be cooked and eaten like spinach.

24 oz. tofu, mashed
2 cups mashed, cooked
  sweet potatoes
¼ cup chopped onion
½ tsp. salt
Pepper
1 cup dried bread crumbs
Oil

Combine tofu, sweet potatoes, onion, salt and pepper. Form into l-inch balls and roll in bread crumbs. Remove excess crumbs, then let stand on paper towel for 10 minutes. In wok, heat cooking oil to 350° F — hot but not smoking — then deep-fry balls until golden brown.

Serves 8 to 10 as an appetizer.

—Colin Webster

Scalloped Yams & Apples

2 lbs. yams, peeled & sliced
6 medium apples, peeled &
  cut into thin wedges
Juice of 1 lemon
⅓ cup brown sugar
⅓ cup butter
¼ tsp. nutmeg
Salt & pepper

Arrange half the yams, cut side down in greased, shallow, 2-quart casserole dish. Add half the apples. Mix remaining ingredients and sprinkle half on mixture. Repeat layers, cover and bake at 350° F for 1 hour.

Serves 6 to 8.

—Judy Morrison-Cayen

Sweet Potato Soufflé

5 sweet potatoes, quartered
2 apples, peeled, quartered &
  cored
4 eggs, separated
1 tsp. vanilla
1 Tbsp. butter

Place sweet potatoes in large saucepan with water to cover and simmer until tender about 30 minutes. Let cool and peel. Place apples in a saucepan, cover with water and simmer for about 8 minutes, until just tender. Put potatoes and apples through a food mill together or purée together in food processor. Transfer to large mixing bowl and stir in egg yolks. In another bowl, beat egg whites until stiff peaks form. Fold into sweet potato/apple mixture. Beat in vanilla.

Place mixture in buttered, 2-quart soufflé dish. Dot with butter and bake at 350° F for 45 to 60 minutes, or until hot and bubbly and lightly browned on top.

Serves 6 to 8.

—Sue Summers

Baked Swiss Chard

This is an excellent way to use an overabundance of chard during the summer. The recipe may be varied by adding mushrooms, tomatoes, olives and chopped bacon.

1 lb. Swiss chard
¼ cup butter
1 large onion, sliced
2 eggs
Salt & pepper
¾ cup grated Cheddar
  cheese

Cut stems from chard, then cut stems into ¼-inch pieces and leaves into 1-inch strips. Melt butter, add onion and stems and cook until onion is transparent. Add leaves and cook for 3 minutes. Place in greased, 2-quart baking dish. Beat eggs, add salt and pepper and then pour over chard. Sprinkle with grated cheese and bake at 400° F for 10 minutes.

Serves 2 to 4.

—Sandra Lintz

Green Tomato Curry

This recipe provides a delicious use for end-of-the-season unripe tomatoes. It can be frozen very successfully and does not take a great deal of time to prepare.

¼ cup butter
2 medium onions, chopped
4 Tbsp. curry powder
1 tsp. cumin
1 cup water
8 cups green tomatoes
½ cup brown sugar
2 Tbsp. lemon juice
½ tsp. paprika
Salt

Sauté onions in butter for 10 minutes. Add curry powder and cumin and cook for 5 minutes longer. Stir in water and remaining ingredients. Simmer for 30 minutes, stirring occasionally and adding more water if necessary. Serve over rice.

Serves 4.

—*Leslie Gent*

Zucchini French Fries

4 medium zucchini
1½ cups flour
Salt
2 eggs
1½ Tbsp. water
1 cup Parmesan cheese
Garlic salt
Oil

Wash zucchini and remove ends, but do not peel. Cut into shoestring strips approximately 3 inches long. Sprinkle well with salt and roll lightly in ½ cup flour. Shake off excess flour and drop strips, several at a time, into eggs beaten lightly with 1½ Tbsp. water.

In wide, shallow pan, combine remaining 1 cup flour with Parmesan cheese and garlic salt. Roll zucchini in flour mixture to coat evenly and spread on paper towels to dry. Heat oil to 375° F. Fry strips, a handful at a time, until crisp and golden. Drain on paper towels and keep warm until all are fried.

Serves 4 to 5.

—*Barb Krimmer*

Scalloped Tomatoes with Herbs

2 medium onions, sliced
½ green pepper, diced
2 stalks celery, diced
¼ cup butter, melted
¼ tsp. pepper
½ tsp. thyme
2 cups coarse, soft bread crumbs
2 Tbsp. chopped parsley
1 tsp. chopped chives
3 cups peeled & chopped tomatoes
2 Tbsp. butter

Sauté onions, green pepper and celery in butter with pepper and thyme. Cook, stirring occasionally, until onions are transparent and remove from heat.

Combine bread crumbs, parsley and chives. Stir half this mixture into onions.

Arrange alternate layers of chopped tomatoes and onion-bread crumb mixture in a greased casserole dish, ending with tomatoes. Sprinkle with remaining bread crumbs and dot with 2 Tbsp. butter.

Bake at 350° F for 45 minutes.

Serves 4.

—*Cathy Gordon*

Zucchini Sour Cream Casserole

3 medium zucchini, sliced
3 Tbsp. butter
¼ cup sour cream
1 Tbsp. grated Cheddar
  cheese
½ tsp. salt
⅛ tsp. paprika
1 egg yolk, beaten
1 Tbsp. chopped chives
½ cup cracker crumbs

Cook zucchini in steamer or small amount of boiling, salted water until tender but crisp. Drain and place in a greased, 1½-quart casserole dish.

Melt 1 Tbsp. butter in small saucepan. Stir in sour cream, cheese, salt and paprika. Cook over low heat, stirring constantly and without boiling, until cheese is melted. Remove from heat and stir in egg yolk and chives. Stir into zucchini. Toss cracker crumbs with remaining 2 Tbsp. melted butter. Cover zucchini with crumb mixture. Bake, uncovered, at 350° F for 20 to 25 minutes.

Serves 3 to 4.

—Diane Cancilla

Stuffed Zucchini Blossoms

The blossoms that fall off squash vines without maturing are the male flowers not retained for seed development. They make decorative as well as edible cases for almost any type of stuffing — bread, meat or vegetable. Open each blossom and lightly stuff, then close the petals. Place on greased baking dish and cook at 350° F until thoroughly heated.

Zucchini Lasagne

2 cups cottage cheese
1 cup cooked, chopped
  spinach
1 lb. mozzarella cheese,
  grated
1½ lbs. ground beef
1 small onion, chopped
8-oz. can tomato sauce
½ tsp. salt
½ tsp. pepper
½ tsp. oregano
½ tsp. thyme
2½ lbs. zucchini, thinly
  sliced lengthwise

Combine cottage cheese, spinach and half the mozzarella cheese in a bowl. Brown ground beef and onion, drain off excess fat, then add tomato sauce, salt, pepper, oregano and thyme. Simmer for 5 minutes.

In a greased 9" x 13" casserole dish, layer half the meat mixture, half the zucchini, all of the spinach-cheese mixture, the rest of the zucchini, the rest of the meat and top with remaining ½ lb. of mozzarella cheese. Cover and bake at 350° F for 30 minutes. Uncover and bake for another 45 minutes.

Serves 6.

—Christine Peterman

Zucchini Parmigiana

6 small zucchini
1 egg
1 Tbsp. water
¼ cup oil
1 medium onion, chopped
2 cloves garlic, finely
  chopped
13-oz. can tomato paste
1½ cups water
1 Tbsp. basil
Salt & pepper
1 cup Parmesan cheese
1 lb. mozzarella cheese,
  grated

Slice zucchini lengthwise ¼-inch thick. Combine egg and water and coat slices in mixture. Cook in hot oil until golden brown, then remove. Cook onion and garlic in remaining oil until tender. Combine with tomato paste, water and seasonings.

In a lightly greased 9" x 13" casserole dish, arrange half the zucchini. Spoon over half the tomato mixture and cover with half the cheese. Repeat layers.

Bake at 350° F for 30 to 45 minutes, until heated through and golden.

Serves 4 to 6.

—Jane Durward

Cabbage Tomato Casserole

This is an excellent recipe for the fall, when fresh cabbage and tomatoes are plentiful.

3 cups finely shredded
    cabbage
1½ cups peeled & coarsely
    chopped tomatoes
¾ tsp. salt
¼ tsp. paprika
1 cup grated Cheddar cheese
1 cup bread crumbs
2 strips bacon, finely
    chopped

Boil cabbage in salted water for 5 minutes, then drain well. Heat tomatoes and add salt and paprika.

Place alternating layers of tomatoes and cabbage, beginning with tomatoes, in a greased baking dish. Sprinkle each layer with grated cheese and bread crumbs.Top casserole with chopped bacon. Bake at 350° F until crumbs are brown — about 30 minutes.

Serves 6.

—Janeen Clynick

Italian Vegetable Medley

This recipe is really just a guideline. Almost any garden-fresh vegetable can be added or substituted — it is the banana pepper and garlic which give the dish its distinctive flavour.

3 Tbsp. oil
4 medium onions, cut in half
    & sliced lengthwise
1 banana pepper, sliced
6 cloves garlic, crushed
1 tsp. finely chopped ginger
2 Tbsp. curry
2 sweet peppers, thinly
    sliced lengthwise
Juice of 1 lemon
8 tomatoes, peeled &
    chopped
1 cup bean sprouts

Sauté onions, banana pepper, garlic and ginger lightly in hot oil. Add curry and sweet peppers. When vegetables are cooked, but still crunchy, add tomatoes and lemon juice. Cook over low heat until tomatoes are soft. Add bean sprouts and toss. Serve with pasta or rice.

Serves 4.

—Sandra Hunter

Vegetable Medley with Beer Sauce

1 medium eggplant, peeled &
    cut into ½-inch slices
2 medium zucchini, cut into
    ½-inch slices
2 eggs
2-3 Tbsp. butter
13-oz. can tomato paste
½ lb. mushrooms, sliced
14½-oz. can stewed
    tomatoes
½ cup beer
½ green pepper, diced
1 medium onion, diced
2 tsp. oregano
½ tsp. basil
1 tsp. salt
4 oz. cream cheese, softened
    or sliced
4 oz. Monterey jack cheese,
    sliced
4 oz. Cheddar cheese, sliced

Dip eggplant and zucchini slices in beaten eggs and sauté for approximately 5 minutes on each side.

Make the beer sauce by combining the tomato paste, mushrooms, stewed tomatoes, beer, green pepper, onion, oregano, basil and salt in a saucepan. Bring to a boil and simmer for 10 minutes.

Assemble the casserole in a greased 9" x 13" pan as follows: half the eggplant, all of the cream cheese, half the zucchini, one-third of the beer sauce, the rest of the eggplant, half of the Monterey jack and Cheddar cheese, one-third of the beer sauce, the rest of the zucchini, the rest of the beer sauce and the rest of the cheeses.

Bake at 350° F for 45 to 50 minutes.

Serves 6.

—Francie Goodwin-Rogne

Tomato Squash Casserole

1 large onion, chopped
1 green pepper, chopped
1 large butternut squash, cubed
3 Tbsp. brown sugar
3 Tbsp. flour
28-oz. can tomato sauce
Salt & pepper

Sauté onion and green pepper. Add squash, sugar, flour, tomato sauce and salt and pepper and mix well. Place in buttered casserole dish and bake at 350° F for 40 minutes.

Serves 4.

—Valerie Repetto

Simple Summer Casserole

2 ears corn
4 very ripe tomatoes
2 onions
4 stalks celery
½ cup cooked rice
2 cloves garlic, crushed
1½ tsp. chili powder
¾ tsp. salt
Pepper
2-2½ cups grated Cheddar cheese

Cut corn from cob, peel and chop tomatoes coarsely, slice onions in rings and cut celery into bitesized pieces.

Place vegetables in 9-inch round casserole dish. Add rice, garlic, seasonings and 1 cup grated cheese. Stir until well mixed and press to form even top. Sprinkle remaining cheese over top. Bake at 350° F for 45 to 50 minutes.

Serves 4.

—Linda Page

Cheese Tomato & Corn Scallop

2 cups bread crumbs
2 cups canned tomatoes
2 cups whole kernel corn
¼ cup butter
1 tsp. salt
1 cup grated Cheddar cheese

Combine bread crumbs, tomatoes, corn, butter, salt and ⅔ cup cheese. Pour into greased, shallow baking dish. Sprinkle remaining cheese on top. Bake at 350° F for 20 to 30 minutes, or until brown on top.

Serves 4.

—Helene Conway-Brown

Tomato Alfalfa & Cheese Pie

Pastry for double 9-inch pie shell
¼ cup finely chopped celery
½ tsp. parsley
½ tsp. basil
¼ tsp. salt
2 Tbsp. butter
2 cups peeled & sliced tomatoes
4 oz. alfalfa sprouts
1 cup grated Cheddar cheese
½ cup mushrooms, sliced
¼ cup bread crumbs

Sauté celery, parsley, basil and salt in butter until celery is limp. Line pie plate with half of pastry, then layer tomatoes, sprouts, cheese, mushrooms, bread crumbs and celery/herb mixture. Add top crust and bake at 375° F for 45 minutes.

—Tracy Brown

Moroccan Tagine

The contributor learned how to make this dish while living in Morocco. The word "tagine" refers to the covered clay pot in which the vegetables and tomato sauce were simmered over an open fire.

1 parsnip
1 potato
1 carrot
1 eggplant
1 zucchini
3 tomatoes
1 onion, chopped
1 clove garlic, chopped
2 tsp. cumin
½ tsp. turmeric
½ tsp. cayenne
5-6 prunes
5-6 olives

Chop or slice parsnip, potato, carrot, eggplant and zucchini. Steam tomatoes to remove skins and then mash with fork. In saucepan, sauté onion and garlic; add tomatoes and spices. Layer vegetables over tomato sauce as follows — parsnip, potato, carrot, eggplant, zucchini, tomatoes. Add a little water and the prunes and top with olives.

Cover and simmer on medium heat for about 30 minutes or until vegetables are tender.

Serves 2 to 3.

—Sylvia Dawson

Colache

This mixed vegetable dish is a Mexican recipe dating from the days of the Aztecs.

1 cup chopped onion
2 medium tomatoes, peeled
   & coarsely chopped
1 green or red pepper, diced
2 cups diced zucchini
½ cup green beans
½ cup wax beans
2 cups corn
½ cup vegetable stock
1 tsp. oregano
⅛ tsp. chili powder
⅛ tsp. pepper
Salt

Cook onion and tomatoes in heavy pot until softened. Add green or red pepper, zucchini and beans and cook over medium-high heat, stirring, for 5 minutes. Add corn, stock, oregano, chili powder, pepper and salt and simmer for 10 minutes.

Serves 4 to 6.

—*Heather Quiney*

Gui Ding

This Chinese vegetable dish can be accompanied by rice and sweet and sour spareribs for a complete meal.

2 carrots
2 stalks celery
1 can bamboo shoots
1 can water chestnuts
4 green onions
2 Tbsp. plus
   1 tsp. peanut oil
½ lb. cashews
2 Tbsp. cornstarch
¾ cup water
½ tsp. garlic powder
1¼ tsp. soya sauce
1 tsp. sugar
2 drops sesame seed oil

Cut carrots, celery, bamboo shoots, water chestnuts and green onions into ½-inch pieces. Cook carrots and celery in 2 Tbsp. peanut oil for 1 minute. Add bamboo shoots, water chestnuts, green onions and cashews and continue to cook over high heat, stirring frequently.

Meanwhile, combine cornstarch, water, garlic powder, soya sauce, sugar, remaining 1 tsp. peanut oil and sesame seed oil. Pour over vegetables and fry for another minute until well mixed and slightly thickened.

Serves 6.

—*Mary Giesz*

Vegetable Pot Pie

This is a delicious alternative to the traditional beef or chicken pot pie.

Pastry for 9-inch pie shell
6 small white onions or 1
   medium onion, cut into
   eighths
2 cups chopped cauliflower
1 cup sliced carrots
1 cup quartered mushrooms
1 cup peas
½ cup slivered almonds
3 Tbsp. butter
4 Tbsp. flour
1 cup milk
1 Tbsp. parsley
Salt & pepper

Cook onion, cauliflower and carrots until just tender. Drain and save 1 cup liquid. Arrange cooked vegetables in greased 8" x 8" baking dish along with mushrooms, peas and almonds.

To make sauce, melt butter, stir in flour, then gradually add cooking liquid and milk. Continue to stir and cook, adding parsley and salt and pepper, until sauce is thickened. Pour over vegetables. Top with pie crust and bake at 425° F for 20 to 25 minutes, or until crust is lightly browned. Cool for 10 minutes before serving.

Serves 4.

—*Julie Pope*

Layered Vegetable Cheese Bake

1 Tbsp. oil
1 large onion, coarsely
  chopped
1 large green pepper, cut into
  squares
1 small eggplant, peeled &
  cut into small cubes
½ lb. mushrooms, halved
1 large tomato, peeled &
  chopped
1 cup bread crumbs
1 tsp. salt
¾ tsp. thyme
⅛ tsp. pepper
2 cups grated Swiss cheese

Heat oil over medium heat,
add onion and green pepper and
sauté for 3 minutes. Add
eggplant and mushrooms and
sauté for another 3 minutes,
stirring constantly. Add tomato
and cook for 1 minute.

Mix bread crumbs with salt,
thyme and pepper. Spread on
bottom of greased casserole dish.
Top with half the vegetable
mixture, then half the cheese.
Repeat. Bake at 350° F for 30 to
40 minutes.

Serves 2.

—Christine Davidson

Kohlrabi Carrot Bake

3 medium kohlrabi, peeled &
  sliced into ½-inch fingers
4 medium carrots, sliced
  diagonally
¼ cup chopped onion
2 Tbsp. butter
2 Tbsp. flour
½ tsp. salt
Pepper
1½ cups milk
¼ cup parsley
1 Tbsp. lemon juice
¾ cup bread crumbs
1 Tbsp. melted butter

Cook kohlrabi in small
amount of water for 15 minutes.
Add carrots and cook for another
10 to 12 minutes until
vegetables are tender. Drain.

Cook onion in butter until
tender. Blend in flour, salt and
pepper. Add milk and cook,
stirring, until bubbly. Stir in
vegetables, parsley and lemon
juice. Turn into greased, 1-quart
casserole dish. Combine bread
crumbs and butter and sprinkle
over casserole. Bake at 350° F
for 20 to 25 minutes.

Serves 6.

—Valerie Gillis

Lentil Kale & Mushroom Stew

*This dish can be served as a
vegetable accompaniment or as
a main course.*

3 potatoes, cubed
6-8 dried Chinese
  mushrooms
2 carrots, sliced
½ cup lentils
1 clove garlic, crushed
4 Tbsp. butter
¼ cup soya sauce
1 bunch kale, chopped

Combine all ingredients except
soya sauce and kale in large,
heavy pot. Cover with water and
simmer for several hours. Add
soya sauce and kale and cook
for another hour.

Serves 4.

—Arlene Pervin

Ploughman's Platter

This dish uses up leftover vegetables in a delicious and easy-to-prepare meal. You may use more or less vegetables, depending on your preference and what you have available.

1½ cups vegetables
2 slices onion, chopped
½ clove garlic, chopped
3 Tbsp. soya sauce
2 potatoes, cooked & sliced
½ cup grated Cheddar
　 cheese
Yogurt

Steam or fry vegetables, onion and garlic until tender, then toss with soya sauce.

Place potatoes in a single layer to cover bottom of greased, shallow baking dish. Place vegetable mixture on top of potatoes in another layer. Cover with grated cheese.

Broil until cheese is bubbly and dish is steaming hot. Serve with yogurt garnish.

Serves 2.

—Jane Lott

Buttered Green Beans with Cashews

1½ lbs. green beans
3 Tbsp. butter
¼ tsp. salt
½ tsp. pepper
¼ cup chopped parsley
1 cup roasted unsalted
　 cashews

Trim beans and blanch in boiling water. Meanwhile, melt butter and stir in salt, pepper and parsley. Drain beans and place in warm bowl. Sprinkle with cashews and then pour butter over. Toss well.

Serves 6 to 8.

—Kristine Mattila

Tamari Almond Green Beans

2-3 cups French-cut green
　 beans
1 small onion, chopped
1 clove garlic, minced
4 Tbsp. butter
½ cup slivered almonds
3 Tbsp. tamari

Cook beans, drain and set aside. In large saucepan, fry onion and garlic in butter until almost transparent. Add almonds and stir-fry for a minute or two longer. Stir in green beans and add tamari. Mix well and serve when heated through.

Serves 4.

—Mikell Billoki

Fried String Beans

"During a rather hard winter, we lived mostly on our canned food, frozen fruits, vegetables and meats, plus potatoes, carrots and onions. We made many interesting and different dishes. This was one we really liked."

¼ lb. bacon
½ cup chopped onion
1 quart canned beans
salt & pepper

Fry bacon until crisp, then set aside. Drain most of bacon fat off, leaving about 4 Tbsp. in pan. Cook onion in bacon fat until soft. Add drained beans and fry until lightly browned about 20 minutes. Add bacon and salt and pepper. Heat and serve.

Serves 4.

—Irene Whetson

Lemon-Buttered Cabbage

Serve this fresh-tasting cabbage with roast pork for flavours that complement one another well.

¼ cup butter
1 head cabbage, shredded
½ tsp. grated lemon rind
2 Tbsp. lemon juice
½ tsp. celery seed
½ tsp. salt
¼ tsp. pepper

Melt butter in large skillet. Add shredded cabbage, cover and cook over medium heat stirring occasionally, for 8 to 10 minutes, or until just tender. Add remaining ingredients. Stir to combine and serve at once.

Serves 6 to 8.

—Holly Andrews

Maple-Glazed Carrots

1½ lbs. whole baby carrots
3 Tbsp. butter
½ cup maple syrup
½ tsp. salt
2 Tbsp. chopped parsley or
mint

Cook carrots in boiling, salted water until almost tender. Drain, reserving ¼ cup liquid. Melt butter and roll carrots in it. Add reserved liquid, maple syrup and salt. Cook, uncovered, until liquid is thickened and carrots are tender — about 10 minutes. Sprinkle with parsley or mint.

Serves 6.

—Lynn Tobin

Almond Butter Carrots

Carrots deserve better treatment than the slicing and boiling they generally get. This is a simple but tasty method of dressing up the nutritious, inexpensive vegetable.

6 carrots, scraped &
julienned
3 Tbsp. butter
⅓ cup slivered almonds
¼ tsp. curry
1 Tbsp. lemon juice

Steam carrots until crispy-tender. Melt butter until lightly browned, add almonds and sauté until golden brown, stirring constantly. Stir in curry and lemon juice and cook over low heat for 1 to 2 minutes. Pour over carrots and serve.

Serves 4 to 6.

—Jayne Simms-Dalmotas

Scalloped Cabbage

"This recipe has been handed down through the family, although I am unaware of anyone ever writing it down. My mother made it on the farm, and her mother before her. My children continue to make it in their own homes, and so, I suppose, in that sense it has become a traditional dish for us."

3½ cups coarsely chopped
cabbage
1-2 onions, chopped
¼ cup butter
¼ cup flour
1 cup milk
½ cup grated Cheddar
cheese
dry bread crumbs
Parmesan cheese

Steam cabbage and onions for 5 to 8 minutes over boiling water. Melt butter, stir in flour and blend to make a smooth paste. Add milk gradually, stirring constantly. Remove from heat when thickened. Add Cheddar cheese and cabbage mixture, blending thoroughly. Pour into greased casserole dish and top with bread crumbs and Parmesan cheese. Bake, uncovered, at 350° F for 25 minutes.

Serves 4 to 6.

—Shirley Fulton

Brussels Sprouts with Bacon Sauce

"Top Brussels sprouts with this creamy bacon sauce and you will elevate them to gourmet status."

1 lb. Brussels sprouts
4 slices bacon
1 small onion, chopped
½ cup sour cream
1 Tbsp. flour
⅛ tsp. salt
pepper

Trim stems and outer leaves from sprouts and cut an x in base. Boil or steam, covered, for 10 minutes, or until crispy-tender. Cook bacon until crisp, remove from pan and drain. Remove all but 1 Tbsp. of fat from pan, then add onion and sauté until tender — about 5 minutes. Combine sour cream, flour, salt and pepper. Stir sour cream mixture into onion; add crumbled bacon and heat sauce through. When sprouts are done, drain well, top with sauce and serve.

Serves 4 to 5.

—Donna Jubb

Fresh Corn Pudding

Freezing fresh-from-the-cob corn is time consuming, but the taste in midwinter makes the work well worthwhile. Blanch the corn on the cob, immerse immediately in ice-cold water, then cut the kernels from the cob with a small, very sharp knife. Bag and freeze.

2½ cups corn
3 eggs, beaten
3 Tbsp. chopped onion
2 Tbsp. melted butter
¼ cup flour
2 cups milk
1 tsp. salt
⅛ tsp. pepper
1 Tbsp. sugar
¼ cup dry bread crumbs
¼ cup Parmesan cheese

Combine corn, eggs, onion, butter, flour, milk, salt, pepper and sugar, and spoon into greased casserole dish. Combine bread crumbs and cheese and sprinkle over corn mixture. Place casserole in pan containing 1 inch hot water and bake, uncovered, at 325° F for 1 hour or until firm.

Serves 6.

—*Terry Braatz*

Spicy Carrots

"This vegetable dish can be served hot or cold and is especially good with lamb. The carrots are aromatic and full of flavour."

2 lbs. carrots, scraped & cut into ½" slices
5 Tbsp. olive oil
½ tsp. salt
½ tsp. pepper
½ tsp. cinnamon
½ tsp. cumin seed
3 cloves garlic, finely chopped
½ tsp. thyme
1 bay leaf
1 Tbsp. lemon juice

Cook carrots until firm but tender — about 15 minutes. Drain, reserving ½ cup liquid, and keep warm. Meanwhile, in large frying pan combine oil and all other ingredients except reserved liquid and lemon juice. Simmer for 10 minutes, then add carrot liquid and carrots, turning carrots frequently to coat well. Cook for 3 to 5 minutes to heat thoroughly. Sprinkle with lemon juice, remove bay leaf and serve.

Serves 6.

—*Judith Almond-Best*

Corn Oysters

⅓ cup cornmeal
⅓ cup flour
2 tsp. salt
¼ tsp. pepper
3 egg yolks, beaten
½ cup melted butter or oil
2 cups corn
3 egg whites, beaten until stiff
oil for cooking

Combine cornmeal, flour, salt and pepper and mix well. Stir in egg yolks and butter or oil. Add corn, then gently fold in egg whites. Drop by spoonfuls into hot oil and fry until golden brown.

Serves 4.

—*Darlene Abraham*

Potato Pancakes (Latkes)

3 eggs, separated
4½ cups grated potatoes, well drained
6 Tbsp. grated onion
1-1½ tsp. salt
¼ tsp. pepper
3 Tbsp. matzo meal or potato flour or dry bread crumbs
oil

Beat together everything but egg whites and oil. Beat whites until stiff, then fold into potato mixture. Fry in about ½ inch hot oil, using a heaping tablespoonful of batter for each pancake. Turn when edges are golden brown. Keep pancakes hot until all are fried.

Makes 14 to 16 pancakes.

—*Lynne Roe*

Corn & Eggplant Casserole

If your garden provides you with an overabundance of eggplant in the fall, bake extras at 350° F. until soft, peel, purée and freeze in plastic bags. To use, thaw and squeeze out excess moisture.

1 eggplant, cubed
3 Tbsp. oil
3 Tbsp. chopped onion
½ cup diced green pepper
¼ cup diced sweet red pepper
¼ cup chopped mushrooms
1 Tbsp. chopped parsley
½ tsp. basil, thyme, oregano, marjoram, tarragon or savory
2 slices bread
¼ cup milk
1 cup cooked corn
1 cup grated Cheddar or Swiss cheese
salt & pepper
2 large eggs
2 Tbsp. bread crumbs
3 Tbsp. grated Cheddar or Swiss cheese
1 Tbsp. melted butter

Place eggplant in saucepan and cover with boiling water; cover and simmer for 15 minutes. Drain, squeezing out liquid gently, then mash.

Heat oil in skillet and sauté onion until clear. Add peppers, mushrooms, parsley, basil and herbs. Sauté for 1 minute, then blend into eggplant. Soak bread in milk for 5 minutes. Squeeze out excess milk, tear bread into small pieces and add to eggplant with corn and 1 cup cheese. Season with salt and pepper. Beat eggs until thick and fold into vegetable mixture.

Pour into greased casserole dish. Combine bread crumbs and 3 Tbsp. cheese and sprinkle over top. Drizzle with melted butter. Bake, uncovered, at 350° F for 1 hour.

Serves 4.

—Ingrid Birker

Greek Eggplant & Cheese

1 large eggplant, sliced ¼" thick
olive oil
1 onion, chopped
1 large clove garlic, minced
28-oz. can tomatoes, drained
2 Tbsp. parsley
⅛ tsp. cinnamon
⅛ tsp. pepper
1½ cups cottage cheese
¼ cup Parmesan cheese
1 egg
1 cup grated Cheddar or mozzarella cheese

Brown eggplant in olive oil and set aside. Sauté onion and garlic in more olive oil. Add tomatoes, parsley, cinnamon and pepper. Simmer, uncovered, for 5 minutes. Spread half the tomatoes in a greased 9" x 13" baking pan. Mix cottage and Parmesan cheeses together and beat in egg. Spread this over the layer of tomatoes.

Arrange eggplant slices, overlapping, on top of cheese, then spread remaining tomatoes over eggplant. Top with grated Cheddar or mozzarella. Cover tightly and bake at 375° F for 30 minutes. Uncover and bake for another 10 to 15 minutes. Let stand for 10 minutes before serving.

Serves 4 to 6.

—Susan O'Neill

Vinny's Eggplant Italiano

1 eggplant
6 eggs
1¼ cups Parmesan cheese
1¼ cups bread crumbs
1 lb. spinach
salt & pepper

Peel eggplant carefully from top to bottom, reserving the peels, and cube. Boil eggplant and peels for 15 to 20 minutes in water to cover.

Meanwhile, beat eggs, add cheese and bread crumbs and mix well. Cook spinach for 3 to 4 minutes, drain well and chop. Drain eggplant and peels. Mash eggplant, add spinach and mix well. Add to egg mixture and mix well. Season with salt and pepper.

Grease a 9" x 9" baking pan and spread peels shiny side down on bottom. Fill with eggplant mixture and bake, uncovered, at 350° F for 40 to 45 minutes.

Serves 10 to 12.

—Lisa Caggiula-Duke

Minted New Peas

"My grandmother was from England, and she kept a big, sprawling patch of mint tucked behind her beloved roses. Her peas with fresh mint was one of my favourite dishes as a child — to this day, the odour of a rose or of a sprig of mint reminds me of her garden."

½ cup chopped green onions
3 Tbsp. butter
2 cups fresh peas
1 Tbsp. finely chopped mint
1 tsp. sugar
1 tsp. lemon juice
¼ tsp. salt
¼ tsp. rosemary

Cook onions in butter until tender. Add remaining ingredients and 2 Tbsp. water. Cover and cook until peas are tender. Garnish with lemon twist and fresh mint leaves, if desired.

Serves 4.

—Alyson Service

South-of-the-Border Eggplant Casserole

1 large eggplant, sliced
¾ cup olive oil
28-oz. can tomato sauce
4-oz. can green chilies
½ cup sliced green onions
2 cloves garlic, crushed
½ tsp. cumin
1 cup pitted black olives
1½ cups grated Cheddar cheese
½ cup sour cream

Brush eggplant with oil and place on baking sheet. Bake at 450° F for 10 to 20 minutes, or until soft. Combine tomato sauce, chilies, onions, garlic, cumin and olives in saucepan and simmer for 10 minutes.

Grease shallow casserole dish and layer eggplant, sauce and cheese, ending with cheese. Bake, uncovered, at 350° F for 25 minutes. Serve with sour cream.

Serves 6 to 8.

—Sybil D. Hendricks

Stuffed Onions "Au Four"

"On Sundays, when my father took over cooking duties, he loved to create this special dish. In my European family, onions were always an integral part of a meal."

8 large onions
1 Tbsp. butter
5 Tbsp. dry rice
4 oz. ham, chopped
½ red pepper, chopped
4 oz. mushrooms, chopped
1 cup white wine
1 cup chicken stock
4 oz. mozzarella cheese, cubed
1 bundle chives, chopped
salt & pepper
1 cup heavy cream

Peel onions and cut off crowns. Cook in boiling salted water for 10 minutes, then rinse until cold. Hollow out onions, then chop removed centre parts. Melt butter and sauté chopped onions, rice, ham, red pepper and mushrooms. Add ½ cup wine and chicken stock, cover and simmer for 20 minutes, or until all liquid is absorbed. Add cheese, chives and salt and pepper.

Stuff hollowed onions with rice mixture, place in greased casserole dish and bake, uncovered, at 450° F for 10 minutes. Pour remaining ½ cup wine over onions and bake for 15 to 20 minutes more. When onions are crisp and light brown, add cream and heat through.

Serves 4 to 6.

—Inge Benda

Champ

"Champ is a very old and very popular Irish dish. I don't think a week passed that we didn't have this for our main course at dinnertime at least one day when I was a child. It's economical and was a favourite Friday dish for those who kept Lent. My father's book of Irish Country Recipes *says, 'In a farmhouse, 2 stones (28 lbs) or more of potatoes were peeled and boiled for dinner. Then the man of the house was summoned when all was ready, and while he pounded this enormous potful of potatoes with a sturdy wooden beetle, his wife added the potful of milk and nettles or scallions or chives or parsley, and he beetled it till it was smooth as butter, not a lump anywhere. Everyone got a large plateful, made a hole in the centre and into this put a large lump of butter. Then the champ was eaten from the outside with a spoon or fork, dipping it into the melting butter in the centre. All was washed down with new milk or freshly churned buttermilk.'"*

9 potatoes
6 green onions, chopped
1¼ cups milk
salt & pepper

Peel potatoes and boil in salted water until tender. Drain and mash. When free from lumps, beat in green onions and milk. Season with salt and pepper and beat until creamy. Champ must be kept very hot and be served on hot plates.

Serves 6 to 8.

—Hazel R. Baker

Baked Hash Browns

"This is an easy way to make delicious, crispy hash browns. I serve it for special breakfasts or brunch with eggs and broiled tomatoes. It is also good for supper with smoked pork chops."

4 slices bacon
4 potatoes, grated
1 onion, grated
⅓ cup bread crumbs
1 egg
⅛ tsp. pepper
⅛ tsp. salt

Cook bacon lightly, so that fat is cooked out but bacon is not yet crisp. Drain, reserving fat. Dice bacon. Put bacon fat into a 9" x 9" baking pan. Heat at 400° F.

Combine remaining ingredients, including bacon, and spread in the hot dish. Bake at 400° F, uncovered, for about 45 minutes.

Serves 2.

—Ruth Ellis Haworth

Indian Spiced New Potato Fry

3 Tbsp. oil
1 tsp. mustard seed
1 lb. small, even-sized new potatoes, boiled & peeled
1 tsp. chili powder
1½ tsp. coriander
¼ tsp. turmeric
½ tsp. salt
3 sprigs coriander, chopped
lemon juice

Heat oil in wok and add mustard seed and potatoes. Stir-fry over low heat until lightly browned. Sprinkle with chili powder, coriander, turmeric and salt and continue to stir-fry for 5 to 6 minutes. Remove from heat and sprinkle with coriander and lemon juice.

Serves 2 to 4.

—Lynn Andersen

Spinach Mould

This vegetable dish can be cooked ahead of time. It freezes well and holds its shape when sliced.

½ cup flour
1 tsp. salt
1 tsp. baking powder
3 eggs
1 cup milk
1 lb. mild Cheddar cheese, grated
2 pkgs. spinach, chopped
½ cup finely chopped onion

Combine flour, salt and baking powder and mix well. Beat eggs. Add flour mixture and milk to eggs, beating well. Add cheese, spinach and onion and mix well. Pour into greased, small tube pan and bake, uncovered, at 350° F for 35 minutes. Leave in pan to cool and set. Serve warm or cool.

Serves 4 to 6.

—*Evelyn M Grieve*

Italian Spinach Dumplings

1 pkg. spinach
4 tsp. salt
½ tsp. ground nutmeg
¼ tsp. pepper
1 egg, lightly beaten
½ cup ricotta cheese
6 Tbsp. flour
1 Tbsp. butter

Cook spinach and drain thoroughly, pressing with spoon to squeeze out all liquid. Chop finely or purée. Combine spinach, 1 tsp. salt, nutmeg, pepper, egg and ricotta cheese in large bowl. Gradually add flour, using enough to make a firm mixture. Shape into 1-inch balls. Place on a plate and chill for at least 30 minutes.

Combine 8 cups water, butter and remaining 3 tsp. salt in large saucepan. Bring to a boil. Drop balls gently into water, several at a time, and cook, uncovered, for 8 minutes, or until balls rise to top and are tender. Lift out with a slotted spoon and keep warm.

Serves 4.

—*Ingrid Birker*

Swiss Chard Rolls

There are many variations to this recipe. Add walnuts to the filling, or use other vegetables. Sprinkle the casserole with grated cheese and then bake.

1 cup dry brown rice
4 Tbsp. oil
2 stalks celery, chopped
12 large mushrooms, sliced
2 onions, chopped
12 large Swiss chard leaves
4 cups spicy tomato sauce

Cook rice and set aside until cool. Heat oil and sauté celery, mushrooms and onions. Mix with rice.

Fill leaves with vegetable mixture and roll up, folding in ends. Place in 9" x 13" baking pan and pour tomato sauce over. Bake, covered, at 350° F for 15 to 20 minutes.

Serves 12 as a side dish, 4 as a main dish.

—*Arlene Pervin*

Orange Squash

1-2 Tbsp. grated gingerroot
juice and grated rind of 2 oranges
1 Tbsp. coriander
¼ cup butter, softened
salt
3 small squash, halved & seeded

Combine ginger, orange rind, juice of 1 orange, coriander, butter and salt and mix well. Place in squash halves. Bake in covered casserole dish with juice of other orange at 350° F for 45 minutes.

Serves 6.

—*Wendy Vine*

Squash with Garlic, Goat Cheese & Walnuts

'This is a great fall recipe. It smells wonderful when baking. Use any kind of squash and while firm goat cheese is preferable, a creamy variety will do."

1 medium squash, peeled & halved
3 Tbsp. butter
2 cloves garlic, crushed
2 Tbsp. flour
1 cup light cream
½ cup whipping cream
salt & pepper
nutmeg
½ cup crumbled goat cheese
TOPPING:
2 Tbsp. Parmesan cheese
2 Tbsp. bread crumbs
1 Tbsp. butter, softened
¼ cup chopped walnuts

Seed squash and cut into ¾-inch cubes. Cook in boiling water until tender — 6 to 8 minutes — then drain and keep warm in a bowl.

Melt butter over medium heat, sauté garlic for 1 minute, then stir in flour and cook for 2 minutes. Remove from heat and gradually whisk in creams, salt and pepper and nutmeg. Return to heat and cook, stirring, until thickened. Remove from heat and stir in cheese until it melts. Pour over squash, toss, then turn into greased casserole dish.

Combine topping ingredients and sprinkle over squash. Bake, uncovered, at 425° F for 10 to 12 minutes or until brown and bubbling.

Serves 4 to 6.

—Terry Seed

Stuffed Pumpkin

This is an ideal holiday dish for non meat-eaters. Tasty and colourful, no one will miss the turkey.

1 pumpkin
6 Tbsp. oil
2 onions, chopped
2 cloves garlic, chopped
2 stalks celery, chopped
1 green pepper, chopped
1 lb. mushrooms, chopped
1 cup cooked, chopped spinach
4 cups cooked rice
salt & pepper
1 tsp. sage
¾ tsp. thyme
½ tsp. rosemary
½ tsp. basil
½ tsp. oregano

Wash pumpkin and slice off top as you would for a jack-o'-lantern. Scoop out seeds and rinse inside of pumpkin.

Heat oil and sauté onions, garlic, celery, green pepper and mushrooms for 10 minutes. Combine with remaining ingredients and place in pumpkin. Replace lid so it is not tightly sealed.

Bake at 350° F in baking dish with 1 inch water for approximately 1½ hours, or until pumpkin flesh is soft.

Serves 6.

Spinach with Peanut Sauce

Even children liked spinach cooked this way when we tested this recipe, so it must be good. See page 328 for directions to make coconut milk.

2 lbs. spinach
2 Tbsp. butter
1 large onion, chopped
crushed hot red peppers
1 Tbsp. whiskey
1 tsp. soy sauce
½ cup coconut milk
½ cup crushed unsalted peanuts

Cook spinach without water until limp. Cool, then squeeze to remove all moisture. Melt butter and sauté onion and pepper until onion is soft. Stir in remaining ingredients and cook, stirring, for 2 to 3 minutes. Add spinach, stir and heat through.

Serves 6.

—Ingrid Birker

Rutabaga Bharta

"Rutabagas are one of our favourite vegetables, so we always grow a lot. We are constantly looking for new things to do with them. This recipe came from a small East Indian store in Edmonton."

1 lb. rutabagas
2 Tbsp. oil
½-inch piece gingerroot, finely chopped
1 onion, finely chopped
2 tsp. aniseed or fennel
1 tsp. fenugreek
½ tsp. pepper
½ tsp. paprika or chili powder
½ tsp. garam masala
1 tsp. salt
1 tsp. brown sugar

Peel rutabagas and cut into small pieces. Boil in minimum water until soft, then mash. Heat oil and sauté ginger and onion. Add spices, mashed rutabagas, salt and sugar. Mix well and cook gently until excess moisture has been driven off.

Serves 6.

—*Barbara Prescott*

Zucchini Pancakes

Freeze shredded zucchini when you think you cannot possibly eat another one, and use through the winter for this recipe, soups, breads, et cetera. Just be sure to drain well before using. Small amounts of grated zucchini can be added to almost any soup, stew or casserole recipe without altering the flavour or texture. It is a good way to allow zucchini haters the benefit of eating this nutritious vegetable.

2 cups grated zucchini
2 eggs, beaten
¼ cup chopped onion
½ cup flour
½ tsp. baking powder
½ tsp. salt
savory
oil

Drain zucchini in strainer, pressing out as much liquid as possible, then combine with eggs and onion. Mix remaining ingredients, except for oil, in separate bowl. Stir dry ingredients into zucchini mixture, then drop by spoonsful into hot oil and fry until lightly brown.

Serves 4.

—*Darlene Abraham*

Very Different Turnips

A sure way to get turnip into turnip haters, this recipe takes the bitter taste out of turnips.

2 lbs. turnips, peeled & cubed
1 onion, minced
½ cup butter
1½ cups grated sharp Cheddar cheese
½ cup milk
salt & pepper

Cook turnips for 20 to 30 minutes, or until tender, then mash. Cook onion in 4 Tbsp. butter until soft. Add turnip, remaining butter, cheese and milk. Heat until cheese melts, then season with salt and pepper.

Serves 6.

—*Mary M. Loucks*

Turnips & Apples

1 large turnip
1 Tbsp. butter
2 apples
¼ cup brown sugar
½ tsp. cinnamon
CRUST:
⅓ cup flour
⅓ cup brown sugar
2 Tbsp. butter

Cook turnip, then mash with butter. Peel and thinly slice apples. Toss with sugar and cinnamon. In greased casserole dish, arrange turnip and apples in layers, beginning and ending with turnip.

Combine crust ingredients until texture is crumbly. Pat on top of turnip. Bake, uncovered, at 350° F for 45 minutes.

Serves 4.

—*Pat de la Ronde*

Stuffed Sunburst Squash

8-10 'Sunburst' squash
3 eggs, beaten
½ cup Parmesan cheese
½ cup ricotta cheese
½ cup grated mozzarella
   cheese
4 Tbsp. chopped basil
½ lb. Italian sausage,
   browned & crumbled

Parboil whole squash for 8 minutes. Drain, then cut off tops of squash and scoop out seeds. Combine remaining ingredients and mix well. Stuff into squash and replace tops. Place in shallow pan with ½ inch water and bake, uncovered, at 350° F for 30 minutes, or until filling is set.

Serves 4 to 5.

—Laurie D. Glaspey

Sweet Potatoes à l'Orange

4 sweet potatoes
2 cups orange juice
2 oranges, peeled & sliced,
   rind reserved
1 tsp. cinnamon
2 tsp. cornstarch

Peel sweet potatoes, cut into quarters and place in greased casserole dish.

In saucepan, heat orange juice, rind from oranges, cinnamon and cornstarch until thick, stirring often. Pour sauce over potatoes and top with orange slices. Bake, covered, at 350° F for 45 minutes to 1 hour.

Serves 4 to 6.

—Beth Armstrong-Bewick

Zucchini Enchiladas

The Vermont staff gave these enchiladas a resounding "yes" when they tasted them — a wonderful way to use up zucchini. They were definitely one of the most popular test lunches and were surprisingly easy to make. The ambitious cook could make his or her own tortillas, although there are many good commercial varieties available — the frozen ones are generally fresher-tasting than those in cans. Increase the chilies to suit personal taste buds — the amount listed gives a delicate hot taste.

1 zucchini, grated
1 onion, chopped
2 canned green chilies,
   drained & chopped
12 corn tortillas
8 oz. sour cream
½ lb. Monterey Jack cheese,
   grated
2 cups tomato sauce

Combine zucchini, onion and chilies and mix well. Heat tortillas a minute on each side to soften in hot, dry skillet. Keep warm.

To assemble, spread each tortilla with sour cream. Place 2 to 3 Tbsp. zucchini mixture in middle, 2 Tbsp. cheese on this and roll up. Place seam side down in greased 9" x 9" casserole dish. Pour tomato sauce over the enchiladas and top with remaining cheese. Bake, uncovered, at 350° F for 30 minutes.

Serves 4.

—Leslie Pierpont

Zucchini Cheese Casserole

"Very quick and easy, this is a tasty way to subdue the always overpopulated zucchini patch."

4 medium zucchini, sliced
½ cup chopped onion
2 Tbsp. oil
1 lb. cottage cheese
1 tsp. basil
⅓ cup Parmesan cheese

Sauté zucchini and onion in oil. Whip cottage cheese with basil in blender. Place alternating layers of zucchini and cheese in 1½-quart casserole dish; top with Parmesan cheese. Bake, uncovered, at 350° F for 25 to 30 minutes.

Serves 6.

—Sandra K. Bennett

Tomato Curry

This curry can also be made with half ripe and half unripe tomatoes, although the result will not be as smooth. Serve with rice, noodles, meatloaf, fish or hard-cooked eggs.

2 Tbsp. oil
2 onions, chopped
1 Tbsp. chopped coriander
1 tsp. toasted cumin seed
2 cloves garlic, crushed
2 lbs. ripe tomatoes, peeled
　& chopped
1 Tbsp. brown sugar
salt

Heat oil and sauté onions until golden. Add coriander and cook, stirring, for 1 minute, then add remaining ingredients. Cook for 30 minutes over medium heat.

Serves 6 as a sauce.

—Ethel Hunter

Herbed Tomatoes

4 ripe tomatoes
salt
¼ cup butter
⅛ tsp. pepper
1 tsp. brown sugar
1 Tbsp. lemon juice
½ cup diced celery
3 Tbsp. finely chopped
　chives or green onion
3 Tbsp. chopped parsley
½ tsp. oregano

Core tomatoes and sprinkle with salt. Melt butter in frying pan, add pepper and brown sugar, then place tomatoes in pan, cored side down. Cover and simmer slowly for 5 minutes. Turn tomatoes over and spoon butter mixture into hollow. Add remaining ingredients to pan and sauté for 2 minutes. Cover and simmer until tomatoes are just tender — 8 minutes. Spoon mixture into tomatoes and lift carefully from pan. Pour any remaining pan liquids over tomatoes and serve.

Serves 4.

—Lynn Tobin

Zucchini Custard

"Light and fluffy—almost like a soufflé," raved our Vermont testers.

2 lbs. zucchini, coarsely
　grated
1 onion, minced
1 clove garlic, crushed
3 Tbsp. olive oil
⅓ cup minced parsley
⅛ tsp. thyme
⅛ tsp. rosemary
1 tsp. salt
⅛ tsp. pepper
5 eggs
½ cup flour
¾ cup Parmesan cheese

Stir-fry zucchini, onion and garlic in oil in large, heavy skillet over medium heat for 10 to 12 minutes, or until zucchini is tender. Mix in parsley, thyme, rosemary, salt and pepper. Beat eggs until frothy, then mix in flour and Parmesan cheese. Stir zucchini mixture into eggs, spoon into greased 1½-quart casserole dish, and bake, uncovered, at 300° F for 1 to 1¼ hours, or until knife inserted in centre comes out clean.

Serves 4 to 6.

—Doreen Deacur

Spiced Cauliflower & Potatoes

1 cauliflower
6 potatoes, peeled
5 Tbsp. oil
1 tsp. fennel seed
1 tsp. cumin seed
¼ tsp. mustard seed
¼ tsp. fenugreek
1 dried red chili pepper,
  crushed
1 tsp. salt
1 tsp. cumin
1 tsp. coriander
2 tsp. turmeric pepper
1 tsp. garam masala

Break cauliflower into florets and dice potatoes. Heat oil in large heavy skillet until oil is smoking. Add fennel seed, cumin seed, mustard seed and fenugreek and cook, shaking skillet, until seeds begin to pop. Add chili pepper, then stir in cauliflower and potatoes.

Reduce heat to medium and add salt, cumin, coriander, turmeric and pepper. Sauté for 10 minutes, stirring and adding oil if needed. Stir in garam masala and 3 Tbsp. water. Cook, covered, over low heat for 15 minutes. Stir. Add water (just a bit) if needed and cook for 20 minutes more, or until vegetables are tender.

Serves 6.

—Cynthia R. Topliss

Tofu with Mustard & Tamari Sauce

Beautiful to look at and full of flavour, this is a good dish for people unfamiliar with tofu.

⅓ cup peanut oil
¼-½ cup dark mustard
¼ cup tamari
1 lb. firm tofu, rinsed &
  drained
4 cups chopped vegetables
  (peppers, bok choy,
  mushrooms, snow peas)
3 cups cooked brown rice,
  kept warm

Heat oil, stir in mustard and tamari and mix well. Quarter tofu and carefully place in sauce. Cook, turning frequently, for 10 to 15 minutes. Cover and set aside.

Meanwhile, steam vegetables until crispy-tender. Place rice on serving platter, surround with vegetables and top with tofu and sauce.

—Janice Baldrate & Anne Kress

Tofu Ratatouille

This makes a tasty side dish, or it can be served over pasta as the main meal.

3 cloves garlic, crushed
⅓ cup olive oil
1 onion, chopped
1½ green peppers, chopped
2 zucchini, sliced
1 eggplant, cubed
1 cup sliced mushrooms
1 block tofu
1 tsp. basil
1 tsp. oregano
1 tsp. salt
1½ cups tomato juice

Sauté garlic in oil. Add onion, peppers, zucchini, eggplant and mushrooms, one vegetable at a time, and stir after each addition. Sauté for 10 minutes, then add tofu and sauté for 5 minutes more. Add basil, oregano, salt and tomato juice, and simmer for 10 minutes.

Serves 4.

—Shiela Alexandrovich

Russian Vegetable Pie

Pastry for double-crust
   9-inch pie
1 onion, chopped
3 cups grated cabbage
3 Tbsp. butter
⅛ tsp. basil
⅛ tsp. marjoram
⅛ tsp. tarragon
salt & pepper
⅛ tsp. dill
½ lb. mushrooms, sliced
4 oz. cream cheese, softened
4-5 hard-cooked eggs

Line pie plate with pastry. Sauté onion and cabbage in 2 Tbsp. butter. Add basil, marjoram, tarragon, salt and pepper and dill and cook until onion and cabbage are soft. Set aside.

Melt remaining 1 Tbsp. butter and sauté mushrooms. Spread cream cheese on pastry, then slice eggs over this. Add vegetable mixture and mushrooms and top with pie crust. Bake at 400° F for 15 minutes; reduce heat to 350° F and cook for 20 to 25 minutes more.

Serves 4 to 6.

—Lyette Sausoucy

Calzone

Calzone is basically a pizza turnover. It can be made as one large turnover or as individual turnovers. The filling possibilities are limited only by the cook's imagination — try pesto, chicken cacciatore, seafood, a meat spaghetti sauce, ricotta cheese and spinach and so on. For this version, we suggest a combination of onion, mushrooms, olives and zucchini. Calzone can also be eaten cold, without the sauce, as picnic fare.

SAUCE:
8-oz. can tomato sauce
6½-oz. can tomato paste
¼ cup minced onion
3 cloves garlic, crushed
¼ tsp. pepper
¼ tsp. oregano
¼ tsp. basil
10 fennel seeds, crushed
CRUST:
½ tsp. sugar
½ tsp. pepper
½ tsp. parsley
1½ tsp. yeast
1 egg, beaten
2-3 cups flour
FILLING:
4 cups partially cooked
   vegetables
1 tsp. parsley
1 tsp. basil
1 tsp. oregano
1 cup grated mozzarella
   cheese
1 egg, beaten

Combine sauce ingredients in saucepan and simmer for 45 minutes.

For crust: Mix ⅔ cup hot water with sugar, pepper and parsley. Add yeast and beaten egg. Stir in flour to make a soft dough and set in warm place to rise.

Toss vegetables in lightly oiled skillet with parsley, basil and oregano for 10 minutes. Stir in cheese.

Shape dough into oval the thickness of pizza crust. Lay half on and half off a greased cookie sheet. Mix filling ingredients together and arrange on half of dough that is on cookie sheet. Trickle ¼ cup sauce over filling. Fold dough over and pinch edges closed. Bake calzone at 350° F for 3 minutes. Remove from oven and glaze with beaten egg. Cut steam vents and bake for 30 minutes, then broil until golden. Serve with sauce.

Serves 4 to 6.

—E. K. Molitor

Vegetables Parmigiana

2 Tbsp. oil
1 Tbsp. butter
1 lb. eggplant, peeled &
   sliced ½" thick
1 lb. zucchini, sliced ½"
   thick
1 onion, halved & sliced
1 tsp. salt
1 tsp. oregano
½ tsp. pepper
1½ cups tomato sauce
2 cloves garlic, crushed
½ lb. mozzarella cheese,
   sliced
2 Tbsp. Parmesan cheese

Heat oil and butter and sauté eggplant, zucchini and onion for 10 minutes. Stir in salt, oregano and pepper, then spoon into greased 2-quart baking dish. Mix tomato sauce with garlic and pour over vegetables. Tuck mozzarella cheese slices into vegetables so half of each slice is on surface. Sprinkle with Parmesan cheese and bake, uncovered, at 375° F for 25 minutes.

Serves 4.

—Nancy R. Franklin

Greens with Deep-Fried Chèvre

"Absolutely fantastic! This is easy to make and it tastes delicious. If you prefer a less robust cheese, use brie," says our Camden East tester.

½ lb. chèvre
½ cup fine dry bread crumbs
salt & pepper
1 egg
½ head radicchio
1 head Belgian endive
1 head Boston lettuce
¼ cup olive oil
⅛ cup lemon juice
½ tsp. basil
½ tsp. thyme
¼ tsp. pepper
1 clove garlic, crushed
1 tsp. dry mustard
oil for cooking

Form cheese into 4 flattened balls. Mix bread crumbs with salt and pepper in flat bowl. Beat egg in another bowl. Dip cheese rounds in bread crumbs, then egg, then crumbs again, coating well. Refrigerate for several hours.

Wash and dry greens and assemble on 4 plates, keeping leaves whole. Combine remaining ingredients, except cooking oil, for dressing. Heat ½ inch of oil in skillet until hot, then fry each cheese round until golden brown, turning frequently to prevent burning. Dress salad, top with cheese rounds and serve.

Serves 4.

—*Lynn Tobin*

Spinach, Watercress & Mushroom Salad

"My aunt and uncle operate a restaurant in Pennsylvania Dutch country. They serve this salad there — it has been in our family for three generations."

2 bunches spinach, washed & torn
1 bunch watercress, washed & torn
½ lb. mushrooms, sliced
½ lb. lean bacon, diced
2 eggs
1 Tbsp. sugar
6 Tbsp. dill vinegar
2 Tbsp. chopped dill

Toss spinach and watercress with mushrooms. Fry bacon until crisp. Whip eggs lightly and stir in sugar, vinegar and dill. Pour off all but 2 Tbsp. bacon drippings, then pour egg mixture into skillet. Cook, stirring, until it thickens. Pour over greens and serve warm.

Serves 4 to 6.

—*Sandy Lance*

Green Salad with Mustard Vinaigrette

1 head Romaine lettuce
1 head Boston lettuce
2 heads endive
DRESSING:
¼ cup olive oil
¼ cup cider vinegar
¾ tsp. marjoram
2 tsp. minced green onion
1 clove garlic, minced
1 tsp. snipped parsley
2 tsp. Dijon mustard
salt & pepper

Tear up lettuces and slice endive thinly. Toss together and chill.

Place oil, vinegar, marjoram, green onion, garlic, parsley and mustard in jar with lid and shake well to mix. Season with salt and pepper. Toss greens with dressing just before serving.

Serves 12.

—*Pam Collacott*

Spinach Gouda Salad

This was submitted to us with the following reprimand: "I sent this recipe to you for the second edition of your cookbook. It must have gone astray or you must have been suffering from sensory overload when you tasted it, because it's one of the tastiest salads around. I'm giving you one more chance!" It did, indeed, go astray last time. Now, tested and tasted, we agree with the contributor.

DRESSING:
⅓ cup oil
1 Tbsp. cider vinegar
1 clove garlic, minced
½ tsp. salt
¼ tsp. pepper
1 tsp. dill weed
10 oz. spinach, washed & torn
8-10 mushrooms, sliced
6 pieces bacon, chopped & cooked until crisp
¼ cup chopped green onion
1 cup grated Gouda cheese

Combine dressing ingredients and mix well. Toss remaining ingredients in a bowl with dressing.

Serves 6 to 8.

—*Colleen Suche*

Spinach Salad with Tangy Creamy Dressing

This recipe was a salad category winner in a local cooking contest. Inspired by the contributor's love of quiche, it combines ingredients available year-round.

6 cups spinach
4 slices bacon, chopped & cooked until crisp
1 hard-cooked egg, chopped
1 small red onion, sliced
½ cup sliced mushrooms
1 orange, peeled, seeded & chopped
⅔ cup grated Swiss cheese
DRESSING:
½ cup light cream
4 Tbsp. vinegar
1 tsp. dry mustard
1 Tbsp. chopped parsley
½ tsp. sugar (optional)
salt & pepper

Wash spinach and pat dry. Tear into bite-sized pieces and toss with remaining salad ingredients. Shake all dressing ingredients together. Toss lightly with salad.

Serves 6 to 8.

—*Sandy Robertson*

Fantastic Spinach Salad

1 lb. spinach, washed & torn
½ cup diced, cooked bacon
1 cup sliced green onions
½ lb. mushrooms, sliced
2 cloves garlic, crushed
1½ tsp. salt
¼ cup lemon juice
½ cup olive oil
¼ tsp. pepper
¼ tsp. dry mustard
¼ tsp. Tabasco sauce
2 egg yolks

Mix spinach with bacon, onions and mushrooms. Combine remaining ingredients and shake in jar to make a creamy dressing. Toss with salad and serve.

Serves 6 to 8.

—*Trudy McCallum*

Spinach Salad with Sour Cream Dressing

1 pkg. fresh spinach, washed & dried
1 small onion, sliced into thin rings
6 slices bacon, cooked crisp & crumbled
1 cup sliced mushrooms
2 eggs, hard-cooked & chopped
1 cup sour cream
2 Tbsp. lemon juice
1 Tbsp. grated onion
white pepper
1 tsp. Worcestershire sauce
¼ tsp. salt
1 tsp. sugar

Tear spinach and toss with onion, bacon, mushrooms and eggs. Combine remaining ingredients, blend well and chill for 30 minutes. Toss with salad.

Serves 4 to 6.

—*Donna Parker*

Kale Salad

"This recipe makes use of a vegetable many people overlook, yet kale is available in most markets and can be grown easily. It lasts long into the winter, even under the snow, and in spring it sprouts new green top growth for early salads."

4 slices bacon, chopped
⅓ cup sugar
½ tsp. salt
1 Tbsp. cornstarch
1 egg, beaten
¼ cup cider vinegar
1 head kale
1 onion, chopped
3 hard-cooked eggs, chopped
pepper

Fry bacon slowly until crisp. Mix together sugar, salt and cornstarch, then add egg, vinegar and 1 cup water and stir until smooth. Remove all but 1 to 2 Tbsp. drippings from pan, then stir liquid ingredients into pan and cook over medium heat, stirring, until thickened. Cool slightly.

Wash kale, remove heavy centre rib and tear leaves into bite-sized pieces. Place in large bowl, add onion, eggs and pepper and toss with dressing. Serve warm or chilled.

Serves 6.

—Harriet Felguieras

Celeriac, Pepper & Chicken Salad

Celeriac, a turnip-rooted celery, absorbs a lot of liquid. If more than indicated is required, use some of the water in which the celeriac was cooked. Strain well before using, however, as celeriac has a lot of soil in it.

¼ cup raisins
1 celeriac
2 chicken breasts, cooked & chopped
½ red pepper, diced
½ green pepper, diced
2 Tbsp. apple cider vinegar
2 Tbsp. olive oil
chopped parsley
salt & pepper

Soak raisins in ½ cup water for 2 hours. Drain and reserve liquid. Cook celeriac (in skin) in water until tender. Save cooking liquid. Peel and dice celeriac.

Toss all ingredients, including raisin liquid, adding cooking liquid if needed.

Serves 4.

—Gabriele Klein

Carrot Sprout Salad

"We live on a trapline for most of the year, quite a distance from town, so we can only take in vegetables that store well in the root cellar, such as carrots and potatoes. The special appeal of this salad to us is that we can have fresh salad all year round."

2 cups grated carrots
2 cups alfalfa sprouts
⅓ cup raisins
2 Tbsp. toasted sunflower seeds
½ tsp. salt
pepper
1 clove garlic, crushed
1 Tbsp. vinegar
1 Tbsp. oil

Combine carrots, sprouts, raisins and sunflower seeds. Combine salt, pepper, garlic, vinegar and oil and pour over salad. Mix well and serve immediately.

Serves 4.

—Beth Hunt

Snow Pea & Red Pepper Salad

"This is a colourful salad, suitable for any festive occasion, but a great favourite with our family any time. Quick and easy to make too."

1½ lbs. snow peas
1 lb. mushrooms
2 sweet red peppers
2 cloves garlic, finely
  chopped
3 Tbsp. white wine vinegar
3 Tbsp. lemon juice
1 Tbsp. sugar
1 tsp. salt
pepper
1 cup oil
⅓ cup toasted sesame seeds

Remove tops and strings from snow peas. Blanch for 1 minute in large pot of boiling water. Drain immediately and plunge into iced water to chill quickly. Drain again and dry on paper towels. Slice mushrooms. Cut peppers into ½-inch dice. Using a food processor or bowl with a whisk, combine garlic, vinegar, lemon juice, sugar, salt and pepper. While beating, slowly add oil to make a smooth dressing. In salad bowl, toss vegetables together; just before serving, add dressing and sesame seeds and toss well.

Serves 12.

—*Margaret Brister*

Luxembourg Salad Dressing

4 cloves garlic, minced
⅓ cup vinegar
2 Tbsp. lemon juice
1½ Tbsp. Dijon mustard
1½ Tbsp. mixed salad herbs
  (parsley, chives, tarragon,
  chervil)
1 cup olive oil
salt & pepper

Whisk garlic, vinegar, lemon juice and mustard together. Whisk in herbs, then gradually whisk in oil. Season with salt and pepper.

Makes about 1½ cups.

—*Kristine Mattila*

Sweet & Sour Onion Salad Dressing

⅓ cup cider vinegar
1 tsp. dry mustard
½ tsp. salt
1 tsp. celery seed
1 Tbsp. sugar
1 onion, chopped
1 cup oil

In blender, mix together vinegar, mustard, salt, celery seed and sugar. Add onion, then add oil in steady trickle.

Makes 2 cups.

—*Linda Fritz*

Ginger Salad Dressing

½ cup coarsely chopped
  onion
¼ cup coarsely chopped
  carrot
2 tsp. coarsely chopped
  celery
1½ tsp. minced gingerroot
1¼ cups oil
¾ cup soy sauce
½ cup vinegar
¼ cup lemon juice
1½ tsp. tomato paste
salt & pepper
Tabasco sauce

Purée onion, carrot, celery and ginger in blender or food processor. Add remaining ingredients.

Makes 2 cups.

—*Mary Hewson*

Creamy Caesar Salad Dressing

It is important to use freshly grated Parmesan cheese in this dressing to fully appreciate its flavour.

3 oz. olive oil
1 large clove garlic, minced
1 Tbsp. wine vinegar
½ tsp. salt
½ tsp. pepper
8 drops Worcestershire sauce
3 drops Tabasco sauce
½ tsp. anchovy paste
1 egg
¼ cup Parmesan cheese

Place all ingredients except egg and Parmesan cheese in blender. Cook egg in boiling water for 1 minute, add to blender and blend for 1 minute at high speed. Add Parmesan cheese and blend again.

—*Colleen Suche*

Chinese Beef and Broccoli in Oyster Sauce, page 347

Manicotti, page 418

Fresh Raspberry Pie, page 530; Fresh Blueberry Tart, page 532; Pecan Pie, page 534

Raspberry Bombe, page 524

Blueberry Muffins, page 442; Poppy Seed Muffins, page 442

Raspberry Bars, page 467; Chocolate Chip Cookies, page 460; Oatmeal Chocolate Chip Cookies, page 460

Hot Cranberry Wine Cup, page 568

Assorted Preserves, pages 509–520

J.B.'s Coleslaw

The pineapple juice and sour cream give this coleslaw a light creamy taste.

¼ cup sour cream
¼ cup mayonnaise
¼ cup pineapple juice
1 Tbsp. lemon juice
1 Tbsp. sugar
½ tsp. salt
⅛ tsp. pepper
5 cups shredded cabbage
1 apple, diced
1 stalk celery, diced

Combine sour cream, mayonnaise, pineapple and lemon juices, sugar, salt and pepper and mix well. Toss together cabbage, apple and celery and then toss with dressing.

Serves 6 to 8.

—*June Plamondon*

Tomato Green Pepper Salad

1 large onion, finely chopped
2-3 green peppers, thinly sliced
½ tsp. basil pepper
3 Tbsp. red wine vinegar
3-4 Tbsp. olive oil
4-5 tomatoes, sliced

Toss together onion and peppers. Combine basil, pepper, vinegar and oil and pour over onion and peppers. Toss, then chill for 1 to 2 hours. Stir in tomatoes just before serving.

Serves 6.

—*Trudi Keillor*

Vietnamese Coleslaw

"Because of the quantity of garlic, this salad is not for the faint of heart, but it's the garlic that makes it authentic." Dress this salad only when you are ready to serve — it does not keep well once dressed.

1 head Napa cabbage
3 large carrots, peeled & grated
1 large red onion, finely chopped
1 chicken, cooked, meat removed from bone & chopped
1 cup rice wine vinegar
⅓ cup fish sauce
½-1 tsp. pepper
10 cloves garlic, minced
1 tsp. sugar
½ cup peanuts

Slice cabbage finely (do not grate). Mix with carrots, onion and chicken. Chill. Meanwhile, prepare dressing. Combine vinegar, fish sauce, pepper, garlic and sugar and mix well. Toss with salad when ready to serve. Garnish with peanuts.

Serves 6.

—*Donna J. Torres*

Green Coleslaw

"Wonderful colour, light and tasty—one of the best coleslaws I've tasted," says our Vermont tester.

12 cups slivered cabbage
1 large green pepper, chopped
1 onion, chopped
1 cup sugar
1 cup vinegar
¾ cup oil
1 Tbsp. dry mustard
1 Tbsp. celery seed
1 Tbsp. salt

Toss together cabbage, pepper and onion. Sprinkle with sugar and toss. Combine remaining ingredients in saucepan and bring to a boil. Pour over slaw and toss. Chill.

Makes 14 cups.

—*Shirley Morrish*

Onion & Olive Salad

Serve this as a spicy side dish in small quantities.

1 bunch green onions,
  coarsely chopped
1 Spanish onion, sliced
  paper-thin
½ cup wine vinegar
1 tsp. salt
1 cup sliced green olives
  with pimiento
1½ cups sliced black olives
1 clove garlic, minced
1 cup olive oil
pepper

Place onions in bowl, pour vinegar over, sprinkle with salt and place in refrigerator for at least 1 hour. Add olives and garlic, then toss with olive oil and grind black pepper over to taste. Allow to marinate for at least ½ hour.

Serves 8.

—*Ingrid Birker*

Danish Vegetable Salad

The dressing for this salad would also work well on any leftover, lightly cooked vegetable.

½ lb. asparagus, sliced into
  ½" lengths & cooked
2 carrots, pared, sliced ¼"
  thick & cooked
1 cup snow peas, snapped in
  half & steamed
10-12 mushrooms, quartered
  & steamed
2 Tbsp. capers
3 Tbsp. mayonnaise
3 Tbsp. sour cream
2 tsp. lemon juice
½ tsp. Dijon mustard
salt & pepper
2 cups halved cherry
  tomatoes

Toss vegetables, except tomatoes, together. Mix remaining ingredients, except tomatoes, for dressing. Pour over vegetables and stir gently to coat evenly. Garnish with tomatoes and chill for 2 to 4 hours.

Serves 6 to 8.

—*Lynne Roe*

Mushroom Cheese Salad

1 small red onion, thinly
  sliced
1 lb. fresh mushrooms,
  sliced
⅓ cup olive oil
¼ cup red wine vinegar
½ tsp. salt
½ tsp. sugar
½ tsp. chervil
tarragon
cayenne
¼ lb. sharp Cheddar cheese,
  cubed
½ cup watercress leaves &
  top sprigs
lettuce

Separate onion into rings. Toss with mushrooms in medium bowl. Shake oil, vinegar, salt, sugar, chervil, tarragon and cayenne together in jar. Pour over mushroom mixture and toss to blend. Cover and chill for several hours.

Add cheese cubes and watercress to salad at serving time and toss to blend. Serve on lettuce.

Serves 6.

—*Mary Hewson*

Greek Cucumber Yogurt Salad

For those not troubled by the digestive difficulties often associated with North American cucumbers, substitute them for a fresher, less expensive salad.

1 large English cucumber
¼ cup plain yogurt
1 green onion, sliced
1 large clove garlic, minced
½ tsp. dried mint
1½ tsp. cider vinegar
¼ tsp. salt
white pepper

Slice cucumber as thinly as possible. Mix together remaining ingredients and add cucumber slices. Refrigerate for at least 1 hour before serving.

Serves 2 to 4.

—*Susan O'Neill*

Curried Apple, Beet & Cabbage Salad

This salad has a tangy sweet and sour flavour with a mild, pleasant curry taste.

4 cups shredded red cabbage
2 cups julienned cooked beets
3 large green apples, grated
⅔ cup mayonnaise
1 tsp. Dijon mustard
1 tsp. curry
salt & pepper
¼ cup chopped parsley

Toss cabbage, beets and apples in large bowl. Combine mayonnaise, mustard and curry and toss with salad. Add salt and pepper to taste. Chill for 1 hour. Garnish with parsley.

Serves 8 to 10.

—*Ingrid Birker*

Green Bean & Artichoke Salad

Prepare the dressing and keep at room temperature; cook the beans ahead of time, so they are chilled when it is time to assemble the salad. Serve immediately once it is assembled.

¾ cup light olive oil
⅓ cup red wine vinegar
3 Tbsp. chopped chives
½ tsp. salt
2 tsp. basil
2 tsp. oregano
¾ tsp. dry mustard
¾ tsp. pepper
¼ tsp. cayenne
¼ cup chopped parsley
3 cups sliced green beans, cooked
2 cups quartered artichoke hearts
1 lb. mushrooms, sliced
2 green peppers, chopped
4 stalks celery, sliced
4 green onions, chopped

Combine oil, vinegar, chives, salt, basil, oregano, mustard, pepper, cayenne and parsley. Whisk well and set aside. Toss vegetables with dressing and serve.

Serves 10 to 12.

—*Judith Christensen*

Zesty Rutabaga Salad

1 rutabaga, thinly sliced
3 carrots, cut into ¼" slices
½ small head cauliflower, broken into florets
1 small green pepper, cut into strips
1 tsp. salt
DRESSING:
½ cup vinegar
¼ cup oil
⅓ cup sugar
¼ tsp. curry powder
1 tsp. salt
¼ tsp. pepper

Cut rutabaga slices in wedges. Drop all vegetables into boiling salted water in large saucepan. Boil, uncovered, for 5 minutes or until crispy-tender. Drain. Chill in cold water, then drain again. In screw-top jar, combine dressing ingredients. Cover and shake. Pour over vegetables and toss lightly. Refrigerate, covered, for several hours or overnight, tossing occasionally.

Serves 6.

—*Donna Jubb*

Antipasto Salad

10 leaves Romaine lettuce
8 slices Genoa salami,
    julienned
1 carrot, shredded
1 Tbsp. chopped capers
2 Tbsp. chopped pitted black
    olives
1 red onion, sliced in rings
1 stalk celery, sliced
½ green pepper, julienned
1 Tbsp. Romano cheese
salt & pepper
1 Tbsp. olive oil
1 Tbsp. red wine vinegar

Tear lettuce into bite-sized
pieces. Toss with salami, carrot,
capers, olives, onion, celery and
green pepper. Sprinkle with
cheese and salt and pepper.
Drizzle oil, then vinegar over all
and toss lightly.

Serves 4.

—Sandy Robertson

Summer Bean Salad

*A well-rounded and appealing
salad—the beans complement
each other in colour and flavour
without compromising texture.*

2 cups cooked sliced green
    beans
2 cups cooked sliced wax
    beans
2 cups cooked kidney beans
2 cups cooked chickpeas
½ red onion, chopped
2 Tbsp. chopped parsley
1 stalk celery, chopped
1 cup quartered artichoke
    hearts
6 Tbsp. peanut oil
3 Tbsp. cider vinegar
1 clove garlic, minced
salt & pepper

Combine beans, chickpeas,
onion, parsley, celery and
artichoke hearts in large bowl.
Combine remaining ingredients
and toss with salad. Chill for at
least 2 hours to blend flavours.

Serves 6 to 8.

—Lynne Roe

Lima Bean & Tuna Salad

*"This recipe was given to me by
a close friend in 1976. She
knew that I did not like lima
beans and assured me that I
would like this recipe. To my
surprise, she was right."*

1 lb. dry baby lima beans
2 Tbsp. olive oil
2 7-oz. cans tuna
½ green pepper, chopped
1 onion, minced
2 cups diced celery
½ tsp. salt
⅛ tsp. pepper
2 Tbsp. lemon juice
2 Tbsp. chopped parsley
mayonnaise

Cover washed beans with
water, bring to a boil and boil for
2 minutes. Cover and let stand
for 1 hour, then cook until
tender. Drain and cool.

Add remaining ingredients and
toss. Chill well.

Serves 8.

—Judy Sheppard-Segal

Mom's Potato Salad

"Our family of 11 children grew up on this. With so many people, it was easiest to have buffet-style meals. This dish is easy to enlarge."

6 potatoes, cooked & diced
5 hard-cooked eggs, diced
1 cup chopped parsley
2 stalks celery, chopped
½ cup chopped chives
½ cup chopped radishes
¼ cup chopped red onion
DRESSING:
¼ cup sugar
¼ cup flour
2 tsp. salt
1½ tsp. dry mustard
¾-1 tsp. cayenne
4 egg yolks, lightly beaten
1½ cups milk
½ cup vinegar
1 Tbsp. butter

To make dressing: In top of double boiler, mix sugar, flour, salt, mustard and cayenne. Stir in yolks and milk and cook, stirring, until thickened. Add vinegar and butter, mix well, then cool. Combine remaining ingredients and toss with cooled dressing. Chill.

Serves 8 to 10.

—Penny Tognet

Pennsylvania German Potato Salad

This piquant sweet and sour dressing makes a tasty change from more common mayonnaise- based dressings for potato salad.

6 large potatoes, cooked & diced
1 cup chopped celery
½ cup minced onion
3 hardcooked eggs, diced
chopped chives
DRESSING:
½ cup sugar
1 Tbsp. flour
1 tsp. Dijon mustard
1 Tbsp. salt
2 eggs, lightly beaten
⅔ cup vinegar

To make dressing: In top of double boiler, mix sugar, flour, mustard and salt. Add eggs, vinegar and 2 Tbsp. water and cook, stirring, over boiling water until thickened. Combine potatoes, celery, onion and eggs and toss with dressing. Garnish liberally with chives.

Serves 4 to 6.

—Janet Jokinen

Green Bean & Potato Salad

4 large russet potatoes
¾ lb. green beans, snapped in half
⅓ cup olive oil
¼ cup cider vinegar
1 clove garlic, crushed
½ tsp. basil
¼ tsp. thyme
salt & pepper
½ tsp. dry mustard
⅓ cup Parmesan cheese

Scrub and dice potatoes. Cook in boiling water. Steam green beans until bright green and crispy-tender. Combine potatoes and beans. Mix together oil, vinegar, garlic, basil, thyme, salt and pepper and mustard. Toss with vegetables. Sprinkle with cheese. Serve warm or at room temperature.

Serves 4 to 6.

—Nancy R. Franklin

Marinated Mushrooms

"Pungent mushrooms, great garlic flavour and nice texture. This makes a wonderful addition to a relish or pickle platter." If small button mushrooms are available, they can be left whole.

1½ lbs. mushrooms, halved
¼ onion, chopped
2 cloves garlic, crushed
2 sprigs parsley
½ cup olive oil
¼ cup dry white wine
¼ cup cider vinegar
1 Tbsp. lemon juice
½ tsp. salt
pepper

Boil mushrooms for 5 minutes. Meanwhile, combine remaining ingredients in large jar. Add drained mushrooms and marinate for 24 hours. Mushrooms will keep for 1 week.

—*Mary Rogers*

Town Hall Supper Salad

"A much-requested salad favourite at our community suppers and luncheons, this is a nutritious as well as a tasty salad."

¼ cup dry wild rice
4 cups broccoli florets
4 cups cauliflower florets
2 cups raisins
1⅓ cups roasted, salted peanuts
½ lb. bacon, fried crisp & crumbled
¼ cup toasted wheat germ
4 green onions, thinly sliced
2 cups mayonnaise
¼ cup sugar
1½ Tbsp. raspberry vinegar
pepper

Cook rice until tender, drain well and set aside. Blanch broccoli and cauliflower, drain, then rinse in cold running water. Combine with rice, raisins, peanuts, bacon, wheat germ and onions. Beat together mayonnaise, sugar, vinegar and pepper until smooth. Toss with salad ingredients. Chill well.

Serves 12.

—*Ellen Ross*

Rice & Vegetable Salad

"An A-1 salad!" says our Vermont tester. It has a wonderful fresh taste, good texture and tangy flavour."

1 cup dry rice
2 cups peas
1½ cups chopped celery
½ cup minced green onions
½ cup toasted almonds
½ cup oil
2 Tbsp. vinegar
2 Tbsp. soy sauce
2 tsp. curry
½ tsp. salt
½ tsp. sugar
½ tsp. celery salt

Cook rice, then mix with peas, celery, onions and almonds. Combine remaining ingredients, pour over salad and toss. Chill before serving.

Serves 4 to 6.

—*Greta Bacher*

Millet Vegetable Salad

This makes a colourful, tasty, nutritious summer vegetarian salad.

2½ cups cooked millet
4 tomatoes, chopped
½ cup diced green pepper
¾ cup sliced zucchini
½ cup chopped scallions
2 Tbsp. chopped parsley
1 tsp. basil
¼ cup mayonnaise
1 tsp. Dijon mustard
¼ tsp. pepper
2 Tbsp. lemon juice

Combine millet, tomatoes, pepper, zucchini, scallions and parsley. Whisk remaining ingredients together until smooth, then toss with salad.

Serves 4 to 6.

—*Ingrid Birker*

Beans
& Grains

Zucchini & Barley Casserole

2 medium zucchini, sliced
1 small onion, chopped
1 clove garlic, crushed
½ tsp. oregano
½ tsp. basil
2 Tbsp. butter
1 cup pot barley, cooked & cooled
1 apple, cored & diced
1 green pepper, chopped
½ lb. mushrooms, sliced
2 stalks celery, sliced
10-oz. can tomatoes
1 cup grated Cheddar cheese

In a casserole dish combine zucchini, onion, garlic, oregano, basil and butter. Bake, covered, at 350° F for 15 minutes.

Remove from oven and add cooked barley, apple, green pepper, mushrooms and celery. Partially drain tomatoes, then chop them. Stir into casserole.

Bake at 350° for 45 minutes. Top with cheese and return to oven for 5 minutes.

Serves 4 to 6.

—Diane Schoemperlen

Barley Pilaf

2 Tbsp. butter
2 Tbsp. oil
¼ cup chopped onions
6 mushrooms, sliced
¾ cup uncooked barley
2½ cups stock
¼ cup diced salami or fried bacon
¼ cup finely chopped parsley
Salt & pepper

Heat butter and oil in frying pan. Add onions and cook for 5 minutes over low heat, stirring constantly. Add mushrooms and cook for 3 minutes longer.

Remove vegetables, leaving 1½ Tbsp. drippings in pan. Add barley and cook over low heat for 10 minutes or until well browned, stirring often. Place barley in casserole dish. Stir in onions, mushrooms, salt, pepper and stock. Cover and bake at 350° F for 45 minutes. Add salami or bacon, cover and bake for another 25 minutes. Toss with parsley and serve.

Serves 3 to 4.

—Jo Belicek

Bandersnatch Barley

1 cup uncooked barley
2 cups stock
4 oz. cream cheese
1 egg
½ cup sour cream
¼ tsp. salt
Pepper
3 tsp. dill
½ cup Parmesan cheese

Cook barley in stock. Bring to a boil, then simmer for 25 minutes. Mix remaining ingredients except Parmesan cheese into barley.

Put into a greased casserole dish and sprinkle with cheese.

Bake at 350° F for 20 to 25 minutes, then broil for 2 minutes.

Serves 4.

—Dee Lowe

Mushroom Barley Casserole

½ lb. mushrooms
1 large onion, chopped
1 cup pot barley
¼ cup butter
½ tsp. salt
⅛ tsp. pepper
4 cups chicken stock

Sauté mushrooms, onion and barley in melted butter. Place in a casserole dish and add remaining ingredients. Mix well.

Bake, covered, 1½ hours at 350° F. If there is too much liquid, remove lid for last 20 minutes.

Serves 6 to 8.

—Eileen Deeley

Quilter's Stew

1 cup lentils
6 cups water
1 cup tomato sauce, page 414
1 bay leaf
2 tsp. salt
1 tsp. pepper
1 potato, chopped
2 stalks celery, chopped
1 tsp. basil
2 Tbsp. brown sugar
1 cup uncooked small
   noodles

Combine all ingredients except noodles in a stew pot and cook for 30 minutes over medium heat.

Add noodles and cook for 10 minutes longer.

Serves 8.

—Marie Yoder Dyck

Soybean Pizza Casserole

1½ cups dry soybeans
Water to cover
2 Tbsp. oil
1 cup tomato sauce, page 414
½ cup grated mozzarella
   cheese
⅓ cup raw wheat germ

Soak soybeans in water overnight. With oil, cook in a pressure cooker with water to cover for 40 minutes or until tender. Drain.

Mix with tomato sauce and place in a casserole dish. Bake, covered, at 375° F for 20 minutes.

Combine cheese and wheat germ, pour over casserole and bake 10 minutes longer.

Serves 4.

—Kristine Reid

Refried Beans

2 Tbsp. oil
5 cups cooked kidney beans
1½ Tbsp. oregano
1½ Tbsp. minced garlic
1 Tbsp. crushed chili peppers
½ lb. Cheddar cheese, grated

Place oil, beans, oregano, garlic and chili peppers in a heavy, deep frying pan. Simmer for 10 minutes. Mash until all the beans are broken up.

Stir in cheese and cook until it melts. Serve in tortillas.

Serves 6 to 8.

—Donna Schedler

Polenta

This variation of a traditional Italian dish, polenta, with a mush-like consistency, is good topped with cheese and stew.

5 cups water
1 tsp. salt
3 cups cold water
3 cups corn meal

Bring 5 cups of salted water to a boil. Combine cold water with corn meal and add to boiling water. Cook, stirring, over medium heat for 30 minutes — until mixture thickens.

Serves 4.

—Anne Erb Panciera

Soybean Casserole

1 onion, sliced
1 clove garlic, crushed
1 green pepper, sliced
1 cup chopped celery
1 lb. fresh mushrooms,
   sliced
1 tomato, chopped
Safflower oil as needed
1 Tbsp. brewer's yeast
¼ cup wheat germ
6-oz. can tomato paste
1 cup stock
Cayenne pepper
½ tsp. thyme
½ tsp. basil
1 cup cooked soybeans
⅓ cup grated Cheddar cheese
2 Tbsp. sesame seeds

Lightly sauté onion, garlic, pepper, celery, mushrooms and tomato in oil for approximately 5 minutes. Remove from heat, add yeast and wheat germ and mix lightly.

In a separate bowl, mix the tomato paste with the stock and seasonings.

In a casserole dish, layer soybeans and vegetables. Pour tomato stock over the casserole and top with grated cheese. Sprinkle with sesame seeds.

Bake at 350° F for 30 minutes.

—Dena Ross Reuben

Felafel

This traditional Middle Eastern "hamburger" can be made more or less spicy to taste, depending on the amount of garlic, cumin and coriander used. For those who really like hot food, crushed chili peppers may be added. Garlic may also be added to the yogurt topping.

1 lb. uncooked chick peas
4 onions, sliced
4 cloves garlic
½ cup chopped parsley
2 tsp. cumin
2 tsp. coriander
1 tsp. baking powder
Salt & pepper
Cayenne

Cook chick peas in water to cover, adding more water as needed, until just tender but not soft. Grind with onions and garlic.

Mix in a bowl with remaining ingredients. Chill for 1 hour, form into small balls and deep fry. Serve in pita bread (page 454) with chopped lettuce and yogurt.

Serves 8.

—*Bryanna Clark*

Creamy Bulgur & Cheese Casserole

1 medium onion, chopped
1 clove garlic, minced
2 Tbsp. oil
1 cup uncooked bulgur
2 cups water
Salt & pepper
1 large tomato, peeled & thinly sliced
1 cup cottage cheese
1 egg, beaten with ½ cup water
2 Tbsp. fresh parsley, chopped
½ cup grated Cheddar cheese

Sauté onion and garlic in oil until onion is translucent. Add bulgur and cook, stirring, for 2 minutes. Add water, bring to a boil, cover and simmer for 15 minutes.

Place two-thirds of the bulgur in a greased casserole dish. Add salt and pepper to taste, and cover with sliced tomato. Mix cottage cheese with egg and stir in parsley. Pour over tomato and top with remaining bulgur. Cover with grated cheese. Bake for 30 minutes at 350° F.

—*Carol Bomke*

Broccoli & Chick Peas

½ cup water
½ tsp. salt
1 lb. broccoli, cut into 1-inch pieces
2 cups cooked & drained chick peas
2 Tbsp. chopped red pepper
1 tsp. lemon juice
½ tsp. basil
Salt & pepper
Artichoke hearts (optional)

In medium-sized saucepan, bring water and salt to boil. Add broccoli and cook for 4 minutes. Add remaining ingredients.

Toss gently and cook until heated through. Serve hot or cold.

Serves 4.

—*Ingrid Birker*

Bulgur-Nut Pilaf

This is one of many variations of traditional rice pilaf. Other possibilities include the addition of meat or seafood, or, for a fancier meal, a topping of grated cheese.

1 cup uncooked bulgur
1 onion, chopped
1 Tbsp. butter
2 cups broth
2 medium carrots, shredded
½ tsp. salt
½ cup chopped almonds

Sauté bulgur and onion in butter for 5 minutes. Stir in broth, carrots and salt. Cover and bake at 350° F for 25 minutes. Stir in nuts.

Serves 4.

—*Marva Blackmore*

Pickled White Beans

16 oz. navy beans
Pinch baking soda
¾ cup sugar
1 tsp. salt
½ tsp. pepper
⅔ cup vinegar
⅓ cup vegetable oil
1 green pepper, chopped
1 onion, chopped
Parsley

Soak beans in water overnight. Bring beans and baking soda to a boil (add more water if necessary), and then simmer until beans are soft. Cool.

Mix together remaining ingredients and combine well. Chill overnight.

Bean Filling
for Pita Bread

4 cups cooked white navy
   beans
5 Tbsp. oil
2 Tbsp. lemon juice
1 tsp. oregano
½ tsp. salt
½ tsp. cumin
¼ tsp. ground pepper
4 oz. cream cheese, cubed
2 medium tomatoes, chopped
1 medium cucumber, diced
2 Tbsp. chopped parsley
Pita bread for 4 (page 454)

Toss beans, oil, lemon juice and spices in a large bowl. Gently stir in cheese, tomato and cucumber. Cover and chill for 2 hours.

Cut bread in half and fill with bean mixture. Sprinkle with parsley.

Serves 4.

—Margaret Silverthorn

Tabouleh

Of Middle Eastern origin, tabouleh makes a delicious light lunch in the heat of summer.

1 cup uncooked bulgur
4 bunches parsley, chopped
2 medium tomatoes, chopped
1 medium onion, chopped
1 cucumber, diced
1 green pepper, diced
2 green onions, chopped
Juice of 1 lemon
¾ cup olive oil
Salt

Cover bulgur with boiling water and soak until softened. Drain, add remaining ingredients and toss. Chill well.

Serves 6.

—Glenn Countryman

Betty's Baked Beans

1 cup navy beans
1 tsp. dry mustard
1 tsp. salt
¼ tsp. pepper
¾ cup brown sugar
2 cups tomato juice
½ cup chopped onion
1 cup bacon pieces
3 medium-sized apples

Cook beans in boiling water until tender. Add mustard, salt, pepper, brown sugar, tomato juice, onion, bacon and apples.

Place in bean pot or casserole dish, cover and bake at 300° F for 1 hour.

Serves 4.

—Catherine Rupke

Spanish Bulgur

Bulgur, which is cracked wheat, can be substituted for rice in many recipes, including this one which is generally thought of as a rice dish. It cooks very quickly and has a pleasant nutty flavour.

1 clove garlic, minced
½ cup green onions, chopped
½ green pepper, diced
1¼ cups uncooked bulgur
   wheat
2 Tbsp. cooking oil
1 cup cooked lima beans
1 tsp. paprika
1 tsp. salt
⅛ tsp. ground pepper
Dash of cayenne pepper
28-oz. can tomatoes

Sauté garlic, onions, pepper and bulgur in oil for 5 minutes. Add remaining ingredients, cover and bring to a boil. Simmer 15 minutes or until liquid is absorbed and bulgur is tender. If necessary, add more liquid.

Serves 4 to 6.

—Laura Poitras

Soy Millet Patties

These patties are good served hot as a hamburger substitute, or cold in a sandwich with alfalfa sprouts and mayonnaise.

2 cups cooked soybeans
2 Tbsp. oil
½ cup water
2 Tbsp. chopped onion
1½ tsp. celery seed
1½ tsp. oregano
1 tsp. salt
3 Tbsp. soya sauce
1½ cups cooked millet
¼ cup raw ground cashews
¼ cup raw ground sunflower
   seeds
1 cup bread crumbs

Blend in a mixing bowl, soybeans, oil, water, onion, celery seed, oregano, salt and soya sauce. Add remaining ingredients. Mix well and form into patties.

Fry in butter until cooked through and lightly browned, about 20 minutes.

Serves 6.

—*Andrea Stuart*

Lentil Burgers

1 cup uncooked lentils,
   rinsed
½ cup uncooked rice
3 cups water
1½ Tbsp. salt
1 cup bread crumbs
½ cup wheat germ
1 large onion, chopped
½ tsp. celery seed
½ tsp. marjoram
¼ tsp. thyme
1 tsp. salt
½ tsp. pepper
1 Tbsp. chopped fresh parsley
Wheat germ

Combine lentils, rice, water and salt in a saucepan. Bring to a boil, lower heat, cover and simmer for 35 to 45 minutes or until rice is tender. Remove from heat, let stand 10 minutes and then mash together with any remaining liquid in pan.

Place in a large bowl with bread crumbs, wheat germ, onion, celery seed, marjoram, thyme, salt, pepper and parsley. Mix well and shape into patties.

Coat with wheat germ and fry in vegetable oil until golden brown on both sides.

Makes 24 patties.

—*Barbara J. Spangler*

Hummus

A chick pea paté of Middle Eastern origin, hummus makes a flavourful and protein-rich sandwich spread or appetizer dip.

2 cups cooked chick peas
⅓ cup water
Juice of 2 lemons
½ cup tahini
   (ground sesame seeds)
2 cloves garlic, crushed
½ tsp. salt
Cayenne pepper

Whir all ingredients in a blender until smooth. Serve as a dip for pita bread or raw vegetables.

Makes 2½ cups.

—*Sandra James-Mitchell*

Vegi-Burgers

There are many good recipes for meatless burgers. Most grains can be used, but it is important to add sufficient seasoning, otherwise the finished product will be bland and pasty. Toppings can include regular hamburger sauces, sprouts, yogurt, chili sauce and so on.

1 cup grated Cheddar cheese
1 cup sunflower seeds
2 cups bread crumbs
¼ cup bran
¼ cup wheat germ
¼ cup oats
1 cup onion, finely chopped
1 tsp. salt
1 tsp. sage
6 eggs

Mix all ingredients together and form into patties. Fry on both sides in vegetable oil. Makes 12 patties.

—*Brenda Kennedy*

Soya-Seed Loaf

¼ cup roasted sesame seeds
¼ cup roasted sunflower
  seeds
⅓ cup roasted wheat germ
1 onion, chopped
1 clove garlic, minced
1 Tbsp. oil
½ tsp. sage
½ tsp. oregano
2 cups cooked soybeans
1 egg
1 tsp. salt
1 cup grated zucchini

Grind seeds and wheat germ into a fine meal.

Sauté onion and garlic in oil until onion is translucent. Add sage and oregano and cook for 1 minute. Remove from heat.

Place soybeans in a blender with a small amount of liquid and blend until a thick paste is formed.

Mix all ingredients together and place in greased loaf pan. Bake at 350° F for 50 minutes.

Serves 4 to 5.

—Shan Simpson

Cheese Nut Loaf

1 medium onion, chopped
1 clove garlic, chopped
3 Tbsp. oil
1 cup cooked rice
½ cup wheat germ
½ cup chopped walnuts or
  cashews
½ cup thinly sliced
  mushrooms
¼ tsp. salt
¼ tsp. pepper
½ lb. Cheddar cheese, grated
2 eggs, beaten

Sauté onion and garlic in oil. Combine with rice, wheat germ, nuts, mushrooms, salt, pepper and all but half a cup of cheese. Mix well, add eggs and mix again.

Place in a greased loaf pan and bake at 350° F for 50 minutes. Sprinkle with remaining cheese after 30 minutes.

Serves 4.

—Carol Bomke

Sunflower-Sprout Loaf

1½ cups stale bread crumbs
1½ cups milk
½ green pepper, chopped
1 stalk celery, chopped
1 small onion, chopped
2 cloves garlic, minced
2 Tbsp. oil
2 cups bean sprouts
¼ cup sunflower seeds
1 cup grated cheese
½ cup powdered milk
2 eggs
1-2 Tbsp. tamari sauce
Tarragon
Pepper

Soak the bread crumbs in milk until softened. Lightly sauté pepper, celery, onion and garlic in oil. Combine with remaining ingredients in a mixing bowl.

Bake in a greased loaf pan at 350° F for 1 hour, or until firmly set and bubbly.

Serves 4 to 6.

—Anna Lee

Nut Loaf

2 cups uncooked red
   river cereal
1 cup boiling water
1 cup light cream
1 small onion, chopped
1 cup Cheddar cheese,
   cubed
1 cup walnuts, chopped
3 Tbsp. Worcestershire
   sauce
1 tsp. sage
1 egg

Pour boiling water over the cereal, stir in the cream and let stand.

Combine remaining ingredients, add to cereal mixture, and pack into a loaf pan coated with ⅛-inch of vegetable oil.

Bake at 350° F for 1 hour.

Serves 4.

—Norma Stellings

Meatless Stuffed Cabbage Rolls

1½ lbs. mushrooms
1 medium onion, chopped
2 Tbsp. cooking oil
½ tsp. salt
¼ tsp. pepper
½ tsp. marjoram
1 cup cooked rice
¼ cup grated Cheddar
   cheese
1 head cabbage
Boiling water
2 cups tomato sauce, page 414
1 Tbsp. lemon juice
¼ cup brown sugar
1 cup water

Sauté mushrooms and onions in oil. Add salt, pepper, marjoram, rice and cheese. Blend well. Cut core out of cabbage and pour in boiling water to separate the leaves. Divide rice mixture into 6 portions and roll in 6 large outside leaves. Chop rest of cabbage and add to the remaining ingredients in a large saucepan. Place cabbage rolls on top and simmer, covered, for 30 minutes, or until tender.

Makes 6 cabbage rolls.

—Merilyn Mohr

Rice-Spinach-Cheese Bake

2 cups cooked brown rice
1 cup cottage cheese
2 eggs, beaten
10 oz. spinach
½ cup chopped green pepper
2 cups grated Cheddar cheese
1 tsp. salt
⅛ tsp. pepper
3 Tbsp. bread crumbs
Melted butter or olive oil

Combine all ingredients except bread crumbs and butter. Pour into a buttered baking dish. Sprinkle top with bread crumbs, then drizzle with butter or olive oil.

Bake at 350° F for 30 minutes, or until bubbly hot.

Serves 4 to 6.

—Jacqueline L. Dysart

Rice with Sour Cream & Green Chilies

1 cup uncooked rice
4-oz. can green chilies,
   chopped & drained
8 oz. sour cream
Salt & pepper
½ lb. Cheddar cheese, grated
2 Tbsp. butter

Cook rice and combine it with the green chilies, sour cream, salt, pepper and three-quarters of the cheese.

Place in a 2-quart casserole dish, sprinkle with remaining cheese and dot with butter.

Bake, uncovered, at 350° F for 30 minutes.

Serves 2 to 4.

—Liz Eder and Paul Jett

Bean & Rice Casserole

4 cups cooked kidney or
    pinto beans
4 cups cooked rice
3 cups tomato sauce, page 414
1 large onion, finely chopped
1 cup corn meal
1⅔ cups boiling water
⅔ cup powdered milk
5 Tbsp. vegetable oil
5 Tbsp. honey
1 egg, beaten
1¼ cups flour
4 tsp. baking powder
½ tsp. salt
1 cup grated Cheddar cheese

Combine beans, rice, tomato sauce and onion, mix well and place in a 9" x 13" casserole dish. The mixture should be quite liquidy — add additional tomato sauce if necessary. Bake at 375° F for 25 minutes or until bubbly.

Meanwhile, combine corn meal, boiling water and powdered milk and let sit 10 minutes. Stir in oil, honey and egg.

Combine flour, baking powder, salt and cheese and add to corn meal mixture. Stir until just mixed.

Remove beans from oven and raise heat to 400°. Top casserole with corn meal mixture and bake for 20 minutes.

Serves 6 to 8.

—Sandy McCallum

Cheesy Rice Casserole

1¼ cups uncooked rice
2 Tbsp. soy grits
2 Tbsp. butter
2 small onions, chopped
2 stalks celery, diced
1 green pepper, diced
1 large carrot, chopped
¼ cup sunflower seeds
6 mushrooms, sliced
½ tsp. thyme
Dash cayenne
½ cup grated Cheddar cheese
¼ cup grated Parmesan
    cheese

Cook the rice and soy grits in simmering water for about 25 minutes. Drain.

Melt butter in a frying pan. Sauté the onion, celery, green pepper, carrot and sunflower seeds until the onion softens. Add the mushrooms and seasonings and sauté a few minutes longer. Add the drained rice and soy grits and mix thoroughly. Stir in the Cheddar cheese.

Turn the mixture into a greased casserole dish and top with Parmesan cheese. Bake at 350° F for 30 minutes, or until heated through.

Serves 4 to 6.

—Janet Flewelling

Cheese, Broccoli & Rice Casserole

1 cup chopped onion
1 Tbsp. butter
1½ cups white sauce, page 132
½ cup sliced mushrooms
Salt & pepper
2 tsp. tamari sauce
1 cup grated Cheddar cheese
1 cup cooked rice
½ tsp. dry mustard
4 hard-boiled eggs, quartered
1 bunch broccoli, cooked

Sauté onion in butter until soft, then gradually stir in white sauce, mushrooms, salt, pepper and tamari sauce. Add cheese, rice and mustard and cook, stirring, until cheese is melted. Fold in quartered eggs.

Place broccoli in greased 2-quart baking dish and pour sauce over it.

Bake at 350° F for 20 minutes.

Serves 6 to 8.

—Signe Dickerson

Buster's Red Beans & Rice

1 smoked pork hock
Oil for frying
4 cups uncooked small red
    beans
Cold water to cover
4 large onions, sliced
1 bulb garlic, broken into
    cloves & chopped
Salt
4 cups raw rice, cooked

Cut pork hock in half, fry in oil and place in a large pot. Add beans and cold water to cover. Fry onions in oil, add to pot and bring mixture to a boil. Simmer, covered, for 5 to 6 hours or until beans are tender. Let cool. Remove pork hock from pot, discard bone and fat and return meat to pot. Add garlic and simmer 1 more hour. Add salt to taste. Serve over a bed of rice. Serves 10.

—Cathy Reed

Garden Rice

1½ cups green beans, cut in
    1-inch lengths
1 cup shelled green peas
1 small bunch broccoli, cut
    up
2 small zucchini, thickly
    sliced
½ cup rice
1 cup water
3 ripe tomatoes, cubed
8 Tbsp. butter
2 cloves garlic, crushed
¼ lb. sliced mushrooms
1 tsp. dried basil
Salt & pepper
¼ tsp. crushed chili peppers
¼ cup chopped parsley
½ cup cream
⅓ cup Parmesan cheese

Place 1 inch of water in a large saucepan and add peas and beans. Place vegetable steamer on top and add broccoli and zucchini. Cook until vegetables are crispy-tender. Meanwhile, cook rice in 1 cup of water.

In a large frying pan, sauté tomatoes in 6 Tbsp. of butter. Add garlic, mushrooms, basil, salt, pepper, chilies and parsley. When mushrooms are done, add the cooked vegetables and simmer while making the sauce.

To make sauce, melt remaining 2 Tbsp. butter in small saucepan, add cream and cheese and cook over medium heat until cheese melts and sauce is smooth.

Add rice and sauce to vegetables and mix well. Cook over low heat until everything is heated through.

Serves 2 to 3.

—Kynda Fenton

Swiss Brown Rice

2 cups sliced onion
3 stalks celery, sliced
½ lb. mushrooms, sliced
½ cup chopped parsley
2 Tbsp. oil
1 clove garlic, minced
1½ tsp. paprika
1 tsp. salt
½ tsp. black pepper
½ tsp. ginger
3 cups cooked rice
1 lb. Swiss cheese, grated
Chopped parsley to garnish

Sauté onion, celery, mushrooms and parsley in oil. Add garlic and seasonings and mix well.

Layer the rice, vegetables and cheese in a shallow casserole dish and bake at 350° F for 20 to 25 minutes. Garnish with parsley.

Serves 8 to 10.

—Water St. Co-op

Browned Rice

2 cups uncooked rice
¼ cup butter
1 cup sliced mushrooms
¼ cup chopped green onions
½ lb. slivered almonds
3 cups chicken stock

Brown rice in butter in large saucepan. Sauté mushrooms, onion and almonds in butter in a frying pan. Boil stock and pour over rice. Boil again, reduce heat, cover and cook for 15 minutes.

Add mushrooms, onions and almonds and leave on low heat until ready to serve.

Serves 8 to 10.

—Jacquie Gibson

Mushroom Brown Rice

1 cup bread crumbs
1½ cups melted butter
2 cups mushrooms, sliced
6 cups cooked brown rice
Salt & pepper
1 cup grated Cheddar cheese
¼ cup minced parsley

Sauté bread crumbs in ½ cup melted butter. Remove crumbs from pan, then sauté mushrooms.

Place rice in a casserole dish and toss lightly with remaining butter. Add mushrooms, bread crumbs and salt and pepper to taste. Mix well and top with cheese and parsley.

Bake at 350° F for 20 to 30 minutes.

Serves 8 to 10.

—*Winona Heasman*

Herbed Rice

3 Tbsp. butter
¼ cup finely chopped chives
   or green onions
1 cup uncooked rice
½ tsp. marjoram
½ tsp. rosemary
½ tsp. salt
2 cups chicken stock

In a heavy saucepan, melt butter and sauté chives or onions until softened. Add rice and cook, stirring constantly, until the rice is lightly browned. Add the herbs, salt and chicken stock.

Cover tightly and bring to a boil, then lower heat and simmer until rice is tender.

Makes 3 cups.

—*Kathy Christie*

Spanish Rice

Quickly and easily assembled, this dish can be served as a meatless main dish or as a side dish.

1 cup uncooked brown rice
2 cups water
1 onion
1 green pepper
3 stalks celery
3 cloves garlic
4 Tbsp. oil
28-oz. can tomatoes
1 tsp. salt
Dash of pepper
3 whole cloves or ½ tsp.
   ground cloves
1 cup grated Cheddar cheese

Cook rice in boiling water for 45 minutes. Meanwhile, chop onion, green pepper and celery and sauté with garlic in oil until onion becomes translucent. Add tomatoes and seasonings to vegetables and simmer for 10 minutes.

Combine with cooked rice in casserole dish and top with grated cheese. Bake at 350° F for 15 to 20 minutes.

Serves 4.

—*Rae Anne Huth*

Donna's Rice Pilaf

2 cups beef stock
1 cup rice
½ tsp. salt
1 onion, chopped
1 stalk celery, chopped
¼-½ cup chopped
   mushrooms
1 small green pepper, chopped

Bring stock to a boil and add rice and salt. Stir, cover, return to a boil, then reduce heat to minimum. Simmer until rice is cooked.

Sauté onion, celery, mushrooms and pepper in a frying pan. When rice is cooked, add vegetables, stir, and replace lid. Turn heat off but leave pot on warm burner for another 5 minutes.

Serves 4.

—*Donna Gordon*

Curried Rice Salad

1½ cups uncooked rice
2 Tbsp. diced green pepper
2 Tbsp. raisins
1 small onion, finely chopped
2 Tbsp. snipped parsley
⅔ cup olive oil
⅓ cup wine vinegar
Salt & pepper
½ tsp. dry mustard
1 clove garlic, mashed
1 Tbsp. curry powder
Green pepper rings & tomato
    wedges to garnish

Cook rice and cool. Add green pepper, raisins, onion and parsley and mix well.

Combine oil, vinegar, salt, pepper, mustard and garlic in a small bowl.

When ready to serve, pour dressing over salad, add curry powder and mix well. Garnish with green pepper rings and tomato wedges.

Serves 6.

—Sandra Kapral

Parmesan Rice Crust

1 egg, beaten
¼ cup Parmesan cheese
Juice of 1 lemon
Pepper
2 cups cooked rice
2 Tbsp. melted butter
¼ cup sesame meal

Mix together egg, cheese, lemon juice and pepper. Toss rice with butter and sesame meal and stir into egg-cheese mixture.

Press into 9-inch pie pan and bake at 350° F until it becomes crusty — about 15 minutes. Use for quiches.

—Kathie Reid

Rice Salad

2 small onions
1 green pepper
3 cups chilled cooked rice
1 cup uncooked peas
1 cup mayonnaise, page 132
Salt
Green onions, radishes &
    parsley to garnish

Dice onions and green pepper. Add to rice along with peas, mayonnaise and salt. Mix well. Garnish with sliced green onions, radishes and chopped parsley.

Serves 6.

—Carolyn Somerton

Curried Rice & Fried Eggs

1 cup uncooked rice
½ tsp. salt
1 Tbsp. curry powder
¼ tsp. ground Jamaican
    ginger
1 onion, coarsely chopped
½ cup slivered almonds
5-6 mushrooms, thinly sliced
4 eggs
Pepper

Cook rice in 2 cups boiling water with curry powder, salt and ginger. When rice is cooked, remove from heat, stir in onion, almonds and mushrooms, replace lid and let sit.

While rice is sitting, gently fry eggs.

To serve, place rice on plate, top with eggs and sprinkle with pepper.

Serves 2.

—Steve Pitt

Chinese Rice Salad

1 cup cold cooked rice
1 cup cooked peas
¼ cup chopped green onion
½ cup shrimp
1½ cups chopped celery
1 tsp. salt
1 Tbsp. soya sauce
3 Tbsp. vinegar
1 tsp. curry powder
⅓ cup oil
½ tsp. sugar

Combine rice, peas, onion, shrimp and celery.

Combine remaining ingredients to make a dressing and pour over rice mixture. Mix well and refrigerate for several hours.

Serves 6 to 8.

—Beth Hopkins

Manitoba Wild Rice Casserole

1 cup wild rice
¼ tsp. basil
½ tsp. pepper
½ tsp. salt
1 tsp. thyme
1 tsp. sage
3 cups beef stock
8 slices bacon
1 onion, chopped
½ lb. mushrooms, sliced

Soak rice overnight, wash and drain. Place rice, basil, salt, pepper, thyme, sage and beef stock in the top of a double boiler and cook, covered, over boiling water for 45 minutes or until tender.

Meanwhile, chop and fry bacon. Add onion and mushrooms, and stir until cooked.

Combine rice and bacon mixtures in a greased casserole dish. Bake at 350° F for 20 to 25 minutes.

Serves 6.

—Joan Hoepner

Rice Cakes

2 eggs, well beaten
3 cups cooked brown rice
3 Tbsp. flour
2-3 Tbsp. finely chopped onion
½ cup milk
1 tsp. salt
1-2 tsp. parsley

Blend eggs into cooled rice. Add flour, onion, milk and seasonings. Mix well.

Drop by spoonfuls onto hot frying pan. Flatten, brown and flip.

—Pat Dicer

Cinnamon Granola

1½ tsp. vanilla
¾ cup oil
1 cup honey
1 cup rolled oats
1 cup bran
1 cup wheat flakes
½ cup wheat germ
½ cup sesame seeds
½ cup coconut
½ cup sunflower seeds
½ cup cashews
½ cup rye flakes
1 cup powdered milk
1 tsp. cinnamon
½ tsp. nutmeg
2 cups raisins
¾ cup chopped dried apricots

Combine vanilla, oil and honey and heat.

Mix oats, bran, wheat flakes, wheat germ, sesame seeds, coconut, sunflower seeds, cashews, rye flakes, powdered milk, cinnamon and nutmeg. Add honey mixture and blend thoroughly with fingers.

Place in two 9" x 13" pans and bake at 325° F for 30 to 45 minutes.

Remove from oven and add raisins and apricots. Store in refrigerator.

Makes 9 cups.

—Shirley Thomlinson

Crunchy Granola

1 cup butter
½ cup honey
1 Tbsp. milk
1 tsp. salt
4 cups rolled oats
1 cup wheat germ
1 cup coconut
¼ cup sesame seeds
½ cup sunflower seeds
½ cup raisins

Heat butter, honey, milk and salt. Combine rolled oats, wheat germ, coconut, sesame seeds and sunflower seeds. Mix in honey-butter mixture until well combined.

Place in a large shallow pan and bake at 350° F for 20 minutes, stirring from time to time.

Stir in raisins and cool.

Makes 7 cups.

—Carol Frost

Al Taylor's Granola

½ cup oil
½ cup honey
1 Tbsp. milk
4 cups rolled oats
1 cup rolled wheat flakes
1½ cups wheat germ
1 cup sesame seeds
1 cup sunflower seeds
1 cup coconut
¼ cup flax seeds
¼ cup poppy seeds
½-1 cup chopped almonds or
    cashews
1 tsp. salt
1 cup raisins

Combine and heat oil, honey and milk. Mix remaining ingredients, except raisins, and spread in a large shallow pan. Dribble oil-honey mixture over cereal and mix in. Bake at 350° F for 15 minutes, stir well and bake another 15 minutes. Remove from oven and stir in raisins. Cool and store in airtight containers. Makes 11 to 12 cups.

—Paddy & Daryl Taylor

Sesame Cereal

1½ cups water
¼ tsp. salt
1 Tbsp. soy grits
1 cup rolled wheat
2 Tbsp. roasted & ground
    sesame seeds

Bring water to a boil, add salt, soy grits and wheat. Cook over low heat until thick. Stir in sesame seeds.

Serves 2.

Wheat Berry Muesli

Served with milk, muesli makes an unusual and wholesome breakfast.

¼ cup oatmeal
½ cup water
1 cup raisins
1 cup steamed wheat
1 cup yogurt
3-4 Tbsp. honey
1 tsp. lemon juice
1 apple, unpeeled & chopped
1 banana, sliced

Soak oatmeal in ½ cup water for 30 minutes. Simmer raisins until tender, then drain. Combine oatmeal, raisins and remaining ingredients and chill. Muesli will keep for several days, refrigerated, in a glass container.

Serves 4.

—Joanne Ramsy

Wheat and Raisins

A hearty, satisfying dish, this is good served hot or cold, as a dessert or a cereal. Dried apricots, prunes or peaches can be substituted for raisins.

1 cup raisins
2 cups water
1 Tbsp. vinegar
3 Tbsp. honey
1 Tbsp. butter
2 Tbsp. cornstarch
4 cups cooked whole wheat

Simmer raisins in water until soft. Add vinegar, honey and butter. Add cornstarch and cook, stirring, until thickened. Add wheat and serve.

Serves 6.

—Joanne Ramsy

Hot Cereal

1 heaping Tbsp. buckwheat
    groats
1 heaping Tbsp. hulled millet
1 Tbsp. sesame seeds
1 Tbsp. safflower oil
Raisins
¼ tsp. kelp
1¼-1½ cups water
1 Tbsp. brewer's yeast
1 Tbsp. lecithin granules

Place all ingredients in top of double boiler and soak for at least 12 hours. Using only top of double boiler, bring cereal to a boil, reduce heat and cook gently, stirring frequently, for 8 to 10 minutes. Meanwhile, heat water in the bottom of the boiler. Place top over bottom, cover and let stand until ready to serve, about 10 minutes. Just before serving, stir in brewer's yeast and lecithin granules. Serve with milk.

Serves 2.

—John Osborne

Cinnamon Oat Wheat Cereal

3½ cups water
½ tsp. salt
2 Tbsp. cinnamon
¾ cup raisins
4 Tbsp. soy grits
1⅓ cups rolled wheat
1⅓ cups rolled oats
2 cups milk

Bring water, salt, cinnamon and raisins to a boil. Add soy grits and rolled oats, stirring well. Cook over low heat, uncovered, until water is absorbed and oats are tender. Serve with milk and honey.
Serves 6.

Mixed Baked Beans

3 cups cooked white beans,
   with cooking liquid
   reserved
1½ cups cooked red kidney
   beans, with cooking liquid
   reserved
1½ cups cooked soy beans
   with cooking liquid
   reserved
½ cup chopped onion
½ cup ketchup
¼ cup brown sugar
¼ cup molasses
1½ tsp. salt
1 tsp. dry mustard
¼ tsp. pepper
¼ lb. salt pork or bacon, cut
   into pieces

Combine beans, onion, ketchup, brown sugar, molasses, salt, mustard and pepper. Spread half of pork in casserole dish, add bean mixture and top with remaining pork. Add enough reserved cooking liquid to cover.

Cover and bake at 350° F for 2 hours, adding liquid as needed. Remove cover and bake for an additional 30 minutes.

Serves 4.

—Elizabeth Clayton-Paul

Sweet & Sour Beans

½ cup maple syrup
¼ cup lemon juice
3 Tbsp. soya sauce
1 cup unsweetened
   pineapple chunks, drained
   with juice reserved
2-3 Tbsp. cornstarch
1 cup thinly sliced carrots
1 cup thinly sliced celery
1 onion, thinly sliced
2 cups cooked kidney beans
2 cups cooked garbanzo
   beans
Salt
4 cups steamed rice

Combine maple syrup, lemon juice and soya sauce with reserved pineapple juice in a saucepan. Add cornstarch dissolved in 2-3 Tbsp. water. Heat, stirring, until mixture boils. Add carrots and celery and simmer, covered, for 10 minutes, or until vegetables are tender but still crisp. Stir in pineapple, onion and beans and heat through. Season with salt to taste. Serve on rice.

Serves 4 to 6.

—Patricia McKay

Vegetarian Chili

1 cup pinto beans
1 cup navy beans
1 cup kidney beans
9 cups water
1 large onion, chopped
2 cloves garlic, minced
2 Tbsp. oil
2 stalks celery, chopped
1 large green pepper, chopped
2 26-oz. cans tomatoes
1 cup chopped mushrooms
Chili powder

Soak beans in water overnight. Sauté onion and garlic in oil. Add celery and green pepper and cook for 5 minutes. Add tomatoes, mushrooms and beans, bring to a boil and simmer for at least 2 hours. Season with chili powder to taste.

Serves 6.

—Lynn Bakken

Refritos Negros

1 Tbsp. lard or bacon fat
¼ cup chopped onion
2 cloves garlic, minced
2 Tbsp. diced, seeded
   jalapeño peppers
½ tsp. cumin
¼ tsp. cinnamon
⅛ tsp. cloves
½ tsp. salt
2 cups cooked black beans,
   drained with cooking
   liquid reserved

Melt lard or bacon fat and cook onion and garlic until onion is soft but not browned. Add peppers and spices and cook for a few minutes longer.

In food processor or blender, process spice mixture with beans, adding cooking liquid as needed to make a soft, moist mixture. Return mixture to saucepan and cook, stirring constantly, until heated through.

Serves 2.

—Karen Kadlee

Navy Bean Paté

8 cups cooked navy beans
3 cups roasted hazelnuts or
   walnuts
6 onions, chopped
2 cups chopped mushrooms
Butter
2 tsp. thyme
1 tsp. white pepper
1 tsp. nutmeg
1 tsp. cloves
1 tsp. ginger
1 bunch parsley, finely
   chopped
Salt
Tamari sauce
8 eggs
2 cups cream

Grind together navy beans and nuts. Sauté onions and mushrooms in butter, then add to bean mixture. Add thyme, pepper, nutmeg, cloves, ginger, parsley, salt and a dash of tamari sauce.

Beat eggs with cream and blend into above ingredients. Turn into 2 well-greased baking pans. Cover with buttered wax paper and bake at 350° F for 45 to 60 minutes. Serve either hot or cold.

Makes 2 loaves.

—Deborah Washington

Bean Lentil Stew

This vegetarian stew is flavourful and hearty. It is very easy on the budget, especially in summer, when fresh vegetables are in abundance.

1 cup navy beans, rinsed
1 cup brown lentils, rinsed
28 oz. canned tomatoes
2 onions, chopped
2 stalks celery, chopped
½ cup diced green pepper
1-2 cloves garlic, minced
1 Tbsp. butter or oil
3 large carrots, cut into
   chunks
1 large potato, cut into
   chunks
1 cup diced turnip
2 tsp. salt
¼ tsp. pepper
1 tsp. crushed savory
½ tsp. crushed basil
¼ cup finely chopped parsley

Place navy beans in a large pot, cover with 4 cups water and bring to a boil. Boil for 2 minutes, turn off heat and let sit for 1 hour. Then simmer beans gently for about 2 hours, or until almost tender. Add lentils and tomatoes.

In heavy pan, sauté onions, celery, green pepper and garlic in oil. Add this to the bean mixture. Add remaining ingredients and simmer until lentils and vegetables are cooked, adding liquid as necessary.

—Jan Gilbert

Black Bean Dinner

1 cup black beans
4 cups water
6-oz. can tomato paste
2 cloves garlic
1 Tbsp soya sauce
Oregano
1 tsp. chili powder
2 onions, chopped
2 ribs celery, chopped
2 green peppers, chopped
1 Tbsp. grated ginger root

Boil beans in water for 2 hours. Add remaining ingredients and simmer until flavour is well blended. Serve with baked potatoes, pasta or brown rice.

Serves 4.

—Kathe Lieber

Hot Curried Garbanzo Beans

1½ cups garbanzo beans
2 cups water
2 tsp. curry
1 tsp. turmeric
⅛ tsp. chili peppers
Salt & pepper
2 Tbsp. cornstarch
3 green onions, chopped

Soak garbanzo beans in water for 24 hours. Simmer in 2 cups water for approximately 1½ hours. Add curry, turmeric and chili peppers. Season with salt and pepper to taste. If sauce is too thin, thicken with 2 Tbsp. cornstarch dissolved in ¼ cup of water. Stir in green onions. Serve over millet or rice.

Serves 2.

—Joanne Lavallée

Black Turtle Beans

Many countries of the world include black beans and rice as a daily dietary staple. The legume and rice combination forms a complete protein, one that is much more economical than meat. Serve this dish with stir-fried mustard greens or collards.

1 lb. black turtle beans
Stock
2 cloves garlic
1 tsp. salt
1 Tbsp. oil

Rinse beans thoroughly and cover by at least 1 inch with stock. Cook gently for 1½ to 2½ hours, or until tender.

Crush garlic with salt in mortar and pestle until paste is formed. Heat oil in small skillet and sauté garlic until lightly browned.

Remove large spoonful of beans from pot and mash into garlic-oil mixture until beans are well puréed. Return to bean pot. Simmer gently for another half-hour, adding water if beans become too thick. Serve with rice.

Serves 6 to 8.

—Mrs. J.E. Tilsley

Indonesian Fried Rice

For a vegetarian meal, the meat can be easily omitted from this recipe.

1 onion, chopped
3 cloves garlic
½ tsp. ginger
½ tsp. cardamom
½ tsp. turmeric
½ tsp. crushed red pepper
1 tsp. salt
¼ tsp. pepper
2 Tbsp. oil
2 Tbsp. lemon juice
1 Tbsp. soya sauce
1 cup cubed, cooked meat
3 Tbsp. chopped green pepper
3 Tbsp. chopped celery
¼ cup coconut milk
4 cups cooked rice

Crush together onion, garlic, ginger, cardamom, turmeric, red pepper, salt and pepper. Sauté in oil for 2 to 3 minutes. Add lemon juice, soya sauce and meat and cook for a few minutes longer. Add green pepper, celery, coconut milk and rice. Stir-fry until hot.

—Susan Bates Eddy

Curried Rice Salad

1 carrot
2 stalks celery
3 green onions
1 cucumber
10 mushrooms
3 cups cooked brown rice,
    cooled
½ cup mayonnaise
½ cup yogurt
2 tsp. curry powder
2 Tbsp. parsley
Salt & pepper

Slice vegetables thinly and combine with rice. Mix together mayonnaise, yogurt, curry powder, parsley and salt and pepper. Toss with rice-vegetable mixture until all ingredients are coated. Chill well and serve.

Serves 8 to 10.

—Avril Houstoun

Rosemary's Rumbletum Rice

This recipe and the previous one are two examples of rice salads. The possible additions and combinations are limited only by the cook's imagination. This dish makes use of rice, olives, raisins, nuts and corn — an unusual but tasty mix.

2 cups cooked rice
¼ lb. olives, coarsely
    chopped
½ cup raisins
½ cup mixed nuts
1½ cups corn
1 small onion, finely chopped
Salt & pepper
Olive oil

Combine all ingredients, using just enough oil to bind them together. Chill thoroughly before serving.

—Mary Flegel

Ravishing Rice

This rice is a meal-in-a-dish — with the cottage cheese and tamari sauce providing protein.

1 cup raw rice, cooked
1 clove garlic
2 green onions, chopped
½-1 cup sliced mushrooms
3 Tbsp. butter
2 Tbsp. sesame seeds
1 cup cottage cheese
2 Tbsp. tamari sauce

As rice is cooking, sauté garlic, green onions and mushrooms in butter. Add sesame seeds, stirring until they coat mushrooms.

Add cottage cheese, tamari sauce and mushroom mixture to cooked rice and heat through.

Serves 3 to 4.

—Helene Dobrowolsky

Sesame Rice

This is a slightly dressed-up version of fried rice. Cashews or other nuts or seeds may be used in place of sesame seeds.

1½ cups sesame seeds
½ tsp. cayenne
1 bay leaf
4 Tbsp. butter
1 tsp. salt
4 cups cooked rice
Juice of ½ lime

Sauté sesame seeds, cayenne and bay leaf in butter until seeds are golden. Stir in salt and rice and cook over high heat, stirring constantly, until rice is heated through. Sprinkle with lime juice and serve.

Serves 4.

—Susan Bates Eddy

Spinach & Brown Rice Casserole

1 cup brown rice
2½ cups water
2 Tbsp. oil
1 cup sliced mushrooms
½ cup chopped green onions
¼ cup roasted sunflower
   seeds
1 lb. spinach, chopped
¾ cup grated jack cheese
2 cups cubed, cooked chicken
6-oz. jar marinated artichoke
   hearts, drained
¾ cup grated Cheddar cheese

Cook rice in boiling water until tender. Remove from heat, uncover and cool slightly. Heat oil in small saucepan over medium heat. Add mushrooms and green onions and sauté until mushrooms are golden. Set aside.

Mix sunflower seeds into rice, then spread in a greased, shallow 2-quart casserole dish. Layer spinach, then jack cheese, then chicken over the rice. Spread mushroom mixture over this, then arrange artichokes. Sprinkle with Cheddar cheese and bake, covered, at 350° F until bubbly and cheese has melted — about 45 minutes.

Serves 6.

—Julianne Ourom

Indonesian Rice Salad

2 cups cooked brown rice
½ cup raisins
2 green onions, chopped
½ cup chopped onion
½ cup toasted sesame seeds
½ cup toasted almonds or
   cashews
½ cup sliced water
   chestnuts
1-2 cups bean sprouts
1 green pepper, chopped
1 red pepper, chopped
1-2 stalks celery, chopped
DRESSING:
Parsley
¾ cup orange juice
½ cup oil
Juice and chopped peel of 1
   lemon
2 cloves garlic, crushed
1 Tbsp. sesame oil
4 Tbsp. soya sauce
2 Tbsp. sherry

Combine rice, raisins, onions, seeds, nuts and vegetables. Blend remaining ingredients well to make dressing. Pour over rice-vegetable mixture and stir to coat. Chill several hours or overnight.

Serves 6 to 8.

—Megan Sproule

Curried Rice & Artichoke Salad

6-oz. jar marinated artichoke
   hearts
2-3 stalks celery
½ green pepper
1 green onion
1 cup pitted black olives
4 Tbsp. slivered almonds
1 cup mayonnaise
½ tsp. curry powder
Salt & pepper
2 cups cooked rice

Chop artichoke hearts, reserving liquid from jar. Chop celery, green pepper, onion and olives. Combine all ingredients and mix well. Chill before serving.

—Elizabeth Lettic

Kusherie

This is a traditional Egyptian recipe for rice and lentils. It is served with a tomato sauce, fried onions and yogurt.

2 Tbsp. oil
1¼ cups lentils
4 cups boiling water
Salt & pepper
1½ cups rice
SAUCE:
¾ cup tomato paste
3 cups tomatoes
1 green pepper, chopped
1 stalk celery, chopped
1 Tbsp. honey
1 tsp. cumin
¼ tsp. cayenne
Fried onions
Yogurt

Heat oil in heavy saucepan. Add lentils and cook over medium heat for 5 minutes, stirring often. Add 3 cups of boiling water and salt and pepper to taste. Cook for 10 minutes, uncovered, over medium heat. Stir in rice and remaining 1 cup water, cover and simmer for 25 minutes without stirring.

For sauce, combine tomato paste, tomatoes, green pepper, celery, honey, cumin and cayenne. Bring to a boil, reduce heat and simmer for 20 to 30 minutes.

Serve grains topped with tomato sauce and fried onions, with yogurt as an accompaniment.

Serves 4 to 6.

—*Chris Nofziger*

Bulgur Burgers

1 cup bulgur
2 cups brown rice
1 cup wheat germ
1 cup soy flour
½ cup oil
3 tsp. turmeric
2 tsp. salt
Cheese

Bring bulgur and rice to a boil in 7 cups water. Lower heat and simmer, covered, until water is absorbed — about 45 minutes. Add wheat germ, soy flour, oil, turmeric and salt and mix well. Shape into burgers and place on baking sheet. Bake at 350° F for 15 minutes, top each burger with a slice of cheese and bake for 5 minutes more.

Makes approximately 18 burgers.

—*Kristine Reid*

Nut Rissoles

1½ cups ground brazil nuts
1½ cups ground cashews
⅔ cup whole wheat flour
½ tsp. salt
1 small onion, grated
1 cup grated old Cheddar cheese
Bread crumbs
Cooking oil

Combine all ingredients in a bowl and stir in enough water to make a stiff dough. Shape into patties and roll in bread crumbs. Fry in oil until golden.

Makes 12 patties.

—*Leslie Gent*

Brown Rice Burgers

This basic rice burger recipe can be added to in a number of ways. Mushrooms, peas, green pepper, celery or almost any other vegetable, finely chopped, can be added, as can thyme or sage. Cornmeal or wheat germ can replace the oatmeal.

3 cups cooked rice
½ bunch parsley, finely chopped
3 carrots, grated
1 onion, chopped
1 clove garlic, minced
2 eggs
¼ cup oatmeal
¾ cup flour
Salt
1 tsp. dill weed

Combine all ingredients. Shape into patties and fry in oil.

Serves 4.

—*Dixie Yeomans*

Barley Casserole

½ lb. bacon, finely chopped
½ cup finely chopped onion
1 cup finely chopped celery
½ lb. fresh mushrooms, sliced
1 cup pearl barley
3 cups beef stock
¼ cup finely chopped fresh parsley **or** 1 Tbsp. dried parsley

Sauté bacon and onion and place in casserole dish with other ingredients. Cover and bake at 350° F for 2 hours, or until liquid is absorbed and barley is tender.

—*Devon Anderson*

Lentil Barley Stew

¾ cup brown lentils
¾ cup chopped onion
¼ cup butter
6 cups water
28 oz. tomatoes
¾ cup barley
2 tsp. salt
¼ tsp. pepper
½ tsp. rosemary
½ tsp. garlic salt
Cayenne pepper
¾ cup chopped cabbage
½ cup grated carrots

Rinse lentils in warm water. Sauté onion in butter in large saucepan. Add water and lentils and cook for 20 minutes. Add tomatoes, barley, salt, pepper, rosemary, garlic salt, cayenne and cabbage. Simmer for 45 to 60 minutes. Add grated carrots and cook for 5 minutes longer.

Serves 6.

—Teri McDonald

Herbed Rice & Lentil Casserole

2⅔ cups water
¾ cup lentils
¾ cup chopped onion
½ cup rice
¼ tsp. salt
⅛ tsp. garlic powder
⅛ tsp. pepper
¼ tsp. oregano
2 Tbsp. chopped dill weed
1 cup grated Cheddar cheese

Combine all ingredients in a greased casserole dish and bake at 325° F for 1½ to 2 hours, stirring twice.

Serves 2.

—Rose Strocen

Spanish Bulgur Casserole

This delicious casserole can be frozen successfully, either cooked or uncooked, so it makes a handy dish to keep on hand for unexpected guests.

4 Tbsp. oil
1 cup chopped celery
1 cup chopped green pepper
½ cup chopped onion
3 cloves garlic, finely chopped
¼ lb. mushrooms, sliced
1½ cups raw bulgur
1 cup sliced black olives
2 cups tomatoes
½ cup sherry
½ cup water
2 tsp. oregano
Salt & pepper
2 cups grated Cheddar cheese
Parsley
Paprika

Heat oil in a large skillet. Sauté celery, green pepper, onion, garlic and mushrooms until limp. Add bulgur, olives, tomatoes, sherry, water, oregano, salt and pepper. Mix well and bring to a boil.

Pour into a large, greased casserole dish. Bake, covered, at 375° F for 20 minutes. Uncover and sprinkle with cheese, parsley and paprika. Bake 15 minutes longer.

Serves 6 to 8.

—June Countryman

Kibbi

This ancient Lebanese dish is a good meat extender as a little goes a long way. Ground lamb may also be used. Cold kibbi stuffed in pita bread and topped with yogurt, chopped lettuce and tomato is a delicious variation.

1½ cups raw bulgur
1 lb. ground beef
1 small onion, grated or finely chopped
1 Tbsp. salt
Cumin, pepper, allspice, cinnamon
Butter

Soak bulgur in cold water for 15 minutes. Drain, then squeeze dry with hands. Mix all ingredients very well, either kneading by hand or running several times through meat grinder. Pat into square cake pan. Score to bottom of pan in diamond pattern.

Bake at 350° F for 45 to 60 minutes. Drain any excess grease.

Serves 8.

—Sandra Wikeem

All in-one Cereal

2 cups cracked wheat
1 cup rolled oats
½ cup toasted wheat germ
½ cup raw wheat germ
½ cup soy grits
½ cup wheat germ
1 cup coarse cornmeal

Combine all ingredients and store in cool place in jar with tight-fitting lid.

To cook, use 1 cup cereal to 4 cups water, adding ¼ to ½ tsp. salt to taste for each cup of grain. Bring salted water to a boil and stir in cereal slowly. Cook and stir for 1 to 2 minutes, then cover and cook on very low heat for 20 to 25 minutes.

Makes 6 cups of dry cereal.

—*Kathy Cowbrough*

Slow-Cooker Cereal

What could be better on a busy morning than getting up to a flavourful breakfast of nutritious whole grains? This cereal is the old-fashioned kind that sticks to the ribs. The apples, raisins and coconut provide natural sweetening so the addition of honey or sugar is unnecessary.

¼ cup rye berries
¼ cup rolled oats
¼ cup corn meal
¼ cup brown rice
¼ cup sunflower seeds
¼ cup soy grits
2 Tbsp. flax seeds
¼ cup shredded coconut
¼ cup raisins
¼ cup chopped, dried apples
¾ tsp. salt
5 cups water

Combine all ingredients in slow cooker and cook overnight on low.

Serves 6 to 8.

—*Jan Gilbert*

Glazed Dinner Loaf

1½ cups oatmeal
1 cup wheat bran
¼ cup wheat germ
¼ cup peanuts, coarsely ground
¼ cup almonds, coarsely ground
¼ cup tamari sauce
¼ cup sesame oil
2 eggs
½ cup tomato juice
1 onion, chopped
Oregano
Basil
Salt
GLAZE:
½ cup tomato juice
1 Tbsp. dry mustard
2 Tbsp. honey
1 tsp. lemon juice
1 Tbsp. cornstarch

Combine all loaf ingredients and mix well. Place in greased loaf pan. Bake at 350° F for 30 minutes.

To make glaze, heat tomato juice, dry mustard, honey and lemon juice in small saucepan. Mix cornstarch with a little bit of water and stir in. Continue cooking until thick.

Cover loaf with glaze and bake for 15 minutes longer.

Serves 6.

—*Joanne Lavallée*

Healthy Breakfast Cookies

These cookies are sold at the Saturday morning Kamloops farmers' market. Packed full of grains and nuts, they provide a nutritious, if unusual, breakfast.

½ cup butter or oil
½ cup peanut butter
1½ cups honey
2 eggs
½ tsp. vanilla
1½ cups flour
1 tsp. salt
1 tsp. baking soda
3 cups rolled oats
1 cup coconut
¾ cup bran
¼ cup wheat germ
1 cup raisins
½ cup chopped peanuts

Cream butter or oil, peanut butter and honey. Add eggs and vanilla, then beat well. Stir in flour, salt and baking soda until very smooth. Add remaining ingredients and blend well.

Drop by teaspoonful onto greased cookie sheets. If a large, meal-sized cookie is desired, use ¼ cup of dough for each cookie. Bake at 375° F for 10 to 20 minutes, depending on size of cookies.

—Dianne Lomen

Almond Butter Rice

"This is especially good served with shish kebabs and Greek salad. It is, to those in our house, the best way to cook rice."

½ tsp. salt
1 cup dry basmati rice
½ cup butter
1 onion, finely chopped
1 clove garlic, crushed
½-1 tsp. turmeric
2 cups strong chicken stock
½ cup chopped parsley
½ cup slivered almonds, toasted

Combine salt with 2 cups water. Bring to a boil, then pour over rice. Let stand for 30 minutes, then rinse rice with cold water and drain well. Meanwhile, melt butter and sauté onion and garlic for 2 minutes. Stir in turmeric and rice. Cook, stirring, over medium heat until butter is absorbed — 5 minutes.

Place in greased casserole dish and stir in stock. Bake, covered, at 325° F for 45 minutes. Stir in parsley, sprinkle with almonds and bake, uncovered, for 15 more minutes.

Serves 4.

Vegetable Paella

There are as many paella recipes as there are Spanish cooks. The essential ingredients are rice and saffron — after that, it is up to the imagination of the cook and the ingredients that are available. Almost all paellas include chicken and seafood (we include such a recipe on page 263); we present this as a tasty vegetarian alternative.

2 cups dry basmati rice
4 Tbsp. olive oil
2 onions, sliced fine
4 cloves garlic, crushed
3 green peppers, sliced
2 tomatoes, sliced
1 bay leaf
½ tsp. saffron threads
salt
2 cups snow peas, steamed just until colour changes
2 pimientos, diced

Boil rice until tender but firm. Meanwhile, heat oil in large heavy pot, then sauté onions, garlic, peppers and tomatoes. Combine rice with vegetables, add 2½ cups water, bay leaf, saffron and salt. Cover and cook over low heat until water is almost absorbed. Add peas and pimientos and heat through.

Serves 4.

Vegetable Rice Pilaf

This pilaf is foolproof, attractive and flavourful.

½ cup butter
½ cup chopped onion
½ cup chopped celery
½ cup thinly sliced green
    pepper
½ cup grated carrot
salt & pepper
1 cup dry basmati rice
1 cup water
1 cup chicken stock
¼ cup chopped parsley

Melt ¼ cup butter in skillet and sauté onion, celery, green pepper and carrot until tender. Add salt and pepper. Place in greased casserole dish. Melt remaining butter and cook rice, stirring, until brown. Add rice to casserole along with water, stock and parsley. Cover and bake at 375° for 30 minutes. Stir, replace cover and bake for 30 minutes longer.

Serves 4.

—Evelyn M. Grieve

Brown Basmati Rice with Fruits, Flowers & Vegetables

Brown basmati rice, readily available in most health-food stores, has a nutty flavour. The calendula petals add flavour and colour. Serve this rice with fish, poultry or meat.

½ cup dry brown basmati
    rice
1 Tbsp. oil
1 Tbsp. butter
¼ cup thinly sliced green
    beans
¼ cup grated carrot
3 Tbsp. drained crushed
    pineapple
1 Tbsp. calendula petals
½ Tbsp. snipped chives
pepper

Bring 1 cup water to a boil in heavy saucepan. Add rice, stir, reduce heat and simmer, covered, for 45 minutes, or until water is absorbed and rice is tender. Remove from heat and set aside.

Put oil, butter and 1 Tbsp. water in small skillet. Heat over medium heat, then add beans and carrot. Cook just until beans turn bright green. Add rice, pineapple, calendula petals, chives and pepper. Heat through, stirring gently.

Serves 2 to 3.

—Ellen Ross

Persian Rice

4 cups dry basmati rice
4 potatoes, peeled & thinly
    sliced
6 Tbsp. butter
½ cup currants
⅛ tsp. saffron, soaked in ¼
    cup hot water
salt & pepper

Cook rice until tender but firm. Rinse while still warm with cold water to remove starchiness. Place potato slices in bottom of greased casserole dish. Dot with 2 Tbsp. butter. Spread rice over potatoes, then sprinkle with currants and saffron water. Melt remaining butter and pour over casserole. Add salt and pepper.

Cover and bake at 350° F for 15 minutes. Remove from oven, shake gently and let stand, uncovered, for 10 minutes. Discard potatoes when serving.

Serves 8.

Oriental Rice Salad

⅓ cup oil
2 Tbsp. orange juice
1 Tbsp. brown sugar
2 tsp. soy sauce
½ tsp. dry mustard
salt & pepper
1 cup dry rice, cooked
4 green onions, sliced
1 cup chopped water
    chestnuts
2 cups sliced celery
1 tomato, chopped

Combine oil, orange juice, sugar, soy sauce, mustard and salt and pepper in large bowl and mix well. Stir in warm rice. Add onions, water chestnuts, celery and tomato and toss lightly. Chill well.

Serves 4 to 6.

—Rose Strocen

Cabbage & Rice

This was a big hit — even with the doubters in the crowd — when we tested it in our Vermont office. It is easy to prepare and has a subtle sweetness.

3 Tbsp. oil or butter
6 cups chopped cabbage
1 onion, chopped
1½ cups cooked brown rice
¾ cup grated Swiss cheese
¾ cup sliced mushrooms, sautéed
½ tsp. savory
1 egg
½ cup wheat germ
2 Tbsp. butter, melted

Heat oil or butter in heavy pot and sauté cabbage and onion until cabbage is tender. Keep covered with the heat low. Combine remaining ingredients except wheat germ and melted butter. Layer half cabbage mixture in greased casserole dish. Spread rice mixture over this. Top with remaining cabbage.

Combine wheat germ and melted butter and drizzle over casserole. Bake, uncovered, at 350° F for 30 to 40 minutes.

Serves 3 to 4.

—Susan O'Neill

Swiss Chard & Rice Casserole

Incredibly quick and easy to prepare, this casserole helps use up that ever bountiful Swiss chard.

3 cups cooked rice
2 eggs, beaten
salt
19-oz. can tomatoes, drained & diced
1 lb. Swiss chard leaves, torn up
½ lb. mild Cheddar cheese, grated

Combine rice, eggs, salt, tomatoes and chard in greased casserole dish and mix well. Stir in half the cheese. Sprinkle remaining cheese over top. Cover and bake at 350° F for 30 minutes.

Serves 4 to 6.

—Julie Herr

Wild Rice

6 Tbsp. butter
½ cup chopped parsley
½ cup chopped onion
1 cup sliced celery
1½ cups dry wild rice
3 cups hot chicken stock
1 tsp. salt
½ tsp. marjoram
½ cup sherry

Combine butter, parsley, onion and celery in heavy skillet and cook for 10 minutes, or until soft but not brown. Add remaining ingredients except sherry. Bring to a boil, reduce heat, cover and cook for approximately 45 minutes, stirring occasionally. Add hot water if mixture gets too dry. When rice is tender, stir in sherry and cook, uncovered, for 5 more minutes.

Serves 6 to 8.

—Rose Strocen

Wild Rice Baron

2 lbs. ground beef
1 lb. mushrooms, sliced
½ cup chopped celery
1 cup chopped onion
½ cup butter
2 cups sour cream
¼ cup soy sauce
¼ tsp. pepper
1 cup dry wild rice, cooked
1 cup dry basmati rice,
  cooked
½ cup slivered almonds,
  browned in butter

Brown ground beef. Sauté mushrooms, celery and onion in butter until limp. Combine sour cream, soy sauce and pepper. Add rice, beef, vegetables and ¼ cup almonds. Toss lightly. Place in greased casserole dish and bake, uncovered, at 350° F for 1 hour, stirring occasionally and adding water if necessary. Garnish with remaining almonds.

Serves 12.

—*Ingrid Magnuson*

Cashew Nut Fried Rice

This is a wonderful dish — beautiful to look at, full of different textures and very tasty. It does not take long to prepare once the rice is cooked.

6 Tbsp. peanut oil
8 eggs
½ head cabbage, shredded
6 green onions, sliced
½ lb. bacon, fried &
  crumbled
1½ cups roasted cashews
2 slices gingerroot
3 Tbsp. sesame oil
3 Tbsp. soy sauce
3 Tbsp. sherry
2 cups cooked brown rice
2 cups cooked basmati rice
2 cups cooked wild rice

Heat wok, then add peanut oil. Add eggs, stir quickly to scramble, then remove and keep warm. Stir-fry remaining ingredients until crispy-tender and heated through. Remove ginger slices and add eggs.

Serves 10.

—*Sandra K. Bennett*

Festive Rice Ring

Serve this as an edible centrepiece for a special buffet. When the centre of the ring is filled with colourful vegetables, it is very attractive. If desired, a combination of wild, basmati and brown rices can be substituted for the brown rice.

6 Tbsp. butter
3 large onions, diced
3 cloves garlic, crushed
1½ cups sliced mushrooms
½ lb. spinach, chopped
½ lb. watercress, chopped
2 cups dry brown rice, cooked
1 cup milk
3 eggs, beaten
2 cups grated sharp Cheddar
  cheese
soy sauce
cayenne

Heat butter in heavy skillet and sauté onions, garlic and mushrooms. Stir in spinach and watercress and cook until spinach is wilted.

Combine rice with milk, eggs, cheese, soy sauce and cayenne. Stir in vegetables. Place in greased tube pan and bake at 350° F for 1 to 1½ hours. Let stand for 10 minutes, then invert onto platter and garnish with colourful vegetables if desired.

Serves 12 to 15.

—*Michael & Dyan Walters*

Broccoli Nut Casserole

1½ cups dry brown rice
2-3 Tbsp. oil
1 large onion, chopped
2 cloves garlic, crushed
½ tsp. dill
1 tsp. thyme
1 tsp. oregano
½ bunch parsley, chopped
½ lb. mushrooms, sliced
1 green pepper, sliced
1 head broccoli, cut into
  florets
½ cup cashews
½ lb. Swiss or Gruyère
  cheese, grated
2 Tbsp. Parmesan cheese

In heavy pan with tight-fitting lid, combine rice, 3 cups water and dash of salt. Bring to a boil, reduce heat and simmer, covered, until water is absorbed — about 45 minutes. Heat oil in large skillet. Add onion, garlic, dill, thyme and oregano and cook until onions are limp. Add parsley, mushrooms, green pepper and broccoli and cook, stirring often. When broccoli becomes deep green but is still crisp, toss in nuts and remove from heat. Spread rice in greased casserole dish. Cover with vegetable-nut mixture, mix well and sprinkle with cheeses. Bake, uncovered, at 350° F for 15 minutes, or until bubbly.

Serves 8.

—Sandra K. Bennett

Broccoli & Brown Rice Casserole

2 lbs. broccoli
3 Tbsp. butter
½ lb. mushrooms, sliced
3 Tbsp. flour
1 cup milk
½ cup chicken stock
1 tsp. thyme
2 Tbsp. soy sauce
salt & pepper
¾ cup grated Cheddar cheese
9-oz. can tuna
2 cups dry brown rice,
  cooked

Cut broccoli into spears, lightly steam, then set aside. Melt butter in heavy skillet and sauté mushrooms until limp. Stir in flour until smooth. Gradually add milk and chicken stock, stirring well. Add thyme, soy sauce and salt and pepper. Cook over medium heat, stirring, until thickened. Stir in ½ cup cheese and the tuna and continue cooking until cheese melts.

Assemble casserole by layering rice, broccoli and tuna mixture in greased casserole dish. Top with remaining cheese. Bake, covered, at 350° F for 30 minutes.

Serves 6.

Fiesta Pilaf

¼ cup butter
3 cloves garlic, finely chopped
1 cup finely chopped green
  onions
1 cup sliced mushrooms
½ cup diced red pepper
½ cup diced green pepper
1 cup dry wild rice
¼ tsp. thyme
⅛ tsp. cloves
4 cups chicken stock
pepper

Melt butter and add garlic, onions and half the mushrooms. Cook over low heat for about 3 minutes. Add peppers and remaining mushrooms. Increase heat and cook for 2 to 3 minutes. Stir in wild rice, coating well with buttery mixture. Season with thyme and cloves. Pour in stock and bring to a boil; cover and simmer over low heat for 45 to 50 minutes. Season with pepper.

Serves 4.

—Mo'e Howard-Samstag

Wild & Fruity Dressing

½ cup sliced celery
¼ cup minced onion
2 Tbsp. butter
½ cup chopped dried apricots
1 cup orange juice
1 cup dry wild rice, soaked
　　overnight & drained
2 tsp. grated orange peel
½ tsp. sage
1 cup chicken or vegetable
　　stock
salt & pepper

Sauté celery and onion in butter until crispy-tender. Soak apricots in orange juice, then add to celery-onion mixture. Add remaining ingredients and bring to a boil. Reduce heat, cover and simmer for 25 minutes, or until rice is tender and all liquid is absorbed. Season to taste with salt and pepper.

Stuffs 1 large chicken or 8 pork chops, with enough left for a side dish.

—Mo'e Howard-Samstag

Mushroom Rice

Equally delicious as a side dish or as a poultry stuffing, this will keep you from ever using commercially prepared rice dishes. For a 12-to-14-lb. turkey, double the recipe.

2 Tbsp. butter
1 onion, chopped
6 mushrooms, sliced
⅔ cup dry brown rice
⅓ cup dry wild rice
2 cups hot chicken stock
1 Tbsp. chopped parsley
¼ tsp. thyme
pepper to taste

In heavy pot with tight-fitting lid, melt butter over medium heat. Sauté onion and mushrooms until limp. Add rice. Cook, stirring, until rice browns. Pour in stock. Stir in parsley, thyme and pepper. Cover pot and bring to a boil. Reduce heat and simmer for 35 to 45 minutes. Turn off heat and let stand, covered, for 10 minutes.

Serves 4 to 5.

—Lynne Roe

Indonesian Rice Salad

2 cups cooked rice
　　(basmati, brown, wild or a
　　combination)
¼ cup raisins
3 green onions, chopped
¾ cup sliced water chestnuts
1 cup bean sprouts
1 green pepper, chopped
2 stalks celery, chopped
1 cucumber, chopped
⅓ cup sliced radishes
⅓ cup sesame seeds, toasted
⅓ cup cashews, toasted
DRESSING:
¾ cup oil
⅓ cup lemon juice
2 tbsp. soy sauce
1 tbsp. sherry
2 cloves garlic, crushed
1 slice gingerroot
salt & pepper

Combine salad ingredients and toss gently. Place dressing ingredients in jar with lid and shake until blended. Pour over salad and toss. Chill well.

Serves 6.

Swiss Cheese, Rice & Bulgur

½ cup butter
½ cup chopped onions
½ cup dry white wine
1½ cups strong chicken stock
½ tsp. salt
¾ cup dry brown rice
½ cup bulgur
¼ lb. Swiss cheese, grated

Melt butter in heavy pot, then sauté onions until limp. Add wine, stock, salt and rice, then cover. Bring to a boil, reduce heat and simmer until rice is almost tender — about 20 minutes. Add bulgur and cook until it is tender — 5 to 10 minutes. Stir in cheese and let stand for 5 minutes. Stir and serve.

Serves 4 to 6.

—Linda Giesecke

Wild Rice Cake

"My friend Grace Milashenko of Saskatoon presented me with a gift of Saskatchewan wild rice, and I set forth to experiment. The wild rice cake was daring in that, if it didn't work, I would have wasted many expensive ingredients. Fortunately, it produced a moist, delightful cake with a curious tang of the outdoors."

1 cup dry wild rice, washed, soaked in cold water overnight & drained
2-3 strips orange zest
1 tsp. sugar
1 pkg. yeast
¼ cup melted butter
½ cup maple syrup
1 tsp. salt
½ tsp. cinnamon
2 eggs
½ cup brown sugar
1½ cups whole wheat flour
2 cups unbleached white flour
¼ cup wheat germ
⅓ cup buttermilk or sour milk
handful crushed walnuts

Cook drained rice in 2½ cups water, adding zest strips when water comes to a boil. Reduce heat to medium and cook for 45 minutes to 1 hour, or until rice is fluffy.

Mix sugar with ½ cup warm water. Stir in yeast and set aside for 10 minutes. Meanwhile, combine melted butter, maple syrup, salt and cinnamon with cooked rice. Beat in eggs, then add brown sugar. Stir in flours, wheat germ and buttermilk. Add walnuts. Stir in yeast mixture. Mix well and let rise for 1 hour.

Stir down dough. Grease tube pan and pour in dough. Let rise for another hour. Bake at 400° F for 15 minutes, lower heat to 375° and bake for an additional 45 minutes, or until done. Let cool slightly and top with praline topping.

PRALINE TOPPING:
¼ cup brown sugar
½ cup chopped walnuts
¼ tsp. nutmeg
1 Tbsp. melted butter
2 Tbsp. cream

Mix all ingredients together. Pour over hot or cooled cake. Broil about 3 inches from direct heat for 2 to 3 minutes, or until amber-brown.

—Mo'e Howard-Samstag

Herbed Lentil & Rice Casserole

The aroma of this casserole is just as satisfying as the actual taste.

2⅔ cups chicken stock
¾ cup dry lentils
¾ cup chopped onions
½ cup dry brown rice
¼ cup dry white wine
½ tsp. basil
¼ tsp. salt
¼ tsp. oregano
¼ tsp. thyme
1 clove garlic, crushed
pepper
½ lb. Cheddar cheese, grated

Combine all ingredients except cheese. Stir in half the cheese. Mix well, then place in ungreased casserole dish and bake, covered, at 350° F for 1½ to 2 hours, or until lentils and rice are cooked, stirring twice during cooking. Uncover, top with remaining cheese and bake 3 to 5 minutes longer.

Serves 4 to 6.

—Connie Holck

Millet Casserole

"We first served this as part of a vegetarian Thanksgiving meal with friends. It was one of the favourite dishes and elicited many requests for its recipe. Yeast flakes, often identified as 'good-tasting' or 'delicious nutritious' yeast, can be bought at natural-food stores."

1 cup dry millet
4 Tbsp. oil
1 tsp. basil
1 tsp. cumin
1 tsp. curry
2 cloves garlic, crushed
3 onions, chopped
2 stalks celery, chopped
½ green pepper, chopped
1 cup wheat germ
1 cup yeast flakes
28-oz. can tomatoes
6½-oz. can tomato paste
1 cup grated Cheddar cheese

Cook millet in 4 cups water until tender — 30 minutes. Meanwhile, heat oil and sauté basil, cumin, curry, garlic, onions, celery and green pepper for 2 to 3 minutes. Remove from heat. Stir in wheat germ, yeast, tomatoes and tomato paste. Combine with cooked millet. Place in greased casserole dish and bake, covered, at 350° F for 45 minutes, then sprinkle with cheese and cook, uncovered, for a further 15 minutes.

Serves 6 to 8.

Vegetarian Couscous

Cook couscous by pouring 4 cups boiling water over 2 cups dry couscous. Cover and let stand for 5 minutes. Mix in 4 tablespoons butter and fluff up with a fork.

3 Tbsp. oil
1 onion, chopped
1 red pepper, chopped
1 green pepper, chopped
1 tsp. allspice
2 sweet potatoes, peeled & cubed
2 tomatoes, peeled & chopped
1 Tbsp. lemon juice
½ tsp. saffron threads
4-5 cumin seeds
2 cups cooked chickpeas
salt
2 zucchini, chopped
4 cups hot cooked couscous
hot pepper sauce

Heat oil over medium heat. Add onion, peppers and allspice and cook until onion is soft — 5 minutes. Stir in sweet potatoes and cook, stirring often, for 2 minutes. Add tomatoes, ¼ cup water, lemon juice, saffron, cumin and chickpeas. Season with salt, cover, reduce heat and simmer for 15 minutes. Mix in zucchini and cook for 5 minutes more.

To serve, spread couscous around edge of deep platter and spoon vegetables into centre. Serve with hot pepper sauce.

Serves 6

—*Helene Gaufreau*

Kibbeh

Serve this warm or cold, as a main dish or as a sandwich filling in pita bread. It is delicious dipped in yogurt. The filling can be omitted and the kibbeh baked plain.

FILLING:
2 Tbsp. butter
2 onions, finely chopped
½ cup pine nuts
KIBBEH:
4½ cups dry bulgur
3 lbs. ground lamb or beef
3 onions, finely chopped
1 Tbsp. salt
1 tsp. pepper
¾ tsp. cinnamon
½ tsp. allspice
¼ cup ice water
oil

Prepare filling by melting butter, then sautéing onions until limp. Add pine nuts, mix well and set aside.

For kibbeh: Wash bulgur in cold water. Drain well by squeezing out excess water. Combine meat, onions, salt, pepper, cinnamon and allspice. Mix well. Add bulgur and knead well, adding ice water by the tablespoonful to keep mixture cold.

Grease a 9" x 12" baking dish. Smooth half the meat mixture evenly in the pan. Spread filling over meat, then smooth remaining meat mixture over this. Make deep lines through kibbee to form diamond shapes. Dribble oil over top. Bake, uncovered, at 350° F for 30 minutes, or until brown.

Serves 8 to 10.

—*Katherine S. Jones*

Potatoes & Farina

Farina is more commonly known as cream of wheat. This dish, however, resembles not breakfast cereal but a fine barley. it makes a tasty side dish to either a meat or a vegetarian entrée.

2 potatoes, peeled & diced
½ cup oil
2 cups dry farina
salt & pepper

Boil potatoes in 1 cup salted water. Do not drain. Heat oil, add farina and sauté over medium-low heat until farina is golden brown. Mash potatoes in cooking water, adding salt and pepper. Add farina, mix, cover and cook over low heat until farina is tender — 10 to 15 minutes.

Serves 4.

Couscous with Vegetables

1½ lbs. couscous
1½ lbs. pumpkin, cut into chunks
4 green peppers, quartered
4 stalks celery, sliced
1 turnip, chopped
2 onions, chopped
2 cups cooked chickpeas
1 tsp. salt
1 tsp. hot paprika
1 tsp. cumin
½ tsp. dry mustard
½ tsp. chili peppers
1 tsp. curry
2 cloves

Soak couscous in hot water to cover for 10 minutes. Put 3 quarts liquid (water, stock or bean liquid) in cooking pot, bring to a boil and add remaining ingredients. Add couscous, cover and cook for 15 minutes. Stir well, recover and cook for 15 minutes more.

Serves 6.

Soybean Baked Beans

Chili sauce is the unusual ingredient here. This is a delicious way to eat the nutritious, but often disliked, soybean. For vegetarians, the bacon can be omitted and the beans will still have a rich flavour.

3 cups dry soybeans
1 tsp. salt
2 Tbsp. oil
1 tsp. dry mustard
½ cup brown sugar
¼ cup molasses
⅓ cup maple syrup
1 onion, chopped
½ cup chopped celery
½ cup tomato paste
¼ cup chili sauce
¼ lb. bacon, chopped
1½ tsp. salt

Wash soybeans. Soak overnight in 9 cups cold water. Drain. Place in heavy pot with salt, oil and enough water to cover beans generously. Bring to a boil, reduce heat, cover and simmer for 3 hours.

Place drained beans in greased casserole dish and add remaining ingredients. Mix well. Cover and bake at 300° F for 3 hours, stirring occasionally and adding liquid if necessary.

Serves 10.

—Barbara Curtis

Caribbean Beans & Rice

2 cups dry kidney beans
1 Tbsp. salt
3 Tbsp. butter
2 cloves garlic, crushed
4 green onions, chopped
1 tomato, chopped
⅛ tsp. cloves
2 Tbsp. chopped parsley
salt & pepper
1 tsp. chili powder
2 cups dry rice

Soak beans overnight. Add salt and 6 cups water. Bring to a boil, reduce heat, cover and simmer until tender — 40 to 60 minutes. Drain, reserving liquid.

Heat butter in heavy covered skillet. Add garlic, onions, tomato, cloves, parsley, salt and pepper and chili powder and sauté for 5 minutes. Add beans, rice and 4 cups liquid reserved from cooking beans (add water if necessary). Bring to a boil, reduce heat, cover and simmer, without stirring, for 20 to 25 minutes.

Serves 8.

Tabouli

This is a delicious version of tabouli. We had not tried one before that did not cook the bulgur, but our concern was unnecessary. The bulgur "cooks" by soaking overnight in the dressing.

½ cup dry bulgur
3 cups packed, chopped parsley
6 4" mint tops (leaves only), chopped
½ cucumber, chopped
1 onion, chopped
2-3 tomatoes, chopped
½ green pepper, chopped
juice of 2 lemons
1 shallot, chopped
½ cup oil
salt & pepper

Combine all ingredients and mix well. Let stand, refrigerated, overnight. Toss gently before serving.

Serves 6 to 8.

—Penny Tognet

Many-Bean Baked Beans

The different tastes and textures of five kinds of beans are what make this bean dish special. Beans can be cooked ahead of time and frozen, making the assembly of this dish much quicker.

2 cups cooked black turtle
  beans, cooking liquid
  reserved
2 cups cooked pinto beans,
  cooking liquid reserved
2 cups cooked navy beans,
  cooking liquid reserved
2 cups cooked lima beans,
  cooking liquid reserved
2 cups cooked kidney beans,
  cooking liquid reserved
8 slices bacon, diced
2 cups chopped onions
½ cup brown sugar
1 tsp. salt
1½ tsp. dry mustard
2 cloves garlic, minced
½ cup vinegar
½ cup tomato paste

Combine beans, reserving cooking liquid separately, in large greased casserole dish. Fry bacon until crisp. Set aside. Fry onions in bacon fat, then add bacon and remaining ingredients. Cook for 5 minutes and pour over beans. Add reserved bean liquid to just cover beans.

Bake, uncovered, at 325° F for 1½ to 2 hours, adding liquid if necessary.

Serves 10.

Soybean Nut Loaf

4 cups cooked soybeans
1 cup ground almonds
½ cup sesame seeds
3 Tbsp. butter
2 stalks celery, chopped
2 cloves garlic, chopped
2 onions, chopped
½ green pepper, chopped
1 tsp. cayenne
1 tsp. oregano
1 tsp. basil
1 tsp. cumin
3 Tbsp. peanut butter

Purée soybeans, almonds and sesame seeds. Melt butter and sauté celery, garlic, onions and green pepper. Stir into soybean-nut mixture. Add spices and peanut butter and mix well. Place in greased loaf pan and bake at 350° F for approximately 1 hour.

Serves 6.

Mexican Bean Dip

½ cups dry pinto beans,
  cooked, drained & mashed
3 cloves garlic, minced
1 cup minced onion
1 tsp. salt
pepper
½ tsp. crushed hot red
  peppers
⅓ tsp. cumin
¼ tsp. dry mustard

Combine all ingredients and mix well. Chill.

Makes approximately 3 to 4 cups.

Black Bean Soup with Ham

3 cups dry black turtle beans
2 large onions, chopped
5 stalks celery, chopped
1 bay leaf
4 ham hocks
3 Tbsp. butter
3 Tbsp. flour
3 Tbsp. red wine vinegar
salt & pepper

Place beans, onions, celery, bay leaf and ham in large heavy pot. Add 10 to 12 cups water. Bring to a boil, reduce heat, cover and simmer until beans are tender — 3 hours.

Remove ham and set aside. Discard bay leaf. Purée soup. If too thick, add liquid. Cut meat from bone, dice and return to soup. Mash together butter and flour, adding a little water if needed. Stir into soup. Add vinegar and salt and pepper.

Serves 10 to 12.

Black Bean & Tomato Salad

1 cup cooked black turtle
  beans
1 Tbsp. cider vinegar or
  lemon juice
2 Tbsp. olive oil
salt & pepper
1 large onion, chopped
2 large tomatoes, chopped, or
  1½ cups cherry tomatoes
2 cloves garlic, chopped

While beans are still warm, mix with vinegar, oil and salt and pepper. Chill, then add onion, tomatoes and garlic, combining well. Chill overnight.

Serves 4.

—Judith Almond Best

Teresita's Beans

"This recipe came to me from a Mexican friend. It is a favourite at outdoor summer parties. Leftover beans may be mashed and thinned with water and red wine to make an excellent soup."

2¼ cups dry black beans
1 lb. boneless pork, cut into
   bite-sized pieces
4 Tbsp. oil
1 large green pepper, chopped
1 large onion, chopped
4-oz. can jalapeño peppers,
   chopped
⅓ cup sherry
1 Tbsp. cumin
salt & pepper
6-oz. can tomato sauce
1 bay leaf
4 cloves garlic, crushed

Soak beans in cold water overnight. Drain, then cover with cold water and cook over low heat until crispy-tender — about 3 hours.

Meanwhile, brown pork in oil. Add green pepper and onion and cook until soft. Add to cooked, drained beans along with remaining ingredients. Cook over low heat — 1 hour for chewy beans, 2 hours for very soft beans.

Serves 8.

—*Rebecca Quanrud*

Baked Beans with Pizzazz

2 cups dry navy beans
4 Tbsp. butter
2 large onions, chopped
4 cloves garlic, crushed
½ tsp. salt
1 tsp. allspice pepper
2 tsp. dill
5 Tbsp. light molasses
5 Tbsp. Poupon mustard
4 cups tomato juice
2 Tbsp. lemon juice
1 Tbsp. soy sauce
1 green pepper, chopped
1 stalk celery, chopped
2 carrots, diced

Cover beans with water. Bring to a boil, reduce heat, cover and simmer for 1 to 2 hours, or until beans are tender. Add water during cooking if necessary. When cooked, drain.

Meanwhile, melt butter and sauté onions and garlic until limp. Add salt, allspice, pepper, dill, molasses, mustard, tomato juice, lemon juice and soy sauce. Bring to a boil, reduce heat and simmer, covered, for 45 minutes.

In large, greased casserole dish, combine beans, sauce and vegetables. Bake, covered, at 325° F for 1 to 2 hours, or until liquid is absorbed.

Serves 6 to 8.

Pesto Bean Salad

"Pesto adds a wonderful flavour to almost everything. It is most commonly associated with pasta, but I developed this easy salad one summer day, when confronted with leftover pesto and beans."

3 cups cooked navy beans
2 cups cooked white kidney
   beans
¾ cup garlic mayonnaise
PESTO:
1 cup fresh basil
1 clove garlic
¼ cup parsley
¼ tsp. salt
¼ cup olive oil
¼ cup Parmesan cheese
2 Tbsp. pine nuts
salt & pepper

Combine beans and mayonnaise and toss to coat beans completely.

Make pesto by placing first seven ingredients in blender or food processor and processing to make a chunky paste. Toss into salad. Add salt and pepper and chill thoroughly.

Serves 6 as a side dish.

Bean Tortilla Casserole

If cooked beans are kept on hand, this dish can be assembled quickly as a tasty, vegetarian casserole.

2 cups chopped onion
2 cloves garlic, crushed
1 cup chopped red or green
　　pepper
4-6 Tbsp. oil
6-oz. can tomato sauce
12-oz. can tomatoes
¾ tsp. salt
1 tsp. oregano
1 tsp. basil
¼ tsp. cayenne
½ cup dry pinto beans, cooked
½ cup dry kidney beans,
　　cooked
4 corn tortillas
2 cups grated Cheddar cheese

Sauté onion, garlic and pepper in oil until limp. Stir in tomato sauce, tomatoes, salt, oregano, basil and cayenne and simmer for 30 minutes.

After cooking beans, drain but reserve liquid. Mash beans with ¼ cup cooking liquid and 1 cup tomato-vegetable sauce, but do not purée. Assemble casserole in greased 9" x 9" baking pan. Place one-third of sauce in bottom of pan, then 2 tortillas, then half the mashed beans, then one-third of the cheese. Repeat. Place remaining sauce and cheese over top.

Bake, uncovered, at 350° F for 30 to 40 minutes.

Serves 6.
　　　　　　—Rhoda Mozorosky

Haricots Bretonne

Surpassed only by soybeans and chickpeas, lima beans rank high in the biological value of legumes. Biological value is a measure of the proportion of absorbed protein that is retained by the body.

1 lb. dry lima beans
2 carrots, quartered
1 onion, studded with
　　2 cloves
1 bay leaf
salt & pepper
2 cups chopped onions
1 clove garlic, minced
1 tsp. thyme
4 Tbsp. butter
4 tomatoes, chopped
4 Tbsp. tomato paste
¼ cup chopped parsley

Sort and rinse lima beans. Place in soup pot with 8 cups water, bring to a boil and cook for 10 minutes. Remove from heat and let stand for 30 minutes. Drain, then return to pot with 8 cups fresh water. Add carrots, whole onion, bay leaf and salt and pepper. Bring to a boil, reduce heat, cover and simmer for 30 minutes. Remove bay leaf and set mixture aside.

Sauté chopped onions, garlic and thyme in butter until limp — about 5 minutes. Add tomatoes and cook for 10 minutes, stirring occasionally. Add tomato paste and salt and pepper to taste. Cover and simmer for 20 minutes.

Remove carrots and whole onion from beans. Chop and add to tomato mixture. Drain beans and reserve liquid. Add beans to tomato mixture with 1 cup liquid and parsley. Simmer, uncovered, for 15 minutes.

Serves 8 to 10.
　　　　　　—Ingrid Birker

Tofu in Peanut Sauce

Piquant and crunchy, this is a wonderful way to present tofu to those who do not like its texture. Rich in protein, tofu is soybean curd. It is soft and bland in its basic form, so lends itself to all kinds of cooking. It has no cholesterol, is low in calories and is very inexpensive. Add it anonymously to soups or salad dressings, or feature it by spicing it up as we have done in this recipe.

½ cup hot vegetable stock
½ cup peanut butter
½ tsp. crushed hot red
　　peppers
2 Tbsp. honey
5 Tbsp. soy sauce
¼ cup red wine vinegar
¾ lb. snow peas
4 Tbsp. oil
4 slices gingerroot, chopped
4 cloves garlic, crushed
1 lb. tofu, drained & cubed
6-8 green onions, sliced
1 cup chopped peanuts

Prepare sauce by mixing together stock and peanut butter until smooth. Stir in crushed peppers, honey, 2 Tbsp. soy sauce and vinegar and set aside. Snap ends off snow peas and set aside.

Heat 2 Tbsp. oil in wok. Add half the ginger and garlic and sauté for 30 seconds. Add tofu and stir-fry for approximately 5 minutes. Add it to peanut sauce, mix gently and set aside.

Return wok to stove. Add remaining oil and sauté remaining ginger and garlic. Add onions, peanuts and snow peas, and sauté for 2 to 3 minutes, stirring frequently. Add remaining 3 Tbsp. soy sauce.

Meanwhile, gently heat tofu-peanut butter mixture. Pour sauce over snow peas and mix gently to coat well. Serve over rice.

Serves 6.

Curried Lentils

The aroma given off while these lentils are cooking is most enticing. Serve this dish hot as a main course or cold as a sandwich spread in pita bread. We suggest that it be served with raita — a cooling yogurt, cucumber, sweet pepper and tomato salad.

3 Tbsp. oil
1 onion, quartered & sliced
2 cloves garlic, minced
2 Tbsp. chopped gingerroot
2 bay leaves, crumbled
8 cloves
2 tomatoes, chopped
4 Tbsp. hot curry powder
1 tsp. cinnamon
crushed chilies
1 tsp. turmeric
3 cups dry green lentils
salt & pepper
fresh coriander for garnish

Heat oil in soup pot and sauté onion. Add garlic, ginger, bay leaves and cloves. Cook, stirring, for 1 minute. Add tomatoes and continue cooking.

Mix curry powder, cinnamon, chilies and turmeric with ¼ cup water. Add to pot and cook, stirring, for 2 to 3 minutes. Add lentils and salt and pepper and cook for 2 more minutes. Add 6 cups water, bring to a boil, reduce heat, cover and simmer for 45 minutes to 1 hour, adding water if needed. Serve garnished with fresh coriander.

Serves 6.

—Wendy Vine

Sweet & Sour Lentil Bake

What a wonderful combination of flavours—the zest of curry, zing of cayenne and sweetness/pungency of apple and sausage.

½ lb. pork sausage
4 cups cooked lentils
2 Tbsp. butter
1 tsp. curry cayenne
1 onion, chopped
1 carrot, chopped
1 tart apple, chopped
2 cloves garlic, chopped
1 Tbsp. cornstarch
¼ cup brown sugar
¼ cup cider vinegar
2 tsp. Worcestershire sauce
½ cup chicken stock

Brown pork sausage, breaking it up as it cooks. Drain and add to lentils. Melt butter and sauté curry and cayenne for 2 minutes. Add onion, carrot, apple and garlic and sauté for 5 minutes.

Combine cornstarch and brown sugar. Slowly pour in vinegar, mixing until smooth, then add Worcestershire sauce and stock. Combine all ingredients in greased casserole dish and mix well. Bake, uncovered, at 350° F for 45 minutes, or until bubbly.

Serves 4.

—Gretchen Sonju

Curried Lentil Spaghetti Sauce

Despite our initial hesitation about this recipe—primarily because it does not call for browning the beef and vegetables — this spaghetti sauce was delicious and the hit of the Camden East lunchroom. It can be assembled first thing in the morning and left to simmer all day, with only an occasional stir.

2 28-oz. cans tomatoes
1 cup dry lentils
1 lb. ground beef
½ cup tomato paste
1 clove garlic, crushed
½ cup chopped green pepper
½ cup chopped mushrooms
1 onion, chopped
1½ Tbsp. curry
2 tsp. cumin
1 tsp. oregano
1 tsp. basil
1 Tbsp. parsley
salt & pepper

Combine all ingredients in heavy pot. Bring to a boil, stir thoroughly, reduce heat to lowest setting, cover and simmer for 1½ to 2 hours.

Serves 6 to 8.

—Judie Wright

Fish & Seafood

Salmon Mediterranean

1 qt. tomatoes
¼ cup olive oil
4-6 cloves garlic, minced
1 Tbsp. basil
1 tsp. oregano
Salt & pepper
Large bunch parsley, chopped
4 lbs. salmon, cut into 1½
    inch steaks
2 onions, thinly sliced
1 large lemon, thinly sliced

Combine tomatoes, olive oil, garlic, basil, oregano, salt, pepper and parsley in a saucepan and cook for 15 minutes. Transfer to a baking dish.

Place salmon steaks in baking dish so that at least half of each steak is submerged in sauce. Arrange onion and lemon slices among the steaks. Cover and bake at 325° F for 30 minutes, uncover and bake a further 30 minutes.

Serves 6 to 8.

—Chris Ferris

Salmon Supper Casserole

2 cups cooked salmon
1 large onion
4 medium potatoes
Salt & pepper
1 cup milk
Flour

Remove bones and flake the salmon. Spread one half in buttered casserole, cover with thin slices of onions and a generous layer of sliced raw potatoes. Sprinkle with salt, pepper and flour. Repeat these layers, then pour milk over all.

Dot with butter and bake at 400° F for about 50 minutes, or until potatoes are tender.

Serves 4.

—Mrs. Fred Smith

Spring Salmon with Cream & Chive Sauce

1 large head romaine lettuce
2-3 stalks celery
1-2 carrots
1 leek
2 Tbsp. butter
3 cups fish stock
1 cup white wine
Salt & white pepper
1 onion, chopped
Juice of ½ lemon
4 slices fresh salmon fillets
1 bunch chives
2 cups light cream
¼ cup butter

Dip lettuce leaves in boiling water and rinse in cold water. Cut celery, carrots and leek in julienne style. Blanch for 2 minutes in boiling water, then sauté in 2 Tbsp. butter for 3 or 4 minutes. Combine stock, wine, salt, pepper, onion and lemon juice.

Spread out lettuce leaves, grouping 3 or 4 together to form one serving. Salt and pepper salmon and place on lettuce leaves. Spread vegetables on top and fold as for cabbage rolls. Simmer in fish stock for 10 to 15 minutes.

Remove rolls from stock and keep warm. Reduce stock to one-third, add chives and cream and heat until slightly thickened. Whisk in butter and pour sauce around salmon. Garnish with parsley.

Serves 4.

—Ascona Place Restaurant

Canadian Smoked Salmon

1 lb. smoked salmon
Juice of 1 lemon
2 Tbsp. mayonnaise, page 132
1 dill pickle, finely chopped
1 large green onion, finely
    chopped
Salt & pepper
Salad greens
Tomato, radishes,
    cucumbers & green
    peppers to garnish.

Slice salmon thinly, removing bones and skin. This is most easily done if the salmon has been placed in the freezer for a few hours first.

Toss in lemon juice and mayonnaise. Add dill pickle, onion, salt and pepper. Toss again and refrigerate.

Serve on a bed of greens, garnished with raw vegetables.

Serves 6 as an appetizer.

—Nita Hunton

Salmon à la King

2 cups cooked salmon
⅓ cup chopped green pepper
1 tsp. grated onion
¼ cup chopped pimento or
   red pepper
¼ cup butter
¼ cup flour
1 tsp. salt
Dash pepper
2 cups milk
2 beaten egg yolks
1½ cups sliced mushrooms

Drain fish and flake. Sauté green pepper, onion and pimento in butter until tender. Blend in flour, salt and pepper. Add milk and cook until thick and smooth, stirring constantly. Stir a little of this mixture into the beaten egg yolks, then pour egg yolks into sauce, stirring constantly. Add the fish and mushrooms and heat thoroughly. Serve over rice, noodles or puff pastry.

Serves 6.

—Ken Parejko

Salmon Loaf

15-oz. can salmon
1 egg, beaten
½ cup cottage cheese
1 cup cracker crumbs
2 or 3 chopped green onions
½ cup green peas
1 Tbsp. Worcestershire sauce
1 Tbsp. lemon juice
½ tsp. paprika
Salt & pepper
¼ cup milk

Drain salmon, remove bones and break into small pieces. Add remaining ingredients and blend well. Pack lightly into a buttered baking dish and bake at 350° F for 30 minutes.

Serves 4.

—Dawn Hermann

Baked Salmon Cakes

7-oz. can salmon
4 green onions finely
   chopped
½ tsp. salt
¼ tsp. pepper
6 boiled potatoes, mashed
Breadcrumbs

Mix all ingredients together, adding a little salmon juice, if necessary, and form into patties. Cover patties with bread crumbs. Leave in a cool place overnight.

Bake in shallow dish at 350° F for 15 minutes.

Makes 10 to 12 cakes.

—F. Rosati

Salmon Cakes

2 cups cooked salmon
1 medium onion, chopped &
   sautéed
1 egg
¼ cup chopped parsley
1 tsp. dry dill weed
½ tsp. sweet basil
4 Tbsp. flour

Combine all ingredients except flour in a bowl and shape into patties. Coat well with flour. Fry, turning once, until crisp and golden.

Makes 8 large patties.

—Chris Ferris

Poached Cod

1 lb. fish fillets
1¼ cups milk
½ tsp. salt
1 small bay leaf
3 peppercorns
1 whole clove
2 Tbsp. butter
3 Tbsp. chopped green onion
2 Tbsp. flour
⅛ tsp. pepper
2-3 Tbsp. Lemon juice

Cut fish into serving-sized pieces. Heat milk, salt, bay leaf, peppercorns and clove to boiling in a large skillet. Add fish, bring just to a boil, lower heat, cover and simmer until flaky — 5 to 10 minutes. Lift fish out and keep warm.

Meanwhile, melt butter and add onion. Cook, stirring, for 3 minutes. Sprinkle in flour and pepper, stirring to blend. Remove from heat and stir into fish liquid.

Return pan to heat and stir sauce until boiling, thickened and smooth. Add lemon juice. Pour the sauce over the fish and garnish with more green onion.

Serves 4.

—Sharron Jansen

Breaded Cod Fillets

1 lb. cod fillets
1 egg
¼ cup milk
8-10 crushed crackers
¼ tsp. sea salt
Pinch of pepper
¼ tsp. garlic powder
¼ tsp. sweet basil
¼ tsp. dill weed

Dip fillets in egg and milk beaten together. Combine remaining ingredients and coat fillets with this mixture.

Fry fillets in oil for about 5 minutes on each side.

Serves 4.

—Diane Schoemperlen

Baked Cod with Vegetables

2 lbs. frozen cod fillets
2 cups finely chopped tomatoes
½ cup finely chopped onion
¼ cup finely chopped green pepper
1 tsp. salt
⅛ tsp. pepper
½ tsp. basil
¼ tsp. thyme
¼ tsp. tarragon
¼ cup corn oil

Thaw fish until fillets can be separated, and arrange in a shallow greased baking dish. Combine tomatoes, onion, green pepper, seasonings and oil, and spread on top of fish. Bake 10 to 15 minutes at 475° F or until fish flakes when tested with a fork.

Serves 6.

—Shirley Gilbert

Sole Amandine

With its subtle flavours and contrasting textures, this simple but elegant dish can only be described as delectable.

½ cup flour
1 tsp. salt
¼ tsp. pepper
1 tsp. paprika
2 lbs. sole fillets
3 Tbsp. butter
3 Tbsp. slivered almonds
3 Tbsp. lemon juice
1 tsp. grated lemon rind
3 Tbsp. chopped chives
⅓ cup salad oil

Combine flour, salt, pepper and paprika in a flat dish. Cut fish into serving-sized pieces and dip into flour mixture to coat both sides.

Heat butter in a small skillet. Add almonds and cook gently, stirring, until golden. Stir in lemon juice, lemon rind and chives.

Heat oil in large heavy skillet and fry fish quickly on both sides until golden. Lift out onto a hot platter and pour almond mixture over fish. Serve immediately.

Serves 6.

—Patricia Burley

Capers' Sole

1 lb. sole, thinly sliced
1 cup sour cream
1 green onion, chopped
¼ lb. baby shrimp
6 oz. orange juice
Grated Parmesan cheese to garnish

Place half the sole in a greased baking dish. Cover with half the sour cream and half the green onion. Sprinkle with all of the shrimp. Repeat layers of sole, sour cream and green onion. Pour orange juice over all and sprinkle with Parmesan cheese.

Bake at 350° F for 30 minutes.

Serves 2.

—Capers Restaurant

Sole Florentine

1½ lbs. spinach, cooked,
    drained & chopped
2 lbs. sole fillets, wiped dry
3-4 green onions, chopped
2 cups sliced mushrooms
4 Tbsp. butter
½ cup butter
½ cup flour
2 cups milk
Salt & pepper

Place spinach in buttered casserole dish and lay fish fillets on top.

Sauté mushrooms in 4 Tbsp. butter. Sprinkle green onion and mushrooms on top of fish.

Melt remaining ½ cup butter in heavy saucepan. Stir in flour and cook for about 2 minutes. Gradually add milk, stirring constantly. Bring to a boil and cook for 1 to 2 minutes or until thick. Add salt and pepper to taste.

Pour over fish and bake at 425° F for 15 to 20 minutes.

Serves 6.

—Sheila Bear

Haddock Fillets with Mushroom Sauce

2½ lbs. haddock fillets
1 tsp. salt
Pinch pepper
Pinch cayenne
5 Tbsp. flour
5 Tbsp. butter
1 Tbsp. oil
Pinch white pepper
2 cups milk
½ cup finely chopped
    mushrooms
1 tsp. chopped fresh dill

Pat fillets dry with a paper towel, season on both sides with ½ tsp. salt, pepper and cayenne, and dust lightly with 1 Tbsp. flour.

Place 1 Tbsp. butter and oil in a heavy frying pan, heat and brown fillets, one at a time, on both sides. Place on a heated serving platter to keep warm.

Melt 4 Tbsp. butter in heavy saucepan and stir in 4 Tbsp. flour, white pepper and remaining salt. Slowly stir in milk until sauce is smooth and creamy. Add mushrooms.

Pour mushroom sauce over fish and garnish with dill.

Serves 4 to 6.

—Brenda Eckstein

Tuna Casserole

3 Tbsp. butter
3 Tbsp. flour
1 cup milk
Pinch each: celery salt, dry
    mustard, paprika
¼ tsp. garlic powder
¼ tsp. basil
½ cup grated Cheddar cheese
1 cup uncooked macaroni
1 small onion, chopped
1 green pepper, chopped
2 stalks celery, chopped
½ cup chopped mushrooms
1 large tin tuna

Melt butter, blend in flour and cook on low heat for 5 minutes. Slowly blend in milk and seasonings. Add cheese and cook, stirring, until thick and smooth. Remove from heat and set aside.

Cook macaroni in boiling water until tender.

In a casserole dish, mix together the vegetables, macaroni, cheese sauce and tuna. Bake at 350° F for 45 minutes.

Serves 6.

—Diane Schoemperlen

Baked Fish Alaska

2 lbs. fish fillets
1 cup sour cream
½ cup chopped green onion
    tops
Salt
⅓ cup grated Parmesan cheese
Paprika

Place fillets in well greased baking pan. Combine cream, onion tops, salt and cheese, and spread over fillets. Bake at 350° F for 20 to 25 minutes or until fish flakes easily when tested with a fork. Sprinkle with paprika and serve.

Serves 4.

—J. Bertrand

Baked Fish

2-3 lbs. fish fillets
1 cup milk
1 tsp. salt
Pepper
Paprika
1 Tbsp. lemon juice
3 Tbsp. butter
4 slices bacon
Fine dry bread crumbs

Cut fillets into serving-sized pieces and arrange in a greased casserole dish. Pour milk over fish. Add salt, pepper, paprika and lemon juice. Dot with butter. Arrange bacon slices on fish, cutting them in half if necessary. Sprinkle with bread crumbs. Bake at 425° F until fish flakes easily when tested with a fork — 15 to 20 minutes.

Serves 4 to 6.

—Johanna Vanderheyden

Stir-Fried Fish

Safflower oil or unsalted butter
1 onion, diced
1 green pepper, diced
½ lb. mushrooms, diced
1½ lbs. fish, boned
1½ cups hot water with 1 soya cube added **or** 1½ cups vegetable stock
4 tsp. flour
1 tsp. soya sauce
½ tsp. ginger
2 Tbsp. sherry (optional)

Coat wok with oil or butter. Sauté vegetables quickly in the order listed, placing each new vegetable in centre of wok.

Cut fish into bite-sized pieces and sauté quickly. Add remaining ingredients and stir together.

Serves 4.

—Trish Hines

Oven-Fried Fillets

½ cup fine dry bread crumbs
½ tsp. salt
⅛ tsp. pepper
1 Tbsp. parsley flakes
1 tsp. paprika
2 Tbsp. vegetable oil
2 lbs. sole or perch fillets

Combine bread crumbs, salt, pepper, parsley flakes and paprika in a bowl. Add oil and blend with fork until thoroughly combined. Spread on wax paper.

Separate fish fillets carefully. Press into crumb mixture to coat both sides. Place on greased cookie sheet and bake at 450° F for 12 minutes, or until fish flakes easily.

Serves 6.

—Helen Potts

Fillets au Gratin

2 Tbsp. butter
2 Tbsp. flour
½ tsp. salt
1 cup milk
1 cup grated cheese
1 lb. fish fillets
1 cup bread crumbs tossed with 4 Tbsp. melted butter

Melt butter, remove from heat, blend in flour and salt. Add milk slowly. Return to heat when well blended. Cook until smooth and thickened. Add cheese and remove from heat.

Meanwhile, steam the fillets gently for about 5 minutes. Break them up into a baking dish. Pour cheese sauce over fish. Sprinkle with bread crumbs. Bake at 350° F for 20 minutes.

Serves 4.

—Anne White

Fish in Beer Batter

12-14 oz. flat beer
3 Tbsp. Thousand Island dressing
Whole wheat flour
White flour
1 tsp. baking powder
¼ tsp. tarragon
¼ tsp. paprika
¼ tsp. parsley
¼ tsp. dill
Salt & pepper
9 fillets fish (bass, perch, pickerel)

Pour beer into a large mixing bowl, add the dressing and beat until it breaks into tiny particles.

Slowly mix in flour, using white and whole wheat in proportion to suit your taste, breaking up lumps until batter is thick, not runny, and adheres to a wooden spoon. Add baking powder and seasonings and let sit for 30 minutes.

Dip fillets in batter and fry or deep fry until golden brown and crisp. Drain well and serve.

Serves 4.

—Roly Kleer

Boatman's Stew

2 lbs. white fish
Salt
2 Tbsp. butter
2 medium onions, sliced
6-oz. can tomato paste
3 cups water
¼ tsp. red pepper
¼ tsp. black pepper
1 cup chopped fresh parsley
⅓ cup dry white wine
  (optional)

Cut fish into 2-inch chunks. Sprinkle with salt and let stand for 1 hour. Melt butter in a heavy saucepan and brown onions. Pour off fat and stir in tomato paste, water, pepper, parsley and wine. Simmer for 30 minutes. Drain fish and add to onion/tomato paste mixture. Simmer for 10 minutes.

Serves 6.

—Wendy Searcy

Anchovy Dip

8 oz. cream cheese
1 cup sour cream
1 can anchovies
¼ cup sweet pickled cocktail
  onions
2 cloves garlic

Cream together cheese and sour cream. Mince anchovies, onions and garlic finely. Stir into cheese mixture. Serve with fresh raw vegetables.

Makes 2 cups.

—Maureen Johnson

Salmon Cheese Ball

2 6½-oz. cans salmon
8 oz. cream cheese, softened
1 Tbsp. lemon juice
2 tsp. grated onion
¼ tsp. salt
Dash Worcestershire sauce
6 Tbsp. mayonnaise, page 132
3 Tbsp. snipped fresh
  parsley

Drain and flake salmon, removing bones. Mix all ingredients thoroughly except the parsley. Chill several hours. Shape into a ball or log, roll in parsley and chill.

Makes 2½ cups.

—Marva Blackmore

Sweet & Sour Fish

2 lbs. fish fillets
2 Tbsp. cornstarch
2 Tbsp. oil
1 small onion, chopped
1 clove garlic, minced
1 slice ginger
3 Tbsp. soya sauce
2 Tbsp. sherry (optional)
½ cup honey
4 Tbsp. vinegar
½ tsp. sesame oil (optional)
1 cup chicken stock

Cut fish into 2-inch chunks and shake in cornstarch to coat. Heat oil in wok and fry fish until golden brown, stirring frequently. Remove from pan.

Add chopped onion, garlic and ginger and fry until golden brown.

Combine remaining ingredients, add to wok and bring to a boil. Lower heat and cook until thickened. Add fish and simmer 1 minute.

Serves 6.

—Brigitte Wolf

Creamy Tuna Filling

1 cup cottage cheese
½ cup mayonnaise, page 132
1 small can tuna, drained &
  flaked
¼ cup sliced stuffed olives
Few drops Tabasco sauce

Combine cottage cheese and mayonnaise and blend until smooth. Add tuna, olives and Tabasco sauce. Combine thoroughly.

Chill and use for sandwiches.

Makes 2 cups.

—Donna Jubb

Kipper Paté

1 lb. kipper fillets
4 Tbsp. butter
1 onion, peeled & finely
    chopped
Black pepper

Cook kippers by gently poaching in water.

Melt butter in pan and fry onion until very soft but not brown. Add kippers. Flake and mix well with onion and pepper to taste.

Remove from heat. Mash well with fork until quite smooth.

Put into earthenware dish or other container suitable for serving. Press down. Cover and refrigerate until served.

—*Sheila Bear*

Hot Seafood Cocktail Spread

8 oz. cream cheese
1 Tbsp. milk
7½-oz. tin shrimp
2 tsp. Worcestershire sauce
2 Tbsp. green onion

Soften cream cheese and combine with milk. Crumble shrimp and add to cheese mixture. Add Worcestershire sauce and green onion and mix well.

Turn into greased 8-inch pie plate and bake at 350° F for 15 minutes. Spread on crackers and serve hot.

Makes 1½ cups.

—*Olga Harrison*

Crab Delight

8 oz. cream cheese, softened
1 Tbsp. milk
6 oz. cooked crabmeat
1 Tbsp. finely chopped green
    onion
Pinch Dijon mustard
Pinch salt

Cream cheese with milk until soft and smooth. Add crabmeat, onion, mustard and salt. Blend well.

Refrigerate 3 to 4 hours. Serve with crackers or bite-sized fresh vegetables.

—*Brenda Watts*

Shrimp Dip

8 oz. cream cheese
Juice of 1 lemon
½ cup mayonnaise, page 92
2 Tbsp. ketchup
1 small onion, grated
Dash Worcestershire sauce
Dash salt
1 cup chopped shrimp

Cream cheese with lemon juice and add remaining ingredients. Chill well before serving.

Makes 2 cups.

—*A. H. McInnis*

Bethany Peppers

4 large green peppers
2 Tbsp. butter
1 onion, chopped
1 clove garlic, minced
1 tsp. minced parsley
2 cups canned tomatoes,
    drained
¼ cup wheat germ or fine
    bread crumbs
Salt & pepper
1 egg, beaten
1 cup cooked shrimp
½ cup bread crumbs tossed
    with 3 Tbsp. butter

Split in half and seed green peppers. Steam for 5 minutes and set aside.

Sauté onion in melted butter. Add garlic, parsley, tomatoes and wheat germ or bread crumbs. Cook, stirring, until soft and well mixed. Season with salt and pepper, then stir in egg and shrimp.

Stuff peppers with this mixture and sprinkle with bread crumbs. Bake at 350° F for 20 minutes.

Serves 4.

—*Bryanna Clark*

Scalloped Crab

2 Tbsp. butter
2 Tbsp. flour
1 cup light cream
Salt & pepper
½ tsp. paprika
2 cups crabmeat
⅔ cup bread crumbs
2 Tbsp. melted butter
Paprika

Melt the butter, add flour and cook a few minutes. Add cream and cook, stirring, until smooth and thick. Season with salt, pepper and paprika.

In an ovenproof dish place half the sauce, the crabmeat, the rest of the sauce, then the bread crumbs. Drizzle the melted butter over all and dust with paprika. Bake for about 25 minutes at 350° F.

Serves 4.

—*Irene Louden*

Baked Scallops

1 cup bread crumbs
Salt & pepper
1 lb. scallops
½ cup melted butter

Butter a casserole dish and layer the crumbs, seasoned with salt and pepper, and scallops, finishing with a layer of crumbs. Pour melted butter over all and bake at 375° F for 15 to 20 minutes.

Serves 2.

—*Audrey Moroso*

Shrimp Tarts

Pastry for 9-inch pie crust
1½ cups shrimp
½ cup chopped green onion
½ lb. Swiss cheese, grated
1 cup mayonnaise, page 92
4 eggs
1 cup milk
½ tsp. salt
½ tsp. dill weed

Roll out pastry and cut into six 4-inch circles. Place in muffin tins. Combine shrimp, green onion and cheese and place in pastry shells. Beat together mayonnaise, eggs, milk, salt and dill weed. Pour over mixture in shells.

Bake at 400° F for 15 to 20 minutes.

Makes 6 tarts.

—*Linda Fahie*

Crab Tarts

2 loaves thin sandwich bread
½ cup melted butter
3 Tbsp. butter
¼ cup flour
1½ cups milk
1 cup grated Cheddar cheese
6-oz. can crabmeat, drained & flaked
1 Tbsp. green onion, finely chopped
1 Tbsp. lemon juice
2 Tbsp. minced parsley
1 tsp. Worcestershire sauce
1 tsp. prepared mustard
½ tsp. salt
Dash Tabasco sauce

To make toasted shells, cut circle out of bread using a medium-sized cup. Brush melted butter on both sides of the bread circles. Press bread gently into muffin tins to form a shell. Bake at 425° F for 5 minutes, or until edges are crisp and golden brown.

To make filling, melt butter in medium saucepan over medium heat. Let butter bubble, then stir in flour to form a smooth paste. Let bubble and add milk. Bring to a boil, stirring frequently, then turn heat to low. When mixture forms a thick, creamy sauce, add the cheese, stirring until melted.

Add the remaining ingredients one at a time, stirring after each addition. Remove from heat. Spoon filling into toasted shells and place on a cookie sheet. Bake at 350° F for 15 minutes.

Makes 3 dozen.

—*Cathy Davis*

Clam Crisp

1¼ cups flour
1 tsp. baking powder
¼ tsp. cayenne
2 eggs
½ cup milk
2 cans minced clams
1 green onion, chopped
Parsley
1 celery stalk, chopped
Salt & pepper

Mix flour, baking powder and cayenne in a bowl. Beat eggs and milk together, then beat in flour mixture until smooth. Let stand for 30 minutes.

Add clams, onion, parsley, celery, salt and pepper. Drop by spoonfuls into hot oil and cook until golden brown.

—Jane Guigueno

Seafood Casserole

1 lb. scallops
2 cups milk
¼ cup butter
¼ cup flour
½ tsp. salt
Pepper
1 tsp. curry powder
1 can cream of shrimp soup
½ cup shrimp

Cover scallops with milk and simmer for 10 minutes. Drain and reserve 1½ cups of milk.

Meanwhile, melt butter and stir in flour and seasonings. Add reserved milk and cook, stirring, until thickened. Stir in curry powder and shrimp soup.

Pour into serving dish and add shrimp and scallops.

Serves 4.

—J.E. Riendl

Coquilles St. Jacques

1 lb. scallops
½ cup white wine
¼ cup water
1 small onion, chopped
Salt & pepper
Bouquet garni (small cheesecloth bag containing 1 bay leaf, 6 sprigs parsley, chopped celery stalk & 6 peppercorns)
¼ lb. mushrooms
Juice of 1 lemon
3 Tbsp. butter
3 Tbsp. flour
1 cup light cream
1 egg yolk
¼ cup bread crumbs
2 Tbsp. melted butter
2 Tbsp. Parmesan cheese

Wash scallops and simmer slowly in wine and water with onion, salt, pepper and bouquet garni. Drain, reserving liquid. Place liquid back on stove, boil down to ½ cup and set aside.

Slice mushrooms, combine with lemon juice and cook 4 minutes. Set aside.

Melt butter, stir in flour and cook until smooth. Stir in cream and cook slowly, stirring constantly, until mixture thickens. Stir in scallop liquid. Beat egg yolk and pour sauce over it slowly, stirring constantly.

Combine scallops, drained mushrooms and sauce. Pour into a casserole dish or scallop shells. Sprinkle with bread crumbs, melted butter and Parmesan cheese. Brown under broiler and serve immediately.

Serves 6 as an appetizer.

—Margaret Silverthorn

Shrimp Curry

1 stalk celery, finely chopped
½ green pepper, finely diced
2 green onions, finely chopped
¼ cup butter
1 lb. shrimp, cleaned & deveined
¼ cup flour
2 cups light cream
Salt & pepper
2 Tbsp. curry powder

Sauté celery, green pepper and onions in butter. When celery is slightly softened, stir in shrimp and continue to sauté, stirring constantly, until shrimp is bright pink. Remove shrimp and vegetables from pan.

Stir flour into remaining liquid, adding butter, if needed, to make a roux. Slowly stir in cream to make a thick cream sauce. Add salt, pepper and curry powder. Return shrimp and vegetables to sauce and heat through.

Serves 2.

Shrimp & Scallop Tilsit

12 oz. scallops
1½ tsp. lemon juice
1 tsp. salt
⅓ lb. small mushrooms,
   halved
1 Tbsp. diced green pepper
7 Tbsp. butter
6 Tbsp. flour
1½ cups milk
8 oz. Tilsit cheese, diced
¼ tsp. garlic powder
¼ tsp. white pepper
¼ tsp. dry mustard
1 tsp. ketchup
8 oz. cooked shrimp
2 Tbsp. sherry
Patty shells **or** homemade
   cream puff shells

Cover scallops with water, add ½ tsp. lemon juice and ¼ tsp. salt and simmer 10 minutes. Drain, reserving ¼ cup of the stock.

Cook mushrooms and green peppers in 2 Tbsp. butter for 5 minutes. Add remaining butter, stir in flour, then slowly add milk and stock. Stir in cheese until melted, add remaining lemon juice and seasonings. Add scallops, shrimp and sherry. Heat through and serve in patty shells.

Serves 4.

—*Dorothy Hurst*

Shrimp in Beer Creole

½ cup sliced blanched
   almonds
3 Tbsp. butter
1 Tbsp. oil
Salt
2 lbs. shrimp, shelled &
   deveined
¼ cup butter
¼ cup minced scallions
1 green pepper, cut into
   strips
½ lb. small mushrooms,
   cleaned
1 Tbsp. paprika
Salt & pepper
1 tsp. tomato paste
1 cup light beer
¾ cup heavy cream

In a small skillet, sauté the almonds in 1 Tbsp. of butter and the oil until golden. Drain on paper towels, sprinkle with salt and set aside.

Cook the shrimp in ¼ cup butter over medium heat, stirring, until they turn pink. Transfer the shrimp and pan juices to a bowl and reserve.

Add 2 Tbsp. butter to saucepan and sauté scallions and green pepper until softened. Add mushrooms, paprika, salt and pepper and cook until mushrooms are tender. Stir in tomato paste, beer and pan juices and reduce liquid over high heat to ½ cup. Reduce heat to low, add cream and shrimp and simmer until hot.

Serve over rice pilaf and garnish with almonds.

Serves 4.

—*Veronica Green*

Turkey Oyster Pie

1 onion, diced
2 stalks celery, diced
1 small green pepper, diced
2 Tbsp. butter
2 cups diced cooked turkey
2 cups fresh oysters, lightly
   poached
1½ cups cream of
   mushroom sauce, page 132
Dash Worcestershire sauce
Pepper
3-4 cups mashed potatoes

Sauté onion, celery and green pepper in butter. Place in casserole dish and add turkey, oysters, mushroom sauce, Worcestershire sauce and pepper. Combine well and top with mashed potatoes.

Bake at 350° F for 30 to 40 minutes.

Serves 6.

—*The Sword Restaurant*

Crabmeat Mousse

2 tsp. gelatin
¼ cup cold water
¼ cup boiling water
¾ cup mayonnaise, page 132
1 cup flaked crabmeat
½ cup chopped celery
2 Tbsp. chopped parsley
½ cup chopped cucumber
2 Tbsp. chopped olives
1-2 Tbsp. lemon juice
Shredded lettuce

Soften gelatin in cold water and then dissolve in boiling water. Add mayonnaise, then crabmeat, celery, parsley, cucumber, olives and lemon juice and mix well.

Place in a wet mould and chill until firm. Unmould onto lettuce.

Serves 6.

Crab Louis

2 tsp. chili sauce
2 tsp. chopped green onion
1 tsp. vinegar
1 tsp. horseradish
1 tsp. mustard
½ tsp. sugar
¼ tsp. paprika
Salt & pepper
½ cup mayonnaise
½ cup sour cream
1 lb. crabmeat, cooked and
 cut into chunks
1 head lettuce
2-3 hard-boiled eggs, sliced
1 cucumber, sliced

Combine chili sauce, green onion, vinegar, horseradish, mustard, sugar, paprika, salt, pepper, mayonnaise and sour cream. Toss with crabmeat.

Shred lettuce and line serving bowl with it. Top with crabmeat mixture and surround with egg and cucumber slices.

Serves 6.

—J. Bertrand

Shrimp Salad

1½ cups cooked rice
1½ cups raw peas
1½ cups chopped celery
¼ cup chopped green onion
1 cup shrimp
½ cup salad oil
1 Tbsp. soya sauce
1 tsp. celery seed
2 Tbsp. cider vinegar
Salt
½ Tbsp. sugar

Combine rice, peas, celery, onion and shrimp. For dressing, blend remaining ingredients well. Pour over shrimp mixture. Toss and chill.

Serves 4.

—Trudy Mason

Seafood in Filo Pastry

2 Tbsp. butter
½ cup thinly sliced celery
½ cup chopped onions
1 cup sliced mushrooms
4 Tbsp. flour
1 tsp. salt
1½ cups milk
½ cup white wine
2 Tbsp. lemon juice
¼ cup grated Parmesan
 cheese
½ lb. cooked shrimp
½ lb. cooked sole
1 lb. cooked salmon
8 sheets filo pastry
¾ cup melted butter

Melt butter in large, heavy saucepan. Add celery and onion and cook until tender. Add mushrooms and continue cooking. Stir in flour and salt. Add milk slowly, stirring constantly, and cook until slightly thickened. Stir in wine, lemon juice and cheese. Cook until thickened, stirring constantly. Remove from heat and add seafood.

Grease a 9" x 13" baking dish. Brush each sheet of pastry with melted butter and layer in dish. When all 8 sheets are buttered and in dish, spoon a row of filling down the middle of pastry.

Fold both sides in, so they overlap. Flip gently so seam is facing down. Tuck ends under and brush top with remaining butter.

Bake at 375° F for 45 minutes or until crisp and golden brown.

Serves 8.

—Susan Gillespie

Scallops Mornay

2 lbs. scallops, cut in half
1 onion
Bouquet garni of bay leaf,
 parsley & thyme
1-2 cups white wine
Salt & pepper
¼ cup butter
¼ cup flour
1 cup cream
½ cup grated Swiss cheese

Combine scallops, onion, bouquet garni, salt and pepper in saucepan and add enough white wine to cover. Gently bring to a boil and simmer for 2 minutes. Drain and reserve 1 cup stock.

In a separate pan, melt butter, add flour and cook for 2 minutes. Slowly add cream, stirring constantly. Add stock, bring to a boil and cook gently for 2 minutes. Add Swiss cheese and cook until melted. Add scallops and stir well.

Pour into greased casserole dish and top with a sprinkling of bread crumbs, grated Swiss cheese and a drizzle of melted butter. Brown in oven and serve.

Serves 6.

—Sheila Bear

Seafood Salad

Equally good hot or cold, this dish can be made with fresh, frozen or canned seafood.

¼ cup butter
¼ cup chopped onion
¼ cup chopped green & red
  peppers
2 cups crabmeat, drained &
  rinsed if canned
10 oz. large shrimp, drained
  & rinsed if canned
1 cup mayonnaise, page 132
1 tsp. Worcestershire sauce
2 tsp. mustard
Salt & pepper
Parsley
Lemon wedges

In a small skillet, melt butter, add onions and peppers, and cook until onions are translucent. Pour into lightly greased baking dish. Add remaining ingredients except parsley and lemon. Mix well. Bake at 350° F for 20 minutes, sprinkle with parsley, layer lemon over top and serve.

Serves 4.

—C. Majewski

Herring Salad

Herring is a traditional Yuletime dish for many, and this salad provides a colourful and flavourful method of serving it. Milter herring are the male fish during breeding season.

6 milter herring
1 cup dry red wine
2 hard-boiled eggs, cubed
1 cup cooked veal, cubed
2 cups pickled beets, cubed
½ cup chopped onion
2 stalks celery, chopped
½ cup chopped boiled
  potatoes
3 cups diced apples
1 cup shredded almonds
1 cup sugar
2 Tbsp. horseradish
2 Tbsp. parsley
Olives to garnish

Soak the herring in water for 12 hours. Skin them and remove the milt and bones. Rub the milt through sieve with wine.

Cube the herring and mix with eggs, veal, beets, onion, celery, potatoes, apples and almonds.

Combine milt mixture with sugar, horseradish and parsley. Pour over salad and mix well. Shape into mound and garnish with olives.

Serves 12.

Lobster Mould

1 lb. cooked lobster
1 Tbsp. capers
⅓ small onion
3 Tbsp. whipping cream
⅓ cup butter, softened
2 Tbsp. anisette
Dash Tabasco sauce
1 tsp. salt
1 tsp. fresh tarragon
Whipped cream & grapes to
  garnish

Grind together the lobster, capers and onion. Add whipping cream, butter, anisette, Tabasco sauce, salt and tarragon. Mix well and pack into a mould. Refrigerate for several hours before unmoulding.

Place unmoulded salad on a bed of lettuce, cover with whipped cream and garnish with green grapes.

Serves 4.

Salad Niçoise

2 cloves garlic, peeled
6 anchovy fillets, coarsely
  chopped
6-oz. can tuna, drained
2 tomatoes, peeled &
  quartered
1 cucumber, peeled & finely
  chopped
12 black olives, pitted &
  chopped
1 cup Bibb lettuce, torn up
1 cup romaine lettuce, torn up
French dressing, page 133

Rub salad bowl with garlic and discard garlic. Combine anchovy fillets, tuna, tomatoes, cucumber, olives and lettuces. Toss gently with dressing to coat. Chill well before serving.

Serves 2 as a main course, 4 as a salad.

Chinese Tuna Salad

2 6½-oz. cans tuna
2 cups coarsely shredded
 lettuce
¼ cup chopped onion
½ cup chopped parsley or
 watercress
¼ tsp. grated lemon rind
½ tsp. ground coriander
¼ cup sesame seeds
¼ cup toasted slivered
 almonds
3-oz. pkg. chow mein
 noodles
1 Tbsp. lemon juice
3 Tbsp. soya sauce
1 Tbsp. oil

Combine all but last 3
ingredients. Mix together lemon
juice, soya sauce and oil, pour
over salad and toss.

Serves 6.

—Anna J. Lee

Cottage
Salmon Casserole

1 cup cooked salmon
2 cups cottage cheese
1 Tbsp. minced onion
1 egg
½ cup bread crumbs
1 tsp. salt
Paprika

Combine all ingredients,
reserving ¼ cup bread crumbs
for topping. Place in greased
casserole dish and top with
reserved crumbs and a
sprinkling of paprika. Bake at
350° F for 30 minutes.

Serves 2.

—Isabell Lingrell

Sole Swirls
in Tropical Sauce

2 lbs. sole fillets
Salt
1 cup coarsely grated carrot
¼ cup finely chopped onion
½ cup melted butter
½ tsp. salt
1 cup crushed pineapple,
 drained & juice reserved
SAUCE:
1 cup pineapple juice
2 Tbsp. vinegar
1 Tbsp. brown sugar
1 Tbsp. cornstarch
2 tsp. soya sauce
½ medium green pepper,
 chopped

Sprinkle fillets with salt. Sauté
carrot and onion in ¼ cup
melted butter until tender, then
add salt. Combine pineapple
with vegetables and stuff fillets.
Place in greased baking dish and
drizzle with remaining butter.
Bake for 20 to 30 minutes at
450° F.

Combine and heat ingredients
for sauce until thickened. Pour
over fish and serve.

Serves 6.

—Gillian Richardson

Fillets of Sole
with Leeks & Shrimp

2 cups sliced leeks, white
 part only
½ cup butter
8 oz. shrimp, cooked,
 shelled & chopped
2 Tbsp. chopped dill weed
1 cup whipping cream
⅔ cup dry white wine
Salt & white pepper
Lemon juice
4 sole fillets
Flour

Cook leeks in ¼ cup butter
over medium heat for 5 minutes.
Stir in shrimp and dill and cook
for 1 minute. Add cream, wine,
salt and pepper and lemon juice
to taste and simmer for 10
minutes, or until thickened. Set
aside and keep warm.

Dust sole with flour and sauté
in remaining ¼ cup butter over
medium-high heat until golden
and flaky. Transfer to heated
platter and pour sauce over.

Serves 4.

—Pam Collacott

Creamy Fillet of Sole

4 sole fillets
1 green onion, chopped
1 Tbsp. chopped parsley
6 large mushrooms, sliced
1 tsp. salt
⅛ tsp. pepper
3 Tbsp. apple juice
2 Tbsp. butter, cut into
    pieces
3 Tbsp. cream
1 tsp. lemon juice

Place sole in buttered dish. Sprinkle with onion and parsley. Top with mushrooms and salt and pepper. Add apple juice and dot with 1 Tbsp. butter. Top with a piece of brown paper and bake at 500° F for 15 minutes. Drain liquid and reduce to half by cooking over high heat. Add cream, lemon juice and remaining 1 Tbsp. butter. Mix and pour over fillets and place in hot oven or under broiler for 5 minutes to brown.

Serves 4.

—Andrea Stuart

Sole Gratinée aux Champignons

1½-2 lbs. sole fillets
½ cup dry white wine
Salt
4 Tbsp. butter
1/2 lb. mushrooms, sliced
2 Tbsp. lemon juice
3 Tbsp. flour
⅓ cup light cream
⅛ tsp. nutmeg
¾ cup grated Swiss cheese

Arrange fish in greased, shallow baking dish so that fish is no more than 1-inch and no less than ½-inch thick. Pour white wine over fish and sprinkle with salt. Cover and bake at 400° F for 6 to 10 minutes, depending on thickness. Drain off juices and measure, adding water to make I cup. Place fish in baking dish and set aside.

In skillet, melt 2 Tbsp. butter and add mushrooms and lemon juice. Cook over high heat, stirring, until mushrooms are cooked and juice is evaporated. Let cool, then remove mushrooms from pan.

Melt remaining 2 Tbsp. butter in pan and stir in flour. Remove from heat and gradually add 1 cup fish stock, cream and nutmeg. Return to heat and cook, stirring, until thickened.

Cover fish evenly with mushrooms and sauce and top with cheese. Bake, uncovered, at 400° F for 10 to 15 minutes, or until hot.

Serves 4 to 6.

—Heather Petrie

Stuffed Sole

1 clove garlic, finely chopped
3 mushrooms, finely chopped
¾ cup finely chopped spinach
1 Tbsp. butter
6 medium shrimp, chopped
3 medium-sized sole fillets
Salt & pepper

Cook garlic, mushrooms and spinach in butter until soft. Add shrimp and stir to mix. Season fillets with salt and pepper. Place one-third of mixture on each fillet, roll up and secure with toothpick. Place in buttered baking dish, cover and bake at 350° F for 15 to 20 minutes.

Serves 3.

—Gail Walter

Scrumptious Sole

1 head broccoli, chopped &
    parboiled
1 lb. sole fillets
4 oz. shrimp
1 cup sliced mushrooms
2 cups cream of mushroom
    sauce (page 132)
¼ cup Parmesan cheese
½ tsp. chopped dill weed
½ tsp. salt
½ tsp. pepper
¼ tsp. nutmeg
1 Tbsp. lemon juice
1 Tbsp. Worcestershire sauce

Line a 9" x 13" baking pan with foil. Place broccoli in bottom and cover with fillets. Top with shrimp and mushrooms. Combine mushroom sauce, cheese, dill, salt, pepper, nutmeg, lemon juice and Worcestershire sauce and pour over fish. Close and seal foil and bake at 350° F for 1 hour.

Serves 4.

—Karen Havelock

Babine River
Salmon Royal

3-4 lbs. filleted salmon, char
   or rainbow trout
Salt
¼ cup butter
2 cups soft bread crumbs
¾ tsp. salt
½ tsp. pepper
1 Tbsp. finely chopped
   parsley
1½ Tbsp. lemon juice
1 cup drained baby clams
1 tsp. tarragon or dill
DRAWN BUTTER SAUCE:
3 Tbsp. butter
3 Tbsp. flour
1½ cups boiling water
¼ cup butter, cut into
   ½-inch cubes
½ tsp. salt
1 Tbsp. lemon juice
1 Tbsp. parsley
Lemon wedges

Sprinkle fillets with salt. Melt butter and combine with remaining ingredients. Lay one fillet, skin side down, on large piece of foil and shape foil up sides of fish. Pile stuffing evenly over fish and top with the other fillet. Bring foil up to overlap edges so that no open flesh is showing, only skin. Place on baking sheet and bake for 10 minutes per stuffed inch at 450° F.

To make sauce, melt butter over low heat and stir in flour to make thick roux. Add boiling water gradually and stir constantly until smooth. Add the chopped butter gradually, stirring well after each addition. Season with salt and add lemon juice and parsley. Place on platter garnished with parsley and lemon wedges and serve with sauce.

Serves 6 to 8.

—Lori Messer

Orange Curried
Fish Steaks

Although halibut is a white-fleshed fish and salmon a pink, either one can be used equally successfully in this recipe.

4 halibut or salmon steaks,
   1-inch thick
Oil
Salt & pepper
¾ cup mayonnaise
¼ cup catsup
2 tsp. grated orange peel
2 Tbsp. orange juice
¼ tsp. curry
1 orange, cut into wedges
Parsley

Brush fish steaks lightly with oil and sprinkle with salt and pepper. Place on well-oiled broiler and barbecue over moderately hot coals for 5 to 7 minutes on each side, brushing occasionally with additional oil.

Meanwhile, make the sauce by combining mayonnaise, catsup, orange peel, orange juice and curry.

Remove fish to serving plate, garnish with orange wedges and parsley and serve with the sauce.

Serves 4.

—Irene Louden

Baked Sole
with Currants

½ cup currants
¾ cup white wine
1-1½ lbs. sole
Salt & pepper
Juice of 1 lemon
2 green onions, sliced
2 cloves garlic, crushed
3 Tbsp. oil
1 9-oz. can tomatoes
2 whole cloves
3 Tbsp. chopped parsley
2 Tbsp. flour

Soak currants in wine for at least 15 minutes. Place fish in greased baking pan and sprinkle with salt, pepper and lemon juice. Sauté onions and garlic in oil over low heat for about 3 minutes. Add remaining ingredients except flour and simmer for 10 minutes. Make a smooth paste of flour mixed with sauce juices and stir into sauce. Pour over fish and bake at 400° F for 30 minutes.

Serves 4.

—Marjorie Moore

Smoked Salmon

Smoked salmon can serve as the base for a number of delicious hors d'oeuvres. Of course, it is best known served as lox, with bagels and fresh cream cheese. Smoked salmon should be pale pink and should not be salty in taste. If it is red in colour and tastes salty, a smoke salt extract has been used in the processing.
It is easiest to slice smoked salmon if it is partially frozen — it should be sliced across the grain as thinly as possible. A few suggestions for serving smoked salmon as a canape follow.

1. Place on crackers or squares of toast, dust with freshly ground pepper and sprinkle with lemon juice.
2. Top salmon with a slice of stuffed olive.
3. Top with guacamole and serve on toast.

Smoked Salmon Caribbean

1½ lbs. smoked salmon
4 Tbsp. olive oil
1 Tbsp. lime or lemon juice
¼ tsp. pepper
½ Tbsp. Tabasco sauce
½ cup chopped green onions
½ cup chopped onions
2 tomatoes, chopped
1 ripe avocado, chopped
½ cup cooked garbanzo
    beans
½ cup chopped sweet red
    peppers
½ cup chopped artichoke
    hearts
Romaine lettuce

Chop salmon into bite-sized pieces. In a bowl, combine oil, lime or lemon juice, pepper and Tabasco sauce. Add salmon, onions, tomatoes, avocado, garbanzo beans, peppers and artichoke hearts. Toss and serve on lettuce leaves.

Serves 4.

—Noel Roberts

Stuffed Snapper with Orange & Lime

4 Tbsp. butter
5 oz. shrimp, sliced
1 cup sliced mushrooms
2 green onions, finely chopped
2 stalks celery, chopped
½ tsp. tarragon
½ tsp. basil
½ tsp. thyme
1 pineapple, half sliced &
    half diced
5-6 lbs. red snapper fillets
Juice of 1 lime
Juice & zest of 3 oranges
2 Tbsp. flour
1 cup whipping cream
2 Tbsp. sherry
Pepper

Melt 2 Tbsp. butter and sauté shrimp, mushrooms, green onions, celery and herbs. Add diced half of pineapple and sauté for 2 to 3 minutes.

Lay fillets flat and make a slit lengthwise down the centre of each, starting and ending 2 inches from either end and being careful not to cut all the way through. Run knife sideways down the slit out towards the edges of the fillet, creating a pocket. Stuff sautéed mixture into snapper, reserving ¼ cup. Cover with lime and orange juices. Bake, covered, at 350° F for 30 minutes.

Gently mince the reserved stuffing and set aside. Place remaining 2 Tbsp. butter in skillet, add flour and cook until blended. Add cream, stirring until thickened and add reserved stuffing. Stir in sherry, pepper and grated orange zest.

When snapper is cooked, remove from pan to serving dish. Add pan liquid to sauce and reduce by simmering. Surround fish with sliced pineapple and pour sauce over top.

Serves 6 to 8.

—Jan van der Est

Baked Stuffed Arctic Char

The contributor of this and the following recipe lived on Baffin Island for 5 years, where char is fresh and readily available. This recipe is an adaptation of one for stuffed fish that came originally from McGowen House, a fishermen's boardinghouse on Lake Memphramagog in Quebec.

2 cups cracker crumbs
1 small onion, chopped
½ cup chopped parsley
4-5 sweet pickles, chopped
½ cup melted butter
¼ cup pickle juice
1 large Arctic char, cleaned
Soft butter

Combine crumbs, onion, parsley, pickles, melted butter and pickle juice. Stuff fish with this and sew opening together. Rub fish all over with soft butter. Place in foil-lined roasting pan and bake at 400° F for 45 to 60 minutes, or until fish flakes.

Serves 6 to 8.

—*Judith Asbil*

Barbecued Arctic Char

Arctic char, cut into fillets
Soya sauce
Lemon wedges

Marinate char in soya sauce for 1 hour or more, turning occasionally to make sure all parts of fish are covered. Cover barbecue grill with foil and grease lightly. Place drained fillets on grill for 5 minutes. Turn and grill for another 5 minutes, or until fish flakes with a fork. Serve with lemon wedges.

Serves 6 to 8.

—*Judith Asbil*

Red Snapper Vera Cruz

4 tomatoes, peeled & chopped
1 onion, chopped
1 green pepper, sliced
5 Tbsp. butter
½ tsp. thyme
¼ cup white wine
1 bay leaf
1 lemon, quartered
1 tsp. parsley
4 lbs. red snapper, filleted

Make sauce by sautéing tomatoes, onion and green pepper in butter until onion is transparent. Add remaining ingredients except fish and cook for 5 minutes. Place fish in greased casserole dish, top with sauce and bake at 350° F for 35 minutes.

Serves 4.

—*Melody Scott*

Chinese Red Snapper

¼ cup chopped green onions
1 clove garlic, chopped
1-inch piece ginger root, chopped
4 lbs. red snapper
¼ cup sesame seed oil
½ cup soya sauce

Combine green onions, garlic and ginger root and rub over fish, placing some inside fish. Bake at 400° F for 1 hour. Remove onions, ginger and garlic from fish.

Heat sesame seed oil and soya sauce. Pour over fish and serve.

Serves 6 to 8.

—*Claudette Spies*

Baked Trout with Almond Cream

⅓ cup slivered almonds
3 Tbsp. butter
1 Tbsp. minced green onion
3 rainbow trout, boned
Parsley
6 Tbsp. white wine
½ cup whipping cream
1 Tbsp. sour cream
1½ tsp. cornstarch
Salt & pepper
Lemon juice

Brown almonds in butter and set aside. Butter a piece of aluminum foil large enough to wrap around fish. Sprinkle with green onion and place fish on top. Stuff each fish with parsley, then pour over wine and butter from cooking almonds. Tightly close foil over fish and bake at 425° F for 10 minutes per inch of thickness of fish.

Meanwhile, remove almonds to paper towel. Combine whipping cream, sour cream and cornstarch in saucepan. When fish is cooked, pour fish liquid into cream mixture and bring to a boil, stirring constantly. Cook until thickened and smooth. Add salt and pepper and lemon juice to taste.

To serve, remove parsley from fish. Top each fish with small ribbon of sauce and almonds. Serve remaining sauce separately.

Serves 6.

—*The Art of Cooking School*

Fillets Baked
in Sour Cream

4 tsp. butter
2 lbs. fish fillets (sole,
  haddock or flounder)
1 tsp. salt
½ tsp. Tabasco sauce
1 Tbsp. paprika
¼ cup Parmesan cheese
1 cup sour cream
¼ cup fine bread crumbs
Lemon & parsley

Grease 2-quart casserole dish
with 1 tsp. butter. Arrange fish
in dish. Blend salt, Tabasco
sauce, paprika and Parmesan
cheese into sour cream. Spread
over fish. Top with bread crumbs
and dot with remaining butter.
Bake, uncovered, at 350° F for
30 minutes, or until fish is easily
flaked with a fork. Garnish with
lemon slices and parsley sprigs.

Serves 4 to 6.

—Judy Morrison Cayen

Fish Spinach
Casserole

6 oz. fine egg noodles
3 cups vegetable stock
4 Tbsp. butter
4 Tbsp. flour
½ cup yogurt or sour cream
1½ cups cooked spinach
1 cup cooked, flaked fish
3 eggs, hard-boiled & sliced
5 Tbsp. Parmesan cheese

Cook egg noodles in stock
until just tender. Drain and
reserve liquid.

Melt butter until it foams, add
flour and stir until combined.
Add warm stock and stir until
thickened. Remove from heat
and add yogurt or sour cream.

Assemble in a casserole dish
by layering as follows: noodles,
spinach, half the sauce, fish and
eggs. Add 4 Tbsp. Parmesan
cheese to remaining sauce and
pour over top. Bake at 350° F for
20 minutes. Sprinkle remaining
tablespoon of cheese over top
and broil until browned.

Serves 4.

—Ann R. Jeffries

Curried Almond Cod

1 lb. cod
1 lemon, cut into quarters
1 tsp. salt
½ cup flour
Salt & pepper
1 tsp. paprika
Oil
2 medium onions, chopped
1 Tbsp. curry powder
1 Tbsp. flour
1½ cups stock
½ cup shredded almonds
1 Tbsp. chutney
2 tomatoes

Rub cod with lemon and
sprinkle with salt. Let sit for 30
minutes to lose excess liquid.
Wipe the fish and cut into 2-inch
chunks. Combine flour, salt,
pepper and paprika. Roll fish in
seasoned flour. Fry in oil, drain
and place in serving dish. Keep
warm.

Fry onions in 2 Tbsp. oil until
golden, add curry and cook for a
few more minutes. Add flour and
cook, stirring constantly, for 2
minutes. Stir in stock and
simmer, uncovered, for 15
minutes. Add almonds and
simmer for 15 minutes longer.
Add chutney, salt and pepper.
Add tomatoes and heat through.
Spoon over the cod and serve.

Serves 4.

—Kay Barclay

Greek Pastry Stuffed with Fish & Spinach

This recipe takes a bit of time to prepare, but the resulting dish is well worth the effort. Filo pastry can be found in most Italian and Greek specialty stores. It can be stored in the freezer for several months if necessary.

FILLING:
1½ lbs. spinach, washed & coarsely chopped
Butter
1 bunch green onions, sliced
¾ lb. Boston bluefish, minced
½ green pepper, minced
4 eggs, lightly beaten
¼ cup lemon juice
Salt & pepper
1½ tsp. dill weed
1 tsp. garlic powder
PASTRY:
2 cups butter
⅓ cup lemon juice
1 Tbsp. garlic powder
1 lb. filo pastry

To make filling, sauté spinach in butter until limp. Combine with remaining ingredients in bowl and set aside.

For dough, combine butter, lemon juice and garlic powder in saucepan. Cook over low heat until melted. Unwrap filo dough on large working area. Fold one sheet lengthwise in thirds and brush with butter mixture. Fold and butter a second sheet similarly. Place strips end to end, overlapping by ½ inch. Place 2 Tbsp. filling near one end and fold pastry into triangle shape, folding over and over until all dough is used. Place on greased cookie sheet. Repeat with remaining dough and filling. Drizzle with remaining butter mixture and bake at 350° F for 30 minutes, or until golden brown and puffed.

Makes 12 triangles.

—*Titia Posthuma*

Jamaican Saltfish & Dumplings

2 green peppers
1 sweet red pepper
3 or 4 hot banana peppers
2-3 hot cherry peppers
2-3 cups oil
2 large onions, sliced
1 lb. cooked saltfish
DUMPLINGS:
3 cups flour
1 cup corn meal
½ tsp. salt
1½ tsp. baking powder
1 cup warm water

Cut all peppers into large chunks. Place 2 cups oil in pot over medium-high heat. When oil is hot, add onions. Cook for 3 minutes, then add fish and peppers. Oil should just cover all ingredients. Cook for 5 minutes, then reduce heat to medium and cook a further 25 to 30 minutes.

While saltfish and peppers are cooking, prepare dumplings. In a large bowl, mix together flour, corn meal, salt and baking powder. Add just enough water to make a rather stiff dough. Knead for 1 minute, then shape dough into patties. Place 3 Tbsp. of the oil from the fish and peppers in a frying pan. Fry dumplings at medium heat, turning once, until golden brown on both sides. Drain fish and peppers with slotted spoon and serve with dumplings.

Serves 4 to 6.

—*Ken Williamson*

Herring in Sour Cream

16-oz. jar herring, whole or fillets
6 large onions
6 apples
1 quart sour cream
3 Tbsp. vinegar
Salt & pepper
¼ cup crushed walnuts

Drain liquid from jar of herring, discarding spices, onion rings, etc. Dice herring and place in 4-quart porcelain or glass bowl. Peel onions and apples. Cut onions into thinly sliced rings; core and cube apples into ¼-inch cubes. Add to herring. Pour sour cream over top and mix well. Add vinegar, salt and pepper and walnuts. Cover and let stand for 8 hours at room temperature, then refrigerate.

Serves 12 as an appetizer.

—*Wido J. Heck*

Piraeus Shrimp

Served in bowls with a loaf of Italian bread for dipping, this dish makes a delicious meal in itself. It takes its name from the Greek port where the contributors first tasted it.

2 medium onions, chopped
3 large cloves garlic, chopped
2½ Tbsp. olive oil
28-oz. can tomatoes, lightly chopped
Oregano & basil
Salt & pepper
¼ cup white wine
1 lb. shelled, deveined shrimp
8 oz. feta cheese, crumbled

Sauté onions and garlic in oil for 30 seconds over medium-high heat. Add tomatoes, oregano, basil, salt and pepper. Cook until boiling, then add wine. Stir in shrimp when liquid is boiling. Simmer for 5 minutes, or until shrimp turn pinkish white. Add cheese and cook for another 2 or 3 minutes.

Serves 4.

—*John & Elaine Bird*

Seaside Manicotti

6 manicotti shells
10 oz. spinach
½ cup chopped onion
1 clove garlic
2 Tbsp. butter
3 Tbsp. flour
2 cups milk
1 cup Swiss cheese
¼ cup grated Parmesan cheese
2 Tbsp. butter, melted
½ tsp. salt
1 lb. perch fillets, cooked & flaked
Ground nutmeg

Cook manicotti shells and drain. Cook spinach and drain.

Meanwhile, prepare cheese sauce. Cook onion and garlic in 2 Tbsp. butter until tender but not brown. Blend in flour. Add milk all at once. Cook and stir until thick and bubbly. Stir in Swiss cheese until melted.

Combine ½ cup of sauce with the spinach, Parmesan cheese, 2 Tbsp. melted butter and salt. Fold in flaked fish. Stuff manicotti shells with this mixture.

Pour half of remaining sauce into baking dish. Put manicotti on top and pour remaining sauce over.

Cover and bake at 350° F for 30 to 35 minutes. Sprinkle nutmeg over top before serving.

Serves 6.

—*Mary Ann Vanner*

Barbecued Squid

4 large squid
1 thumb-sized piece fresh ginger
1 clove garlic
2 Tbsp. sake or white wine
2 Tbsp. soya sauce

Clean and peel squid and slice into 1½" x 2½" strips. Peel and grate ginger and garlic. Place squid, ginger and garlic in bowl and sprinkle with sake and soya sauce. Mix, then marinate for 30 minutes in cool place. Place squid in a broiler pan and broil for 3 to 5 minutes, basting with sauce once during cooking.

Serves 4.

—*Isao Morrill*

Marinated Squid

2 lbs. squid, cleaned & sliced into 1-inch strips
⅓ cup oil
¼ cup vinegar
1 Tbsp. lemon juice
¼ tsp. salt
Pepper
1 tsp. chopped chives
1 tsp. chopped sweet pepper
1 tsp. chopped parsley

Simmer strips of squid in boiling, salted water for 1 hour. Drain. Combine other ingredients in a bowl and add squid. Marinate for at least 1 hour in refrigerator.

Serves 6 to 8.

—*Marjorie Bobowski*

Spinach Tuna Paté

Butter
2 lbs. spinach, stemmed &
    washed
¾ cup whipping cream
3 large eggs
4 oz. tuna, drained & flaked
½ cup minced scallions
4 anchovy fillets, drained
1 Tbsp. lemon juice
⅓ cup soft white bread
    crumbs
1 tsp. salt
⅛ tsp. pepper
Lemon wedges
Parsley sprigs

Butter bottom of loaf pan, line with wax paper and butter paper lightly.

Cook spinach in large saucepan of boiling, salted water until tender — about 3 minutes. Drain in colander and rinse under cold, running water to cool. Squeeze spinach with hands to remove as much moisture as possible, then chop coarsely. Set aside.

Purée cream, eggs, tuna, scallions, anchovies and lemon juice in blender or food processor until smooth. Turn tuna mixture into medium bowl. Add bread crumbs, salt, pepper and spinach and stir to mix well.

Pour spinach mixture into prepared pan and cover with aluminum foil. Place loaf pan in larger baking dish or small roasting pan and fill with boiling water halfway up sides of loaf pan. Bake in centre of oven at 375° F until knife inserted in centre of paté comes out clean but wet — about 1 hour. Remove from water bath and cool in pan on rack to room temperature. Refrigerate, covered, until chilled — about 3 hours.

At serving time, remove paté from mould and place on serving platter. Cut into ½-inch slices and garnish with lemon wedges and parsley.

—Erika Maurer

Shrimp in Shells au Gratin

½ lb. uncooked shelled
    shrimp
½ cup dry white wine
5 Tbsp. butter
2 Tbsp. flour
1½ cups light cream
Salt
1 Tbsp. finely chopped
    parsley
½ cup sliced mushrooms,
    sautéed
2 Tbsp. Parmesan cheese
½ cup coarse bread crumbs

Cook shrimp in wine for 5 minutes and set aside, reserving liquid. In heavy saucepan, melt 3 Tbsp. butter and stir in flour, cooking for 2 minutes. Gradually stir in ½ cup shrimp liquid then cream. Bring to a boil, then cook for 2 to 3 minutes, stirring constantly. Add salt to taste. Stir in parsley, mushrooms and shrimp.

Spoon mixture into 2 greased au gratin dishes or scallop shells. Melt remaining 2 Tbsp. butter and stir in Parmesan cheese and bread crumbs. Sprinkle this over each shell and place under broiler until crumbs brown.

Serves 2.

—Valerie Cameron

Stir-Fried Prawns

The prawns are cooked in their shells in this recipe. To enjoy all the delicious flavour, suck the shells before removing them to eat the prawns.

3 Tbsp. peanut oil
2 Tbsp. finely chopped
    ginger root
2 cloves garlic, chopped
1 lb. fresh prawns, deheaded
    & washed
1 Tbsp. soya sauce
1 Tbsp. dry sherry
½ tsp. salt
Pepper
Coriander

Heat oil in wok and stir-fry ginger root and garlic for 30 seconds. Add prawns and cook for 2 more minutes to brown shells lightly. Add soya sauce, sherry, salt and pepper and cook for another 2 minutes. Transfer to warm serving dish and garnish with coriander.

Serves 3 to 4.

—Helen Campbell

Shrimp Cooked in Beer

This dish makes an excellent cold appetizer or party snack.

2 bottles beer
2 bay leaves, crumbled
½ tsp. crushed red pepper
½ tsp. cayenne
2 Tbsp. mustard seeds
1½ lbs. jumbo shrimp, shelled & deveined
¼ cup wine vinegar
1 large clove garlic, peeled

Combine beer, bay leaves, red pepper, cayenne and mustard seeds in saucepan. Bring to a boil and simmer for 5 minutes. Add shrimp and simmer for 8 to 10 minutes, or until shrimp turns pink.

Remove from heat and add vinegar and garlic. Let stand for 30 minutes. Strain and chill well before serving.

Serves 8 to 10 as an appetizer.

—*Mary Carney*

Sweet & Sour Shrimp

1½ cups orange juice
1 Tbsp. soya sauce
2 Tbsp. vinegar
2 Tbsp. currant jelly
1 tsp. dry mustard
¼ tsp. ginger
1 Tbsp. cornstarch
1 Tbsp. water
1½ cups pineapple chunks
1 green pepper, cut into chunks
6 water chestnuts, sliced
1½ lbs. shrimp, cleaned & cooked

In heavy saucepan, combine orange juice, soya sauce, vinegar, jelly, mustard and ginger and heat just to boiling. Dissolve cornstarch in water and stir into hot mixture until thickened. Add pineapple, green pepper and water chestnuts and cook, stirring, for 1 minute. Add shrimp and remove from heat. Let stand for a few minutes and serve.

Serves 4 to 6.

—*Christine Fordham*

Shrimp Marseillaise

3 cups shrimp
½ cup butter
Salt & pepper
6 green onions, minced
1 clove garlic, minced
1 large tomato, peeled & chopped
¼ cup brandy
¼ cup white wine
1 Tbsp. Worcestershire sauce
1 Tbsp. lemon juice
1 Tbsp. parsley
½ tsp. basil
Coriander
Mace
Dill weed
4 dashes Tabasco sauce
1 bay leaf

Sauté shrimp in butter until pink. Salt and pepper lightly, add onions and sauté for 1 minute. Add garlic and cook for 30 seconds, then add tomato and cook for 1 minute. Add brandy and wine and ignite. Allow to burn for 30 seconds to 1 minute, then extinguish flame. Add remaining ingredients and heat through.

Serves 4 to 6.

—*Marney Allen*

Mama's Scampi

1½ lbs. shrimp
½ cup melted butter
½ tsp. salt
Pepper
1 clove garlic, chopped
1 cup sliced mushrooms
¼ cup chopped parsley
¼ cup chopped chives

Shell and devein shrimp. In large heavy pot, melt butter and sauté shrimp for 5 minutes, or until shrimp are pink. Sprinkle with salt and pepper, place on heated platter and keep warm. Sauté garlic and mushrooms for 1 to 2 minutes, then add parsley and chives and cook for 1 minute longer. Pour over shrimp. Serve with rice.

Serves 4.

—Kirsten McDougall

Guyanese Cook-up

Make the coconut milk for this recipe by combining 3 cups boiling water with 1 cup grated coconut — preferably fresh. When mixture is cool enough to handle, squeeze out all the liquid and discard the coconut.

1½ cups raw brown rice
3 cups coconut milk
½ tsp. salt
¾ cup sliced green beans
½ cup shrimp

Cook rice in coconut milk with salt for 25 minutes. Place green beans and shrimp on top of rice to steam for remaining cooking time — about 20 minutes. Stir when cooked and serve.

Serves 4.

—Shiela Alexandrovich

Manicotti with Shrimp Filling

18 manicotti noodles
2 cups ricotta cheese
1½ cups cottage cheese
½ cup Parmesan cheese
2 eggs
1 green pepper, chopped
3-4 green onions, chopped
¼ cup finely chopped fresh
  parsley
½ tsp. salt
½ tsp. pepper
1½ cups shrimp
2 cups white sauce (page 132)

Cook noodles in boiling water for 6 minutes, stirring so they do not stick to one another.

Combine cheeses, eggs, green pepper, onions, parsley, salt, pepper and shrimp. Carefully stuff the manicotti shells with this mixture. Arrange filled noodles in single layers in two greased 9" x 13" baking pans. Pour one cup of white sauce over each.

Bake, covered, at 350° F for 45 minutes.

Serves 4 to 6.

—Lorraine McFarland

Prawns with Cheese Sauce

24 prawns in shell
1 Tbsp. butter
1 Tbsp. flour
1 cup milk
1 cup grated Cheddar cheese
Salt & pepper
Garlic powder
2 Tbsp. chopped green onion
½ cup bread crumbs

Remove heads from prawns and place prawns in pot of boiling, salted water for 30 seconds. Plunge immediately into cold water and shell.

Melt butter and blend in flour. Slowly add milk, stirring constantly. Cook until thickened, then add cheese, seasonings and green onions.

Place prawns in greased baking dish and pour cheese sauce over. Top with bread crumbs. Bake at 375° F for 20 minutes — until hot and bubbly.

Serves 4.

—Carol Swann

Shrimp Fondue

2 lbs. shrimp, cleaned &
   deveined
2 cups white wine
1 clove garlic
1 lb. Swiss cheese, cubed
3 Tbsp. cornstarch
½ tsp. Worcestershire sauce
1 tsp. salt
Pepper
1¼ tsp. nutmeg

Boil shrimp for 3 minutes,
drain and keep warm. Heat 1½
cups wine and garlic in top of
double boiler. Remove garlic and
stir in cheese until melted.
Combine remaining ½ cup wine,
cornstarch, Worcestershire
sauce, salt, pepper and nutmeg.
Stir into cheese and cook until
smooth. Pour into fondue pot
and dip shrimp.

Serves 6.

—Audrey Moroso

Shrimp & Artichoke Tarts

Pastry for 24 tart shells
2 cups cooked shrimp,
   drained
1 can artichoke hearts,
   drained
1 can smoked oysters,
   drained
2 cups grated jack cheese
4 green onions, chopped
1½ cups milk
4 eggs
2 Tbsp. chopped dill weed
Salt & pepper
Paprika
Olives, sliced
4 Tbsp. Parmesan cheese

Combine shrimp, artichokes,
oysters, jack cheese and onions
and place in pastry-lined muffin
tins.

Combine milk, eggs, dill and
salt and pepper and beat well.
Pour over mixture in shells. Top
with paprika, olives and
Parmesan cheese and bake at
375° F for 20 minutes. Let sit for
10 minutes before serving.

Serves 6 to 8.

—Gillian Barber-Gifford

Shrimp Paté

1 lb. shelled small shrimp,
   cooked
½ lb. butter, softened
Juice of 1 lemon
1 small clove garlic, minced
1 Tbsp. Madeira wine
Nutmeg
Salt & pepper
Crackers

In food processor or blender,
combine shrimp, butter (broken
into pieces], lemon juice, garlic
and wine and process with
on/off motion until blended but
not puréed. Season with nutmeg
and salt and pepper.

Pile paté into individual servings
or a serving crock, cover tightly
and chill. Serve with crackers.

Serves 8.

—Francie Goodwin-Rogne

Scallops in Wine

2 lbs. scallops
2 cups white wine
¼ cup butter
4 shallots, finely chopped
24 mushroom caps, finely
   sliced
2 Tbsp. parsley
2 Tbsp. flour
2-4 Tbsp. whipping cream
½-1 cup bread crumbs
Butter

Wash scallops and simmer in
wine for 5 minutes. Drain and
reserve liquid.

Melt butter and sauté shallots,
mushroom caps and parsley. Stir
in flour. Add reserved liquid and
whipping cream and cook until
slightly thickened. Stir in
scallops and place in greased,
shallow casserole dish. Top with
bread crumbs and dot with
butter. Broil until golden brown.

Serves 4.

—Kathy Payette

Crab Potato Cakes

1 medium onion, finely
  chopped
2 Tbsp. butter
2 cups mashed potatoes
1 cup crabmeat, flaked
1 egg
¼ cup milk
½ tsp. parsley
½ tsp. pepper
¼ cup corn meal

Sauté onion in 1 Tbsp. butter.
Combine potatoes, crabmeat,
egg, milk, parsley and pepper to
form a stiff, slightly sticky
dough. Add onions, form into
cakes and dredge in corn meal.
Melt remaining 1 Tbsp. butter in
heavy pan and cook cakes over
medium heat until golden.

Serves 4 to 6.

— *Nancy Chesworth Weir*

Crab Vermicelli

2 cups chopped onion
½ lb. mushrooms, sliced
2 cloves garlic, minced
½ cup butter
½ lb. vermicelli, cooked
2-3 cups flaked crabmeat
½ cup sliced stuffed green
  olives
½ lb. Cheddar cheese, grated
½ cup sour cream
12-oz. can stewed tomatoes,
  drained
1½ tsp. salt
1½ tsp. basil

Sauté onion, mushrooms and
garlic until onion is translucent.
Add remaining ingredients, place
in greased casserole dish and
bake at 350° F for 45 minutes.

Serves 4 to 6.

— *Anita DeLong*

Scallops Compass Rose

*This recipe comes from a guest
house on Grand Manan Island
in the Bay of Fundy. As the
owners say, "It helps when you
can scoop the fresh scallops
from the fishermen's boats at
$3.50 a pound!"*

1½ Tbsp. oil
1½ lbs. scallops, each cut
  into 4 thin slices
2 tsp. salt
1 green onion, sliced
  diagonally
2 slices ginger root
1 Tbsp. cornstarch,
  dissolved in 4 Tbsp. water

Heat oil in skillet. Add scallops
and cook for 1 minute. Add salt,
onion and ginger root and cook
for 2 minutes. Add
cornstarch-water mixture and
cook, stirring, until juices
thicken — about 1 minute.

Serves 4.

—*Linda L'Aventure &
Cecilia Bowden*

Curried Crab

2 coconuts
1 cup water
1 small onion, chopped
2 cloves garlic, minced
1 inch ginger, peeled &
  grated
2 Tbsp. olive oil
Salt
1 Tbsp. curry
2 or more crabs, cleaned

Crack coconuts and save milk.
Chop or shred coconut meat and
place in blender. Add ¾ cup
water and blend thoroughly.
Remove from blender and
squeeze all liquid from pulp,
save and add to coconut milk.
Replace pulp in blender and add
remaining ¼ cup water. Blend,
save liquid and discard pulp. Fry
onion, garlic and ginger in oil
until light brown. Add coconut
liquid, pinch of salt and curry.
Add crabmeat, bring liquid to
boil, then reduce heat and cook
until liquid thickens about 10
minutes.

Serves 2.

—*Pieter Timmermans*

Spicy Clams

4 Tbsp. olive oil
2 cloves garlic, chopped
½ tsp. chili peppers
2 Tbsp. wine
2 Tbsp. soya sauce
⅓ cup fish stock
Green onion, chopped
24 clams, cleaned, steamed
   & chopped

Heat oil in wok. Add garlic, chili peppers, wine, soya sauce, stock and onion and stir-fry briefly. Add clams and heat thoroughly.

Serves 4.

—Wendy Neilson

Oystacado

2 avocados
¼ cup mayonnaise
1 tsp. Dijon mustard
Salt & pepper
1 can smoked oysters,
   drained & chopped
1 Tbsp. lemon juice
1 cup sour cream
4 almonds

Cut avocados in half, scoop out pulp and mash. Add mayonnaise, mustard, salt and pepper, oysters and lemon juice. Fill each avocado shell with mixture and top with dollop of sour cream and an almond.

Serves 4.

—Gillian Barber-Gifford

Lasqueti Oyster Sauté with Tarragon

24 oysters
Seasoned flour
¾ cup butter
Buttered toast
Tarragon mayonnaise
Lemon slices

Shuck oysters, discard liquor and pat dry. Dredge in flour, shaking off excess. Heat butter until foamy, add oysters and sauté on both sides over high heat until lightly browned.

Arrange on buttered toast and top with a spoonful of tarragon mayonnaise and a lemon slice.

Serves 4 to 6.

—Katherine Dunster

Angels on Horseback

12 oysters, shucked & rinsed
Flour
Salt & pepper
12 strips bacon, fried until
   almost crisp

Dust oysters with flour and salt and pepper. Wrap bacon strip around each oyster and hold together with a toothpick. Broil for 4 to 6 minutes, or until bacon is crisp.

Serves 3.

—Nina Christmas

Smoked Oyster Dip

1 can smoked oysters, finely
   chopped & juice reserved
¾ cup chopped celery
½ cup chopped onion
4 slices crisp bacon,
   crumbled
8 soda crackers, crumbled
2-3 Tbsp. bacon drippings
2 eggs, hard-boiled & finely
   chopped
6 Tbsp. mayonnaise
Juice of 1 lemon

Combine all ingredients, mix well and refrigerate for 24 hours. Serve with vegetable sticks and crackers.

Makes approximately 3 cups.

—Cynthia Gilmore

Marinated Oysters

10 oysters
3 Tbsp. olive oil
2 Tbsp. tarragon vinegar
2 Tbsp. lemon juice
3-4 Tbsp. diced onions
2 Tbsp. chopped parsley
2-3 Tbsp. chopped chives
1 Tbsp. grated lemon peel
1 tsp. salt
½ tsp. white pepper
1-2 cloves garlic, crushed
Pumpernickel bread

Steam oysters in salt water until plump — 5 to 10 minutes — then cut into quarters. Combine remaining ingredients, except bread, for marinade and pour over oysters. Refrigerate for at least 4 hours. Serve on pumpernickel bread.

Serves 4.

—Berit Christensen

Oyster Crêpes

Crêpe batter (page 29)
FILLING:
¼ lb. bacon, chopped
1 onion, chopped
1 clove garlic, crushed
Salt & pepper
2 Tbsp. butter
2 cups oysters
¼ cup white wine
Parsley
SAUCE FONDUE:
2 tsp. butter
2 Tbsp. flour
1 cup cream
1 cup white wine
2 cups grated Swiss cheese

Prepare and cook crêpes as recipe directs. Set aside and keep warm.

Cook bacon until crisp; drain and set aside. Sauté onion, garlic and salt and pepper in butter. Add oysters and cook for 3 to 5 minutes. Add bacon, wine and parsley and simmer for 10 minutes.

To make sauce, melt butter, then add flour, stirring constantly. Gradually add cream, stirring, until well blended. Stir in wine. Add cheese and cook until melted and thickened.

To assemble, place filling in crêpes, roll up and top with sauce. Bake at 350° F for 15 minutes.

Serves 4.

—Audrey Alley

Clam or Mussel Pie

Pastry for double 9-inch pie shell
1½ cups clams or mussels
¾ cup diced potatoes
1 onion, chopped
2 cloves garlic, chopped
¼ cup chopped celery
3 Tbsp. butter
2 Tbsp. flour
Thyme
Salt & pepper

Scrub clams or mussels and cook in boiling water for 10 minutes, then shuck. Reserve liquid. Cook potatoes in fish liquid. Remove and set aside. Sauté onion, garlic and celery in butter. Stir in flour, thyme, salt and pepper and cook for 2 minutes. Slowly add cooking liquid and cook until thickened. Add potatoes and clams or mussels.

Place in pastry-lined pie plate and top with pastry. Bake at 400° F until crust is browned.

Serves 4.

—Rachelle Poirier

Moules Grillée

2 dozen mussels
Lemon juice
Garlic powder
Butter
Thyme
Parsley

Scrub mussel shells and remove byssus threads. Open by inserting a small, sharp knife between shells on flat side one-third of the way from the pointed end. Cut through to the wide end and spread the shell open. Remove meat from one shell to the other so that all the mussel is on one side. Break shells apart and place shells containing meat on ovenproof serving dishes. Squirt with lemon juice and sprinkle with garlic powder. Dot with butter and top with thyme and parsley. Broil for 5 minutes and serve.

Serves 4 to 6.

—Nancy Witherspoon

Seafood Casserole

¾ cup crabmeat, cooked
¾ cup small shrimp, cooked
    & shelled
2 Tbsp. grated sharp
    Cheddar cheese
2 sole fillets, split in half
    down the centre
1½ cups white sauce
    (page 132)
1 Tbsp. Parmesan cheese
1 Tbsp. parsley

Toss crabmeat and shrimp with cheese and place half in each of two greased individual casserole dishes. Mound mixture into loaf shapes and place one half split fillet on each side of each mound. Cover with warm white sauce and sprinkle with Parmesan cheese and parsley. Bake at 325° F for 20 minutes.

Serves 2.

—*June McKinnell*

Seafood Spaghetti Sauce

1 cup water
1 cup dry white wine
1 bay leaf
Cloves
1 medium onion, finely
    chopped
1-2 cloves garlic, finely
    chopped
Salt & pepper
½ lb. shrimp
½ lb. squid, cut into small
    pieces
1 lb. sole fillets, cut into
    1-inch pieces
3 Tbsp. butter
4 Tbsp. flour
2½ cups fish liquid
½ cup whipping cream
½ tsp. lemon juice
2 Tbsp. chopped parsley
1 tsp. tarragon
1 tsp. thyme

Bring water, wine, bay leaf, pinch of cloves, onion, garlic and salt and pepper to a boil. Add fish one type at a time and cook for 3 to 4 minutes each. Remove from liquid and set aside. Strain and reserve liquid.

Melt butter in double boiler, add flour and cook, stirring, for 5 minutes. Add 2½ cups reserved fish liquid while stirring, bring to a boil and simmer for a few minutes. Add cream, lemon juice, parsley, tarragon and thyme. Add fish, heat to boiling point and serve.

Serves 6.

—*Harvey Griggs*

Paella

An elegant party dish, this version of paella uses only seafood, whereas there are some that also include chicken. After the baking, any clams and mussels that did not open should be discarded.

4-5 cups stock, half clam &
    half chicken
1 tsp. saffron
⅓ cup oil
2 cloves garlic
1 large onion, finely chopped
1 green pepper, cut into thin
    strips
2 lbs. white fish, cut into
    2-inch pieces
Salt & pepper
2 cups raw rice
2 large tomatoes, peeled,
    seeded & diced
12 shrimp, shelled &
    deveined
12 scallops
1-2 cups partially cooked
    vegetables (peas, green
    beans, zucchini, artichoke
    hearts)
12 mussels or clams,
    scrubbed in shells

Bring stock to a boil, add saffron and set aside. In a large casserole dish, heat ¼ cup oil, fry garlic until browned, then remove and discard. Add onion, green pepper and white fish and cook until slightly browned. Season with salt and pepper. Add remaining oil and the rice and cook, stirring, for 2 to 3 minutes until rice is slightly browned. Add tomatoes and simmer for 2 to 3 minutes. Add stock and stir once.

Bury shrimp and scallops in rice, then add vegetables. Arrange mussels or clams around edge of dish, cover and simmer for 15 minutes, or until rice is cooked, adding stock as necessary. Uncover and bake at 450° F for 10 minutes.

Serves 8.

—*Alice J. Pitt*

Company Seafood Bake

¼ cup butter
1½ cups rice
3 cups chicken stock
2½ tsp. salt
⅜ tsp. pepper
12 Tbsp. butter
1½ cups sliced mushrooms
2 tsp. curry
½ tsp. ginger
2 6-oz. cans crabmeat,
  drained
5-oz. can lobster, drained
¼ cup dry sherry
¼ cup flour
¼ tsp. dry mustard
3 cups light cream
1 cup grated Swiss cheese

Heat ¼ cup butter in large saucepan, add rice and cook gently, stirring, until rice is golden brown. Add chicken stock, bring to a boil, turn down heat and simmer, covered, for 40 minutes, or until rice is tender and liquid absorbed. Add 1½ tsp. salt and ¼ tsp. pepper and stir together lightly with a fork. Spread rice mixture in bottom of greased, 9" x 13" baking dish.

Melt 6 Tbsp. butter in large skillet. Add mushrooms, curry and ginger and cook gently for 3 minutes, stirring. Remove from heat. Add crabmeat, lobster, ½ tsp. salt and sherry and blend lightly. Spoon over rice.

Melt remaining 6 Tbsp. butter in saucepan. Sprinkle in flour, ½ tsp. salt, ⅛ tsp. pepper and mustard and let bubble. Remove from heat and add cream all at once, stirring to blend. Return to moderate heat and cook, stirring, until thickened. Pour over seafood evenly and sprinkle with cheese. Bake at 400° F for about 25 minutes, or until very hot.

—Karen Havelock

Shrimp & Crabmeat Crêpes

Crêpe batter (page 29)
6 Tbsp. butter
3 Tbsp. flour
1 cup milk
¼ tsp. garlic powder
¼ tsp. basil
¼ lb. mushrooms, finely
  chopped
1 small onion, finely
  chopped
6 oz. can crabmeat, drained
1 cup small shrimp, cooked

Prepare and cook crêpes as recipe indicates. Cover, set aside and keep warm.

Make a white sauce by melting 3 Tbsp. butter. Blend in flour and cook over low heat for 5 minutes. Slowly add milk, garlic powder and basil. Set aside.

Sauté mushrooms and onion in remaining 3 Tbsp. butter. Add crabmeat and shrimp and heat through. Add to white sauce, fill crêpes, place in a greased, shallow baking dish, cover and bake at 300° F for 30 minutes.

Serves 2 to 3.

—Diane Schoemperlen

Steamed Red Snapper with Ginger Sauce

2-3 lbs. red snapper, cleaned
& scaled but left whole
SAUCE:
2 Tbsp. vinegar
1 Tbsp. sugar
1 Tbsp. soy sauce
4 tsp. sesame oil
½ tsp. pepper
1 Tbsp. cornstarch
1 cup chicken stock
VEGETABLE GARNISH:
1 cup sliced green pepper
1 cup sliced red pepper
⅓ cup grated gingerroot
1 cup sliced green onions
1 Tbsp. oil

Steam fish for 15 to 25 minutes until flaky.

Meanwhile, combine sauce ingredients and cook over medium heat until thickened. Sauté all but a bit of each vegetable in oil until slightly soft. Add sauce and pour over fish. Garnish with remaining vegetables.

Serves 4 to 6.

—Billie Sheffield

Salmon Seviche

This cold fish dish makes a wonderfully refreshing appetizer. The contributor serves it on a bed of Boston lettuce with pickled cucumber.

3 lemons
3 oranges
3 cloves garlic
3 green onions
2 Tbsp. sugar
½ tsp. salt
1 Tbsp. red peppercorns
  (optional)
⅛ tsp. white pepper
1½ lbs. fresh red salmon

Squeeze juice of lemons and oranges into medium-sized bowl. Slice garlic and onions and add to juices. Add remaining ingredients except fish and stir to dissolve sugar. Thinly slice salmon into marinade. Marinate for at least 4 hours before serving. The fish will be opaque and look cooked when it is ready to eat.

Serves 6 to 8 as an appetizer.

— *Janet Jokinen*

Fresh Salmon Paté

"My recipe was inspired by a salmon paté I had at The Pilgrim's Inn, Deer Isle, Maine. Their version was coated with finely chopped pistachios." This paté has a delicate flavour — be sure to serve with a light, mild cracker.

⅔-lb. salmon steak
salt
4 oz. cream cheese
1 Tbsp. heavy cream
1 tsp. lime juice
¼-½ tsp. dill
pepper
⅓ cup whole almonds
⅓ cup parsley

Poach salmon in 2 Tbsp. water with dash of salt until just done — pink through. Cool slightly, then remove bones and skin. Crumble salmon into bowl. Add cream cheese and mix thoroughly. Add cream, stirring until smooth. Add lime juice, dill and pepper and mix well. Chill for 1 to 2 hours.

To serve, finely chop almonds and parsley in shallow bowl. Spoon chilled paté into centre. Pat into ball, then turn to coat with almonds and parsley.

Serves 8 to 10 as an appetizer.

—*Jane Crosen*

Scalloped Salmon

"Fast and simple but with an outstanding flavour, this is firm and slices well, hot or cold," comments our Camden East tester.

½ cup chicken stock
2 eggs, beaten
½ cup milk
2 Tbsp. chopped parsley
1 Tbsp. minced onion
½ tsp. dry mustard
16-oz. can salmon
2 cups bread crumbs
1 tsp. sage
1 cup grated Cheddar cheese

Combine all ingredients and mix well. Pour into greased 9-inch pie pan. Bake, uncovered, at 350° F for 35 to 40 minutes.

Serves 4.

—*Ingrid Magnuson*

Salmon Barbecue

1 cup dry vermouth
¾ cup oil
⅓ cup lemon juice
2 Tbsp. chopped chives
½ tsp. celery salt
½ tsp. thyme
1½ tsp. salt
½ tsp. pepper
4 salmon steaks

Combine all ingredients except salmon steaks and mix well. Pour over salmon and marinate, refrigerated, for 4 hours. Barbecue for approximately 10 minutes on each side, depending on thickness of steaks.

Serves 4.

—*Debra Gaudreau*

Salmon Mousse

Although somewhat time-consuming to prepare, this mousse is well worth the effort. For a beautiful presentation, pipe the mousse into artichoke hearts. Garnish with a dollop of mayonnaise and a caper.

1 lb. fresh salmon
¼ cup chopped celery with
    leaves
1½ tsp. chopped onion
¾ tsp. salt
⅛ tsp. pepper
small piece bay leaf
¼ cup butter, softened
1 Tbsp. egg white
2 tsp. lemon juice
½ tsp. salt
white pepper
cayenne
tarragon
1 tsp. unflavoured gelatin
¼ cup whipping cream
¼ cup mayonnaise

Place salmon on large piece of foil. Sprinkle with celery, onion, ¾ tsp. salt, ⅛ tsp. pepper and bay leaf. Wrap foil securely around fish and place in boiling water. Boil for 10 minutes per inch of thickness of fish. Remove from water and cool. Remove skin and bones. Discard bay leaf. Grind fine.

Add butter and egg white and blend well. Add lemon juice, ½ tsp. salt, white pepper, cayenne and tarragon.

Soak gelatin in ¼ cup cold water for 5 minutes, then set in small pan of hot water and heat until gelatin dissolves — 5 minutes. Cool but do not chill. Whip cream until stiff. Beat gelatin into mayonnaise, then beat into salmon. Fold in whipped cream. Pipe into artichoke hearts, if desired

Serves 8 as an appetizer.

Poached Fish Japanese Style

1 cup soy sauce
sugar
1 tsp. grated gingerroot
½ cup sherry
1 clove garlic, slashed
1 trout, cleaned but left
    whole

Combine soy sauce, sugar, ginger, sherry, garlic and 2 cups water in a skillet and bring to a boil. Add trout and poach for 3 minutes on each side, turning only once.

Serves 1.

—Jan Iwanik

Baked Whitefish

½ cup milk
2 tsp. Dijon mustard
4 tsp. mayonnaise
20 oz. whitefish fillets
1 clove garlic, crushed
¼ tsp. salt
⅛ tsp. thyme
white pepper
½ tsp. tarragon
½ tsp. chopped chives

Pour milk in bottom of greased casserole dish. Combine mustard and mayonnaise and spread over fish. Sprinkle with garlic, salt, thyme, pepper, tarragon and chives. Place fillets in casserole and bake, covered, at 400° F for 20 to 25 minutes, or until fish flakes easily.

Serves 4.

—Linda Humphrey

Seviche

This is a Central/South American dish. The citric acid in the lime or lemon juice "cooks" the fish.

1½ lbs. fresh firm white fish
    fillets
1 cup lime or lemon juice
½ cup olive oil
2-3 cloves garlic, crushed
½ tsp. thyme
1 tsp. oregano
¼ tsp. coriander
1 small hot pepper, chopped
1 red pepper, cut in strips
1 green pepper, cut in strips
2 green onions, chopped
1 tomato, chopped

Cut fish into thin strips. Cover with juice and chill for at least 1½ hours.

Meanwhile, combine olive oil, garlic, thyme, oregano, coriander and hot pepper. Once fish has turned white, pour this mixture over it. Add red and green peppers, onions and tomato. Mix gently. Chill 1 hour more before serving.

Serves 6 to 8 as an appetizer.

—Cary Elizabeth Marshall

Haddock in Fennel & Yogurt

Fried coconut flakes are available in cans in many ethnic food stores. If not available, simply dry-roast coconut flakes in a heavy saucepan.

3 Tbsp. olive oil
2 onions, chopped
2 cloves garlic, minced
1 small hot green chili, chopped
1 Tbsp. fennel seeds, crushed
2 Tbsp. fried coconut flakes
1 cup plain yogurt
½ tsp. salt
2 lbs. haddock fillets, cut into 2-3" pieces
2 sprigs coriander, chopped

Heat oil in heavy pot and sauté onions, garlic and chili until mixture turns light brown. Add crushed fennel and coconut and sauté for 3 minutes more.

Lightly beat together yogurt with 1 cup water. Add to pot and stir. Add salt and simmer for 5 minutes. Add fish and simmer for 5 to 7 minutes, or until fish is tender and flaky. Garnish with coriander.

Serves 4.

— *Ingrid Birker*

Steamed Sole with Tomato Coulis

2 carrots
2 zucchini
3 purple & white turnips
3 Tbsp. butter
1 large tomato
3 sprigs lemon thyme or ½ tsp. thyme + ½ tsp. sage
salt & pepper
juice of 1 lemon
4 fillets sole

Grate or julienne into 2-inch strips, carrots, zucchini and turnips. Melt 1 Tbsp. butter with 3 Tbsp. water in skillet. Toss vegetables in skillet to coat and mix. Remove from heat.

Purée tomato, including skin, with herbs and remaining 2 Tbsp. butter. Season with salt and pepper.

Arrange sole on top of vegetables, brush with lemon juice and season lightly with salt and pepper. Cover skillet tightly, place over medium heat and steam for 6 minutes, or until fish is white.

Place one quarter of the vegetables on each of 4 plates and top with a fillet of sole. Pour tomato purée into skillet, boil over high heat for 1 minute, then pour in a ribbon around each mound of vegetables.

Serves 4.

— *The Art of Cooking School*

Fish Duet Ring Mould

Our Camden East tester comments, "The subtle flavours of salmon, sole and broccoli come together extremely well in this dish."

3 Tbsp. butter
1 small onion, finely chopped
5 Tbsp. flour
1 cup milk
1 tsp. salt
½ tsp. white pepper
4 eggs, separated
6 sole fillets
1 lb. salmon, ground
½ tsp. paprika
½ tsp. chervil
1 head broccoli, cooked & chopped
½ tsp. nutmeg

Melt butter and sauté onion until golden. Stir in flour, then add milk gradually and cook over medium-low heat, stirring, until sauce thickens. Add salt and pepper.

Beat egg yolks and blend in a little cream sauce. Stir in remaining sauce and set aside to cool.

Grease a 2-quart ring mould. Line bottom and sides with sole fillets, skin side up, with tips of fillets draped over edge of mould. Place salmon, paprika and chervil in one bowl and broccoli and nutmeg in another. Divide cream sauce evenly between them. Mix well and season to taste.

Beat egg whites until stiff. Add half to salmon and half to broccoli. Fold in gently.

Spread broccoli mixture onto fillets, then salmon mixture. Fold fillet tips over. Place buttered round of waxed paper on top. Bake in a water bath at 375° F for 45 minutes. Siphon off excess fluid, unmould and serve hot or cold.

Serves 10 to 12 as an appetizer.

—*Lillian Steinfeld*

Malpeque Oyster Stew

¾ cup unsalted butter
1 cup finely chopped celery
1 cup thinly sliced leeks
1 cup finely grated carrots
1 onion, finely chopped
½ cup whole wheat flour
2 cups light cream
2 cups milk
1 cup minced clams with
  liquor (about 5 large
  clams)
2 cups shucked oysters with
  liquor (about 30 oysters)
pepper
fresh coriander or parsley

Melt ½ cup butter in saucepan, stir in vegetables, cover tightly and cook over low heat for 30 minutes, stirring occasionally.

Meanwhile, in medium saucepan, melt remaining butter, whisk in flour and cook over medium heat for 2 to 3 minutes, but do not brown. Remove from heat and gradually whisk in cream and milk. Return to heat and cook until sauce is smooth and thickened, whisking constantly. Stir sauce into vegetables in large saucepan.

In another saucepan, combine clams and oysters with liquors. Cook, uncovered, over low heat for 10 minutes or until oysters just start to curl. Stir seafood into vegetable mixture and heat through gently. Season with pepper to taste and garnish each serving with a sprig of coriander or parsley.

Serves 8.

—Tyne Valley Tea Room

Shrimp-Stuffed Sole

1 clove garlic, minced
1 large shallot, diced
3 Tbsp. butter
⅔ cup chopped parsley
⅛ tsp. dill
3 fresh basil leaves, chopped
juice of ½ lemon
salt & pepper
¼ cup bread crumbs
1 cup cooked, chopped
  shrimp
1 tomato, peeled, seeded &
  diced
4 sole fillets
2 tsp. butter
6 thin slices lemon
3 Tbsp. chicken stock
2 Tbsp. white wine

Sauté garlic and shallot in 3 Tbsp. butter, but do not brown. Add ⅓ cup parsley, dill, basil, lemon juice and salt and pepper, and cook gently for 2 minutes. Stir in bread crumbs and shrimp and let stand for 2 minutes. Stir in tomato.

Place sole in greased shallow casserole dish, with half of each fillet lining pan edge. Place ⅓ to ½ cup stuffing on each fillet. Fold other half of fillet over stuffing and tuck end under. Dot fish with 2 tsp. butter, lay lemon slices on top and sprinkle with remaining ⅓ cup parsley. Combine stock and wine and pour over fillets.

Bake, covered, at 350° F for 20 minutes, or until flaky but still moist

Serves 4.

—Laurie D. Glaspey

Szechuan Shrimp

1 lb. small shrimp, peeled &
  deveined
1½ Tbsp. cornstarch
1 egg white
¼ cup diced bamboo shoots
¼ cup chopped green onions
¼ cup chopped green pepper
½ tsp. crushed hot red
  pepper
1 clove garlic, minced
1 Tbsp. grated gingerroot
½ cup chicken stock
5 Tbsp. tomato paste
½ tsp. soy sauce
2 Tbsp. dry sherry
½ tsp. sesame oil
2 cups plus 2 Tbsp. peanut oil
salt

Rinse shrimp in cold water and pat dry. Combine cornstarch and egg white and mix well. Add shrimp and stir to coat. Let stand for 5 hours. Combine bamboo shoots, green onions, green pepper, hot red pepper, garlic and ginger. Set aside.

Blend together stock, tomato paste, soy sauce, sherry and sesame oil. Set aside. Heat 2 cups peanut oil in wok. Cook shrimp for 1 minute, then remove shrimp from oil. Drain oil from wok. Heat remaining 2 Tbsp. oil in wok. Cook shrimp and vegetable mixture quickly over high heat. Add tomato paste mixture and cook until shrimp are coated and mixture is heated through. Add salt to taste.

Serves 2.

—Trudy McCallum

Seafood-Stuffed Avocados

This was a big hit with our testers. The textures and flavours complement each other perfectly

2 Tbsp. butter
1 onion or 3 green onions, chopped
1 stalk celery, finely chopped
6-8 large mushrooms, chopped
6 oz. light cream
2 Tbsp. flour
4 oz. dry white wine
4 oz. lobster, cooked & chopped
4 oz. shrimp, cooked & chopped
4 oz. crabmeat, cooked & chopped
2 large avocados, halved
salt & pepper
sweet paprika

In large skillet, melt butter and sauté onions, celery and mushrooms. When just limp, blend cream and flour together and add to vegetables. Cook slowly, stirring, and add wine. When hot, add seafood and remove from heat. Mound in avocado halves and sprinkle with salt and pepper and paprika.

Serves 4.

— *Linda Powidajko*

Seafood Casserole

½ lb. crabmeat
½ lb. shrimp
½ lb. scallops
⅓ cup butter
½ lb. mushrooms, sliced
2 onions, chopped
½ cup flour
1 tsp. dry mustard
2 cups milk
1 cup heavy cream
salt & pepper
2 Tbsp. sherry
1 cup grated Swiss cheese

Boil crabmeat, shrimp and scallops together for 5 minutes. Drain and set aside.

Melt butter, then sauté mushrooms and onions until tender. Stir in flour and mustard, and cook for 1 to 2 minutes. Slowly stir in milk and cream and cook until thickened. Add salt and pepper, seafood and sherry. Remove from heat and allow to cool. Spoon into greased casserole dish and cover with grated cheese.

Bake, uncovered, at 300° F until browned — 30 minutes.

Serves 4.

Steamed Oysters on the Half Shell

Shuck oysters, saving the juice. Place oysters in half shell on baking dish. To each oyster add salt, small piece of minced garlic and a dab of butter. Cover with ½ slice bacon. Bake at 350° F for 15 minutes, or until bacon is cooked.

—*John Isenhower*

Crabmeat & Watercress Salad with Kiwi Vinaigrette

This is a very quick salad to assemble, but it looks and tastes exotic.

2 bunches watercress, stemmed
6 oz. crabmeat, cooked
6 Tbsp. oil
4 Tbsp. white wine vinegar
2 tsp. Dijon mustard
4 tsp. puréed kiwi fruit
salt & pepper
1 kiwi, chopped

Arrange watercress on 2 plates. Place crabmeat on top. Combine oil, vinegar, mustard, puréed kiwi and salt and pepper and mix thoroughly. Pour over salad. Garnish with chopped kiwi.

Serves 2.

—*Lynn Tobin*

Sesame Shrimp & Asparagus

Serve this dish over rice accompanied by a salad of mixed greens.

1 Tbsp. sesame seeds
⅓ cup oil
1½ lbs. asparagus, cut into 2" pieces
2 small onions, sliced
1½ lbs. shrimp
4 Tbsp. soy sauce

Toast sesame seeds until golden in dry skillet over medium heat. Set aside.

Heat oil and cook asparagus, onions and shrimp for 5 minutes over medium-high heat. Stir in sesame seeds and soy sauce.

Serves 4.

Paella

Like most regional dishes, paella varies in ingredients from cook to cook. This version combines meat and seafood in a colourful, festive presentation. Other possible ingredients include sausage, octopus, clams and crayfish or lobsters.

2 cups fresh peas or green
  beans
2 lbs. halibut, cut into
  chunks
1 lb. mussels, scrubbed
1 lb. shrimp, shelled &
  deveined
½ lb. squid, cleaned & cut
  into rings
1 tsp. saffron threads
½ cup olive oil
½ lb. ham, cubed
1 whole chicken breast,
  boned & cut into chunks
2 tomatoes, sliced
1 large clove garlic, sliced
2 Tbsp. sweet paprika
3 cups dry rice
2 red peppers, roasted,
  peeled & cut into strips

Cook peas or beans in water until just tender. Drain, saving water. Add enough water to vegetable water to make 5 cups, bring to a boil, add fish, mussels, shrimp and squid and simmer for 5 minutes. Remove mussels and set aside.

Lift out remaining seafood and set aside. Add saffron to cooking water and let stand. In large ovenproof skillet, heat olive oil. Sauté ham and chicken until just done and set aside. In same oil, sauté tomatoes and garlic. Add paprika and cook gently for a couple of minutes. Sprinkle rice into pan, cover with peas or beans, halibut, shrimp, squid, ham and chicken. Pour water with saffron over top and bring to a boil. Continue boiling while arranging mussels and strips of pepper on top.

Bake, uncovered, at 400° F for 15 minutes. Remove from oven and cook on top of stove for 1 to 2 minutes.

Serves 8.

Cheesy Crab in Filo

Made as directed, in two long rolls, this works well as a main course. To serve as an appetizer, cut the filo and roll individually. Leftover filo dough can be well wrapped and frozen.

½ cup chopped green onions
½ cup butter
1 cup dry white wine
12 oz. crabmeat
4 oz. cream cheese
¼ cup chopped parsley
4 egg yolks, lightly beaten
1 tsp. salt
½ tsp. pepper
1 pkg. filo dough
melted butter
1 egg, beaten

Sauté onions in butter for 3 to 4 minutes. Add wine and bring to a boil. Boil for 3 to 5 minutes until liquid is reduced by half, then remove from heat. Stir in crabmeat, cheese, parsley, egg yolks, salt and pepper. Stir until cheese is melted, then set aside to cool.

Place 1 filo leaf on waxed paper. Brush with melted butter. Repeat 3 more times. Place half the crab mixture on the filo, close to the bottom, leaving a 2-inch border. Roll up, folding in ends. Repeat with more filo and remaining crab mixture.

Place on greased cookie sheet. Brush with beaten egg. Bake at 350° F for 15 minutes, then at 450° F for 10 minutes.

Serves 4 to 6.

—Nancy Blenkinsop

Scallops Provençale

Since sea scallops are larger than bay scallops, the cooking time will need to be adjusted accordingly if one is substituted for the other.

2 Tbsp. peanut oil
1 lb. Atlantic scallops
1 tsp. butter
1 Tbsp. finely chopped
  shallots
1 clove garlic, crushed
1 cup sliced mushrooms
½ cup diced tomato
sesame oil
1 tsp. Pernod
½ tsp. paprika
juice of ½ lemon
garnish of chopped green
  onion & dill

Heat oil until very hot. Add scallops and sauté for 1 minute. Drain off all liquid, then add butter, shallots and garlic. Sauté for 1 minute more, then add mushrooms and tomato. Season with sesame oil, Pernod, paprika and lemon juice and cook until liquid is reduced. Serve in scallop shells with garnish.

Serves 2.

—A. Camm

Prawns in Coconut Milk

"My husband and I work at a large open-pit coal mine. This recipe came from a Fijian family working at the mine. We serve it with basmati rice, raita and chutney. Coconut milk can be bought at specialty food marts and ethnic food stores. It can also be made by pouring hot milk over grated coconut."

½ cup butter
1 onion, chopped
3 large cloves garlic, crushed
2 tsp. coriander
2 tsp. turmeric
½ tsp. cayenne
1 tsp. chili powder
½ tsp. ginger
salt & pepper
2 Tbsp. white vinegar
1 cup coconut milk
1½ lbs. large prawns, shelled
   & deveined

Melt butter in a wok and add the onion and garlic. Sauté over low heat until soft. Mix spices and vinegar into a paste with mortar and pestle. Add to mixture in pan and sauté for another few minutes, stirring constantly. Add coconut milk and turn up heat. Cook until thickened — 5 minutes. Add prawns and stir until coated. Simmer for a few minutes until prawns are just cooked.

Serves 4 to 5.

— *Tracy Carroll*

Avocado Filled with Crab & Almonds

The differing textures of crunchy apples, toasted almonds and smooth avocado combine with the crab to create an unusual and special dish.

2 avocados
lemon juice
2 Tbsp. mayonnaise
½ cup heavy cream, whipped
2 drops Tabasco sauce
½ tsp. anchovy paste
2 Tbsp. almonds, toasted
3 oz. crabmeat
salt & pepper
½ apple, finely chopped

Halve and pit the avocados and sprinkle with lemon juice. Combine mayonnaise, whipped cream, Tabasco sauce, anchovy paste, almonds, crabmeat and salt and pepper. Mix well, then fold in apple. Spoon into avocado halves.

Serves 4.

— *Sandy Campisano*

Broiled Lemon Sole with Cucumber Dill Topping

2 lbs. lemon sole
1 cup mayonnaise
½ cup chopped cucumber
1 Tbsp. chopped dill
3 green onions, sliced
Tabasco sauce
salt & pepper

Arrange fish in single layer on greased tray. Combine remaining ingredients and spread evenly over fish. Broil 3 to 5 inches from heat for 5 to 7 minutes.

Serves 4.

Crab Hors d'Oeuvres

2 Tbsp. butter
2 Tbsp. flour
½ cup milk
½ lb. crabmeat, cooked &
   chopped
cayenne
3 green onions, chopped
4 Tbsp. chopped parsley
1 cup cracker crumbs
2 eggs, beaten with 1 Tbsp.
   water
oil for frying

Melt butter, stir in flour, then milk and cook over low heat until thickened — 3 to 5 minutes. Add crabmeat, cayenne, green onions and parsley. Chill for 2 hours, then roll into balls, using 1 Tbsp. for each ball. Roll in crumbs, eggs, then crumbs again. Fry in oil until browned, turning once.

Makes approximately 20 balls.

— *Billie Sheffield*

Tarragon Mussels

For tarragon lovers only, this dish makes a tasty appetizer. "I am a potter and I made some pots to serve this dish in. Just an ordinary pot with a lid, but the lid serves as a bowl in which to discard the shells."

4 Tbsp. butter
4-5 green onions, chopped
4 dozen mussels, scrubbed
2 tsp. flour
½ cup white wine
2 tsp. tarragon
cayenne

Melt butter and sauté green onions. Add mussels, then stir in flour, wine, tarragon and cayenne. Cover and cook over medium heat for 6 minutes.

Serves 8 as an appetizer.

— *Doris McIlroy*

Poultry & Game

Chicken Breasts in Maple Syrup

4 chicken breasts, boned
Seasoned flour
3 large mushrooms, finely
 chopped
½ cup finely diced ham
½ tsp. dried chives
2 Tbsp. butter
¼ cup butter
1 cup thinly sliced onion
Savory
4 Tbsp. maple syrup

Roll each breast in seasoned flour. Fry mushrooms, ham and chives in 2 Tbsp. butter for 2 to 3 minutes or until mushrooms are tender.

Slit thick portion of each breast and insert spoonful of ham mixture. Pinch edges together to seal. Brown stuffed breasts in ¼ cup butter. Remove from pan, add onion to pan and fry until golden brown.

Arrange breasts in casserole dish. Top with onion and sprinkle with savory. Spoon maple syrup over chicken breasts. Rinse frying pan with ½ cup water, then pour over chicken.

Bake, uncovered, at 350° F for 30 minutes.

Serves 4.

—Mary Rogers

Chicken Breasts Alfredo

3 eggs, beaten
3 tsp. water
½ cup grated Romano cheese
¼ cup snipped parsley
½ tsp. salt
3 whole chicken breasts,
 split & boned
½ cup flour
1 cup fine dry bread crumbs
3 Tbsp. butter
3 tsp. oil
1 cup whipping cream
¼ cup water
¼ cup butter
½ cup grated Romano cheese
¼ cup snipped parsley
6 slices mozzarella cheese

Mix together eggs, water, Romano cheese, parsley and salt. Dip chicken in flour, then egg mixture and then bread crumbs.

Melt butter and oil in large skillet. Cook chicken over medium heat until brown — about 15 minutes. Remove to baking dish.

Heat cream, water and butter in 1-quart saucepan until butter melts. Add cheese, cook and stir over medium heat for 5 minutes. Stir in parsley. Pour over chicken.

Top each piece with a slice of mozzarella cheese. Bake at 425° F until cheese melts and chicken is tender, about 8 minutes.

Serves 4 to 6.

—Pam Collacott

Parmesan Chicken

1 cup bread crumbs
1½ cups grated Parmesan
 cheese
3 Tbsp. parsley
¼ tsp. salt
1 tsp. dry mustard
½ tsp. Worcestershire sauce
¼ tsp. garlic salt
½ cup melted butter
8-10 boned chicken breasts

Combine bread crumbs, cheese, parsley and salt and set aside. Combine remaining ingredients except chicken. Dip chicken, one piece at a time, into butter mixture, then into bread crumbs.

Place in shallow baking pan and bake at 350° F for 40 to 50 minutes. Garnish with pitted, sliced black olives and sliced mushrooms.

Serves 4 to 5.

—Barbara Johnson

Chicken in Bacon Roll with Cheese

4 whole chicken breasts,
 skinned & boned
4 slices ham
4 2-inch cubes mozzarella
 cheese
12 slices bacon

Pound chicken breasts between sheets of wax paper until quite thin — ¼ inch.

Wrap each piece of cheese in a slice of ham and place in the centre of each breast. Fold edges of chicken over ham and cheese. Wrap 3 slices of bacon around each breast.

Place on a baking sheet and bake at 375° F for 30 minutes.

Serves 4.

—Kathee Roy

Rolled Chicken Washington

½ cup finely chopped fresh
   mushrooms
2 Tbsp. butter
2 Tbsp. flour
½ cup light cream
1¼ cups shredded sharp
   Cheddar cheese
¼ tsp. salt
Cayenne pepper
6 chicken breasts
Flour
2 eggs, slightly beaten
¾ cup fine dry bread crumbs

Cook mushrooms in butter for 5 minutes. Blend in flour and stir in cream and cheese. Add salt and cayenne pepper. Cook over low heat, stirring constantly, until cheese is melted. Turn mixture into pie plate and cover. Chill until cheese is very firm and then cut into 6 equal portions.

Remove skin and bones from chicken breasts. Pound to a thickness of ½-inch. Sprinkle with salt. Place piece of cheese mixture on each breast and roll up, tucking in sides. Press to seal well.

Dust chicken rolls with flour. Dip in slightly beaten egg, then roll in bread crumbs. Cover and chill for at least 1 hour.

Fry in butter at 350° F, turning occasionally, until golden brown on the outside and meat is cooked through.

Serves 6.

—Martha Brown

Creamy Breast of Chicken with Shrimp

2 large chicken breasts
Salt
Pepper
Nutmeg
1 clove garlic, minced
½ cup flour
¼ cup butter
½ cup celery
1½ cups fresh mushrooms,
   sliced
½ cup chopped onions
¾ cup dry white wine
1½ cups shrimp
2 Tbsp. chopped parsley
½ cup sour cream

Cut each breast into bite-sized pieces. Sprinkle with seasonings and garlic and let sit for half an hour. Coat chicken pieces with flour and brown in half the butter until crisp. Add celery, mushrooms, onions and white wine. Simmer, covered, for 30 minutes.

Sauté shrimp in remaining butter for 5 minutes and add to chicken mixture. Add parsley and sour cream and bring to a boil.

Serve over rice.

Serves 4.

—Shirley Gilbert

Coated Chicken Breasts

¾ cup sour cream
¼ tsp. sage
½ tsp. salt
¼ tsp. thyme
¼ tsp. basil
Freshly ground pepper
2 tsp. grated onion
½ tsp. lemon juice
1 cup fine bread crumbs
½ cup grated Cheddar cheese
½ tsp. paprika
12 chicken breasts, boned
½-1 cup flour

Combine sour cream, seasonings, onion and lemon juice in a bowl. Combine crumbs, cheese and paprika in a flat dish. Dip chicken in flour to coat both sides, then in sour cream mixture, then in crumb mixture. Place in greased baking dish. Cover with foil and bake at 350° F for 30 minutes. Uncover and bake until tender, about 15 minutes more.

Serves 6 to 8.

— Shirley Hill

Cranberry Glazed Chicken

3 lbs. frying chicken, cut into pieces
1 cup flour
2 tsp. paprika
Garlic salt
Pinch rosemary, thyme & sage
2 Tbsp. brown sugar
¼ tsp. ginger powder
½ cup cranberry jelly
¼ cup orange juice
1 Tbsp. Worcestershire sauce
1 tsp. grated orange rind

Rinse and pat dry chicken. Coat with flour, mixed with paprika, garlic salt, rosemary, thyme and sage. Bake at 400° F for 35 minutes.

Combine sugar, ginger, cranberry jelly, orange juice, Worcestershire sauce and orange rind in small saucepan. Bring to a boil, stirring constantly. Spoon over chicken and bake 10 to 15 minutes longer until chicken is tender.

Serves 4.

—Mrs. K. Love

Chicken Divan

1 cup white sauce, page 132
1 egg yolk
2 Tbsp. cream
2 Tbsp. grated Parmesan cheese
2 Tbsp. grated Gruyère cheese
3 Tbsp. sherry
3-4 lbs. chicken breasts, skinned & boned
2 lbs. broccoli
Parmesan cheese to garnish

Warm the white sauce. Beat together the egg yolk and cream until well blended. Add a little of the warm sauce to the egg and cream, stir, then return mixture to the rest of the sauce. Heat through, then add cheeses and sherry and continue cooking and stirring until sauce thickens. Set aside.

Poach chicken breasts until tender but still juicy. Cook broccoli until crispy-tender. Drain.

Arrange broccoli on a heatproof platter. Place chicken pieces on top of the broccoli and pour the sauce over it all. Sprinkle with Parmesan cheese.

Bake at 350° F for 20 minutes, or until bubbly.

Serves 6.

—Cary Elizabeth Marshall

Chicken Kiev

½ cup soft butter
2 Tbsp. chopped parsley
1 clove garlic, chopped
2 Tbsp. lemon juice
¼ tsp. cayenne pepper
6 chicken breasts, skinned & boned
½ cup flour
2 eggs, beaten
½ cup bread crumbs

Combine butter, parsley, garlic, lemon juice and pepper. Mix well and chill until firm.

Halve chicken breasts and flatten. Salt and pepper lightly. Place a piece of butter mixture on each chicken breast, roll and secure with toothpicks. Coat each roll with flour, dip in beaten eggs and then bread crumbs.

Chill for 1 hour, then deep fry until golden — 15 minutes.

Serves 6.

—Marney Allen

Chicken Royale

2 chicken breasts, boned
2 pork sausages
¼ cup oil
3 potatoes, thinly sliced
2 cups broccoli pieces

Stuff boned chicken breasts with sausages, roll and fasten with a toothpick. Heat oil in an electric frying pan and brown breasts. Lower heat, add vegetables and cook for 20 minutes.

Serves 4.

—Hazel R. Baker

Yogurt Marinated Chicken

The marinade for this dish produces pleasantly mild flavoured chicken which remains moist after baking. The chicken is delicious cold as well as warm.

1 broiler chicken, cut into
   serving-sized pieces
2 Tbsp. lemon juice
1 cup yogurt
¼ inch fresh ginger, minced
2 cloves garlic, minced
½ tsp. ground cardamom
½ tsp. chili powder
½ tsp. cinnamon

Combine all ingredients except chicken. Marinate chicken in yogurt mixture overnight. Bake at 375° F for 30 to 45 minutes, basting occasionally.

Serves 6.

—*Ingrid Birker*

Lemon Chicken

This dish may be assembled up to one day ahead and refrigerated until ready to cook.

2 lbs. chicken pieces
¼ cup lemon juice
2 Tbsp. melted butter
1 small onion, chopped
½ tsp. salt
½ tsp. celery salt
½ tsp. pepper
½ tsp. rosemary
¼ tsp. thyme

Arrange chicken in a baking dish. Mix together remaining ingredients and pour over chicken. Marinate for three hours, then bake at 325° F, covered, for 45 minutes to 1 hour.

Serves 4.

—*Gena Hughes*

Baked Chicken with Apples

3 lbs. chicken pieces
Seasoned flour
2 Tbsp. butter
2 Tbsp. oil
1 clove garlic, crushed
3 apples, cored & quartered
2 Tbsp. brown sugar
½ tsp. ginger
1½ cups unsweetened apple
   juice
½ cup water or dry sherry
2 Tbsp. cornstarch
¼ cup cold water

Dredge chicken in flour. Brown in butter and oil with garlic. Remove chicken and discard garlic. Add apples to drippings. Sprinkle with brown sugar and brown the apples.

Place chicken and apples in a casserole dish, sprinkle with ginger and pour drippings, apple juice and water or sherry over them. Cover and bake for 45 minutes at 350° F.

Remove chicken from sauce and keep warm. Blend cornstarch with water and stir into pan juices. Cook over high heat, stirring until thickened. Pour over chicken and serve.

Serves 4 to 6.

—*Bryanna Clark*

Sweet & Sour Orange Chicken

5-6 lb. chicken, cut up
1 cup flour
6 Tbsp. oil
1½ cups orange juice
3 medium onions, thinly
   sliced
4 cloves garlic, crushed
⅓ cup soya sauce
⅓ cup cider vinegar
3 Tbsp. honey
2 Tbsp. water
1 large green pepper, sliced

Dredge chicken pieces in flour. Heat oil in deep frying pan and brown chicken slowly over medium heat.

Transfer to a casserole dish. Add orange juice, onions and garlic. Cover and cook at 350° F for 20 minutes. Mix together soya sauce, vinegar, honey and water and pour over chicken. Add sliced pepper. Cover and continue cooking for 25 minutes.

Serves 6.

—*Ingrid Birker*

Hawaiian Chicken

1 Tbsp. oil
1 cup uncooked rice
2 cups chicken stock
1 cup coarsely chopped
    onion
½ cup chopped green pepper
2 cups chopped celery
1½ cups cooked chicken
1 Tbsp. soya sauce
1 cup pineapple juice
Salt & pepper
1 cup pineapple chunks

In a heavy frying pan, brown rice in oil, stirring frequently, for about 12 minutes. Add chicken stock, cover and cook for about 3 minutes. Add remaining ingredients, except pineapple chunks, mix well and spoon into casserole dish. Top with pineapple chunks. Bake at 350° F for 30 to 35 minutes.

Serves 4.

—A.H. McInnis

Chicken with Sour Cream

¼ cup flour
1 tsp. salt
Pepper
1 tsp. paprika
½ tsp. poultry seasoning
1½ lbs. boned chicken, cut
    into bite-sized pieces
Cooking oil
1 cup soft bread crumbs
2 Tbsp. butter
½ cup grated Parmesan
    cheese
¼ cup sesame seeds
½ cup hot water
1½ cups cream of
    mushroom sauce, page 132
1 cup sour cream

Mix flour, salt, pepper, paprika and poultry seasoning. Dredge meat in this mixture and brown slowly in hot oil. Arrange meat in baking dish. Combine bread crumbs, butter, cheese and sesame seeds. Spoon over meat. Stir water into meat drippings. Pour around meat. Bake at 350° F until tender — 45 to 50 minutes. Heat mushroom sauce and blend in sour cream. Serve with chicken.

Serves 4.

—Elizabeth Clayton

Chicken with Pineapple

The delightful idea of combining pineapple with meat is popular in many parts of the world — even in areas where only the tinned variety is regularly available.

8-oz. can pineapple tidbits
¼ cup brown sugar
2 Tbsp. cornstarch
½ cup water
1 Tbsp. cider vinegar
1 Tbsp. soya sauce
4 lbs. chicken pieces

Drain pineapple and reserve syrup. Combine sugar, cornstarch and syrup in medium saucepan. Blend in water, vinegar and soya sauce.

Cook over low heat until thick and bubbly, stirring occasionally.

Place chicken pieces in a baking dish and cover with sauce. Add the pineapple tidbits. Bake at 350° F for 40 to 45 minutes, basting chicken with sauce at 10 minute intervals.

Serves 4.

—Christine Collis

Orange-Ginger Chicken

4 Tbsp. frozen orange juice
    concentrate, thawed
4 tsp. soya sauce
Salt
1 tsp. powdered ginger
4 chicken breasts

Combine juice, soya sauce, salt and ginger. Place chicken breasts in a shallow pan and brush with sauce. Bake at 350° F, basting frequently, until tender — 30 to 40 minutes.

Serves 4.

—Pat Bredin

Chicken with Olives & Lemon

1 large onion, thinly sliced
1 clove garlic, minced
1 Tbsp. minced parsley
1 Tbsp. ground coriander
1 tsp. salt
½ tsp. pepper
⅛ tsp. turmeric
2-3 Tbsp. olive oil
2½-3 lbs. chicken pieces
⅓ cup sliced green olives

Sauté onion, garlic, parsley, coriander, salt, pepper and turmeric in olive oil. Add chicken and brown. Place lemon slices on top of chicken. Cover and simmer for 30 minutes. Stir in olives.

Remove chicken to a platter and keep warm. Boil down juices and pour over chicken.

Serves 4 to 6.

—Bryanna Clark

Chicken with White Wine

3 lbs. chicken pieces
Salt & pepper
3 Tbsp. cooking oil
Few pinches basil
½ cup dry white wine
4 cups cooked rice

Season chicken pieces with salt and pepper and brown in oil in large skillet. Sprinkle with basil. Cover and cook for 30 minutes on low heat. Pour wine over chicken and cook, covered, until chicken is very tender.

Remove chicken and keep warm. Reduce pan juices and stir in rice, scraping bottom of pan. Add chicken and mix well.

Serves 4 to 6.

—Bryanna Clark

Chicken Marengo

3 lbs. chicken pieces
1 cup flour
Salt & pepper
¼ cup olive oil
1 clove garlic, crushed
1 small onion, chopped
4 tomatoes, quartered
1 cup dry white wine
1 bay leaf
Pinch thyme
1 Tbsp. minced parsley
¼ lb. mushrooms, sliced
2 Tbsp. butter
½ cup sliced olives
2 Tbsp. flour
½ cup cold broth

Dredge chicken in flour seasoned with salt and pepper. Brown in oil. Add garlic, onion, tomatoes, wine, bay leaf, thyme and parsley. Cover and simmer for 30 minutes.

Meanwhile, sauté mushrooms in butter. Add to chicken after 30 minutes along with olives. Discard bay leaf and remove chicken mixture to warm platter. Keep warm.

Thicken liquid with flour mixed with broth. Boil for 3 to 5 minutes, stirring, until thickened. Return chicken to sauce and simmer for 10 minutes.

Serves 4 to 6.

—Bryanna Clark

Chicken Cacciatore

4-lb. chicken, cut up
3 Tbsp. flour
2 Tbsp. chopped onion
1 clove garlic, minced
¼ cup olive oil
¼ cup tomato paste
½ cup white wine
1 tsp. salt
¼ tsp. pepper
¾ cup chicken stock
1 bay leaf
⅛ tsp. thyme
½ tsp. basil
⅛ tsp. marjoram
½ tsp. oregano
2 Tbsp. chopped parsley
Parmesan cheese

Dredge chicken pieces with flour and brown with onion and garlic in oil. Add remaining ingredients except cheese. Simmer, covered, for 1 to 2 hours. Serve over spaghetti or baby potatoes and top with grated Parmesan cheese.

Serves 6.

—Carolyn Hills

Paprika Chicken

4 Tbsp. butter
1 large onion, chopped
2 Tbsp. paprika
2½-3 lbs. chicken pieces
Salt
2 green peppers, chopped
2 tomatoes, chopped
2 Tbsp. flour
½ cup cold water
½ cup sour cream

Heat butter in casserole dish, add onion and fry until translucent. Sprinkle with paprika and stir. Add a few tablespoons of water and cook until liquid is almost evaporated.

Add the chicken and salt and cook for 5 minutes, stirring frequently. Add a little water and cover. Continue cooking over low heat. Add peppers and tomatoes after 20 minutes. Continue cooking until chicken is tender, about 20 minutes.

Stir flour into ½ cup cold water and mix with sour cream. Add to chicken and stir until smooth. Cook for 5 more minutes.

Serves 6.

— Anton Gross

Chicken Egg Foo Yung

3 Tbsp. oil
1 lb. chopped chicken meat
2½ Tbsp. soya sauce
1 tsp. sugar
Salt
½ cup chopped celery
½ cup chopped onion
½ cup peas
1 lb. bean sprouts
½ cup chopped mushrooms
½ tsp. pepper
12 eggs
2-3 green onions, diced

Heat 2 Tbsp. oil in a skillet. Add the chicken when oil smokes. Sauté for a few seconds, then add ½ Tbsp. soya sauce, sugar and salt. Sauté for a few more seconds. Add celery, onion, peas, sprouts and mushrooms. Mix well and stir in 2 Tbsp. soya sauce and pepper. Cover and cook until it boils for 30 seconds.

Beat eggs, add green onions and combine with cooked mixture. Mix well.

To a clean, hot skillet over medium-high heat, add 1 Tbsp. oil. Place large spoonfuls of mixture in hot oil and fry patties until well cooked.

Serves 6.

—Brenda Watts

Honey Mustard Chicken

Quick and easy to prepare, this chicken dish has a slightly sweet-and-sour flavour.

¼ cup butter
½ cup honey
¼ cup prepared mustard
10 chicken drumsticks
Salt & pepper

Melt butter, honey and mustard together. Dip chicken pieces into the mixture, then bake in a shallow casserole dish at 350° F for 35 minutes.

Serves 5.

—Ingrid Birker

Soya Butter Baked Chicken

3 Tbsp. soya sauce
1 tsp. crushed chili peppers
⅛ tsp. pepper
1½ tsp. lemon juice
½ cup butter
⅓ cup water
½ tsp. salt
3 lbs. chicken, cut up

Combine all ingredients except the chicken in saucepan, bring to a boil, reduce heat and simmer for 10 minutes.

Place chicken in single layer in baking dish. Pour sauce over chicken and bake at 400° F for 45 to 55 minutes, basting occasionally and turning chicken once.

Serves 4 to 6.

—June Plamondon

Florida Fried Chicken

This recipe produces golden delicious pieces of honey fried chicken. Just make sure that the oven is not too hot after the sauce is added or the honey will burn.

½ cup flour
1 tsp. salt
¼ tsp. pepper
2 tsp. paprika
4-6 lb. frying chicken, cut up
⅓ cup butter
¼ cup butter
¼ cup orange blossom
  honey (or any pure honey)
⅕ cup orange juice

Combine flour, salt, pepper and paprika in a clean paper bag. Add chicken 1 piece at a time and shake to coat well. Melt ⅓ cup butter in a large shallow baking dish in the oven at 400° F. Remove from oven and roll coated chicken pieces in butter. Leave in pan, skin side down. Bake for 30 minutes at 400°, then cool oven to 300° while making sauce.

In a small saucepan, melt ¼ cup butter, stir in honey and orange juice. Remove chicken from oven, turn pieces of chicken skin side up and pour sauce over all. Continue cooking another 30 minutes or until chicken is done.

Serves 6.

—Cheryl Suckling

Chicken-Artichoke Casserole

1½ tsp. salt
¼ tsp. pepper
½ tsp. paprika
3-lb. fryer, cut up
6 Tbsp. butter
¼ lb. chopped mushrooms
2 Tbsp. flour
⅔ cup chicken stock
3 Tbsp. sherry
12- or 15-oz. jar marinated
  artichoke hearts, drained

Sprinkle salt, pepper and paprika over chicken pieces. Brown in 4 Tbsp. of the butter, then place in a large casserole dish.

In the remaining 2 Tbsp. of butter, sauté the mushrooms for 5 minutes. Sprinkle flour over them and mix it in. Add chicken stock and sherry and stir. Cook for 5 minutes.

Arrange artichoke hearts among the chicken pieces. Pour the mushroom-sherry sauce over them and bake, covered, at 375° F for 40 minutes.

Serves 4 to 6.

—Carrie Spencer

Chicken Casserole

1 large chicken
6 onions, chopped
1 bunch celery, chopped
1 lb. mushrooms, chopped
1 green pepper, chopped
1 can pimento
¼ lb. butter
3 cups tomato sauce, page 414
Salt, pepper & any other
  seasoning desired
8-oz. package egg noodles
  (medium-sized)

Boil chicken, half-covered with water, until tender. Cool slightly, remove meat from the bones and cut into bite-sized pieces. Reserve broth.

Sauté onions, celery, mushrooms, green pepper and pimento in butter until vegetables are tender. Add tomato sauce, seasonings and chicken. Cook noodles in boiling salted water, drain and add to mixture.

Bake at 375° F until hot and bubbling — 20 to 30 minutes.

Serves 6.

—J. Elizabeth Fraser

Jambalaya

3-lb. roasting chicken, cut up
1 onion, finely chopped
1 green pepper, finely
   chopped
1 clove garlic, finely chopped
1 carrot, thinly sliced
19-oz. can tomatoes, cut up
½ tsp. oregano
½ tsp. basil
1 tsp. salt
½ tsp. pepper
8-oz. tin of shrimp
2 cups cooked rice

Combine chicken, onion, green
pepper, garlic, carrot, tomatoes,
oregano, basil, salt and pepper
in a slow cooker. Cover and cook
on low for 8 hours.

Approximately 1 hour before
serving, add shrimp and rice.
Cover and continue cooking for 1
hour or until heated through.

Serves 4.

—Ruth Faux

Chicken, Rice & Dumplings

1½ cups cooked rice
2 cups diced cooked
   vegetables
2 cups chicken broth or
   gravy
1 cup diced cooked chicken
1 cup flour
2 tsp. baking powder
½ tsp. salt
1 egg
¼ cup cold milk
Parsley
Pepper

Combine rice and vegetables
with broth. Simmer for 5
minutes. Add chicken.

To make dumplings, mix flour,
baking powder and salt together.
Beat egg, mix with milk and add
to dry ingredients. Stir until all
the flour is moistened.

Dip a spoon into the broth,
then take a spoonful of the
batter and drop it onto the top of
the broth. Repeat, leaving a
small space between each
dumpling, until the batter is
gone.

Cover and simmer for 10 to 15
minutes, or until dumplings are
cooked. Sprinkle with parsley
and pepper and serve.

Serves 4.

—Joan Southworth

French Potted Chicken

4-6 lb. stewing chicken
¼ cup drippings
1 onion, chopped
1 cup chopped celery
1 cup sliced peeled carrots
2-3 cups chicken stock
2 whole cloves
1 tsp. salt
¼ tsp. thyme
Parsley

Brown chicken in drippings in
heavy saucepan and remove
from pan. Briefly sauté onions,
celery and carrots.

Return chicken to pan. Add
stock, cloves, salt and thyme.
Cover and simmer 3 to 4 hours,
adding more stock or water as
needed.

Garnish with parsley before
serving.

Serves 6 to 8.

—Jean Stewart

Crispy Chicken

½ cup flour
¼ cup corn meal
2 Tbsp. soy flour
2-3 Tbsp. wheat germ
½ tsp. sage
½ tsp. thyme
Curry powder
Pepper
1 egg, beaten
½ cup milk
1 chicken, cut up

Combine dry ingredients and
liquid ingredients separately. Dip
chicken pieces in liquid then
coat with flour mixture. Place on
a cookie sheet and bake at 375°
F for 45 minutes to 1 hour.

Serves 4 to 6.

—Karen Armour

Blanketed Chicken

4-6 lbs. chicken, cut up
2 Tbsp. finely chopped green
   pepper
Salt & pepper
1 Tbsp. finely chopped chives
6 strips bacon
4 Tbsp. flour
1½ cups light cream

Place chicken pieces in roasting pan and add green pepper, salt, pepper and chives. Cover with bacon. Bake at 400° F for 40 to 50 minutes. Combine 3 Tbsp. fat from roasting pan, flour and cream and cook slowly until thickened. Season with salt and pepper. Place chicken in serving dish and cover with sauce.

Serves 6.

—Judy Bell

Country Chicken

¾ cup sour cream
1 Tbsp. lemon juice
1 tsp. salt
1 tsp. paprika
½ tsp. Worcestershire sauce
Garlic powder
2½-3 lb. chicken, cut up
1 cup fine dry bread crumbs
¼ cup butter

Combine sour cream, lemon juice, salt, paprika, Worcestershire sauce and garlic powder.

Dip chicken in mixture, roll in bread crumbs and place in shallow baking dish. Dot with butter.

Bake, covered, at 350° F for 45 minutes. Remove cover and cook 45 to 50 minutes longer.

Serves 5 to 6.

—Donna Jubb

Chicken Curry

An excellent authentic Indian recipe for an easy popular dish, this can be made with leftover chicken meat, chicken pieces or a whole chicken.

4-lb. stewing chicken
1½ cups ghee (clarified
   butter)
1½ lbs. onions, sliced
1 cup chopped fresh ginger
1 head garlic (7 or 8 cloves)
2½ cups water
2 tsp. turmeric
2 tsp. garam masala
1 Tbsp. salt
1 Tbsp. cumin
½ tsp. ground black pepper
1 tsp. hot chili powder
10 cardamoms
10 cloves
4 bay leaves
5 sticks cinnamon
1¼ cups yogurt

Skin chicken and cut into pieces.

Melt ghee in large heavy saucepan, add half the onions. While they are frying on low heat, liquidize in a blender the ginger, garlic and remaining onions with water. When the onions are fried to golden brown, add spice mixture and stir over low heat for 10 minutes.

Add turmeric, garam masala, salt, cumin, pepper, chili powder, cardamoms, cloves, bay leaves and cinnamon. Cook, stirring, for a further 10 minutes.

Add chicken pieces and yogurt. Cover the pan and cook on low heat for 3 hours.

Serves 6 to 8.

—Sheila Bear

Chicken Hearts with Mushrooms

¼ cup uncooked rice
¼ cup uncooked bulgur
4 Tbsp. oil
1 cup boiling water
Salt to taste
2 Tbsp. soya grits
½ lb. mushrooms, chopped
1 lb. chicken hearts
2 cloves garlic, minced
1 cup cottage cheese
½ cup yogurt
1 stalk leafy celery, chopped
Pinch thyme & sage
Flour

Sauté rice and bulgur in oil until browned. Combine with boiling water, salt and soya grits in a saucepan. Simmer, covered, over low heat for 15 to 20 minutes, or until cooked. Set aside and keep warm.

Meanwhile, sauté mushrooms, hearts and garlic in oil until hearts turn pink. Remove from heat and keep warm.

Combine and heat cottage cheese, yogurt, celery and herbs. If necessary, thicken with a little flour. Add hearts, mushrooms and garlic.

Serve over rice-bulgur mixture.

Serves 3.

—Nicol Séguin

Poulet aux Tomates

1 or 2 chickens, cut up
Flour, salt & pepper to coat
  chicken
¼ cup butter
1 cup finely chopped onion
1 green pepper, cut in strips
1 clove garlic, minced
½ cup celery, finely chopped
½ lb. mushrooms, chopped
5 cups canned tomatoes
2 tsp. salt
½ tsp. pepper
½ tsp. thyme
1 Tbsp. parsley

Coat chicken with seasoned flour. Brown in melted butter. Add onion, green pepper, garlic, celery and mushrooms and sauté for 5 minutes. Add remaining ingredients and simmer for 10 minutes.

Place in a Dutch oven or casserole dish and bake at 350° F for 1 hour.

Serves 6 to 8.

—*Jolaine Wright*

Crusty Chicken Pie

¼ cup butter
2¼ cups flour
1⅔ cups milk
1 cup chicken stock
2 cups diced cooked chicken
½ cup diced celery
1 cup cooked carrots
½ cup chopped mushrooms
¾ tsp. salt
4 tsp. baking powder
½ tsp. salt
⅓ cup cold butter
1 cup grated Cheddar cheese

Melt ¼ cup butter and stir in ¼ cup flour. Add 1 cup milk and chicken stock. Cook until thick, stirring constantly. Add meat, vegetables and ¾ tsp. salt and heat thoroughly. Place in casserole dish and keep warm.

Sift 2 cups flour, baking powder and ½ tsp. salt into bowl. Cut in butter until it is the size of peas.

Pour ⅔ cup milk into centre of flour mixture and stir until mixture comes away from sides of bowl. Knead gently on floured surface for 1 minute then roll out to ¼-inch thickness. Sprinkle with grated cheese. Roll as for jelly roll and cut in ½-inch slices. Place on top of hot chicken.

Bake at 425° F for 20 minutes.

Serves 6.

—*Shirley Thomlinson*

Old-Fashioned Chicken Pot Pie

3-lb. chicken
3 cups water
2 tsp. salt
½ tsp. peppercorns
1 medium onion, chopped
⅓ cup butter
¼ cup flour
¼ tsp. celery salt
⅛ tsp. pepper
1 cup cooked peas
1 cup cooked carrots
2 cups mashed potatoes

Cut chicken into pieces. Place in a large pot with water, 1 tsp. of salt and peppercorns. Bring to a boil, then simmer for 45 minutes, or until tender. Remove chicken. Strain broth and discard peppercorns. Cool the chicken, remove skin and bones and cut up the large pieces. Sauté onion in butter in a medium saucepan until tender. Add flour and blend well. Cook for 1 minute. Gradually add 2 cups of broth, stirring until smooth. Cook over low heat, stirring constantly until thickened and bubbly. Add 1 tsp. salt, celery salt and pepper. Remove from heat.

Arrange chicken, peas and carrots in a 2½-quart casserole dish. Spoon sauce over and top with mashed potatoes.

Bake at 425° F for 20 minutes.

Serves 4.

—*Sharron Jansen*

Barbecued Chicken

¼ cup vegetable oil
1 tsp. minced garlic
2 medium onions, finely
   chopped
6-oz. can tomato paste
¼ cup white vinegar
1 tsp. salt
1 tsp. basil or thyme
¼ cup honey
½ cup beef stock
½ cup Worcestershire sauce
1 tsp. dry mustard
1 chicken, cut up
Salt & pepper
2 Tbsp. oil
1 clove garlic, crushed

Heat oil in a 12-inch skillet. Add minced garlic and onions and cook, stirring frequently, until onion is soft. Lower heat and add remaining ingredients, except chicken, salt, pepper, garlic, and oil. Simmer, uncovered, for 15 minutes.

Season chicken with salt, pepper and garlic. Brown in oil at a high temperature. Remove to a large deep, cast-iron frying pan. Pour barbecue sauce over the chicken, cover and cook over medium heat until sauce is lightly boiling. Reduce heat and simmer for 1½ to 2 hours.

Makes 2½ cups.

—Marilyn & Patricia Picco

Cold Barbecued Chicken

4-lb. broiler, cut in pieces
4 Tbsp. salad oil or
   shortening
1 large onion, sliced
3 Tbsp. brown sugar
3 Tbsp. cider vinegar
¼ cup lemon juice
1 cup ketchup or tomato
   sauce
3 Tbsp. Worcestershire
   sauce
1 Tbsp. prepared mustard
½ cup diced celery
1¼ cups water
½ tsp. salt
½ tsp. oregano
¼ tsp. pepper

In a large frying pan, brown the chicken in salad oil. As pieces are done, place them in a 3-quart casserole dish.

Add remaining ingredients to pan and bring to a boil. Pour sauce over chicken. Cover and bake for 1 hour at 350° F. Cool. Uncover and refrigerate until needed. Serve at room temperature.

Serves 4.

—Mrs. J. Hall-Armstrong

Chicken Beer Barbecue

3 lbs. chicken pieces
12 oz. beer
1 tsp. salt
¼ tsp. pepper
2 Tbsp. lemon juice
½ tsp. orange extract
1 tsp. grated orange rind
1 Tbsp. brown sugar
1 Tbsp. dark molasses
Generous dash Tabasco
   sauce

Place chicken in large bowl. Mix together remaining ingredients. Pour over chicken and marinate for several hours or overnight. Barbecue over hot coals, brushing frequently with marinade.

Serves 4 to 6

—Cynthia Stewart

Chicken Enchiladas

12 tortillas
3 cups chopped cooked chicken
¾ cup sliced almonds
2 cups shredded Jack cheese
3 cups chicken stock
2 Tbsp. cornstarch
½ tsp. chili powder
¼ tsp. garlic powder
¼ tsp. cumin

Fry tortillas quickly on both sides in hot oil. Stack and keep warm. Combine chicken, almonds and ½ cup cheese.

To make sauce, bring chicken stock to a boil. Mix cornstarch with a little cold water and stir into stock. Add seasonings and boil for 1 minute.

Add ½ cup of sauce to chicken mixture. Dip each tortilla in sauce to soften, put some chicken mixture on it and roll up. Place tortillas in greased casserole dish in a single layer. Top with remaining 1½ cups cheese and pour remaining sauce around tortillas.

Bake at 350° F for 20 to 25 minutes.

Serves 4.

—Linda Townsend

Chicken Wings in Beer

36 chicken wings
¼ cup sugar
2 Tbsp. minced onion
1 clove garlic, minced
½ tsp. ginger
1 cup beer
1 cup pineapple or orange juice
¼ cup vegetable oil

Cut tips off wings and discard. Wash wings well. Marinate, refrigerated, in remaining ingredients overnight, turning a few times.

Place in baking pan with marinade and bake, uncovered, for 2 hours at 350° F.

Serves 8.

—Anne Lawrence

Chicken Wings

5 lbs. chicken wings
2 Tbsp. vegetable oil
1 medium onion, chopped
2 cloves garlic, minced
½ cup brown sugar
1 cup chili sauce
1 Tbsp. Worcestershire sauce
½ cup lemon juice
½ cup water
2 Tbsp. vinegar

Cook wings in oil in casserole dish at 350° F for 30 minutes. Remove wings from oven. Combine remaining ingredients and pour over wings. Return to oven for 1 to 1½ hours.

Serves 4 to 6.

—Reo Belhumeur

Cantonese Chicken Wings

3 lbs. chicken wings
1 Tbsp. cooking oil
1 Tbsp. soya sauce
½ tsp. salt
¼ cup brown sugar
1 tsp. chili powder
¾ tsp. celery seed
¼ cup vinegar
1 cup tomato sauce, page 414

Pat chicken wings dry. Place on broiler pan. Mix oil and soya sauce and brush over each wing. Mix salt, sugar, chili powder and celery seed and sprinkle over top. Place 5 inches below broiler and cook for approximately 10 minutes.

Remove from oven, place in casserole dish. Combine vinegar with tomato sauce and pour over casserole.

Bake at 350° F for 1 hour.

Serves 4.

—Irene MacPhee

Pauline's Chicken Wings

4 lbs. chicken wings
½ tsp. salt
½ tsp. garlic powder
¼ tsp. pepper
½ cup brown sugar
½ tsp. cornstarch
¼ cup vinegar
2 Tbsp. ketchup or tomato paste
½ cup chicken stock
1 Tbsp. soya sauce

Combine all ingredients but chicken and pour over wings. Bake, uncovered, at 400° F for 35 to 40 minutes, glazing every 10 minutes.

Serves 4.

—Mary Anne Vanner

Chicken Chow Mein

2 Tbsp. butter
¼ cup chopped onion
½ cup celery
4 cups bean sprouts
1 cup diced cooked chicken
½ cup water
4 cups Chinese noodles
Salt & pepper

Melt butter in a large pot and add onion and celery. Sauté for 3 to 5 minutes. Add bean sprouts, chicken, water, noodles and seasonings. Stir. Place in casserole dish and bake at 325° F for 30 minutes.

Serves 2.

Almond Chicken

½ cup whole almonds
2-3 Tbsp. butter
3-4 stalks celery, thinly
　sliced
1 onion, sliced
1 green pepper, cut in strips
1½ cups peas
1 cup sliced mushrooms
2 cups cooked chicken, cut
　into bite-sized pieces
1 tsp. sugar
2 Tbsp. cornstarch
1½ cups chicken stock
1 tsp. soya sauce

Brown almonds in butter and set aside. To the remaining butter, add celery, onion and green pepper and brown slightly. Add peas. Cook about 1 minute, then stir in mushrooms and chicken. Blend sugar, cornstarch and stock. Add to pan, cooking until clear. At the last moment before serving, add soya sauce and almonds. Serve with rice.

Serves 4 to 6.

—*Adele Dueck*

Chicken Cantaloupe Salad

2 cups diced cooked chicken
1 cup sliced celery
¼ cup chopped green pepper
1½ Tbsp. lemon juice
2 Tbsp. French dressing,
　page 133
2 Tbsp. mayonnaise, page
　132
½ tsp. salt
1 cantaloupe
Lettuce
⅓ cup slivered almonds

Combine chicken, celery and green pepper with lemon juice, French dressing, mayonnaise and salt. Chill. Halve cantaloupe, place on lettuce leaf and fill with chicken mixture. Garnish with almonds.

Serves 2.

—*Laura Wilson*

Chicken Salad

½ cup mayonnaise, page 132
1 Tbsp. fresh lemon juice
¼ tsp. salt
⅛ tsp. pepper
⅛ tsp. diced marjoram
2 Tbsp. heavy cream
3 cups chopped chicken, in
　large pieces
Ripe olives
Tomato slices

Combine mayonnaise with lemon juice, salt, pepper, marjoram and cream, mix chicken into dressing. Arrange on plate with olives and tomatoes.

Serves 4.

—*Winona Heasman*

Chicken Tetrazzini

1 cup sliced mushrooms
1 cup chopped celery
½ cup chopped green pepper
1½ cups slivered almonds
¼ cup butter
¼ cup flour
1 cup chicken stock
2 cups light cream
Salt & pepper
1 cup grated Swiss cheese
3-4 cups cooked chicken,
　cut into bite-sized pieces
12 oz. spaghetti, cooked
½ cup Parmesan cheese

Sauté mushrooms, celery, green pepper and 1 cup almonds in butter for 5 minutes. Remove with slotted spoon. To butter in frying pan, add flour and stir until smooth. Slowly add chicken stock and cream, stirring constantly. Cook until slightly thickened. Add salt, pepper and cheese.

When sauce has thickened, remove from heat. In large casserole dish, combine cooked spaghetti, vegetables, chicken and sauce. Mix well and top with Parmesan cheese and remaining almonds.

Bake at 350° F for 20 to 30 minutes.

Serves 8 to 10.

Rice Turkey Dressing

⅔ cup butter
¾ cup chopped onion
1 cup chopped celery
4 oz. mushrooms, sliced
4 oz. raisins (optional)
6-8 slices bread, cubed
1 cup uncooked brown or
   wild rice
1 Tbsp. savory
1½ Tbsp. chopped parsley
1½ cups hot water

Heat butter in skillet, add onion and celery and sauté over low heat for 15 minutes. Add mushrooms and raisins. Pour mixture over bread cubes, rice and seasonings. Add hot water and mix. Spoon into turkey using just enough to fill. Because stuffing swells during baking or roasting, pack it very loosely. (Extra stuffing can be added during the last half hour of cooking the turkey, or cooked separately in a covered casserole dish.) Pull flap of neck skin gently over stuffing and fasten with a skewer, then truss the legs of the bird.

Bake at 350° F for 15 minutes per pound plus 15 minutes more. Grease skin thoroughly with butter before baking, place in a shallow pan, and cover loosely with foil. Do not allow the foil to touch the skin and remove for the last 15 minutes.

—*Trish Hines*

Sage Dressing

4 cups dry bread crumbs
2 cups mashed potatoes
½ cup melted butter
½ cup minced onion
1 tsp. salt
4 Tbsp. powdered sage
½ tsp. pepper

Mix all ingredients in bowl.

Makes enough dressing to stuff a 15-lb. bird.

—*Barb Curtis*

Russian Turkey Dressing

With the consistency of a very firm paté, this rich stuffing is thick enough to be sliced and makes fine leftover sandwich fare.

3 medium onions, chopped
3 stalks celery, chopped
½ cup butter
½ tsp. pepper
2 Tbsp. salt
2 Tbsp. poultry seasoning
10 cups bread crumbs
12 eggs
1 lb. chopped chicken livers
2 Tbsp. dried parsley
Milk to moisten dressing

Sauté onions and celery in butter and let cool. Mix remaining ingredients together and moisten with milk. Add onions and celery.

Makes enough stuffing for a 12- to 14-lb. turkey.

—*Anne Lawrence*

Turkey Squares

1 onion, chopped
2 Tbsp. oil
2 cups cooked rice
2 cups diced leftover turkey
¾ cup gravy
2 eggs, well beaten
1 tsp. salt
½ cup chopped celery
½-1 cup grated cheese

Sauté onion in oil. Combine with all remaining ingredients, except cheese, in a casserole dish. Bake for 40 minutes at 350° F. Top with cheese and return to oven for another 5 minutes.

Serves 4.

—*Louise Jackson*

Mushroom Sausage Dressing

¾ cup chopped mushrooms
¾ cup chopped onion
⅓ cup chopped celery
⅓ cup butter
½-¾ cup crumbled cooked
   sausage meat
4 cups dry bread cubes
1 Tbsp. parsley
1 tsp. salt
Pepper
Savory
Thyme
Chicken stock to moisten
   dressing

Sauté vegetables in butter. Add sausage meat, bread cubes and seasonings. Taste and adjust seasoning if necessary. Add enough stock to moisten.

Makes enough dressing to stuff a 10- to 12-lb. bird.

—*Lynn Shelley*

Orange Cranberry Dressing

10-12 cups coarse bread
    crumbs
1 Tbsp. grated orange rind
2 oranges in segments
1 cup thick cranberry sauce
1 cup finely chopped celery
1 cup finely chopped onion
2 tsp. salt
½ tsp. pepper
½2 cup soft butter

Toss all ingredients together lightly.

Sufficient to stuff a 10- to 12-lb. turkey.

—*Sherri Dick*

Breading for Fried Chicken

2 cups flour
1 tsp. salt
1 Tbsp. celery salt
1 Tbsp. pepper
2 Tbsp. dry mustard
2 Tbsp. paprika
2 Tbsp. garlic powder
1 tsp. ginger
½ tsp. thyme
½ tsp. sweet basil
½ tsp. oregano

Mix thoroughly and store tightly sealed. Coat chicken pieces before frying.

Makes 2½ cups.

—*Shirley Morrish*

Sausage Dressing

1 lb. sausage meat
3 Tbsp. minced onion
4 Tbsp. minced parsley
4 Tbsp. minced celery
3 Tbsp. melted butter
Salt & pepper
5-6 cups bread crumbs

Fry sausage meat just until it loses the pink colour, and drain. Combine with remaining ingredients and mix well.

Makes enough dressing to stuff a 14- to 17-pound bird.

—*Mary Reid*

Rice Dressing

2 cups cooked rice
2-3 green onions, chopped
1 cup mushrooms, chopped
½ tsp. thyme
½ tsp. sage

Combine all ingredients and place in an ovenproof dish. When poultry is nearly cooked, take 2 Tbsp. of drippings from roasting pan and add to dressing to moisten. Cover and bake for 30 minutes.

Serves 4.

—*Lydia Nederhoff*

Oyster Dressing

2 dozen large oysters,
    shucked
Seasoned flour
2 eggs, beaten with 1 Tbsp.
    oil & ½ tsp. Tabasco sauce
Cracker crumbs
¾ cup butter
1 cup chopped onion
¼ cup oil
¼ cup chopped celery
2 cups dry bread crumbs
1½ tsp. salt
½ tsp. thyme
⅛ tsp. each pepper &
    rosemary
1 Tbsp. chopped parsley

Dip the oysters into the seasoned flour, then into the egg mixture. Roll in cracker crumbs and let stand about 10 minutes. Melt 3 to 4 Tbsp. butter until bubbling and fry the oysters until golden brown — about 1 minute on each side. Drain.

Sauté the onion in oil and remaining butter until brown. Add the celery and cook for about 3 minutes more. Add all remaining ingredients except oysters, and toss thoroughly.

Stuff bird alternately with the crumb mixture and the fried oysters.

Makes about 8 cups.

—*Nina Kenzie*

Chicken Liver Paté Casanova

½ cup butter
4 oz. cream cheese
½ lb. chicken livers
1 small onion, quartered
6 Tbsp. chicken broth
2 Tbsp. brandy or cognac
½ tsp. paprika
½ tsp. salt
Cayenne pepper

Remove butter and cream cheese from refrigerator about 1 hour before starting.

Clean and quarter livers, sauté in skillet or saucepan with the onion, chicken broth and brandy for 5 minutes.

Empty mixture, including liquid, into blender container. Add paprika, salt and cayenne. Cover and blend on high speed. Slice in butter and cream cheese, scraping down mixture with rubber scraper if necessary.

Pour into small crock and chill for at least 2 hours. Serve with garnish of chopped hardboiled eggs.

Makes 2½ cups.

—*Erika Johnston*

Chicken Liver Mousse

This rich paté may be unmoulded and served with crackers or dark rye bread as an appetizer or sliced for sandwiches.

1 lb. chicken livers
2 Tbsp. minced shallots
2 Tbsp. butter
⅓ cup Madeira or cognac
¼ cup whipping cream
½ tsp. salt
⅛ tsp. allspice
⅛ tsp. thyme
⅛ tsp. pepper
¼ cup butter

Cut livers into ½-inch pieces. Sauté with shallots in 2 Tbsp. butter until rosy. Scrape into blender.

Boil down Madeira or cognac rapidly and add to liver. Add cream and seasonings and blend to a smooth paste.

Melt ¼ cup butter, add and blend. Force through a fine sieve with a wooden spoon. Correct seasoning.

Spoon into a mould, cover and chill for 2 to 3 hours.

Makes 2 cups.

—*Susan Bates Eddy*

Chicken Liver Paté

1 cup chicken livers
1 medium onion, chopped
2 Tbsp. Worcestershire sauce
1 Tbsp. lemon juice
2-4 cloves garlic, crushed
Salt & pepper
Pinch nutmeg
1 cup bread crumbs

Place all ingredients, except bread crumbs, in a small saucepan and add approximately ¼ cup water. Bring to a boil, then simmer for 10 minutes. Allow to cool slightly.

Add bread crumbs and place mixture in blender or food processor. Blend to a smooth paste. Refrigerate to chill and serve with crackers.

Makes 2 cups.

—*Nicolle de Grauw*

Goose Liver Paté

2 Tbsp. bread crumbs
1 Tbsp. white flour
1 cup whipping cream
1 goose liver
1 egg
1 Tbsp. chopped onion
Salt & pepper
1 Tbsp. butter, melted & cooled

Mix bread crumbs and flour and soak them in the cream. Scrape the liver. Add to liver, egg, onion, salt and pepper. Stir in bread crumb mixture. Force through a sieve, or put through a food processor. Add cooled butter. Taste for seasoning.

Pour mixture into a greased ovenproof dish or pan. Cover with aluminum foil and cook in a water bath at 350° F for about 40 minutes.

Serves 4.

—*Sherrie Dick*

Delicious Onion Quiche, page 40

Indonesian Rice Salad, page 211

Dilled Tomato Soup, page 88

Chicken Pinwheels, page 300

Vegetable Pasta, page 419

Old Fort Henry Brown Bread, page 477

Castilian Hot Chocolate, page 571

Pavlova and Yogurt Chantilly, page 545

Liver Paté

1 medium onion, chopped
1 clove garlic, chopped
2 eggs
1 lb. chicken livers
¼ cup flour
½ tsp. ginger
½ tsp. allspice
1 cup heavy cream
1 Tbsp. salt
1 tsp. pepper
¼ cup butter

Blend onion, garlic and eggs in a blender for 1 minute. Add liver and blend for 2 more minutes. Remove to a large bowl. Combine remaining ingredients, then add to liver mixture.

Place in greased loaf pan and cover with butter. Butter aluminum foil and cover pan with it. Set in a larger pan of water and bake at 325° F for 3 hours.

Remove paté from pan and cool. Wrap and refrigerate.

—Lisa Brownstone

Sidney Bay Rabbit

¼ cup butter
¼ cup honey
1 Tbsp. soya sauce
3-4 lbs. rabbit, cut up
2 Tbsp. chopped ginger root

Melt butter, honey and soya sauce together. Spread half this mixture over rabbit in a roasting pan.

Cover with foil and bake for 45 minutes at 375° F. Remove foil, add ginger root, turn rabbit over and add remaining sauce.

Bake for 1 more hour, basting frequently, until rabbit is tender and sauce is thick and shiny.

Serves 4 to 6.

—Helen Campbell

Rabbit Paté Camille

2-lb. rabbit with liver reserved
1 Tbsp. butter
1 tsp. salt
½ tsp. pepper
4 slices bacon
2 chicken livers
1 large shallot, finely chopped
⅛ tsp. allspice
¼ cup bread crumbs
2 large egg yolks
4 Tbsp. brandy
Fatback slices to line small casserole dish
¼ tsp. thyme
1 bay leaf

Cut rabbit meat from the bones in chunks. Coarsely chop and sauté in butter for a few minutes. Lightly salt and pepper then set aside.

Cut bacon into small pieces. Finely chop rabbit and chicken livers. Combine livers and bacon in bowl with shallots, salt, pepper, allspice, bread crumbs, egg yolks, brandy and rabbit meat. Mix thoroughly.

Line 3-cup terrine or small casserole dish with fatback. Spoon in paté mixture and press down well. Sprinkle with salt, pepper and thyme. Place bay leaf on top, cover with more fatback and cover casserole dish.

Cook in a water bath at 300° F for 3 hours. After removing from oven, put a weight on top of the paté to compress and allow to cool. Refrigerate overnight.

Makes 3 cups.

—Sheila Bear

Rabbit with Dressing

2-3 lbs. rabbit meat, cut up
1 onion, sliced
5-6 cups chicken stock
3 peppercorns
¼ cup minced onion
⅓ cup butter, melted
6 cups dry bread cubes
½ tsp. sage
Salt & pepper
4 Tbsp. butter
¾ cup flour
4 egg yolks, well beaten

Place rabbit pieces, onion slices, chicken stock and peppercorns in heavy saucepan. Simmer, covered, for 1½ hours, or until rabbit is tender. Remove rabbit from broth and cool. Set broth aside. Bone meat, cut up and arrange in a 3-quart casserole dish.

Sauté minced onion in melted butter. Combine with bread cubes, sage, salt and pepper and mix lightly. Sprinkle over rabbit pieces.

Strain broth. Heat 4 Tbsp. butter in skillet, stir in flour and blend in broth. Cook, stirring constantly, until thickened. Pour a little sauce into the egg yolks, then stir yolks back into the hot mixture. Cook for 1 minute, then pour over casserole.

Bake at 375° F for 35 minutes or until dressing is set and golden brown.

Serves 8.

—Charlene Bloomberg

Rabbit Casserole

2 rabbits, cut up
½ cup flour
1 Tbsp. salt
1 tsp. pepper
½ cup oil
1 clove garlic, chopped
1 cup chopped onion
1 cup chopped celery
1 green pepper, chopped
½ lb. mushrooms
Thyme
Cayenne
Bay leaf
4 large tomatoes, quartered
1 cup dry white wine
½ lb. shrimp

Coat rabbit in mixture of flour, salt and pepper. Brown in oil, then place in a casserole dish. Sauté garlic and onion, then stir in celery, green pepper and mushrooms. Cook, stirring, over medium heat for 5 minutes. Add what is left of the flour mixture, thyme, cayenne, bay leaf, tomatoes and wine. Bring to a boil. Pour over rabbit and bake at 350° F for 40 minutes. Add shrimp, cover and cook for another 20 minutes.

Serves 6 to 8

—Gail Cool

Rabbit in Sour Cream & Mustard

2 medium onions, chopped
Olive oil
2-3 lb. rabbit, cut up into
  serving pieces
Dijon mustard
Water
1 cup sour cream

Sauté the onions in 2 Tbsp. olive oil, then put in a heavy saucepan. Coat the rabbit pieces generously with the mustard and fry gently in olive oil, being careful not to burn them. Place the meat on top of the onions. To drippings in pan, add just enough water to simmer the rabbit. Pour over rabbit and cook gently until it is done — about 2 hours.

Meanwhile, fry the liver and kidney. Add them to the rabbit mixture 10 minutes before it is done.

When the rabbit is cooked, remove the meat from the sauce and arrange on a serving dish. Keep warm. Add sour cream to the sauce and mix well while heating it, but do not let it boil. Pour sauce over meat and serve immediately.

Serves 4.

—Eila Belton

Roast Rabbit

Soak rabbit overnight in salted water. Drain and wipe dry. Rub shortening all over it and season with salt and pepper. Sprinkle rosemary and a sliced clove of garlic into the cavity.

Bake in a roasting pan at 300° F for 2 hours. Increase the temperature to 350° and roast for 1 more hour. Turn the rabbit over for the last 30 minutes, so that both sides will be brown and crisp.

Serves 4.

—F. Rosati

Rabbit Sausage Casserole

1 rabbit
Flour
4 Tbsp. oil
1 lb. pork sausage
1 cup beer
¼ cup cider vinegar
1 cup chicken stock
1 cup browned bread crumbs
1 tsp. caraway seeds
1 tsp. grated lemon peel
1 tsp. brown sugar
Salt & pepper

Skin, clean and cut up the rabbit. Dust with flour and brown in hot oil. Place in a large, deep pot and add remaining ingredients. Bring to a boil, reduce heat, cover and simmer gently for 2 hours. If a thicker sauce is desired, blend 2 Tbsp. flour into a little water and stir into sauce.

Serves 6.

—Carolyn Hills

Barbecued Wild Duck

¾ cup oil
½ cup vinegar
¼ cup soya sauce
1 sprig rosemary
1 Tbsp. celery seed
1 tsp. salt
¼ tsp. pepper
4 small wild ducks, cleaned,
　　dressed & cut up

Combine all ingredients except ducks and simmer for 10 minutes. Put duck pieces in sauce and simmer for another 10 minutes, turning so that all sides are covered. Place in roasting pan and roast, uncovered, at 350° F for 50 to 60 minutes, basting often.

Serves 4

—Adele Moore

Smothered Pheasant

Salt
Pepper
Thyme
Basil
Seasoned salt
½ cup flour
2 or 3 pheasants, cut up
Oil
1 cup sliced onions
1 cup chopped mushrooms
1½ cups cream of
　　mushroom sauce, page 132
1 pint sour cream

Add seasonings to flour and coat pheasant. Brown in oil. Put in roaster and top with onions, mushrooms and mushroom sauce. Cook for 1 hour at 350° F. Add sour cream and cook for another 30 minutes.

—Gail Cool

Glazed Duck

½ cup butter
½ cup lemon juice or wine
　　vinegar
2 cups hot water
1 duck
Flour
2 Tbsp. cranberry jelly
Water
Salt & pepper

Combine butter, lemon juice and hot water. Pour over duck in roasting pan. Cover and bake at 350° F for 20 minutes per pound, basting several times.

For gravy, cool drippings and remove fat. Blend remaining juices with flour to make a paste, then add cranberry jelly and water until desired consistency is reached. Add salt and pepper to taste.

Serves 4.

—Goldie Connell

Grouse à la David

8 grouse breasts
Flour
Salt & pepper
Oil
¼ cup red wine

Remove breast meat from bone. Pound each breast and coat with flour. Sprinkle with salt and pepper. Fry pieces in cooking oil until golden brown on both sides, about 5 minutes. Pour wine over meat. Cover and cook for 5 more minutes.

Serves 4.

—Ronald Manuel

Roast Duck or Goose

Stuff duck or goose with whole apples. Place on rack in roaster and keep about half an inch of water in bottom of roaster while baking, to prevent fat drippings from burning.

Bake at 400° F, uncovered, until done, turning every half hour or so. After the first half hour, prick the skin liberally with a fork to let the fat run out. Skim off excess fat. Sprinkle with salt, pepper and caraway seeds.

Simmer the heart and gizzard separately in water until tender and add to the roasting pan, along with the liver, during the last hour of baking.

When done, cut the bird into serving-sized portions with poultry shears and serve with the apples that were baked in it.

If gravy is desired, separate the fat from the broth in the roasting pan and thicken the broth with cornstarch mixed with a little cold water. Season with salt and pepper.

Serves 4.

—Tonya Bassler

Moose Steak Roast

½ cup flour
Salt & pepper
2 medium-sized moose
 steaks
2 eggs, beaten
1 cup bread crumbs
Oil
1 cup tomato juice
2 onions, chopped
Dash soya sauce
Stalk of celery, chopped
½ green pepper, chopped

Combine flour, salt and pepper and sprinkle on both sides of meat. Pound with a meat hammer. Continue to sprinkle and pound until flour mixture is used up. Brush both sides of meat with eggs, then coat in bread crumbs. Sear gently in oil. Place meat in roasting pan and pour tomato juice over it. Sprinkle remaining ingredients on top. Roast at 350° F until tender. Baste frequently and add more tomato juice if necessary.

Serves 2 to 4.

—H. Miller

Gourmet Venison Chops

6 venison chops
½ cup brandy
½ cup olive oil
1 clove garlic, crushed
Freshly ground pepper

Marinate chops in brandy for 2 to 3 hours, turning once so brandy has a chance to soak into both sides. Combine olive oil and garlic and let sit while the meat is marinating.

Discard garlic and heat olive oil in a large frying pan. Sprinkle chops with pepper and brown in oil at a high temperature. Turn heat down to medium-low and cook, covered, for 5 minutes on each side. Serve immediately.

Serves 6.

—Nancy Russell

Roast Venison

Be sure the meat has been properly hung and aged. Wipe the roast with a damp cloth. Make several cuts in the top and insert pieces of salt pork, bacon or fat.

Bake in roasting pan in moderate oven, allowing 40 minutes per pound. Baste occasionally. Sprinkle with salt and pepper 30 minutes before time is up. To brown, raise the temperature to 450° F for the last 10 minutes of cooking time.

—Goldie Connell

Grouse Fried Rice

4 grouse, cut into bite-sized
 pieces
Garlic powder
Ginger
Salt & pepper
1 large onion, chopped
4 carrots, thinly sliced
 diagonally
1 bunch celery stalks &
 leaves, sliced
3 cups cooked rice
Curry powder
3 tomatoes, cut in wedges

In large frying pan, sauté grouse in oil over medium-high heat. Season with garlic powder, ginger, salt and pepper.

When meat is browned, add onion and carrots. Stir-fry until onions are almost soft, about 5 minutes, then add celery and cook for another 2 minutes.

Add ½ cup water and simmer, covered, for 20 minutes. Add rice, curry powder and tomato wedges and cook, stirring constantly, until heated through.

Serves 6 to 8.

—Lois Pope

Roast Canada Goose

Cut off the oil sack, then wash and dry the goose. Brush the cavity with lemon juice. Insert stuffing and close cavity.

Brush 2 Tbsp. seasoned melted butter over skin of goose. Pour water into base of roasting pan and place goose on tray. Bake at 450° F for 15 minutes, reduce heat to 350° and roast 20 minutes per pound.

If the goose is very fatty, pierce the flesh several times during roasting to drain excess fat.

—Goldie Connell

Curried Moose

2 Tbsp. butter
1 medium onion, chopped
2 cups beef stock
2-lb. moose roast, cubed
   while still partly frozen
12 oz. tomato paste
3 Tbsp. curry powder
Handful dark raisins
2 medium potatoes, cubed

Melt butter in skillet, sauté onion in it, then combine onion with beef stock in a large saucepan.

Sear meat in skillet until brown on all sides, about 10 minutes, then add to stock and onion in saucepan, leaving juices in skillet.

Combine tomato paste and curry powder in skillet. Cook briefly, stirring, over medium heat, then add to contents of saucepan.

Stir in raisins and simmer for 2 to 3 hours. Add potatoes, and continue to simmer for another 1½ hours.

Serves 2 to 4.

—John Mortimer

Corned Moose

4 qts. hot water
2 cups coarse salt
¼ cup sugar
2 Tbsp. mixed pickling spice
3 cloves garlic
5 lbs. moose meat

Combine hot water, salt, sugar and pickling spice. When cool, add garlic and pour mixture over meat. Cure in refrigerator or cool place for 3 weeks. Cook in boiling water until tender (5 to 8 hours).

Serves 10.

—Pat McCormack

Moose Heart & Tongue Creole

1 moose heart
1 moose tongue
Salt & pepper
2 onions, chopped
4 Tbsp. butter
2 cloves garlic, minced
28-oz. can tomatoes
1 green pepper, chopped
1 bay leaf
2 Tbsp. chopped parsley
2 Tbsp. sherry or wine
Pinch thyme
2 Tbsp. sugar
1 cup sliced mushrooms
¼ cup chili sauce

Wash heart and tongue well. Place in pot, cover with water, add salt, pepper and 1 onion. Bring to a boil, lower heat and simmer until very tender — 3 to 5 hours. Peel tongue. Cut tongue and heart into thick slices. Set aside.

Melt butter, add remaining onion and garlic and cook, covered, for 2 minutes.

Add remaining ingredients and cook for approximately 1 hour. Add meat and heat through.

Serves 6 to 8.

—Mrs. T. Cushman

Moose Pepper Steak

Cooking oil
1 onion, chopped
1 stalk celery, thinly sliced
   diagonally
2 lbs. moose meat
3 or 4 carrots, thinly sliced
   diagonally
1 potato, diced
Salt & pepper
1 cup chopped mushrooms
2 cups snow peas
2 Tbsp. tapioca, softened in
   2 Tbsp. water

Pour a few teaspoons of oil into a heated wok. Add onions and celery, and stir until the onions are transparent. Add the meat and stir until browned. Stir in carrots, potato, salt and pepper.

Add about ½ cup water and cover until steam rises around edges of lid. Stir in mushrooms and snow peas, then tapioca. Cook, stirring, only until vegetables are glossy and sauce thickens. Serve immediately over cooked rice.

Serves 4.

—Angela Denholm

Moose Ribs

1 clove garlic
3 Tbsp. cooking oil
3 lbs. moose ribs, cut into
    serving-sized pieces
3 medium onions, sliced
1 cup tomato paste or
    ketchup
½ cup vinegar
1 tsp. curry powder
1 tsp. paprika
¼ tsp. chili powder
1 Tbsp. brown sugar
1 cup beef stock
½ tsp. salt
Pinch of pepper
½ tsp. dry mustard

Brown garlic in oil in a heavy frying pan. Remove garlic from oil and reserve. Brown ribs quickly in oil.

Place meat and garlic in a 2-quart baking dish. Layer onions on top. Combine remaining ingredients and pour over meat.

Cover and bake at 350° F for 1 hour. Remove lid and continue baking at 300° for another hour, or until meat is tender. Serve over rice.

Serves 4 to 6.

—*Florence Hutchison*

Roast Wild Boar

The preparation of young wild boar is very similar to that of suckling pig. Properly presented, with head intact and garnished, it makes a spectacular Christmas or New Year's dinner.

Flour
2 cups boiling chicken stock
Apple, cranberries &
    watercress to garnish
1 dressed boar,
    approximately 12 pounds
3 qts. stuffing, page 281
Butter

Stuff boar with dressings and sew it up. Place a block of wood in the mouth to hold it open. Skewer legs into position.

Rub with butter and dredge with flour. Cover tail and ears with foil and bake, uncovered, at 450° F for 15 minutes. Reduce heat to 325° and bake a further 25 minutes per pound. Baste every 15 minutes with the stock and pan drippings.

To serve: Remove foil and place boar on a platter. Remove wood from boar's mouth and replace with an apple. Place cranberries in eyes and garnish neck and platter with watercress.

Serves 12.

Saddle of Elk

6-lb. saddle of elk
Salted pork, cut into 2-inch
    strips
Garlic, peeled & cut in half
Butter

Preheat oven to 550° F.

Lard the elk with pork strips — draw through meat surface with a larding needle, or make slits with a knife and insert pork.

Rub elk with garlic and then butter. Place, fat side up, in a roasting pan in oven, reduce heat to 350° F and bake for 20 minutes per pound.

Serve with wild rice and gravy.

Serves 8.

Stewed Beaver

Remove as much fat as possible, especially the little kernels, then sear and brown the meat in a deep iron skillet. Season as you would rabbit or chicken. Add a little water and simmer until the meat falls from the bones, adding water as required. Cook until it is as dry and brown as possible without burning. Serve hot.

—*Goldie Connell*

Supremes de Volailles aux Quatres Fromages

Contributed by a London, Ontario, restaurant, this recipe for Deboned Chicken Breasts With Four Cheeses is incredibly rich, but delicious. It is relatively simple to prepare and can be assembled hours in advance — the final cooking stage takes only 5 minutes. Because it is so rich, it is best served with a salad or cooked vegetable and a light dessert of fruit.

¼ lb. plus 3 Tbsp. butter
6 chicken breasts, deboned, trimmed & pounded
Flour
Salt & pepper
1 cup flour
3 cups milk
2½ cups grated Jarlsberg cheese
1 cup plus 1 Tbsp. Parmesan cheese
¼ tsp. nutmeg
1 egg
1 cup grated white Cheddar cheese
1 cup grated old Gouda cheese

Melt 3 Tbsp. butter on high heat. Dredge chicken in flour and sauté. Season with salt and pepper and set aside.

In medium saucepan, melt ¼ lb. butter. Add 1 cup flour and stir over medium heat for 2 minutes. Pour in milk, stirring constantly, and bring to a boil. When sauce boils, lower heat, add 1½ cups Jarlsberg, 1 Tbsp. Parmesan, nutmeg, egg and salt and pepper. Continue cooking and stirring until cheese is melted. Mix together remaining cheeses.

To assemble, place chicken in shallow baking dish or in individual gratin dishes. Pour sauce over each breast, then sprinkle each with one-sixth of cheese mixture. Bake at 400° F for 5 minutes, then broil to brown the top.

Serves 6.

—Auberge du Petit Prince

Wild Chili

6 cups water
2 lbs. chicken necks
2 bay leaves
¾ tsp. rosemary
Freshly ground pepper
1 cup chopped celery & leaves
2 medium carrots, cut in half
¾ cup cubed turnip
1-1½ lbs. ground moose meat
1½ medium onions, chopped
2 cloves garlic, minced
½ lb. mushrooms, in thick slices
20-oz. can tomatoes
6-oz. can tomato paste
1½ cups cooked chick peas or kidney beans
2 cups cranberries
3 Tbsp. chili powder
Salt
½ cup uncooked bulgur
1 medium zucchini, sliced

In water, simmer chicken necks, bay leaves, rosemary, pepper, celery, carrots and turnip for about 2½ hours or until chicken comes away from the bone. Remove bay leaves and necks and let broth cool in refrigerator overnight. Remove excess fat and put broth and vegetables through blender.

Cook ground moose meat, onion, garlic and mushrooms in large casserole dish. Add broth and remaining ingredients. Simmer for 1½ to 2 hours.

Serves 8.

—Nicol Séguin

Chicken Madagascar

This recipe was developed by the contributor when he was the teaching chef in a Victoria, British Columbia, high school. In his words, "When the budget got tight, I decided I could not afford beef tenderloin for pepper steak. I used chicken, and this recipe evolved." Deglazing the pan is simply adding liquor and/or stock to the concentrated juices in which the meat has been cooked to dilute them.

2 chicken breasts
2 Tbsp. unsalted butter
2 cloves garlic, minced
2 Tbsp. minced shallots
½ Tbsp. green peppercorns
Worcestershire sauce
1 oz. brandy
1 oz. strong chicken stock
½ cup whipping cream
Salt

Debone and skin chicken breasts. Pound between wax paper until meat is of even thickness. Melt butter and sauté garlic and shallots. Add chicken and brown lightly, but do not overcook. Remove meat and keep warm. Add peppercorns and Worcestershire sauce and mash peppercorns. Add brandy and chicken stock and cook over high heat to reduce liquid and deglaze pan. Reduce heat, add cream and salt and simmer, stirring constantly, until cream begins to thicken. Return chicken and continue to simmer until chicken is heated through.

Serves 2.

—Wayne Smith

Shrimp Stuffed Chicken

1¼ cups chopped, cooked
  shrimp
¼ cup chopped celery
1 tsp. salt
¼ cup chopped onion
½ cup softened butter
3 chicken breasts, deboned,
  skinned & halved
1 cup cream of mushroom
  sauce (page 132)
½ cup chicken stock
½ cup sherry

Combine shrimp, celery, salt, onion and butter and divide evenly among chicken breasts. Roll up and secure with toothpicks.

Combine mushroom sauce, stock and sherry and blend well. Arrange chicken rolls in shallow baking dish and pour sauce over top. Bake at 350° F for 1 hour.

Serves 6.

—Jane Falls

Chicken Lemonese

4 chicken breasts
1 egg, beaten with 2 Tbsp.
  water
½ cup flour
½ cup grated Monterey jack
  cheese
½ cup Parmesan cheese
Garlic powder
¼ cup chopped parsley
1 tsp. paprika
Salt
3 Tbsp. butter
1 clove garlic, minced
3 lemons

Skin, debone and cut chicken breasts into bite-sized pieces. Place egg and water in shallow bowl. Mix together flour, cheeses, garlic powder, parsley, paprika and salt in another shallow bowl. Drop chicken pieces first into flour-cheese mixture, then into egg mixture, then back into flour-cheese mixture, coating well.

Melt butter and add garlic. Sauté chicken pieces until golden brown on both sides. Remove from pan and set aside. To liquid in pan add the juice of 2 lemons and simmer briefly. Add 1 sliced lemon, pour over chicken and serve.

Serves 4.

—Francie Goodwin-Rogne

Chicken Bolero

2 chicken breasts
1 large green pepper
1 large onion
3 Tbsp. oil
1½ Tbsp. dill weed
2½ cups sour cream
Salt & pepper
4 cups cooked rice

Debone chicken and slice into narrow strips. Slice pepper and onion into narrow strips. Sauté in hot oil until chicken is golden and vegetables are tender. Add dill weed, sour cream and salt and pepper. Cook over low heat for 10 minutes without boiling. Serve with rice.

Serves 3 to 4.

—Katie Larstone

Dijon Chicken

3 Tbsp. milk
2 Tbsp. Dijon mustard
2 chicken breasts
¼ cup bread crumbs
1 tsp. tarragon leaves,
  crushed or crumbled

Whisk milk and mustard together. Dip chicken in mixture, then coat with mixture of bread crumbs and tarragon. Place in shallow baking dish and bake at 375° F for 30 minutes, covered, then 15 minutes, uncovered.

Serves 2.

—Beth Rose

Brandied Chicken Breasts

4 chicken breasts, skinned,
   deboned & halved
¼ cup brandy
Salt & pepper
Marjoram
Thyme
6 Tbsp. unsalted butter
½ cup dry sherry
4 egg yolks
2 cups light cream
Nutmeg
Grated Gruyère cheese

Soak chicken in brandy, seasoned with salt and pepper, marjoram and thyme, for about 20 minutes.

Heat butter in large skillet and sauté chicken over medium heat for 6 to 8 minutes on each side. Remove to heated ovenproof platter and keep warm. To remaining butter in pan add sherry and the brandy that the chicken soaked in. Simmer over low heat until reduced by half.

Beat egg yolks into cream and add to pan juices, stirring constantly. Season with salt, pepper and nutmeg and cook, stirring, until slightly thickened. Pour sauce over chicken breasts, sprinkle with cheese and brown under broiler.

Serves 4.

—Jim Boagey

Herbed Chicken Breasts

2 chicken breasts, deboned
   & halved
1 Tbsp. flour
¼ cup plain yogurt
¼ tsp. lemon juice
1 tsp. grated onion
Sage, thyme & basil
¼ tsp. salt
Pepper
3 Tbsp. grated Cheddar
   cheese
¼ tsp. paprika
⅓ cup fine cracker crumbs

Sprinkle chicken with flour to lightly coat both sides. Mix yogurt, lemon juice, onion, spices and salt and pepper in a bowl. Mix cheese, paprika and crumbs in a flat dish.

Dip chicken in yogurt mixture, then in crumb mixture to coat all sides. Put in greased baking dish, cover with foil and bake at 350° F for 30 minutes. Uncover and bake until tender — about 15 minutes.

Serves 2.

—Maureen Thornton

Mandarin Chicken Breasts

¼ cup flour
½ tsp. paprika
½ tsp. salt
6 chicken breasts, deboned
2 Tbsp. butter
1¾ cups chicken stock
1 Tbsp. minced onion
2 Tbsp. lemon juice
1 bay leaf
1 Tbsp. cornstarch
1 cup seedless grapes
1 can mandarin oranges

Mix flour, paprika and salt in pie plate. Dip chicken into mixture to coat, then brown slowly in butter. Stir in chicken stock, onion, lemon juice and bay leaf. Heat to boiling, cover and reduce heat. Simmer for 25 minutes, then remove bay leaf. Mix cornstarch with a little water to make a paste and stir into gravy. Cook, stirring constantly, for 3 minutes. Stir in grapes and oranges and heat until bubbly. Serve over rice.

Serves 6 to 8.

—Marsha Plewes

Chicken with Peaches & Cream

3 whole chicken breasts
Garlic powder
1 cup raw rice
1 head broccoli
1 cup sour cream
½ cup mayonnaise
3 peaches, sliced
1 cup grated Cheddar cheese

Bake or broil chicken, seasoned with garlic powder, until tender. While chicken is baking, cook rice and place in greased casserole dish.

Steam broccoli pieces until barely tender and layer over rice. Blend sour cream and mayonnaise together and carefully fold in peach slices and drained, cooked chicken. Layer on top of broccoli, top with Cheddar cheese and bake at 350° F until cheese is hot and bubbly — 20 minutes.

Serves 3.

—Annette Laing

Chicken Breasts à la Walper

This recipe originated with the contributor's grandmother who operated the Walper Hotel, now called the Dominion Hotel, in Zurich, Ontario.

6 chicken breasts, skinned, deboned & cut in pieces
Seasoned flour
12 slices Swiss cheese
6 cups sauerkraut, well drained
1 cup sour cream or yogurt
2 Tbsp. butter

Arrange chicken breasts in well-greased, shallow baking dish. Sprinkle with seasoned flour. Top with 6 slices of Swiss cheese, then sauerkraut. Spoon sour cream over this and place remaining Swiss cheese over sour cream. Dot with butter and bake at 325° F for 45 to 50 minutes, or until chicken is tender.

Serves 6 to 8.

—E.K Walper

Chicken Breasts & Vegetables

This is an excellent and economical family dinner that is easy to prepare. If the honey and barbecue sauce are not to your liking, the chicken can be floured and sautéed in butter (rather than being put in the oven) for a different but just as satisfying result.

2 chicken breasts, deboned & halved
4 carrots, sliced
2 stalks celery, sliced
1 small onion, chopped
½ tsp. rosemary
½ tsp. thyme
½ tsp. parsley
½ tsp. marjoram
½ tsp. salt
½ cup white wine
¼ cup honey
¼ cup barbecue sauce

Place chicken, carrots, celery, onion, seasonings and wine in large saucepan. Cover with water and cook over medium heat for 30 minutes. Remove from heat and keep warm. Combine honey and barbecue sauce. Place chicken in shallow ovenproof dish and brush with honey-barbecue sauce mixture. Bake at 325° F for 15 to 20 minutes. Serve with drained vegetables and mashed potatoes.

Serves 4.

—Edwina Johnson

Forty Garlic Cloves Chicken

⅔ cup olive oil
4 stalks celery, chopped
Parsley
1 Tbsp. tarragon
Salt & pepper
Nutmeg
½ cup Cognac
40 cloves garlic, peeled but
    not cut
2 chickens, cut up

Place oil, celery, parsley, tarragon, salt and pepper, nutmeg, cognac and garlic in heavy enamel cooker. Add chicken. Cover tightly with foil or with lid glued on with a paste of flour and water. Bake at 350° F for 2 hours.

Serves 4 to 6.

—Marie-Paula Chartier

Sesame Yogurt Chicken

½ cup yogurt
2 Tbsp. Worcestershire
    sauce
2 Tbsp. lemon juice
½ cup sesame seeds
½ cup bread crumbs
½ tsp. paprika
Salt & pepper
6 chicken legs or breasts

Combine yogurt, Worcestershire sauce and lemon juice in shallow bowl. In another bowl, mix sesame seeds, bread crumbs, paprika and salt and pepper.

Dip chicken in yogurt mixture, then coat with crumb mixture. Place in greased shallow pan in a single layer. Bake at 350° F for 50 to 60 minutes, or until chicken is tender and surface crisp.

Serves 6.

—Jane Lott

Chicken Larousse

3 large chicken breasts, cut
    in half
Salt
Paprika
1 cup Parmesan cheese
1 lb. green beans, trimmed &
    Frenched
½ cup slivered almonds
1½ cups raw wild rice
¾ cup butter
1 small onion, chopped
1 small green pepper,
    chopped
1 cup chopped celery
Mushrooms, halved
Pepper
1 cup dry white wine

Sprinkle chicken with salt and paprika, roll in Parmesan cheese and set aside. Place green beans and almonds in shallow casserole dish. Cook wild rice according to package directions. Melt ½ cup butter, add onion, green pepper and celery and sauté until soft. Stir in mushrooms, wild rice and salt and pepper to taste. Place chicken over beans and almonds and spoon wild rice mixture around sides of casserole. Pour white wine over all, dot chicken with remaining butter and bake at 350° F for 45 to 50 minutes.

Serves 6.

—Sandra Binnington

Golden Popover Chicken

1 chicken, cut up
2 Tbsp. oil
Salt & pepper
3 eggs
1½ cups milk
1 Tbsp. oil
1½ cups flour
¾ tsp. crushed dried parsley
MUSHROOM SAUCE:
1 cup cream of mushroom
    sauce (page 132)
½ cup white wine
1 Tbsp. parsley
½ cup sliced mushrooms

Brown chicken pieces in oil, then season with salt and pepper and place in 9" x 13" casserole dish.

Blend remaining ingredients together in order given and pour over chicken. Bake at 350° F for 55 to 60 minutes, or until chicken is cooked and batter has puffed up and turned golden brown.

Meanwhile make sauce. Combine all ingredients in saucepan and cook over low heat. Serve with chicken.

Serves 4.

—Marcy Goldman-Posluns

Chicken Parmesan

2 chickens, cut up
Oil
1 small onion, grated
4 Tbsp. butter
3 Tbsp. flour
1 cup Parmesan cheese
2 cups milk
2 egg yolks

Lightly brown chicken in hot oil, but do not cook right through. Remove from oil, drain on paper towels, then place in large baking dish.

Cook onion in butter, add flour and stir in well. Add ¾ cup cheese, then gradually stir in milk and cook over low heat, stirring constantly, until sauce is thick. Beat egg yolks slightly and add a little of the sauce to the yolks. Stir back into sauce gradually. Cook over low heat for 10 minutes, pour over chicken and sprinkle with remaining ¼ cup cheese. Bake, covered, at 325° F for 1 hour.

Serves 6.

—Dorothy Hurst

Crispy Wheat Germ Chicken

¼ cup soya sauce
2 Tbsp. oil
1 clove garlic, minced
3 lbs. chicken pieces
½ cup wheat germ
¼ cup dry bread crumbs
2 Tbsp. sesame seeds
½ tsp. pepper
½ tsp. paprika

Combine soya sauce, oil and garlic. Arrange pieces of chicken in single layer in broad, shallow baking dish. Pour soya mixture over top and let stand for 10 minutes, turning chicken pieces several times to coat all sides.

Meanwhile, mix together wheat germ, bread crumbs, sesame seeds, pepper and paprika. Lift chicken pieces from marinade, drain briefly, then turn over in wheat germ mixture to coat all sides evenly. Arrange chicken, skin side down, on well-greased, rimmed baking sheet. Bake, uncovered, at 350° F for about 1 hour, or until done, turning after 30 minutes.

Serves 4.

—Lisa Reith

Chicken Puff

1½ cups flour
2 tsp. baking powder
½ tsp. salt
2 eggs, separated & beaten
1 cup milk
1 cup chopped, cooked chicken
2 tsp. chopped onion
¼ cup grated, raw carrot
2 Tbsp. melted butter
Chicken gravy

Mix together flour, baking powder and salt. Add beaten egg yolks and milk and mix well. Add chicken, onion, grated carrot and melted butter and mix well. Fold in stiffly beaten egg whites. Bake in greased baking dish at 400° F for about 25 minutes. Serve with hot chicken gravy.

Serves 2.

—Cathy Royer

Southern Baked Chicken

½ cup butter
1 small onion, finely chopped
1 clove garlic, finely chopped
¼ cup Parmesan cheese
¾ cup bread crumbs
¾ cup corn meal
3 Tbsp. minced fresh parsley
1 tsp. salt
1 tsp. pepper
2 chickens, cut up

Melt butter and sauté onion and garlic until tender. Combine cheese, bread crumbs, corn meal, parsley, salt and pepper. Dip chicken in butter and then roll in coating.

Bake at 350° F for 1 hour.

Serves 8.

—Valerie Marien

Italian Style Chicken Casserole

1 onion, sliced
6-8 medium potatoes, peeled & sliced
1 chicken, cut up
1 head broccoli, cut into bite-sized pieces
1 green pepper, sliced
19-oz. can tomatoes
¼ tsp. oregano
¼ tsp. basil
¼ tsp. parsley
¼ tsp. pepper
½ tsp. salt

In greased casserole dish, arrange layers of onion, potatoes, chicken and broccoli. Cover with slices of green pepper and tomatoes. Sprinkle with spices. Cover and cook at 350° F for about 2 hours. Remove cover for last 10 minutes to brown meat and potatoes.

Serves 4 to 6.

—Julie Herr

Balkan Chicken Stew

4-5 lbs. chicken pieces
Salt & pepper
3 medium onions, thinly sliced
1 clove garlic, crushed
4 Tbsp. butter
1 cup white wine
2 cups sour cream
1 cup pitted ripe olives

Pat chicken dry and season with salt and pepper. Sauté onions and garlic in butter until transparent. Remove onions, add chicken and sauté until brown. Return onions to skillet, add wine and simmer for 1 hour. Cool to room temperature, then stir in sour cream and olives. Simmer gently for 20 minutes.

Serves 5 to 6.

—Midge Denault

Spanish Chicken

¼ cup chopped onion
1 Tbsp. brown sugar
½ tsp. salt
1 tsp. prepared mustard
1 Tbsp. chili sauce
1 tsp. Worcestershire sauce
¼ cup vinegar
1 cup tomato juice
¼ cup water
½ cup sliced, stuffed green olives
Flour
Salt & pepper
3½ lbs. chicken pieces
½ cup butter

Combine onion, sugar, salt, mustard, chili sauce, Worcestershire sauce, vinegar, tomato juice and water. Cook over low heat for 10 minutes, then add olives.

Meanwhile, combine flour and salt and pepper. Dredge chicken pieces in this. Melt butter, add chicken and brown well.

Arrange chicken in 9" x 13" baking dish and cover with sauce. Cover and bake at 350° F for 45 minutes.

Serves 4.

—Barbara Taylor

Skier's Orange Chicken

A delightful meal to return home to after a winter day's outside activity, this dish can be assembled in the morning and popped into the oven at the last minute. Serve with rice pilaf and a tossed salad.

1 cup orange marmalade
1 Tbsp. curry
1 tsp. salt
½ cup water
3 lbs. chicken pieces

Combine marmalade, curry, salt and water. Place chicken cut side down in greased 9" x 13" baking pan. Spoon marmalade mixture over chicken.

Bake, uncovered, at 350° F for 45 minutes, spooning sauce over chicken several times. If sauce begins to stick to bottom of pan, add ¼ cup water.

Serves 4.

—Mrs. E. Louden

Chicken Supreme

1 chicken, cut up
Juice of 1 lemon
¼ cup flour
¼ cup butter
1 clove garlic, minced
3 carrots, sliced
2 onions, sliced
1 stalk celery, sliced
¼ cup white wine or chicken
   stock
1 cup cream sauce
½ tsp. paprika
¼ tsp. basil
¼ tsp. rosemary
2 Tbsp. parsley
Salt & pepper

Brush chicken with lemon juice and coat with flour. Melt butter and brown chicken in skillet. Place in casserole dish and top with vegetables.

Pour wine into skillet with chicken drippings, add sauce and seasonings, mix well and pour over chicken. Bake at 350° F for 1½ hours.

Serves 4.

—*Pat Dicer*

Casserole Roast Chicken

5 lbs. chicken pieces
2 tsp. salt
1 tsp. pepper
2 tsp. paprika
2 large cloves garlic, minced
4 Tbsp. butter
12 small white mushrooms
12 small onions
3-5 potatoes, quartered
5 carrots, quartered
   lengthwise
1 cup chicken stock
Parsley

Wash and dry chicken pieces. Combine salt, pepper, paprika and garlic and rub the chicken with this mixture. Melt the butter in a casserole dish and brown the chicken. Add the mushrooms, onions and potatoes and brown lightly. Add the carrots. Mix in the stock, cover and bake at 375° F for 1 hour or until tender, basting frequently. Serve garnished with fresh parsley.

Serves 4 to 6.

—*Maureen Marcotte*

Poulet Gratine au Fromage

3-4 lbs. chicken pieces
Salt
Melted butter
1 cup grated Gruyère or
   Swiss cheese
1 Tbsp. dry mustard
¾ cup whipping cream

Place chicken pieces on rack in roasting pan and salt lightly. Bake, uncovered, at 350° F for about 1 hour, or until well browned. Brush the chicken once with melted butter while it is cooking. When done, place the chicken in a shallow, heat-resistant serving dish. Sprinkle with ½ cup of the grated cheese. Return to the oven and turn off the heat.

Skim and discard fat from chicken juices in roasting pan. Stir dry mustard and whipping cream into juices. Bring to a boil on high heat and stir until shiny bubbles form — about 3 to 4 minutes. Remove from heat, stir in remaining ½ cup grated cheese and keep warm.

Broil chicken 4 to 5 inches from heat for about 1 minute, or until cheese bubbles. Pour sauce around chicken.

Serves 4.

—*Anne Calverley*

Chicken & Shrimp Casserole

10 oz. raw shelled shrimp
2 cups chicken stock
½ cup plus 1 Tbsp. butter
½ cup flour
1 cup whipping cream
2 egg yolks
½ cup plus 2 Tbsp.
  Parmesan cheese
Salt & pepper
2 tsp. parsley
3 cups chopped cooked
  chicken
2 Tbsp. ground almonds
¼ cup bread crumbs

Combine shrimp and ½ cup stock and boil for 1 minute. Drain, reserving stock. Melt ½ cup butter, add flour and stir to mix. Stir in all stock and cook until thickened. Add cream and bring to a boil. Lower heat and simmer, stirring, for 5 minutes. Beat egg yolks, stir in a little of the sauce, then return to pan. Add ½ cup cheese, salt and pepper and 1 tsp. parsley. Mix in shrimp and chicken and place in greased casserole dish. Combine remaining 1 tsp. parsley, 2 Tbsp. Parmesan cheese, 1 Tbsp. butter, almonds and bread crumbs until crumbly and sprinkle over casserole. Bake at 400° F for 30 to 35 minutes.

Serves 4.

—Linda Townsend

Baked Almond Chicken

3½ lbs. chicken pieces
Flour
1 tsp. celery salt
1 tsp. paprika
1 tsp. salt
½ tsp. curry
½ tsp. oregano
½ tsp. freshly ground pepper
7 Tbsp. melted butter
¾ cup sliced almonds
1½ cups light cream
½ cup sour cream
3 Tbsp. fine, dry bread crumbs

Coat chicken pieces with flour. Blend celery salt, paprika, salt, curry, oregano and pepper with 6 Tbsp. melted butter. Roll chicken pieces in this, coating all sides. Arrange chicken in single layer in 9" x 13" baking dish and sprinkle evenly with almonds. Pour light cream between pieces.

Bake, covered, at 350° F for 45 minutes. Uncover, add about ½ cup sauce from pan to sour cream, mix together and pour evenly over chicken. Combine bread crumbs with remaining 1 Tbsp. melted butter and sprinkle over chicken. Bake, uncovered, for 15 minutes longer, or until chicken is tender.

Serves 6.

—Marilyn Nichols

Sherried Chicken

1 chicken, cut up
½ tsp. salt
⅛ tsp. pepper
½ tsp. paprika
Butter
1 cup chicken stock
½ cup sherry
Savory
Thyme
Rosemary
Parsley
Marjoram
1 bay leaf
¼ cup butter
1 cup sliced mushrooms

Sprinkle chicken on both sides with salt, pepper and paprika and brown in butter. Add stock and sherry and sprinkle with herbs. Cover and simmer for 45 minutes, turning chicken over during cooking. Add a little water if too dry. Stir in mushrooms 5 minutes before serving.

Serves 4.

—Lori Davies

Murray Bay Nasturtium Chicken

This recipe comes from the collection of the contributor's grandmother, and brings back memories of summertime family reunions on the lower St. Lawrence River. As she recalls, "Lunches and dinners for 20 to 30 people were not unusual. When the chickens were all cooked, cooled and smelling of lemon, laid out on beds of lettuce and garnished with nasturtium flowers, they were indeed a sight to behold."

½ cup butter
2 Tbsp. lemon juice
1 tsp. salt
1 clove garlic, mashed
⅛ tsp. pepper
½ tsp. paprika
Handful mushrooms, sliced
1 Tbsp. nasturtium seeds
2-3 lbs. chicken pieces
Lettuce
Nasturtium flowers

Place butter, lemon juice, salt, garlic, pepper, paprika, mushrooms and nasturtium seeds in skillet and bring to a boil. Add chicken, cover and simmer for 30 minutes, turning chicken several times.

Remove from heat, and as the chicken cools spoon butter mixture over it. When thoroughly cooled, place on bed of lettuce, garnish with flowers and serve.

Serves 3 to 4.

—Katherine Mackenzie

Gallino en Chicha

This recipe for chicken in wine sauce is of El Salvadoran origin. Planning ahead is required as some of the ingredients will involve a trip to a specialty food shop.

5 lbs. chicken pieces
2 large onions
2 Tbsp. sesame seeds
2 dried sweet red peppers
2 peppercorns
4 small bay leaves
1 small Italian loaf of bread, soaked in sweet red table wine
1 cup apple cider vinegar
1 tsp. pepper
1 cup sweet red table wine
1 Tbsp. Worcestershire sauce
24 dried prunes
1 cup olives, pitted
½ cup capers
6-oz. can tomato paste
12-oz. jar pimentos

Simmer chicken slowly with onions in salted water, using just enough water to cover bottom of skillet. Add water as needed while cooking.

Grind the sesame seeds, red peppers, peppercorns, laurel leaves and bread into a paste.

When chicken is soft, add vinegar, pepper, wine, Worcestershire sauce, prunes, olives, capers, tomato paste, pimentos and sesame seed paste. Cover and cook slowly on top of stove for 1 hour.

Serves 6.

—Kathy Cowbrough

Jefferson Chicken

4 chicken breasts, deboned & cut in half
Butter
2 Tbsp. sherry
½ cup white wine
¼ cup lemon juice
Grated rind of 1 lemon
Grated rind of 1 orange
1 cup light cream
Parmesan cheese
Orange & lemon slices

Brown chicken in butter, cover, lower heat and stew until cooked through. Remove chicken from pan and place on serving dish.

Combine sherry, wine, lemon juice and rinds. Add to juices in pan and bring to a boil. Lower heat and slowly stir in cream.

Sprinkle cheese over chicken and brown briefly under broiler. Pour sauce over chicken, garnish with orange and lemon slices and serve.

Serves 4.

—Elizabeth Ballantyne

Chicken Adobe

1 chicken, cut up
2-3 cloves garlic
Soya sauce
15-20 peppercorns
2-3 bay leaves
½ onion, finely chopped
⅓ cup vinegar
Flour

Place chicken in pot and cover with water. Heat water to boiling, add garlic, soya sauce, peppercorns and bay leaves. Cover and simmer for 30 minutes. Add onion and vinegar. Use sufficient flour to thicken the water to a gravy and simmer for another 20 minutes.

Serves 4.

—Bette Warkentin

Eggplant & Chicken

1 chicken, cut up
2 Tbsp. oil
2 cloves garlic, minced
1 unpeeled eggplant, cut into
   1-inch cubes
1 onion, diced
6 tomatoes, peeled & sliced
½ cup dry red wine
1 tsp. oregano
1 tsp. basil
¼ tsp. pepper
Salt

In large pan, brown chicken on all sides in oil with garlic. Add eggplant and onion and sauté for 5 minutes. Add tomatoes, wine and spices, cover and let simmer for about 1 hour, stirring occasionally.

Serves 4 to 6.

—Julie Herr

Chicken with Lemon-Mustard Sauce

1 chicken, cut up
2 Tbsp. oil
2 Tbsp. flour
½ tsp. salt
⅛ tsp. pepper
1½ cups chicken stock
2 Tbsp. Dijon mustard
1 tsp. tarragon
½ lemon, thinly sliced

Brown chicken in hot oil in large skillet and move to one side. Stir in flour, salt and pepper, then stock, mustard and tarragon until well blended. Cover and simmer for 30 minutes. Add lemon slices; cover and simmer 5 minutes longer or until chicken is tender. Serve over rice or noodles.

Serves 4.

—Rosy Hale

Poulet Framboise

2 medium onions, thinly
   sliced
2 Tbsp. water
3 Tbsp. unsalted butter
2-3 lbs. chicken pieces
Salt & pepper
1 large tomato, peeled,
   seeded & chopped
2 cloves garlic, crushed
2 cups raspberry vinegar
1 cup whipping cream
2 Tbsp. Cognac or Armagnac

Cook onions, water and 1 Tbsp. butter in large frying pan over low heat for 30 minutes. While onions are cooking, season chicken pieces with salt and pepper. Heat remaining 2 Tbsp. butter in another frying pan and cook chicken until golden on both sides. Add tomato and garlic to onions. Place chicken pieces on top of onion mixture and cook, covered, over low heat for 30 minutes, or until chicken is tender.

Remove any excess butter from pan used to brown chicken. Add raspberry vinegar and simmer gently until only ½ cup remains. Place cooked chicken on a warm serving platter. Purée the onion and tomato mixture and add to reduced vinegar in frying pan. Place chicken in the pan and reheat with vinegar mixture for 10 to 15 minutes. Stir in cream and liquor and serve.

Serves 4.

—Ingrid Birker

Mexican Chicken Pie

Quite different from the usual crusted chicken pie, this is a flavourful and multi-textured dish.

3 lbs. chicken pieces
12 corn tortillas
3 cups cream of mushroom
   sauce (page132)
7-oz. can green chili salsa
1 cup grated Cheddar cheese

Bake chicken pieces, covered, at 400° F for 1 hour in a 9" x 13" casserole dish. Remove chicken and debone. Do not wash dish.

Break up 4 tortillas into 2-inch pieces and place in bottom of same casserole dish. Place half the chicken on the tortillas. Combine mushroom sauce with green chili salsa, then pour one-third of this over the chicken. Cut 4 more tortillas into 2-inch pieces and place on top of sauce. Top with remaining chicken and another third of sauce. Cut up remaining tortillas and place on top of sauce. Top with remaining sauce and the cheese. Bake at 375° F for 1 hour.

Serves 6.

—Linda Stanier

Chicken Rice Pie

2 cups cooked rice
⅓ cup butter, melted
1 tsp. salt
¼ tsp. pepper
2 Tbsp. flour
1 cup milk
2 cups diced, cooked
  chicken
2 large tomatoes, peeled &
  chopped
3 stalks celery, chopped
1 small green pepper,
  chopped
3 Tbsp. dry bread crumbs

Combine rice, 2 Tbsp. butter, half the salt and half the pepper and mix well. Press into deep pie plate to form shell and set aside.

Melt 2 Tbsp. butter, stir in flour and cook until bubbly. Gradually stir in milk until thickened and smooth. Season with remaining salt and pepper. Stir in chicken, tomatoes, celery and green pepper. Pour into rice shell. Mix bread crumbs with remaining melted butter and sprinkle over pie. Bake at 350° F for 25 minutes, or until golden brown.

Serves 6.

—Inez Atkins

Chicken, Leek and Sausage Pie

This delicious modification of an old Basque recipe makes a substantial dinner. It is easily assembled, especially if one has pastry on hand.

Pastry for double 9-inch pie
  shell
½ lb. sausage meat
2 Tbsp. oil
2 whole leeks, chopped
2 Tbsp. flour
2 cups chicken stock
2 cups cooked chicken, cut
  into bite-sized pieces

Shape sausage meat into ¾-inch balls and fry in oil until golden. Remove from pan. Pour out all but 2 Tbsp. of oil. In this, sauté leeks for 1 minute. Sprinkle flour on top and stir to blend well. Slowly pour in chicken stock and cook until thickened.

Place cooked sausage balls in bottom of pastry-lined pie plate. Put chicken on top of sausage and pour sauce over top. Cover with pastry and make a slit to allow steam to escape. Bake at 400° F for 35 to 40 minutes, or until golden brown.

Serves 4.

—Terri d'Aoust

Chicken Pinwheels

These pinwheels are delicious served hot or cold. For a special occasion, make a cream of mushroom sauce (page 132) and pour over the pinwheels. Serve with stir-fried snow peas.

1 cup white flour
½ cup whole wheat flour
3 Tbsp. bran
2 Tbsp. wheat germ
⅓ cup skim milk powder
4 tsp. baking powder
1 tsp. salt
⅓ cup lard or shortening
⅔ cup water
1 Tbsp. butter
2 Tbsp. flour
¼ cup chicken stock
¼ cup milk
2 cups chopped, cooked
  chicken
¼ cup chopped chives or
  green onions
Sage
¾ cup grated Cheddar cheese

Mix flours, bran, wheat germ, milk powder, baking powder and ½ tsp. salt. Cut in lard to form a coarse meal. Add water to make a soft dough. Roll on a floured board to a 12-inch by 15-inch rectangle.

Melt butter and stir in flour. Gradually add stock and milk to make a thick cream sauce. Mix with chicken, chives, sage and cheese.

Spread chicken mixture on dough, leaving ½ inch of dough uncovered around the edges. Roll up like a jelly roll and slice every ¾ inch. Place on ungreased cookie sheet.

Bake at 425° F for 12 to 15 minutes or until golden brown.

Makes 12 pinwheels.

—Heather Quiney

Gougère de Gibier

Gougère is a rich choux-like pastry which originated in Burgundy, France. It can be filled in a variety of ways — this recipe called originally for game (gibier) but has been adapted to use chicken.

FILLING:
1 small onion, chopped
1 Tbsp. butter
1 Tbsp. flour
⅓ cup chicken stock
¼ cup chopped mushrooms
1 cup diced, cooked chicken
Salt & pepper
½ tsp. thyme
¼ tsp. sage
PASTE:
¼ cup butter
½ cup water
½ cup flour
2 eggs
⅛ tsp. prepared mustard
Salt & pepper
⅔ cup grated Cheddar cheese
⅓ cup dry bread crumbs

To make filling, fry onion slowly in butter. Stir in flour, then stock and mushrooms. Boil, stirring frequently, until thick, then add chicken. Season with salt and pepper, thyme and sage. Cool.

For paste, measure butter and water into heavy pot. Bring to a boil until butter melts, then remove from heat. Add flour and beat until smooth. Cool, then beat in eggs. Add mustard, salt and pepper and ⅓ cup cheese.

Spread half of paste in greased pie plate, working it ½ inch up sides. Add filling and spread evenly. Cover with remaining paste, sprinkle with remaining cheese and bread crumbs and bake at 425° F for 25 minutes. Reduce heat to 375° and bake for another 10 minutes.

Serves 4.

—*Judy McEwen*

Hot Chicken Legs

3 Tbsp. flour
Salt & pepper
2 tsp. turmeric
1 Tbsp. cumin
1 tsp. garlic powder
6 chicken legs
3 hot peppers, sliced, including seeds
3 onions, coarsely chopped
½ cup coarsely chopped Italian parsley
Chunks of Chinese lettuce or celery
2 cups chicken stock

Combine flour with salt and pepper, turmeric, cumin and garlic powder in large plastic bag. Shake chicken pieces in bag to coat them and brown with fat in skillet over high heat. Place in casserole dish and add peppers, onions, parsley and lettuce. Combine stock with 1 heaping Tbsp. coating mixture to thicken and pour over chicken. Cover and bake at 325° F for 1 hour.

Serves 6.

—*Harvey Griggs*

Skillet Chicken

6 chicken legs
2-3 Tbsp. oil
1 cup tomato sauce (page 414)
2 Tbsp. finely chopped onion
1 Tbsp. vinegar
2 tsp. Worcestershire sauce
2 tsp. prepared mustard
¼ cup molasses
½ cup water

Split chicken legs in half through joint. Heat oil and brown chicken gently on all sides. Combine tomato sauce, onion, vinegar, Worcestershire sauce, mustard, molasses and water. Drain off excess fat from skillet and add sauce. Cover and simmer gently for 35 minutes, turning occasionally. Remove chicken to warm platter and boil sauce briskly to reduce and thicken it. Pour over chicken and serve.

Serves 4 to 6.

—*Linda Russell*

Chinese Walnut Chicken

1 cup coarsely broken walnuts
¼ cup oil
2 chicken breasts, deboned and cut into thin strips
½ tsp. salt
1 Tbsp. cornstarch
¼ cup soya sauce
2 Tbsp. sherry
1¼ cups chicken stock
1 cup onion slices
½ cups celery slices, cut diagonally
1½ cups mushrooms
5-oz. can water chestnuts, drained & sliced

In skillet, toast walnuts in hot oil, stirring constantly, then remove and drain on paper towels. Place chicken in skillet and sprinkle with salt. Cook, stirring frequently, for 5 to 10 minutes, or until tender. Remove chicken.

Make sauce by combining cornstarch, soya sauce and sherry in skillet and gradually adding chicken stock. Cook for 2 to 3 minutes until sauce begins to thicken. Add chicken, onion, celery, mushrooms and water chestnuts and cook for 5 minutes, or until vegetables are slightly tender. Stir in toasted walnuts. Serve with hot rice.

Serves 4 to 6.

—Donna Petryshyn

Chicken Wokeries

Chinese 5-spice powder, a pungent, somewhat sweet mixture of ground spices, is readily available in Chinese specialty shops, but it is also very simple to make oneself. Simply grind into a fine powder equal amounts of Chinese star anise, fennel, pepper, cloves and cinnamon. Store in a small jar with a tightly fitting lid.

2 Tbsp. whole wheat flour
2 chicken breasts, deboned & cut into pieces
3 Tbsp. soya oil
2 onions, thickly sliced
1 cup mushrooms, halved
1 green pepper, thickly sliced
2 cups peas
1 cup chopped broccoli
1 cup sliced celery
¼ cup sliced water chestnuts
3-4 cloves garlic, sliced
2-3 Tbsp. soya sauce
½ cup chicken stock
¼ tsp. Chinese 5-spice powder
¼ tsp. grated ginger root

Place flour in plastic bag, add chicken pieces and shake bag until chicken is coated. Heat oil in wok, add chicken and cook for 1 or 2 minutes. Set chicken aside. Stir onions, mushrooms, green pepper, peas, broccoli, celery, water chestnuts and garlic into wok, adding more oil if necessary. Cook for 2 minutes, stirring occasionally. Stir in soya sauce, stock, 5-spice powder and ginger root. Add chicken, heat and serve.

Serves 3 to 4.

—Joanne Marcil

Chicken Wings

48 chicken wings
½ cup honey
1 cup soya sauce
6 cloves garlic, minced
⅓ cup cornstarch
½ tsp. pepper
1 cup water

Cut chicken wings in half, discarding tip of wing. Mix honey, soya sauce, garlic, cornstarch and pepper and pour over wings. Marinate for minimum of 1 hour.

Drain wings, keeping marinade to one side. Fry wings in hot, shallow oil until golden brown on both sides. Place wings, marinade and water in baking dish and bake at 350° F for 15 to 20 minutes.

Serves 12.

—Andrew Camm

Honey Garlic Chicken

½ cup honey
½ cup soya sauce
2 cloves garlic, crushed
¼ cup butter
1 chicken, cut up

Combine honey, soya sauce, garlic and butter in a saucepan. Bring to a boil, reduce heat and simmer for 5 minutes.

Place chicken in a shallow pan and bake at 375° F for 15 minutes. Cover with sauce and continue baking, turning chicken occasionally, until sauce is absorbed and chicken cooked.

Serves 4.

—Louise Olson

Turmeric Chicken & Rice Bake

1 cup uncooked rice
2 cups boiling water
2 tsp. salt
1½ tsp. turmeric
¼ tsp. pepper
1 bay leaf
2 Tbsp. chopped onion
1 Tbsp. lemon juice
3 lbs. chicken pieces

Mix all ingredients except chicken in 2-quart casserole dish, stir well, then add chicken pieces. Cover and bake at 325° F for 1½ hours.

Serves 5 to 6.

—Mary Barrett

Chicken Tandoori

This is an East Indian recipe traditionally served with curried rice, crisp vegetables and yogurt shakes.

2 cups yogurt
2 tsp. chili powder
6 cloves garlic, crushed
¼-½ tsp. red pepper
6 tsp. vinegar
Juice of 1 lime
1 tsp. salt
1 tsp. ginger
1 tsp. coriander
1 tsp. cumin
1 tsp. cardamom
2 tsp. honey
Pepper
4-5 lbs. chicken pieces

Combine all ingredients except chicken and mix well. Marinate chicken in this mixture for about 8 hours, turning frequently. Remove from marinade and bake at 375° F for 60 to 75 minutes, basting with marinade.

Serves 4 to 6.

—Randi Kennedy

Khaeng Khieu Wan Kai

A visit to a Chinese or Indian specialty store may be necessary to purchase some of the ingredients for this curry, but the resulting flavour is well worth the effort.

GREEN CURRY PASTE:
1 large, fresh green chili
1 tsp. peppercorns
1 small onion, chopped
1 Tbsp. chopped garlic
2 Tbsp. chopped fresh coriander
2 tsp. chopped lemon rind
1 tsp. salt
2 tsp. ground coriander
2 tsp. dried shrimp paste
1 tsp. ground turmeric
1 Tbsp. oil
CHICKEN:
3 cups coconut milk
3 Tbsp. green curry paste
3 lbs. chicken pieces
2 Tbsp. lemon rind
½ tsp. salt
2 Tbsp. oyster sauce
2 Tbsp. finely chopped red chilies
4 Tbsp. finely chopped fresh basil

Prepare paste by chopping green chili, seeds and all, and blending with remaining ingredients to a smooth paste. Add additional oil or water if necessary to make paste smooth.

Prepare chicken by heating the green curry paste and half the coconut milk in saucepan until oil separates — about 10 minutes. Add chicken pieces and cook over medium-low heat for 10 minutes. Blend in remaining coconut milk, lemon rind, salt and oyster sauce. Cook, covered, for 30 minutes. Add red chilies and basil just before serving.

Serves 6.

—Ingrid Birker

Chicken Talunan

This Philippine dish originally utilized the tough meat of the losing rooster (called the talunan) in a cockfight. The sauce and lengthy stewing time serve to tenderize the meat.

2 cakes tofu
1 cup vinegar
½ cup brown sugar
4 cups water
3½ lbs. chicken pieces
2 lbs. pigs' feet, or other pork bits
1 clove garlic, crushed
1 cucumber, sliced
1 bay leaf
1 Tbsp. oregano
1 whole clove
1 star anise
1 stick cinnamon

Mash tofu and mix with vinegar and sugar. Combine water, chicken, pigs' feet and tofu mixture in large saucepan. Simmer until meat is tender and remove meat.

Add garlic, cucumber, bay leaf, oregano, clove, star anise and cinnamon to stock, cover and simmer until thick. Place meat on serving dish and pour sauce over.

Serves 6.

—P.S. Reynolds

Indian Chicken Curry

1 chicken
Salt & pepper
Cornstarch
Oil
1 Tbsp. soya sauce
4 onions, chopped
6 cloves garlic, minced
1 green pepper, chopped
3 cups mushrooms, sliced
3 tomatoes, peeled &
   chopped
4 Tbsp. curry

Cut chicken into small pieces, season with salt and pepper and dust with cornstarch. Brown in hot oil and set aside.

In chicken drippings and soya sauce, brown onions and garlic. Add green pepper and mushrooms and cook for 4 minutes. Add tomatoes and cook for 2 more minutes. Return chicken to pot, sprinkle with curry and cook for 10 minutes, turning chicken frequently. Add ½ cup boiling water, cover, reduce heat and simmer for 1 hour.

Serves 4 to 6.

—Judith Goodwin

Curried Chicken with Shrimp

3 lbs. chicken pieces
Salt & pepper
2 Tbsp. butter
¾ cup finely chopped onion
½ cup finely chopped celery
1 tsp. finely minced garlic
2 Tbsp. curry
1 bay leaf
1 cup cubed apple
⅓ cup diced banana
2 tsp. tomato paste
1½ cups chicken stock
½ cup whipping cream
12 large shrimp

Sprinkle chicken with salt and pepper and brown in butter. Add onion, celery and garlic and cook briefly. Add curry, bay leaf, apple and banana. Cook for 5 minutes, then stir in tomato paste. Add stock and stir to blend. Cover and cook for 20 minutes longer, or until chicken is tender.

Remove chicken. Strain sauce through fine sieve. Reheat with cream. Return chicken along with shrimp to sauce and simmer until shrimp are pink.

Serves 6.

—Linda Thompson

Chicken Apple Curry

½ cup chopped onion
1 clove garlic, minced
3 Tbsp. butter
1 Tbsp. curry
1 cup chopped apple
½ cup chopped celery
¼ cup flour
1 cup chicken stock
¾ cup milk
½-¾ tsp. salt
2 cups cooked, diced chicken

Sauté onion and garlic in butter with curry until onion is tender. Add apple and celery and cook for about 3 minutes longer. Stir in flour, then stock, milk and salt. Stir while heating until mixture boils. Add chicken; heat and serve over rice.

Serves 4.

—Jane Lott

Curried Fruit Chicken

4 pieces chicken
½ cup oil
½ cup brown sugar
4 tsp. curry
1 Tbsp. flour
2 peaches, pitted & cubed
2 pears, pitted & cubed
2 plums, pitted & cubed

Brown chicken in ¼ cup of oil. Arrange the chicken, skin side up, in a baking dish. Combine the sugar, curry, flour and remaining oil and stir into the fruit. Let stand for 15 minutes, stirring occasionally. Spread fruit over chicken. Cover and bake at 350° F for 30 minutes. Uncover and bake until the chicken is tender — about 50 minutes.

Serves 4.

—Maureen Marcotte

Chicken Satay

1 cup finely chopped onion
1 clove garlic, crushed
¼ cup soya sauce
¼ cup oil
¼ cup peanut butter
2 Tbsp. brown sugar
3 Tbsp. lemon juice
¼ tsp. cayenne
1 tsp. coriander
1 chicken, cut up

Blend all ingredients, except chicken, until smooth. Marinate chicken in mixture for at least 2 hours, then bake at 350° F for 30 to 45 minutes.

Serves 4.

—Cynthia Gilmore

Chicken with Raisins & Almonds

5-lb. chicken
2 onions, chopped
¼ cup honey
1 Tbsp. butter
1 tsp. cinnamon
1 tsp. turmeric
Ginger
½ cup raisins
1 cup almonds, blanched, peeled & toasted

Place chicken in pot with water to half cover. Add remaining ingredients except raisins and almonds, bring to a boil and cook until chicken is done — about 1 hour. Add raisins and almonds and boil until liquid is about 1 to 2 inches deep. Place chicken in serving dish and pour sauce over it.

Serves 4.

—Dale Fawcett

Chicken with Dates

2 chickens, deboned & cut up
2 Tbsp. butter
2 Tbsp. oil
Salt & pepper
1 cup orange juice
2 cups chicken stock
3 Tbsp. cornstarch
1 tsp. salt
½ tsp. pepper
1 tsp. curry
1 medium onion, chopped
Juice of 1 lemon
Pitted dates
Green pepper rings
Orange slices

Brown chicken in butter and oil. Place in casserole dish and sprinkle with salt and pepper. Place orange juice, stock, cornstarch, salt, pepper, curry, onion and lemon juice in pot where chicken was browned. Heat to boiling, stirring constantly, until slightly thickened sauce results. Pour over chicken and bake at 350° F for 35 minutes. Arrange dates, pepper rings and orange slices on casserole and bake for 10 more minutes.

Serves 6.

—Eleanor Wallace Culver

Barbecued Chicken Burgers

3 lbs. chicken, skinned & deboned
1-2 strips bacon
1-2 slices dry whole wheat bread
Salt & pepper
4 slices mozzarella cheese
4 sesame seed buns

Put chicken meat through meat grinder along with bacon. When all meat has been ground, put bread through grinder and add to meat. Season with salt and pepper, mix gently and form into 4 patties. Grill over hot coals, turning when well-browned on one side. Place a slice of cheese on each patty and continue grilling until other side is browned. Serve on toasted buns with your choice of toppings.

Serves 4.

—Karen Ritchie

Chicken Loaf

1½ lbs. finely ground,
  cooked chicken
¼ cup Parmesan cheese
½ cup bread crumbs,
  softened with ½ cup water
1 small onion, minced
½ tsp. basil
½ tsp. garlic powder
Salt & pepper
1 Tbsp. parsley
½ cup milk
3 eggs, lightly beaten
¼ cup melted butter

Mix together chicken,
Parmesan cheese, bread
crumbs, onion, basil, garlic
powder, salt and pepper and
parsley. Blend milk, eggs and
melted butter together, then add
to above mixture. Pat down
lightly into greased loaf pan and
bake at 350° F for 45 minutes.
Invert on a meat platter and slice
to serve.

Serves 4 to 6.

—*Judy Black*

Hot Chinese Chicken Salad

8 chicken thighs, skinned,
  boned & cut into 1-inch
  chunks
¼ cup cornstarch
¼ cup oil
⅛ tsp. garlic powder
1 large, ripe tomato, cut into
  chunks
4-oz. can water chestnuts,
  drained & sliced (optional)
½ cup sliced mushrooms
1 bunch green onions,
  coarsely chopped
1 cup celery, sliced
  diagonally
¼ cup soya sauce
2 cups finely shredded
  lettuce

Roll chicken in cornstarch.
Heat oil over high heat, add
chicken and brown quickly.
Sprinkle with garlic powder and
stir in tomato, water chestnuts,
mushrooms, onions, celery and
soya sauce. Cover and simmer
for 5 minutes, then toss in
lettuce. Serve hot with rice.

Serves 6.

—*Carol Weepers*

Chicken Salad Veronique

2½ cups diced, cooked
  chicken
2½ tsp. lemon juice
1¼ cups diced celery
⅔ cup green seedless grapes
3 hard-boiled eggs, cut into
  quarters
¾ cup slivered, toasted
  almonds
⅔ cup mayonnaise
Bibb lettuce
Paprika

Combine chicken, lemon juice,
celery, grapes, eggs, almonds
and mayonnaise and mix well.
Heap in bowl lined with lettuce
and sprinkle with paprika.

Serves 6.

—*Nan & Phil Millette*

Hot Chicken Salad

2 cups cooked chicken
  pieces
1 cup diced celery
½ cup slivered almonds
1 Tbsp. lemon juice
3 hard-boiled eggs, sliced
1 cup cream of mushroom
  sauce (page 132)
2 tsp. minced onion
1 tsp. salt
¼ tsp. pepper
½ cup mayonnaise
2 cups cracker crumbs

Combine all ingredients,
except cracker crumbs, in
greased casserole dish. Top with
crumbs and bake at 350° F for
20 minutes.

Serves 4.

—*Ingrid Magnuson*

Chicken Salad

Either yellow summer squash or zucchini can be used successfully in this recipe. Yellow beets are advised as they do not bleed and therefore result in a more attractive presentation.

2 cups cooked chicken
3-4 radishes
1 cup green or yellow beans
1 cup snow peas
1 small summer squash
6 pickling-sized yellow beets, cooked until tender
1 onion
1 head lettuce
½ cup mayonnaise
4 leaves red cabbage

Chop chicken and vegetables, except cabbage, into bite-sized pieces. Toss together. Add mayonnaise and mix well. Place in serving bowl lined with cabbage.

Serves 4 to 6.

—*Cindy Majewski*

Chicken Liver & Corn

2 Tbsp. flour
½ tsp. salt
¼ tsp. savory or rosemary
1½ lbs. chicken livers
2-3 Tbsp. butter
1 cup corn
½-1 cup water

Mix together flour, salt and seasoning. Rinse liver in very cold water and drain. Melt butter and add liver so pieces are lying flat. Sprinkle with half the seasoned flour, turn and sprinkle with remainder. Fry until lightly browned, then add corn and water and simmer until just tender, about 10 to 15 minutes. Add more water, if necessary, to make a light gravy.

Serves 4.

—*Rose Hurlbut-Wilson*

Chicken Livers in Beer Sauce

2 lbs. chicken livers, rinsed & drained
4 Tbsp. butter
4 Tbsp. flour
1 cup chicken stock
1 medium onion, finely chopped
1 clove garlic, crushed
2 Tbsp. chopped parsley
½ cup sliced mushrooms
Salt & pepper
¼ tsp. thyme
½-¾ cup beer (or red wine)

Sauté livers in butter for 5 minutes on medium-high heat, then set aside. Lower heat, add flour to remaining juices and stir to make a smooth paste. Add chicken stock gradually, stirring over medium heat until a thickened sauce forms. Add onion, garlic, parsley, mushrooms and seasonings, and simmer for 5 minutes, stirring occasionally. Add beer or wine and livers; simmer for a few more minutes until livers are done. Do not overcook.

Serves 6.

—*Janet Drew*

Chicken Giblet Curry

2 lbs. chicken giblets
2-3 onions, chopped
Butter
1-2 tsp. garlic powder
1 tsp. salt
½ tsp. crushed red pepper
1 tsp. ground coriander
12 cloves
4-5 bay leaves
1 tsp. finely chopped ginger root
2 tsp. cumin
12 peppercorns
3-4 cardamom seeds
1 tsp. turmeric
1 tsp. cinnamon
3-4 tomatoes, peeled & chopped
1 cup water

Cut giblets into small pieces. Brown onions in butter, then add giblets, garlic powder and salt. Cook for 5 minutes, add remaining spices and cook for a few minutes. Add tomatoes and water, lower heat and simmer for 45 minutes.

Serves 4 to 6.

—*Sue Griggs*

Sweet & Sour Rabbit

3 lbs. rabbit pieces
Flour
1 tsp. salt
¼ tsp. pepper
1 cup pineapple juice
¼ cup vinegar
1 cup pineapple chunks
1 green pepper, cut into
  chunks
½ red pepper, cut into chunks
1 cup bean sprouts
1 cup diced celery
1½ Tbsp. cornstarch
½ cup brown sugar
½ cup water

Roll rabbit pieces in flour and brown. Add salt, pepper, pineapple juice and vinegar and simmer until tender — about 40 minutes. Add pineapple, green and red peppers, bean sprouts and celery. Simmer for 10 minutes. Mix cornstarch and sugar and stir into water. Gradually stir this mixture into liquid containing rabbit. Cook slowly until thickened about 5 minutes.

Serves 4 to 6.

—Marian Page

Chicken Paté with Sorrel & Dill

1 lb. ground white chicken
  meat
½ cup diced fresh sorrel
1 tsp. freshly ground pepper
½ tsp. dry mustard
1 tsp. finely chopped fresh
  dill weed
1 cup dry white wine
1 egg
2 sprigs fresh dill

Mix chicken, sorrel, pepper, mustard and chopped dill and pour white wine over mixture. Cover and refrigerate for at least 4 hours.

Drain wine from mixture. Beat egg and mix into meat. Using a deep, narrow baking pan, place 1 sprig of dill on bottom, fill with chicken mixture and place remaining sprig of dill on top. Cover with aluminum foil and bake in water bath at 325° F for 1 hour.

Remove pan from water bath and uncover. Drain any liquid that has accumulated. Leaving paté in pan, place weight on top, cover and refrigerate for at least 4 hours.

To serve, remove paté from pan and discard dill from top and bottom. Remove any gelatin that has formed. Slice very thinly and arrange on a bed of fresh sorrel and garnish with sprigs of fresh dill.

Makes 25 thin slices.

—Arthur Grant

Mother's Gehackte Leber

This is a basic traditional recipe for chopped liver.

1 lb. chicken livers
2 onions, coarsely chopped
1 hard-boiled egg
1 slice bread
1 Tbsp. brandy
Dry mustard
Salt & pepper
Mayonnaise

Fry chicken livers and 1 onion until liver is cooked. Put through meat grinder with remaining onion, egg and bread. Mix in brandy, a little mustard and salt and pepper to taste. Add enough mayonnaise to hold mixture together. Chill and serve with crackers.

Makes approximately 2 cups.

—Jeannie Rosenberg

Turkey Ring

3 cups diced, cooked turkey
1 cup soft bread crumbs
1 Tbsp. oil
½ tsp. salt
⅛ tsp. pepper
1 cup hot milk
2 eggs, beaten
¼ cup finely chopped celery
2 Tbsp. finely chopped green
  pepper
2 Tbsp. finely chopped
  pimento

Combine all ingredients and mix thoroughly. Pour into greased ring mould and bake at 350° F for 35 to 40 minutes. Let stand for 5 minutes; remove from mould.

Serves 6.

—Christine Curtis

Rabbit Pie

Work on this dish must begin a day ahead as the cooked rabbit and stock need to be refrigerated overnight.

Pastry for double 9-inch pie
   shell
5-6 lb. rabbit
1 Tbsp. salt
½ tsp. pepper
1 cup chopped celery leaves
1 large onion, quartered
½ tsp. crumbled savory **or**
   thyme
1 bay leaf
6 cups boiling water
3 cups sliced carrots
2 cups diced celery
12-24 small white onions
¾ cup butter
¾ cup flour
2 cups milk
1 cup whipping cream
1 Tbsp. lemon juice
½ cup minced parsley

Place rabbit in large pot with salt, pepper, celery leaves, onion, savory or thyme, bay leaf and boiling water. Cover and simmer over low heat until rabbit is tender — 1½ to 2 hours. Leave rabbit in stock until cool enough to handle. Pull meat off bones and place in a large bowl. Put bones back in pot and boil stock, uncovered, until reduced to two-thirds its original quantity. Strain stock over rabbit, cover and refrigerate overnight.

The next day, place carrots and celery in bowl and cover with boiling water. Let stand for 1 hour. Peel onions and boil for 15 minutes.

Heat rabbit just until stock can be strained, measure out 3 cups. Melt butter, add flour and stir until blended. Add milk, cream and 3 cups stock and cook until sauce is creamy. Add drained onions, carrots, celery, rabbit, lemon juice and parsley. Place in deep pie plate lined with pastry. Top with pastry, crimp edges, make steam holes and bake at 400° F for 40 to 50 minutes, or until golden brown.

Serves 6 to 8.

—Marian Page

Turkey Artichoke Pie

1 lb. spinach, steamed &
   chopped
2 cups cooked rice
4 Tbsp. butter
¼ cup chopped toasted
   almonds
15-oz. can artichoke hearts,
   drained
1½ cups chopped, cooked
   turkey
1 cup grated jack cheese
¼ lb. mushrooms, sliced
2 Tbsp. flour
½ tsp curry
½ tsp. garlic powder
1 tsp. dry mustard
Salt & pepper
1 cup milk
Paprika

Combine spinach, rice, 2 Tbsp. butter and almonds and press into greased pie plate. Chill for 1 hour. Arrange artichokes, turkey and cheese in shell.

Melt remaining 2 Tbsp. butter and sauté mushrooms. Stir in flour, curry, garlic powder, mustard, salt and pepper and milk and cook until thickened. Pour over pie and top with paprika. Bake at 350° F for 45 minutes.

Serves 6.

—Gillian Barber-Gifford

Spicy Rabbit

This recipe results in a flavourful, aromatic dish that needs only a bowl of rice and a salad to make a full meal.

2 Tbsp. oil
2 Tbsp. butter
1 large onion, thinly sliced
1 large clove garlic, minced
1 tsp. ginger
1½ tsp. cumin
1 tsp. salt
½ tsp. paprika
½ tsp. pepper
⅛ tsp. saffron
⅛ tsp. cayenne
1 rabbit, cut up
¾ cup pitted prunes
1 Tbsp. honey
1-2 Tbsp. lemon juice
2 Tbsp. toasted sesame
   seeds
Chopped coriander

Heat oil and butter in heavy pot with tightly fitting lid. Add onion and sauté until translucent, then add garlic. Combine ginger, cumin, salt, paprika, pepper, saffron and cayenne and add. Stir in rabbit pieces. Place lid on pot, reduce heat and simmer for 1 hour, turning meat occasionally and adding water if meat becomes too dry. Add prunes and cook for 15 minutes longer. Gently stir in honey and cook for 5 more minutes. Remove meat and prunes and keep warm. Raise heat to high and reduce liquid to thick sauce. Stir in lemon juice, pour over meat and sprinkle with sesame seeds and coriander leaves.

Serves 4 to 6.

—Ann Jeffries

Lapin au Citron

Developed by the contributor for a potluck supper in hopes of increasing sales for her rabbit business, this dish, presented to the guests as chicken lest they be squeamish about eating rabbit, was the pièce de résistance of the meal.

4-5 lbs. deboned rabbit
   pieces
2 Tbsp. butter
1 Tbsp. olive oil
Juice & grated rind of 2
   lemons
1 tsp. salt
Pepper
2 Tbsp. chopped parsley
2 Tbsp. chopped chives
1 tsp. marjoram
1 Tbsp. paprika
Butter
1 cup chicken stock
¼ cup dry vermouth
2 Tbsp. cornstarch dissolved
   in 3 Tbsp. cold water

Brown rabbit pieces over medium heat in butter and oil. Transfer rabbit with butter and oil to large, shallow baking dish. Add lemon juice and rind, salt and pepper. Cover and bake at 350° F for 45 minutes. Add herbs, dot with butter and broil for 5 minutes. Pour juices into saucepan, add stock and vermouth and bring to a boil. Add cornstarch-water mixture and simmer until thickened — about 5 minutes. Pour over rabbit.

Serves 6 to 8.

—*J.M. Bowden*

Brandied Orange Rabbit with Chanterelles

Chanterelles, known in France as girolles, are edible mushrooms, impossible to confuse with any other. They are formed in the shape of a cup with a frilled edge and are the colour of egg yolk. The stalks are so short as to be nonexistent in some cases. Regular mushrooms can be substituted in this recipe.

4 lbs. rabbit pieces
½ cup brandy
½ cup frozen orange juice
   concentrate
4 Tbsp. butter
2 cups sliced chanterelles
1 Tbsp. cornstarch dissolved
   in ½ cup orange juice
2 cloves garlic, crushed
Curry
Salt & pepper
4 carrots, sliced julienne
   style

Marinate rabbit in brandy and orange juice concentrate overnight. Melt butter and sauté chanterelles until tender. Thicken juices with cornstarch-orange juice mixture.

Arrange rabbit in baking dish. Add marinade to chanterelle mixture along with garlic, curry and salt and pepper. Bake, uncovered, at 325° F for 1 hour. Add carrots and cook for 1 more hour.

Serves 4 to 6.

—*Dianne Radcliffe*

Rabbit Diable

2-3 lbs. rabbit pieces
4 Tbsp. butter
½ cup honey
¼ cup prepared mustard
1 tsp. salt
1 tsp. curry

Wash rabbit pieces and pat dry. Melt butter in shallow baking pan. Stir in remaining ingredients and roll rabbit in mixture to coat all sides. Bake at 375° F for 1 hour.

Serves 4.

—*Barbara Wilkinson*

Yogurt Baked Rabbit

⅓ cup flour
1 tsp. salt
1 tsp. paprika
½ tsp. thyme
½ tsp. cayenne
½ tsp. pepper
¾ cup chopped celery
½ cup chopped onion
2 cups sliced mushrooms
Butter
1½ cups plain yogurt
Shortening
2½-3 lbs. rabbit pieces

Combine flour, salt, paprika, thyme, cayenne and pepper in plastic bag and set aside. Cook celery, onion and mushrooms in butter until tender. Add yogurt and place in casserole dish.

Heat shortening so there is ¼ inch in skillet. Shake rabbit pieces in flour mixture to coat evenly, then brown in hot shortening. Place in casserole dish with sauce and bake at 375° F for 1 hour.

Serves 6.

—*Diane G. Michaud*

Cornish Game Hens Indienne

6 Cornish game hens
1½ tsp. salt
1 tsp. pepper
1 tsp. thyme
½ cup butter, melted
6 strips bacon
3 medium onions, chopped
5 Tbsp. flour
3 Tbsp. sugar
2 Tbsp. curry
2 cups apricot nectar
Juice from 1 lemon
Juice from 1 orange
STUFFING:
½ cup brown & ½ cup wild
   rice, cooked in chicken
   stock
½ cup chopped mushrooms
2 Tbsp. butter
⅛ cup dry red wine

Wipe hens inside and out. Combine 1 tsp. salt, pepper and thyme and sprinkle ½ tsp. inside each hen. Place hens, breast side up, in pan and brush with ¼ cup melted butter. Roast at 375° F for 50 to 60 minutes, basting with remaining ¼ cup butter and pan drippings.

Meanwhile, sauté bacon until crisp. Drain and crumble. Stir chopped onions into bacon drippings and sauté until soft. Blend in flour, sugar, curry and remaining ½ tsp. salt. Heat, stirring constantly, to boiling point. Stir in apricot nectar, lemon and orange juice, bacon and onions. Bring to a boil and simmer for 5 minutes.

Prepare stuffing by combining cooked rice, mushrooms, butter and wine. Remove hens from pan and discard drippings. Stuff hens, return to pan, pour sauce over top and roast for 10 minutes.

Serves 6.

—Mary-Lee Chase

Coq au Cambertin

This recipe calls for a demi glace. Traditionally, making this is a fairly complex procedure involving many steps, but for the purposes of this recipe, a somewhat simplified process is provided. The dedicated chef may consult any book of traditional French cooking for more detailed instructions.

2 Cornish game hens
Oil
1 onion, chopped
1 lb. mushrooms, sliced
¼ lb. bacon, chopped
3 cloves garlic, crushed
1 cup dry red wine
2 cups demi glace
Salt & pepper
3 bay leaves
1 tsp. tarragon
½ tsp. thyme
DEMI GLACE:
Shoulder of veal
Beef stock
Chicken stock
½ cup butter
½ cup flour
Parsley
Green onions
½ bay leaf
Thyme

To make demi glace, cover veal with beef stock and cook over high heat until stock is reduced to coating on bottom of pot. Cool. Refill saucepan with chicken stock, heat slowly to boiling point and skim fat. Remove veal and allow stock to cool slightly.

Make a roux by melting butter and stirring in flour. Cook slowly for 2 minutes. Gradually pour stock into roux, stirring constantly. Add parsley, green onions, bay leaf and thyme. Bring to a boil, lower heat and simmer for 1 hour. Skim. Simmer for 30 minutes and skim again. Strain and set aside. This is the demi glace.

Cut hens in half and remove breast and back bones. Braise lightly in a little oil and set aside. In same pan, sauté onion, mushrooms, bacon and garlic. Add wine and demi glace. Add salt and pepper, bay leaves, tarragon and thyme. Place chicken in sauce, cover and cook for 25 minutes.

Serves 4.

—Anne McKenzie

Braised Duck

Whether made from wild or domestic duck, this dish has a deliciously delicate flavour. Of course, wild duck will result in a stronger, gamier taste.

4½-lb. duck, skinned &
   quartered
¼ cup soya sauce
¼ cup vinegar
½ cup water
1 small onion, finely
   chopped
1 tsp. butter
Salt & pepper
2 Tbsp. red currant jelly
2 bay leaves
1 cup chicken stock
1 tsp. ground ginger
½ cup green or red grapes

Marinate duck in soya sauce, vinegar and water for at least 2 hours or overnight. Sauté onion in butter. Add duck and brown. Add marinade plus salt and pepper, jelly, bay leaves, stock and ginger. Cover and simmer until duck is tender — approximately 1 hour.

Remove duck and reduce sauce to ¾ cup over high heat. Strain sauce over duck and add grapes.

Serves 4.

—Dianne Baker

Pheasant with Rice Stuffing

2 Tbsp. butter
½ cup rice
1 cup chicken stock
¼ tsp. salt
½ cup chopped onion
2 Tbsp. chopped parsley
3 Tbsp. chopped celery
2 pheasants
6 slices bacon

In heavy saucepan, melt 1 Tbsp. butter, add rice and stir constantly for 2 to 3 minutes until most of rice has turned opaque. Pour in chicken stock, add salt and bring to boil. Cover, reduce heat and simmer for 15 minutes, or until rice has absorbed all the liquid.

Sauté onion in remaining 1 Tbsp. butter for 5 to 6 minutes. Add parsley and celery, then combine with cooked rice.

Sprinkle body cavities of pheasants with salt. Stuff and truss. Cover tops with bacon and cook at 350° F for 1 hour, remove bacon and cook until done.

Serves 2.

—Margaret Fredrickson

Sweet & Sour Partridge

The contributor of this recipe spent the fall and winter of 1981 trapping in northern Ontario. Fresh game was scarce, and, in her words, "It was a special occasion and a real treat, so we turned our plain old partridge into a gourmet meal."

1 partridge
½ cup brown sugar
1 Tbsp. cornstarch
⅓ cup vinegar
⅓ cup pineapple juice
1 Tbsp. soya sauce
¼ tsp. garlic powder
½ cup chopped pineapple

Clean and debone partridge, wrap in foil and refrigerate overnight. Cut into 1-inch cubes, place in pot and cover with water. Cover pan and simmer until tender — 30 minutes.

To make sauce, combine sugar and cornstarch in saucepan. Stir in vinegar, pineapple juice, soya sauce and garlic and cook until thick. Add pineapple and simmer for 2 more minutes. When partridge is cooked, pour off excess liquid and add sauce. Cook for 5 to 10 minutes.

Serves 2.

—Jane Kavelman

Shanghai Duck

6 green scallions
2 slices ginger root
4-6 lb. duck
1 Tbsp. sherry
¾ cup soya sauce
½ cup sugar
½ cup water
Anise seeds

Lay scallions and ginger root in bottom of large pan. Place duck on top, breast down. Pour sherry, soya sauce, sugar and water over duck and sprinkle with anise. Bring to a boil, then simmer for 45 minutes, turn duck over and simmer for another 45 minutes. Remove duck, skim fat off gravy and reduce to a thick sauce.

Serves 6.

—Anne Morrell

Partridge Pie

Pastry for 9-inch pie shell
3-4 bush partridges, cleaned, skinned & cut up
Salt & pepper
Flour
6 hard-boiled eggs, sliced
1 egg yolk, beaten

Cook partridges in salted water until tender. Cool enough to be handled easily and debone. Place in deep pie dish and add salt and pepper. Thicken liquid in pot with flour, then pour over meat. Cover with egg slices and top with pastry. Slash pastry to allow steam to escape and brush with beaten egg yolk. Bake at 375° F for 40 to 50 minutes, or until golden brown.

Serves 4 to 6.

—Janet Bantock

Pheasant Breast aux Valden

Originally a native of the Caspian region of eastern Europe, the pheasant is now found in many parts of the world. It is considered a food for the real gourmet and is described as follows by French gastronome Brillat-Savarin, Eaten at precisely the right moment, its flesh is tender, sublime and highly flavoured, for it has at once something of the flavour of poultry and of venison. This ideal moment is when the pheasant begins to decompose."

½ lb. lean bacon
2 medium pheasant breasts
½ cup plus 2 Tbsp. flour
2 tsp. garlic powder
2 medium-sized onions
½ tsp. dill weed
1 tsp. ground ginger
¼ tsp. pepper
1 cup water
¼ cup red table wine
¾ cup whipping cream
2 Tbsp. brandy

Cut bacon into ½-inch pieces and place in a 4-quart, stoneware or cast-iron oven pan. Fry the bacon on medium heat sufficiently to melt down the fat. Using a slotted spoon, remove the bacon and place on paper towels to drain.

Split pheasant breasts and wash under cold water. Pat dry and place in a paper bag containing ½ cup flour and 1 tsp. garlic powder. Shake to cover. Brown evenly in bacon fat and remove from pan.

Finely chop onions and fry in bacon fat until just turning brown. In small bowl, mix remaining 1 tsp. garlic, dill weed, ginger, pepper, remaining 2 Tbsp. flour and 1 cup water. Add this mixture to onions, stirring constantly as mixture thickens. Add cooked bacon.

Place browned pheasant breasts in roasting pan and coat evenly with sauce. Bake at 350° F for 1 hour, turning over after half an hour.

Remove breasts from pan and mix cream and brandy into sauce. Place on serving platter and pour sauce over the breasts.

Serves 4.

—*Valerie Rudyke*

Pheasant in Cream Sauce

1½-2 lbs. pheasant pieces
1 medium onion, sliced
2 stalks celery with tops
1 tsp. salt
⅛ tsp. pepper
1 cup whipping cream
1½ Tbsp. flour
2 Tbsp. cold water
2-3 Tbsp. red wine

Combine pheasant, 2 cups boiling water, onion, celery, salt and pepper and simmer, covered, for about 45 minutes, or until pheasant is tender.

Remove pheasant from stock and take meat off bones, leaving it in large pieces. Strain stock and boil down to ½ cup. Add cream to this and heat to boiling. Stir in blended flour and cold water and cook, stirring, until mixture thickens. Add pheasant and heat through. Add red wine and serve immediately.

Serves 3 to 4.

—*Tracy Cane*

Orange Grouse

2 grouse, cut up
Flour, seasoned with salt & pepper
2 Tbsp. butter
2 Tbsp. oil
1½ cups white wine
½ cup orange juice
½ tsp. rosemary
½ tsp. dry mustard
Cayenne

Dredge grouse in seasoned flour and brown in butter and oil mixture in heavy skillet. Add wine, orange juice, rosemary, mustard and cayenne. Cover and simmer for 1½ hours, adding a little water if necessary. Thicken with flour and water paste and serve over hot buttered noodles.

Serves 2.

—*Judy Cushman*

Black Bear Stew

1½ lbs. lean bear meat, cubed
2 quarts water
½ cup vinegar
Salt & pepper
½ small onion, chopped
½ green pepper, chopped
2 medium potatoes, cubed
2 cups diced carrot
3 stalks celery, cut into
   ½-inch pieces
18-oz. can tomatoes
2 Tbsp. cornstarch

Wash meat in cold water, then soak for 15 minutes in water and vinegar. Dry meat in towel and fry with salt and pepper, onion and green pepper. When well fried, add potatoes, carrot, celery and tomatoes. Simmer for 45 minutes. While simmering, add the cornstarch dissolved in a few tablespoons of water.

Serves 2 to 4.

—Ken Laninga

Corned Bear

Served either hot with boiled potatoes, hot mustard and horseradish, or cold on a sandwich, corned bear is a delicious and unusual alternative to other corned meats.

4 quarts hot water
2 cups coarse salt
¼ cup sugar
2 Tbsp. mixed whole spice
5-lb. piece bear meat
3 cloves garlic, peeled

Combine hot water, salt, sugar and whole spice. When cool, pour over bear meat and garlic. Place in enamelled pot, stoneware or glass jar. Weight meat to keep it submerged. Let marinate for 3 weeks in a cool place, turning every few days.

To cook, rinse meat under cold water, cover with boiling water and simmer for 4 hours, or until meat is tender.

—Kass Bennett

Moose Meat Pies

Pastry for 6 double 9-inch
   pie shells
7 lbs. ground pork
3 lbs. ground moose meat
3 medium cooking onions
4 cups sliced mushrooms
2 tsp. cloves
2 tsp. ground cinnamon
¼ tsp. ground mace
3-4 bay leaves
½ tsp. celery seed
2 Tbsp. sherry
¼ tsp. allspice
Salt & pepper
½ tsp. nutmeg

Combine all ingredients except pastry in large pot. Bring to a boil and simmer until meat turns white. Fill pastry-lined pie plates with meat mixture and cover with top crust. Bake at 425° F for 15 minutes and then at 350° for 30 minutes.

Makes 6 pies.

—Diane Ladoucer

Elk Meatballs

1 lb. minced elk meat
½ cup cracked wheat
½ tsp. garlic powder
1 onion, minced
2 cups chicken stock
2 cups water
2 Tbsp. tamari sauce
3 Tbsp. cornstarch

Combine meat, wheat, garlic and onion and form into walnut-sized balls. Bring stock, water and tamari sauce to a boil. Simmer meat for 15 minutes. Remove and keep warm. Reduce stock to 2½ to 3 cups. Mix cornstarch and a little cold water and add to stock. Boil for 5 minutes, then pour over meatballs.

Serves 4.

—Linda Townsend

Tjalknol Fran Medelpad

This recipe comes from the province of Medelpad in Sweden — Tjäl-Knöl means frost-chunk. It can be made from any kind of roast, but is particularly tasty when made with elk.

3-4 lb. frozen elk roast
2½ cups water
5 oz. salt
1 tsp. sugar

Place frozen roast on rack and bake at 150° F for 12 hours. Place meat in plastic bag and add water, salt and sugar. Force out air, tie bag and let roast marinate for 5 hours. Cut in thin slices and serve with potato salad.

Serves 8 to 10.

—Maria Ehnes

Venison Patties

1 lb. ground venison
½ lb. bacon, chopped
½ tsp. salt
⅛ tsp. pepper
⅛ tsp. thyme
⅛ tsp. marjoram
½ tsp. grated lemon peel
1 egg, beaten
1 cup cracker crumbs

Combine all ingredients and mix well by hand. Form into roll 2 to 3 inches diameter. Chill or freeze, then cut into slices and fry.

Serves 4.

—Taya Kwantes

Chicken Gismonda

⅛ cup bread crumbs
⅛ cup Parmesan cheese
¼ cup melted butter
¼ cup dry sherry
2 chicken breasts, skinned & boned
1 egg, beaten with 1 Tbsp. milk
1 lb. fresh spinach
nutmeg
½ lb. mushrooms, sliced
1 clove garlic, minced
1 cup grated Cheddar cheese

Combine bread crumbs with Parmesan cheese. Set aside. Combine butter with sherry and set aside.

Dip chicken in egg-milk mixture, then coat with bread crumbs and Parmesan cheese. Sauté in one-half of the butter and sherry until brown on both sides. Rinse and trim spinach. Sprinkle lightly with nutmeg. Cover and steam until limp. Sauté mushrooms and garlic in remaining butter-sherry mixture.

To serve: Place chicken breasts on a bed of spinach, top with mushrooms, sprinkle with Cheddar cheese and bake, uncovered, for 20 minutes at 350° F.

—Barbara Denz

Madeira Chicken

Simple but elegant, with a rich, creamy flavour.

flour for dredging
2 chicken breasts, skinned & boned
2 Tbsp. butter
2 Tbsp. minced shallots
½ cup Madeira
½ cup heavy cream
parsley
sautéed mushrooms (optional)

Lightly flour chicken, then sauté in butter for about 5 to 10 minutes per side. When done, remove and keep warm. Add shallots and sauté, stirring constantly, for 2 to 3 minutes. Add Madeira and bring to a hard boil. Add cream slowly and, stirring occasionally, reduce until thick. Serve over chicken, garnishing with fresh parsley and sautéed mushrooms.

Serves 2.

—Lori Messer

Wolfe Island Buttermilk Chicken

"My husband developed this recipe—it is the crispiest chicken you'll ever taste, even when reheated."

6 chicken breasts, halved
salt & pepper
2 cups flour
2 cups buttermilk
oil for frying

Season breasts with salt and pepper (and any other desired herbs). Coat with flour, dip in buttermilk, then coat again with flour.

Heat oil in deep skillet to 350° F, then reduce heat to keep oil at 325°. Cook chicken, a few pieces at a time, for 10 minutes, turning once.

Serves 6.

—*Lorraine Smythe*

Chicken with Tarragon & Pears

2 whole chicken breasts, split, skinned & boned
2-4 Tbsp. butter
1 small onion, diced
brandy or white wine
1 cup heavy cream
2 pears, sliced thickly
Sauce:
¼ cup butter
1 clove garlic, minced
1 Tbsp. tarragon
1-2 Tbsp. lemon juice
1 tsp. parsley

Brown chicken in butter. Remove from pan and keep warm. Sauté onion, adding butter if needed. Remove and place with chicken. Deglaze pan with brandy or wine. Return chicken and onion to pan, then stir in cream and pears. Simmer until chicken is cooked.

Meanwhile, prepare sauce: Melt butter and briefly sauté garlic. Stir in tarragon, lemon juice and parsley and cook for 1 minute. Set aside, then add to chicken 5 to 10 minutes before serving.

Serves 4.

—*Kathy Payette*

Whiskey Chicken

"Golden pieces of chicken surrounded by green peas, all glistening with buttery sauce, and the delicate aroma of whiskey are seductive enough to bring strong people to their knees."

4 boneless chicken breasts
juice of one lemon
flour for dredging
4 Tbsp. butter
salt & pepper
2 oz. (or more) whiskey
1 cup peas

Pound chicken breasts flat and thin between sheets of waxed paper. Pour lemon juice over meat in shallow glass container. Marinate for at least 1 hour, turning once or twice. Remove from juice and dredge with flour. Melt butter in large skillet and allow butter to foam. Add chicken and cook over medium heat for 2 minutes. Turn chicken over and sprinkle with salt and pepper. Pour 1 oz. whiskey over and slosh it around chicken pieces by shaking pan. Add 1 oz. more whiskey and flame it. Stand back. When flames die down, add peas and shake pan so peas heat in sauce. Cook a minute or so longer, until thoroughly heated.

Serves 3 to 4.

—*Barbara Sharp*

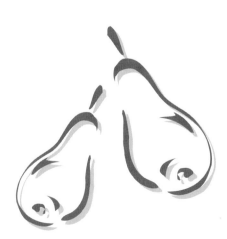

Vegetable & Ham Stuffed Chicken Breasts

This makes a tasty and elegant "company" dish and, since it freezes successfully, can be made ahead of time. The concept is similar to a "cordon bleu" recipe, but the addition of hazelnuts and vegetables makes this dish much richer.

1 onion, finely chopped
2 carrots, finely chopped
1 stalk celery, finely chopped
4 slices bacon, chopped
4 Tbsp. butter
1 head broccoli, chopped
1 cup chopped hazelnuts
8 oz. cream cheese
4 whole chicken breasts, halved, skinned, boned & pounded flat
8 thin slices ham
1 cup chicken stock
1 cup dry white wine
2 Tbsp. flour
1 cup light cream
parsley

Sauté onion, carrots, celery and bacon in 2 Tbsp. butter until onions are transparent and vegetables are cooked. Add broccoli, ¾ cup hazelnuts and cream cheese and sauté until blended. Line inside of each chicken breast with slice of ham. Spoon stuffing into centre of ham and fold meat over. Lay breast with fold underneath in glass baking dish.

Combine chicken stock and wine, pour over chicken, cover and bake for 1 hour at 350° F. Remove liquid, strain and reserve. Melt remaining 2 Tbsp. butter and mix in flour. Add cream and 1 cup reserved cooking liquid, whisking constantly until it thickens. Do not boil.

Place chicken breasts on serving platter and pour sauce over them. Sprinkle with remaining hazelnuts and parsley.

Serves 8.

—Linda Powidajko

Chicken with Tomatoes & Cream

When made with homegrown tomatoes and basil, this is especially good as a light summer supper. Home-frozen tomatoes and basil (just wash, dry thoroughly, chop the basil and freeze in plastic bags) will also result in a fresh summery taste in midwinter.

2 whole chicken breasts, halved
3 Tbsp. butter
1 clove garlic, minced
1 small onion, minced
3 Tbsp. flour
¼ cup white wine
1 cup chopped tomatoes
½ cup light cream
¼ cup chopped fresh basil & parsley, mixed
salt & pepper

Poach chicken breasts in enough salted water to cover, until tender — about 20 minutes. Remove, reserving liquid. Skin and bone chicken and set aside. In large pan, melt butter and sauté garlic and onion. Add flour and stir well. Whisk in ½ cup stock and wine and cook over high heat until sauce is reduced, stirring constantly. Reduce heat to medium, add tomatoes, cream and basil-parsley mixture and cook for 4 to 5 minutes. Fold in chicken. Add salt and pepper. Serve on toast, over rice or in pita pockets.

Serves 4.

—Susan S. Hubbard

Stuffed Chicken Breasts

2 whole chicken breasts, halved, skinned & boned
4 slices ham
4 oz. Swiss or Gruyère cheese, grated
flour
1 egg, beaten with ¼ cup milk
⅔ cup fine dry bread crumbs
¼ cup butter
1 clove garlic, minced
2 Tbsp. oil

Pound chicken breasts between sheets of waxed paper to ¼" thickness. In centre of each chicken piece, place 1 slice ham and ½ of the cheese. Fold chicken over to make a flat rectangle and coat with flour. Dip each piece in egg-milk mixture, then roll in bread crumbs. Place pieces gently on rack and let coating set for at least 30 minutes.

Melt butter, then add garlic and oil. Add chicken and cook over medium heat for about 10 minutes on each side, or until done.

—Pamela Swainson

Sesame Baked Chicken

"The sesame coating on this chicken delights everyone's taste buds. My dad and I used to race to see who could scrape out the most leftover 'crispies' from the bottom of the pan."

½ cup butter
1⅓ cups fine cracker crumbs
½ cup toasted sesame seeds
2-3-lb. fryer chicken, cut up
⅓ cup evaporated milk

Melt butter in 9" x 13" baking pan in the oven. Combine cracker crumbs and sesame seeds. Dip chicken pieces in evaporated milk, then roll in cracker mixture to cover. Dip skin side of chicken pieces in butter, turn over, and arrange in baking dish. Bake, uncovered, at 350° F for 1½ hours.

Serves 4.

—LaRae DuFresne Bergo

Hearty Harvest Casserole

Garlicky chicken combined with readily available winter vegetables produce a substantial, tasty, yet low-fat meal.

8 chicken thighs, skin removed
12 cloves garlic, halved
2 large potatoes, cubed
6 oz. mushrooms, sliced
3 onions, quartered
1 tsp. tarragon
1 tsp. basil
1 small acorn squash, cut into eighths
4 canned tomatoes, halved, liquid reserved
½ cup apple cider
⅓ cup red wine
salt & pepper

Make 3 cuts in each thigh and insert a garlic half in each slit. Place one-third of potatoes, one-third of mushrooms and one-third of onions in large casserole dish. Lay 4 thighs on this and sprinkle with half the tarragon and basil. Next, layer half the squash, one-third of each of potatoes, mushrooms and onions, remaining chicken and remaining tarragon and basil. Cover with remaining squash, potatoes, mushrooms and onions. Arrange tomatoes over this.

Combine ½ cup tomato liquid with cider and wine and pour over everything. Sprinkle with salt and pepper. Cover and bake at 375° F for 1 hour. Let rest out of oven, still covered, for 10 to 15 minutes before serving.

Serves 4.

—Dayna Lee Burnett

Down-Home Chicken & Dumplings

Exquisitely light dumplings and a flavourful sauce make this a special treat.

1 cup flour
1 tsp. paprika
1 frying chicken, cut up
3 Tbsp. oil
1 cup chicken stock
½ cup white wine
1 tsp. curry
½ tsp. tarragon
DUMPLINGS:
1½ cups flour
1 Tbsp. baking powder
½ tsp. salt
1 cup milk

Place flour and paprika in plastic bag. Add chicken pieces and shake to coat. Heat oil in heavy pan with tight-fitting lid. Fry chicken pieces until golden, removing to platter as they brown.

To liquid in pan, add stock, wine, curry and tarragon. Add chicken and simmer, covered, until tender — about 1½ hours.

For dumplings: Sift flour and measure, then resift with baking powder and salt. Add milk and stir just until dry ingredients are dampened. Batter will be slightly lumpy. Dip a tablespoon into the hot chicken liquid to keep batter from sticking to the spoon. Drop by spoonfuls on top of chicken pieces. Cover and cook for 12 minutes, turning heat up slightly. Do not raise cover.

Put dumplings on a heated platter and surround them with chicken pieces. Serve gravy separately.

Serves 4.

—Edie Spring

Chicken Breasts with Spinach Stuffing & Asiago Cheese Sauce

Asiago is a hard cow's-milk cheese that is sharper and saltier than Parmesan. Look for it in specialty cheese displays.

STUFFING:
⅓ cup butter
¾ cup chopped green onions
½ pkg. fresh spinach
¼ lb. Black Forest ham
salt & pepper
½ tsp. fennel
¾ cup bread crumbs
½ cup Parmesan cheese
1 tsp. tarragon
nutmeg
1 egg yolk
2 whole chicken breasts, halved, skinned & boned
1 tsp. thyme
ASIAGO SAUCE:
1½ cups milk
2 Tbsp. butter
2 Tbsp. flour
salt & pepper
1 cup grated Asiago cheese
¼ cup dry white wine
1 Tbsp. chopped parsley
lovage (optional)

In heavy pot, melt ¼ cup butter, add onions and cook until soft. Wash, trim and coarsely chop spinach. Add to butter and onions and cook until leaves are limp, 2 to 3 minutes. Chop ham finely, add to pot and cook for 30 seconds. Remove pan from heat. Mix in salt and pepper, fennel, bread crumbs, Parmesan cheese, tarragon and nutmeg. Set aside to cool, then blend in egg yolk.

Cut a pocket on the thick breastbone side of each chicken breast. Spoon in stuffing, skewer opening shut and press gently to flatten breast. Set in single layer in ovenproof dish. Melt remaining butter, brush over breasts and season with salt and pepper and thyme. Cover with foil and bake at 400° F for 40 minutes or until firm to the touch. Uncover and brown for 5 minutes.

For sauce: Scald milk. Melt butter, stir in flour and cook for 2 to 3 minutes. Pour in hot milk and beat vigorously to make a smooth sauce. Season with salt and pepper and blend in cheese. Just before serving, add wine and parsley. Add lovage if available. To serve, place chicken breasts on hot plate and top with sauce.

Serves 4.

—Tracy Cane

Lemon Maple Chicken

The exceptional flavour belies the speed and ease of assembling this dish.

4 chicken legs
½ cup maple syrup
½ cup Dijon mustard
¼ cup fresh lemon juice
1 Tbsp. grated lemon rind
1 tsp. cinnamon

Cut chicken legs at the joint but do not separate. Place in casserole dish. Combine remaining ingredients and pour over chicken. Bake at 375° F for 30 minutes. Baste with pan drippings, then cook for 20 minutes longer or until done. Serve over rice using the degreased pan juices as sauce.

Serves 4.

—Gail Driscoll

Chicken & Bell Peppers

Make this with as many colours of bell peppers as are available to produce a colourful dish.

4 chicken breasts, skinned & boned
2 Tbsp. seasoned flour
2 Tbsp. butter
2 Tbsp. oil
2 cloves garlic, crushed
1 onion, sliced
12 large mushrooms, sliced
1 cup sliced artichoke hearts
1½-2 cups sliced bell peppers
2 oz. white wine
2 oz. white rum
2-3 tomatoes, peeled & chopped
½ tsp. dried basil

Dredge chicken breasts in seasoned flour. Heat butter and oil in skillet and sauté chicken breasts for 2 to 3 minutes on each side. Add garlic, onion, mushrooms and artichoke hearts and cook for 5 minutes. Add peppers, wine, rum and tomatoes, simmer for 6 minutes, then sprinkle with basil and simmer for about 2 minutes more. Serve over fresh noodles or rice.

Serves 4.

—Jim & Penny Wright

Belgian Chicken

3-4 lbs. chicken pieces
flour
salt & pepper
3 Tbsp. butter
½ cup chopped onion
1 cup dry white wine
1 cup chopped mushrooms
½ cup golden raisins
¾ cup light cream
chopped parsley

Coat chicken pieces in flour seasoned with salt and pepper. Sauté in butter until light brown. Add onion and cook until tender. Add wine and mushrooms, cover and simmer for 30 to 35 minutes. Add raisins and cook for 5 minutes. Remove chicken pieces and place in a warmed dish. Add cream to the gravy, reheat and pour over chicken. Sprinkle chicken with chopped parsley and serve over rice or noodles.

Serves 4.

—Joanne Avelar

Chicken Cacciatore

Spicy and highly flavourful, this chicken cacciatore is an interesting departure from traditional cacciatore recipes.

2-3 lbs. chicken pieces
28-oz. can tomatoes
7-oz. can tomato sauce
1 cup chopped onions
½ cup chopped green pepper
2 stalks celery, chopped
2 carrots, chopped
4 cloves garlic, minced
½ cup dry red wine
1 tsp. salt
½ tsp. allspice
2 bay leaves
½ tsp. thyme
pepper
cayenne

Remove skin from chicken pieces, then cut meat into serving-sized pieces. Combine remaining ingredients in large pot and bring to a boil. Add chicken, cover, reduce heat and simmer for about 2 hours, or until chicken and carrots are tender. Remove bay leaves. The cover may be removed for the last half hour of cooking to reduce and thicken sauce slightly. Serve with rice or noodles.

Serves 4.

—Judith Asbil

Raspberry Chicken

4 chicken breasts or legs
¼ tsp. salt
⅛ tsp. pepper
2 Tbsp. butter
2 Tbsp. oil
1 pint fresh raspberries
3 Tbsp. white or rosé wine
1 small clove garlic, crushed
1 Tbsp. minced parsley
¼ cup chicken stock
1 tsp. crushed green
  peppercorns
2 Tbsp. butter, cut into
  pieces
sliced, sautéed mushrooms
  (optional)

Sprinkle chicken with salt and pepper. Heat butter and oil in large frying pan and brown chicken on all sides. Mash half the berries through a sieve to remove seeds. Refrigerate the remainder. In small bowl, combine mashed berries, wine, garlic, parsley and stock. Pour over chicken, cover and cook for 15 minutes, or until chicken is tender. Remove chicken to serving dish and keep warm. Stir crushed peppercorns into sauce. Remove pan from heat and stir in butter pieces until they melt and sauce is well blended. Pour sauce over hot chicken and garnish with reserved raspberries and mushrooms.

Serves 4 to 6.

—Mr. & Mrs. Dale Brooks

Chicken Fricassee

½ cup flour
1 tsp. salt
½ tsp. freshly ground pepper
¼ tsp. mace
¼ tsp. nutmeg
5-lb. frying chicken, cut up
⅓ cup oil
½ lb. mushrooms, sliced
1 large onion, sliced
3 cups chicken stock
¼ cup sour cream
¼ cup white wine
¼ tsp. prepared mustard
1 tsp. tomato paste

Mix flour, salt, pepper, mace and nutmeg. Roll dampened pieces of chicken in flour mixture to coat on all sides. Heat oil in large skillet over high heat. Brown chicken, then remove to a plate. Reduce heat, add mushrooms and onion and cook until soft. Add chicken and stock and bring to a boil. Reduce heat, cover, and simmer until very tender — 1 to 2 hours.

Just before serving, skim off fat and stir in a mixture of sour cream, wine, mustard and tomato paste.

Serves 4.

—Norma Somers

Chicken Mandarin

2½-3 lbs. chicken, cut up
flour, seasoned with salt & pepper
1 Tbsp. oil
1 cup chicken stock
2 Tbsp. Worcestershire sauce
⅓ cup orange juice
2 tsp. cornstarch
1 can mandarin orange segments, drained
2-3 cups 'Sugar Snap' or edible pod peas

Coat chicken with flour and brown in oil in large skillet. Add chicken stock, Worcestershire sauce and orange juice. Cover and simmer for 1 hour or until tender. Remove chicken and cut meat from bones. Blend cornstarch with 2 tsp. cold water; stir into pan liquids. Bring to a boil, stirring until thickened. Add oranges, peas and boneless chicken. Cover and heat until peas have just changed colour — 3 to 5 minutes. Serve over rice or noodles.

Serves 4.

—Roseann LaPlace

Chicken & Apricots

3 lbs. chicken pieces, skin removed
4 Tbsp. butter
2 large onions, sliced
2 Tbsp. flour
¼ tsp. nutmeg
paprika
salt & pepper
1 cup apricot juice
1 cup chicken stock
1 green pepper, sliced
1 lb. dried apricots, soaked overnight

Lightly brown chicken pieces in butter and remove from pan. In same pan, sauté onions until soft. Add flour, nutmeg, paprika and salt and pepper. Cook for one minute. Add apricot juice and chicken stock and bring to a boil, stirring constantly. Return chicken pieces to pan. Lower heat, cover and simmer for 30 minutes. Add green pepper and apricots. Simmer for another 15 minutes. Serve over brown rice.

Serves 6 to 8.

—Patricia Daine

African Chicken

¼ cup butter
1 small onion, diced
1 Tbsp. ground coriander
1½ tsp. salt
3-lb. chicken, cut up
½ cup chicken stock
1 Tbsp. lemon juice
2 Tbsp. flour
1 cup yogurt

Combine butter, onion, coriander and salt. Roll chicken in this mixture. Place in slow cooker, then pour chicken stock and lemon juice over. Cover and cook on low setting for 8 hours or less. Stir flour into yogurt, then stir into chicken just before serving.

Serves 4.

—Midge Denault

Baked Chicken Rosemary

The tangy barbecue-style sauce works well over pork, lamb or chicken.

1 frying chicken, cut up
salt & pepper
1 clove garlic, minced
1 tsp. paprika
1 Tbsp. onion, finely minced
½ cup vinegar
½ cup tomato sauce
½ cup water
1 tsp. rosemary leaves
1 Tbsp. prepared mustard
2 Tbsp. brown sugar or
    honey
1 tsp. soy sauce

Arrange chicken pieces one layer deep in 9" x 13" baking pan. Sprinkle with salt and pepper, garlic, paprika and onion. Combine remaining ingredients and pour over chicken. Bake at 325° F until fork-tender — about 1 hour. Serve with rice.

Serves 3 to 4.

—Mary Irwin-Gibson

Poule au Pot (French Stewed Chicken)

1 cup bread crumbs
2 cloves garlic, chopped
½ onion, chopped
2 slices ham, chopped
giblets, chopped
1 tsp. thyme
½ tsp. basil
½ tsp. sage
2 eggs, beaten
4-6-lb. stewing chicken
10 cups seasoned chicken
    stock
2 leeks
1 Spanish onion studded
    with 2 cloves
3 carrots, halved
2 turnips, halved
4 potatoes, quartered
1 small cabbage, quartered
½ cup barley flour

Combine bread crumbs, garlic, onion, ham, giblets, thyme, basil and sage. Mix well, then stir in eggs. Place stuffing in chicken. Place chicken and chicken stock in large heavy pot. Bring to a boil, reduce heat, cover and simmer for 1 hour. Add vegetables and barley and simmer for 40 minutes more.

Remove chicken and vegetables to serving dish and keep warm. Thicken gravy with flour (mix a bit of gravy with flour, then stir into pot) and pour over chicken and vegetables.

Serves 6.

—Malcolm Flowerday

Mexican Spiced Chicken

This is a spicy, hot chicken dish with lots of sauce.

4 Tbsp. olive oil
3 lbs. chicken, cut up
2 cloves garlic, chopped
1 thin slice white bread
1 onion, chopped
2 or more canned serrano chilies
⅛ tsp. cloves
⅛ tsp. cinnamon
3 large tomatoes or 1 cup canned tomatoes
1 cup chicken stock
salt & pepper
½ cup dry sherry (optional)

Heat oil in skillet and sauté chicken until golden. Remove and keep warm. In same skillet, sauté garlic and bread, then onion. Break up bread and place with onion, garlic, chilies, cloves, cinnamon, tomatoes and a little chicken stock in blender or food processor and purée. Pour sauce into nonferrous skillet with a lid. Simmer for a few minutes, adding remaining stock. Add chicken pieces, cover and simmer until chicken is tender — about 1 hour. Salt and pepper to taste and add sherry just before serving.

Serves 3 to 4.

—*Beth Toron*

Chicken Stroganoff

3 Tbsp. oil
4 chicken breasts, skinned, boned & cut into thin strips
½ tsp. salt
1 tsp. pepper
1 clove garlic, minced
3 onions, sliced
1 cup sliced mushrooms
3 Tbsp. flour
6 Tbsp. white wine
2 cups chicken stock, heated
⅔ cup sour cream
1 Tbsp. tomato paste

Heat oil in heavy pan. Sear chicken pieces, season with salt and pepper and remove. Mix chicken with garlic and keep warm. Cook onions and mushrooms in pan until onions are transparent. Add extra oil if needed. Stir in flour to make a roux. Add wine, hot stock, sour cream and tomato paste, stirring it into a smooth mixture. Add chicken and garlic. Simmer gently for 20 minutes, or until chicken is tender. Serve in a ring of hot buttered noodles.

Serves 4.

—*Ann Coyle*

Chicken in Mustard Sauce

1½ lbs. chicken pieces
¼ cup flour
½ tsp. salt
1 clove garlic, crushed
2 Tbsp. grated onion
2 Tbsp. butter
½ Tbsp. lemon juice
¾ tsp. dry mustard
1 tsp. sugar
½ Tbsp. cornstarch

Coat chicken pieces in mixture of flour, salt, garlic and onion. Fry in butter until lightly browned. Add ½ cup water, cover and cook for 30 minutes. Combine remaining ingredients and add to liquid in pan. Turn pieces to coat with sauce, cover and cook for an additional 30 minutes or until tender. Uncover and place under hot broiler for a few minutes before serving.

Serves 2.

—*Rose Strocen*

Lemon Chicken

4 chicken breasts, skinned
   & boned
1 egg
flour
2 Tbsp. peanut oil
2½ Tbsp. cornstarch
¼ cup lemon juice
grated rind of 1 lemon
⅓ cup sugar
¼ tsp. ginger
rind of ½ lemon, cut into
   thin strips

Cut chicken into 1-inch strips. Beat egg with 2 Tbsp. water. Dip chicken in this, then dredge in flour. Heat peanut oil in skillet or wok and fry chicken, removing pieces once they are cooked. Mix remaining ingredients except strips of lemon rind. Bring to a boil in skillet. Add chicken and lemon rind to the mixture and heat for 5 minutes.

Serves 4.

—Mary-Lee Judah

Oven-Crisp Chicken

Our Vermont tester says, "Hurrah! This chicken has an unusual and flavourful coating; it is very tender and moist and not at all greasy."

¾ cup cracker crumbs
½ cup Parmesan cheese
½ cup ground pecans
2 eggs
1 cup buttermilk
3-4-lb. broiler chicken, cut up
melted butter

Combine cracker crumbs, cheese and pecans. Beat together eggs and buttermilk. Roll chicken pieces in crumb mixture until evenly coated, dip in egg mixture, then roll in crumbs again. Place a single layer in lightly oiled 9" x 13" baking dish. Brush lightly with melted butter.

Bake, brushing occasionally with more butter, at 400° F for 1 hour.

Serves 4.

—Nancy R. Franklin

Chicken with Broccoli

"This is a family favourite. Baked in a 'raw cookware' clay pot, it has a wonderful, almost smoky flavour. It's good served with buttered noodles or baked potatoes to soak up the extra sauce."

2 Tbsp. flour
1½ tsp. salt
pepper
½ tsp. tarragon
3-lb. chicken, cut into
   serving pieces
2 Tbsp. olive oil
juice of ½ lemon
1 cup sour cream
2 oz. grated Cheddar cheese
1 head broccoli, broken into
   florets

Presoak clay pot in water for 15 minutes.

Combine flour, salt, pepper and tarragon in plastic bag. Add chicken pieces two at a time and shake to coat. Brown chicken quickly in oil, then arrange in pot. Squeeze lemon juice on top of chicken.

Add sour cream and rest of flour mixture to drippings in frying pan. Stir, then pour over chicken. Sprinkle cheese over top. Place covered pot in cold oven, then set temperature at 450° F and cook for 35 minutes. Add broccoli, then cook for an additional 10 minutes.

Serves 4.

—Susan Holec

Chicken in Parmesan Sauce

"Easy to make and very good," reports the Vermont test kitchen.

3 lbs. chicken breasts, skinned & boned
salt & pepper
3 Tbsp. oil
3 Tbsp. butter
3 Tbsp. flour
1½ cups milk
¼ cup dry white wine
1½ Tbsp. lemon juice
½ cup Parmesan cheese
3 egg yolks, beaten
½ cup bread crumbs
½ tsp. rosemary

Cut chicken into strips, sprinkle with salt and pepper and brown in oil in hot skillet. Remove chicken and set aside. Melt butter in same skillet and blend in flour. Add milk and whisk over low heat until smooth and thickened. Add wine and lemon juice, and increase heat to medium-high. When mixture begins to boil, reduce heat to low and add ¼ cup cheese. Once cheese has melted, add egg yolks and stir well.

Place ⅛ cup cheese and ¼ cup bread crumbs in bottom of flat casserole dish. Arrange chicken on top followed by sauce, then remaining bread crumbs and cheese. Sprinkle with rosemary. Bake at 375° F for 20 minutes, covered, and 10 minutes uncovered.

Serves 4 to 6.

—Mary-Lee Judah

Stir-Fry Chicken & Snow Peas

1 cup boned, cubed, raw chicken
2 Tbsp. oil
3 Tbsp. soy sauce
¼ tsp. pepper
1 cup snow peas
6 scallions, sliced diagonally
2 carrots, grated
2 Tbsp. cornstarch
1 cup chicken stock

Stir-fry chicken in hot oil in wok or skillet until almost done — about 2 minutes. Add soy sauce and pepper and stir. Add snow peas and stir-fry for about 2 minutes. Add scallions and carrots, stir, cover, and cook for another 3 minutes, stirring frequently. Mix the cornstarch and chicken stock and add to wok, stirring until the sauce thickens. Serve over hot rice.

Serves 4.

—Barry LeClair

Tropical Chicken

2 whole chicken breasts, skinned & boned
2 Tbsp. oil
¼ cup soy sauce
2 cloves garlic, crushed
1 tsp. finely chopped fresh gingerroot
pepper
1 cup peeled, ripe papaya slices
1 large green pepper, sliced
cooked rice

Cut chicken into 1-inch pieces. Heat oil in large frying pan. Add chicken pieces and brown on all sides. Pour off fat and add soy sauce. Add garlic, ginger and pepper to taste.

Cover and cook over low heat until almost tender. Add papaya and pepper slices and cook just until heated through — about 5 minutes. Serve over hot rice.

Serves 4.

—Irene Louden

Chinese-Style Asparagus Chicken

4 chicken breasts, boned &
   cut into 1" cubes
¼ cup cornstarch
4 Tbsp. oil
1 Tbsp. chopped onion
1 lb. fresh asparagus, cut
   into 1" pieces
4 large mushrooms, sliced
¼ cup slivered almonds
2 Tbsp. soy sauce
1 Tbsp. freshly grated
   gingerroot
1 cup chicken stock

Shake chicken in cornstarch
to coat. In wok or heavy frying
pan, brown chicken in oil. Add
vegetables, almonds, soy sauce
and ginger. Cook, stirring, for 2
minutes. Add chicken stock and
stir for an additional 2 minutes.
Spoon over rice.

Serves 4.

—Ingrid Magnuson

Cashew Chicken

*This dish, often with almonds
replacing the cashews, is a
standard in Cantonese Chinese
restaurants. It is quick and
simple to prepare at home.*

2 Tbsp. plus 2 tsp. cornstarch
1 cup chicken stock
5 Tbsp. soy sauce
2 lbs. chicken breasts,
   skinned & boned
4 Tbsp. oil
4 stalks celery, sliced
2 cups sliced mushrooms
½ lb. snow peas
1 onion, sliced
1 clove garlic, minced
1 cup cashews
cooked rice

Combine 2 tsp. cornstarch
with chicken stock and 1 Tbsp.
soy sauce. Set aside.

Slice chicken into strips. Blend
remaining 2 Tbsp. cornstarch
with remaining 4 Tbsp. soy
sauce in a bowl and stir in
chicken. Heat 2 Tbsp. oil in large
frying pan or wok, add chicken
and stir over medium head for 3
minutes. Remove chicken. Add
remaining 2 Tbsp. oil and reheat
pan. Add remaining ingredients,
except cashews and rice, cover
and cook over medium heat for 1
minute, shaking the pan several
times. Uncover and cook for
another 2 to 4 minutes, stirring
occasionally. Add chicken-
cornstarch mixture, and stir
over medium heat until the
sauce thickens — about 3
minutes. Stir in most of the
cashews just before serving,
reserving a few for garnish.
Serve over rice.

Serves 6.

— Diane Milan

Almond Gai Ding

*"I enjoyed this so much when I
had it in a restaurant that I
developed my own recipe for it
at home. Its success depends
upon fresh vegetables."*

1 egg white
1 Tbsp. light soy sauce
sesame oil
2 chicken breasts, skinned,
   boned and cut into bite
   size pieces
3 Tbsp. oil
½ cup slivered almonds
1 clove garlic, minced
2 thin slices gingerroot
1 onion, chopped
2 stalks celery, sliced
   diagonally
1-2 carrots, sliced diagonally
1 cup cauliflower florets
1 cup sliced mushrooms
½ can water chestnuts, sliced
1 Tbsp. cornstarch

Combine egg white, soy sauce
and a few drops sesame oil.
Marinate chicken in this while
continuing with recipe.

Heat 1 Tbsp. oil in wok and
brown almonds. Remove
almonds and set aside. Add
another tablespoon of oil to wok
and sauté garlic and ginger for a
few seconds. Add chicken. Stir-
fry until just cooked — 2 to 3
minutes — then remove from
wok.

Add remaining 1 Tbsp. oil to
wok. Stir-fry onion, celery and
carrots until carrots are just
crisp-tender — 5 to 8 minutes.
Add cauliflower, mushrooms and
water chestnuts.

Continue cooking, stirring
frequently, until vegetables
reach desired doneness. Stir in
chicken. Dissolve cornstarch in
2 Tbsp. water, stir in. Cook until
thickened.

Serves 4.

—Adele Dueck

Millionaire Chicken

It is almost impossible to describe how good this dish is. Serve it as is, over rice, or dress it up by also stir-frying snow peas, baby corn and mushrooms. It makes a sensational company meal when served over fried noodle cakes. (Take small bunches of fresh vermicelli noodles and place in wok with a generous amount of hot peanut oil. Pat down to form a pancake and fry, turning once, long enough to stick noodles together and until both sides are golden brown. Drain well before serving.) Tofu can be substituted for the chicken in this dish with an equally tasty result.

4 Tbsp. soy sauce
2 Tbsp. honey
1 clove garlic, crushed
2 whole chicken breasts, skinned, boned & cut into bite-sized pieces
3 Tbsp. oil
2 scallions, chopped
4 slices gingerroot, minced
½-1 tsp. crushed Szechuan pepper
¼-½ tsp. crushed hot red pepper

Combine soy sauce, honey and garlic and pour over chicken. Let marinate for at least 1 hour.

Heat oil in wok and rapidly sauté scallions, ginger and peppers for 2 to 3 minutes. Reduce heat slightly and add chicken and marinade. Cook, stirring, until chicken is done — 5 minutes. The sauce may be thickened with cornstarch.

Serves 4.

—Evelyn Gervan

Wrong Wong's Chicken

"A family favourite for years, this marinade and sauce recipe can also be used with firm-fleshed fish."

2 chicken breasts, skinned & boned
MARINADE:
1 egg white
2 tsp. cornstarch
1 Tbsp. cold water
SAUCE:
1 Tbsp. soy sauce
1 Tbsp. cold water
1 Tbsp. white wine vinegar
1 Tbsp. white sugar
1 Tbsp. cornstarch
2 whole dried red peppers
3 scallions, minced
1 large clove garlic, crushed
½" gingerroot, chopped
2½ Tbsp. peanut oil

Slice chicken into 2-by-¼-inch strips. Mix marinade ingredients, add chicken, stir to coat and set aside for 30 minutes. Combine sauce ingredients in small bowl and set aside. Assemble peppers, scallions, garlic and ginger.

Heat 1½ Tbsp. oil in wok until smoking hot. Add chicken and stir quickly. Chicken will separate and turn white within a few minutes. Remove chicken and drain on towelling. Add 1 Tbsp. oil to wok, heat, then add peppers, scallions, garlic and ginger. Stir-fry for 30 seconds. Add chicken and toss well. Stir sauce and pour over chicken. Stir-fry over high heat until sauce thickens. Serve immediately.

Serves 2.

—Keith McLaren

Festive Stir-Fry

Quick, simple and healthy, this dish looks really pretty with the bright red and green of the pepper and broccoli.

3 Tbsp. oil
1 large clove garlic, minced
2 chicken breasts, skinned, boned & cubed
1 small head broccoli, cut into florets
1 sweet red pepper, diced
1 small onion, diced
½ lb. mushrooms, sliced
¼ cup sherry
¼ cup soy sauce
2 Tbsp. vinegar
2 Tbsp. brown sugar
1 tsp. ground ginger
1 Tbsp. cornstarch
½ cup water

Heat oil in wok or heavy skillet. Add garlic and chicken. Cook, stirring, over high heat for 3 to 5 minutes. Remove chicken and reheat oil if necessary. Add vegetables and stir-fry for another 3 to 5 minutes. Combine all remaining ingredients, mixing well, and stir into wok. Add chicken, stir until hot and sauce has thickened. Serve over rice.

Serves 2 to 3.

—Penny Rioux

Drumsticks Bernard

Chicken wings have become a North American institution over the past few years, often appearing on bar snack menus. Cut chicken wings into two sections to make mini drumsticks if this is to be served as a finger food. Otherwise, use regular drumsticks, allowing 2 to 3 (6 to 8 minis) per person. This glaze will do approximately 36 drumsticks.

36 drumsticks or 48 wings
  cut in half
1 cup honey
⅔ cup soy sauce
2 Tbsp. whiskey
2 cloves garlic, crushed
1" gingerroot, slivered
sesame seeds

    Arrange drumsticks in deep saucepan, 12 at a time. Combine honey, soy sauce, whiskey, garlic, ginger and 1 cup water and pour over chicken. Simmer for 20 to 30 minutes, remove legs and repeat with same marinade until all legs are cooked.

    Refrigerate overnight. Sprinkle with sesame seeds and reheat at 325° F. Reheat and reduce marinade for dipping sauce.

    Serves 12 as an appetizer.

                —*Patricia Daine*

A Simple Chicken Curry

"When I was living in Bombay, I was part of a culture-sharing organization comprising American, Canadian, British and Indian women. This is one of the many interesting recipes that were exchanged." Either buy commercial canned coconut milk, or make it by pouring 2 cups hot milk over 2 cups dried coconut. Let stand for 1 hour, then strain, pressing the coconut hard to release all the milk. Feed the coconut to the birds and use the milk.

2 Tbsp. butter
1 onion, chopped
2 cloves garlic, chopped
1 Tbsp. ground coriander
1 tsp. mustard seed
1 tsp. cumin seed
1 tsp. turmeric
½ tsp. ground ginger
½ tsp. dry crushed chilies
1 frying chicken, cut up
2 cups coconut milk
2 tsp. lime juice

    Melt butter, then saute onion and garlic until golden. Add coriander, mustard, cumin, turmeric, ginger and chilies and cook gently, stirring, for 3 minutes. Add chicken and cook until lightly browned. Add coconut milk and simmer until chicken is cooked through. Season with a little salt and lime juice and serve over rice.

    Serves 4 to 5.

                —*Ethel Hunter*

Chicken Curry

Not a curry you would find in a small, rural Indian village, this is a very rich dish. Serve the delicately flavoured curry with an assortment of condiments — roasted cashews, diced green pepper and celery, mandarin oranges, bananas, coconut, raisins and plain yogurt.

5-6-lb. chicken
1 onion
3 celery tops
1 Tbsp. salt
1 bay leaf
4 cloves
2½ cups hot milk
3 cups coconut
½ cup butter
2 cloves garlic, chopped
1½ cups chopped onion
¼ tsp. ginger
1½-3 Tbsp. curry
½ cup flour
1 tsp. salt
1 Tbsp. lemon juice
1 cup light cream

    Place chicken, whole onion, celery tops, salt, bay leaf and cloves in large stockpot with 12 cups water. Bring to a boil, reduce heat and simmer, covered, for 2 hours. Remove chicken and set aside to cool, then remove meat from bones and chop. Strain stock and reserve 2 cups for use in curry.

    Pour hot milk over coconut and let stand for 45 minutes. Melt ¼ cup butter in heavy skillet, then sauté garlic, chopped onion, ginger and curry for 3 to 5 minutes. Stir in 2 cups stock, then coconut and milk. Reduce heat and simmer for 1 hour, stirring occasionally Strain and press, reserving liquid and discarding coconut.

    Melt remaining ¼ cup butter, stir in flour, salt and lemon juice. Gradually stir in cream and simmer for 5 minutes. Add chicken and curry sauce and gently heat through.

    Serves 8.

Debbi's Chicken Curry with Saffron Rice

An excellent curry with multileveled seasonings and just a touch of sting.

CURRY:
1 lb. chicken breasts, cut into 1" cubes
¼ cup oil
1 cup finely chopped onion
1 clove garlic, crushed
1 tsp. freshly grated gingerroot
½ tsp. ground cumin
½ tsp. turmeric
1 tsp. ground coriander
½ tsp. hot red pepper
¼ tsp. fennel
1 tsp. garam masala
1 cup tomatoes, peeled & chopped
½ cup plain yogurt
1½ tsp. lemon juice
SAFFRON RICE:
1 cup dry basmati rice
½ tsp. saffron threads
1 cinnamon stick
2 whole cloves
½ cup finely chopped onion
3 Tbsp. butter
½ tsp. brown sugar
½ tsp. salt
2 cardamom pods, ground

For curry: Sauté chicken in oil until just cooked. Remove and keep warm. In same pan sauté onion, garlic and ginger. Reduce heat and add spices. Sauté for 1 minute. Add tomatoes and ¼ cup water and bring to a boil. Reduce heat and simmer for 30 minutes. Add meat and heat through. Add yogurt and lemon juice.

For saffron rice: Wash rice in cold water. Soak saffron in 2 Tbsp. boiling water for 10 minutes, reserving liquid. Fry cinnamon, cloves and onion in butter for 8 minutes. Add rice and fry for an additional 5 minutes. Add 2 cups boiling water, sugar, salt, cardamom, saffron and soaking liquid. Cover and remove from heat. Let sit undisturbed for 30 to 40 minutes, or until rice is cooked.

Serves 4.

—Heidi Juul

Sweet & Sour Chicken Wings

When we tested these wings in our Vermont kitchen, they were very popular. The meat was falling-off-the-bone tender, and the sauce adhered well to the wings.

16-20 chicken wings
2 cups brown sugar
2 Tbsp. vinegar
4 Tbsp. soy sauce
1 tsp. chopped garlic

Cut tips off wings. (Freeze tips and add to soup stock the next time you make it.) Place wings in large shallow baking dish. Mix remaining ingredients together and pour over wings. Cover and bake at 350° F for 1 hour, remove cover, turn wings and bake for 40 to 60 minutes more.

Serves 4 to 6.

—Jan Higenbottam

Sesame Chicken Wings

Good, crunchy wings. Serve with dips for a delicious snack to have with drinks on a summer afternoon or evening.

3-4 lbs. chicken wings
2 cups flour
½ cup sesame seeds
1 tsp. ginger
1-1½ cups melted butter

Wash and dry wings and cut off tips. Combine flour, sesame seeds and ginger and mix well. Dip wings in butter and shake off excess, then roll in flour mixture. Place on cookie sheet and bake for 45 to 60 minutes at 350° F. Place under broiler briefly to brown.

Serves 12 as an appetizer.

—Gail Driscoll

Creamed Horseradish Sauce

2 Tbsp. butter
2 Tbsp. flour
1¼ cups light cream
salt
white pepper
3 Tbsp. vinegar
2 Tbsp. sugar
2-3 Tbsp. freshly shredded
   horseradish

Melt butter in small saucepan. Add flour and stir for a few minutes. Add cream, a little at a time, while stirring. Add salt, white pepper, vinegar, sugar and horseradish. Stir until thickened.

Serve over boiled, boned chicken meat.

—*Erik Panum*

Curried Lemon Dip

This recipe and the two that follow make good dips for chicken wings. They can also be used as basting sauces.

2 Tbsp. butter
4 cloves garlic, minced
½ tsp. salt
½ tsp. pepper
1 tsp. hot curry
2 Tbsp. freshly grated lemon
   peel
½ cup lemon juice

Melt butter and sauté garlic for 3 minutes. Stir in all other ingredients and simmer for 5 minutes.

Spicy Wing Sauce

1 onion, finely chopped
2 Tbsp. olive oil
2 tsp. coriander
1 tsp. cumin
1 tsp. cinnamon
1 tsp. ground cardamom
¼ tsp. cloves
¼ tsp. cayenne
2 Tbsp. white wine vinegar
1 Tbsp. tomato paste
1 tsp. salt
¼ cup water

Sauté onion in olive oil until transparent. Add remaining ingredients and stir well.

Satay Sauce

½ cup smooth peanut butter
⅓ cup soy sauce
⅓ cup lemon juice
⅓ cup sherry
2 Tbsp. brown sugar
1 tsp. Tabasco sauce
2 cloves garlic, finely minced

Combine all ingredients and mix well. Serve warm or at room temperature.

Best Ever Barbecue Sauce

"We use this sauce on almost everything: beef, pork, poultry. It's great on chicken wings."

2 Tbsp. butter
1 onion, finely chopped
2 cloves garlic, minced
juice of 1 orange
1 Tbsp. raisins
2 Tbsp. cider vinegar
2 Tbsp. oil
grated zest of 1 orange
1 cup molasses
1 cup tomato sauce
2 tsp. chili powder
⅛ tsp. allspice
1 tsp. prepared mustard
1 tsp. Worcestershire sauce
2 tsp. crushed hot red pepper
½ tsp. salt

Melt butter and add onion and garlic. Cook for 5 minutes. Combine orange juice, raisins, vinegar and oil in food processor or blender until smooth. Add processed ingredients and remaining ingredients to onion-garlic mixture. Heat until boiling, reduce heat and simmer uncovered, for 15 minutes.

Makes enough sauce for 36 wings.

—*Mary-Eileen Clear*

Cold Chicken Loaf

4-lb. chicken
2 onions, halved
2 stalks celery, chopped
1 carrot, chopped
10 peppercorns
2 tsp. salt
¼ cup parsley
2 cups bread crumbs
1 cup milk
2 large eggs, lightly beaten
1 onion, finely chopped
1¼ tsp. salt
¼ tsp. pepper
½ cup chicken stock

Place chicken, onions, celery, carrot, peppercorns, salt and parsley in stockpot. Add water to cover chicken and simmer until tender. Remove chicken from bones and grind or chop in food processor. Strain stock, reserving ½ cup.

In large bowl, combine bread crumbs, milk, eggs, onion, salt and pepper. Add ground chicken and stock and mix well. Line bottom of loaf pan with waxed paper. Butter paper and sides of pan. Fill with chicken mixture. Press mixture down and smooth top. Cover with foil. Poach in a larger pan with 1 inch of water at 375° F for 1 hour. Remove foil and cook an additional 10 minutes. Cool and chill thoroughly before turning out. Tastes best made a day ahead.

Serves 6.

—Kathryn MacDonald

Hickory Hollow Giblet Stew

Light, and a good source of iron, this stew is a tasty way to get giblets into the mouths of giblet-haters.

4 Tbsp. olive oil
1 lb. chicken giblets, diced
1 onion, chopped
1 stalk celery, chopped
4 Tbsp. flour
1 tsp. salt
pepper
1 bay leaf
2 Tbsp. parsley
1 tsp. dill
4 cups chicken stock
8-10 potatoes, diced
4 carrots, julienned
1 parsnip, julienned
1 cup puréed zucchini

Heat olive oil and brown giblets, onion and celery. Remove from pot and set aside. Stir flour, salt and pepper into oil until smooth. Add bay leaf, parsley, dill and chicken stock and bring to a boil. Return giblet mixture to pot and add vegetables. Bring to a boil, reduce heat, cover, and simmer for 1 hour. Remove bay leaf. Thicken gravy with flour, if desired.

Serves 4 to 6.

—Helen Shepherd

Bitochki (Russian Chicken Burgers)

1½ lbs. chicken breasts, skinned & boned
1 cup fine bread crumbs
⅓ cup heavy cream
cayenne
½ tsp. salt
½ tsp. pepper
⅛ tsp. nutmeg
2 Tbsp. oil

Cut chicken into chunks and grind in food processor or blender until it is slightly coarse in texture. Put meat into mixing bowl and add ½ cup bread crumbs, cream, cayenne, salt, pepper and nutmeg. Blend thoroughly with hands.

Divide mixture into 6 equal portions. Shape into balls. Roll each ball in remaining crumbs. Press down on balls to form flat patties. Heat oil in frying pan and brown patties on both sides — 10 to 12 minutes. Serve in hamburger buns with tartar sauce or mayonnaise and shredded lettuce.

Serves 4 to 6.

—Barbara J. Kirkland

Chicken Broccoli Salad

Perfect picnic fare, this salad can be adapted to make use of a variety of green vegetables — use whatever is in season. Homemade mayonnaise could be spiced up with garlic or blue cheese to give more zest to the dressing.

1 whole chicken breast, cooked & chopped
1 head broccoli, cut into florets & steamed
1 avocado, chopped
3 green onions, chopped
2 cups dry macaroni shells, cooked & cooled
1 tsp. lemon juice
1 cup mayonnaise
½ tsp. dry mustard
1 tsp. basil
Salt & pepper

Combine chicken, broccoli, avocado, onions and macaroni. Sprinkle with lemon juice. Add mayonnaise, mustard, basil and salt and pepper, and toss lightly. Chill.

Serves 6.

Pojarskis

Croquettes, as the name implies, should be crunchy on the outside but have a creamy interior texture. The chilling time before cooking is very important to bind the filling so that it does not fall apart in the frying process. These turkey croquettes are distinctive due to the use of nutmeg and the large proportion of onion.

CROQUETTES:
1 cup soft bread crumbs
½ cup milk
2 cups ground, cooked turkey
½ cup chopped onion
½ tsp. salt
¼ tsp. pepper
1 tsp. nutmeg
flour
¼ cup butter
WHITE SAUCE:
2 Tbsp. butter
2 cups sliced mushrooms
2 Tbsp. flour
Salt & pepper
1 cup milk

Knead bread crumbs with milk, then add ground turkey, onion, salt, pepper and nutmeg. Shape into 4 patties, roll in flour and refrigerate for 1 hour to set shape. Cook in butter for 10 minutes on one side and 5 minutes on the other. Transfer to serving platter and keep warm.

For sauce: Melt butter and briefly sauté mushrooms. Stir in flour, salt and pepper. Gradually stir in milk and cook over medium heat until thickened and smooth. Pour over the patties.

Serves 4.

—Rose Strocen

Chicken or Turkey Divan

A standby to use up leftover poultry, this is a good hot supper—a biscuit-topped meal in one dish. It is also a recipe that an inexperienced cook would be able to prepare with confidence and serve with pride.

FILLING:
1 onion, chopped
2 stalks celery, chopped
1 clove garlic, minced
2 Tbsp. butter
1 cup chicken stock
3-4 carrots, diced
½ small turnip, diced
4 potatoes, diced
parsley
savory
2 cups chopped cooked chicken or turkey
2 Tbsp. cornstarch mixed with ½ cup water
CRUST:
2 cups flour
4 tsp. baking powder
1 tsp. salt
¼ cup cold shortening
¼ cup cold butter
2 Tbsp. Parmesan cheese
1 cup milk

Brown onion, celery and garlic in butter. Add stock and simmer until vegetables are transparent. Add carrots, turnip, potatoes and water to cover. Bring to a boil and cook until crispy-tender. Add parsley, savory, chicken and cornstarch mixture and cook, stirring, until thickened. Pour into greased casserole dish and set aside.

For crust: Sift together flour, baking powder and salt. Cut in shortening and butter, then add cheese and milk. Mix lightly, then knead 6 to 8 times on floured surface. Roll out and cut into 2-inch biscuits. Place on chicken.

Bake, uncovered, at 375° F for 18 to 20 minutes or until bubbly and browned.

Serves 6.

—Donna Parker

Curried Kiwi & Chicken Salad

A light, refreshing summer salad with a very successful combination of textures and flavours. Serve as a luncheon dish with fresh biscuits or muffins, or use as part of a cold dinner buffet.

½ cup olive oil
2 Tbsp. vinegar
2 Tbsp. lemon juice
½ tsp. paprika
½ tsp. curry
1 clove garlic
¼ tsp. salt
¼ tsp. pepper
4 cups cubed, cooked
  chicken
⅓ cup toasted slivered
  almonds (optional)
⅓ cup dark raisins or currants
¼ cup flaked coconut
3 kiwi fruit, peeled & thinly
  sliced

Combine oil, vinegar, lemon juice, paprika, curry, garlic, salt and pepper until well blended. Let sit for 30 minutes, then remove the garlic clove.

Toss chicken in a bowl with almonds, raisins and coconut. Just before serving, line a glass serving bowl with the sliced kiwi fruit. Mix chicken mixture with dressing and pile in centre of bowl. Garnish with kiwi slices.

Serves 4 to 6.

—Irene Louden

Rich Chicken Liver Paté

I make this smooth, rich paté at Christmas and give it away in small, earthenware pots."

1 Spanish onion, finely
  chopped
4 Tbsp. melted chicken fat
4 Tbsp. rich chicken stock
1 lb. chicken livers
cinnamon, nutmeg & cloves
½ cup heavy cream
2 eggs, lightly beaten
1 Tbsp. cornstarch
4 Tbsp. dry sherry
melted butter

Simmer onion in fat and chicken stock until golden. Add livers and spices. Cover and simmer until tender. When livers are firm, drain and put through food processor. Add cream and eggs. Dissolve cornstarch in sherry and mix thoroughly with livers. Pack into loaf pan or small pots and cook in a water bath at 325° F for 1½ to 2 hours or until firm. Cover top with melted butter and chill for at least 3 days before using.

—Crissie Hunt

Paté à l'Orange

A delicious paté, this recipe eliminates the need for eggs, pork fat and a long cooking time but retains the rich, luxurious taste.

1 lb. poultry livers
1 lb. lean ground pork
1 onion, chopped
1½ cups butter
1 tsp. coriander
¼ cup Cointreau or orange
  liqueur
½ tsp. pepper
grated orange peel

Sauté livers, pork and onion in ¾ cup butter until cooked through. Put meat mixture, remaining butter, coriander, Cointreau and pepper in blender or food processor. Chop until mixture is smooth. (It may be slightly soupy but will become firm when chilled.) Place in mold and chill for at least 4 hours.

To serve, cut into thin slices and garnish with grated orange peel.

Serves 12 to 16.

—J.R. Galen

Butter-Braised Pheasant

2 2-3-lb. pheasants
2 cups red wine
2 bay leaves
¼ cup oil
1 Tbsp. juniper berries
¼ tsp. peppercorns
3 Tbsp. butter

Clean and quarter pheasants, then rinse well in cold water. Combine wine, bay leaves and oil. Coarsely crush juniper berries and peppercorns and add to marinade. Place pheasant in shallow dish, pour marinade over, cover, and refrigerate for 3 days, turning several times.

In Dutch oven, brown pheasants in butter. Remove from heat, add marinade and bake, covered, at 400° F for 1 to 1½ hours, or until tender.

Serves 6 to 8.

—J.R. Galen

Chicken Liver Pâté

"This is a recipe which originated with an Austrian friend. It is excellent, smooth and buttery and keeps well in the refrigerator for about 3 weeks."

2 onions, chopped
1 clove garlic, chopped
1 Tbsp. butter
nutmeg
salt & pepper
2 cups chicken livers
1 cup butter
2 Tbsp. brandy

Sauté onions and garlic in butter until golden brown. Add nutmeg and salt and pepper. Add chicken livers and cook until liver is firm and not pink. While still hot, put mixture into blender or food processor. Add butter and brandy, and blend until smooth.

Makes approximately 3 cups.

—Joan Morrison

Chicken with Mushrooms, Pine Nuts & Feta

2 Tbsp. olive oil
¼ lb. mushrooms, sliced
3 Tbsp. pine nuts
1 clove garlic, minced
½ lb. feta cheese, crumbled
1 Tbsp. minced parsley
pepper
3-lb. chicken
salt & pepper
¼ cup butter, melted
3 Tbsp. lemon juice
1 tsp. Dijon mustard

Heat oil, then add mushrooms, pine nuts and garlic. Sauté for 5 minutes, then stir in feta cheese, parsley and pepper. Remove from heat and cool.

Sprinkle chicken with salt and pepper. Fill with cooled stuffing. Combine butter with lemon juice and mustard, then brush over chicken. Roast chicken for 5 minutes on each side at 425° F, reduce heat to 350° F and roast, breast side up, for 30 to 40 minutes.

Serves 4.

Self-Basting Roast Turkey

1 turkey, stuffed with your
  favourite dressing
6-8 strips bacon

Attach strips of bacon evenly over turkey breast, fastening with toothpicks. Place turkey, breast up, on rack in roasting pan. Place roasting pan and turkey inside 2 large brown-paper grocery bags — one from each end.

Preheat oven to 450° F. Place turkey in oven and immediately reduce heat to 350° F. Roast for 18 to 20 minutes per pound of turkey. If not browned enough, remove bags for last 30 to 40 minutes of cooking time.

—*Kathleen S.H. Moore*

Turkey Dressing

2 cups dry brown & white rice
½ lb. bacon
1½ cups dried fruit (peaches,
  pears, apples)
¾ cup butter
2 cups diced celery
1 cup diced leeks
1½ tsp. salt
2 Tbsp. tarragon
1 Tbsp. mint
½-1 cup sliced mushrooms

Cook rice in 4½ cups water for 45 minutes. Fry bacon and crumble. Soak dried fruit in ⅔ cup boiling water. Melt butter in large heavy pan, and sauté celery and leeks. Add salt. Remove from heat and stir in rice, bacon, fruit, seasonings and mushrooms. Stuff bird and cook as usual.

Enough stuffing for a 12-pound bird.

—*Diane Ladouceur*

Wild Rice, Sausage & Almond Stuffing

This is a wonderfully crunchy stuffing for chicken, goose, duck or even pork. It can be baked in a greased casserole dish by itself, if you wish, to accompany pork chops or baked chicken breasts.

½ cup dry wild rice
½ lb. sausage meat
1 small onion, chopped
½ cup chopped celery
½ cup sliced mushrooms
½ cup coarsely chopped
  almonds
3 slices dry whole wheat
  bread, cubed
½ tsp. salt
½ tsp. pepper
¼ tsp. sage
savory
thyme

Place wild rice in strainer and rinse thoroughly under cold water. Drain well. Place in saucepan and pour 1½ cups boiling water over. Return to boil. Reduce heat and simmer for 45 minutes, or until tender but not mushy. Drain well and transfer to a large bowl.

In large skillet, cook sausage meat over medium heat until no longer pink, breaking it up as it cooks. Stir in onion, celery and mushrooms, and cook until tender — about 5 minutes.

With slotted spoon, transfer sausage-vegetable mixture to wild rice. Add remaining ingredients, stirring gently. Taste and adjust seasoning. Pack loosely into the cavity of a 10-lb. bird, or place in greased casserole dish and bake, covered, at 350° F for 45 minutes.

—*Sandy Robertson*

Stuffed Cornish Game Hens with Orange Sauce

4 Cornish game hens
STUFFING:
1 cup sliced mushrooms
4 Tbsp. butter
1 cup chopped spinach
¼ cup sliced green onion
¼ cup chopped parsley
1 cup cooked white rice
1 cup cooked wild rice
1 cup mandarin orange
  sections
¼ cup walnut pieces
SAUCE:
2 Tbsp. sugar
1 cup water
2 Tbsp. grated orange peel
½ cup frozen orange juice
  concentrate
1½ Tbsp. cornstarch, mixed
  with 2 Tbsp. water
2 Tbsp. Grand Marnier or
  orange flavoured liqueur

To make stuffing, brown mushrooms in 2 Tbsp. butter. Add spinach, onion and parsley and cook for 1 minute. Remove from heat. Add rices, orange sections and walnuts. Spoon into hens, then arrange hens in shallow baking dish and dot with remaining butter. Roast at 400° F for 45 minutes, basting occasionally with pan drippings.

Meanwhile, prepare orange sauce. Combine sugar, water, orange peel and orange juice in heavy pot and bring to a boil. Stir cornstarch mixture into sauce, and cook, stirring, until thickened. Stir in liqueur. Roast hens for 15 minutes more, basting with orange sauce.

Serves 4.

—*Laura Rance*

Wild Game Steakettes

2 lbs. venison or moose
   steaks, sliced ½" thick
½ cup flour
1½ cups bread crumbs
salt & pepper
¼ tsp. thyme
¼ tsp. sage
¼ tsp. celery salt
½ tsp. basil
2 eggs
2 Tbsp. milk
oil for cooking
2 onions, sliced

Pound steaks to tenderize.
Combine flour, bread crumbs,
salt and pepper, thyme, sage,
celery salt and basil. Beat eggs
and milk together. Dip meat into
egg mixture, then into bread
crumbs. Fry in hot oil until
crisp, remove from pan and set
aside. Place onions in skillet,
reduce heat to low, then return
meat to pan. Cook for 7 to 10
minutes.

Serves 4.

—*Stella Zachkewich*

Vermont Style Skillet-Roasted Duck

*"Everything about this is
wonderful," says our Vermont
tester. "The skin is crispy and
sweet, the meat is moist, and
there is a natural congruity to
the flavours."*

4-5-lb. duck
salt & pepper
3 'MacIntosh' apples
   (1 whole; 2 peeled, cored
   & sliced)
1 cup maple syrup
½ cup diced raw bacon
juice of ½ lemon

Remove excess fat from duck,
rub inside with salt and rinse
well in cold water. Place whole
apple inside and truss legs. Rub
with salt and pepper and place
in hot cast-iron skillet. Sear on
all sides until well browned.

Heat oven to 400° F. Roast
duck, in skillet, for about 1½
hours. For the last 30 minutes,
reduce temperature to 325° F
and brush with maple syrup,
two or three times, using about
¼ cup. When duck is done and
drumstick wiggles freely, remove
from skillet and stand on end to
drain fat.

In skillet, cook bacon until
crisp, remove excess fat and add
sliced apples. Toss for a few
seconds, then add remaining
maple syrup and lemon juice.
Cut duck in half and spoon
bacon and apples over duck.

Serves 2.

—*James F. Lehane*

Stuffed Duck with Apple-Cinnamon Glaze

*"This glaze has a very
flavourful, mildly spicy, apple
taste. Its sweetness goes well
with the duck. It is easy to
prepare, as both stuffing and
sauce can be made ahead of
time and refrigerated."*

STUFFING:
1 onion, chopped
1 stalk celery & leaves,
   chopped
1 cooking apple, cored &
   diced
4 Tbsp. butter
2 cups mashed potatoes
1½ cups bread crumbs
1 tsp. savory
½ tsp. marjoram
¾ tsp. salt
¼ tsp. pepper
GLAZE:
½ cup apple juice or cider
¼ cup apple jelly
1 Tbsp. cider vinegar
¼ tsp. cinnamon
¼ tsp. salt
⅛ tsp. dry mustard
1 Tbsp. cornstarch mixed
   with 1 Tbsp. water
4-5-lb. duck, wings tied back

For stuffing: Combine onion,
celery, apple and butter in
saucepan. Sauté until
translucent. Mix with potatoes,
bread crumbs, savory, marjoram,
salt and pepper. Stuff duck.
Bake, uncovered, at 350° F for
2¾ to 3 hours, occasionally
removing excess fat.

Meanwhile, prepare glaze. Heat
juice, ½ cup water, jelly, vinegar,
cinnamon, salt and mustard.
Blend cornstarch mixture slowly
into sauce and cook until
thickened. After about 2¾
hours, brush duck generously
with glaze. Bake for 20 to 25
minutes longer or until duck is
done. Serve with extra sauce.

Serves 3 to 4.

—*Madonna Levesque*

Canard à l'Orange

2 ducks
2 tsp. salt
2 tsp. grated orange peel
½ tsp. thyme
½ tsp. pepper
2 Tbsp. finely chopped onion
¼ tsp. sage
BASTING SAUCE:
wing tips & giblets
2 Tbsp. butter
2 Tbsp. finely chopped onion
1 tsp. dried parsley
1 bay leaf
3 Tbsp. sugar
¼ cup vinegar
1 tsp. grated orange peel
2 Tbsp. cornstarch
½ cup port wine

Remove giblets, wash and dry ducks and cut off wing tips at the first joint. Reserve, with giblets, for sauce. Combine salt, orange peel, thyme, pepper, onion and sage. Rub mixture on skin and inside the cavity of each duck. Tie legs together, then place ducks on rack in roasting pan. Roast at 350° F for 2½ to 3 hours, or until drumstick moves and skin is crisp and golden.

Meanwhile, prepare sauce. Brown wing tips and giblets in butter. Add onion and cook until lightly browned. Add parsley, bay leaf and 3 cups water. Cover and simmer for 1 hour. Strain and cook liquid until reduced to 2 cups. Combine sugar and vinegar and cook until sugar caramelizes to a dark brown. Add stock, orange peel and cornstarch mixed with ¼ cup of port wine. Cook, stirring, until thickened.

About half an hour before ducks are done, remove them from pan. Drain off the fat and add ¼ cup port to pan. Heat and scrape browned particles into liquid. Add this to basting sauce. Replace ducks and baste until done. Serve extra sauce over sliced duck.

Serves 4 to 6.

—Laurie Noblet

Duck with Blueberries & Vegetables

Our Camden East tester raved about this recipe. Although unusual, the flavour combinations were most successful and the appearance of the completed dish was very attractive.

3-lb. duck
salt
1 Tbsp. butter
¼ cup sugar
1 cup orange juice
½ cup red wine vinegar
1 cup blueberries
½ cup small white onions
½ cup baby carrots
1 cup whole green beans
2 potatoes, scooped into balls
butter

Place duck on rack in roasting pan and tie legs and wings to body. Sprinkle with salt, then bake, uncovered, at 500° F for 25 minutes. Reduce heat to 400° F and bake for another 45 minutes.

Melt butter and sugar, stirring until caramelized. Add orange juice and continue cooking until reduced. Add red wine vinegar and continue to reduce until consistency of marmalade. Add blueberries and baste duck once or twice with this.

Steam vegetables until just cooked, then sauté lightly in butter and keep hot.

Carve duck, arranging slices of meat on platter with vegetables around duck. Place sauce in gravy boat and serve.

Serves 2.

—Billie Sheffield

Venison Stroganoff

"Wondering how to prepare the piece of venison you've been presented with need never be a problem again. This simple recipe does not require the extensive marinating often called for when cooking game. Venison should be well trimmed of all fat and strong membrane before use."

1-lb venison steak
flour
4 Tbsp. butter
½ cup chopped onion
1 clove garlic, minced
½ lb. mushrooms, sliced
3 Tbsp. flour
1 Tbsp. tomato paste
1½ cups beef stock
2 Tbsp. white wine
1 cup sour cream
cooked noodles

Cut meat into ¼-inch strips, against the grain, and dust with flour. Heat 2 Tbsp. butter in large skillet. When foam dies down, add meat and brown quickly. Add onion, garlic and mushrooms, adding more butter if necessary. Sauté for 3 to 5 minutes, or until onion and mushrooms are tender. Remove meat mixture and add 2 Tbsp. butter to pan. Blend in flour and tomato paste. Stir in stock and cook, stirring, until thickened. Return meat mixture to skillet. Stir in wine and sour cream. Heat gently but do not boil. Serve over hot buttered noodles.

Serves 4.

—Susan Baker

Breaded Venison Steaks

1½ lbs. boneless venison
    steak
½ cup flour
½ tsp. salt
⅛ tsp. pepper
¾ tsp. paprika
1 egg, lightly beaten
1 Tbsp. milk
1 cup fine dry bread crumbs
2 Tbsp. grated onion
1 clove garlic, crushed
½ tsp. basil
½ tsp. thyme
½ cup oil

Pound steaks to tenderize.
Combine flour, salt, pepper and
¼ tsp. paprika in one bowl, egg
and milk in a second and bread
crumbs, onion, garlic, basil,
thyme and remaining ½ tsp.
paprika in a third.

Dip meat first in flour, then
egg, then bread crumb mixtures.
Be sure entire surface of meat is
covered. Sauté steak in oil to
desired doneness.

Serves 2.

—Dorothy Cage

Beer-Braised Rabbit

1½-2 lbs. rabbit, cut up
salt & pepper
3 Tbsp. oil
3 potatoes, peeled & halved
2 cups carrots, cut into 1"
    pieces
1 onion, sliced
1 cup beer
¼ cup chili sauce
1 Tbsp. brown sugar
½ tsp. salt
1 clove garlic, minced
⅓ cup water
3 Tbsp. flour

Generously season rabbit with
salt and pepper. Heat oil in
10-inch skillet and brown rabbit.
Add potatoes, carrots and onion.
Combine beer, chili sauce,
brown sugar, salt and garlic and
pour over rabbit. Bring to a boil;
cover, reduce heat and simmer
for 45 minutes or until tender.
Remove rabbit and vegetables to
a serving platter and keep warm.

Measure pan juices, adding
additional beer or water if
needed to make 1½ cups liquid.
Return pan juices to skillet.
Blend ⅓ cup water into flour
and stir into juices. Cook,
stirring, until thickened and
bubbly. Continue cooking for 1
to 2 minutes more. Serve with
rabbit.

Serves 4.

—Kristine Mattila

Rabbit, Asparagus & Apple Salad

*Serve this salad on a bed of
greens and top with a few
alfalfa sprouts.*

⅓ cup cooked, chopped
    rabbit
½ cup steamed asparagus,
    cut into 1" pieces, cooking
    water reserved
¼ cup diced apple
DRESSING:
1 Tbsp. cider vinegar
1 Tbsp. oil
1 tsp. honey
salt
chopped parsley

Combine rabbit, asparagus
and apple. Mix together vinegar,
oil, honey, salt and parsley. Toss
with salad, adding a little
asparagus water if needed.

Serves 2.

—Gabriele Klein

Yogurt Fried Rabbit

¼ cup whole wheat flour
1 tsp. thyme
salt & pepper
1 rabbit, cut up
3 Tbsp. oil
½ cup yogurt
1 egg, beaten
1 tsp. basil
⅛ cup heavy cream

Combine flour, thyme, salt and
pepper. Dust rabbit with flour
mixture. Heat oil and fry rabbit
until golden. Cover pan tightly
and simmer for 30 minutes or
until meat is tender. Remove
meat and keep warm.

Combine yogurt and egg, then
stir into pan juices to blend. Add
basil, then cream. Pour over
rabbit and serve.

Serves 4.

—Helen Campbell

Covey Hill Braised Rabbit

Hesitant friends will be converted to the joy of eating rabbit once they have tasted this moist, tender preparation. Fresh herbs provide a flavour bonus, but if only dried are available, use ½ tsp. of each.

1 cup flour
1 tsp. paprika
¼ tsp. salt
¼ tsp. pepper
1 tsp. each chopped savory,
   basil, parsley & thyme
3-4-lb. rabbit, cut up
1 onion, chopped
2 cloves garlic, crushed
⅓ cup oil
1 bay leaf
2-3 carrots, chopped
2 stalks celery, chopped

Mix flour and seasonings in plastic bag. Moisten rabbit with water or milk and shake in flour mixture until each piece is well coated. Brown onion and garlic in oil in heavy skillet. Brown rabbit pieces, adding oil if needed. Place in clay baker or covered casserole dish with bay leaf. Add remaining flour mixture to skillet and add 2 to 3 cups water. Heat and stir until gravy has thickened. Arrange carrots and celery around rabbit, then cover with gravy.

Bake, covered, at 300° F for 2 to 3 hours, turning the pieces every 45 minutes or so. More liquid may be added if gravy becomes too thick. Uncover for the last half hour of cooking. Remove bay leaf before serving.

Serves 4.

—E. Ransom Hodges

Herbed Rabbit

Similar in aroma to gin, juniper berries are prized for seasoning game and bean dishes.

MARINADE:
3 Tbsp. olive oil
3 Tbsp. red wine vinegar
1 onion, sliced
8 peppercorns
8 juniper berries, crushed
1 tsp. rosemary
1 tsp. salt
¼ cup butter
½ cup chopped ham or bacon
2 onions, sliced
1 cup chopped celery
1 cup sliced carrots
3 Tbsp. flour
2 cups rabbit or chicken
   stock
¼ cup apricot jelly
¼ cup white wine
1 tsp. lemon juice
1 rabbit, cut into 8 pieces

Combine marinade ingredients. Add rabbit and marinate overnight. Drain and dry rabbit pieces, saving marinade.

Melt butter and fry rabbit until browned, then remove and set aside. Fry ham, onions, celery and carrots until onions are limp — 8 minutes. Add flour, stirring well. Remove from heat and stir in marinade. Return to heat, bring to a simmer and add rabbit and stock to cover.

Cover and cook over low heat for 2½ to 3 hours or until tender. Stir in jelly, wine and lemon juice.

Serves 4.

—Gabriele Klein

Michigan Dutch-Style Rabbit

Despite its simplicity, this dish is full of flavour. Serve over mashed potatoes.

1 cup flour
salt & pepper
1 rabbit, cut into
   serving-sized pieces
¼ cup butter
½ tsp. thyme
1 cup heavy cream

Combine flour and salt and pepper in paper bag. Place one piece of rabbit in bag at a time and shake to coat completely. Melt butter in deep, heavy skillet that has a lid, and brown meat on both sides. Sprinkle with thyme and add cream. Cover and simmer over very low heat for about 1½ hours or until tender. If cream gets too thick, stir in a little water.

Serves 4.

—Teresa Carel

Meat

Sauté of Veal
with Herbs

2 lbs. veal, cut into 1½" cubes
Salt & pepper
2 Tbsp. butter
2 Tbsp. oil
½ lb. mushrooms, sliced
1 medium onion, chopped
¾ cup chopped celery
1 clove garlic, minced
½ cup dry white wine
¼ cup flour
1½ cups chicken stock
1 cup crushed tomatoes
½ tsp. dried rosemary
2 sprigs parsley
1 bay leaf
2 medium onions, quartered

Sprinkle meat with salt and pepper, heat butter and oil in skillet and brown meat, a few pieces at a time. Set aside.

Add mushrooms, chopped onion, celery and garlic to skillet and cook until onion is soft. Add wine, and cook to evaporate.

Return meat to skillet and sprinkle with flour. Gradually add the stock, stirring to blend. Add the tomatoes, rosemary, parsley and bay leaf and cover. Cook over low heat for about 1 hour. Add the quartered onions and cook 45 minutes longer. Serve sprinkled with parsley.

Serves 4 to 6.

—Shirley Hill

Veal Marengo

½ cup flour
1 tsp. salt
½ tsp. pepper
1 tsp. tarragon
3 lbs. veal, in thin slices or cutlets
½ cup olive oil
1 cup dry red wine
2 cups canned tomatoes
1 clove garlic, crushed
8 mushrooms, sliced
Snipped fresh parsley

Combine flour, salt, pepper and tarragon and dredge meat in it. Save leftover flour. Brown meat in oil in large skillet, then remove to a casserole dish.

Add reserved flour to pan juices, stirring quickly. Add the wine. Cook until sauce is thick and smooth, then pour it over the meat. Add tomatoes, garlic and mushrooms.

Cover and bake at 350° F for 45 minutes or until tender. Garnish with parsley.

Serves 6.

—Cary Elizabeth Marshall

Veal Parmesan

3 Tbsp. butter
½ cup fine bread crumbs
¼ cup grated Parmesan cheese
½ tsp. salt
Dash pepper
1 lb. veal cutlets
1 egg, slightly beaten
1 cup tomato sauce, page 414
1 cup grated mozzarella cheese

Melt butter in 8-inch square baking dish. Combine crumbs, Parmesan cheese, salt and pepper. Cut veal into serving-sized pieces. Dip first into egg and then into crumb mixture. Place in baking dish and bake at 400° F for 20 minutes, turn and bake for another 15 minutes.

Pour tomato sauce over meat and top with mozzarella cheese. Return to oven to melt cheese — about 3 minutes.

Serves 4.

—Mrs. W. Atkins

Jellied Veal Loaf

3 lbs. lean veal with bones
1 qt. water
1 medium onion
1 carrot
1 stalk celery
1 bay leaf
½ tsp. salt
Pepper
2 envelopes unflavoured
    gelatin
1 Tbsp. lemon juice
1 Tbsp. parsley

In a heavy saucepan, place veal, water, onion, carrot, celery, bay leaf, salt and pepper. Simmer until tender — 2 hours. Strain. Cool stock and set aside.

Remove fat and skin from meat and discard. Put meat through food processor or meat grinder.

Soften gelatin in cold stock, then simmer, stirring. Remove from heat and add lemon juice. Add meat and parsley. Pour into a mould which has been lightly greased with vegetable oil. Refrigerate until set.

—Margaret Burrow Robbins

Boeuf en Daube

In this recipe, the beef is cooked in one piece surrounded by vegetables, but the final result is essentially a stew.

2½ lbs. rump of beef
2 Tbsp. butter
2 Tbsp. cooking oil
½ lb. onions, finely sliced
1 lb. carrots, finely sliced
½ lb. salt pork, cubed
1 cup dry white wine
½ cup beef stock
1 tsp. dried basil
½ tsp. dried rosemary
1 bay leaf
½ tsp. curry powder
Salt & pepper
6 black olives

Wrap string around beef to prevent it from falling apart. Brown quickly in butter and oil to seal. Drain and place in a casserole dish. Fry onions, carrots and salt pork until golden brown. Drain and place around beef. Pour wine and stock over everything in the casserole and add seasonings. Bring to a boil, cover, then bake at 325° F for 2½ to 3 hours or until tender. Add olives 30 minutes before serving.

Serves 4 to 6.

—Sheila Bear

Beef Wellington

5 lb. fillet of beef
1 tsp. dry mustard
Fat back to cover beef
4 chicken livers
½ lb. mushrooms
¼ lb. cooked ham
1 small clove garlic
2 Tbsp. butter
⅓ cup sherry
1 Tbsp. meat extract
1 Tbsp. tomato purée
Puff pastry

Sprinkle beef with mustard and cover with fat back. Roast at 400° F for 25 minutes. Cool and remove fat. Sauté chicken livers, chop finely and set aside. Finely mince mushrooms, ham and garlic and sauté for 5 minutes in butter. Add chicken livers, sherry, meat extract and tomato purée. Mix well and remove from heat. Roll out puff pastry in a large enough sheet to enclose the fillet. Lay the fillet in centre of pastry and spoon mushroom mixture over and around it. Carefully wrap pastry around fillet, turning in the ends and pressing all the seams together firmly. Lay fillet seam-side down in a baking dish. Bake at 350° F for 30 to 35 minutes, until crust is lightly browned.

Serves 8 to 10.

—Cary Elizabeth Marshall

Oven Stew

This stew can be assembled in a matter of minutes early in the day and left to simmer, unwatched, until dinner time. To use a slow cooker, start stew 10 to 12 hours before serving time.

2 lbs. stewing beef, cut into
    bite-sized pieces
1 onion, chopped
4 carrots, chopped
4 celery stalks, chopped
½ green pepper, chopped
¼ cup quick-cooking tapioca
¼ cup dry bread crumbs
1 cup mushrooms, chopped
Salt
28-oz. can tomatoes
¼ cup water
½ cup red wine

Combine ingredients, cover and cook for 4 hours at 300° F.

Serves 4 to 6.

Lazy Man's Roast

This recipe is also easily adapted to a slow cooker— simply allow 2 hours more cooking time.

3-4 lb. rump roast
1 cup red wine
1½ tsp. salt
10 whole peppercorns
1½ Tbsp. brown sugar
2 bay leaves
½ tsp. dried sage

Trim most of fat from roast and place meat in a casserole dish. Add wine, salt, peppercorns, sugar and herbs. Cover tightly and cook for 4 hours at 275° F. Remove pan from heat and let meat sit in its liquid for 1 hour before serving.

Serves 6.

—Kathleen Fitzgerald

Yorkshire Pudding

This traditional British accompaniment to roast beef can be prepared as the roast cooks and baked while the roast rests before carving.

¼ cup hot drippings from
    roast
1 egg, well beaten
½ cup milk
½ cup flour
¼ tsp. salt

Divide drippings among 6 large muffin tins.

Beat egg and milk together until light. Gradually beat in flour and salt, and continue beating until batter is smooth.

Pour into muffin tins and let stand for 30 minutes. Bake at 450° F for 15 to 20 minutes.

Serves 6.

—Mrs. W. Atkins

Corned Beef

4-lb. rump roast
8 cups water
4 Tbsp. sugar
2 bay leaves
10 peppercorns
4 tsp. mixed pickling spice
2 cloves garlic, minced
1 cup salt

Place meat in a crock. Combine the remaining ingredients and pour over meat. Weight the meat down in the brine and cover. Let stand in a cool place for 5 to 7 days. Remove meat from brine and place in cold water. Bring to a boil. Remove scum from the surface. Cover and simmer for 5 hours.

Serves 6.

—Pam McFeeters

New England Boiled Dinner

4 lbs. corned beef brisket
Salt to taste
6 medium-sized carrots,
    diced
1 turnip, halved
1 small cabbage, quartered
6 medium potatoes, diced

Cover meat with cold water, bring to a boil, then lower heat and simmer gently for 2 hours.

Skim off fat. Add salt, carrots, turnip, cabbage and potatoes. Continue to cook for 1 more hour.

Serves 6 to 8.

—Shirley Morrish

Marinated Beef

½ cup soya sauce
½ cup lemon juice
2 cloves garlic, crushed
1 lb. chuck, blade or round
    steak cut into thin strips

Mix soya sauce, lemon juice and garlic. Pour over beef and marinate for 4 hours, turning once. Drain and dry beef, reserving marinade. Fry or broil beef at a high temperature, so that it cooks quickly.

Serve with rice, using marinade as a sauce.

Serves 3 to 4.

—Judy Wuest

Stir-Fried
Meat & Vegetables

1 green pepper, cut in strips
2 stalks celery, cut in strips
1 cup thinly sliced onions
1 cup sliced mushrooms
4 Tbsp. butter
2 cups green beans, cut in
  pieces
½ cup leftover gravy
⅛ tsp. pepper
3 cups cooked meat, cut in
  1-inch pieces
3 Tbsp. soya sauce
2 cups fresh bean sprouts

Brown green pepper, celery, onions and mushrooms in butter. Add green beans and stir gently. Then add remaining ingredients except for the bean sprouts and stir. Heat thoroughly. Stir in bean sprouts when ready to serve.

Serves 6.

—Ruth Anne Laverty

Wine Beef Stew

The flavour of beef simmered slowly in red wine is difficult to surpass. This recipe adds potatoes and carrots to provide a complete meal in one dish.

6 Tbsp. oil
3 lbs. beef chuck, cut into
  ½-inch cubes
1 cup chopped onion
1 cup sliced celery
2 Tbsp. parsley
1 clove garlic, finely chopped
1½ Tbsp. salt
¼ tsp. pepper
⅛ tsp. thyme
1 bay leaf
1 cup tomato sauce, page 414
2 cups beef stock
1 cup dry red wine
6 medium potatoes, diced
6 medium carrots, sliced
1-2 Tbsp. flour
2 Tbsp. cold water

In hot oil, brown beef well on all sides. Remove and set aside. Add onion and celery and sauté until tender — about 8 minutes. Return beef to pan. Add parsley, garlic, salt, pepper, thyme, bay leaf, tomato sauce, beef stock and wine. Bring to a boil. Reduce heat and simmer, covered, for 1¼ hours. Add potatoes and carrots. Simmer, covered, 1 hour longer, or until tender. Remove from heat and skim off fat. Mix flour with cold water and stir into beef mixture. Return to stove and simmer, covered, for 10 minutes.

Serves 6.

—Myrna Henderson

Steak & Kidney Pie

For an unusual version of this traditional dish, add a pint of fresh oysters and a bay leaf.

Pastry for double 9-inch pie
  crust
1½ lbs. sirloin or round steak
1 lb. kidneys
2 tsp. salt
1 tsp. pepper
¼ cup flour
3 Tbsp. butter & 1 Tbsp. oil
1 cup sliced mushrooms
½ cup chopped onion
1½ cups water
¼ cup dry red wine
1 Tbsp. chopped parsley
¼ tsp. thyme
¼ tsp. Worcestershire sauce

Cut steak and kidney into cubes and dry with paper towels. Sprinkle with 1 tsp. salt and ½ tsp. pepper. Toss in a bowl with the flour.

Melt the butter and oil in a pan. Brown a few of the meat cubes at a time and transfer to a large casserole dish.

Stir the mushrooms and onion in the same pan for 2 to 3 minutes, then add to the meat.

Pour the water into the frying pan, bring to a boil, stirring to pick up the residues, and pour into casserole dish. Add wine, parsley, thyme, Worcestershire sauce and the rest of the salt and pepper. Stir gently.

Cover with pastry. Brush with water and bake at 425° F for 30 minutes, reduce heat to 350° and bake for 30 minutes longer.

—Carolyn Hills

Swiss Steak

¼ cup flour
1 tsp. salt
1 lb. round steak
3 Tbsp. oil
1½ cups tomato sauce
1½ cups water
1 medium onion, sliced
1½ cups sliced carrots
1½ cups Brussels sprouts
1 tsp. salt
1 tsp. parsley
1 tsp. Worcestershire sauce
Dash pepper & garlic powder

Combine flour and salt. Cut meat into serving-sized pieces and coat with flour mixture. Brown in oil in large frying pan.

Reduce heat and add remaining ingredients. Cover and simmer for 1½ hours or until meat is tender.

Serves 4.

—Helen Eagles

Boeuf à la Creole

This beef dish is delicious with saffron rice and a tossed green salad.

4 Tbsp. olive oil
2 onions, peeled & sliced
1½ lbs. stewing beef
1 Tbsp. tomato sauce, page 414
1 clove garlic, sliced
1 sprig thyme
1 sprig parsley
Few pinches saffron

Pour olive oil into heavy casserole dish and top with onions. Cut beef into serving-sized pieces and place on top of onions. Add remaining ingredients, cover and simmer for 3 to 4 hours.

Serves 4.

Cornish Pasties

Individual, moon-shaped meat and vegetable pies, pasties are equally delicious hot or cold.

Enough pastry for 2-crust pie
1 lb. stewing beef, cut in small cubes
Salt & pepper
2 medium onions, thinly sliced
4 small carrots, thinly sliced
4 small potatoes, thinly sliced
2 cups sliced turnip

Roll pastry into 4 circles with 7-inch diameters.

On one half of each piece of pastry, place meat, then sprinkle with salt and pepper. Place onions on top of the meat and the other vegetables on top of the onions.

Fold the other half of the pastry over filling and press edges down. Trim with a knife to within ½ inch of the contents. Moisten edges slightly with water and turn over to seal.

Make a small hole in the top and pour in 2 teaspoons of water.

Bake at 450° F for 15 minutes. Reduce heat to 375° and continue baking for another 45 minutes.

Serves 4.

—Elizabeth Mitchell

Barbecued Beef Braising Ribs

3½ lbs. beef braising ribs
3 Tbsp. oil
1 clove garlic, minced
¼ cup white vinegar
1 cup tomato paste
1 cup water
1 Tbsp. Worcestershire sauce
¼ cup brown sugar
½ cup minced onion
½ tsp. salt
¼ tsp. pepper
1 Tbsp. butter

Brown ribs in oil with garlic. Transfer ribs and drippings to roasting pan.

Combine remaining ingredients in a saucepan and simmer for 15 minutes. Pour over ribs and bake, covered, at 350° F for 1½ to 2 hours, stirring after 1 hour.

Serves 6.

—Diane Cane

Boeuf au Vin

¼ lb. bacon, finely chopped
1 clove garlic, finely chopped
1 onion, chopped
6 carrots, cut in spears
1 lb. round, chuck or blade
   steak, cubed
1 tsp. thyme
1 bay leaf
1 cup dry red wine
Parsley, finely chopped
½ lb. mushrooms, sliced

Cook bacon in a heavy frying pan until crisp. Remove with slotted spoon and reserve. Sauté garlic, onion and carrots in bacon fat until slightly browned. Remove and set aside.

Brown beef in remaining bacon fat. Add garlic, onion, carrots and bacon. Sprinkle with thyme and crumbled bay leaf. Add wine. Cover and simmer for 1½ hours. If necessary, add water during cooking. Add mushrooms and parsley and cook for another 10 minutes.

Serves 3 to 4.

—Judy Wuest

Boeuf Bourbonnais

Seasoned flour
2½ lbs. round steak, cubed
2 Tbsp. oil
2 cups beef stock
1 cup red wine
1 bay leaf
1 Tbsp. tomato paste
10-15 small onions
½ lb. mushrooms, halved
1-2 Tbsp. flour
2 Tbsp. water

Place seasoned flour in small bag. Add meat in small amounts and shake to coat. Brown meat in oil.

Add all remaining ingredients except mushrooms, flour and water. Bring to a boil, then turn heat low and cover. Simmer for 1½ hours, or until meat is tender. Cool quickly, uncovered, in the refrigerator.

An hour or so before serving, skim fat from top and heat mixture to a boil. Add mushrooms and thicken with flour mixed with cold water. Cook and stir until thickened.

Serves 8.

—Donna Gordon

Beef Curry

3 lbs. stewing beef, in 1-inch
   cubes
1 cup chopped onion
1 cup chopped apple
3 cloves garlic, minced
½ cup butter
1 Tbsp. turmeric
2 bay leaves, crumbled
1 inch fresh ginger, minced
2 tsp. coriander
2 tsp. cumin
½ tsp. cardamom
½ tsp. ground mustard seed
½ tsp. cinnamon
½ tsp. ground fenugreek
4 hot chilies, crushed
Salt & pepper
3 cups coconut milk

Sauté meat, onion, apple and garlic in the butter. Combine spices and add to meat when well browned. Cook briefly, stirring.

Add coconut milk and simmer until meat is very tender — 3 to 6 hours.

Serve over rice with any or all of: fresh fruit, nuts, chopped celery, green peppers, coconut, raisins and yogurt.

Serves 8 to 10.

—Ingrid Birker

Chinese Beef & Broccoli in Oyster Sauce

1 lb. round steak
2 Tbsp. soya sauce
1 tsp. cornstarch
1 large onion
1 head broccoli
3 Tbsp. oil
1 clove garlic
1 thin slice ginger
3-4 Tbsp. bottled oyster
   sauce
Brown sugar
Salt
½ cup cold water
1 Tbsp. cornstarch

Slice steak very thinly. Place in a bowl with soya sauce, cornstarch and a few drops of water. Mix well and set aside.

Slice onion very thinly. Cut broccoli into small pieces and steam until partly cooked. Drain and set aside.

Heat oil in skillet until very hot. Add garlic and ginger. Cook 1 minute, then remove. Add meat and fry until meat sweats, then add onion and broccoli. Stir-fry until vegetables are crispy-tender.

Stir in oyster sauce, a pinch of brown sugar, salt and ½ cup cold water with 1 Tbsp. cornstarch dissolved in it. Stir and cook until sauce is thickened. Serve with rice.

Serves 4.

—Bryanna Clark

Red Eye Stew

3 lbs. stewing beef, cut into
   1-inch pieces
¼ cup flour
2 Tbsp. salt
1 tsp. pepper
¼ cup oil
4 large onions, sliced
1 clove garlic
12 oz. beer
1 Tbsp. soya sauce
1 Tbsp. Worcestershire sauce
1 Tbsp. tomato paste
½ tsp. thyme
2 bay leaves
2-3 cups tomato juice
3 potatoes, peeled & diced
2 cups peas

Dredge meat in flour mixed with salt and pepper. Brown in hot oil.

Add onions and garlic and cook until onions are transparent. Add beer, soya sauce, Worcestershire sauce, tomato paste, thyme and bay leaves. Bring to a boil, then reduce heat and simmer for 1 hour.

Add tomato juice and simmer for 30 minutes. Add potatoes, cook 20 minutes, then peas, and cook until tender. Remove bay leaves and serve.

Serves 10 to 12.

—Barbara Smith

Hungarian Goulash

Almost any meat can be used in goulash; vegetables or red wine may be added. The one constant is sweet paprika, available from specialty stores.

2 lbs. round steak
¼ cup butter
1½ cups chopped onion
1 cup boiling tomato juice
1 tsp. salt
½ tsp. Hungarian paprika
Cornstarch
6 cups cooked noodles

Cut beef into 1-inch cubes. Melt butter and brown meat on both sides. Add onion and sauté. Add tomato juice, salt and paprika. Cover and simmer for 1½ to 2 hours. Remove meat from pot and keep warm. To thicken gravy, mix cornstarch with a small amount of cold water and stir rapidly into hot gravy. Bring to a boil and cook until desired consistency is reached. Place meat on noodles and pour thickened gravy over all.

Serves 6.

Round Steak with Orange Slices

3 Tbsp. soya sauce
1 clove garlic, minced
1½ lbs. round steak
2 Tbsp. oil
2 onions, sliced & separated into rings
1 large orange, peeled & cut into slices

Blend soya sauce and garlic in large flat baking dish, add steak, cover and marinate in refrigerator several hours or overnight, turning a few times.

Heat oil in large skillet and cook steak for 4 minutes on each side, or until browned. Remove to warm platter.

Add onion and any remaining marinade to skillet and sauté for a few minutes. Cover and simmer for 5 minutes. Add orange slices and heat through. Cut steak crosswise in thin slices and top with orange and onion mixture.

Serves 6.

—Shirley Gilbert

Italian Steak

2 lbs. round steak
1 cup bread crumbs
1 cup Parmesan cheese
2 eggs, beaten
4 Tbsp. cooking oil
¾ cup chopped onion
2 cups tomato sauce, page 414
¼ cup water
¼ tsp. salt
⅛ tsp. pepper
1 tsp. oregano
¼ lb. mozzarella cheese, grated

Trim fat from meat and cut into serving-sized pieces. Combine bread crumbs and Parmesan cheese. Dip meat in egg and then in cheese mixture. Brown on both sides in 2 Tbsp. oil.

Sauté onion in remaining oil until tender — about 3 minutes. Stir in tomato sauce, water, seasonings and bring to a boil. Reduce heat and simmer for 10 minutes, stirring occasionally.

Arrange meat in a shallow baking dish, cover with three-quarters of sauce, spread with mozzarella and add remaining sauce.

Bake at 300° F for 30 to 45 minutes, until meat is tender.

Serves 6.

—John & Leone Lackey

Beef Stroganoff

1½ lbs. round steak, cut in narrow strips
¼ cup flour
4 Tbsp. butter
1 onion, diced
½ cup dry red wine
½ lb. mushrooms, sliced
2 green onions, chopped
1 tsp. salt
¼ tsp. chervil
1 cup sour cream

Dredge meat in flour and brown in butter. Add onion and cook until translucent. Add wine and simmer, covered, for 30 minutes. Add mushrooms, green onions, salt and chervil. Cook 2 to 3 minutes. Stir in sour cream and heat through but do not boil.

Serves 4.

Chili for Twenty

3-3½ lbs. lean ground beef
2 medium onions, chopped
2 medium green peppers, chopped
5 stalks celery, chopped
Salt & pepper
Crushed chilies to taste
15 cups cooked kidney beans
2 28-oz. cans tomatoes

Brown meat, onions, green peppers and celery. Add salt, pepper and chilies and cook for a few minutes. Add kidney beans and tomatoes and simmer for 3 hours. The flavour of this dish improves with 1 or 2 days of ageing.

Serves 20.

—Janice Touesnard

Aberdeen Roll

This chilled roll has the texture of a rough paté. The combination of bacon and ground beef gives an attractive marbled look to the completed dish.

½ lb. ground beef
½ lb. bacon, minced
1 large egg, beaten
1½ cups coarse bread crumbs
Salt & pepper
Pinch dry mustard
Pinch garlic powder
1 shake Tabasco sauce
2 small onions, finely
    chopped

Blend all ingredients together and shape into a roll. Cover tightly with tin foil. Boil for 2 hours. Chill and serve sliced.

—Wendy Wallace

Meat Loaf

2 eggs, slightly beaten
¼ cup milk
¼ cup ketchup
¾ cup onion, minced
¾ tsp. dry mustard
2 tsp. salt
2 cups soft bread crumbs
2 lbs. ground beef

Combine eggs, milk, ketchup, onion, mustard, salt and bread crumbs. Let stand for 10 minutes. Add beef and mix well. Place in loaf pan.

Bake at 350° F for 35 minutes, then lower heat to 325° and bake 1 hour longer.

Serves 8.

—Joanne Ramsy

Spoonbread Chili Pie

This recipe tops a basic chili with a corn meal cheese biscuit.

½ lb. ground beef
1 medium onion, chopped
¼ green pepper, chopped
1 clove garlic, minced
1 tsp. chili powder
1¼ cups canned tomatoes
1½ cups kernel corn
1 tsp. salt
Pepper
2 cups cooked kidney beans
1¼ cups milk
1 Tbsp. butter
½ tsp. salt
¼ cup corn meal
½ cup grated Cheddar cheese
1 egg, beaten

Cook ground beef, onion, green pepper and garlic over medium heat for 8 minutes. Stir in chili powder and cook for another minute.

Stir in tomatoes, corn, salt and pepper. Cover and simmer for 5 minutes. Add kidney beans and cook for another 5 minutes. Turn into casserole dish and set aside.

Scald milk with butter and salt. Gradually add corn meal while stirring. Cook until thickened — 4 minutes. Remove from heat and stir in cheese and egg.

Spread topping over casserole. Bake at 375° F for 35 minutes or until topping has set.

Serves 6.

—Nel vanGeest

Beef & Potato Pie

1 partially baked pie shell
1 large onion, chopped
1 clove garlic, minced
1 stalk celery, chopped
½ cup minced celery leaves
4 Tbsp. oil
2 lbs. ground beef
1½ cups beef stock
2 Tbsp. cornstarch
1 tsp. salt
Dash pepper
Dash Worcestershire sauce
Dash Tabasco sauce
½ tsp. chili powder
1½ cups grated Cheddar
    cheese
8 potatoes, boiled
1 egg, beaten
½ cup milk
⅛ tsp. salt
1 tsp. butter

Cook onion, garlic, celery and leaves in oil until tender. Remove from pan. Cook ground beef until browned and drain. Combine beef, vegetables, stock, cornstarch, salt, pepper, Worcestershire sauce, Tabasco sauce, chili powder and cheese. Simmer until thick, then place in pie shell. Whip potatoes until fluffy. Add remaining ingredients and spread over pie. Bake at 350° F for 30 minutes.

Serves 4 to 6.

—Jaine Fraser

Swedish Meatballs

1 lb. ground beef
1 cup soft bread crumbs
½ cup milk
1 egg, well beaten
2 medium onions, finely
    chopped
2 tsp. salt
⅛ tsp. pepper
½ tsp. nutmeg
Oil
1 cup hot water
1 Tbsp. flour
2 Tbsp. cold water

Mix beef, bread crumbs, milk, egg, onions, salt, pepper and nutmeg. Form into 1-inch balls. Heat a little oil in skillet and brown balls on all sides. Remove and keep warm.

Add hot water to meat drippings and stir. Mix flour and cold water well and add to drippings. Bring to a boil, stirring until thick. Return meatballs to skillet, cover and cook for 30 minutes, adding more water if necessary.

Serves 4 as a main course, 12 as hors d'oeuvres.

—Peter Suffel

Sweet & Sour Meatballs with Sausages

2 onions, chopped
1-2 Tbsp. cooking oil
1 lb. ground beef
1½ cups water
Salt & pepper
1 lb. sausages
1 cup ketchup
4 Tbsp. brown sugar
4 Tbsp. cider vinegar
1-2 tsp. Worcestershire
    sauce

Sauté onions in oil over low heat until transparent. Remove from pan. Mix one-quarter of onions with ground beef, ½ cup water, 1 tsp. salt and pepper. Shape into 1-inch meatballs and brown in pan used for onions. Place in casserole dish. Deglaze pan with 1 cup water, reducing liquid to ⅓ cup. Set aside.

Cut sausages in half crosswise. Brown and place in casserole dish with meatballs.

Combine remaining onions, liquid from pan, ketchup, brown sugar, vinegar, Worcestershire sauce, ½ tsp. salt and pepper. Pour over meat.

Bake at 325° F, covered, for 45 minutes. Remove lid and continue baking for another 15 minutes.

Serves 6 to 8.

—Mrs. Garnet Baker

Tomato Meat Loaf

1½ lbs. ground beef
1 egg, beaten
1 cup fresh bread crumbs or
    wheat germ
1 medium onion, chopped
1¼ tsp. salt
¼ tsp. pepper
1 cup tomato sauce, page 414
2 Tbsp. vinegar
1 cup water
2 Tbsp. brown sugar

Combine beef, egg, bread crumbs, onion, salt, pepper and ½ cup tomato sauce and mix well. Place in loaf pan and bake at 350° F.

Meanwhile, combine remaining tomato sauce, vinegar, water and brown sugar. Pour over meat loaf after it has cooked for 30 minutes, then bake 1 hour more.

Serves 6.

—Laura Poitras

Pita Tacos

Pita bread for 4
½ lb. ground beef
1 small onion, chopped
½ cup kidney or pinto
    beans, mashed
½ tsp. ground pepper
Salt
2-3 Tbsp. chili powder
Dash Tabasco sauce
6-oz. can tomato paste
½ lb. grated Cheddar cheese
Lettuce & tomato

Slit bread to form a pocket and warm in oven. Sauté beef and onion until brown. Drain. Add remaining ingredients except lettuce and tomato. Stuff into bread. Garnish with lettuce and tomato.

Serves 4.

—Melody Scott

Beef Enchiladas

Olive oil
1 lb. ground beef
1 onion, chopped
1 green pepper, chopped
1 tsp. parsley flakes
2 cloves garlic, crushed
¾ tsp. chili powder
½ tsp. cumin
½ tsp. dried chilies
Salt & pepper
½ cup kernel corn
1 tomato, chopped
2-4 Tbsp. sour cream
3½ cups tomato sauce, page 414
1 Tbsp. white vinegar
½ tsp. oregano
½ tsp. basil
½ tsp. rosemary
½ tsp. garlic powder
1 tsp. brown sugar
6 tortillas
2 cups grated Cheddar cheese

In olive oil, fry ground beef, onion and green pepper. Season with ½ tsp. parsley, garlic, ½ tsp. chili powder, ¼ tsp. cumin, chilies and salt and pepper. Add corn, tomato, sour cream and ½ cup tomato sauce. Cook for 15 minutes. Combine remaining ingredients, except for tortillas, to make sauce. Fill tortillas with beef mixture. Cover with sauce and top with cheese. Bake, covered, at 350° F for 45 minutes.

Serves 6.

—Diane Schoemperlen

Shepherd's Pie

1 lb. ground beef or 3 cups
    leftover meat
¼ cup chopped green pepper
¼ cup chopped onion
1 Tbsp. shortening
1 Tbsp. flour
1 tsp. salt
½ tsp. chili powder
Dash pepper
½ cup tomato sauce, page 414
1 cup water
½ cup cooked carrots
½ cup peas
½ cup cooked celery
½ cup chopped mushrooms
3 cups seasoned hot mashed
    potatoes
Paprika

Sauté ground beef, green pepper and onion in shortening until meat is browned and pepper tender. Drain off any excess fat. Sprinkle next four ingredients in. Stir in tomato sauce, water, carrots, peas, celery and mushrooms. Combine well and cook until mixture thickens.

Place mixture in 2-quart casserole dish. Top with potatoes and sprinkle with paprika. Place under broiler to brown, or bake at 425° F for 15 minutes.

Serves 6.

—Mrs. W. Atkins

Cabbage Rolls with Sour Cream

1 large cabbage
1 cup raw rice
1 lb. ground beef
1 large onion, chopped
8 oz. can stewed tomatoes
1 pint sour cream

Peel leaves from cabbage and place in boiling water until limp. Drain and remove centre vein.

Mix together rice, ground beef and chopped onion. Place about 2 Tbsp. of mixture on each cabbage leaf and roll up, envelope fashion. Line baking dish with remaining leaves. Place cabbage rolls in layers and pour the stewed tomatoes over them. Add tomato juice, if necessary, to cover.

Bake at 350° F for approximately 2 hours. Remove from oven and spread sour cream over rolls. Return dish to oven for 5 minutes, then serve.

Serves 4 to 6.

—Paula Gustafson

Chinese Meatballs

1½ lbs. ground beef
½ cup chopped onion
Salt & pepper
3 Tbsp. soya sauce
2 Tbsp. cornstarch
½ cup pineapple juice
2 Tbsp. brown sugar
1 tsp. soya sauce
2 Tbsp. vinegar
1 Tbsp. cornstarch dissolved
   in ⅔ cup water
1 cup pineapple chunks

Combine beef, onion, salt, pepper, 3 Tbsp. soya sauce and 2 Tbsp. cornstarch and shape into balls.

Fry until brown, remove from pan and set aside. Discard all but 2 Tbsp. of drippings.

To drippings add pineapple juice, brown sugar, 1 tsp. soya sauce and vinegar. Thicken with cornstarch mixture. Add pineapple and meatballs and cook until heated through.

Serves 4.

—Velma Hughes

Beef Noodle Bake

1 lb. ground beef
¼ cup butter
2 onions, thinly sliced
1 stalk celery, chopped
1 clove garlic
1½ tsp. salt
⅛ tsp. pepper
1½ tsp. chili powder
6-oz. can tomato paste
1 cup tomato sauce, page 414
2 cups water
2 cups uncooked noodles
1½ cups shredded Cheddar
   cheese

Brown meat in butter, then add onions, celery and garlic. Fry until onions are translucent. Add remaining ingredients except for noodles and cheese. Cover and simmer for 30 minutes. Remove garlic.

In a greased 2-quart casserole dish, layer the ingredients: first, half the noodles, then half the meat mixture, and finally one-third of the cheese. Repeat.

Bake at 325° F for 30 to 35 minutes. Sprinkle with remaining cheese and brown under broiler.

Serves 4 to 6.

—Maud Doerksen

Crustless Pizza

1 lb. minced beef
¼ cup bread crumbs
½ tsp. garlic salt
¼ tsp. pepper
⅔ cup milk
⅓ cup minced onion
1½ cups tomato sauce, page
   414
¼ tsp. oregano
¾ cup sliced mushrooms
1½ cups grated cheese

Combine minced beef, bread crumbs, garlic salt, pepper, milk and onion. Flatten mixture into a greased 9-inch square pan. Cover with tomato sauce. Sprinkle with oregano. Distribute mushrooms evenly over sauce, then top with grated cheese.

Bake at 400° F for 30 to 45 minutes.

—Heather Rochon

Cheese Stuffed Meatballs

1½ lbs. medium ground beef
¾ cup fine bread crumbs
1 egg, lightly beaten
1 tsp. salt
1 small onion, minced
4 tsp. Worcestershire sauce
¼ lb. Cheddar cheese, cubed
12 slices bacon, cut in half

Combine beef, bread crumbs, egg, salt, onion and Worcestershire sauce. Roll into 24 small balls and push a cube of cheese into the centre of each one. Wrap a bacon slice around each meatball.

Place on a broiler pan and bake at 375° F for 20 to 25 minutes.

—Margaret Bezanson

Baked liver

1 lb. liver, sliced
⅓ cup flour
Salt & pepper
½ tsp. dry mustard
1 large onion, sliced
8-10 slices bacon
1½ cups tomato juice
1 Tbsp. ketchup

Coat liver slices in flour mixed with salt, pepper and mustard. Place in baking dish and cover with sliced onion and bacon. Mix together tomato juice and ketchup and pour over meat. Bake at 300° F for 1 hour.

Serves 3 to 4.

—Albert Sauer

Polynesian Liver

2 lbs. liver, cut in strips
⅔ cup pineapple juice
4 Tbsp. tomato paste
1 Tbsp. soya sauce
2 Tbsp. brown sugar
½ cup water
1 onion, sliced into rings
2 Tbsp. cornstarch dissolved
   in ¼ cup cold water
1 green pepper, cut in strips
1½ cups pineapple chunks

Combine liver, pineapple juice, tomato paste, soya sauce, brown sugar, water and onion in frying pan. Bring to a boil and simmer for 3 minutes.

Add cornstarch dissolved in water and cook until thickened. Add green pepper and pineapple, cover, lower heat and simmer for 5 minutes.

Serves 4.

—Catherine Cole

Venetian Liver

1 Tbsp. flour
1 tsp. salt
¼ tsp. pepper
1 tsp. paprika
1 lb. beef liver, cut in strips
1 Tbsp. vegetable oil
2 medium onions, sliced
1 stalk celery, chopped
1 green pepper, cut in strips
1 tomato, cut in wedges
¾ cup beef stock
¼ tsp. basil

Put flour, salt, pepper and paprika in a bag and coat liver strips by shaking them in the flour mixture. Sauté liver in oil in a large frying pan, about 3 minutes on each side. Remove to serving platter and keep warm in oven.

Sauté onions, celery and green pepper until soft and golden. Add tomato and cook for another 2 minutes. Arrange vegetables on top of liver.

In the frying pan, combine stock and basil, and bring to a boil. Simmer, uncovered, for about 2 minutes. Pour over liver and serve at once.

Serves 4.

—Diane Wilson-Meyer

Sautéed Lemon Liver

1 lb. liver, thinly sliced
½ cup milk
⅓ cup butter
3 onions, sliced
¼ cup flour
¼ tsp. paprika
¼ tsp. salt
1 peeled & cored apple, cut
   in thin wedges
1 green pepper, cut in thin
   strips
½ lemon

Cover liver with milk and refrigerate for at least 2 hours or as long as overnight. Drain.

Melt butter in a large frying pan. Add onions and cook until soft. Remove from pan. Lightly coat liver with a mixture of flour, paprika and salt. Cook in hot butter until lightly browned. Return onions to pan, along with apple and green pepper. Sprinkle lightly with about 1 Tbsp. of lemon juice. Cover and cook for 5 minutes, or until pepper is done as you like it.

Serves 4.

—Diane Wilson-Meyer

Orange Pork

2 lbs. pork tenderloin, cut
  into 6 pieces
½ cup flour
¼ cup oil or bacon drippings
Salt & pepper
2 large onions, chopped
½ lb. mushrooms, sliced
3 Tbsp. flour
2 cups orange juice

Coat pork with ½ cup flour,
then brown in oil. Sprinkle with
salt and lots of pepper. Remove
to shallow casserole dish,
reserving pan drippings. To pan
drippings, add onions and cook
lightly. Add mushrooms and stir
briefly. Sprinkle with 3 Tbsp.
flour and mix. Gradually add
orange juice, stirring constantly,
to make a smooth sauce. Taste
and adjust seasoning. Pour
sauce over pork and cover with
foil. Bake at 350° F for 1 hour,
checking occasionally. Add more
juice if necessary. Serve,
garnished with orange segments,
strips of orange rind or fresh
mint.

Serves 6.

—Nita Hunton

Jager Schnitzel

*This pork in mushroom and
cream sauce dish can also
make use of veal.*

2 10-oz. pork fillets
1 Tbsp. seasoned flour
3 Tbsp. oil
½ cup butter
½ lb. mushrooms, sliced
1 Tbsp. flour
4 Tbsp. chicken stock
4 Tbsp. dry white wine
Pinch grated nutmeg
Salt & pepper
4 Tbsp. whipping cream

Halve each fillet lengthwise,
leaving attached at one side.
Open out and pound until flat
and thin.

Toss in seasoned flour, then
fry gently in 2 Tbsp. oil and ¼
cup butter until golden brown.

Meanwhile, gently fry
mushrooms in remaining butter
and oil. Add flour and cook for 2
minutes. Gradually add stock,
wine and seasonings, stirring all
the time. Bring to a boil, and
cook gently for 2 to 3 minutes,
stirring. Remove from heat and
stir in cream.

Pour sauce over meat.

Serves 4.

—Sheila Bear

Braised Liver
with Vegetables

1 lb. liver, ½ inch thick
¼ cup flour
Salt & pepper
4 Tbsp. cooking oil
1 onion, diced
2 raw carrots, diced
6 raw potatoes, sliced ¼ inch
  thick
1 cup tomato juice
1 cup water or vegetable stock

Cut liver into 1-inch squares.
Roll in flour seasoned with salt
and pepper. Heat oil in heavy
frying pan and brown liver in it.
Add onion and cook briefly. Add
carrots, potatoes, tomato juice
and water. Cover and simmer
gently for 1 hour, adding water if
necessary.

Serves 4 to 6.

Apple & Pork Chop
Bake

4-6 pork chops
4-6 apples, cored & chopped
4-6 onions, peeled & thinly
  sliced
¼ cup brown sugar
2 Tbsp. cinnamon
Water
Butter

Presoak clay baker for 20
minutes. Salt chops, then layer
half of each of the following:
apples, onions, chops, sugar and
cinnamon in baker. Repeat. Pour
in ¼ cup water and dot with
butter.

Cover and bake at 400° F for 1
hour, then uncover and bake for
10 more minutes.

Serves 4 to 6.

—Dorothy Malone

Pork Chop &
Potato Casserole

4 shoulder pork chops
3 cups sliced potatoes
½ onion, sliced
4 tsp. flour
1 tsp. salt
¼ tsp. pepper
1¼ cups milk

Brown chops in frying pan.
Arrange potatoes and onion in
layers in greased casserole dish.
Sprinkle with flour and
seasonings. Top with chops, add
milk and cover.

Bake at 350° F for 45 minutes,
or until tender. Uncover and
continue baking until brown.

Serves 4.

—Maureen Johnson

Pork Chops &
Olives Marsala

¼ cup flour
1 tsp. salt
¼ tsp. pepper
4 shoulder pork chops
1 clove garlic, halved
3 Tbsp. olive oil
½ cup water
½ cup Marsala wine
½ cup sliced pimento stuffed
  olives

Combine flour, salt and
pepper. Rub pork chops with
garlic and dredge in flour
mixture.

Heat oil in a skillet. Brown
chops well on both sides. Pour
water over meat. Reduce heat,
cover tightly and simmer 30
minutes. Add the wine and olives
and continue cooking for
another 30 minutes.

Serves 4.

—Dee Lowe

Italian Pork Chops

1 egg
3 Tbsp. cold water
3 Tbsp. fine bread crumbs
3 Tbsp. grated Parmesan
  cheese
4 pork chops
Flour, seasoned with salt &
  pepper

Beat egg with cold water.
Combine bread crumbs and
cheese. Coat chops with flour.
Dip them into the egg mixture,
then into bread crumbs and
cheese. Place on wax paper and
let stand for 1 hour. Cook in oil,
10 minutes on each side.

Serves 2 to 4.

—Helen Potts

Barbecued
Loin Pork Chops

4 pork chops
3 Tbsp. seasoned flour
2 Tbsp. oil
¼ cup chopped onion
¼ cup diced celery
2 Tbsp. brown sugar
Juice of half a lemon
½ tsp. salt
⅛ tsp. red pepper
½ tsp. dry mustard
½ tsp. chili powder
½ cup water
1 cup tomato sauce

Coat chops in seasoned flour
and brown in oil. Place in
ovenproof dish. Mix remaining
ingredients together and pour
over meat. Cover and bake at
350° F for 1 hour, basting
occasionally.

—Maud Doerksen

Curried Pork
with Peaches

4-6 lean loin chops
¼ cup butter
1 medium onion, minced
¼ cup flour
1 tsp. salt
1 tsp. curry powder
2 cups milk
1 cup button mushrooms
3 peaches, halved

Brown chops in small amount
of butter. Remove from pan, add
remaining butter and sauté
onion. Add flour, salt and curry
powder to butter and onions to
form a paste. Slowly add milk
and stir until smooth. Add
mushrooms and simmer 2
minutes over low heat. Arrange
pork in large shallow pan which
has a tightly fitting lid. Place half
a peach on each chop and pour
curried sauce over. Bake at 350°
F, covered, for 45 minutes, then
for 15 minutes, uncovered.

Serves 4 to 6.

—Judy Parfitt

Pork Stew with Apples & Potatoes

1 lb. lean pork, cut into
   1-inch cubes
2 Tbsp. butter
½ tsp. paprika
¼ tsp. pepper
2 tsp. salt
Dash sage
1 clove garlic, crushed
2 Tbsp. flour
3 onions, sliced
4 large potatoes, cubed
2 apples, cored & cut up
2 Tbsp. dry sherry
1½ cups chicken stock

Brown pork in heavy pot with butter. Add paprika, pepper, salt, sage and garlic and stir well. Sprinkle with flour and add onions, potatoes, apples, sherry and stock.

Cover and simmer 40 minutes.

Serves 4.

—Bryanna Clark

Stuffed Pork Chops

Home butchered pork chops are ideal for this recipe — they are thick enough to allow for stuffing.

4 thick loin pork chops
1 cup dry bread crumbs
¾ cup finely chopped apple
½ tsp. salt
2 Tbsp. minced onion
¼ tsp. sage
2 Tbsp. melted butter
Salt & pepper

Combine all ingredients except chops and moisten slightly with a little water. With a sharp knife, cut pockets in the pork chops. Fill loosely with stuffing, then fasten with toothpicks.

Flour the chops and brown well in hot fat in a skillet. Sprinkle each side with salt and pepper. Add ¼ cup water, cover the pan tightly and simmer over low heat until very tender, about 1½ hours.

Serves 4.

—Sherrie Dick

Pork & Snow Peas

1 tsp. sugar
1 Tbsp. cornstarch
2 Tbsp. soya sauce
3 Tbsp. water
3 Tbsp. oil
1 clove garlic, minced
2 slices candied ginger
Dash salt
1 lb. pork loin, sliced
⅓ lb. snow peas
2 Tbsp. dry sherry
½ cup chicken broth

In a small bowl combine sugar, cornstarch, soya sauce and water and set aside.

Heat 1 Tbsp. oil in wok, add garlic, ginger and salt. Cook, stirring, until garlic is golden. Add pork. Stir-fry until lightly browned and cooked through. Remove to a bowl.

Reheat wok. Add 2 Tbsp. oil, then snow peas and stir-fry until peas turn darker green, about 1 minute. Add meat, sherry and broth. Stir in soya sauce mixture. Cook just until broth is thickened.

Serves 4.

—Barbara J. Spangler

Scrapple

Scrapple, a meatloaf originally made with pork trimmings and scraps, can be served hot with vegetables as a main course, or cold in a sandwich.

1½ lbs. fresh pork shoulder
4 cups cold water
1 tsp. salt
½ tsp. black pepper
1¼ cups corn meal
⅓ cup flour
1 tsp. or more crushed sage
Dash oregano
Dash cayenne pepper

Simmer the pork in the water for about 2 hours. Remove meat from the stock, shred it and set aside.

Strain stock, reserve 1 cup and set aside. Continue to boil the rest of the stock.

In a bowl, combine the rest of the ingredients, then add the cup of reserved stock slowly, while stirring rapidly to avoid lumps.

Add corn meal mixture and shredded meat to the boiling stock. Simmer over low heat for 1 hour, stirring now and again, so that it does not stick to the pan.

Pour into a greased loaf pan and chill. Cut into thin slices and brown on both sides in bacon drippings.

Makes 2 pounds.

—Cary Elizabeth Marshall

Quebec Tourtière

In French Canadian families, this traditional meat pie is eaten hot after midnight mass on Christmas Eve.

Lard pastry for double-crust 9-inch pie
1 lb. lean ground pork
1 medium onion, chopped
Salt & pepper
½ tsp. savory
Pinch ground cloves
¼ cup boiling water

Mix meat, onions and spices in a saucepan. Add boiling water. Simmer, uncovered, for 20 minutes, stirring occasionally. Skim off any fat.

Roll out half the pastry and line a 9-inch pie plate. Place filling in pie plate and cover with the remaining pastry. Prick with a fork. Bake at 375° F for 30 minutes or until golden.

Serve piping hot topped with homemade tomato ketchup or chili sauce.

Serves 4 to 6.

—Nicole Chartrand

Gefullte Paprika

These stuffed peppers may use either green or yellow peppers.

6 green or yellow bell peppers
2 lbs. ground pork
1 cup cooked rice
Salt & pepper
Marjoram
Paprika
¼ cup chopped onion
¼ cup shortening
¼ cup flour
48-oz. can tomato juice

Hollow out peppers and rinse. Mix ground pork with rice, salt, pepper, herbs and onion. Stuff meat mixture into peppers and set aside.

In large, heavy pot, melt shortening and stir in flour until thick. Add tomato juice and cook and stir until thickened and smooth.

Add peppers. Cover and cook slowly, stirring occasionally, 20 to 30 minutes.

Serves 6.

—Kris Brown

Garlic Spareribs

2-3 cloves garlic, crushed
2 Tbsp. brown sugar
½ cup honey
¼ cup soya sauce
¼ cup vinegar
6 lbs. pork spareribs, cut
   into 2-inch pieces
1 cup tomato sauce
2 tsp. salt

In a large bowl, combine garlic, sugar, honey, soya sauce and vinegar. Add spareribs and marinate in refrigerator for several hours or overnight, turning meat several times. Drain and reserve marinade.

Combine marinade with tomato sauce and salt in a heavy saucepan. Simmer for 10 minutes.

Bake ribs at 400° F for 30 minutes. Reduce heat to 325° and bake 1 hour, basting frequently with sauce.

Serves 10 to 12.

—Margaret Silverthorn

Terrine of Pork

Terrine originally meant the dish in which patés were cooked; it has come to mean the paté itself.

3-4 strips bacon
1 lb. lean pork, minced
8 oz. pork sausage meat
4 oz. rolled oats
Rind & juice of 1 lemon
Salt & pepper
½ Tbsp. sage
1 grated onion
1 egg, beaten

Stretch bacon to line a loaf pan. Combine remaining ingredients. Press meat mixture into pan and level the top.

Cover with foil, set in a large shallow baking dish containing 1 inch of water and cook 1½ hours at 350° F.

Remove from oven and pour off grease but leave loaf in pan. Weight down the top and leave overnight before removing from pan.

Serve cold, sliced.

—Wendy Wallace

Sweet & Sour Spareribs

2 lbs. spareribs
⅓ cup flour
1 tsp. dry mustard
⅓ cup soya sauce
1 tsp. vegetable oil
1 clove garlic, crushed
1 inch fresh ginger
⅓ cup vinegar
1½ cups water
½ cup brown sugar
1 tsp. salt
1 small onion, diced

Chop ribs into small pieces. Mix flour, mustard and soya sauce and marinate ribs in this mixture for 30 minutes to 1 hour.

Heat oil. Add crushed garlic and ginger. Brown ribs, add vinegar, water, sugar, salt and onion. Simmer for 1 hour.

Serves 4 to 6.

—Pieter Timmermans

Stuffed Spareribs

2 racks pork ribs
Garlic powder
½ cup wild rice
¼ cup chopped onion
½ cup chopped mushrooms
½ apple, peeled & chopped
¼-½ tsp. Worcestershire
   sauce
¼ tsp. pepper
1 tsp. basil

Roll ribs into a circle, tie with string and sprinkle inside and out with garlic powder. Set aside.

Cook rice in boiling water for 20 minutes. Drain. Add remaining ingredients and mix well. Loosely stuff into ribs.

Bake at 375° F for 1½ hours.

Serves 2.

—Cheryl Lockhart

Ginger Pork Roll

Although this dish requires a fair amount of preparation, the final flavour of pork, crabmeat and seasonings encased in a rich cream cheese pastry makes it all worthwhile.

1 cup butter
4 oz. cream cheese
½ tsp. salt
2 cups flour
1 egg yolk
2 tsp. cream
1 lb. ground pork
½ cup flaked crabmeat
1 tsp. salt
½ cup minced water
    chestnuts
2 green onions, minced
2 tsp. grated ginger root
2 Tbsp. soya sauce
1 clove garlic, crushed
1 egg
¼ cup fine dry bread crumbs

Beat butter, cheese and salt together until completely smooth. Work in flour to make a smooth dough. Flatten in foil to form an 8" x 6" rectangle. Chill overnight. Remove from refrigerator 10 minutes before rolling. Divide into 4 portions, roll each piece between 2 sheets of floured wax paper to form a 9" x 12" rectangle.

Cook and stir pork until white but not dry. Add remaining ingredients, mix well and cool thoroughly.

Cut each pastry rectangle in half lengthwise and spread with filling. From long side, roll tightly like a jelly roll. Moisten edge and press to seal. Place seam-side down on an ungreased cookie sheet. Chill 1 hour. Bake at 375° F for 30 to 35 minutes. Cool and cut into 1-inch slices. Serve hot or cold.

Makes 8 dozen slices.

—Irene Simonson

Stuffed Peppers

There are many ways of preparing stuffed peppers. The fillings can contain everything from pork, as in this recipe, to beef, lamb or seafood. Methods of preparation also vary — these peppers are cooked on top of the stove, but they may also be baked.

2 Tbsp. shortening
¼ cup flour
8-oz. can tomato paste
2 cups stock
Salt
2 small onions, chopped
Celery leaves
¼ cup raw rice
8 green peppers
1 lb. minced pork
Small bunch fresh parsley
1 egg
Salt & pepper
Marjoram

Heat 1 Tbsp. shortening in a deep saucepan and stir in flour until light brown. Add tomato paste and stir until smooth. Add stock, salt, 1 onion and celery leaves, and bring to a boil. Cook over medium heat, stirring occasionally to keep from burning.

In the meantime, cook rice in boiling water until half done, and cool. Seed and core peppers and wash them thoroughly. Sauté remaining onion in the rest of the shortening. Combine meat, onion, parsley, rice and egg in a bowl. Add salt, pepper and marjoram to taste. Mix well and stuff into peppers.

Place peppers in a large saucepan and pour sauce over them. Bring to a boil, cover and cook over medium heat until done — 25 to 30 minutes.

Serves 4.

—Anton Gross

Tangy Pork

2 medium onions, finely
    chopped
2 cups cooked pork, cut in
    cubes
2 medium carrots, cubed
2 cups tomato juice
½ cup chopped cabbage
2 apples, peeled & chopped
¼ cup brown sugar
¼ cup vinegar
½ tsp. salt
½ tsp. pepper
1 tsp. Worcestershire sauce
1 Tbsp. soya sauce

Fry onions in a small amount of oil until golden. Place in a heavy pot with remaining ingredients. Simmer for 45 minutes on top of stove.

Serves 4.

—Louise R. Taylor

Baked Cottage Roll

4 slices cottage roll
4 Tbsp. brown sugar
1 Tbsp. dry mustard
½ cup orange juice

Place slices of meat in baking dish. Combine remaining ingredients and pour over meat. Bake at 350° F for 1 hour, basting once or twice.

Serves 4.

—Paula Gustafson

Ham & Rice Skillet

1 cup cooked ham
1 cup sliced mushrooms
½ onion, finely chopped
2 cloves garlic, crushed
⅓ cup chopped raisins
Butter
½ tsp. paprika
½ tsp. Worcestershire sauce
½ tsp. basil
½ tsp. dry mustard
½ tsp. curry powder
Salt & pepper
1 cup cooked rice
2 eggs, slightly beaten

Sauté ham, mushrooms, onion, garlic and raisins in butter until mushrooms are nearly cooked. Add seasonings and rice. Cook over low heat about 10 minutes. Turn up heat, add eggs and stir-fry until eggs are done.

Serves 2.

—Kynda Fenton

Sausage, Bacon & Tomato Pie

1 lb. sausages
4 slices bacon
1 medium onion, chopped
4 tomatoes
2 Tbsp. flour
Salt & pepper
2 lbs. potatoes, cooked
Butter & milk

Fry sausages, bacon and onion. Place in greased casserole dish. Fry tomatoes and arrange on top of sausage mixture.

Add flour to remaining fat in pan and cook for a minute or two. Make a thick gravy by adding about 1 cup water. Pour on top of meat and tomatoes.

Mash potatoes, adding milk and butter to taste. Spread on top of casserole and dot with more butter. Bake at 400° F for 20 to 30 minutes until golden brown on top.

Serves 4.

—Sheila Bear

Pork Balls in Wine Sauce

1½ lbs. minced pork
8 oz. lean bacon, ground
2 cups fresh bread crumbs
1 large egg
1 tsp. salt
½ tsp. black pepper
½ tsp. ground allspice
2 Tbsp. fresh chopped parsley
1 cup dry sherry
1 cup chicken stock
2 Tbsp. wine vinegar
1 Tbsp. sugar
1 tsp. salt
4 tsp. cornstarch, dissolved
   in 3 Tbsp. water

In a large mixing bowl, combine the pork, bacon, bread crumbs, egg, salt, pepper, allspice and parsley. Using your hands, knead the ingredients until they are well combined. Shape into 12 balls. Place the balls, in one layer, in a large baking dish. Set aside.

In a small saucepan, combine the sherry, stock, vinegar, sugar and salt over low heat, stirring constantly. When the sugar has dissolved, increase the heat to high and bring the mixture to a boil. Reduce the heat to low and stir in the cornstarch mixture. Cook, stirring constantly, until the sauce has thickened slightly.

Remove pan from heat and pour sauce over meatballs. Place meatballs in the oven and bake for 1½ hours, basting occasionally with sauce.

Serves 4.

—Dolores de Rosario

Ham & Potato Casserole

4 or 5 boiled potatoes
¼ cup butter
¼ cup flour
½ tsp. salt
2 cups milk
½ tsp. Worcestershire sauce
2 cups cubed cooked ham
½ cup grated Cheddar cheese

Slice or dice the potatoes and set aside. In a saucepan, melt the butter and add the flour and salt. Stir until blended. Slowly add the milk, stirring constantly, until smooth and thickened. Stir in Worcestershire sauce, potatoes and ham.

Spoon into 1½-quart baking dish. Sprinkle with cheese. Bake at 350° F for 30 to 40 minutes.

Serves 4 to 5.

—Dianne Orlowski

Stuffed Ham

12-lb. ham
2 heads cabbage
2 lbs. kale
2 large onions
1½ small red peppers
Salt & pepper

Wash ham. Cut up vegetables, mix and season to taste. Parboil, saving water for cooking ham.

Make deep slits across top and down sides of ham with sharp knife. Stuff vegetables into slits, piling any leftover mixture on top of the ham.

Sew ham in cheesecloth to hold dressing in place and cook slowly in vegetable water until meat is tender.

—Judy Lord

Ragoût De Pattes

This is a very inexpensive stew, using pork hocks and root vegetables.

2 pork hocks, washed & scraped to remove hair
4 potatoes, chopped
4 carrots, chopped
1 small turnip, chopped
Salt & pepper
4 Tbsp. flour
½ cup water

Put meat in a large saucepan, cover with water and simmer until tender, about 1 hour. Then add vegetables and salt and pepper. Simmer for another hour.

Brown flour in frying pan, being careful not to burn it. Add water to flour and mix well. Pour into meat mixture and cook until broth thickens.

Serves 2 to 4.

—Emilia Ouellette

Chinese Hot Sausages

1 lb. pork sausage links
1 Tbsp. vegetable oil
7½-oz. can tomato sauce
¼ cup brown sugar
1 Tbsp. soya sauce
1 tsp. Worcestershire sauce
¼ tsp. garlic powder
Generous pinch of salt

Prick sausage skin in several places. Heat oil in a frying pan just large enough to hold the sausages. Add sausages and brown evenly. Pour off fat.

Stir remaining ingredients together and pour into frying pan. Roll sausages until coated with sauce. Cover, reduce heat to medium-low and simmer for 20 minutes. Stir occasionally. Serve in crusty rolls, or with rice or baked potatoes.

Serves 4.

—Diane Wilson-Meyer

Weeping Lamb

6-8 lb. leg of lamb
Cloves of garlic, sliced
Salt & pepper
1 tsp. rosemary
8 potatoes, unpeeled & sliced
Butter
2 large onions, sliced
1 cup chicken stock

Pierce lamb at 2-inch intervals and insert slices of garlic. Rub with salt, pepper and rosemary.

Grease a roasting pan and place one layer of potatoes in it. Dot with butter, add another layer of potatoes and the onion. Dot with butter and add chicken stock.

Place lamb on top of this and roast at 325° F for approximately 2 hours.

Serves 8.

—Mary Reid

Head Cheese

Traditionally, this recipe is made using a whole pig head. The substitution of pork hocks provides an easier and tidier method of preparation, but still produces the authentic flavour.

5 pork hocks
2 cloves garlic
3 whole cloves
1 stick cinnamon
2 Tbsp. salt
2 large onions, cut in half
2 large carrots, sliced
½ tsp. pepper

Wash hocks well. Tie in a clean white cotton cloth along with all the remaining ingredients. It is important that the hocks are completely covered by the cloth. Place in a large pot, cover with cold water and bring to a slow boil. Simmer for 3 hours.

Unwrap hocks and discard spices and vegetables. Cut the meat into small pieces or put through a coarse food grinder. Include every piece of meat and skin. Strain the broth, return the meat to it and boil for 10 minutes.

Ladle into straight-sided glass or plastic bowls. Cool and refrigerate. To serve, unmould and garnish with greens. Good with potato salad and coleslaw.

—Aurora Sugden

Herbed Leg of Lamb

Work on this dish must begin 24 hours before it is to be served. Once the marinade is assembled and the lamb placed in it, however, no more labour is required until baking time. The herb combination and the cooking method produce a moist, flavourful leg of lamb.

2 cups red wine
½ cup vinegar
1 cup cooking oil
Parsley
Thyme
4 bay leaves
6 cloves garlic
3 onions, finely chopped
Pinch of nutmeg
2 Tbsp. sugar
1 tsp. salt
6-8 lb. leg of lamb
½ cup finely chopped parsley
1 carrot, finely chopped
1 stalk celery, finely chopped
4 Tbsp. butter
1 cup beef stock
¼ tsp. basil
⅛ tsp. oregano
Salt & pepper

Stir together 1 cup red wine, vinegar, oil, parsley, thyme, bay leaves, 2 cloves garlic (crushed), 2 chopped onions, nutmeg, sugar and salt. Marinate lamb in this mixture for 24 hours, turning frequently.

On day of cooking lamb, make the herb sauce by sautéing parsley, carrot, remaining onion and celery in butter until soft. Place in bottom of roasting pan, along with leftover marinade. Slice remaining garlic into slivers. Pierce the leg of lamb at 3-inch intervals and insert garlic slivers. Roast the lamb at 450° F for 15 minutes. Meanwhile, combine remaining wine, beef stock, basil, oregano, salt and pepper. Pour mixture over lamb, reduce heat to 350° F and continue roasting 15 to 20 minutes per pound. Serve with herb mixture.

Serves 8 to 10.

—Anne Morell

Couscous

This is a traditional North African stew making use of native vegetables.

3 cups couscous (semolina)
1½ tsp. salt dissolved in 1½
   cups cold water
1 Tbsp. oil
½ cup oil
2 lbs. lamb, cut into 2" chunks
3 cups finely chopped onion
1½ Tbsp. salt
1 Tbsp. black pepper
¼ tsp. allspice
2 cinnamon sticks
¾ tsp. turmeric
1 tsp. chopped parsley
4-5 tomatoes, quartered
1 cup raw chick peas, cooked
1 lb. carrots
1 lb. turnips
1 lb. zucchini
½ lb. pumpkin
4 potatoes, peeled & quartered
1 chili pepper
Handful raisins

Spread couscous evenly in large, shallow pan. Sprinkle with salted water and 1 Tbsp. oil, then rub grains between fingers, dropping back into pan until water and oil are completely absorbed. Cover with plastic wrap and set aside for 15 minutes.

Meanwhile, in a deep pot, heat ½ cup oil until light haze forms above it. Add meat, onions, salt and pepper. Fry over high heat for 6 to 8 minutes, until browned. Add spices, parsley, tomatoes, chick peas and 3 cups cold water, and stir until mixture boils. Reduce heat to low and simmer, covered, for 1 hour.

Steam couscous in a large sieve over rapidly boiling water for 20 minutes. Do not cover pot, or couscous will get sticky.

Prepare vegetables: scrape carrots and turnips and cut into 1½-inch lengths. Cut zucchini into quarters. Peel and cut pumpkin into 2-inch pieces.

After meat broth has cooked for 1 hour, add carrots and turnips and cook 30 minutes more, adding more water if necessary.

Half an hour before serving time, add potatoes, zucchini, pumpkin, chili and raisins to lamb broth, bring to a boil and simmer. Steam couscous another 30 minutes. Serve lamb mixture over couscous.

Serves 6.

—Ann Simpson

Hungarian Baked Lamb Chops

6 loin lamp chops, 1½
   inches thick
1½ tsp. salt
½ tsp. freshly ground pepper
1 tsp. paprika
2 cups sliced green onions
½ cup sour cream
3 Tbsp. grated Parmesan
   cheese

Brown chops on both sides in a skillet and pour off fat. Place in a shallow casserole dish and season with salt, pepper and paprika, spread green onions over them and add the sour cream.

Bake at 350° F for 30 minutes. Sprinkle with cheese and bake 30 minutes longer.

Serves 6.

—Brenda Eckstein

Navarin d'Agneau

This lamb stew uses carrots and turnip, but other root vegetables may be substituted.

2 lbs. shoulder of lamb, cut
   into chunks
2 Tbsp. butter
1 large onion, chopped
1½ lbs. carrots, sliced
1 lb. turnip, peeled & diced
1 clove garlic, crushed
1 Tbsp. tomato purée
1 Tbsp. flour
3 cups chicken stock
1 bay leaf
Pinch thyme
Salt & pepper
8 small potatoes, peeled

Fry lamb in butter until golden. Discard all but 1 Tbsp. of fat. Stir in onion, 2 slices carrot, 2 pieces turnip, garlic, tomato purée and flour. Gradually add stock, stirring all the time. Add bay leaf, thyme and seasonings, cover and simmer gently for 1½ hours.

Add remaining vegetables and cook for a further 25 to 30 minutes or until cooked.

Serves 4 to 6.

—Sheila Bear

Lamb with Green Peppers

2 lbs. lamb
Salt & pepper
Flour
3 Tbsp. olive oil
2 cloves garlic
1¼ cups white wine
6 green peppers
½ lb. tomatoes
1 bay leaf

Cut meat into 1-inch pieces, sprinkle with salt and pepper and dust with flour.

Heat oil in wide-mouthed casserole dish, crush in peeled garlic, add meat and fry until lightly browned, stirring frequently. Add wine, and boil rapidly until reduced by a third.

Cut peppers lengthwise into quarters, discard seeds and pith and rinse in cold water. Peel and quarter tomatoes. Add peppers, tomatoes and bay leaf to lamb. Cover and simmer gently for about 45 minutes. Check seasoning and serve.

Serves 4.

—Sheila Bear

Spiedies

A shish kebob of Italo-American origin, spiedies (pronounced speedees) come in varying degrees of spiciness, and this recipe may be altered to suit.

1 lb. beef, lamb or pork
¼ cup red wine vinegar
¼ cup vegetable oil
3 Tbsp. lemon juice
1 Tbsp. oregano
1 Tbsp. minced onion
½ tsp. minced garlic flakes
¼ tsp. dried mint flakes
¼ tsp. salt
⅛ tsp. pepper

Cut meat into bite-sized pieces and set aside. Combine remaining ingredients and mix well. Let stand for 10 minutes, then pour over meat. Cover and refrigerate overnight. Thread meat onto metal skewers and broil over hot charcoal fire for about 10 minutes for beef and a little longer for lamb or pork, turning often.

Serve on buttered Italian bread.

Serves 2.

—Melchiore Curatolo

Lamb Korma

A spicy lamb casserole, this dish is similar to curry.

½ tsp. saffron
¼-⅓ cup boiling water
½ cup unsalted cashews
3 green chilies
1½ Tbsp. chopped fresh ginger
1-inch stick cinnamon
½ tsp. cardamom seed
6 cloves
3 cloves garlic
2 tsp. coriander
½ tsp. cumin
1¼ cups water
½ cup ghee (clarified butter)
1 large onion, sliced
1 tsp. salt
1¼ cups yogurt
1 lb. lamb, cut into chunks
1 Tbsp. chopped fresh coriander
2 tsp. lemon juice

Place saffron in a bowl, pour water over it and let sit for 10 minutes. Put cashews, chilies, ginger, cinnamon, cardamom, cloves, garlic, coriander, cumin and water into blender. Blend until smooth — about 2 minutes.

Heat ghee and fry onion until golden. Stir in salt, blended spices and yogurt. Cook gently for 5 minutes, stirring occasionally. Add meat and toss to coat all sides. Add saffron mixture and cook gently, covered, for 20 minutes. Add fresh coriander and cook 10 minutes more. Add lemon juice and serve.

—Sheila Bear

Dolmathes with Augolemono Sauce

A Greek variation of cabbage rolls, dolmathes traditionally make use of grape leaves, but maple may be substituted.

48 edible leaves, grape or
    maple
2 cups cooked rice
1 lb. cooked lamb, finely
    chopped
Mint
Rosemary
Olive oil
3 large eggs
½ cup lemon juice
1 cup hot chicken stock
Salt & pepper

If using fresh leaves, blanch and cut woody stems off. If using tinned leaves, wash well.

Mix rice, meat and seasonings and add oil to make mixture stick together. Place leaves shiny side down, put 2 Tbsp. stuffing at base and roll, tucking in sides. Place rolls seamside down in large pot. Add 1 cup water and place a weight on top. Simmer until heated through.

Meanwhile beat eggs until thick and foamy, then add lemon juice slowly. Add hot chicken stock in a steady stream and season with salt and pepper. This sauce will thicken as it is being beaten. Serve over dolmathes.

Serves 6.

—Glenn Countryman

Veal Rolls Divan

3 slices bacon
1½ cups dry herbed dressing
¼ cup butter
6 thin veal steaks, pounded
Salt
1 Tbsp. oil
2 heads broccoli, chopped &
    parboiled
½ cup chicken stock
1 cup cream of mushroom
    sauce (page 132)
½ cup cooked shrimp

Cook bacon until crisp and drain. Combine dressing and butter and crumble bacon into mixture.

Sprinkle veal with salt. Place ⅓ cup dressing on each steak, roll and tie securely. Heat oil in skillet and brown veal. Arrange veal and broccoli in greased, shallow baking dish.

Pour chicken stock over casserole, cover and bake at 350° F for 1 hour. Combine mushroom sauce with shrimp in saucepan and heat through. To serve, remove ties from meat and pour sauce over casserole.

Serves 6.

—Tracy Cane

Massale Darh Kababs

This is a shish kabab variation which makes use of ground meat and is coated with yogurt.

1 Tbsp. green ginger
1 Tbsp. turmeric
1 Tbsp. coriander
3 peppercorns
1 tsp. chili powder
Salt
2 lbs. lamb or beef, ground
3 medium onions, chopped
2 Tbsp. butter
Yogurt
2 Tbsp. rice flour

Grind well all spices and salt. Combine with meat and onions and mix thoroughly. Add half the butter and enough yogurt to moisten. Mix well.

Roll into sausage shapes, powder lightly with flour and dip in yogurt. Fry in remaining butter in a heavy skillet. Handle very gently. When kababs are set, turn them over to brown on the other side.

Serves 4.

—Betty Ternier Daniels

Seasoned Flour

Particularly tasty for coating pork chops, this coating can be quickly assembled and stored for several months.

2 cups flour
2 Tbsp. salt
1 Tbsp. celery salt
1 Tbsp. pepper
2 Tbsp. dry mustard
4 Tbsp. paprika
2 Tbsp. garlic powder or salt
1 tsp. ginger
½ tsp. thyme
½ tsp. sweet basil
½ tsp. oregano

Sift all ingredients together and store in refrigerator. Use to coat pork chops.

Makes 2½ cups.

—J. Hall-Armstrong

Barbecue Sauce

5½-oz. can tomato paste
½ cup vinegar
1½ Tbsp. dry mustard
3 Tbsp. corn syrup
½ tsp. garlic powder
1 tsp. onion powder
½ tsp. celery salt
⅛ tsp. cayenne pepper
½ tsp. salt
1 Tbsp. brown sugar

Mix all ingredients and store in covered container in refrigerator.

—Angela Denholm

Meat Coating

This recipe provides a healthy, homemade alternative to commercial Shake 'n' Bake.

½ cup wheat germ
½ cup corn meal
1 cup triticale flour
Salt & pepper

Mix until well blended and store in covered container until ready to use.

—Angela Denholm

Brown Sugar Mustard

½ cup lemon juice
¼ cup corn oil
⅛ tsp. Tabasco sauce
½ tsp. coarse salt
¼ tsp. black pepper
¼ tsp. marjoram, crushed
1½ cups well-packed brown sugar
4 oz. dry mustard

Combine lemon juice, oil, Tabasco sauce, salt, pepper, marjoram and brown sugar in blender. Cover and blend at high speed for about 12 seconds, or until the ingredients are thoroughly mixed.

Add about half of the mustard, cover and blend at medium speed for 10 seconds, or until smooth. Repeat with remaining mustard, adding it in 3 parts.

Spoon mustard into jars and seal with plastic wrap.

—V. Alice Hughes

Steak Sauce

6 qts. tomatoes, cooked & strained
2 lbs. brown sugar
1 lb. granulated sugar
1 cup flour
2 tsp. ginger
2 tsp. cinnamon
Cayenne pepper
2 tsp. ground cloves
2 Tbsp. dry mustard
¼ cup salt

Combine all ingredients and mix well. Boil 20 minutes, stirring constantly. Pack in hot sterilized jars and seal. Serve with hot or cold meats or as a barbecue marinade.

—Marilyn Fuller

Veal & Ham Pie

PASTRY:
½ tsp. salt
⅓ cup very cold water
2 cups flour
1 egg
⅔ cup butter, softened
FILLING:
2 lbs. cooked veal
1 lb. cooked ham
2 eggs, hard-boiled & peeled
1¾ cups veal stock
1 egg yolk, beaten
1 envelope gelatin

To make pastry, dissolve salt in water. Sift flour into a ring on working surface and place egg, butter and salt water in centre. Mix these together, then work in flour to make dough. Wrap in wax paper and refrigerate for 2 hours. Line a greased, 9-inch cake pan with two-thirds of the pastry.

Cut veal and ham into bite-sized pieces and place in pie shell in alternate layers, packing around eggs. Add 3 to 4 Tbsp. stock.

Top with remaining one-third of pastry. Make central hole to allow steam to escape. Brush with egg yolk and bake at 375° F for 1 to 1½ hours. Cool.

Dissolve gelatin in remaining stock. Pour stock carefully into pie through central hole. Refrigerate. When jelly is set, remove pie from dish and serve.

Serves 4.

—Ruth Leir

Veal Casserole

2 lbs. boneless veal, cut into
    1-inch cubes
1 Tbsp. oil
1 Tbsp. butter
½ cup chopped onion
½ cup chopped celery
¼ cup diced green pepper
14-oz. can tomatoes, drained
    with juice reserved
Chicken stock
½ cup white wine
1 Tbsp. parsley
Thyme
Garlic powder
Salt & pepper
½ cup sliced mushrooms

Brown veal in oil and butter in 2-quart casserole dish, removing pieces as they are done. Cook onion and remove from pan. Drain fat from pan and replace meat and onion. Add celery, green pepper and tomatoes.

Add chicken stock to reserved tomato juice to make 1 cup and bring to a boil in a small saucepan. Cool slightly and add wine. Pour over casserole and add seasoning.

Cover and bake at 325° F for 1¾ hours. Add mushrooms and bake for a further 15 minutes.

Serves 4.

—Florence Hutchison

Wiener Schnitzel

6 veal scallops
Salt & pepper
2 eggs, slightly beaten
Flour
3 Tbsp. bacon drippings
Juice of 1 lemon
1 Tbsp. flour
1 cup sour cream
Lemon slices

Sprinkle veal with salt and pepper. Dip into beaten eggs then into flour. Brown on both sides in hot bacon drippings, then cover and cook slowly until chops are tender — about 1 hour. Sprinkle with lemon juice and arrange on hot platter.

Blend 1 Tbsp. flour with fat in pan, add sour cream and cook for 3 minutes, stirring constantly. Season with salt and pepper and serve with chops. Garnish with lemon slices.

Serves 6.

—Lorraine Murphy

Korean Vegetables & Beef

3-4 Tbsp. soya sauce
1 Tbsp. oil
1 tsp. honey
1 clove garlic, crushed
½ lb. beef, thinly sliced
Sesame oil
1 onion, chopped
2½ cups chopped assorted
  vegetables (green beans,
  zucchini, cauliflower,
  broccoli)
3 Tbsp. crushed sesame
  seeds

Combine soya sauce, oil, honey and garlic. Marinate beef in this for 15 minutes.

Heat oil in wok. Stir-fry drained beef and onion. Add vegetables and fry until bright in colour. Add sesame seeds and leftover marinade. Heat through and serve with rice.

Serves 3 to 4.

—Gwen Miller

Carbonnade of Beef

⅓ cup flour
1 tsp. salt
¼ tsp. pepper
3 lbs. round, chuck or blade
  steak, cut into stewing
  pieces
¼ cup oil
¼ cup butter
6 large onions, thinly sliced
1½ bottles beer
2 cloves garlic, crushed
2-3 bay leaves
¼ tsp. thyme
¼ tsp. basil
¼ tsp. marjoram
Parsley
½ tsp. salt

Combine flour, salt and pepper in plastic bag. Place meat, a few pieces at a time, into bag to coat with flour. Heat oil and butter in heavy casserole dish and add meat, browning on all sides. Add onions and cook until limp. Add any extra flour and the beer. Add spices and mix thoroughly. Bring to a boil, cover and place in oven. Cook at 300° F for 2 hours.

Serves 6.

—Sheri Lemire

Braised Beef with Tomatoes & Herbs

3 lbs. lean chuck steak, cut
  into ½-inch cubes
Salt & pepper
3 Tbsp. olive oil
2 Tbsp. finely chopped garlic
½ lb. onions, chopped
½ lb. whole mushrooms
¼ cup flour
1 cup dry red wine
2 cups canned tomatoes
24 pitted, stuffed green olives
1 bay leaf
½ tsp. thyme
Cayenne
1¼ cup finely chopped
  parsley

Trim fat off meat and sprinkle with salt and pepper. Heat oil in large pan, add beef and cook, stirring often. Add garlic, onions and mushrooms and stir. Sprinkle with flour and stir to coat evenly. Add wine, tomatoes, olives, bay leaf, thyme, cayenne, salt and pepper. Cover and simmer on low heat for 1½ hours. Sprinkle with parsley and serve.

Serves 6.

—Linda Hodgins

Steak with Green Peppers

1½ cups raw rice, cooked
1 lb. lean steak
1 Tbsp. paprika
2 Tbsp. butter
2 cloves garlic, crushed
⅛ tsp. cayenne
½ tsp. salt
1½ cups beef stock
1 cup sliced green onions
2 green peppers, cut into
   strips
2 Tbsp. cornstarch
¼ cup water
½ cup soya sauce
2 large tomatoes, cut into
   eighths

While rice is cooking, thinly slice steak across grain. Sprinkle meat with paprika and let sit for a few minutes. Brown in butter in large skillet. Add garlic, cayenne, salt and beef stock. Cover and simmer for 30 minutes. Add green onions and green peppers, cover and cook for 5 more minutes. Blend together cornstarch, water and soya sauce and stir into meat. Cook, stirring, until stock is clear and thickened — about 2 minutes. Add tomatoes and serve over rice.

Serves 3.

—Janice Hyatt

Gingered Beef with Raisin Sauce

1½ lbs. round steak
2 Tbsp. flour
1½ tsp. ground ginger
1 tsp. paprika
1 tsp. minced garlic
3 Tbsp. oil
3 Tbsp. catsup
½ cup raisins
2 Tbsp. butter
1 Tbsp. soya sauce
½ cup chicken stock

Cut steak in thin strips. Combine flour, ginger, paprika and garlic, and dredge steak in this mixture.

Heat oil in frying pan and fry steak quickly, stirring constantly, until meat loses pink colour. Remove from pan and keep warm.

Add to pan catsup, raisins, butter, soya sauce and chicken stock, stirring well to combine. Simmer for 10 minutes, return meat to pan and heat through. Serve with rice.

Serves 4 to 6.

—Irene Louden

Greek Slipper Steak

4½-lb. steaks
8 Tbsp. chopped, lightly
   toasted almonds
4 Tbsp. chopped stuffed
   olives
2 tsp. minced hot Greek
   pickled pepper
1 tsp. minced garlic
½ tsp. cinnamon
Salt & pepper
Butter
Red wine
Onion slices

Slice a pocket in one side of each steak, cutting to within ¼ inch of the edges. Combine remaining ingredients, except butter, wine and onion slices, and stuff steaks. Stitch opening shut.

Sear steaks in butter in frying pan. When cooked, place on warm platter in oven. Deglaze pan with a little red wine. Add onion slices and sauté briefly. Garnish steaks with onion and spoon pan juices over them.

Serves 4.

—Elizabeth Ballantyne

Girardi Steaks

2 lbs. round or sirloin steak
Salt & pepper
Oil
1 medium onion, sliced
½ cup white wine
1 cup beef stock
6 slices bacon
½ lb. mushrooms
1 small onion
1 Tbsp. chopped parsley
1 tsp. capers
1 tsp. lemon rind
1 Tbsp. flour
½ cup sour cream

Season steaks with salt and pepper, sear on both sides in hot oil and set aside.

In remaining oil, add sliced onion, white wine and beef stock. Replace steaks and allow to simmer.

Meanwhile, mince bacon, mushrooms, onion, parsley, capers and lemon rind. Fry all together, sprinkle with flour and stir in cream. Add this to steaks and simmer until tender.

Serves 4.

—Claudette Spies

Beef Parmigiana

1½ to 2 lbs. round steak
3 Tbsp. flour
Salt & pepper
½ cup fine dry bread crumbs
¼ cup Parmesan cheese
¼ tsp. basil
1 egg, beaten with 1 Tbsp. water
4 Tbsp. oil
2 cups tomato sauce, page 414
1 clove garlic, crushed
½ tsp. oregano
6 slices mozzarella cheese

Cut steak into 4 serving-sized pieces. Combine flour with salt and pepper and dredge meat in it. Pound both sides of meat. Combine bread crumbs with Parmesan cheese and basil. Dip each piece of meat into egg-water mixture and then dredge in crumbs. Brown meat lightly in oil and place in greased 9" x 13" baking dish.

Combine tomato sauce, garlic and oregano and pour over meat. Cover with foil and bake for 1 hour or until very tender. Place a slice of cheese on each piece of meat. Bake for a few minutes longer, until cheese is melted.

Serves 4.

—Laurie Gillespie

Bulkoki

5 tsp. soya sauce
7 Tbsp. oil
3 Tbsp. sherry
3 cloves garlic, crushed
½ cup chopped onion
1 Tbsp. sugar
2 Tbsp. peppercorns, coarsely ground
¼ cup chopped scallions
2 tsp. dill seed
1-1½ lbs. beef, cut into thin strips

Combine soya sauce, 5 Tbsp. oil, sherry, garlic, onion, sugar, peppercorns, scallions and dill seed and marinate beef in this, covered, for 2 to 3 hours. Sauté in remaining 2 Tbsp. oil over high heat for 3 to 4 minutes.

Serves 4.

—Sheila Livingston

Steak Teriyaki

¾ cup oil
¼ cup soya sauce
¼ cup honey
2 Tbsp. cider vinegar
2 Tbsp. finely chopped green onion
1 large clove garlic, chopped
1½ tsp. ground ginger
2 lbs. flank steak

Mix together oil, soya sauce, honey, vinegar, onion, garlic and ginger and pour over meat. Let marinate, turning occasionally, for several hours.

Broil or cook over coals, basting with marinade.

Serves 4.

—Michèle Raymond

Beef and Pork Curry

4 Tbsp. oil
1½ lbs. round steak, cubed
1½ lbs. pork butt or
    shoulder, cubed
2 onions, peeled & chopped
3 cloves garlic, crushed
2 potatoes, peeled & cubed
4 Tbsp. curry
2 tsp. salt

Sauté beef and pork in oil until browned.

Add onions and garlic and cook until soft. Add curry powder and salt and continue cooking, stirring frequently, for one minute. Add potatoes and cover with water. Let simmer on low heat with lid slightly ajar for 1½ to 2 hours. Serve on bed of rice.

Serves 6.

—Terry Pereira

Tomatoes and Bulgur

¾ lb. ground beef
1 tsp. salt
½ tsp. pepper
½ tsp. cinnamon
1 medium onion, chopped
¾ lb. tomatoes, peeled &
    chopped
2 Tbsp. tomato paste
1 cup water
1 cup bulgur

Brown beef with spices. Add chopped onion and cook until soft. Add tomatoes, tomato paste and water and bring to a boil.

Add bulgur, cover and simmer until bulgur is soft, about 20 minutes. Stir occasionally and add water if necessary to prevent sticking.

Serves 4.

—Moira Abboud

Rouladen

The ideal meat for rouladen, or beef rolls, can be bought in most European butcher shops, but an almost-frozen roast of beef slices easily with excellent results.

⅛-inch-thick slices of beef,
    4-5 inches wide by 8
    inches long
Hot mustard
Salt & pepper
Paprika
Thinly sliced onion
Chopped raw bacon
Dill pickle spears
Oil
Bay leaf
Water
Cornstarch

Spread each beef slice thinly with hot mustard and sprinkle with salt and pepper, paprika, onion and bacon. Place dill pickle spear at one end of slice and roll up lengthwise over pickle. Insert toothpicks right through the roll or tie with string to keep from unrolling. In deep, heavy pan containing a little oil, over high heat, darkly brown rolls on all sides almost to the point of burning. Cover with water, add bay leaf and salt and pepper to taste. Bring to a boil, cover and simmer for about 30 minutes. Thicken gravy with cornstarch before serving.

Allow 1 to 2 rolls per person.

—Mary Dzielak

Italian Steak

3 lbs. steaks
¾ cup bread crumbs
1 Tbsp. oregano
1 egg, beaten
Seasoned flour
Oil
28-oz. can tomatoes
1 green pepper, chopped
1 clove garlic, minced
1 large onion, thinly sliced
1 cup sliced green olives
1 cup sliced black olives
1 lb. mushrooms, sliced
Chopped capers

Cut steak into serving-sized pieces. Combine bread crumbs and oregano. Dip meat in egg, flour, egg again, then bread crumbs. Brown in oil in heavy skillet.

Blend remaining ingredients together. Place meat and sauce in alternating layers in greased casserole dish. Bake at 350° F for 1 hour.

Serves 6.

—Marni Olson

Oriental Beef Pot Roast

4-lb. roast of beef
1 tsp. garlic powder
½ tsp. dry mustard
¼ tsp. pepper
2 Tbsp. oil
¾ cup water
3 Tbsp. honey
2 Tbsp. soya sauce
1 Tbsp. vinegar
1½ tsp. celery seed
½ tsp. ginger
1 Tbsp. cornstarch,
    dissolved in 2 Tbsp. water

Rub roast with mixture of garlic powder, mustard and pepper. Heat a 6-quart roasting pan, add oil and brown roast well on all sides. Combine water, honey, soya sauce, vinegar, celery seed and ginger and pour over meat. Cover and roast at 325° F for 2½ hours. Transfer roast to heated platter and thicken gravy with cornstarch-water mixture.

Serves 8.

—*Midge Denault*

Crab Apple Pot Roast

3 Tbsp. flour
1½ tsp. salt
¼ tsp. pepper
¼ tsp. allspice
4-lb. beef pot roast
2 Tbsp. butter
14-oz. jar spiced crab apples
2 Tbsp. lemon juice
¼ cup raisins

Combine 1 Tbsp. flour, salt, pepper and allspice. Dredge meat in mixture. In heavy saucepan, heat butter and brown meat on all sides.

Drain crab apples, reserving juice. Add enough water to juice to make 1 cup, then add to meat along with lemon juice. Cover and simmer for 3 hours or until tender. About 15 minutes before meat is done, add crab apples and raisins.

To serve, place meat and crab apples on platter. Blend remaining 2 Tbsp. flour with ½ cup cold water and stir into liquid. Let boil for a few minutes to thicken and serve with meat.

Serves 8.

—*Mary Hewson*

Beef Macintosh

4 cups dry apple cider
1 cup cider vinegar
2 cloves garlic, minced
2 Tbsp. chopped ginger
2 Tbsp. dry mustard
1 apple, diced
6 prunes, diced
5-lb. roast of beef
2 large onions, sliced
Butter

Combine cider, vinegar, garlic, ginger, mustard, apple and prunes. Marinate roast in this, covered, overnight in the refrigerator.

Take out of refrigerator and allow to come to room temperature. Brown onions in butter and transfer to deep saucepan just large enough to hold roast. Take beef out of liquid and pat dry. Brown on all sides in butter and place in saucepan. Add marinade. If beef is not covered by liquid, add cider to cover. Bring to a boil and simmer gently for 3 or 4 hours. Remove from heat and let stand until cool enough to handle. Remove beef, strain out onions and fruit and degrease stock. Pour back into pot with beef and heat through. Serve with broth, onions and fruit.

Serves 8.

—*Elizabeth Ballantyne*

Roti

This version of a West Indian dish is essentially beef curry wrapped in fried pastry. The amount of curry powder used can vary according to personal taste — that listed below produces a medium-hot curry.

3-4 Tbsp. oil
1 lb. beef, cubed
2 cloves garlic, crushed
6 curry leaves (optional)
½ cups chopped onion
½ cup chopped celery
2 heaping Tbsp. curry
Seeds of 2 cardamom pods
1 heaping tsp. cumin seed
1 heaping tsp. ground
   turmeric
1 heaping tsp. coriander seed
¼ cup vinegar
2 cups peeled, cubed potatoes
3 cups flour
¼ tsp. salt
¼ tsp. baking powder
⅓ cup lard
½ cup milk
½ cup water
Cornmeal
Oil

Heat oil in heavy skillet. Brown meat, garlic and curry leaves. Add onion and celery and sauté until onion is soft.

Crush curry, cardamom, cumin, turmeric and coriander in mortar with pestle or grind in blender. Mix with vinegar and add to meat. Stir and fry for a few minutes. Add water to cover and simmer for 30 minutes. Add potatoes along with more water if necessary.

Bring to a boil, reduce heat and simmer until potatoes are tender. Salt to taste. Cool slightly before putting on wrap.

Meanwhile, make pastry wraps. Combine flour, salt and baking powder in bowl. Cut in lard until mixture resembles coarse crumbs. Mix together milk and water and add to lard mixture. Stir with fork until dough clumps together. Gather dough and knead for 3 minutes until smooth. Let sit, covered, for 30 minutes.

Cut dough into 10 pieces and form each into a ball. Keep balls covered. Roll each ball into 8-inch circle on a lightly floured board sprinkled with cornmeal. Stack wraps with wax paper in between.

To cook, heat a large heavy pan until hot. Cook one wrap at a time in oil until it bubbles and puffs. Brown spots will appear. Flip over and cook for a few minutes on other side. Wraps should be soft and pliable. Stack, covered with a damp cloth.

To serve, spoon ½ cup meat mixture into the centre of each wrap. This can be topped with a dollop of yogurt or sour cream. Fold up wrap and eat like a sandwich.

Serves 4 to 5.

—Anne MacDonald

African Beef

2 lbs. stewing beef
2 large onions, sliced
1½ cups chopped celery
10-oz. can tomato paste
19-oz. can tomatoes
¼ tsp. pepper
⅓ cup brown sugar
1 tsp. ginger
1 tsp. Worcestershire sauce
¼ cup vinegar
Garlic, mushrooms & green
   peppers to taste

Brown meat. Add remaining ingredients. Cover and bake for 3 hours at 325° F. Serve with rice.

Serves 6.

—Valerie Moore

Meat in Yogurt Sauce

This Lebanese variation of Beef Stroganoff is quickly assembled and much lighter.

1 Tbsp. oil
2 lbs. beef or lamb, cubed
1 medium onion, chopped
½ tsp. each salt, pepper &
   cinnamon
1 Tbsp. cornstarch
1 quart plain yogurt

Brown meat in oil. Add onions and spices and cook until onion is soft. Set aside.

Mix cornstarch with a little water, then mix with yogurt and pour into a 2-quart saucepan. Bring to a boil over medium-high heat, stirring constantly. When the sauce comes to a boil, reduce heat, cover and simmer for 5 minutes.

Add meat and continue to simmer for 10 to 15 minutes. Serve with rice.

Serves 6.

—Moira Abboud

Green Pepper Steak

4 Tbsp. clarified butter
1 lb. lean stewing beef, cut
  into 1-inch cubes
1 large onion, chopped
½ lb. mushrooms, thinly
  sliced
1 large green pepper, diced
1 tsp. garlic powder
1 tsp. salt
1 tsp. pepper
4 cups beef stock
2 Tbsp. cornstarch
¼ cup dry vermouth

Heat butter in heavy pot, add meat and cook until browned on all sides. Add onion, mushrooms, green pepper, garlic, salt and pepper and cook for 3 to 5 minutes, stirring occasionally.

Add stock and bring to a boil, reduce heat and simmer for 10 minutes. Blend cornstarch with vermouth and stir into pot. Cook for 2 more minutes until sauce thickens. Bring to a boil, reduce heat and cook, covered, for 1 hour.

Serves 4.

—Joyce Hall

Texas Chili

2 Tbsp. oil
3 lbs. boneless chuck, cut
  into 1-inch cubes
2-3 cloves garlic, chopped
4-6 Tbsp. chili powder
2 tsp. cumin
3 Tbsp. flour
1 Tbsp. oregano
3 cups beef stock
Salt & pepper
Sour cream
Lime wedges

Heat oil in 4-quart pot over medium heat. Add beef and cook, stirring frequently, until meat changes colour but is not browned. Lower heat and stir in garlic. Combine chili powder, cumin and flour and sprinkle over meat, stirring until meat is evenly coated. Crumble oregano over meat. Add 2 cups stock and stir until liquid is well blended. Add salt and pepper and bring to a boil, stirring occasionally.

Reduce heat and simmer, partially covered, for 1½ to 2 hours, stirring from time to time. Add remaining 1 cup stock and cook for 30 minutes longer. Cool thoroughly, cover and refrigerate overnight. Reheat and serve with sour cream and lime wedges.

Serves 8.

—Joan Hampton

Beef and Mushroom Ragoût

This French-style ragoût is as easy to make as an everyday beef stew, but is impressive enough for an elegant dinner. Serve with a tossed salad of mixed greens topped with finely chopped hard-boiled eggs, warm French bread, and complete the meal with a crème caramel.

3 Tbsp. oil
2 lbs. stewing beef
2 large onions, chopped
1 cup sherry or red wine
1 cup water
2 large carrots, finely sliced
1 bay leaf
2 cloves garlic, whole &
  unpeeled
1 lb. mushrooms, finely
  sliced
Salt & pepper
4 cups cooked rice

In a large, deep pan, heat oil and cook meat over medium-high heat, removing pieces as they become well-browned. In same pan, brown onion. Return meat to pan, add sherry or red wine and boil gently until alcohol has evaporated. Add water, carrots, bay leaf and garlic. Cover and simmer for 2 to 3 hours until meat is tender. Add mushrooms and simmer for 15 more minutes. To thicken, uncover and bring to a boil. Remove garlic and bay leaf and adjust seasoning with salt and pepper.

To serve, place cooked rice around the outside of a large platter. Remove the meat and vegetables from the pot with a slotted spoon and place in the centre of the platter. Serve the sauce in a gravy boat.

Serves 4.

—Sandra James-Mitchell

Oxtail Stew

Oxtail soup is the most common use to which oxtails are put. This recipe is another delicious possibility. They can also be stuffed and braised or grilled. Usually sold skinned, it is possible to buy unskinned oxtails, so this should be checked at the time of purchase.

6 lbs. oxtails
Salt & pepper
½ cup oil
1½ cups diced onions
1 cup diced carrots
¼ cup flour
1 tsp. salt
½ tsp. thyme
½ tsp. pepper
5 cups beef stock
2 cups dry red wine
1 lb. carrots
4 small turnips

Trim excess fat from oxtails and sprinkle with salt and pepper. In large, heavy skillet, brown oxtails in oil over high heat and transfer to a large casserole dish. Sauté onions and carrots in remaining oil in skillet, stirring occasionally, until lightly browned. Place in casserole dish and sprinkle with flour, salt, thyme and pepper. Stir gently to coat. Bake at 450° F, stirring once, for 20 minutes. Remove from oven, add stock and wine and bring to a boil over medium-high heat. Return to oven at 325° F and bake for 3 hours.

Meanwhile, quarter carrots lengthwise and cut into 1 ¼-inch lengths. Peel and quarter turnips. Mix vegetables into stew. Bake for another 30 minutes.

Let stew cool, chill it, then skim off fat. Bring stew to a boil, heat through and serve.

Serves 8 to 10.

—*Mary Lighthall*

Muriel's Short Ribs and Beans

2 cups dry pinto or kidney
  beans
2½-3 lbs. meaty beef short
  ribs
3-4 Tbsp. oil
2 medium onions, thickly
  sliced
2 cloves garlic, minced
¾ cup tomato paste
Salt & pepper
1 tsp. chili
2 cups stewed tomatoes

Cook beans until barely tender, then drain, reserving liquid. Trim excess fat from short ribs and cut into serving-sized pieces. Brown short ribs in hot oil in large, heavy pot. Remove and set aside. Add onion and garlic and sauté until tender. Return short ribs to pot and add beans. Mix tomato paste with 1 cup of bean liquid and stir in seasonings. Pour over beans and meat. Add tomatoes and mix slightly. Add bean liquid until mixture is barely covered. Bake, covered, at 275° F for 3 to 4 hours, or until short ribs are tender. Stir occasionally and add more liquid if necessary. Uncover during last 15 to 20 minutes.

Serves 4 to 6.

—*A. Dianne Wilson-Meyer*

Oven Beef Burgundy

2 Tbsp. soya sauce
2 Tbsp. flour
2 lbs. stewing beef
4 carrots
2 large onions
1 cup sliced celery
1 clove garlic, minced
¼ tsp. marjoram
¼ tsp. thyme
Salt & pepper
1 cup dry red wine
1 cup sliced mushrooms

Blend soya sauce with flour in a casserole dish. Cut meat into 1½-inch cubes and add to soya sauce mixture. Toss to coat well. Cut carrots into chunks and slice onions. Add to meat along with celery, spices and wine. Cover and bake at 325° F for 1 hour. Add mushrooms and stir gently. Cover and cook for another 1½ to 2 hours.

Serves 4.

—*Juliana Crawford*

Sicilian Meat Roll

2 eggs, beaten
½ cup tomato juice
¾ cup soft bread crumbs
2 Tbsp. chopped parsley
½ tsp. oregano
¼ tsp. salt
¼ tsp. pepper
¼ tsp. garlic powder
2 lbs. ground beef
4-6 oz. thinly sliced ham
6 oz. sliced mozzarella
   cheese

In a bowl, combine eggs and tomato juice. Stir in bread crumbs, parsley, oregano, salt, pepper and garlic. Add ground beef and mix well. On wax paper, pat meat into an 8" x 10" rectangle. Arrange ham slices on top of meat, leaving a small margin around edges.

Reserve 1 slice of cheese. Tear up remaining cheese and sprinkle over ham. Starting from short end, carefully roll up meat, using paper to lift. Seal edges and ends. Place roll, seam side down, in a 9" x 13" baking pan.

Bake at 350° F for about 1¼ hours. Centre of roll will be pink due to ham. Cut reserved cheese slice into 4 triangles, overlap atop meat and return to oven until cheese melts.

Serves 8.

—Patricia A. Leahy

Lihapirukas Muretainas

This Estonian recipe produces mild-flavoured meat tarts with sour cream crusts. They can be eaten hot or cold and the individual-sized tarts are easily handled.

5 cups flour
2 tsp. salt
1½ cups butter
1 cup sour cream
2 eggs
4 Tbsp. butter
¾ cup finely chopped
   mushrooms
⅓ cup finely chopped onion
4 cups ground beef
1 cup grated Cheddar cheese
Dill
Salt & pepper
½ cup milk
1 egg

Sift flour with salt. Cut in chilled butter until mixture resembles coarse meal. Add sour cream and eggs and work until dough is pliable. Chill for at least one hour.

Melt butter in saucepan. Add mushrooms and cook until golden brown. Remove from pan, add onions and ground beef and sauté until beef is cooked. Add mushrooms, cheese, dill and salt and pepper. Mix thoroughly over medium heat until cheese is melted.

Roll pastry out thinly and cut into 4-inch circles. Place 2 tsp. of meat on each circle. Combine milk and egg. Fold circles in half and seal with milk-egg mixture.

Place on greased cookie sheet and bake at 350° F for 15 to 20 minutes.

Makes 36 tarts.

—Donna Hert

Boboti

1 medium onion, minced
2 Tbsp. oil
½ tsp. nutmeg
½ tsp. cinnamon
1 tsp. coriander
1 tsp. cumin
1 tsp. garam masala
1 tsp. turmeric
1½ lbs. ground beef
¼-½ cup water
¼ cup raisins
Dash nutmeg

Sauté onion in oil. Add spices and stir into onions. Add ground beef and cook until browned, stirring frequently. Stir in water and raisins. Turn into greased casserole dish. Smooth surface and sprinkle with nutmeg.

Bake at 350° F for 15 to 20 minutes.

Serves 6.

—Pamela Morninglight

Roast Pork Stuffed with Apples & Prunes

1 onion, chopped
1 apple, chopped
½ cup chopped, pitted prunes
3 Tbsp. apple butter
1 clove garlic, chopped
½ tsp. thyme
½ tsp. rosemary
Pepper
4-lb. pork loin roast,
   deboned

Mix together onion, apple, prunes, apple butter, garlic and seasonings. Stuff the roast with this mixture, place in roasting pan and bake at 325° F for 2 hours.

Serves 6 to 8.

—Lynn Biscott

Samosas

It takes a bit of time and effort to roll this dough as thin as it should be, so some people may wish to substitute commercial won ton or egg roll wrappers. Available now in most grocery store produce sections, they can be frozen successfully. Samosas also make excellent party fare, as they are delicious hot or cold. When they are to be eaten with the fingers, make them bite-sized. Deep-fry and keep warm in the oven — they will stay very crispy.

DOUGH:
3 cups flour
2 tsp. salt
1 tsp. cumin seeds
Water
FILLING:
2 onions, chopped
Oil
2 lbs. ground beef
½ lb. peas
3 potatoes, chopped
Cayenne
2 tsp. curry
2 cloves, crushed
1 cinnamon stick, crushed
½ tsp. crushed cardamom
½ clove garlic, crushed
4 dried hot chilies, crushed

Combine flour, salt, cumin and water to make a stiff, elastic dough. Roll very thinly and cut into 8-inch triangles.

Make filling by frying onions in oil until browned. Add beef, peas, potatoes and spices. Sauté until meat is well cooked.

Place a spoonful of filling in centre of each triangle. Overlap 3 corners to form a smaller triangle. Seal with water. Deep-fry until golden brown.

Serves 6.

—Ingrid Birker

Canadian Ski Marathon Sauce

Developed to feed hungry cross-country skiers on the Lachute-to-Ottawa marathon, this spaghetti sauce makes use of sausage meat as well as ground beef. Once cooked, it can be left to simmer for several hours if desired, or it can be frozen for later use.

1 lb. spicy Italian sausage
1 lb. lean ground beef
½ cup finely chopped onion
2 cloves garlic, crushed & minced
1 Tbsp. salt
2 tsp. basil
½ tsp. fennel
¼ tsp. pepper
¼ cup chopped parsley
28-oz. can tomatoes
13-oz. can tomato paste

Remove sausage meat from casings and mix with ground beef and onion. In large heavy pot, over medium-high heat, sauté meat mixture and garlic, stirring frequently, until well browned. Drain fat.

Add salt, basil, fennel, pepper and parsley and mix well. Chop up tomatoes and add with liquid. Stir in tomato paste and ½ cup water. Bring to a boil, reduce heat and simmer, covered, for at least one hour, stirring occasionally. Serve over noodles.

Serves 8.

—Louise McDonald

Apple Meat Loaf

This is a very moist meat loaf with an excellent flavour — a good standby for a cold winter night's supper.

2 cooking apples
1½ lbs. ground beef
1½ cups soft bread crumbs
1 onion, finely chopped
Salt & pepper
1 tsp. Worcestershire sauce
2 eggs
Topping:
⅓ cup catsup
2 Tbsp. maple syrup

Peel, core and grate apples and combine with ground beef, onion, bread crumbs and seasonings. Beat eggs and add to meat mixture. Press into loaf pan. Combine topping ingredients and spoon over the meat loaf. Bake at 325° F for 1¼ hours.

Serves 4 to 6.

—Linda Plant

Burger Trittini

This recipe will help use up an overabundance of beet greens or Swiss chard.

2 lbs. ground beef
1 onion, sliced
2 cups tomato sauce, page 414
13-oz. can tomato paste
1 cup sliced mushrooms
2 tsp. basil
1 tsp. oregano
¼ tsp. pepper
4 cups chopped, cooked beet greens or Swiss chard, very well drained
2 cups cottage cheese
1 cup grated mozzarella cheese

Brown beef and onion. Add tomato sauce, tomato paste, mushrooms, basil, oregano and pepper. Mix greens with cottage cheese.

In greased casserole dish, spoon meat mixture evenly over bottom. Cover with half the mozzarella cheese, then the greens-cottage cheese mixture, then the rest of the mozzarella cheese. Bake at 375° F for 25 to 30 minutes.

Serves 6.

—Paula Compton

East Indian Meatballs

1 large onion, chopped (reserve 2 Tbsp. for meat)
2 Tbsp. butter
½ tsp. cinnamon
½ tsp. mace
¾ tsp. curry
1 tsp. whole peppers in cheesecloth bag
⅓ cup seedless raisins
¼ cup slivered blanched almonds
1½ cups water
1 tsp. salt
½ cup soft bread crumbs
¼ cup milk
1 lb. ground beef
2 Tbsp. chopped parsley
1 egg
1 tsp. Worcestershire sauce
¼ tsp. pepper

In a large skillet, cook onion in butter until lightly browned. Add cinnamon, mace, curry, peppers, raisins, almonds and water and simmer for 15 minutes. Remove pepper bag.

Mix remaining ingredients and shape into 1-inch balls. Brown on all sides in a skillet, using a small amount of fat. Pour off excess fat and add sauce to meatballs. Cover and simmer for 20 minutes.

Serves 4.

—Anita Cunningham

Hot Tamale Pie

FILLING:
1 lb. ground beef
1½ cups corn
2 cups tomatoes
Salt & pepper
¾ cup chopped onion
1 Tbsp. chopped chili pepper
CRUST:
¼ cup shortening
1 egg
1½ cups flour
2 cups corn meal
2 tsp. baking powder
1 cup milk

Combine filling ingredients in a heavy pot and bring to a boil. Reduce heat and simmer until meat is cooked through — 15 to 20 minutes.

To make crust, cream shortening and beat in egg. Combine flour, corn meal and baking powder and stir into creamed mixture. Add milk to make a soft, smooth dough.

Place ground beef filling in greased casserole dish and top with dough. Bake at 400° F for 35 to 40 minutes.

Serves 4.

—Anne McKenzie

Ground Beef & Squash

3 acorn squash, cut in half & cleaned
2 lbs. ground beef
2 eggs
2 tsp. lemon juice
Salt & pepper
2 Tbsp. grated onion
1½ cups cooked rice
6 Tbsp. chili sauce

Bake squash at 250° F for 30 minutes. Combine remaining ingredients, spoon into squash and bake for another 40 minutes.

Serves 6.

—Susan Boehm

Baked Rainbow Trout with Almond Cream, page 245

Assorted Cookies

Roti, page 373

Spinach and Fruit Salad with Piquante Dressing, page 140

Sesame Yogurt Chicken, page 293

Crunchy Broccoli, page 149

Quick Breads and Muffins

From top right: Nanaimo Bars, page 485; Cape House Inn Iced Buttermilk with Shrimp Soup, page 92; Devilled Eggs, page 48; Almond and Mushroom Pâté, page 147; Artichoke Salad, page 136; Watermelon Boat Salad, page 141

Baked Stuffed Liver

½ cup soft bread crumbs
½ Tbsp. diced onion
¼ tsp. sage
Salt
Milk
½ lb. liver, cut into wide slices
2 Tbsp. flour
Butter
1 cup tomato sauce, page 414

Combine bread crumbs, onion, sage, salt and enough milk to moisten. Place on slices of liver, roll up and secure with toothpicks. Roll liver in flour and brown in butter. Place in greased casserole dish. Pour tomato sauce over top. Cover and bake at 350° F for 1 hour.

Serves 3.

—Pat Leary

Egg Dumplings

These dumplings can be added in the last few minutes of cooking in almost any stew.

1⅔ cups flour
3 tsp. baking powder
½ tsp. salt
1 Tbsp. butter
½ cup milk
1 egg, beaten

Blend dry ingredients. Rub in butter with fingers, then stir in milk and egg and drop by large spoonfuls into stewpot, cover and simmer for 12 to 15 minutes. Makes 8 dumplings.

—Robert Brandon

Beef Patties à la Lindstrom

Inspired by the contributor's visit to Scandinavia, this dish has gone on to become a family favourite.

4 oz. cooked beets
2 Tbsp. vinegar
4 oz. cold, boiled potatoes
1½ lbs. lean ground beef
2 egg yolks
Salt & pepper
2 Tbsp. grated onion
2 Tbsp. chopped capers
3 oz. butter
Parsley

Slice beets and marinate in vinegar for 20 minutes. Drain and chop finely. Dice potatoes.

Place meat in bowl and mix in egg yolks and salt and pepper. Stir in potatoes, beets, onion and capers and form into 12 patties.

Fry the patties in butter then pour browned butter over them. Serve with chopped parsley.

Serves 4 to 6.

—Kay Barclay

Pepper Steak Patties

1 lb. lean ground beef
1 Tbsp. cracked peppercorns
½ tsp. salt
1 cup sliced mushrooms
½ cup chopped onion
2 Tbsp. butter
1 tsp. Worcestershire sauce
2 Tbsp. lemon juice
2 Tbsp. Cognac

Shape beef into 4 patties. Spread peppercorns on wax paper, then press patties into pepper until both sides are coated. Sprinkle salt over bottom of heavy skillet. Set over medium-high heat and add mushrooms and onions. Cook patties to suit individual preference.

In a separate pan, heat butter, Worcestershire sauce and lemon juice. Pour off drippings from meat, pour butter mixture over meat and flambé with Cognac. Serve.

Serves 4.

—Nan & Phil Millette

Marinated Pork Roast with Currant Sauce

½ cup soya sauce
½ cup sherry
2 cloves garlic, minced
1 Tbsp. dry mustard
1 tsp. ginger
1 tsp. thyme
4-5 lbs. pork loin roast, deboned, rolled & tied
CURRANT SAUCE:
10 oz. currant jelly
2 Tbsp. sherry
1 Tbsp. soya sauce

Combine soya sauce, sherry, garlic, mustard, ginger and thyme. Place roast in plastic bag in deep bowl. Pour in marinade and close bag. Marinate for 2 to 3 hours at room temperature, pressing bag occasionally. Remove from bag and place in roasting pan with marinade and roast, uncovered, at 350° F for 2½ to 3 hours, basting with marinade during last hour.

Meanwhile, make sauce by melting currant jelly. Add sherry and soya sauce and simmer for 2 minutes. Serve roast with sauce.

Serves 8.

—*Susan Bates Eddy*

Roast Pork & Red Cabbage

¼ lb. bacon, cut into strips 1½ inches long & ¼ inch across
½ cup thinly sliced carrots
1 cup sliced onion
3 Tbsp. butter
3 cups red cabbage, cut into ½-inch slices
2 cups dry red wine or beer
2 cups beef stock
2 apples, diced
2 cloves garlic, crushed
Salt & pepper
3 lbs. deboned & rolled pork loin, tenderloin or shoulder end

Place bacon in saucepan and cover with cold water. Bring to a boil, simmer for 10 minutes and drain. Sauté carrots, onion, bacon and butter in covered pot for 10 minutes. Add cabbage, wine or beer, stock, apples, garlic and salt and pepper and blend; cover and bake at 325° F for 3 hours, stirring occasionally.

After 3 hours, brown the pork loin in small amount of fat and place on cabbage. Cover and return to oven for 2 hours. Remove pork and let sit, covered with foil, for 15 to 20 minutes. Place cabbage on a warm platter, slice pork and arrange on cabbage. Serve with cooking juices in a gravy boat.

Serves 6.

—*Jeff Greenberg*

Pork Tenderloin with Apricot Sauce

1½ lbs. pork tenderloin
Flour
Salt & pepper
2-3 cups herbed bread dressing
5-6 strips bacon
2 Tbsp. butter
2 Tbsp. cornstarch
2 cups apricot juice
6 apricot halves

Flatten pork between 2 layers of wax paper to ¼-inch thickness. Cut into 2½" x 3" rectangles, dredge with flour and sprinkle with salt and pepper.

Place a small amount of dressing on each rectangle and roll up like a jelly roll. Secure with toothpicks. Halve bacon strips and drape over pork rolls. Place on rack in shallow pan and bake at 350° F for 1½ hours.

Meanwhile, make apricot sauce. Over medium heat, melt butter, whisk in cornstarch and add 1½ cups juice. Cook, stirring, until mixture comes to a boil and thickens. If sauce is too thick, add remaining ½ cup juice.

When meat is cooked, pour sauce over each roll and bake for 10 more minutes. Top each roll with an apricot half and baste with sauce. Bake for another 10 minutes.

Serves 4 to 6.

—*Louise Routledge*

Pork and Apple Pie

Pastry for double 9-inch pie
    shell
3 cups diced, cooked pork
5 tart apples, peeled, cored &
    thinly sliced
1-2 medium onions, thinly
    sliced
3 Tbsp. flour
¼ tsp. salt
2 Tbsp. brown sugar
½ tsp. cinnamon
½ tsp. nutmeg
1 Tbsp. lemon juice
Milk

Line pie plate with one-half of
pastry.

Combine pork, apples and
onions in a large bowl. Mix flour,
sugar, salt, cinnamon and
nutmeg. Toss together pork and
flour mixtures with lemon juice.
Spoon into shell. Cover with
second half of pastry, flute edges
and cut slits in top for steam.
Brush with milk.

Bake at 425° F for 45 to 60
minutes.

Serves 4 to 6.

—Janie Zwicker

Apple Glazed
Roast Pork

4-5 lbs. pork roast
1 Tbsp. butter
1 small onion, grated
1 Tbsp. cornstarch
1 Tbsp. brown sugar
1 Tbsp. soya sauce
½ tsp. ginger
1 cup apple juice

Place pork fat side up on rack
in shallow roasting pan. Score
fat layer in diamonds and roast,
uncovered, at 325° F for 1 hour.

While roast is in oven, prepare
glaze. Melt butter in saucepan
and sauté onion until soft.
Thoroughly mix together
cornstarch, brown sugar, soya
sauce, ginger and juice. Pour
into pan with sautéed onions
and cook over low heat, stirring
constantly, until thick. Brush
part of glaze over meat, then
continue brushing every 15
minutes for the next hour, or
until meat is done.

Serves 8.

—Donna Sopha

Sweet Red Curry

1 Tbsp. oil
1 lb. cubed pork
1 medium onion, chopped
1 28-oz. can tomatoes,
    mashed
2 Tbsp. brown sugar
1 tsp. curry
2 Tbsp. water
3 apples, diced
1 cup peas
½ cup shredded coconut
6-8 mushrooms

Heat oil in large skillet and
brown meat. Add chopped onion
and cook, stirring, for 3 minutes.
Add tomatoes. Bring to boil and
add brown sugar. Mix curry with
water and add. Simmer for 30
minutes.

A few minutes before serving,
add diced apples, peas, coconut
and mushrooms and heat
through. Serve over rice.

Serves 4.

—Denise Aspinall

Pork Cubes in Apple Cider

¼ cup flour
½ tsp. salt
¼ tsp. pepper
¼ tsp. paprika
Garlic powder
2 lbs. pork, cubed
¼ cup butter
2 cups chopped onion
2 cups unsweetened apple cider

Mix flour and seasonings in paper bag. Add pork a few cubes at a time and shake to coat. Melt butter in skillet and brown cubes a single layer at a time, placing in an ovenproof casserole dish as they brown. Cook onions until limp but not brown and add to pork cubes. Pour cider over all, cover and bake at 350° F until pork is tender — 1 to 1½ hours.

Serves 4.

—Mary Lennox

Adobong Baboy

This recipe for pork adobo is from the Philippines, where the contributor spent some time on a youth exchange.

6 pork chops
8-10 cloves garlic
1 cup vinegar
1 cup water
1½ tsp. salt
2 bay leaves
½ tsp. pepper
Oil

Cut fat from pork and discard. If chops are large, cut into bite-sized pieces. Place pork and all other ingredients except oil into heavy saucepan and marinate for at least 1 hour. Bring to a boil, then reduce heat and simmer for 40 minutes, or until pork is tender. Remove pork from pan, boil liquid over high heat until reduced and thickened, then strain into small bowl. Place oil in the bottom of skillet and fry meat until evenly browned and crisp. Arrange on heated serving platter, pour sauce over the top and serve with rice.

Serves 6.

—Gemma Laska

Mediterranean Pork Chops

6 large pork butt chops
6 Tbsp. flour
½ tsp. salt
¼ tsp. coarsely ground pepper
¼ tsp. oregano
2 oz. tomato paste
12 leaves fresh sage
2 oz. dry white wine
3 cloves garlic, minced

Remove fat from chops and set aside. Mix together flour, salt, pepper and oregano and coat chops with this mixture. Let sit on a rack for 1 hour to help flour adhere.

Place scraps of fat in large shallow pan which can be tightly covered and heat them until bottom of pan is covered with a thin film of liquid fat. Discard scraps.

Put chops in pan and brown lightly on both sides. Spread tomato paste evenly on top of each chop. Add water to cover bottom of pan and simmer meat for 45 minutes with the lid on the pan. Remove lid, place 2 sage leaves on each chop, add wine and place garlic on bottom of pan. Bring to a boil, then cover, decrease heat, and simmer for an additional 5 minutes. Discard sage and garlic and serve immediately.

Serves 6.

—Glenn McMichael

Devilled Pork Chops

4 very thin pork chops
3 Tbsp. chili sauce
1½ Tbsp. lemon juice
2 tsp. Worcestershire sauce
¼ tsp. paprika
¼ tsp. dry mustard
⅛ tsp. curry
⅛ tsp. pepper
½ cup water

Trim excess fat from chops. Heat strips of fat in large skillet until they liquify. Brown chops well on both sides and pour off fat.

Combine chili sauce, lemon juice, Worcestershire sauce, paprika, mustard, curry, pepper and water and pour over chops. Bring to a boil, lower heat, cover and simmer until chops are tender — about 20 minutes.

Serves 4.

—Jane Morrissey

Pork Chops with Peaches

4 pork chops
¼ cup brown sugar
1 tsp. ginger
1 large onion, sliced
1 cup water
2 Tbsp. soya sauce
¼ cup cider vinegar
1 Tbsp. cornstarch,
   dissolved in cold water
2 fresh peaches, peeled &
   sliced

Brown pork chops in hot pan. Sprinkle sugar and ginger over chops, top with onion slices and cover with water, soya sauce and vinegar. Cover tightly and simmer for 35 minutes, turning chops once. Thicken sauce with cornstarch mixture, add peaches and heat until warm.

Serves 4.

—Judy Wuest

Pork Chops with White Wine & Herbs

1 Tbsp. chopped oregano
1 Tbsp. chopped marjoram
1 clove garlic, chopped
Salt & pepper
4 large pork loin chops
¼ cup butter
½ cup dry white wine
1 tsp. cornstarch
1 Tbsp. chopped parsley

Mix together oregano, marjoram, garlic and salt and pepper. Coat both sides of chops with herb mixture, pressing it on well.

Melt butter and fry chops for 3 minutes on each side. Pour in half of wine and bring to a boil. Cover and cook for 30 to 40 minutes or until tender. Transfer to warmed serving dish and keep hot.

Dissolve cornstarch in remaining wine, stir in a little of the hot liquid, then add to the pan, stirring constantly. Bring to a boil and simmer for 3 to 5 minutes. Pour over chops and sprinkle with parsley.

Serves 4.

—Elizabeth Clayton Paul

Steamed Spareribs with Black Bean Sauce

½ lbs. spareribs, cut into
   2"-3" pieces
4-5 Tbsp. cooked black
   beans
6-10 cloves garlic
1 tsp. salt
3 Tbsp. sherry
3 Tbsp. water
3 Tbsp. vinegar
2 Tbsp. oil
4 Tbsp. sugar
6 spring onions, chopped
   into 1-inch pieces

Boil ribs for 5 minutes and drain. Blend remaining ingredients except onions and pour over ribs. Marinate for 4 hours.

Place ribs in steamer, add onions and steam for 45 minutes.

Serves 6 as an appetizer or 3 to 4 as a meal.

—Harvey Griggs

Herbed Spareribs

3 lbs. spareribs
Salt & pepper
2 Tbsp. oil
1 clove garlic, crushed
½ cup chopped onion
2 Tbsp. brown sugar
1 Tbsp. vinegar
1 Tbsp. lemon juice
1 tsp. dry mustard
½ tsp. salt
⅛ tsp. red pepper
¼ tsp. thyme
¼ tsp. oregano
¼ tsp. basil
½ bay leaf
1 cup tomato sauce, page 414
½ cup water

Cut spareribs into serving-sized pieces and sprinkle with salt and pepper. Heat oil in saucepan and sauté garlic and onion until tender. Add remaining ingredients and simmer for 10 minutes.

Parboil spareribs, then place in shallow pan and cover with sauce. Bake at 375° F until done — about 30 minutes.

Serves 6 to 8.
—Helene Conway-Brown

Favourite Pork Spareribs

The contributor of this recipe says, "This has been a favourite in our family for 30 years. In fact, each of my married children has sent home for the recipe."

4 lbs. pork spareribs, cut up
1 large onion, minced
1 clove garlic, crushed
3 Tbsp. butter
2 Tbsp. cider vinegar
2 Tbsp. orange juice
6 Tbsp. brown sugar
3 tsp. salt
1 Tbsp. mustard
1 tsp. cinnamon
4 Tbsp. Worcestershire sauce
2 cups catsup
1½ cups diced celery
1 cup water
8-oz. can crushed pineapple

Cover ribs with water, boil for 15 minutes and drain. In another pan, simmer onion and garlic in butter until tender. Add remaining ingredients and cook for 5 to 10 minutes. Add ribs and cook gently until meat is tender — about 1 hour.

Place ribs in broiling pan, cover with sauce and broil until brown.

Serves 4 to 6.
—Ritta Wright

Spareribs Cantonese

4 lbs. pork spareribs
1 cup orange marmalade
½ cup soya sauce
½ tsp. garlic powder
½ tsp. ginger
Orange slices

Cut ribs into serving-sized pieces. Arrange in a rectangular casserole dish. Brown at 400° F for 15 minutes. Drain off fat.

In a bowl, combine marmalade, soya sauce, garlic powder, ginger and ¾ cup water. Mix well. Pour over ribs, cover casserole dish and bake at 350° for 1 hour, or until the ribs are done to your liking, basting occasionally.

Place ribs on serving dish and garnish with orange slices.

Serves 4 to 6.
—Irene Louden

Zucchini Pork Bake

1 lb. ground pork
½ tsp. garlic powder
3 Tbsp. Parmesan cheese
½ cup yogurt
4 small zucchini, sliced
½ lb. mozzarella cheese, grated

Fry pork until browned, drain. Add garlic, Parmesan cheese and yogurt.

Place half of zucchini in shallow greased pan, cover with meat and top with remaining zucchini. Cover with grated mozzarella cheese. Bake at 375° F for 20 to 25 minutes.

Serves 4.
—Linda Townsend

Sausage & Spinach Pie

Pastry for 9-inch pie shell
1 lb. sausage meat, cooked
3 large eggs
1 lb. spinach, cooked,
    drained & chopped
½ lb. mozzarella cheese,
    grated
¼ cup cottage cheese
¼ tsp. salt
⅛ tsp. pepper
¼ tsp. garlic powder
½ tsp. oregano

Combine all ingredients and mix well. Pour into unbaked pie shell and bake at 375° F for 1 hour.

Serves 4 to 6.

—J. Kristine MacDonald

Sausage Zucchini Casserole

1½ lbs. garlic sausage
1 large onion, diced
2-3 small zucchini, cubed
4 small potatoes, cooked &
    cubed
1 green pepper, diced
6 small tomatoes, peeled &
    cubed
Pepper
Garlic powder
1 cup grated old Cheddar
    cheese

Remove sausage from casing and sauté until no longer pink. Add onion and zucchini and sauté for a few minutes. Layer this mixture with potatoes, green pepper and tomatoes in greased casserole dish. Sprinkle with pepper and a dash of garlic powder. Cover and cook at 350° F for 30 minutes. Remove cover, sprinkle cheese on top and broil until bubbly.

Serves 4 to 6.

—Doris Hill

Dry Garlic Spareribs

1 lb. pork spareribs, cut into
    1" x 1½" pieces
Salt & pepper
1 Tbsp. soya sauce
½ tsp. sugar
2 Tbsp. cornstarch
2 tsp. oil
2 Tbsp. crushed garlic

Place ribs in bowl and add salt and pepper, soya sauce and sugar. Stir, then add cornstarch and stir to mix. Marinate for at least 15 minutes.

Heat oil until very hot. Add ribs and brown, stirring occasionally. Lower heat, cover and cook for 5 minutes. Drain off excess liquid. Increase heat to high, add garlic and stir-fry until it is golden — about 2 minutes. Transfer to broiler pan and broil until crisp, turning once — 5 to 10 minutes.

Serves 4 as an appetizer.

—Judith & Bob Brand

Lecho

This is a Czechoslovakian meal in itself and is delicious served with a hearty rye bread.

2 lbs. onions, finely chopped
Oil
2 lbs. green peppers, finely
    chopped
2 lbs. tomatoes, chopped
Salt & pepper
1½ lbs. Ukrainian sausage
1 egg, beaten

Place onions in large pot with enough oil to prevent sticking and cook until transparent. Add green peppers and cook until colour changes. Add tomatoes and cook for 1 hour. Season with salt and pepper. Cut sausage into ¼-inch rounds and add. Cook 30 minutes longer. Just before serving time, stir in the beaten egg to thicken.

Serves 6.

—Faye Hugar

Orange Glazed Ham

4-5 lbs. ham
1 Tbsp. grated orange rind
1 cup orange juice
¼ cup brown sugar
1½ Tbsp. soya sauce
½ tsp. ginger
1 Tbsp. cornstarch

Bake ham on rack in roasting pan at 325° F for 45 minutes. Remove excess fat and any rind with a sharp knife, leaving ¼ inch fat layer. Score fat in a diamond pattern. Combine orange rind, juice, sugar, soya sauce and ginger in small bowl. Remove and reserve ⅔ cup for orange sauce.

Brush ham with remaining glaze. Continue roasting, brushing with glaze every 15 minutes for an hour longer. Remove roast from oven to a heated platter.

For orange sauce, combine reserved glaze with ⅔ cup water and the cornstarch in a small saucepan. Heat, stirring constantly, until mixture thickens and bubbles. Cook for 1 minute. Slice ham and serve with sauce.

Serves 6 to 8.

—*Valerie Gillis*

Bacon Wrapped Chutney Bananas

2 bananas
1 lb. bacon
Lemon juice
1 cup mango chutney

Slice bananas into halves lengthwise, then into quarters crosswise. Dip bacon in lemon juice, roll around a piece of banana and secure with toothpick. Repeat until all banana pieces are used up.

Place on cookie sheet and bake at 375° F for 20 minutes. Remove from oven, dip into chutney and bake for another 10 to 15 minutes.

Serves 4 as an appetizer.

—*Joanne McInveen*

Southern Ontario Pig Tails

5 lbs. pig tails
4 Tbsp. sugar
4 Tbsp. vinegar
½ cup chopped onion
2 Tbsp. brown sugar
2 Tbsp. soya sauce
1½ cups tomato juice

Boil pig tails until tender, then cut off most of the fat. Make sauce by combining remaining ingredients and cook until onions are tender.

Place pig tails in a casserole dish, pour sauce over them and bake at 275° F basting occasionally, for an hour.

Serves 6.

—*Linda Halford*

Rumaki

½ lb. pork liver
10-oz. can water chestnuts
½ cup soya sauce
¼ cup firmly packed brown sugar
2 cloves garlic, finely chopped
¼ tsp. ginger
1 Tbsp. tarragon
1 lb. bacon

Rinse liver and pat dry. Slice into 36 thin pieces. Cut water chestnuts into 36 pieces.

Combine soya sauce, sugar, garlic, ginger and tarragon in plastic bowl. Stir in liver and chestnuts. Cover, refrigerate and marinate for at least 2 hours. Drain.

Cut bacon slices in half. Lay a slice of liver and a piece of chestnut on each bacon strip. Roll up and secure with toothpicks. Bake at 400° F for 25 to 30 minutes, turning once. Drain well.

Serves 12 as an appetizer.

Danish Liver Paste

1½ lbs. pork liver
2-3 large onions
1 lb. bacon fat
½ cup butter
½ cup flour
Milk
Salt & pepper
2 eggs

Grind liver, then onions, then bacon fat to desired smoothness. Melt butter, add flour and stir until smooth. Add milk to make a thick gravy. Add salt and pepper and eggs. Stir in meat, mix well and bake in a loaf pan at 325° F for 1¼ hours.

Makes 3 to 4 cups.

—*Mary Alice Self*

Leeks with Ham and Cheese

12 small leeks, cleaned
½ lb. cooked ham, chopped
½ cup grated Swiss cheese
¾ cup whipping cream
Salt & pepper

Simmer leeks in water for 15 minutes and drain. Arrange in greased baking dish. Sprinkle with salt and pepper and cover with chopped ham. Sprinkle with cheese and pour cream over all.

Bake at 400° F for 10 to 15 minutes.

Serves 4.

—Denyse Fournier

Roast Mustard Lamb

4-lb. leg of lamb
12 Tbsp. oil
1 Tbsp. soya sauce
4 Tbsp. mustard
¼ tsp. garlic powder
½ tsp. rosemary

Trim away most of the fat from the leg of lamb and place the lamb in a shallow roasting pan. Mix together remaining ingredients and spread over the surface of the leg. Leave at room temperature for about an hour, then roast at 325° F for 20 to 30 minutes a pound, or until an internal temperature of 175° is reached.

Serves 6.

—Adele Dueck

Cold Ham Pie

This pie is perfect take-along food for a picnic. Served with a salad, it is also delicious summer luncheon fare.

Pastry for double 9-inch pie
    shell, with ½ tsp. mustard
    & pinch thyme added
1 egg
1 tsp. dry mustard
1 cup sour cream
2 lbs. ham, cooked & ground
1½ cups sliced mushrooms,
    cooked
⅔ cup grated Swiss cheese
¼ cup thinly sliced green
    onion
3 Tbsp. minced parsley
1 egg, beaten with a little milk

Beat together egg, mustard and sour cream. Add ham, mushrooms, cheese, onion and parsley and mix well.

Place in pastry-lined pie dish and top with remaining pastry. Slit top crust to allow steam to escape. Brush top with beaten egg and milk. Bake at 425° F for 30 minutes, reduce heat to 350° and bake for 10 minutes longer. Cool, then chill in refrigerator.

Serves 4 to 6.

—Trudy Mason

Mustard Mousse

An elegant accompaniment to baked ham.

¾ cup sugar
3 tsp. dry mustard
4 eggs
½ cup vinegar
1 envelope gelatin
2 Tbsp. cold water
1 cup whipping cream

Combine sugar and mustard and beat in eggs. Add vinegar. Cook in top of double boiler over boiling water, stirring frequently, until mixture coats spoon.

Meanwhile, soak gelatin in water. Add to thickened mustard mixture, stirring until dissolved. Let cool.

Whip cream until soft peaks form, and fold into cooled mustard mixture. Chill well in mould. Serve with ham.

Makes approximately 2 cups.

—Heather Bonham

Honey Soya Leg of Lamb

6-lb. leg of lamb
Salt & pepper
5-6 Tbsp. liquid honey
4-6 Tbsp. soya sauce

Remove fat and membrane from lamb. Liberally salt and pepper the meat, rubbing in well. Place leg of lamb on a rack in roasting pan and apply honey as a glaze. Add 1 inch of water to pan and roast, uncovered, at 425° F for 30 minutes. Reduce heat to 350° and pour 2 Tbsp. soya sauce over lamb. Repeat every 45 minutes. Total roasting time is 2½ hours. Remove lamb to platter and keep warm.

Remove any fat from sauce in roasting pan and serve sauce with lamb.

Serves 8.

—Lynne Zahariuk

Phil's Lamb

6-lb. leg of lamb
6 cloves garlic, peeled & sliced in half
1 lemon
1 orange
1 cup liquid honey
Tarragon
Salt & pepper
1 cup orange juice
1 cup water
1 onion, quartered

Make slits in lamb with sharp knife and place half a clove of garlic in each. Cut lemon and orange in half and rub over meat, squeezing out the juice. Place fruit pieces into roasting pan with lamb. Pour honey over lamb, then sprinkle with a generous amount of tarragon. Add salt and pepper, then orange juice, water and onion. Let marinate, refrigerated, overnight, basting from time to time.

Roast at 325° F for 18 to 20 minutes per pound, basting every 15 minutes.

Serves 8.

—Philip Wood

Leg of Lamb with Coriander & Garlic

6-lb. leg of lamb
6 cloves garlic, peeled
1 Tbsp. crushed coriander seeds
1 tsp. salt
½ tsp. pepper
2 Tbsp. butter

With the tip of a sharp knife, make six incisions in the leg of lamb near the bone. Press the garlic cloves and the coriander into the incisions and rub lamb with salt and pepper. Place meat in medium-sized roasting pan. Cut butter into small pieces and dot it over the meat.

Roast meat at 375° F for 20 minutes per pound, or until juices run out faintly rosy when meat is pierced with the point of a sharp knife.

Serves 8.

—Dolores de Rosario

Lamb Steak Bigarade

2 lamb steaks, cut from the leg
1 tsp. salt
2 unpeeled oranges, sliced
2 Tbsp. brown sugar
1 Tbsp. orange rind
½ tsp. ginger
¼ tsp. ground cloves
1 tsp. dried mint
¼ cup melted butter

Place steaks in a 2-inch-deep baking dish, rub with salt and cover with orange slices.

Mix together remaining ingredients and pour over the orange slices. Bake at 325° F for 40 minutes, basting frequently.

Serves 4.

—Carol Frost

Turkish Glazed Roast Lamb

This unusual glaze imparts almost none of its own flavours to the meat, but heightens the flavour of the meat itself, as well as keeping the meat tender and juicy. It originated among the nomadic shepherds who carried very little food. They took what they needed from the flocks they were tending — fresh milk and meat.

⅔ cup strong coffee
⅔ cup sugar
⅔ cup milk or cream
4-lb. lamb roast

Combine coffee, sugar and milk and brush freely over lamb while cooking at 350° F for 20 minutes a pound.

Serves 6.

—Randi Kennedy

Pineapple Soya Lamb Chops

1 small onion, chopped
2 cloves garlic, chopped
⅓ cup oil
½ cup soya sauce
⅓ cup pineapple juice
Pineapple rings
2 Tbsp. brown sugar
6 2-inch lamb chops

Combine onion, garlic, oil, soya sauce, pineapple juice, pineapple and sugar and marinate meat for at least 4 hours, turning once. Broil for 12 minutes on each side. Serve topped with pineapple rings.

Serves 2 to 3.

—Barbara Littlejohn

Apricot Stuffed Lamb

1 cup dried apricots
2 cups strong, hot tea
2 cups coarse bread crumbs
3 Tbsp. chopped parsley
½ cup coarsely chopped walnuts
1 egg
Grated rind of lime or lemon
1 tsp. salt
½ tsp. pepper
2 Tbsp. gin
6-lb. shoulder of lamb, deboned

Cut apricots into dime-sized pieces and soak in hot tea for 30 minutes. Drain, reserving liquid. Place fruit in a bowl and add remaining ingredients, except lamb. Mix well and moisten with reserved liquid until damp but not soggy. Spread on meat and roll and tie with cotton cord. Secure loose ends with toothpicks, to be removed when roast is firm.

Roast, covered, at 350° F for 30 minutes, then uncovered for a total of 20 minutes per pound. Baste meat with tea if it starts to look dry.

Serves 8.

—Randi Kennedy

Riverslea Shoulder of Lamb

3-4 lbs. boneless shoulder of lamb
1 cup bread crumbs
2 Tbsp. melted butter
1 onion, finely chopped
1 clove garlic, crushed
1 cup dried apricots, chopped and soaked in water to soften
1 Tbsp. parsley
1 egg, beaten
Salt & pepper

Have your butcher debone and roll (but not tie) a shoulder of lamb. Combine all other ingredients, mixing well. Lay the meat out flat and spread the mixture over it. Roll the meat up and tie several times to hold together.

Roast in an open pan at 350° F for about 20 to 30 minutes per pound.

Serves 6.

—Jean Rivers

Mutton Curry

This dish is particularly tasty served over rice, with side dishes of yogurt, almonds, coconut and sliced bananas.

3 Tbsp. oil
2 onions, chopped
2 cloves garlic, chopped
1½ lbs. mutton, cut into
   small pieces
Flour
2 cups boiling water
¼ cup stewed tomatoes
2 tsp. salt
2 tsp. curry
1½ tsp. cumin
1 tsp. ginger
Pepper
1 apple, peeled & diced
½ cup raisins

Heat oil in heavy pot and brown onions and garlic. Dredge meat in flour and brown. Add boiling water, tomato, salt, curry, cumin, ginger, pepper, apple and raisins. Simmer for 2 hours.

Serves 4.

—*Jeannie Rosenberg*

Baked Lamb & Summer Squash Casserole

2-3 small summer squash
1-2 green peppers
1 tomato
1 lb. chopped lamb
1 tsp. salt
¼ tsp. pepper
1 tsp. basil
¼ cup oil
1 clove garlic, crushed
SAUCE:
2 cloves garlic, crushed
1 cup yogurt
Cayenne
Crushed mint leaves

Cut up squash, green peppers and tomato. Toss in a greased casserole dish with lamb, seasonings, oil and garlic. Mix well and bake, uncovered, at 425° F for 45 minutes.

Meanwhile, make sauce. Mix garlic, yogurt and dash of cayenne. Stir into casserole when cooked and sprinkle with mint leaves.

Serves 4.

—*Rhonda Barnes*

Tenderloin with Oyster Sauce

½ cup beer
½ cup oil
2 cloves garlic, chopped
1 medium onion, chopped
½ tsp. dry mustard
1 large bay leaf
Pepper
2 small lamb tenderloins
Oil for cooking
2 stalks celery, diagonally
   sliced
½ cup sliced mushrooms
½ cup sliced green pepper
2 scallions, chopped
2 Tbsp. oyster sauce
3 Tbsp. water
1 Tbsp. cornstarch
Pepper

Combine beer, oil, garlic, onion, mustard, bay leaf and pepper. Cut meat in ¼-inch slices and marinate for 1 hour in above mixture, then drain.

Heat oil in skillet and add meat. Fry until browned, then add vegetables and fry until celery is softened. Combine last 4 items and add to meat, bring back to boil and serve over brown rice.

Serves 3 to 4.

—*Charlene Skidmore*

Moussaka

Of Greek origin, the delicate flavour of the eggplant mingling with the succulence of the spring lamb makes this dish well worth the work.

1½ lbs. potatoes
2 medium eggplants
Olive oil
4 large tomatoes, peeled & thinly sliced
Basil
1 large white onion, thinly sliced
1 lb. ground spring lamb
Mint
Garlic powder
2 Tbsp. butter
2 Tbsp. flour
1 cup milk, heated
½ cup grated Emmenthal cheese

Peel potatoes, slice ¼-inch thick and parboil for 10 minutes. Drain and place half in bottom of greased casserole dish.

Trim eggplant and slice ½-inch thick. Fry a few at a time in oil until lightly browned on both sides. Place half the eggplant over the potatoes. Place half the sliced tomatoes over top of eggplant and sprinkle lightly with basil.

Sauté onion in same skillet as eggplant in small amount of oil until transparent, and top tomatoes with half the onions.

In same skillet, adding more oil if necessary, brown lamb and season lightly with mint and garlic. If meat seems dry, add a few tablespoons water or stock. Spread meat evenly over onions. Add remaining layers in this order: onions, tomatoes sprinkled with basil, eggplant and potatoes.

Melt butter in small saucepan, add flour and stir roux for a minute or so over medium-low heat. Whisk in heated milk over medium heat until thick, then stir in cheese and cook until melted. Pour over casserole and bake at 375° F for 30 to 35 minutes, or until top is lightly browned. Remove from oven and cool for 10 minutes before serving.

Serves 6.

—Veronica Green

Apple Mint Lamb Shanks

These are easy, delicious and economical. The glaze can be used as a marinade, a roasting sauce or a barbecuing glaze and can be used on any cut of lamb with good results.

1 cup boiling water
3 Tbsp. dried or 1 cup fresh mint leaves
6-oz. can frozen apple juice concentrate, thawed
3 Tbsp. honey
4 lbs. lamb shanks

Combine water and mint leaves in a saucepan and let steep for 15 minutes to make a strong tea. Add apple juice and honey and heat gently to blend.

Marinate shanks in this for at least 1 hour and as long as 24 hours. Remove shanks from marinade and roast, uncovered, at 325° F for 1 to 1½ hours, turning and basting frequently.

Serves 4.

—Randi Kennedy

Irish Stew

3-4 Tbsp. shortening
1 medium onion, chopped
1 clove garlic, minced
1-1½ lbs. stewing lamb
1¼ cup flour
1 tsp. salt
¼ tsp. pepper
8-10 medium potatoes, chopped
3 large carrots, cut in strips
¼ large cabbage, chopped

Melt 1 Tbsp. shortening in large pot. Brown onion and garlic and set aside. Melt another tablespoon of shortening. Coat meat with flour, salt and pepper and brown, adding shortening as needed. Combine meat and onion mixture, add water to cover and simmer, covered, for 2 to 3 hours or until tender. Add potatoes and carrots and cook for 30 minutes. Add cabbage and cook until tender. Thicken with a little flour and water mixture if desired.

Serves 4.

—Lucille Kalyniak

Janet's Lamb Kidneys

6 lamb kidneys
3 Tbsp. butter
¼ lb. mushrooms, sliced
¼ cup sherry
2 thick bread slices

Remove outer skin from kidneys, split them lengthwise and remove the Y-shaped ligaments inside with scissors. Melt butter in large skillet and sauté mushrooms until nearly done. Push them to cooler side of pan and add the kidneys, cooking and turning until the red is gone. Push them to cool side of pan. Toast 2 slices of bread. Place mushrooms and kidneys on toast, heat pan up and deglaze with sherry, then pour over toast.

Serves 2.

—Randi Kennedy

Lamb Yogurt Tarts

CRUST:
8 oz. cream cheese
8 Tbsp. unsalted butter
2 cups flour
½ tsp. salt
FILLING:
2 tsp. butter
1 cup finely chopped onions
1 lb. ground lamb
1 cup pine nuts
¼ tsp. salt
½ tsp. pepper
½ tsp. ground allspice
2 Tbsp. chopped parsley
1½ cups unflavoured yogurt

To make crust, blend together cream cheese and butter and work in flour and salt. Wrap in wax paper and chill for at least 2 hours.

Meanwhile, make filling. Melt butter and cook onions until transparent. Add meat and cook until red is gone, but do not brown. Drain and cool.

While filling is cooling, roll out dough and cut to make 24 tart shells. When meat is cool, add remaining ingredients, reserving ½ cup yogurt. Mix until smooth, fill tart shells and bake at 350° F for 30 minutes. Serve with remaining yogurt.

Serves 24 as a party snack, or 8 as a main dish.

—Randi Kennedy

Lamb Loaf

This loaf slices well cold and is delicious on rye bread with alfalfa sprouts and Dijon mustard.

1 lb. ground lamb
⅛ tsp. celery seed
⅛ tsp. cloves
¼ tsp. savory
¼ tsp. cinnamon
⅛ tsp. pepper
¼ tsp. salt
¼ green pepper, diced
1 small onion, diced
1 medium tomato, peeled & diced
2 slices bacon, browned & diced
½ cup oatmeal

Combine all ingredients, mix well and bake at 350° F for 45 minutes to 1 hour.

Serves 6 to 8.

—Kathryn MacDonald

Lamb & Apple Stew

4 Tbsp. oil
1 onion, finely chopped
1½ lbs. lean stewing lamb, cubed
1 tsp. salt
White pepper
Cinnamon
1½ cups water
4 small cooking apples

Heat half the oil in a heavy pot and sauté onion until wilted. Add lamb and brown on all sides. Add seasonings and water and bring to boil. Reduce heat, then cover and simmer for 1 hour. Heat remaining oil in a skillet and sauté apples gently for 2 minutes. Add apples to stew and continue to simmer for 15 minutes.

Serves 4.

—Margaret Babcock

Roast Tenderloin with Lemon-Tarragon Cream Sauce

The shallots and tarragon — both in uncommonly large quantities here — combine to produce a sauce that is rich and tasty. Be sure to use French tarragon — Russian will result in an unpleasantly bitter flavour.

4-lb. veal or beef tenderloin
pepper
2 Tbsp. butter
2 Tbsp. oil
¾ cup minced shallots
1 cup chicken stock
1 cup dry vermouth
2 Tbsp. lemon juice
¼ cup packed, chopped
    tarragon
1½ cups heavy cream
salt

Pat tenderloin dry and season with pepper. Melt butter and oil in large heavy skillet over medium-high heat. Brown tenderloin well on all sides. Transfer to roasting pan.

In tenderloin drippings, cook shallots over low heat until softened — about 5 minutes. Add stock, vermouth, lemon juice and tarragon and boil until reduced to 1 cup. Add 1 cup cream and boil again until reduced to 1 cup. Add salt and pepper.

Roast tenderloin, uncovered, at 450° F for about 15 minutes (for rare). Meanwhile, whip remaining ½ cup cream and fold into warm sauce. Slice meat thinly and pass sauce separately.

Serves 8.

—*Ray Rewcastle*

Veal in Paprika & Cayenne Cream Sauce

The Madeira in this dish adds both flavour and body to the sauce.

paprika
4-6 pieces veal, pounded
    thinly
½ lb. butter
1 large Spanish onion,
    chopped
salt & pepper
¼ tsp. cayenne
2½ cups light cream
2 Tbsp. chopped parsley
2 oz. Madeira

Sprinkle paprika generously on both sides of veal slices, pressing firmly with fingers to make it stick. In heavy skillet, melt ⅓ of butter, add onion and sauté until soft. Set aside and keep warm. Add remaining butter to skillet and sauté veal slices one minute per side, then remove veal and keep warm in oven.

Return butter and onions to butter in skillet, add salt and pepper, cayenne and cream and stir over medium heat for 5 to 10 minutes, allowing cream to reduce and thicken. Add parsley and Madeira, stir and return veal and juices to sauce. Cover meat with sauce. Heat for one minute and serve with hot buttered noodles.

Serves 4 to 6.

—*Nancy Gray*

Chevon Stew

2 lbs. goat meat, cubed
6 Tbsp. olive oil
6 Tbsp. flour
2 tsp. salt
¼ tsp. pepper
2 cloves garlic, crushed
1 bay leaf
2 Tbsp. parsley
2 cups beef stock
2 cups water
1 cup dry red wine
1 cup sliced carrots
1 cup diced potatoes
½ cup diced turnip
½ cup diced parsnip
1 cup peas
6 medium onions, chopped

Brown meat in oil in large pot, then remove and set aside. Stir flour and spices into oil in pot. Gradually stir in beef stock, water and wine, stirring until smooth. Return meat to pot, add onions and simmer for 1 hour. Add remaining ingredients and cook over low heat for 3 to 4 hours.

Serves 4.

—*Maria Nisbett*

Hot Stir-Fried Beef

1 lb. lean beef
2 stalks celery
1 chili pepper
1 Tbsp. cornstarch
1 egg white
oil
1 Tbsp. soy sauce
½ tsp. sugar
1 tsp. hot pepper oil
3 cloves garlic
2 Tbsp. sweet rice wine
1 Tbsp. black bean sauce
½ tsp. minced gingerroot

Cut beef into very thin strips, slice celery and crush chili pepper. Blend cornstarch and egg white, add beef and toss. Heat oil and deep-fry beef for 3 minutes. Remove meat from oil. Heat 1 Tbsp. oil in another skillet. Sauté celery for 2 minutes, stir in beef and remaining ingredients and stir-fry until heated through.

Serves 2.

—Mary-Lee Judah

Bulgogi

This is a traditional Korean stir-fry. Serve over fried noodle pancakes accompanied by stir-fried snow peas and mushrooms. The flavour of this dish is very delicate so it is important not to overcook it.

12-oz. fillet steak, sliced into
  thin strips
MARINADE:
1 Tbsp. chopped leek
1 green onion, chopped
½ shallot, chopped
1 clove garlic, minced
¼ tsp. sugar
½ tsp. salt
4 Tbsp. light soy sauce
1 Tbsp. sesame oil
3-4 drops Tabasco sauce
⅔ cup peanut oil
SAUCE:
¼ tsp. salt
¼ tsp. sugar
1 tsp. bean paste
½ tsp. cayenne
1 tsp. sesame seeds
½ tsp. minced garlic
4 Tbsp. soy sauce
1 Tbsp. sesame oil

Combine marinade ingredients, pour over steak and marinate for 3 to 4 hours. Drain. Combine sauce ingredients and mix well. Stir-fry beef with sauce ingredients.

Serves 2.

—Marney Allen

Netherlands Beef Stroganoff

"This recipe produces a flavourful but light stroganoff with a distinctive peppery taste. It was given to me by a friend who is a doctor. He got it from a grateful patient from the Netherlands."

2 lbs. steak
¼ lb. butter
1 onion, diced
½ tsp. pepper
2 oz. vodka
3 Tbsp. chili sauce
½ Tbsp. tomato paste
1 tsp. paprika
1½ Tbsp. flour
3-4 drops Tabasco sauce
cayenne
2 cups light cream
salt & pepper

Slice steak into small strips. Melt butter and brown meat for 1 minute. Place meat in warm oven.

Sauté onion and pepper in same skillet until onion is transparent. Add vodka, ignite and let all liquid burn out. Add chili sauce, tomato paste, paprika and flour and mix until smooth. Add Tabasco sauce, cayenne and cream. Cook, stirring, for 5 minutes. Season with salt and pepper. Return meat to skillet and mix gently.

Serves 4 to 6.

—William H. Combs

Anglo-Irish Stew

"My mother used wartime rationing as an excuse for not teaching me to cook when I was growing up in England. However, I watched her make Irish Stew so often that I discovered I could make it years later. My recipe has never let me down and has been passed on to sons, daughters-in-law and countless friends."

¾ cup flour
salt & pepper
1-1½ lbs. stewing beef or lamb
3 Tbsp. shortening
beef stock
2 bay leaves
3 large carrots
1 leek (optional)
3 onions
4 large potatoes
small turnip (optional)
thyme
1 tsp. curry powder
2 tsp. Worcestershire sauce

Put flour and salt and pepper into paper bag and shake to combine. Cut meat into cubes approximately 1½ inches square. Toss a few at a time into the bag and shake until coated. Melt shortening in large skillet and brown meat well.

Fill a large heavy pot about two-thirds full with stock or water and bring to a full boil. Add bay leaves and browned meat, including any drippings from the skillet. Bring back to full boil, then simmer for approximately 1 hour.

Slice carrots and leek and chop onions, potatoes and turnip. Add all vegetables to pot. Add remaining ingredients, using at least a teaspoon of whole thyme, more if you like its flavour. Stir well, return to boil and then lower heat until the stew is just bubbling gently. Taste and correct seasoning. Cook for 20 minutes. Serve with dumplings if desired.

Serves 6.

—Barbara Brennan

French Pot Roast

"This fills the house with a wonderful smell and produces tender meat with lots of rich sauce."

4-5-lb. rump or round roast
salt & pepper
2 Tbsp. shortening, lard or suet
2 Tbsp. butter
12-16 small white onions
12-16 small carrots
1 cup dry red wine
2 cups beef stock
2 cloves garlic, crushed
1 small bay leaf
thyme
chopped parsley
4 Tbsp. cornstarch, mixed with 1 cup water

Rub roast with salt and pepper. In large pot, brown roast on all sides in hot shortening. Remove roast and set aside.

Add butter to pot and brown onions and carrots lightly. Remove vegetables and set aside. Return meat to pot, add wine, stock, garlic, bay leaf, thyme and parsley. Cover and cook slowly for about 1½ hours. Add onions and carrots, cover and cook slowly for about 1 hour longer, or until meat is tender. Remove bay leaf and discard.

Transfer meat to warm platter and surround with vegetables. Add cornstarch mixture to liquid in pot and boil until sauce is slightly thickened. Spoon a little sauce over the roast and serve remainder in a gravy boat.

Serves 6.

—Mrs. D.J. Zurbrigg

Maple Stew

This is a rich, hearty stew that can be simmered on the stove or baked in the oven. It has quite a sweet flavour.

¼ cup flour
salt & pepper
1 clove garlic, crushed
¼ tsp. celery salt
1½ lbs. stewing beef, cut into 1" cubes
19-oz. can tomatoes
½ cup dry red wine
¼ cup maple syrup
4 potatoes, diced
2 carrots, sliced

Combine flour, salt and pepper, garlic and celery salt. Toss beef in this. Place in casserole dish or saucepan. Add remaining ingredients and ½ cup water. Cover and simmer over low heat for 2½ to 3 hours, or bake at 300° F for 4 hours.

Serves 4.

—Rosalind Mechefske

Beer Stew

4 slices bacon
2 lbs. stewing beef, cut into
   1" cubes
2½ cups chopped onions
2 cloves garlic, minced
salt & pepper
12 oz. beer
1 cup beef stock
1 Tbsp. vinegar
¼ tsp. thyme
2 Tbsp. flour

Fry bacon until crisp, remove from pan and set aside. Brown meat in bacon drippings with onions, garlic and salt and pepper. Add beer, stock, vinegar, thyme and reserved bacon and simmer for 2½ hours.

Stir a little of the hot juice into the flour until smooth, then stir back into stew, cooking until gravy is slightly thickened.

Serves 4.

—Reo Belhumeur

Beef Rouladen

This rouladen comes from the Harz mountain region of Germany. It is a delicious dish for horseradish lovers. Have your butcher cut the rouladen for you.

8 rouladen, 3/16" thick
¼ cup mustard
¼ cup horseradish
salt & pepper
4 slices bacon, chopped
1½ onions, thinly sliced
oil
½ cup red wine
1 cup beef stock

Pound rouladen with mallet until very thin — almost falling apart. Mix mustard and horseradish together and spread on meat. Sprinkle generously with salt and pepper. Lightly sauté bacon and onions, then place on meat. Roll each piece up tightly, folding in ends. Secure with toothpicks.

Heat oil in large skillet and brown meat very well. Add wine and stock to cover, and simmer, covered, for 2 to 2½ hours, adding liquid as required. Reduce sauce slightly before serving.

Serves 4.

—Mary Rogers

Sauerbraten

A very popular German dish, this is similar in concept to corned beef. The beef needs to marinate for 4 days. Serve with potato pancakes.

4-lb. blade roast
1 large onion, sliced
8-10 peppercorns
3 cloves
2 bay leaves
¼ cup sugar
2 cups vinegar
2 tsp. salt
1 lemon, sliced
2 Tbsp. plus ¼ cup butter
¼ cup flour
½ cup sour cream

Wipe meat and place in deep crock with cover. In stainless-steel or enamel pot, combine 2 cups water, onion, peppercorns, cloves, bay leaves, sugar, vinegar and salt. Heat but do not boil, then pour over meat and cool. Add lemon slices, cover and refrigerate for 4 days, turning daily. Remove meat from marinade and drain well. Strain marinade and reserve.

Heat 2 Tbsp. butter in deep Dutch oven over low heat. Add meat and brown slowly. Gradually add 2 cups marinade and bring to a boil. Reduce heat, cover and simmer for 2½ to 3 hours, or until meat is tender. Add liquid if necessary. Remove meat, set aside and keep warm. Set aside cooking liquid as well.

In same pot, melt ¼ cup butter and blend in flour, cooking until golden. Remove from heat and slowly add 3 cups liquid (cooking liquid, more marinade and hot water if needed). Bring to a rapid boil, stirring constantly, until gravy thickens. Reduce heat and slowly stir in sour cream, making certain it does not curdle. Serve with meat.

Serves 6 to 8.

—Anton Gross

Steak & Kidney Pie

Prepare the filling for this pie a day ahead to allow the flavours to blend together properly. Use beef, veal or lamb kidneys.

FILLING:
1 lb. kidneys
2½ lbs. round steak
½ cup flour
6 Tbsp. oil
1 cup thinly sliced onions
½ lb. mushrooms, sliced
½ tsp. salt
½ tsp. pepper
½ tsp. rosemary
½ tsp. tarragon
1 Tbsp. tomato paste
2 tsp. Worcestershire sauce
1 cup red wine
1 cup beef stock
PASTRY:
1½ cups flour
½ tsp. salt
½ cup shortening
1 egg yolk, beaten

To make filling: Clean kidneys, split, remove fat and soak in salted water for 1 hour. Dry and cube. Cut steak into cubes. Toss steak and kidneys with flour to coat. Heat oil and brown meat, removing it as it browns. Add onions and mushrooms to drippings, adding oil if necessary. Sauté for 5 minutes, until onions and mushrooms are lightly browned, stirring frequently. Return meat to skillet, add remaining filling ingredients and simmer for 2 hours or until meat is tender. Cool, then refrigerate overnight.

To prepare crust: Sift flour and salt into bowl, then cut in shortening until mixture resembles coarse cornmeal. Mix egg yolk with 3 Tbsp. ice water and add to flour, tossing with a fork until particles cling together. Form into a ball and refrigerate overnight.

To assemble: After removing any congealed fat from the surface of the filling, place filling in greased 2-quart casserole dish. Roll out pastry until it is 2 inches larger around than the top of the casserole dish. Place dough on top of filling, turning it under at the edges. Cut steam vents and bake at 400° F for 30 minutes, reduce heat to 350° F and bake for another 15 to 20 minutes.

Serves 4 to 6.

—*Shirley Mullen Hooper*

Sesame Steak

Present this in a terra-cotta dish. It is a nutty, slightly sweet Korean method of preparing meat.

2 lbs. steak
1 Tbsp. toasted & pulverized sesame seeds
3 green onions, finely chopped
4 cloves garlic, crushed
¼ cup plus 1 Tbsp. soy sauce
2 Tbsp. sesame oil
¼ cup sugar
2 Tbsp. sherry
⅛ tsp. pepper

Slice meat thinly, diagonally across the grain; score each piece lightly with an X. Combine remaining ingredients in a bowl, mixing well. Add steak and stir to coat well. Refrigerate for at least 30 minutes. Grill for 2 minutes. Serve with rice.

Serves 4 to 6.

—*J. W. Houston*

Orange Marinated Beef

"This roast is delicious served on a warm platter with buttered yams. But it just might be even better the next day, sliced very thinly and served cold."

4-lb. boneless round or rump roast
½ cup red wine vinegar
2 cups orange juice
2 onions, chopped
1 Tbsp. pickling spice
12 peppercorns
1 bay leaf
2 Tbsp. oil

Pierce roast all over with fork. Combine vinegar, juice, onions, pickling spice, peppercorns and bay leaf and bring to a boil. Simmer for 5 minutes, then cool. Pour marinade over roast. Refrigerate for 48 hours, turning roast frequently.

Remove from marinade and brown in oil in Dutch oven. Pour marinade over beef, cover and cook over low heat for 3 to 3½ hours, turning occasionally.

Serves 6 to 8.

—*Kathryn MacDonald*

London Broil with Lime & Ginger Marinade

Lime and ginger bring an unexpected but delicious flavour to this steak dish.

3 cloves garlic, minced
2-3 pieces gingerroot, minced
½ cup soy sauce
4 tsp. sugar
2 tsp. sesame oil
juice of 1 lime
2 Tbsp. sherry
½ tsp. pepper
2-3 lbs. flank steak

Combine all ingredients except steak and mix well. Pour over meat and marinate for at least 6 hours but preferably overnight. Broil in oven or on grill, about 10 minutes per side.

Serves 4 to 6.

—*Kathy Lempert*

Sweet & Sour Meatloaf

Serve this hot or cold—it makes excellent sandwiches on thick slices of rye bread with mustard.

MEATLOAF:
1½ lbs. ground beef
1 onion, chopped
½ cup tomato sauce
1 cup bread crumbs
¼ tsp. salt
1 egg, beaten
SAUCE:
½ cup tomato sauce
2 Tbsp. vinegar
2 Tbsp. brown sugar
2 Tbsp. Dijon mustard

Combine meat loaf ingredients and mix well. Press into greased loaf pan, leaving 1-inch space on all sides.

Combine sauce ingredients with 1 cup water and mix well. Pour over meat loaf. Bake, uncovered, at 350° F for 1½ hours, basting frequently.

Serves 6.

—*Bette Warkentin*

Tortilla Stack

This results in a layered dish that looks like a torte or crêpe pyramid. The filling tastes wonderful and is very hearty.

1 lb. ground beef
4 oz. canned green chilies, seeded & diced
4 oz. canned jalapeno peppers, seeded & diced
1 onion, diced
2-3 cloves garlic, minced
2 cups tomato sauce
1 Tbsp. cumin
1 Tbsp. coriander
4 cups cooked pinto beans
20 corn tortillas
1 lb. Monterey Jack cheese, grated

Brown ground beef, then add chilies, peppers, onion and garlic and sauté until onion is translucent. Add tomato sauce, cumin, coriander and beans and simmer for 15 minutes.

Quickly fry tortillas on both sides in hot, dry skillet until crisp.

To assemble, coat bottom of greased casserole dish with a little sauce. Layer tortillas, sauce and cheese to top of dish. Bake, uncovered, at 350° F for 15 minutes, or until heated through and cheese is melted.

Serves 6.

—*Sandra Senchok-Crandall*

Chili Cornpone Pie

This makes a hearty meal after a winter day spent outside.

CHILI:
3 onions, chopped
1 lb. ground beef
1 green pepper, chopped
2 stalks celery, sliced
3½ cups tomato sauce
6-8 mushrooms, sliced
2 tsp. chili powder
2 pinches dried chilies
Tabasco sauce
1 tsp. Worcestershire sauce
¼ tsp. pepper
1 tsp. celery seed
1 clove garlic, crushed
1 tsp. basil
1 tsp. thyme
3½ cups cooked kidney beans
TOPPING:
1 cup flour
¾ cup cornmeal
2½ tsp. baking powder
⅛-¼ tsp. curry
1 egg
1 cup milk
¼ cup oil

Sauté onions and ground beef, adding green pepper and celery just as meat is almost cooked. Add 2 to 3 Tbsp. water and simmer until meat is cooked. Add remaining chili ingredients, and simmer for 15 minutes.

Meanwhile, prepare topping: Sift together flour, cornmeal, baking powder and curry. Combine egg, milk and oil and mix gently into dry ingredients.

Pour chili into greased 9" x 13" baking pan. Spread batter on top and bake at 400° F for 40 to 45 minutes.

Serves 4 to 6.

—Shelley Bishop

Saturday Night Pie

A variation of Shepherd's Pie, this recipe bases its crust on cornmeal rather than on mashed potatoes.

FILLING:
1 lb. ground beef
1 cup chopped onion
1 cup chopped green pepper
2 cups tomato sauce
1-2 Tbsp. chili powder
1 tsp. salt
1 tsp. pepper
1 cup corn
TOPPING:
2 eggs
½ cup buttermilk
1 Tbsp. butter
1 Tbsp. flour
1 tsp. baking soda
¼ tsp. salt
¾ cup cornmeal

Brown beef and onion in skillet. Add remaining filling ingredients, bring to a boil, reduce heat, cover and simmer for 15 minutes. Pour into ungreased deep 10" pie plate.

For topping: Beat together eggs, buttermilk and butter. Beat in remaining ingredients until smooth. Spread evenly over filling and bake, uncovered, at 350° F for 20 minutes.

Serves 6.

—Patricia Daine

German Meatloaf

The applesauce glaze on top of this meat loaf makes it really attractive—a good combination of apple, beer and meat.

2 lbs. ground beef
1 lb. ground pork
1 egg
1 small onion, finely chopped
½ cup fine dry bread crumbs
1 medium apple, peeled, cored & chopped
1 tsp. savory
1 tsp. salt
¼ tsp. pepper
1 cup beer
1 cup thick applesauce

Combine all ingredients but applesauce and mix well. Turn into greased shallow baking pan and shape into a loaf. Bake for 45 minutes at 350° F, then spread with applesauce. Bake, uncovered, for another 30 to 45 minutes. Serve hot or cold.

Serves 6 to 8.

—Louise Poole

Swedish Meatballs

¾ cup milk
4 slices bread, crumbled
1 lb. ground steak
½ lb. ground veal
½ lb. ground pork
1 onion, grated
2 tsp. salt
⅛ tsp. nutmeg
⅛ tsp. allspice
1 clove garlic, crushed
¼ tsp. pepper
oil
1½ cups beef stock

Pour milk over bread and beat until consistency of paste. Add remaining ingredients except oil and stock and mix well. Form into meatballs, 1 inch in diameter. Fry in a little oil until browned on all sides. Place in casserole dish, pour stock over and bake, uncovered, at 350° F for 30 minutes.

Makes approximately 36 meatballs.

Beef & Tomato Cobbler

This cobbler topping over a sloppy-joe-type beef mixture is a quick and easy casserole.

3 Tbsp. oil
2 large onions, chopped
2 Tbsp. flour
2 cups tomato juice
2 Tbsp. tomato purée
¼ tsp. thyme
¼ tsp. basil
¼ tsp. oregano
salt & pepper
1½ lbs. ground beef
Cobbler:
1 cup flour
2 tsp. baking powder
salt
3 Tbsp. butter
milk

Heat oil and sauté onions until transparent. Stir in flour and cook for 2 to 3 minutes. Gradually add tomato juice, purée, thyme, basil, oregano and salt and pepper. Add meat and simmer for 10 minutes, breaking up lumps. Transfer to casserole dish, cover and bake at 350° F for 1 hour.

Meanwhile, prepare cobbler: Mix flour, baking powder and salt. Cut in butter to form crumbs, and add milk until dough can be rolled. Roll ½ inch thick and cut into rounds.

Remove cover from casserole dish, place biscuits on meat and bake for 15 minutes more.

Serves 6.

—*Midge Denault*

Pastitsio

A Greek dish, Pastitsio is a macaroni, tomato and meat casserole that is topped with a custard and baked. Ground lamb may be used instead of ground beef, if it is available.

1 lb. ground beef
1 large onion, chopped
1 clove garlic, minced
2 cups canned tomatoes
½ tsp. salt
pepper
⅛ tsp. cinnamon
2 cups dry macaroni, cooked
½ cup Parmesan cheese
3 Tbsp. butter
¼ cup flour
2 cups milk
3 eggs

Cook beef, onion and garlic until meat is browned, then drain. Add tomatoes, ¼ tsp. salt, pepper and cinnamon and simmer for 15 minutes. Add macaroni to meat mixture with ¼ cup cheese. Place in 9" x 13" pan and set aside.

Make a white sauce by melting butter, stirring in flour and remaining ¼ tsp. salt and cooking for 2 to 3 minutes. Stir in milk and cook, stirring, until thickened. Cool slightly, then beat in eggs one at a time, followed by remaining ¼ cup cheese. Pour over meat mixture. Bake, uncovered, at 375° F for 35 minutes, or until knife inserted in the centre comes out clean.

Serves 6.

—*Adele Dueck*

Meatball Stroganoff

1 lb. ground beef
1 clove garlic, crushed
2 Tbsp. oil
1 onion, sliced
¼ lb. mushrooms, sliced
2 Tbsp. flour
1 cup beef stock
2 Tbsp. red wine
2 Tbsp. tomato sauce
¾ tsp. Dijon mustard
½ cup sour cream

Combine beef and garlic and form into meatballs. Heat oil and sauté onion and mushrooms until lightly browned. Set aside, and in the same pan sauté meatballs, turning to brown all sides. Remove meatballs. Stir flour into pan drippings and cook for 3 to 4 minutes. Add stock and cook, stirring, until sauce thickens. Add wine, tomato sauce and mustard and mix well. Return meatballs, onions and mushrooms to skillet. Cover and simmer for 20 minutes. Stir in sour cream and heat through without boiling.

Serves 4.

—Ann Chambers

Italian Meatballs

4 slices stale bread
2 eggs, beaten
1 lb. ground beef
¼ cup Parmesan cheese
2 Tbsp. snipped parsley
1 tsp. salt
¼ tsp. oregano
pepper
2 Tbsp. oil

Trim crusts from bread and soak bread in ½ cup water for 2 to 3 minutes. Wring out bread and discard excess water. Tear bread up into large bowl. Add eggs and mix well with egg beater. Combine with beef, cheese, parsley, salt, oregano and pepper. With wet hands, form into small balls. Brown slowly in hot oil, turning often so they don't stick to the bottom. Add meatballs to your favourite sauce and simmer for 30 minutes. Serve over hot spaghetti. Pass extra Parmesan cheese.

Makes 20 meatballs.

—Joyce M. Holland

Sweet & Sour Meatballs with Prunes

2 lbs. ground beef
2 eggs
1 cup bread crumbs
1 onion, chopped
1 tsp. salt
6 prunes
3 tsp. raisins
8-10 peppercorns
2-3 bay leaves
20 oz. tomato juice
¼ cup sugar
juice of 2-3 lemons
½ cabbage, coarsely chopped

Combine beef, eggs and bread crumbs, mix well and form into meatballs. Bring 4 cups water to a boil, then add onion, salt, prunes, raisins, peppercorns, bay leaves and meatballs. Cook for 20 minutes, then add tomato juice, sugar, lemon juice and cabbage. Simmer, covered, for 1 hour.

Serves 6 to 8.

—Lynn Andersen

Liver with Mushrooms & Bacon

1 lb. calf's liver
8 slices bacon, chopped
10-12 mushrooms, sliced
1 large onion, chopped
1 clove garlic, minced
1-2 tsp. flour
½-1 cup beef stock
salt & pepper
parsley

Slice liver into thin strips and set aside. Sauté bacon, mushrooms, onion and garlic until bacon is quite crisp. Remove from skillet with slotted spoon. Add flour to a very small amount of heated stock. Blend well and continue adding stock until you have ½ cup. Set aside.

Cook liver over medium-high heat in bacon fat until lightly coloured. Add bacon mixture and stock. Cook until thickened, adding salt and pepper and parsley.

Serves 3 to 4.

—Colleen Suche

Bacon & Liver Bake

6 slices bacon, chopped
1 cup chopped onion
½ cup flour
1 tsp. salt
pepper
1 lb. calf's liver, cut into
    serving-sized pieces
1½ cups milk
¼ cup fine bread crumbs
1 Tbsp. butter, melted

Combine bacon and onion in skillet and cook until bacon is crisp and onion is tender.

Remove and set aside, reserving drippings in skillet. Combine flour, salt and pepper, and coat liver with this. Reserve leftover flour mixture. Brown liver in skillet, then remove to baking dish. Blend reserved flour with pan drippings until smooth and bubbly, then add milk. Cook, stirring, until thickened and bubbly. Pour sauce over liver and sprinkle with bacon and onion pieces. Combine bread crumbs with melted butter and sprinkle over all. Bake, uncovered, at 350° F for 25 minutes.

Serves 4.

—LaRae DuFresne Bergo

Liver Stroganoff

1 lb. beef liver
4 bacon slices
1 small onion, chopped
1 cup sliced mushrooms
1 cup beef stock
1 Tbsp. flour
¼ cup sour cream

Cut liver into ½-inch-wide strips and set aside. Cook bacon until crisp, remove from skillet and drain. Cook liver, onion and mushrooms in bacon drippings until liver is lightly browned. Add beef stock and simmer for 20 minutes, or until liver is fork-tender. Stir flour into 3 Tbsp. water until smooth and add to skillet. Cook until thickened. Add crumbled bacon and sour cream.

Serves 2.

—Linda Russell

Pork with Port & Garlic

several cloves garlic
2½-lb. rolled loin of pork
1 Tbsp. oil
1 cup port wine
1 tsp. rosemary
½ tsp. salt
1 Tbsp. butter
1 Tbsp. flour

Cut garlic into slivers and stick into folds of pork loin. In Dutch oven, brown pork on all sides in oil. Pour off fat and add port, rosemary and salt. Bring to a boil. Bake, tightly covered, at 325° F for about 2 hours, adding water if necessary. Soften butter and mix with flour. When pork is tender, remove to a platter and mix butter-flour mixture into pan juices a little at a time, just until sauce begins to thicken. Add salt to taste.

Serves 4 to 6.

—Ruth Ellis Haworth

Sweet & Sour Pork with Peaches

This has a colourful appearance and a nicely balanced flavour, making use of healthful and accessible ingredients.

1½ lbs. boneless pork, cut
　　into 1" pieces
2 Tbsp. soy sauce
3 Tbsp. oil
1 clove garlic pepper
2 onions, cut into eighths
1 green pepper, chopped
½ cup sugar
2 Tbsp. cornstarch
¼ tsp. salt
⅓ cup vinegar
2 Tbsp. tomato paste
2 cups sliced peaches
1 large tomato, cut into
　　small wedges

Toss pork cubes in mixture of soy sauce and 1 Tbsp. oil, then marinate for 15 minutes. In large skillet, brown garlic in 2 Tbsp. oil over medium heat. Remove garlic. Brown pork cubes in garlic-flavoured oil, then reduce heat and cook for 15 to 20 minutes longer, stirring often. Sprinkle with pepper. Add onions and green pepper and stir-fry for 2 to 3 minutes.

While meat and vegetables are cooking, make the sauce in a small saucepan. Mix together sugar, cornstarch and salt. Stir in vinegar, 1 cup water and tomato paste. Bring to boil, stirring, until smooth and clear. Drain any excess fat from the frying pan, add sauce to pork mixture, simmer for a minute, taste and adjust seasoning. Add peaches and tomato, cover pan, and cook gently just until heated through.

Serves 4.

—Mrs. D.J. Zurbrigg

Chinese-Style Liver

Serve this tasty, unusual liver dish on a bed of fried bean sprouts.

3 Tbsp. soy sauce
1 Tbsp. honey
1 Tbsp. brown sugar
2 Tbsp. wine vinegar
1 small piece gingerroot,
　　chopped
1 large clove garlic, minced
1 Tbsp. peppercorns
1 lb. beef liver, sliced in thin
　　strips
1 Tbsp. cornstarch
½ cup chicken stock
2 Tbsp. oil
2-3 onions, quartered
10 mushrooms, sliced

Combine soy sauce, honey, sugar, vinegar, ginger, garlic and peppercorns. Pour over liver and let stand for at least 2 hours but preferably overnight, stirring occasionally.

Remove liver from marinade, then strain marinade. Combine marinade with cornstarch and stock, then set aside.

Heat oil and sauté onions and mushrooms until limp. Add to marinade. Sauté liver until lightly coloured. Pour marinade-onion mixture into pan and cook until thickened, stirring constantly.

Serves 2.

—Colleen Suche

Pork in Red Wine with Apple Rings

Start this the evening before you plan to serve it by soaking the dried apple rings in water overnight.

2 Tbsp. oil
2 onions chopped
2 lbs. pork tenderloin, cubed
1¼ cups red wine
⅔ cup chicken stock
2" cinnamon stick
2 slivers lemon rind
salt & pepper
2-3 Tbsp. tomato paste
2 Tbsp. chopped parsley
½ cup dried apple rings,
　　soaked overnight
2 Tbsp. cornstarch

Heat oil and sauté onions until soft. Add pork and cook until browned. Add wine, stock, cinnamon, lemon rind, salt and pepper and tomato paste. Cover and simmer for 1 hour. Stir in parsley and apple rings and cook for 30 minutes more. Discard cinnamon and lemon rind. Dissolve cornstarch in a bit of the hot liquid, then stir into pot and cook, stirring, until gravy is thickened.

Serves 6.

—Ellen Wicklum

Pepper Pork en Brochette

2 large cloves garlic, crushed
3 Tbsp. soy sauce
2 Tbsp. sherry
1 Tbsp. cracked pepper
1 tsp. coriander
1 tsp. brown sugar
½ tsp. cumin
2 green peppers, diced
2 onions, quartered
2 lbs. lean pork roast, cubed
⅓ cup oil

Combine all ingredients except oil and marinate for 1 to 2 hours. Thread pork and vegetables on skewers and barbecue. Add oil to marinade and baste meat and vegetables. Serve with rice or pita bread.

Serves 4.

—Colleen Bruning Fann

Buttermilk Pork Roast

3-4-lb. boned pork shoulder
salt
2 Tbsp. oil
2 cups buttermilk
2 Tbsp. cider vinegar
1 onion, sliced
1 bay leaf
3 peppercorns, crushed
6 carrots, sliced
2 large potatoes, quartered
6 small white onions
cornstarch

Sprinkle meat with salt. Heat oil in Dutch oven, brown meat well on all sides, and remove excess fat. Add buttermilk, 1 cup water, vinegar, onion, bay leaf and peppercorns. Bring to a boil, cover and simmer for 2 ½ hours, or until meat is tender. Add carrots, potatoes and onions and cook for another 30 minutes. Thicken gravy with cornstarch dissolved in water.

Serves 6 to 8.

—Anna J. Lee

Szekely Goulash

"I acquired this recipe in a cooking course I took in 1977. It was described by the Hungarian instructor as 'chunks of pork in creamy delectable kraut.' I make it frequently, as it is very popular."

2 Tbsp. flour
2 tsp. paprika
1½ lbs. lean pork, cubed
1 onion, finely chopped
2 Tbsp. oil
1 qt. sauerkraut
1½ cups thick sour cream

Combine flour and paprika in plastic bag, then toss pork in this to coat well. Cook onion in oil until soft. Add meat and brown on all sides. Add 2 to 3 Tbsp. hot water, cover and simmer for 45 to 60 minutes, stirring occasionally and adding water as needed. Add sauerkraut and 2 cups hot water. Bring to a boil, cover and simmer for 30 more minutes, or until meat is tender.

Remove from heat. Gradually blend 1½ cups cooking liquid into sour cream, then stir this back into liquid and meat.

Serves 4 to 6.

—Dianne Baker

Carnitas Burritos

"I've developed this recipe over the years I've lived in Arkansas. I'm a lifelong fan of Mexican cooking, and used to have ready access to it when I lived in southern California. I use jalapeño peppers out of my own garden, freezing them in the fall for use over the winter."

2 lbs. cooked pork roast, cut into ½" slices
4 cloves garlic, minced
3 jalapeño peppers
1 lb. dry pinto beans
1 Tbsp. salt
3 Tbsp. bacon fat
oil
tortillas
salsa

Place pork, 2 cloves garlic and 1 jalapeño pepper in heavy pot with enough water to just cover. Bring to a boil, cover tightly and reduce heat to medium-low. Simmer for 2 to 3 hours, stirring occasionally and adding water in small amounts only if meat is in danger of boiling dry. Shred meat and keep covered on low heat. Ten minutes before serving, remove cover, increase heat and cook until all liquid is gone.

Meanwhile, rinse and sort beans. Place in heavy saucepan and cover with water to depth of 3 inches. Bring to a boil and cook for 10 minutes. Add salt, remaining 2 cloves garlic, remaining 2 jalapeño peppers and 2 Tbsp. bacon fat. Cover and reduce heat to medium-low. Boil slowly for 2 to 3 hours, stirring frequently and adding water as needed.

Once beans are tender, heat ¼ inch oil and 1 Tbsp. bacon fat in large skillet. Add beans carefully to hot oil, shaking excess liquid from them first. Fill skillet half full with beans and fry for 1 minute, stirring constantly.

Mash beans in skillet, add more beans and continue the process until all beans are fried and mashed.

Serve refried beans and shredded pork with tortillas and salsa.

Serves 4 to 6.

—Tommie Majors-McQuary

Stuffed Pork Chops

4 pork chops, 1" thick
2 Tbsp. butter
2 Tbsp. chopped onion
1 clove garlic, crushed
1 cup bread crumbs
¼ tsp. savory
¼ tsp. salt
pepper
2-4 Tbsp. orange juice

Trim fat from chops. Melt butter in frying pan and brown chops on both sides. Remove chops and add onion and garlic to pan. Cook until onion is tender, stirring frequently. Add bread crumbs and seasonings and stir together. Remove from heat. Stir in enough juice to make mixture crumbly but not soggy. Scrape pan to remove all drippings. Cut meat to bone to form a pocket, being careful not to tear meat. Pack each chop with ¼ cup stuffing. Wrap in foil and seal tightly.

Bake at 350° F for 1 hour, opening foil for last 15 minutes to brown.

—M. Raven

Pork & Beans Paddington Bear

We all remember Paddington Bear's constant craving for orange marmalade. Here is a baked-bean recipe we are certain he would enjoy — it is rich and hearty and the marmalade adds a pleasant, sweet tang.

1 lb. dried lima beans
2 lbs. lean boneless pork, cubed
3 Tbsp. oil
2 tsp. celery salt
2 bay leaves
1 tsp. rosemary
2 cups tomato sauce
1 cup sliced mushrooms
1 onion, chopped
⅓ cup orange marmalade
2 Tbsp. cider vinegar
1 Tbsp. Worcestershire sauce
2 tsp. dry mustard

Rinse beans, cover with 6 cups water and boil for 2 minutes. Remove from heat, cover and let stand for 1 hour.

Brown pork in oil in heavy skillet. Add beans and cooking liquid, celery salt, bay leaves and rosemary. Cover, bring to a boil, reduce heat and simmer for 2 hours. Remove bay leaves. Stir in remaining ingredients and place in casserole dish. Bake, covered, at 350° F for 1 hour. Uncover, stir well, re-cover and bake for 30 minutes more.

Serves 12.

—Midge Denault

Maple Pork Chops

"I serve this with a creamy squash soup first. Accompany the chops with carrots, oven-browned potatoes and a crunchy green vegetable. End the meal with crème caramel." Made with homegrown pork and thick, fresh maple syrup, this dish turns plain pork chops into company fare.

4 pork chops, 1" thick
¼ cup apricot brandy
½ tsp. dry mustard
2 slices gingerroot
1½ tsp. cornstarch
3 Tbsp. maple syrup
salt & pepper

Brown chops in large frying pan and drain off fat. Pour 2 Tbsp. brandy over top, then add ¼ cup water, mustard and ginger. Cover tightly and simmer, turning occasionally, until tender — about 1 hour.

Remove chops to warm platter. Blend cornstarch with 1 Tbsp. water and stir into remaining sauce in pan along with 2 Tbsp. brandy, maple syrup and salt and pepper. Boil, stirring constantly, until thickened and clear. Pour sauce over chops.

Serves 4.

—*Linda Russell*

Pork Chops with Artichoke Hearts

People often relegate pork chops to the "only when I'm in a hurry and can't think of anything else" category. All of these recipes prove this approach wrong — pork chops can be as elegant as any other meat.

6 loin pork chops, 1" thick
¼ cup butter
2 Tbsp. oil
½ lb. mushrooms, sliced
¼ cup chopped green onions
1 clove garlic, crushed
1 large can artichoke hearts, drained
¼-½ cup sherry
1 tsp. tarragon
½ tsp. basil
salt & pepper

Trim fat from chops. Heat 2 Tbsp. butter and oil in large heavy skillet and brown chops, two at a time, over medium heat, turning once. Remove from pan and set aside.

Add 2 Tbsp. butter to drippings. Over low heat, sauté mushrooms, onions and garlic for 5 minutes, or until mushrooms are golden. Cut artichoke hearts in half, add to skillet and sauté 1 to 2 minutes longer. Stir in sherry, tarragon, basil and salt and pepper.

Return chops to pan. Cover and simmer for 20 to 25 minutes, basting frequently.

Serves 6.

—*Barbara Denz*

Pork Chop Oven Dinner

Tender pork, attractive appearance and a pleasant combination of flavours are produced by this recipe. The initial steps can be done ahead of time — the night before or early in the morning. It is then a simple matter of popping the casserole in the oven for 30 minutes and preparing a salad to accompany it.

3 Tbsp. flour
¾ tsp. salt
pepper
6 pork chops
oil
½ cup cooking sherry
1 Tbsp. parsley
¼ tsp. cloves
3 peppercorns
1 bay leaf
6 carrots, halved & cut in 2" pieces
6-8 small potatoes, halved
1 onion, sliced

Combine flour, salt and pepper in plastic bag, and shake with chops to coat. Brown chops in oil in ovenproof skillet. Set aside. Combine 1 cup water, sherry, parsley, cloves, peppercorns and bay leaf in skillet, bring to a boil, add vegetables and bring back to a boil.

Arrange chops on top of vegetables and bake, covered, at 350° F for 1 hour, then uncovered for 30 minutes.

Serves 6.

—*Ruth Stevens*

Vietnamese Sweet & Sour Pork

The traditional way to serve this dish is to line a large platter with romaine lettuce, add a layer of peeled, sliced cucumber and a layer of sliced tomato. Place pork on top of tomato, garnish with chopped cilantro, and serve sauce in a separate bowl.

SAUCE:
⅓ cup sugar
4 tsp. cornstarch
½ cup rice vinegar
1¼ cups chicken stock
½ cup slivered red or green
 pepper
2 lbs. pork spareribs
1 egg, lightly beaten
1 Tbsp. flour
2 Tbsp. cornstarch
1 tsp. pepper
¼ cup oil
4 or more cloves garlic,
 chopped
⅓ cup fish sauce

Make sauce by mixing sugar and cornstarch in saucepan. Add remaining sauce ingredients and simmer until thickened, stirring, then cook over low heat for a few minutes. Set aside, but keep at room temperature.

Cut ribs into small pieces. Combine egg, 3 Tbsp. water, flour, cornstarch and pepper and mix well. Place ribs in this and turn to coat.

Heat oil in skillet. Fry ribs until batter is crisp. Pour out oil, but do not wipe out pan. Cook garlic briefly — 10 seconds — then add fish sauce. Return ribs and turn to coat with garlic and fish sauce. Stir in sauce and heat through.

Serves 3 to 4.

—Donna J. Torres

Spareribs Barbecue

"This is a recipe I received from a favourite aunt who is an excellent cook. I often substitute pork chops for spareribs, and it is still delicious."

4-6 lbs. spareribs
2 onions
2 stalks celery
1 cup sliced mushrooms
1 green pepper
2 Tbsp. brown sugar
3 Tbsp. vinegar
4 Tbsp. lemon juice
1 Tbsp. Worcestershire
 sauce
1 tsp. prepared mustard
1 cup tomato sauce
½ cup hot water
1 tsp. salt

Cut ribs into pieces of 2 to 3 ribs each and place in roasting pan. Chop onions, celery, mushrooms and green pepper and add to ribs. Combine remaining ingredients and pour over ribs and vegetables. Cover and bake at 350° F for 1½ hours, basting several times.

Serves 4 to 6.

—Lorraine Guilfoyle

Maple Barbecued Spareribs

Tasty and unusual, this is not at all like traditional barbecue or sweet and sour recipes.

3 lbs. spareribs
1 cup maple syrup
1 Tbsp. chili sauce
1 Tbsp. vinegar
1 Tbsp. Worcestershire
 sauce
1 onion, finely chopped
½ tsp. salt
¼ tsp. dry mustard
⅛ tsp. pepper

Roast ribs on rack in roasting pan at 425° F for 30 minutes. Drain fat from pan and cut ribs into serving-sized pieces. Place in 9" x 13" pan.

Combine remaining ingredients in saucepan and boil for 5 minutes. Pour over ribs and bake, uncovered, at 375° F for 1 hour, basting occasionally and turning ribs after 30 minutes.

Serves 4.

—Donna Jubb

Baked Ham with Beer

This recipe produces a dark-skinned ham with a flavour similar to that of Black Forest ham. Save the cooking juice to add to baked beans.

1 large ham
1 cup brown sugar
1 Tbsp. dry mustard
1 pint beer

Place ham in roasting pan with lid. Sprinkle ham with sugar and mustard, then pour the beer over, along with 4 cups water. Bake, uncovered, at 350° F for 2 hours, basting every 30 minutes and adding water if necessary. Cool, covered, before slicing.

—Linda Palaisy

Sparky's Sweet & Sour Ribs

3-4 lbs. pork spareribs
¼ cup vinegar
3 Tbsp. soy sauce
1 tsp. sugar
½ tsp. pepper
4 Tbsp. flour
3 Tbsp. oil
½ cup vinegar
1½ cups brown sugar
1 Tbsp. cornstarch

Parboil ribs in ¼ cup vinegar and water to cover for 1 hour. Drain, leaving ribs in pot. Pour soy sauce, sugar, pepper and flour over ribs, turning to cover each piece.

Heat oil in skillet and brown ribs, then place in large casserole dish.

Combine ½ cup vinegar, brown sugar, 1 cup water and cornstarch dissolved in a bit of water in saucepan. Cook over medium heat until slightly thickened. Pour over ribs and bake, uncovered, at 350° F for 30 to 60 minutes.

Serves 4.

—Pat de la Ronde

Baked Ham with Raisin Sauce

This dish makes excellent "feast fare." It will serve a crowd (just increase the sauce recipe and use a bigger ham) and is fancy enough for a Thanksgiving or Christmas dinner. Serve with scalloped potatoes, broccoli, corn and a salad.

HAM:
4-lb. ham
1 onion, halved
1 carrot, halved
1 stalk celery, chopped
2 sprigs parsley
¼ tsp. thyme
1 bay leaf
⅓ cup brown sugar
¼ tsp. mace
juice & grated rind of 1 orange
1¼ cups apple cider or juice
SAUCE:
½ cup sugar
⅓ cup raisins
1 Tbsp. Worcestershire sauce
2 Tbsp. butter
2½ Tbsp. wine vinegar
Tabasco sauce
salt & pepper
mace
¼ cup red currant jelly

Place ham, onion, carrot, celery, parsley, thyme and bay leaf in saucepan with water to cover ham. Cover and simmer gently for 35 minutes per pound. Drain and remove skin.

Place ham in roasting pan, fat side up. Score in diagonal pattern. Combine sugar, mace, orange juice and rind and brush over ham. Pour cider or juice around ham and bake, covered, for approximately 30 minutes, uncovering for last 5 minutes of cooking time.

Meanwhile, prepare raisin sauce: Dissolve sugar in ½ cup water, then boil for 5 minutes. Add remaining ingredients and simmer until jelly dissolves. Serve warm.

Serves 4 to 6.

—Eleonora MacDonald

Sausage Spinach Stuffed Brioche

The flavour of this spectacular-looking brioche depends very much on the type of sausage used. We recommend a garlic or even hotter sausage, but for a milder brioche, use a regular sausage.

SAUSAGE SPINACH FILLING:
½ lb. garlic sausage, crumbled
1 onion, minced
1 clove garlic, crushed
1 pkg. spinach, chopped
½ tsp. pepper
¼ tsp. salt
¼ tsp. thyme
¼ tsp. hot pepper sauce
1 egg
BRIOCHE:
¼ cup milk
⅓ cup butter, cut up
3 Tbsp. sugar
¼ tsp. salt
1 Tbsp. yeast
¼ cup warm water
2¼-2¾ cups flour
2 eggs

Brown sausage well in large skillet. Remove and set aside. In drippings, sauté onion and garlic until tender, stirring occasionally. Stir in sausage, spinach, pepper, salt, thyme and pepper sauce. Cook, stirring, for 5 minutes. Cool slightly.

Beat egg and set aside 1 tsp. of it. Stir remaining egg into sausage mixture and mix well. Combine 1 tsp. egg with ¼ tsp. water and reserve for glaze.

To make brioche: Scald milk in small saucepan. Add butter and stir until melted. Stir in sugar and salt and cool to lukewarm. In large bowl, dissolve yeast in ¼ cup warm water. Stir in milk mixture and 1 cup flour. Beat well. Add eggs and 1 cup flour, or enough to make thick batter. Beat until well blended. Cover and let rise until doubled — about 1 hour. Stir down.

Place large tablespoonful of dough on heavily floured surface and form into smooth ball with well-floured hands. Set aside.

Place half remaining dough in greased, deep 1½-quart casserole dish. Press some dough evenly against sides of dish to form hollow. Fill with sausage-spinach mixture. Place remaining dough over filling and pat to cover filling evenly. Press edges to seal. Make small indentation in centre and press in dough ball. Cover and let rise until almost doubled — 30 minutes. Brush with egg-water glaze. Bake at 400° F for 25 minutes, covering with foil after 10 to 15 minutes. Loosen sides with spatula and turn out. Serve warm.

Serves 4 to 6.

—*Christine Taylor*

Sausage-Stuffed Apples

8 baking apples
8 mushrooms
1 lb. garlic sausage meat

Wash, dry and core apples. Place in 9" x 13" baking dish. Stem mushrooms, chop stems and mix with sausage meat. Brown over medium heat, then drain fat. Stuff apples with sausage and top with mushroom caps. Bake, uncovered, at 350° F for 30 minutes.

Serves 6.

—*Laurie Bradley*

Apples, Yams & Sausage

The flavours of the sausage, yams and apples combine in a very tasty fashion in this simple dish.

1 lb. bulk sausage
2 yams, peeled & cut into 1" chunks
3 medium apples
1 Tbsp. flour
1 Tbsp. brown sugar
½ tsp. cinnamon
salt & pepper

Brown sausage in skillet, cutting into large chunks. Drain off excess fat and place in 2-quart casserole. Add yams. Peel, core and slice apples, then add to casserole and mix gently.

Combine dry ingredients and add to meat, yams and apples, mixing well. Add ½ cup water, cover, and bake for 50 to 60 minutes at 375° F, or until apples and yams are tender.

Serves 3.

—*Judith Almond-Best*

Baked Ham with Port Wine Sauce

1½ cups firmly packed
   brown sugar
1 Tbsp. wine vinegar
1 Tbsp. prepared mustard
2-3-lb. ham
1 cup white wine
SAUCE:
1 cup currant jelly
1 cup port
1 Tbsp. butter

Make a paste of the brown sugar, vinegar and mustard. Remove skin from ham and spread with paste. Let stand overnight.

Place in roasting pan with wine. Cover and bake at 350° F for 1½ hours, uncover and bake for 30 minutes longer at 400° F. Remove from oven and let stand for 30 minutes.

Meanwhile, prepare sauce. Heat together currant jelly, port and butter, but do not allow to boil. Slice ham and serve with sauce.

Serves 4 to 6.

—Dolores De Rosario

Chili Verde Mexican Salsa

Hot and spicy, this is a wonderful salsa recipe. Serve it on tortillas, potatoes, eggs, whatever. It makes a good dip too. We suggest you start with the smaller quantities of peppers, then add more if you want a hotter taste.

1 Tbsp. shortening
1 lb. pork, diced
2 onions, chopped
2 28-oz. cans tomatoes,
   chopped
10-12 oz. canned green
   chilies, seeded & diced
4-8 oz. jalapeño peppers,
   seeded & diced
2 tsp. salt
½ tsp. pepper
2 cloves garlic, minced
2 Tbsp. oil
2 Tbsp. flour

Melt shortening and brown pork. Add onions and cook until they are translucent. Add tomatoes, chilies, jalapeños, salt, pepper and garlic and simmer. Heat oil in another skillet and stir in flour, cooking until browned. Add to other ingredients, cover and simmer for 3 hours, stirring occasionally.

—Rosemary Huffman

Mustard Marinade for Pork

2-3 Tbsp. Dijon mustard
2 cloves garlic, crushed
2 Tbsp. dry white wine
2 Tbsp. olive oil
½ tsp. pepper

Combine all ingredients and mix well. Brush on meat and let sit at room temperature for at least 30 minutes before proceeding with preparation.

—Trudi Keillor

Herb Marinade for Lamb

2 Tbsp. oil
1 Tbsp. lemon juice
1 clove garlic, crushed
½ tsp. marjoram
½ tsp. rosemary
½ tsp. thyme
½ tsp. sage
½ tsp. mint
½ tsp. pepper
½ tsp. salt

Combine all ingredients and mix thoroughly. This can be brushed on a leg of lamb or added to a marinade for cubed lamb. Let sit at room temperature for at least 30 minutes.

—Trudi Keillor

Kashmiri-Style Leg of Lamb

I discovered this dish while living in Dubai. It is not too hot, just tender and flavourful. Serve it with Spiced Cauliflower and Potatoes." All the work is done two days before serving, which makes this a convenient dish to serve guests.

5-lb. leg of lamb
1 Tbsp. grated gingerroot
4 cloves garlic, crushed
3 tsp. salt
1 tsp. cumin
1 tsp. turmeric
½ tsp. pepper
½ tsp. cinnamon
½ tsp. cardamom
¼ tsp. cloves
½ tsp. chili powder
2 Tbsp. lemon juice
1 cup yogurt
2 Tbsp. blanched almonds
2 Tbsp. pistachios
1 Tbsp. turmeric
3 tsp. honey

Remove excess fat from lamb and make deep slits all over the leg. Place in glass or stainless-steel casserole dish. Combine ginger, garlic, salt, cumin, 1 tsp. turmeric, pepper, cinnamon, cardamom, cloves, chili powder and lemon juice. Rub over lamb, pressing into slits.

Blend together yogurt, almonds, pistachios and 1 Tbsp. turmeric and spread over lamb. Drizzle honey over lamb. Cover and marinate, refrigerated, for 2 days, turning occasionally.

Roast, covered, at 450° F for 30 minutes, reduce heat to 350° F and roast for another 1¾ hours. Uncover and serve at room temperature.

Serves 8.

—Cynthia R. Topliss

Savoury Lamb Shanks

4 lamb shanks
3 large cloves garlic, slivered
salt & pepper
1 tsp. rosemary
2 Tbsp. chopped parsley
1 tsp. oregano
2 onions, thinly sliced
1 lb. fresh Italian plum tomatoes, peeled, seeded & coarsely chopped or 2 cups canned Italian plum tomatoes
¾ cup dry white wine
¾ cup olive oil

Remove excess fat and tendons from shanks. Insert garlic into meat in 2 or 3 crevices, then sprinkle remainder on top. Season with salt and pepper. Arrange shanks in baking dish and roast, uncovered, at 425° F for 20 minutes. Reduce heat to 350° F and sprinkle rosemary, parsley, oregano and onions over meat. Spoon tomatoes over meat and pour wine over all. Drizzle olive oil on top.

Return to oven and cook for 1 to 1½ hours, or until tender. Remove shanks to serving dish. Reduce liquid slightly and season with salt and pepper.

Serves 4.

—Ann L. Combs

Black Bean Sauce with Garlic & Ginger

Keep this sauce on hand to dress up spareribs, shrimp, chicken or tofu if unexpected company drops in. Simply add to cooked meat and heat through, thickening with cornstarch if desired.

3 Tbsp. oil
3-4 cloves garlic, crushed
2 Tbsp. chopped cooked black beans
2-3 onions, quartered
1 cup chicken stock
½ inch gingerroot, grated
2 Tbsp. soy sauce
1 tsp. honey

Heat oil, add garlic and black beans and sauté for 30 seconds. Add onions, sauté for 2 to 3 minutes, then add remaining ingredients. Cover and simmer for 1 to 2 minutes. Cool. Refrigerate if not using immediately.

Makes enough sauce for 2 pounds of spareribs.

—Margaret Graham

Riverslea Lamb Shanks

"Lamb shanks are often boned and used for stew, but the meat is perhaps the most tasty cut of lamb. This delicious recipe makes great use of an inexpensive cut."

4 lamb shanks
flour
oil
1 cup pitted prunes
½ cup brown sugar
½ tsp. cinnamon
½ tsp. allspice
3 Tbsp. vinegar

Dust shanks with flour and brown all over in a little hot oil. Mix remaining ingredients and 1 cup water and pour over shanks. Cover and bake at 350° F for 2 hours, turning shanks over occasionally.

Serves 4.

—*Jean Rivers*

Lamb with Fennel & Tomatoes

Also known as finocchio, fennel is an anise-flavoured vegetable. The root looks much like a celery heart, and the stalks end in dill-like, feathery leaves. It can be eaten raw, made into soup, braised or added to casseroles. If using the leaves for seasoning, be discreet, as the anise flavour is very strong.

5 Tbsp. olive oil
2-lb. boned leg of lamb, cubed
1 onion, chopped
2 cups peeled, seeded & mashed tomatoes
salt & pepper
1½ lbs. fennel, quartered

Heat oil in heavy casserole dish, then brown meat on all sides. Stir in onion and sauté for 5 minutes more, then add tomatoes and salt and pepper. Reduce heat, cover and simmer for 40 minutes, adding water if necessary.

Cook fennel in boiling salted water for 20 minutes. Drain, reserving 1 cup liquid. Add fennel and 1 cup liquid to lamb and cook for 20 minutes more.

Serves 4.

—*Carroll MacDonald*

Green Peppers Stuffed with Pork & Veal

Serve these stuffed peppers with a lightly flavoured tomato sauce if desired—the pepper filling is delicate, so be sure not to overpower it with sauce.

2 Tbsp. plus 1 tsp. butter
4 large green peppers
1 large onion, chopped
½ lb. pork sausage
½ lb. ground veal
1 cup dry bread crumbs
2 Tbsp. milk
1 tsp. salt
½ tsp. pepper
⅛ tsp. nutmeg
½ tsp. thyme

With 1 tsp. butter, grease baking dish large enough to hold peppers. Set aside.

Wash peppers, then slice off and discard 1 inch from tops of peppers. Remove and discard pith and seeds. Melt remaining butter over medium heat. When foam subsides, add onion and cook for 5 to 7 minutes, stirring occasionally, until onion is soft and translucent. Add sausage and veal and stir to break up. Cook, stirring, until meat has lost its pink colour.

Stir in remaining ingredients and cook for another 5 minutes. Spoon filling into peppers, then place peppers in baking dish. Bake, uncovered, at 375° F for 40 to 50 minutes, or until peppers are cooked.

Serves 4.

—*Dolores De Rosario*

Pasta

Egg Noodles

Flour
3 large eggs
Olive oil

Mound flour on large, clean working surface. Make a well in the centre of the flour and break eggs into it.

Take ½ eggshell and measure 3 shellfuls of water and 3 of olive oil into the well.

Using a fork, gently beat the liquids to blend and gradually flick flour from the edges into the centre. Keep beating until mixture becomes very stiff. Sprinkle dough with flour and roll it out, adding flour as necessary to make a very stiff, thin dough. When dough has been rolled as thin as possible, let rest for 10 minutes.

Divide dough into strips 8 inches to 10 inches wide and cut into ¼-inch strips for noodles. Hang over broom handle to dry — 15 to 30 minutes.

To cook, place in boiling water and cook 3 to 7 minutes — until tender. To store, bag and refrigerate for up to 3 days, or freeze.

—Noni Fidler

Pizza

2 Tbsp. yeast
1¼ cups warm water
1 tsp. honey
¼ cup olive oil
1 tsp. salt
3½ cups whole wheat flour
6-8 cups tomato sauce, page 414
3 cups sliced mushrooms
1½ cups chopped green olives
2 green peppers, chopped
1 lb. chopped bacon, cooked to eliminate fat but not until crisp
6 cups grated Swiss cheese
6 cups grated mozzarella cheese
3 cups grated Parmesan cheese

To make dough, dissolve yeast and honey in water. Add oil, salt and flour and mix well. Knead until smooth and elastic. Let rise in a warm place until doubled in size – about 1½ hours. Punch down and knead again briefly.

Divide dough into 3 equal portions. Roll each portion out to a 10-inch circle, ⅛ inch thick. Place crust in pizza pan.

Top each crust with about 2 to 2½ cups tomato sauce, then sprinkle vegetables, olives and bacon over this. Top with grated cheeses.

Bake at 425° F for 15 to 20 minutes, until cheese has melted and crust is golden brown.

Makes 3 10-inch pizzas.

German Pizza Dough

1 cup cottage cheese
2 ¼ cups flour
2 tsp. baking powder
4 Tbsp. milk
4 Tbsp. oil
1 egg, beaten

Mix cottage cheese, flour and baking powder with pastry blender until crumbly. Combine milk, oil and beaten egg and add to dry ingredients. Stir until well combined and roll out on floured surface to fit pizza pan. Makes two 12-inch pizza crusts. Bake with favourite toppings at 400° F for 35 to 40 minutes.

—Joann Hudson

Basic Tomato Sauce

This sauce can be used as a basis for spaghetti, lasagne, canneloni, manicotti or pizza, with or without the addition of ground beef and other vegetables.

¼ cup olive oil
1 clove garlic, minced
2 onions, diced
1 qt. canned tomatoes
½ cup tomato paste
½ cup water
1½ tsp. salt
¼ tsp. pepper
1 tsp. basil
1 tsp. oregano
1 Tbsp. parsley
1 bay leaf
½ cup mushrooms, sliced

Heat olive oil in heavy saucepan. Add other ingredients in order listed. Simmer, uncovered, for 1 to 6 hours.

Add sliced mushrooms for the last 15 minutes.

—Helen Shepherd

Macaroni Salad

2 cups uncooked macaroni
1 cup sliced celery
½ cup chopped green onions
¼ cup sliced radishes
1 cup cubed Cheddar cheese
¾ cup mayonnaise
1 Tbsp. vinegar
1 tsp. mustard
1 tsp. salt
Pepper to taste

Cook the macaroni. Drain and rinse with cold water until cool. Toss together the cooked macaroni, vegetables and cheese.

Mix together the mayonnaise, vinegar, mustard, salt and pepper. Toss dressing together with salad. Refrigerate.

Serves 6 to 8.

—Bertha Geddert

Noodle Casserole

3 Tbsp. butter
2 Tbsp. flour
1 cup milk
¼ cup soya grits, soaked in ¼ cup water
¼ cup vegetable flakes
½ tsp. salt
½ cup chopped parsley
½ cup grated Cheddar cheese
3-4 cups cooked & drained broad egg noodles

Melt butter in heavy saucepan and stir in flour. Cook for 1 minute, then add milk slowly, stirring constantly. Add remaining ingredients except cheese and noodles and simmer for 10 minutes. Mix in cheese, then noodles and place in greased loaf pan.

Bake at 350° F for 30 minutes.

Serves 4 to 6.

—Shiela Alexandrovich

Macaroni & Cheese

The addition of tomato sauce to this traditional macaroni and cheese casserole can provide an interesting variation.

3 Tbsp. butter
3 Tbsp. flour
2 cups milk
½ tsp. salt
Pepper to taste
2 cups grated old Cheddar cheese
2 cups cooked macaroni
¾ cup fine bread crumbs

Melt butter, blend in flour and add milk. Cook and stir over low heat until thick. Add seasonings and 1½ cups cheese. Stir and heat until melted.

Put macaroni in greased baking dish. Pour in sauce and mix well. Mix bread crumbs with remaining ½ cup cheese and sprinkle over top of casserole. Bake at 350° F for 30 to 40 minutes.

Serves 4.

—Mrs. Bruce Bowden

Cottage Cheese & Noodle Bake

½ cup chopped onion
2 Tbsp. butter
2 Tbsp. flour
1 tsp. salt
Pepper
1 cup milk
1 tsp. mustard
1 cup cottage cheese
½ cup Cheddar cheese, grated
2 Tbsp. lemon juice
8 oz. noodles, cooked
Parsley

Sauté onion in butter until tender. Stir in flour, salt and pepper until smooth. Gradually stir in milk and mustard. Cook until thickened. Stir in cheeses, lemon juice, then noodles. Pour into a greased casserole dish. Bake at 350° F for 40 to 45 minutes. Sprinkle with fresh parsley to serve.

Serves 4.

Bountiful Pasta

1 lb. spaghetti
¼ cup butter
2 Tbsp. vegetable oil
1½ cups whole cherry
    tomatoes
1 clove garlic, minced
¼ cup chopped green onion
½ tsp. salt
1 tsp. basil
5 cups broccoli, cut into
    bite-sized pieces
½ cup coarsely chopped
    walnuts
1 cup chicken broth
½ cup Parmesan cheese
2-4 Tbsp. parsley

Boil spaghetti, drain and set aside. Melt half the butter in the skillet and combine with oil. Add tomatoes and sauté for 5 minutes until tender. Stir in garlic, onion, salt and basil, and cook for 2 more minutes. Set aside and keep warm. Meanwhile, steam broccoli until tender. Toast walnuts for 5 minutes and set aside.

Melt remaining butter in a saucepan. Add broth, cheese and parsley and mix well. Add tomatoes, broccoli and spaghetti and toss. Pour onto a warm platter and sprinkle with nuts.

Serves 4.

—Pat Dicer

Clam Sauce for Spaghetti

¼ cup butter
5 cloves garlic, peeled &
    halved
2 Tbsp. whole wheat flour
2 Tbsp. powdered milk
2 5-oz. cans whole baby
    butter clams
Oregano

Melt butter and slowly sauté garlic for 3 minutes. Do not let butter brown. Remove garlic and add flour and milk. Blend well and remove from heat.

Drain clams and add liquid to flour slowly, beating well with a whisk. Return sauce to medium heat and cook until thick (about 4 minutes). Add clams and oregano and pour over spaghetti.

Serves 2.

—Linda Townsend

White Sauce for Spaghetti

2 Tbsp. fresh parsley
2 Tbsp. fresh basil
1 cup butter, melted
⅓ cup grated Parmesan
    cheese
¼ cup olive oil
2 cloves garlic, mashed
8 oz. cream cheese
⅔ cup boiling water

Mix together parsley, basil and butter. Add cheese, then mix in remaining ingredients. Simmer until well blended. Serve over cooked noodles.

Makes 2½ cups.

—Ken Parejko

Vegetable Lasagne

Zucchini and olives provide another interesting variation on the standard lasagne flavour. This recipe, like the others, can be frozen with no detraction from the original flavour.

2 Tbsp. oil
1 large clove garlic, minced
1 large onion, chopped
1 green pepper, chopped
2 stalks celery, chopped
½ tsp. oregano
½ tsp. basil
½ tsp. thyme
1 medium zucchini, coarsely
    grated
1½ cups sliced mushrooms
1½ cups tomato sauce, page
    414
5½-oz. can tomato paste
¼ cup grated Parmesan
    cheese
2 cups cottage cheese, mixed
    with 1 egg
½ cup chopped black olives
2 cups grated mozzarella
    cheese
8 oz. lasagne noodles, cooked
10 oz. spinach, torn into
    1-inch pieces

Sauté garlic in oil for 1 minute. Add onion, green pepper, celery and herbs and cook for 5 minutes. Add zucchini and cook another 5 minutes. Add mushrooms, tomato sauce and tomato paste. Simmer 20 minutes, remove from heat, add Parmesan cheese and mix well.

Spread a small amount of the sauce in the bottom of a greased, 2-qt. casserole dish. Layer in half of each of the ingredients: noodles, sauce, cottage cheese, spinach, mozzarella and olives. Repeat.

Cover and bake for 1 hour at 350° F. Allow to sit for 10 minutes before serving.

Serves 6 to 8.

—Shan Simpson

Lasagne

6 oz. lasagne noodles
2 Tbsp. cooking oil
2 cloves garlic, minced
2 onions, chopped
1 lb. ground beef
½ lb. mushrooms, sliced
2 stalks celery, diced
1 green pepper, diced
12 oz. tomato paste
3 cups stewed tomatoes
1 tsp. salt
¼ tsp. pepper
1 tsp. oregano
1 tsp. basil
2 tsp. parsley
1 bay leaf
1 lb. ricotta cheese
5 oz. spinach
¾ cup Parmesan cheese
1 lb. mozzarella cheese,
    grated

Cook noodles in boiling water until tender. Drain and set aside.

Heat oil in large heavy frying pan. Add garlic and onions and sauté until onion is soft. Add ground beef and continue to sauté, stirring frequently, until beef begins to lose pink colour. Add mushrooms, celery and green pepper. Continue cooking until meat is well browned. Stir in tomato paste, tomatoes and seasonings. Simmer for at least 1 hour or all day. The longer the sauce simmers, the richer the flavour.

To assemble, mix together ricotta cheese, washed and torn spinach and ½ cup Parmesan cheese.

Pour a very thin layer of meat sauce into a 9" x 13" baking dish. This will prevent the casserole from sticking to the dish. Arrange a layer of cooked noodles over sauce. Top with half of meat sauce, half ricotta-spinach mixture and half grated mozzarella cheese. Repeat layers. Sprinkle remaining ¼ cup of Parmesan cheese over top layer.

Bake at 350° F for 35 to 45 minutes.

Serves 8.

—Wanda Mary Murdock

Tofu Lasagne

The substitution of tofu for ground beef in this recipe allows vegetarians to enjoy a delicious, protein-rich lasagne. Wheat germ adds an additional, slightly nutty flavour.

8-oz. package lasagne
    noodles
¼ cup butter
½ lb. fresh mushrooms,
    thinly sliced
3 cloves garlic, finely
    chopped
½ tsp. salt
⅛ tsp. pepper
3 cups spaghetti sauce
½ cup wheat germ
1 cup mashed tofu
¼ cup grated Parmesan
    cheese
½ lb. mozzarella cheese,
    grated
¼ cup chopped fresh parsley

Cook and drain lasagne noodles. Set aside.

Melt butter in large skillet. Add mushrooms, garlic, salt and pepper. Cook until mushrooms are tender. Stir in sauce and wheat germ. Heat through.

Combine tofu and Parmesan cheese in a bowl. Combine mozzarella and parsley in another bowl.

In a 9" x 12" pan, layer half of each of the ingredients: noodles, tofu mixture, sauce and mozzarella mixture. Repeat.

Bake at 350° F for 45 minutes or until hot and bubbly. Let stand for 15 minutes before cutting.

Serves 8 to 10.

—Pat Bredin

Rotini & Sauce

¾ lb. rotini noodles
¾ lb. ground beef
Olive oil
⅔ cup sliced carrots
⅔ cup sliced celery
⅔ cup sliced onion
1½ cups tomato sauce, page
    414
Salt & pepper
1 tsp. oregano
Cayenne pepper
1 clove garlic, minced

Cook rotini noodles in boiling, salted water for about 20 minutes, until tender. Meanwhile, brown beef in a skillet, draining off excess fat. Sauté carrots, celery and onion in oil on low heat for 5 minutes. Add tomato sauce, seasonings and cooked beef. Simmer, covered, for 10 minutes. Drain and rinse rotini and top with sauce and Parmesan cheese. Serves 4.

—Glenn F. McMichael

Szechuan Noodles

1 lb. spaghetti or Chinese
  noodles
2 Tbsp. oil
4 green onions, chopped
½ cup minced cooked ham
¼ cup chopped peanuts
⅓ cup sesame seeds
⅓ cup soya sauce
1 Tbsp. cider vinegar
1 tsp. honey
Tabasco sauce
2 Tbsp. ketchup
⅔ cup chopped cucumber or
  celery

Cook noodles, drain and toss with 1 Tbsp. oil. Set aside.

Stir-fry green onions in remaining oil for 1 minute. Add ham, peanuts, sesame seeds, soya sauce, vinegar, honey, Tabasco and ketchup. Simmer 2 to 3 minutes, add cucumber or celery and cook a few minutes longer.

Add noodles, toss and heat through.

Serves 4.

—Bryanna Clark

Spinach Beef Manicotti

2 cups chopped onion
¼ cup butter
¾ lb. fresh spinach
4 cloves garlic, minced
2 tsp. oregano
1 tsp. salt
¼ tsp. pepper
1 lb. ground beef
2 Tbsp. oil
32-oz. can tomatoes
6-oz. can tomato paste
1 Tbsp. basil
1½ tsp. salt
¼ tsp. pepper
12 manicotti shells, cooked,
  drained & cooled
½ cup grated Parmesan
  cheese

Sauté 1½ cups of the onion in butter for 5 minutes. Tear spinach into 1-inch pieces and add to onion along with 2 cloves garlic, oregano, salt and pepper. Stir-fry 2 to 3 minutes and add ground beef. Cook until beef is thoroughly browned. Set aside.

Sauté remaining onion in oil until soft. Stir in tomatoes, tomato paste, remaining garlic, basil, salt and pepper. Bring to a boil, reduce heat, cover and simmer for 20 minutes.

Stuff noodles with meat filling and place in a shallow baking dish. Cover with tomato sauce and sprinkle with Parmesan cheese.

Bake at 350° F for 30 minutes.

Serves 6.

—Bryanna Clark

Manicotti

Manicotti can be made with homemade crêpes, as this recipe indicates, or with commercial pasta, as in the previous recipe. Canneloni noodles may also be used with either of these fillings and do not need to be pre-boiled.

6 eggs
1½ cups flour
¼ tsp. salt
2 lbs. ricotta cheese
½ lb. mozzarella cheese
⅓ cup grated Parmesan
  cheese
2 eggs
1 tsp. salt
¼ tsp. pepper
1 Tbsp. chopped parsley
¼ cup grated Parmesan
  cheese
2-3 cups tomato sauce,
  page 414

Combine 6 eggs, flour, salt and 1½ cups water in blender. After blending, let stand 30 minutes or longer.

Grease and heat an 8-inch skillet. Pour in 3 Tbsp. of batter, rotating skillet quickly to spread batter evenly. Cook over medium heat until top is dry. Cool on wire rack, then stack with wax paper between them.

For filling, combine all remaining ingredients except the ¼ cup of Parmesan cheese. Beat with a wooden spoon to blend well. Spread about ¼ cup filling down the centre of each manicotti and roll up. Place completed rolls, seam-side down, in a shallow casserole dish, making 2 layers if necessary. Top with homemade tomato sauce and remaining Parmesan cheese.

Bake at 350° F for 30 minutes.

Serves 8.

—Hazel R. Baker

Vegetable Pasta

Almost any cooked, puréed vegetables can be added to basic egg noodle dough. For a green pasta, use broccoli, spinach or peas. Tomatoes or carrots result in a red or orange noodle. Even lemon or orange rind and juice can be added for an unusual, light taste. When puréeing vegetables, leave them coarse enough that the pasta will have texture as well as flavour.

It is possible to make many shapes of noodles as well. With an inexpensive hand-crank pasta machine, it takes almost no effort to roll the dough to the desired thinness. From this point, the dough can be cut either by machine or by hand. Fettuccine is a flat noodle cut about ½-inch wide. Spaghetti is a round noodle, which can be cut only by machine. Pappardelle is similar to fettuccine except that it is cut with a fluted ravioli wheel, which provides a fancier noodle. To make farfalle, or bow ties, simply roll out dough to desired thinness, cut into 2" x 1" rectangles with ravioli wheel and pinch long sides together. Of course, only the cook's imagination is the limit when contemplating flavour and shape possibilities. Here is a basic recipe for vegetable pasta.

3 cups flour
4 eggs
½ cup vegetable purée
1 Tbsp. oil

Place flour in large, flat-bottomed mixing bowl and make a well in the centre. Combine eggs, purée and oil and pour into well. Using a spoon first, then hands, work flour in to form a smooth, not sticky, dough. Additional flour may be necessary. Cover dough and let sit for 30 minutes.

If making pasta by hand, begin rolling, adding flour as needed until dough is thin and translucent. If using a pasta maker, begin with rollers on widest setting and gradually narrow until desired thinness and smoothness are reached. Let dough sit for a few minutes until it is slightly dried out. Cut into desired shape. Place noodles over broom handle until time to cook. Fresh noodles will take only 2 to 3 minutes of cooking in boiling water. If the noodles are to be stored, allow to dry *thoroughly*, then bag and store in refrigerator or freezer.

Makes 3 pounds.

—Linda Palaisy

Basil Butter Balls

Simple it is, but seasoned, buttered pasta is one of the most delicious treats possible. These butter balls can be assembled and stored in the freezer, removed at the last minute and served with cooked fresh pasta for a quick and easy supper. All else that is needed is a tossed salad.

½ cup unsalted butter
10 basil leaves
1 clove garlic
¼ tsp. black pepper

In blender or food processor, purée ingredients. Shape into small balls, place on cookie sheet and freeze. When balls are well frozen, remove from cookie sheet and store in covered container in freezer.

—Louise McDonald

Pesto

2 cups fresh basil
2 cloves garlic
½ cup parsley
½ tsp. salt
⅓-½ cup olive oil
¼ cup Parmesan cheese

Place basil, garlic, parsley, salt and ⅓ cup oil in blender. Process, adding more oil if necessary to make a smooth paste. Add cheese and blend for a few seconds. Serve over cooked, buttered spaghetti.

Serves 4.

Noodle Omelette

2 Tbsp. butter
1 Tbsp. oil
1 cup chopped onion
⅔ cup green pepper, sliced into strips
1 cup grated Swiss cheese
8 eggs, beaten
2½ cups cooked noodles
1 tsp. salt

Melt 1 Tbsp. butter and oil in a heavy frying pan. Sauté onion and green pepper until onion browns. Stir in remaining butter and reduce heat to very low.

Combine remaining ingredients and pour over vegetables. Cover and cook over medium-low heat, without stirring, for 15 to 20 minutes. When puffed and browned around the edges, the omelette is cooked.

Serves 8.

Spinach Sauce

¼ cup butter
10 oz. spinach, finely
   chopped
1 tsp. salt
1 cup cottage cheese
¼ cup Parmesan cheese
¼ cup milk
⅛ tsp. nutmeg

Melt butter, add spinach and salt and cook until spinach is limp – about 5 minutes. Lower heat to simmer, stir in cottage and Parmesan cheeses, milk and nutmeg, and cook, stirring, until mixture is heated through. Serve with cooked spaghetti.

Serves 6.

Spaghetti with Garlic & Oil

Quick and simple, this dish allows the diner to really appreciate the flavours of the pasta and the garlic.

4 oz. spaghetti
½ cup olive oil
4 cloves garlic, peeled &
   crushed
Black pepper

Cook spaghetti in boiling, salted water. When almost cooked, heat oil in heavy pot. Add garlic and cook until browned. Drain and rinse spaghetti. Mix with garlic-oil mixture and serve topped with black pepper.

Serves 2.

Artichoke Heart Sauce for Spaghetti

This is a very spicy topping, particularly good with fresh fettuccine. Served as an appetizer, it provides a tangy beginning to a meal.

1 large tin artichoke hearts,
   sliced
½ cup olive oil
1 tsp. crushed, hot red
   pepper
1 tsp. salt
3 cloves garlic, minced
4 Tbsp. chopped parsley
Juice of 1 lemon
Black pepper
Parmesan cheese

Combine artichoke hearts, oil, red pepper, salt and garlic in heavy pot. Cook, stirring, until hot. Add parsley and lemon juice. Serve over cooked noodles, topped with black pepper and Parmesan cheese.

Serves 4.

Noodle Salad

An excellent and easy way to use up leftover pasta, this dish can even utilize pasta with sauce on it – just rinse thoroughly in cold water before mixing with dressing .

½ cup yogurt
½ cup mayonnaise
1 Tbsp. Dijon mustard
1 Tbsp. dill
3-4 cups cooked pasta

Combine yogurt, mayonnaise, mustard and dill. Mix with rinsed pasta and chill well.

Serves 4.

Fettucini Alfredo

This rich pasta dish is particularly delicious served with veal cooked in a cream sauce or with stuffed zucchini. If spinach noodles are used, the dish will be an attractive green.

½lb. fettucini noodles
¼ lb. butter
1 cup whipping cream
½ cup grated Parmesan
   cheese
½ cup chopped parsley
Salt & pepper

Cook noodles in boiling salted water. Drain. Return to pot. Over low heat, stir in butter, cream and cheese and cook, mixing well, until butter is melted and mixture is hot. Stir in parsley and salt and pepper.

Serves 2 as a main dish, 4 as a side dish.

Marsala Liver Sauce for Pasta

1 small onion, minced
¼ cup minced parsley
¼ lb. bacon, minced
½ lb. rabbit or chicken
   livers, quartered
¼ lb. mushrooms, thinly
   sliced
¼ cup Marsala wine
½ cup tomato paste
½ tsp. ground sage
Salt & pepper

Chop together onion, parsley and bacon to make a paste. Cook for 5 minutes. Add livers and mushrooms and continue cooking until livers are browned.

Add wine, tomato paste and seasonings and simmer for 30 minutes. Serve over spaghetti.

Serves 2.

Pork Meatballs and Spaghetti Sauce

A variation of the traditional beef meatballs, pork meatballs provide a flavourful addition to this spaghetti sauce, which is also enhanced by the addition of zucchini.

MEATBALLS:
1 lb. ground pork
¼ cup Parmesan cheese
¼ cup oatmeal
½ cup chopped onion
3 Tbsp. chopped parsley
1 tsp. oregano
½ tsp. salt
¼ tsp. pepper
2 drops Tabasco sauce
1 Tbsp. oil
SAUCE:
28-oz. can tomatoes
6-oz. can tomato paste
¾ cup chopped celery
½ cup chopped green pepper
½ cup chopped green olives
1 tsp. oregano
1 tsp. basil
2 drops Tabasco sauce
¾ cup grated zucchini
1 cup chopped mushrooms

To make meatballs, combine pork, cheese, oatmeal, onion, parsley, oregano, salt, pepper and Tabasco sauce. Mix well and form into small balls. Refrigerate for 1 hour to allow to set. Heat oil in skillet and brown meatballs on all sides. Drain on paper towels.

For sauce, combine tomatoes and tomato paste in large saucepan. Stir in celery, green pepper, olives, oregano, basil and Tabasco sauce. Bring to a boil, then drop in meatballs, zucchini and mushrooms. Simmer for 10 minutes and serve over cooked spaghetti.

Serves 6 to 8.

Fried Noodles with Beef & Snow Peas

Although generally considered an Italian food, pasta has also been a staple of Chinese cuisine for thousands of years. This dish utilizes fried noodles, rather than just boiled, which provides quite a different texture.

16 oz. fine egg noodles
¾ cup oil
2 lbs. round steak, cut into thin strips
1 medium onion, sliced
2 cups beef stock
1 cup chopped mushrooms
2 Tbsp. dry sherry
2 Tbsp. soya sauce
3 Tbsp. cornstarch
8 oz. snow peas

Cook noodles in boiling, salted water until tender. Drain, rinse and drain again. Heat ½ cup oil in heavy skillet. Add noodles and cook, turning occasionally, until browned about 20 minutes.

Meanwhile, in another skillet, heat remaining ¼ cup oil. When hot, cook steak and onion until meat is browned, stirring constantly. Add stock, mushrooms, sherry and soya sauce. Combine cornstarch with ½ cup cold water and gradually stir into skillet mixture. Cook, stirring, until thickened. Add snow peas and cook until heated through. Serve over noodles.

Serves 6.

Chicken & Vegetable Sauce for Macaroni

1 Tbsp. cornstarch
½ tsp. salt
Pepper
2 Tbsp. soya sauce
½ cup chicken stock
2 Tbsp. vegetable oil
1 clove garlic, peeled
½ lb. raw chicken meat, cut into strips
1 medium onion, sliced
1 cup sliced celery
1 cup sliced mushrooms
2 cups broccoli, cut into florets & steamed until tender-crisp
1 tomato, cut into 8 pieces
2 green onions, chopped

Combine cornstarch, salt, pepper, soya sauce and chicken stock and set aside.

Heat oil in wok or heavy skillet. Sauté garlic until golden, then discard. Add chicken and sauté for 3 or 4 minutes, stirring constantly. Remove and set aside. Add onion, celery, mushrooms and broccoli and sauté until celery is tender - 4 minutes. Add chicken, tomato, green onions and cornstarch mixture. Cook until thickened, stirring constantly. Serve over cooked macaroni.

Serves 4.

Cucumber Clam Spaghetti Sauce

4 Tbsp. olive oil
1 clove garlic, peeled
10-oz. can clams, with juice
   reserved
2 seedless cucumbers,
   sliced
1 tsp. salt
Pepper
1 Tbsp. chopped parsley

Heat oil and sauté garlic until browned, then discard. Drain clam juice into pan, stir in cucumbers, salt and pepper. Cook, uncovered, stirring occasionally, for about 15 minutes. Add clams and cook gently for 5 more minutes. Stir in parsley and cook 1 minute further. Serve over cooked spaghetti.

Serves 4.

—Judith Goodwin

Chicken & Sausage Spaghetti Sauce

3 Tbsp. olive oil
4 cloves garlic, peeled &
   crushed
2 medium onions, chopped
1 lb. hot Italian sausage, cut
   into ½-inch slices
3 stalks celery, chopped
1 green pepper, chopped
6 leaves basil
1-2 tsp. oregano
Salt & pepper
Bay leaf
½ lb. mushrooms, sliced
28-oz. can tomatoes
13-oz. can tomato paste
1 chicken, boiled, removed
   from bones & chopped

Heat oil and fry garlic and onions until onions are limp. Add sausage and cook, stirring occasionally, until browned. Stir in celery, green pepper, basil, oregano, salt and pepper and bay leaf. Cook for 5 to 10 minutes. Add mushrooms and cook for 5 more minutes. Add tomatoes, tomato paste and chicken and mix well.

Lower heat to simmer, cover and cook for at least 1 hour, adding water if sauce becomes too thick. Serve over cooked pasta and top with Parmesan cheese.

Serves 8 to 10.

Fettuccine Primavera

This recipe makes use of early spring vegetables – they must be fresh – in a white sauce. Additions or changes may be made according to personal taste. Green beans and cauliflower are good, as is the addition of shrimp. Because so many vegetables appear in the sauce, it is best to use unflavoured fettuccine noodles.

½ large head broccoli,
   cut into florets
1 zucchini, thinly sliced
½ cup sliced mushrooms
10 snow peas
1 medium onion, sliced
1 carrot, sliced
8 oz. fettuccine
¼ cup butter
2 cloves garlic, minced
2 Tbsp. basil
¼ cup cream
¼ cup white wine
2 Tbsp. parsley
½ cup Parmesan cheese

Steam broccoli, zucchini, mushrooms, snow peas, onion and carrot for 10 minutes. Cook fettuccine in boiling, salted water for 10 minutes.

Meanwhile, prepare sauce. Melt butter and brown garlic. Add remaining ingredients, mix thoroughly and heat through. Remove from heat, and toss with vegetables and fettuccine.

Serves 4.

—Janis Scattergood

Pasta e Piselli

This is a southern Italian recipe for pasta with peas, which has been in the contributor's family for four generations.

2 cloves garlic
⅓ cup olive oil
1 medium onion, sliced
1 lb. tomatoes, coarsely
  chopped
½ lb. fresh peas
½ tsp. oregano
Salt & pepper
Chili pepper flakes
1 lb. bite-sized pasta
2 eggs
½ cup Parmesan or Romano
  cheese
2 Tbsp. milk

Peel garlic and brown in oil in large skillet, then remove garlic and discard. Sauté onion in oil until tender. Add tomatoes, peas, oregano, salt and pepper and chili pepper. Cover and simmer slowly as pasta cooks.

Cook pasta in boiling, salted water. While pasta is cooking, beat eggs in bowl and mix in cheese and milk.

Drain cooked pasta and return to pot. Add vegetable mixture, then egg-cheese mixture and heat slowly, stirring constantly, until eggs are cooked.

Serves 6.

—Anthony Balzano

Linguini with Zucchini al Pesto

2 small zucchini,
  cut into strips
2 Tbsp. butter
½ cup fresh basil
½ cup snipped parsley
3 cloves garlic, crushed
4 Tbsp. pine nuts, lightly
  roasted
Handful Parmesan cheese
1 cup olive oil
6 Tbsp. butter, softened
Salt & pepper
8 oz. linguini

Fry zucchini in oil until limp and golden. Whir in blender basil, parsley, garlic, pine nuts and Parmesan cheese, adding oil and butter a little at a time to keep the sauce thick.

Cook linguini until just tender. Combine linguini, zucchini and sauce. Add salt and pepper to taste.

Serves 4 to 6.

—Cary Elizabeth Marshall

Spaghetti alla Carbonara

1 lb. ham, cubed
2 Tbsp. butter
8 oz. spaghetti
¼ cup butter
1 Tbsp. flour
1 cup whipping cream
4 eggs, beaten
1 cup Parmesan cheese
Freshly ground pepper

Fry ham in 2 Tbsp. butter until crispy and set aside. Cook spaghetti in boiling, salted water.

While spaghetti is cooking, make sauce. Melt ¼ cup butter and stir in flour. Gradually blend in whipping cream and bring almost to a boil. Add eggs and ham and simmer for 2 minutes, stirring constantly. Add Parmesan cheese and pepper, pour over cooked, drained spaghetti and serve.

Serves 4.

—Fern Acton

Zucchini and Spaghetti Casserole

4 medium zucchini, sliced
1 large onion, chopped
4 tomatoes, peeled & chopped
½ cup butter
½ cup grated Parmesan cheese
Salt & pepper
1 lb. spaghetti, cooked
1 lb. mozzarella cheese, grated

Sauté vegetables in butter until tender. In casserole dish, toss with Parmesan cheese, salt and pepper and spaghetti. Top with mozzarella cheese.

Bake at 350° F for 30 minutes, or until cheese is melted and bubbling.

Serves 6 to 8.

—Glenda McCawder

Macaroni with Sausage

1 lb. sausage meat
1 onion, finely chopped
1 clove garlic, chopped
¼ cup sliced mushrooms
1 Tbsp. butter
¼ tsp. savory
¼ tsp. celery seed
¼ tsp. oregano
¼ tsp. chili powder
¼ tsp. pepper
¼ tsp. dry mustard
6-oz. can tomato paste
¼ cup water
3 cups cooked macaroni
1 cup cottage cheese

Sauté sausage meat until lightly browned. Drain off fat, separate meat with fork and set aside. Sauté onion, garlic and mushrooms in butter. Add sausage meat, savory, celery seed, oregano, chili powder, pepper and dry mustard. Stir in tomato paste and water and mix well. Add macaroni and stir.

Arrange alternate layers of macaroni-meat mixture and cottage cheese in greased casserole dish, ending with meat on top. Bake at 350° F for 25 to 30 minutes.

Serves 8.

—Ruth Anne Laverty

Spinach Linguini with Red Clam Sauce

Fresh pasta, easily made at home and increasingly available in specialty stores, offers a flavour and texture that is incomparable to commercial dried noodles. The pasta becomes an integral part of the dish, not just the base for the sauce. Fresh pasta, with a cooking time of less than 5 minutes, is strongly recommended for this recipe.

2 Tbsp. olive oil
2 cloves garlic, minced
1 small onion, chopped
1 tsp. chopped fresh marjoram
1 tsp. chopped fresh basil
3 tomatoes, peeled & chopped
1 Tbsp. tomato paste
4 Tbsp. dry white wine
10-oz. can baby clams
½ lb. spinach linguini
Parmesan cheese

Heat olive oil in heavy pot and sauté garlic and onion for 5 minutes. Add marjoram and basil and sauté for 2 more minutes. Stir in tomatoes, tomato paste, wine and clams, cover and simmer for 20 minutes.

Cook linguini until just tender. Drain, rinse under hot water and serve immediately with clam sauce. Top with Parmesan cheese.

Serves 4.

—Jane Pugh

Karin's Ravioli

PASTA:
5 cups flour
1½ tsp. salt
5 eggs
1 Tbsp. oil
1-1½ cups lukewarm water
FILLING:
1 lb. ground beef
½ large onion, chopped
2 cloves garlic, chopped
2 pinches oregano
1 pinch basil
½ tsp. coriander
2 Tbsp. flour
Salt & pepper
1 tomato, peeled & chopped
½ cup grated hard cheese
SAUCE:
28 oz. stewed tomatoes
1 clove garlic, chopped
½ large onion, chopped
½ green pepper, chopped
2 stalks celery, chopped
Salt & pepper
2 tsp. oregano
1 tsp. basil
1 tomato, peeled & chopped
½ lb. mushrooms, sliced

To make dough, combine flour and salt. Mix together eggs, oil and 1 cup water. Make a well in the middle of the flour mixture and pour in liquid. Stir and then knead by hand to make a firm but pliable dough, adding additional water or flour as necessary. Place in a lightly greased bowl, cover and set aside.

For filling, brown ground beef and drain off fat. Add onion and garlic and continue to cook until onion is limp. Add oregano, basil, coriander, flour, salt and pepper, tomato and cheese. Simmer for 1 to 2 hours, then cool.

Combine sauce ingredients in heavy pot and simmer for 1 to 2 hours.

When filling cools, roll out dough to ⅛-inch thickness and cut into 1½" x 3" rectangles. Place 1 tsp. of filling on each rectangle, fold over and pinch together edges. Cook in boiling, salted water until puffy. Place in simmering sauce and serve with Parmesan cheese .

Serves 6.

—Karin Mayes

Savoury Noodle Bake

2 Tbsp. oil
4 Tbsp. butter
2 onions, finely chopped
1 clove garlic, minced
2 cups canned tomatoes
⅛ tsp. salt
Pepper
¼ tsp. oregano or basil
1 bay leaf
8 oz. egg noodles
3 cups grated Cheddar cheese

Combine oil and 2 Tbsp. butter, place over low heat and, when butter has melted, add onions and garlic. Cook over low heat until soft.

Combine tomatoes, salt and spices. Add to onion mixture; simmer for 15 minutes and discard bay leaf.

Cook noodles until tender; rinse with hot water and drain. Add remaining 2 Tbsp. butter and 2 cups cheese. Add tomato sauce. Turn mixture into greased baking dish and top with remaining 1 cup cheese.

Bake at 350° F for 30 minutes.

—Georgina Mitchell

Neapolitan Lasagne

1 lb. ground beef
2 hot Italian sausages, out of casings
1 large onion, finely chopped
1 stalk celery, finely chopped
2 cloves garlic, minced
4 cups tomato purée
6-oz. can tomato paste
4 oz. dry red wine
1 tsp. marjoram
1 tsp. basil
Fresh parsley
½ tsp. cinnamon
Salt & pepper
2 eggs
2 cups cottage cheese
½ cup Parmesan cheese
½ lb. mozzarella cheese, thinly sliced
1 lb. spinach, cooked, drained & chopped
1 zucchini, thinly sliced
16 lasagne noodles, cooked

In heavy pot, cook beef, sausage meat, onion, celery and garlic until lightly browned. Stir in tomato purée and paste, then wine, marjoram, basil, parsley, cinnamon, salt and pepper. Simmer for 30 minutes. Meanwhile, combine eggs, cottage and Parmesan cheeses.

Place a little sauce on the bottom of greased 9" x 13" pan. Alternate layers as follows: noodles, cheese mixture, spinach and zucchini slices, mozzarella, meat sauce. Repeat. Bake at 375° F for 30 minutes.

Serves 10 to 12.

—Valerie Marien

Lasagne Ham Roll-Ups

8 lasagne noodles
8 thin slices ham
2 Tbsp. prepared mustard
1 cup grated Cheddar cheese
Salt & pepper
2 cups tomato or mushroom
    sauce, pages 414 & 132
2 large tomatoes, sliced
Parsley sprigs

Cook noodles until tender. Drain, rinse and lay on sheet of greased foil. Lay slice of ham on each noodle, trimming to fit. Spread with mustard and sprinkle with cheese and seasonings. Roll up each noodle, enclosing the filling. Place in greased shallow baking dish. Pour sauce over top and arrange tomato slices over this. Bake at 375° F for 30 minutes. Garnish with parsley and serve.

Serves 4.

—Anne Budge

Baked Rigatoni

16 oz. rigatoni noodles
3 Tbsp. butter
8 oz. mozzarella cheese,
    diced
4 cups spaghetti sauce
1 cup sliced mushrooms
¾ cup Parmesan cheese

Cook rigatoni in boiling, salted water and place in greased casserole dish. Add 2 Tbsp. butter, cheese, spaghetti sauce and mushrooms and mix well. Sprinkle with Parmesan cheese and dot with remaining butter. Bake at 350° F for 20 to 30 minutes, or until heated through.

Serves 4 to 6.

—Debbie Anne McCully

Lokshen Kugel

Kugel is a traditional Sabbath dish. This noodle pudding was prepared the day before and slow cooked over a fire until the Sabbath, when fires could not be started. It can also be made as a sweet dish by the addition of raisins and cinnamon.

1 pkg. wide egg noodles
1 sleeve soda crackers
Salt & pepper
3-6 eggs

Cook noodles in boiling, salted water until tender. Drain but do not rinse. Crush crackers and add to noodles. Add salt and pepper to taste. Add eggs one at a time until creamy. Bake in greased, deep baking dish at 400° F for 50 to 60 minutes or until golden brown.

Serves 6.

—Lisa Mann

Creamy Pasta Sauce with Fresh Herbs

1½ cups heavy cream
4 Tbsp. butter
½ tsp. salt
⅛ tsp. nutmeg
cayenne
¼ cup Parmesan cheese
¼ cup chopped mixed herbs
    (basil, mint, parsley, chives)
1 lb. angel hair pasta, cooked,
    drained & rinsed

Combine cream, butter, salt, nutmeg and cayenne in heavy saucepan. Simmer for 15 minutes, or until slightly reduced and thickened. Whisk in cheese and herbs and simmer for 5 minutes. Serve over cooked pasta.

Serves 4.

—Barb McDonald

Pork & Mushroom Spaghetti Sauce

4 lbs. coarsely ground
    Boston butt
2 lbs. mushrooms, sliced
1½ cups chopped celery
1 cup chopped onion
1½ cups chopped green
    pepper
2 Tbsp. salt
3 Tbsp. oregano
3 Tbsp. paprika
1 tsp. pepper
13-oz. can tomato paste
28-oz. can tomatoes

Brown pork in heavy saucepan. Add mushrooms, celery, onion, green pepper, salt, oregano, paprika, pepper and 1 cup water. Bring to a boil. Add tomato paste and tomatoes. Simmer for 1½ hours. Serve over cooked pasta.

Serves 10 to 12.

—Fran Pytko

Pasta

We used this recipe in The Harrowsmith Pasta Cookbook, *but as more people are beginning to make their own pasta, we felt we should run it once more for those who do not have that book.*

2 cups flour
3 eggs
2 tsp. oil
2 Tbsp. water

To make dough by hand, mound flour on work surface, and make a well in the centre. Combine eggs, oil and water, and pour into well. Mix together, using a fork at first and then working by hand. Knead dough for 5 to 8 minutes, or until smooth and elastic. Cover and let stand for 10 minutes.

If using a food processor, place all ingredients in machine and process until a ball forms. Knead for 2 to 4 minutes, or until smooth and elastic. Cover and let stand for 2 minutes.

In either case, if dough is too wet, add flour; if too dry, add an egg.

To roll pasta by hand, divide dough into thirds, and roll on floured board until it reaches desired thinness. Cut as desired. If using a pasta machine, divide dough into thirds, and begin with rollers at first setting, rolling twice through each setting, until desired thinness is attained. Cut by machine or by hand.

Pasta Variations

Vegetable:

Almost any cooked, puréed vegetable can be used. For green pasta, use spinach, broccoli or peas. Tomatoes or carrots result in an orange noodle. For a bright red colour, use beets. Cook vegetables until tender, then purée, leaving vegetables coarse enough that the pasta will have texture as well as flavour.

For the above pasta recipe, use ½ cup cooked, puréed vegetables and one less egg. Prepare dough as directed above.

Herbs:

Wash, dry and chop finely 4 Tbsp. of herb desired (or a combination). Mix with flour before adding remaining ingredients. For a beautiful yellow dough, dissolve a small amount of saffron in 2 Tbsp. boiling water, and use in place of the cold water.

Other Flours:

To make whole wheat pasta, use 1½ cups whole wheat flour and ½ cup unbleached white flour. Other flour options include semolina, buckwheat and triticale.

Smooth Spaghetti Sauce

This recipe is for those who prefer a smooth sauce for spaghetti, lasagne or manicotti. Quick to assemble, it can be left to simmer for hours. The vinegar adds an unusual taste.

2 Tbsp. olive oil
½ cup chopped onion
1 large clove garlic, minced
⅓ cup red wine vinegar
¼ tsp. thyme
½ tsp. basil
½ tsp. oregano
1½ tsp. salt
2 Tbsp. parsley
½ tsp. Worcestershire sauce
¼ tsp. pepper
2 Tbsp. honey
28-oz. can tomatoes
3 6½-oz. cans tomato paste

Heat oil and sauté onion and garlic until onion is translucent. Add remaining ingredients and simmer for 1 hour.

Makes 7 cups.

—Susan O'Neill

White Clam Sauce

Serve this delicate sauce over a spinach or tomato pasta to provide contrast. A thick, flat noodle such as linguine is best to absorb the sauce.

2 Tbsp. oil
1 onion, chopped
1 13-oz. can clams, drained, juice reserved
1½ Tbsp. butter
1½ Tbsp. flour
1½ cups light cream
¼ cup white wine
salt & pepper
parsley

Heat oil and sauté onion until translucent. Add water to clam juice, if necessary, to make ¾ cup. Pour into pot and cook until onion is soft.

Melt butter, stir in flour, then add cream and wine, and cook, stirring, over medium-low heat until thickened and smooth. Pour into onion mixture. Season with salt and pepper and parsley. Add clams and simmer for 20 minutes. Serve over cooked pasta.

Serves 2 to 3.

—*Sharon Moroso*

Mushroom Sauce for Pasta

Top this sauce with Olivade (recipe follows). The mild sweetness of the mushroom sauce complements the olive flavour of Olivade. Either is also delicious served alone with pasta.

3 Tbsp. butter
¼ cup chopped green onion
⅓ cup diced red pepper
1½ cups sliced mushrooms
1 cup heavy cream
salt & pepper

Melt butter, then sauté onion and red pepper for 1 minute. Add mushrooms and sauté for 3 to 4 minutes. Stir in cream and salt and pepper. Heat through.

Serves 3 to 4.

—*Sandra K. Bennett*

Olivade

2 lbs. large Kalamata olives, pitted
½ cup olive oil
1¼ cups chopped walnuts
2 cloves garlic, minced
2 tsp. chopped basil
½ tsp. pepper
1 cup Parmesan cheese
2-4 tsp. red wine vinegar

Combine olives, oil, walnuts, garlic, basil and pepper. Mix well. Add cheese and vinegar to taste. This mixture may be stored, refrigerated, for up to 2 months.

—*Sandra K. Bennett*

Pasta Carbonara

We offer here two carbonara recipes. Although both retain the basic concept of a carbonara, they differ considerably from each other.

1 lb. thickly sliced bacon, diced
1 lb. linguine
3 eggs
⅓ cup chopped Italian parsley
½ cup Parmesan cheese
pepper

Fry bacon until crisp. Drain well on paper towels. Cook linguine until just tender. While this is cooking, beat eggs, then stir in parsley and cheese. Drain and rinse linguine, then mix with egg mixture. Add bacon and pepper and toss again.

Serves 4 to 6.

—*Barb McDonald*

Spaghetti alla Carbonara

1 lb. spaghetti
1 clove garlic, minced
2 Tbsp. olive oil
½ lb. mushrooms, sliced
2 cups diced ham
4 eggs
¼ cup minced parsley
¾ cup Parmesan cheese

Cook spaghetti until just tender. Drain and rinse. Meanwhile, sauté garlic in olive oil for 2 minutes. Add mushrooms and ham and sauté until ham is slightly crisp. Beat eggs lightly, add parsley and cheese and mix with spaghetti. Pour ham mixture over and mix well.

Serves 4 to 6.

—*Diane Pearse*

Creamy Garlic Sauce

The creaminess of this sauce complements its tangy garlic flavour – cottage cheese may be substituted if ricotta is unavailable.

½ cup milk
2 Tbsp. butter
3-4 cloves garlic, crushed
1 lb. ricotta cheese
pasta of your choice, cooked, drained & rinsed
½ cup Parmesan cheese
pepper

Heat milk and butter in heavy pot. Add garlic and simmer for 5 minutes, then remove garlic. Add ricotta cheese and cook, stirring, over low heat until ricotta has melted. Remove from heat and cover. Toss pasta with ricotta mixture, and sprinkle with Parmesan cheese and pepper.

Serves 2 to 3.

—*Irene Louden*

Artichoke Heart Spaghetti Sauce

This is a very spicy topping, particularly good with fresh fettuccine. Served as an appetizer, it provides a tangy beginning to a meal.

1 large can artichoke hearts, sliced
½ cup olive oil
2 tsp. crushed hot red pepper
1 tsp. salt
3 cloves garlic, minced
4 Tbsp. chopped parsley
juice of 1 lemon

Combine artichoke hearts, oil, red pepper, salt and garlic in heavy pot. Cook over medium heat, stirring, until hot. Add parsley and lemon juice. Serve over cooked noodles, topped with pepper and Parmesan cheese.

Serves 4.

Hungarian Stew & Noodles

"I developed this recipe for my daughter's first birthday party, when I was still an inexperienced cook. I wanted something that was tasty but would appeal to people from 1 year old to 80 years old, something I could make ahead of time and something that could be made easily in a large quantity. This was the result, and I've used it for many family gatherings since."

½ cup oil
1 clove garlic, crushed
5 lbs. stewing beef, cut into 1" cubes
4 onions, sliced
18-oz. can tomato paste
2½ cups water
1 Tbsp. paprika
2 tsp. salt
1 tsp. pepper
1 bay leaf
16 oz. noodles
2 Tbsp. butter
1 Tbsp. parsley

Heat oil. Cook garlic for 1 minute, then discard. Add beef and onions, and cook over medium-high heat until meat is lightly browned. Stir in tomato paste, water, paprika, salt, pepper and bay leaf. Bring to a boil, reduce heat to low, cover and simmer for 3 hours.

When stew is nearly done, cook noodles. Toss with butter and parsley. To serve, heap noodles in middle of serving plate and surround with stew.

Serves 10.

Basiled Noodles

1 lb. curly noodles
4 Tbsp. butter
¾ cup chopped walnuts
⅓ cup chopped basil
salt & pepper

Cook noodles in boiling water. Meanwhile, melt butter in small saucepan over medium heat and add nuts. Cook for 3 to 4 minutes. Add basil and cook for 1 minute to soften and to release flavour. Mix with drained noodles and add salt and pepper to taste.

Serves 8 as a side dish.

—*Diane M. Johnson*

Noodles Czarina Casserole

Pasta is one of the world's best "comfort foods" — it always makes the eater feel full, warm and cared-for. This dish is a pleasant combination of tastes and textures.

½ cup chopped onion
2 Tbsp. butter
2 Tbsp. flour
1 tsp. salt
pepper
⅔ cup powdered milk
1 cup water
1 tsp. Dijon mustard
1 cup cottage cheese
½ cup grated Cheddar cheese
2 Tbsp. lemon juice
¾ lb. dry egg noodles, cooked
parsley

Sauté onion in butter until tender. Stir in flour, salt and pepper until smooth. Combine powdered milk with water, then add to roux with mustard. Cook, stirring, until thickened. Stir in cheeses and lemon juice, then noodles. Pour into greased casserole dish and bake, uncovered, at 350° F for 40 to 45 minutes. Sprinkle with parsley.

Serves 4.

Crab Pasta Casserole

"In northern California, Dungeness crabs come on the market between Christmas and New Year's. This casserole provides welcome relief from heavy holiday meals."

3 Tbsp. butter
½ cup chopped onion
1 clove garlic, minced
2½ Tbsp. flour
1½ cups chicken stock
⅓ cup dry white wine
1 Tbsp. chopped basil
1 jar marinated artichoke hearts, drained & chopped
⅛ tsp. cayenne
1 lb. fusilli, cooked, drained & rinsed
1 Tbsp. butter
2 Tbsp. Parmesan cheese
1 lb. crabmeat
1 cup grated Monterey Jack cheese

Melt butter, then sauté onion and garlic until golden. Sprinkle with flour, mix, then add chicken stock and simmer until thickened. Add wine, basil, artichokes and cayenne. Set aside.

Toss pasta with butter and Parmesan cheese. Layer pasta, crabmeat and sauce in greased casserole dish. Top with grated cheese. Bake, uncovered, at 350° F for 30 minutes.

Serves 4.

—Noreen Braithwaite

Spaghetti Balls & Sauce

Delicious nonmeat "meatballs," these are based on cream cheese and walnuts. The spaghetti balls are simmered in the tomato sauce and then poured over cooked pasta.

BALLS:
2 eggs
¾ cup cracker crumbs
¼ cup wheat germ
½ cup ground walnuts
4 oz. cream cheese
1 clove garlic, chopped
oil **or** butter
SAUCE:
3 Tbsp. oil
¼ green pepper, chopped
¼ lb. mushrooms, sliced
1 onion, chopped
salt
¼ tsp. sage
½ tsp. oregano
½ bay leaf
28-oz. can tomatoes
6½-oz. can tomato sauce

Lightly beat eggs, then combine with cracker crumbs, wheat germ, walnuts, cream cheese and garlic. Mix well. Shape into small balls. Chill for 1 hour, then brown in oil or butter.

Meanwhile, make sauce. Heat oil and sauté green pepper, mushrooms and onion. Add salt, herbs, tomatoes and tomato sauce. Add browned spaghetti balls, and simmer for 1 hour.

Serve over spaghetti.

Serves 6.

—Vicky Chandler

Ravioli

If you make ravioli often, you may wish to invest in a ravioli cutter. This looks like a wooden rolling pin with small square indentations. The serrated edges on the squares cut easily through the dough. If you use this, roll the dough out in sheets and then fill, rather than rolling out in strips.

pasta
1 egg, lightly beaten
FILLING:
1½ lbs. ground beef
¼ cup Parmesan cheese
1¼ cups chopped raw
  spinach
2 Tbsp. chopped parsley
½ cup bread crumbs
¼ lb. dry Italian salami,
  chopped
2 eggs, lightly beaten
salt & pepper

Make pasta using basic pasta recipe (page 427); set aside.

Cook beef until well browned. Drain off fat, then mix with remaining filling ingredients. Cool.

Flour a large work surface. Roll out dough until it is very thin. Brush with lightly beaten egg. Cut dough into ½-inch strips. Place filling on alternate strips of dough by teaspoonfuls, about 2 inches apart. Place empty dough strips on top of filled ones. Pinch down sides well with a fork, cut between hills of filling and pinch edges closed.

Cook a few at a time in boiling water for 15 minutes, remove and drain. Serve with tomato sauce, if desired.

Makes approximately 4 dozen.

—Diane Capelazo

Rigatoni with Meatballs

Many of us grew up with canned rigatoni as a lunchtime ritual. Homemade rigatoni provides a tastier, more nutritious alternative and does not take long to make.

1 lb. rigatoni, cooked &
  drained
MEATBALLS:
1 lb. ground beef
salt & pepper
2-3 eggs
bread crumbs
basil, thyme, oregano,
  rosemary, marjoram,
  summer savory
1-2 cloves garlic, crushed
½ cup oil or less
SAUCE:
1 onion, chopped
28-oz. can tomatoes
13-oz. can tomato paste
1 cup sliced mushrooms
basil
oregano

Combine ground beef, salt and pepper, eggs, a pinch of bread crumbs, a small pinch each of desired herbs and garlic. Mix well and form into small meatballs. Brown in oil. Remove from pot and set aside.

Brown onion for sauce in meatball drippings. Add tomatoes, tomato paste, mushrooms, basil and oregano. Bring to a boil, then reduce heat. Return meatballs to pot and simmer for 1 to 1½ hours. Serve over cooked rigatoni.

Serves 4.

—Cary Elizabeth Marshall

Green Spaghetti with Cheese & Tomato Sauces

The contributor tasted this while vacationing in Italy and successfully re-created it upon her return home. This is an attractive dish because of the combination of colours.

1 lb. dry spaghetti, cooked,
  drained & rinsed
TOMATO SAUCE:
4 Tbsp. butter
1 large onion, chopped
½ lb. bacon
4 large tomatoes, peeled,
  seeded & cubed
1 Tbsp. basil
salt & pepper
CHEESE SAUCE:
3 cups sour cream
½ lb. sharp Cheddar cheese,
  grated
1 Tbsp. oregano
salt & pepper
paprika

For tomato sauce: Melt butter, then sauté onion and bacon. Add tomatoes and basil and cook for 5 minutes. Add salt and pepper and keep hot.

For cheese sauce: Heat sour cream slowly. Add cheese and cook, stirring, until melted. Stir in remaining ingredients.

Place spaghetti on plates. Pour tomato sauce over spaghetti and top with cheese sauce.

Serves 4.

—Inge Benda

Curried Pasta Salad

16 oz. dry spiral pasta
¼ cup olive oil
1 green pepper, sliced
1 red pepper, sliced
3-4 stalks celery, chopped
2 cups broccoli florets
1 13-oz. can pitted black
  olives, drained
1 4-oz. can water chestnuts,
  drained & sliced
2 cups chopped purple
  cabbage
DRESSING:
⅔ cup olive oil
3 Tbsp. wine vinegar
1 large clove garlic, crushed
1-1½ Tbsp. curry powder
1 tsp. coriander
⅓ cup Parmesan cheese

Cook pasta in boiling water until soft but not soggy. Rinse in cold water and then toss with olive oil. Add remaining salad ingredients and set aside.

Combine dressing ingredients, except Parmesan cheese. Toss with salad, then allow to sit for 5 to 10 minutes. Add Parmesan cheese, toss and serve.

Serves 8 to 10.

—Colleen Suche

Pasta Patricia

A variation of the classic cream sauce for pasta, this dish has a somewhat thinner result. The addition of cottage cheese makes it an especially good source of calcium and protein. Any pasta is acceptable, but we recommend a thick, flat noodle or a round one to better absorb the sauce.

¼ cup butter
1 onion, chopped
2 cloves garlic, minced
salt
¼ tsp. pepper
¾ tsp. nutmeg
¼ tsp. sweet paprika
1 Tbsp. chopped basil
¾ cup chopped green pepper
1 cup sour cream
¼ cup Parmesan or Romano
  cheese
¾ cup fine-curd cottage
  cheese
¼ lb. ham, julienned
cooked pasta

Melt butter and sauté onion and garlic until onion is translucent. Add salt, pepper, nutmeg, paprika, basil and green pepper and sauté for 2 more minutes. Stir in sour cream and cheeses, then add ham and heat through. Serve over cooked pasta.

Serves 4.

—Patricia Pryde

Cappellettini in Brodo

PASTA:
1 egg
1 egg yolk
1 cup flour
1 tsp. salt
1 Tbsp. water
FILLING:
2 chicken breasts, boned
2 green onions, chopped
2 Tbsp. oil
fresh thyme, oregano, sage &
  parsley
1 clove garlic, crushed
1 egg yolk
Parmesan cheese
salt & pepper
bread crumbs
20 cups rich chicken broth

Combine pasta ingredients. Mix well, cover and set aside.

Sauté chicken breasts and onions in oil until chicken is cooked through but not browned. Grind chicken.

Mix herbs to taste in order given. Blend in garlic, egg yolk, 2 Tbsp. Parmesan cheese, cooked chicken and salt and pepper. Add bread crumbs if necessary to hold mixture together. Roll into pencil-thick coil.

Put pasta through pasta machine at thinnest setting, or roll out until paper-thin. Cut into 1-inch squares.

Pinch off a small piece of the chicken coil, and place in the middle of the pasta square. Press 2 opposite corners of pasta firmly together, making a triangle. Wrap around a finger, press smallest corners together and turn down middle point of triangle. Repeat for remaining pasta.

Poach cappellettini in broth for 15 minutes. Serve garnished with parsley and Parmesan cheese.

Serves 8 to 10.

—Mirella Guidi

Seafood Linguine

2 cups sliced mushrooms
4 shallots or green onions,
  finely chopped
½ cup butter
1½ cups Madeira
1 Tbsp. tomato paste
1 Tbsp. snipped tarragon
¼ tsp. salt
pepper
10 oz. linguine
1½ lbs. shrimp, shelled
1½ cups heavy cream
4 egg yolks, beaten
salt & pepper

Cook mushrooms and shallots in butter, uncovered, over medium-high heat for 4 to 5 minutes, or until vegetables are tender. Remove with slotted spoon and set aside.

Stir Madeira, tomato paste, tarragon, ¼ tsp. salt and pepper into butter in skillet. Bring to a boil, and cook vigorously for 10 minutes, or until mixture is reduced to ½ cup.

Meanwhile, cook pasta. Drain and keep warm. Drop shrimp into boiling water and cook for 1 to 3 minutes, or until shrimp turn pink. Drain and keep warm.

In small bowl, stir together cream and egg yolks. Add Madeira mixture. Return to skillet. Cook and stir until thickened. Stir in shrimp and mushroom mixture and heat through. Season with salt and pepper. Toss with pasta.

Serves 6.

—Kristine Mattila

Turkey-Stuffed Pasta Shells

1 lb. ground raw turkey
1 onion, chopped
2 Tbsp. butter
1 egg, slightly beaten
2 cups cottage cheese
1½ cups grated Cheddar
  cheese
½ tsp. oregano
½ tsp. sage
¼ tsp. pepper
1 lb. spinach, chopped &
  steamed
1 lb. large pasta shells
2-3 cups rich tomato sauce
Parmesan cheese

Brown turkey and onion in butter. Combine egg with cottage cheese, Cheddar cheese, oregano, sage and pepper. Squeeze excess liquid from spinach and stir into cheese mixture along with turkey and onion. Mix well.

Stuff pasta shells with filling. Place 3 to 4 Tbsp. tomato sauce in bottom of greased 9" x 13" baking pan. Arrange shells in pan, then pour tomato sauce over. Sprinkle with Parmesan cheese and bake at 350° F for 50 to 60 minutes.

Serves 6 to 8.

—Lois B. Demerich

Bradford Carrot Alfredo

6 carrots, peeled
12 oz. dry fettuccine or 1 lb.
  fresh fettuccine
½ cup butter
1 cup heavy cream
1 cup Parmesan cheese
½ lb. sliced ham, cut into
  thin strips
½ tsp. nutmeg pepper

Cut carrots lengthwise into strips the same size as the fettuccine. Cook fettuccine, drain and keep hot. Cook carrot strips for 3 minutes, or until crispy-tender. Drain.

Melt butter in large pot over low heat. Whisk in cream and Parmesan cheese. Stir in ham and carrots and heat gently. Add fettuccine, nutmeg and pepper. Toss together well. Cook, stirring, until heated through.

Serves 6 to 8.

—Evelyn Hall

Seafood Pasta Salad with Pesto Dressing

This dressing, with or without pesto, is also excellent with potato salad. This is a good picnic salad.

DRESSING:
2 eggs
½ cup sugar
1 Tbsp. dry mustard
paprika
2 tsp. flour
¾ cup vinegar
1 Tbsp. pesto
SALAD:
½ lb. corkscrew pasta
1 lb. shrimp, shelled & deveined
1 lb. scallops, rinsed
1 cup cooked peas
½ cup diced red pepper
½ cup minced green onion
½ cup chopped celery
1 cup black olives
salt & pepper

For dressing: Beat eggs well. Add sugar, mustard, paprika and flour and beat well. Then add vinegar and ¼ cup water. Cook in double boiler until thickened. Set aside. When cool, stir in pesto.

Meanwhile, prepare salad. Cook pasta, drain and rinse. Cook shrimp and scallops in boiling water for 1 minute. Drain immediately.

Toss all salad ingredients in large bowl, then mix in enough dressing to coat. Chill well, then allow salad to return to room temperature before serving.

Serves 6.

—Diane Pearse

Fried Jao-Tze

Originating in northern China, these are essentially fried dumplings, which may also be steamed or boiled. When they are fried, offer a variety of dips as accompaniment – honey-mustard sauce or soy sauce with ginger, to mention just two.

DOUGH:
1½ cups flour
8 Tbsp. water
FILLING:
6 Chinese mushrooms
⅓ lb. ground pork
½ cup diced bamboo shoots
⅓ cup chopped shrimp
1½ Tbsp. Chinese sherry
1½ Tbsp. soy sauce
1 Tbsp. cornstarch
salt
½ egg, beaten
⅓ cup oil

For dough: Place flour in bowl and add water, mixing until well blended. Knead, cover and let stand for 45 minutes.

For filling: Cover mushrooms with boiling water and let stand for 20 minutes. Drain, then squeeze. Cut off stems, discard, then chop mushroom caps. Combine mushrooms with pork, bamboo shoots, shrimp, sherry, soy sauce, cornstarch, salt and egg and mix well. Refrigerate for several hours.

Place dough on lightly floured board and knead for 5 minutes, or until smooth and elastic. Stretch into sausage shape, then pull off 25 to 30 pieces. Roll into balls, flatten, then roll out into 3-inch circles, covering with damp towel as you make them.

Place 2 teaspoons filling on centre of each circle. Bring edges of dough up and pinch together firmly in the centre, forming a crescent. Seal with water and leave each end open. Make a pleat in one end, then gather up remaining dough on end, making 3 or 4 pleats. Repeat at other end. Keep finished crescents covered.

Heat oil. Cook dumplings until golden brown on bottom – 2 minutes. Pour 1 cup water around dumplings. Cover pot tightly and cook on high heat until water is almost gone – 5 minutes — then reduce heat to low for 5 minutes. Return heat to high just to brown dumplings on bottom. Serve bottom-side up.

Serves 6 as an appetizer.

Macaroni & Cheese Casserole

Tomatoes give this macaroni and cheese casserole an added zing. It was developed by the adopted grandmother of the contributor and can be frozen successfully.

3 cups dry elbow macaroni, cooked & drained
1 lb. sharp Cheddar cheese, grated
28-oz. can tomatoes, including juice
pepper
1 cup chopped onion, sautéed in butter
Parmesan cheese

Combine all ingredients except Parmesan cheese and mix well. Top with Parmesan cheese. Bake, uncovered, at 350° F for 1 hour.

Serves 8.

—Anna J. Lee

Braised Shrimp in Pasta Shells with Piquant Mushroom-Tomato Sauce

"This is a dish to make when the urge to create and to fill your home with a heady aroma calls you into the kitchen for a few hours of satisfying cooking. I developed this particular recipe to combine a love of pasta-making with the intriguing notion of mingling zesty Italian and pungent Indian flavours." When we tested this in our Camden East office, there were many loud cries of "More, please!"

BRAISED SHRIMP:
½ tsp. cumin seed
½ lb. large shrimp, shelled & deveined
2 Tbsp. oil
1 tsp. crushed hot red peppers
1 clove garlic, crushed
½ tsp. crushed black pepper
1 Tbsp. lemon juice
MUSHROOM-TOMATO SAUCE:
1/4 tsp. cumin seed
1/4 tsp. coriander seed
1 tsp. butter
1 tsp. olive oil
1 clove garlic, crushed
2 shallots **or** 1 onion, chopped
½ lb. mushrooms, coarsely chopped
1 Tbsp. capers
1 green chili, roasted, peeled & pounded, **or** ½ tsp. crushed hot red peppers
½ tsp. turmeric
½ tsp. basil
½ tsp. thyme
½ tsp. oregano
salt & pepper
1 cup finely chopped tomatoes & juice
1 pound fresh pasta (uncut)
1 tsp. oil
2 Tbsp. Parmesan cheese

For shrimp: Roast cumin seed in dry, heavy pot until it crackles. Remove from pot. Braise shrimp in oil until they turn pink. When cool, combine with cumin and remaining ingredients. Marinate for at least 2 hours.

Meanwhile, prepare sauce. Roast cumin and coriander seeds in dry, heavy pot until they crackle. Remove from heat, crush finely and set aside. Melt butter in oil, then sauté garlic and shallots or onion over medium heat until pale gold. Turn heat to high, add mushrooms, and cook until soft. Add capers, chili, turmeric, basil, thyme, oregano, salt and pepper, cumin and coriander. Cook for 30 seconds, then add tomatoes and juice. Reduce heat and simmer for 15 to 20 minutes, stirring occasionally.

Now, prepare the pasta. Roll out one half very thinly, then cut into 6-to-8-inch disks. Boil disks in water, 2 at a time, then place in a bowl of ice water with oil. Drain and place between damp towels. Cut remaining pasta dough into fettuccine and cook. Set aside 1 fettuccine for each disk, then stir remaining noodles into tomato sauce. Gently mix in shrimp.

For assembly: Butter individual au gratin diskes (one for each pasta disk). Lightly coat each disk with tomato sauce on both sides, then centre in disk with edges hanging over sides. Place one portion of filling in centre, then sprinkle with Parmesan cheese. Fold edges of disk toward centre, crimping together. Fasten with toothpick, then wind single strand of fettuccine around top.

Bake at 450° F for 5 to 8 minutes, or until a pale golden crust forms. Remove toothpick before serving.

Serves 6, approximately.

—Lesley-Anne Paveling

Noodle Casserole Deluxe

Available in most Oriental supply stores, dried tree ears have a distinctive taste and texture. They are somewhat similar to black Chinese mushrooms, which can be substituted if tree ears are not available.

1 oz. tree ears
1 oz. black Chinese mushrooms
1 lb. mushrooms, quartered
2 Tbsp. lemon juice
3 Tbsp. butter
1 onion, finely chopped
1 bunch parsley, chopped
salt & pepper
¼ tsp. thyme
3 eggs, beaten
1 cup heavy cream
½ cup milk
nutmeg
3 cups dry egg noodles, cooked
5 Tbsp. Parmesan cheese
1 cup buttered bread crumbs

Soak tree ears in warm water for 30 minutes and the Chinese mushrooms for 15 minutes. Drain, then chop. Mix regular mushrooms with lemon juice.

Melt butter and sauté onion for 5 minutes. Add all mushrooms and sauté for 2 minutes longer. Add parsley, salt and pepper and thyme and sauté for 10 minutes.

Mix together eggs, cream, milk, nutmeg and salt and pepper. Place cooked noodles and mushroom mixture in greased 9" x 9" casserole dish. Pour egg mixture over and mix well. Sprinkle with cheese and bread crumbs.

Bake, uncovered, at 400° F for 25 to 30 minutes.

Serves 4.

—Inge Benda

Cheesy Broccoli Casserole

This is a rich, tasty casserole. It feeds a crowd and can be prepared and assembled a day ahead.

3 eggs
2½ cups ricotta cheese
¾ cup sour cream
¼ cup butter
1 lb. mushrooms, sliced
2 heads broccoli, cut into florets
2 onions, chopped
salt & pepper
1 lb. dry egg noodles, cooked, drained & rinsed
2 Tbsp. yeast
½ cup bread crumbs
1 cup grated Swiss cheese

Combine eggs, ricotta cheese and sour cream; mix well. Set aside.

Melt butter in heavy skillet. Sauté mushrooms, broccoli and onions until onions are transparent – 5 to 10 minutes. Sprinkle with salt and pepper.

In greased 9" x 13" pan, combine cooked noodles, egg mixture and vegetables. Add yeast and mix well. Sprinkle with bread crumbs and grated cheese.

Bake, covered, at 350° F for 30 minutes, then uncovered for 15 minutes.

Serves 8.

Lasagne Stuffed with Tiny Meatballs

A lot of work but well worth the effort, this recipe makes enough lasagne to serve 16 people. It can also be frozen and used for a last-minute meal.

1 lb. lasagne noodles
2 cups cottage **or** ricotta cheese, puréed
2 eggs, lightly beaten
1 lb. mozzarella cheese, grated
½ cup Parmesan cheese
SAUCE:
3 Tbsp. oil
2 onions, chopped
½ green pepper, diced
10 mushrooms, sliced
1-2 cloves garlic, minced
3 28-oz. cans tomato sauce
1 Tbsp. chopped parsley
1 tsp. basil
½ tsp. oregano
MEATBALLS:
1½ lbs. ground meat (beef, veal or pork)
¼ cup Parmesan cheese
1 clove garlic, minced
1½ Tbsp. chopped parsley
⅛ tsp. nutmeg
1 tsp. basil
½ tsp. grated lemon rind
¼ tsp. salt
¼ tsp. pepper
⅔ cup dry bread crumbs
1 Tbsp. milk
1 egg

Cook noodles in boiling water, drain, rinse and set aside.

Prepare sauce. Heat oil in large pot. Add onions and sauté until soft. Add green pepper, mushrooms and garlic and cook, stirring, for 3 minutes. Stir in tomato sauce and herbs. Bring to a boil, reduce heat, and simmer while preparing rest of dish.

Combine meat, cheese, garlic, parsley, nutmeg, basil, lemon rind, salt and pepper and mix well. In another bowl, combine bread crumbs, milk and egg. Work this into meat, then chill mixture for 1 hour. Shape into tiny meatballs, keeping your hands damp with cold water. Cook meatballs by steaming over low heat in enough water to prevent sticking. Drop cooked meatballs into tomato sauce, setting aside a small amount of sauce to spread on bottom of lasagne pans.

Combine cottage or ricotta cheese with eggs and mozzarella cheese.

To assemble, grease two 9" x 13" pans. Spread bottom of pans with very thin layer of tomato sauce. On top of this, place a layer of noodles, then half the cheese mixture, then one third the meatballs and tomato sauce. Sprinkle with Parmesan cheese. Repeat. Top with layer of noodles, remaining meatballs and sauce and Parmesan cheese.

Bake, uncovered, at 375° F for 30 minutes, or until bubbling and golden. Let stand for 10 minutes before serving.

Serves 16.

—Lynne Roe

Baking

Poppy Seed Lemon Bread

4 eggs
1½ cups oil
1½ cups light cream
1 tsp. vanilla
½ cup poppy seeds
3 cups flour
2¼ cups sugar
1 tsp. salt
1½ tsp. baking soda
2 tsp. baking powder
Rind & juice of 1 lemon

Combine eggs, oil, cream, vanilla and poppy seeds. Mix together flour, 2 cups sugar, salt, baking soda, baking powder and lemon rind.

Add dry ingredients to egg-cream mixture and blend well. Pour into 2 greased loaf pans and bake at 325° F for 70 minutes.

Meanwhile, mix lemon juice and rind with remaining ¼ cup sugar. Pour over bread while hot and still in pan.

Makes 2 loaves.

—Audrey Moroso

Orange Date Nut Bread

1 cup boiling water
¼ cup orange juice
1 cup chopped dates
1½ cups flour
¼ tsp. cinnamon
¼ tsp. nutmeg
Ground cloves
1½ tsp. baking soda
½ tsp. salt
¼ cup shortening
¾ cup brown sugar
1 egg
1 cup chopped walnuts
2 tsp. grated orange peel

Mix together boiling water, orange juice and chopped dates. Set aside until cooled to room temperature.

Sift together flour, cinnamon, nutmeg, cloves, baking soda and salt and set aside.

Cream together shortening and brown sugar. Add egg, beat well and stir in date mixture. Add dry ingredients and stir batter until moistened. Fold in walnuts and orange peel.

Pour into a greased loaf pan and bake at 325° F for 65 to 70 minutes. Cool bread in pan for 10 minutes, remove and cool completely before slicing.

Makes 1 loaf.

—Kathy & Rhett Hagerty

Blueberry Quick Bread

2½ cups flour
¾ cup sugar
1 Tbsp. baking powder
½ tsp. salt
6 Tbsp. butter
¾ cup chopped walnuts
2 eggs
1 cup milk
1 tsp. vanilla
1½ cups blueberries

In large bowl, mix flour, sugar, baking powder and salt. Cut in butter until fine. Stir in walnuts.

In small bowl, beat eggs lightly and stir in milk and vanilla. Stir into flour just until flour is moistened. Gently stir blueberries into batter.

Spoon batter into greased and floured loaf pan. Bake at 350° F for 1 hour and 20 minutes or until toothpick inserted into centre of loaf comes out clean.

Makes 1 loaf.

Pumpkin Bread

4 eggs
2 cups granulated sugar
1¼ cups oil
2 cups cooked & mashed pumpkin
1 tsp. salt
3 cups flour
2 tsp. baking powder
2 tsp. baking soda
2 tsp. cinnamon
½ cup chopped walnuts
1 cup seedless raisins

Beat eggs and add sugar, oil and pumpkin. Mix dry ingredients together and add to egg mixture. Stir in nuts and raisins. Bake at 350° F for one hour.

Makes 2 large loaves.

—Irene P. Simonson

Banana Nut Bread

2 cups flour
2 tsp. baking powder
1 tsp. baking soda
¾ tsp. salt
½ cup shortening
1 cup sugar
2 eggs, well beaten
1 cup mashed bananas
1 cup chopped walnuts

Sift together flour, baking powder, baking soda and salt. Cream together shortening, sugar and eggs.

Add bananas to creamed mixture alternately with dry ingredients, combining well after each addition. Stir in walnuts.

Spoon into greased loaf pan and bake at 350° F for 1 to 1¼ hours or until straw inserted into centre comes out clean.

Makes 1 loaf.

—Janice Clynick

Cinnamon Bread

2 Tbsp. brown sugar
1 Tbsp. cinnamon
½ cup butter
1 cup granulated sugar
2 eggs
2 cups flour
2 tsp. baking powder
½ tsp. salt
1 cup milk
1 tsp. vanilla

Mix together brown sugar and cinnamon and set aside. Cream butter, granulated sugar and eggs. Combine dry ingredients and add to creamed mixture alternately with milk. Stir in vanilla. Layer batter and brown sugar-cinnamon mixture in a greased loaf pan, ending with batter. Bake at 350° F for 1 hour.

Makes 1 loaf.

—Karen Carter

Date & Nut Loaf

1 cup walnuts
1 cup chopped dates
1½ tsp. baking soda
½ tsp. salt
3 Tbsp. shortening
¾ cup boiling water
2 eggs
1 tsp. vanilla
1 cup granulated sugar
1½ cups flour

Combine walnuts, dates, baking soda, salt, shortening and boiling water. Set aside for 20 minutes. Beat eggs with a fork and add vanilla, sugar and flour. Add to date mixture and blend. Pour into a greased bread pan and bake at 350° F for 1 hour.

Makes 1 loaf.

—Joyce Marshall

Carrot Bread

½ cup oil
1 cup sugar
2 eggs, beaten
1 cup shredded carrots
1½ cups flour
1 tsp. baking powder
1 tsp. baking soda
¼ tsp. salt
1 tsp. cinnamon
½ cup milk

Mix oil and sugar. Add beaten eggs and stir in carrots. Sift flour, baking powder, baking soda, salt and cinnamon.

Add small amounts of dry ingredients to sugar mixture alternately with milk. Bake in greased loaf pan for 55 minutes at 350° F.

Makes 1 loaf.

—Patricia A. Leahy

Orange Raisin Bread

1 large orange, unpeeled
¾ cup boiling water
1 egg
¼ cup vegetable oil
2 cups flour
2 tsp. baking powder
1 tsp. baking soda
½ tsp. salt
¾ cup lightly packed brown
  sugar
¾ cup raisins
½ cup chopped nuts

Cut orange into pieces and remove seeds. Combine in blender with boiling water and blend until almost smooth. Add egg and oil and blend for a few seconds.

Combine remaining ingredients. Add orange mixture and stir just until well blended. Pour into greased loaf pan. Bake at 350° F for 45 to 55 minutes.

Makes 1 loaf.

—Margaret Butler

Zucchini Loaf

2 eggs
1 cup sugar
½ cup oil
1½ cups flour
½ tsp. salt
1 tsp. baking powder
½ tsp. baking soda
1 tsp. cinnamon
1 tsp. vanilla
1 cup finely grated raw
   zucchini
½ cup chopped walnuts

Beat eggs until light and add sugar and oil. Stir together flour, salt, baking powder, baking soda and cinnamon. Add to egg mixture, beating until blended. Mix in vanilla, zucchini and nuts.

Turn into a greased loaf pan and bake at 350° F for 1 hour or until a toothpick inserted in centre comes out clean.

Makes 1 loaf.

—Carolyn Hills

Dill Bread

1 pkg. dry yeast
¼ cup warm water
1 cup cottage cheese
2 tsp. dill weed
2 tsp. salt
¼ tsp. baking soda
1 egg
1 Tbsp. melted butter
1½ tsp. minced onion
2 Tbsp. sugar
2¼-2½ cups flour

Dissolve yeast in water and set aside. Combine in a large bowl, cottage cheese, dill weed, salt, baking soda, egg, butter, onion and sugar. Stir in yeast mixture and then flour.

Knead for 5 to 10 minutes on a floured board. Let rise in a greased bowl until doubled in size — about 1 hour. Punch down. Place in 2 greased loaf pans and let rise for 45 minutes.

Bake at 350° F for 30 minutes. Remove from pans and brush with melted butter.

Makes 1 loaf.

—Pat Bredin

Wheat Germ Loaf

1 cup lukewarm water
1 Tbsp. honey
Salt
1 Tbsp. yeast
2 eggs
1 Tbsp. vegetable oil
⅓ cup soya flour
⅓ cup rice polishings
2 cups bran
3 cups wheat germ
1½ cups water

Combine lukewarm water, honey, salt and yeast and let stand for 20 minutes. Add eggs, oil, soya flour, rice polishings, bran and wheat germ. Mix well and add enough water to make a stiff batter.

Place in a greased loaf pan and let rise in a warm place for 1 hour.

Bake at 325° F for 1¼ to 1½ hours.

Makes 1 loaf.

—Gail Miller

Dutch Pumpernickel Bread

2 Tbsp. molasses
3 cups hot water
3 cups Red River cereal
1 cup whole wheat flour
2 tsp. baking soda
1 tsp. salt

In large mixing bowl, combine water and molasses. Add remaining ingredients. Beat at high speed for 2 minutes. Cover with cloth towel and let stand overnight, then pour into greased loaf pan and smooth top.

Bake at 275° F for 1 hour, reduce heat to 250° and bake 1 hour longer. Store in refrigerator for one day before slicing.

Makes 1 loaf.

—Sandra Binnington

Bran Bread

½ cup brown sugar
2 cups bran
1 cup whole wheat flour
1 cup unbleached white flour
2 Tbsp. wheat germ
1 tsp. salt
2 tsp. baking soda
2 cups buttermilk

Combine dry ingredients. Stir in buttermilk. Spoon into a greased pan and bake at 350° F for 1 hour.

Makes 1 loaf.

—Johanna Genge

Buttermilk Cheese Loaf

1 cup unbleached white flour
1 cup whole wheat flour
1½ tsp. baking powder
½ tsp. baking soda
2 tsp. dry mustard
1 tsp. salt
1 cup grated Cheddar cheese
1 cup buttermilk
¼ cup oil
2 eggs
2 Tbsp. minced onion

Combine flours, baking powder, baking soda, mustard, salt and cheese. Beat together buttermilk, oil, eggs and onion. Add to dry mixture and stir until moist.

Pour into greased loaf pan and bake at 375° F for 45 to 50 minutes. Cool for 10 minutes, then remove from pan.

Makes 1 loaf.

—Pat Dicer

Gougère

A rich bread of French origin, this is tasty served warm as an accompaniment to soup or stew.

½ cup unsalted butter
1 cup water
½ tsp. salt
1½ cups pastry flour
4 eggs
Any chopped fresh herb
4 oz. Gruyère cheese, grated

Combine butter, water and salt in a saucepan and bring to a boil. Remove from heat and stir in the flour. Return to heat for a few minutes, stirring constantly, until mixture is slightly thickened.

Remove from heat and stir in the eggs one at a time. Then beat in herb and all but a little of the cheese.

Drop seven heaping spoonfuls of the mixture onto a greased cookie sheet in the shape of a ring, each mound of batter touching the rest. Sprinkle the remaining cheese on top and bake at 375° F for 40 to 45 minutes, until golden brown.

Serve hot or cold.

—N. Burk

Lemon Bread

1 cup butter
1½ cups sugar
3 eggs
1½ cups flour
1 tsp. baking powder
Salt
½ cup milk
½ cup chopped walnuts
Grated rind & juice of 1 lemon

Cream together butter and 1 cup sugar. Beat in eggs. Combine flour, baking powder and salt. Add to creamed mixture alternately with milk and mix well. Stir in walnuts and lemon rind.

Pour into greased loaf pan and bake at 350° F for 1 hour or until firm on top.

Meanwhile, combine remaining ½ cup sugar with lemon juice. When loaf is baked, spoon lemon sugar over top.

Makes 1 loaf.

—Lily Andrews

Apple Honey Muffins

¼ cup honey
1 egg
¼ cup oil
1 cup apple sauce
⅓ cup orange juice
¾ cup rolled oats
1 cup flour
1 Tbsp. baking powder
½ tsp. cinnamon

In a small bowl, mix honey, egg, oil, apple sauce and orange juice until well combined.

Mix dry ingredients in a large bowl. Make a well in the centre and pour in liquid ingredients, then stir just to moisten.

Spoon into greased muffin tins and bake at 400° F for 25 to 30 minutes.

Makes 12 muffins.

—Carol A. Frost

Orange Oatmeal Muffins

1 whole orange, unpeeled
1 cup rolled oats
½ cup boiling water
½ cup orange juice
½ cup butter
½ cup brown sugar
½ cup granulated sugar
2 eggs, beaten
1 cup flour
1 tsp. baking powder
1 tsp. baking soda
½ tsp. salt
1 tsp. vanilla
½ cup raisins

Place whole orange in blender and purée. Mix with oats, water and orange juice and set aside.

Cream together butter and sugars and add eggs. Combine dry ingredients and add to creamed mixture. Add rolled oat/orange mixture, vanilla and raisins, and stir well.

Bake in greased muffin tins at 350° F for 15 to 20 minutes.

Makes 18 muffins.

—M. Heggison

Poppy Seed Muffins

2 eggs
2 Tbsp. soft butter
¾ cup sugar
½ cup poppy seeds
1 cup sour cream
2 cups flour
½ tsp. baking soda
2 tsp. baking powder

Cream together eggs, butter and sugar. Add poppy seeds and sour cream. Sift together dry ingredients and stir into creamed mixture until just blended.

Pour into greased muffin tins, filling each two-thirds full. Bake at 425° F for 20 minutes.

Makes 12 large muffins.

—Sheri Israels

Blueberry Muffins

1 cup fresh blueberries
1¾ cups flour
¾ tsp. salt
3 tsp. baking powder
2 eggs, well beaten
3 Tbsp. melted butter
¾ cup milk
¼ cup granulated sugar

Mix blueberries and 1 Tbsp. flour. Sift together remaining flour, salt and baking powder. Combine beaten eggs, melted butter, milk and sugar. Beat until foamy. Add dry ingredients all at once and stir quickly.

Fill greased muffin tins one-third full with batter. Put blueberries on top and cover with remaining batter until tins are two-thirds full. Bake at 400° F for 15 to 20 minutes. Makes 12 large muffins.

—Janet Young

Banana Muffins

½ cup shortening
1 cup granulated sugar
1 egg, slightly beaten
1 cup mashed ripe bananas
1 tsp. baking soda
2 Tbsp. hot water
½ tsp. salt
1½ cups flour

Cream shortening and sugar together, blend in egg and mashed bananas. Dissolve soda in hot water and add to creamed mixture.

Combine dry ingredients and stir into creamed mixture until just blended. Pour into greased muffin tins and bake at 375° F for 20 minutes. Makes 12 muffins.

—Helen Potts

Apple Muffins

4 eggs
2 cups milk
4 Tbsp. melted butter
1⅓ cups sugar
4 cups flour
1 tsp. salt
8 tsp. baking powder
1 tsp. cinnamon
½ tsp. nutmeg
4 medium apples, peeled,
   cored & chopped

Beat together eggs, milk, butter and ⅔ cup sugar. Combine flour, salt, baking powder, ½ tsp. cinnamon and nutmeg. Add to egg mixture and fold in apples.

Spoon into greased muffin tins until two-thirds full. Combine remaining ⅔ cup sugar and ½ tsp. cinnamon and sprinkle over muffins. Bake at 375° F for 30 minutes.

Makes 24 large muffins.

Energy Muffins

2 cups finely grated carrots
1 cup chopped walnuts
¾ cup chopped dates
¾ cup raisins, softened in
   water & drained
3 cups flour
¼ cup soya flour
½ cup wheat germ
1 cup rolled oats
1 cup coconut
1 tsp. salt
3 tsp. baking powder
2 tsp. mace
2 tsp. cinnamon
1 tsp. nutmeg
3 eggs, beaten
½ cup safflower oil
½ cup honey
¼ cup molasses
2 cups milk or buttermilk

Combine carrots, walnuts, dates and raisins and set aside. Mix together in large bowl flours, wheat germ, oats, coconut, salt, baking powder, mace, cinnamon and nutmeg. Combine remaining ingredients.

Make a well in the centre of flour mixture and add liquid mixture gradually. If not moist enough, add a small amount of water. Add vegetable mixture and stir in.

Bake in greased muffin tins at 350° F for 25 minutes.

Makes 3 dozen muffins.

—Laura Poitras

Cardamom Muffins

1½ cups raisins
¼ tsp. mace
2 Tbsp. brandy
2 tsp. grated orange rind
Orange juice to cover raisins
¼ cup sunflower oil
½ cup honey
2 eggs
¾ cup milk
½ cup wheat germ
¼ cup bran
1¾ cups flour
1½ tsp. baking powder
½ tsp. baking soda
½ tsp. salt
1 tsp. cardamom
⅛ tsp. allspice

Cover raisins with mace, brandy, orange rind and orange juice and let sit overnight.

Mix oil and honey, add eggs and milk and stir well. Combine remaining ingredients and add to egg mixture. Fold drained raisins into batter.

Spoon into greased muffin tins and bake at 400° F for 15 to 20 minutes.

Makes 24 muffins.

—Jody Schwindt

Buttermilk Bran Muffins

1 cup bran
1 cup wheat germ
2 cups boiling water
1 cup oil
2 cups granulated or brown
   sugar
4 eggs, beaten
5 cups flour
5 tsp. baking soda
1½ Tbsp. salt
4 cups milk
4 cups bran flakes
1-1½ cups raisins

Stir together bran, wheat germ and boiling water. Set aside to cool.

Combine remaining ingredients and mix well. Stir in bran mixture. Let sit for 24 hours before using.

Spoon into well greased muffin tins and bake at 400° F for 15 to 20 minutes. Batter will keep up to a week in the refrigerator.

Makes 4 to 5 dozen muffins.

—Dawn Livingstone

Delicious Muffins

¼ cup butter
½ cup brown sugar
¼ tsp. salt
¼ cup molasses
2 eggs
1 cup milk
½ tsp. baking soda
1 tsp. vanilla
1 cup flour
2 tsp. baking powder
1½ cups bran
2-3 Tbsp. wheat germ

Cream together butter, sugar, salt and molasses. Beat in eggs. Add milk, baking soda and vanilla. Mix slightly. Sift flour and baking powder into creamed mixture, stirring only a little. Add bran and wheat germ. Mix only until all ingredients are moist. Fill greased muffin tins three-quarters full. Bake at 325 to 350° F for 20 to 25 minutes.

Makes 12 large muffins.

—Donna Wallis

Quick Muffins

4 eggs
1½ cups milk
¾ cup oil
1 tsp. orange juice
2 cups white flour
2 cups rye flour
1 cup sugar
2 Tbsp. baking powder
Salt
Cinnamon & nutmeg

Combine liquid ingredients well, add flours, sugar, baking powder, salt and spices and mix until just moist.

Bake in greased muffin tins at 400° F for 20 minutes.

Makes 18 muffins.

—C. Majewski

Corn Muffins

1 cup milk
1 egg
3 Tbsp. oil
¾ cup flour
1 Tbsp. baking powder
3 Tbsp. sugar
1¼ cups corn meal

Beat together milk, egg and oil. Sift together dry ingredients and stir into milk mixture until moist.

Pour into greased muffin tins and bake at 425° F for 20 minutes.

Makes 12 muffins.

—Sheri Israels

Corn Meal Raisin Muffins

1 cup raisins
Boiling water
2 cups corn meal
3 cups buttermilk
2⅔ cups flour
2 tsp. baking powder
1 tsp. salt
2 tsp. baking soda
2 eggs
1 cup oil
1 cup honey

Scald raisins with boiling water and drain well. Combine corn meal and 2 cups buttermilk and set aside.

Mix together flour, baking powder, salt and baking soda. Beat eggs and add oil, honey and remaining 1 cup buttermilk. Add to corn meal-buttermilk mixture and then to flour mixture. Add raisins.

Place in greased muffin tins and bake at 400° F for 20 minutes.

Makes 24 muffins.

—Adella Bragg

Carrot Pineapple Muffins

1½ cups flour
1 cup sugar
1 tsp. baking powder
1 tsp. baking soda
1 tsp. cinnamon
½ tsp. salt
⅔ cup salad oil
2 eggs
1 cup finely grated raw carrot
½ cup crushed pineapple,
    with juice
1 tsp. vanilla

Sift flour, sugar, baking powder, baking soda, cinnamon and salt together in large bowl. Add oil, eggs, carrot, pineapple and vanilla.

Blend on low speed until all is moist, then beat for 2 minutes at medium speed. Half fill greased muffin tins and bake at 350° F for 25 minutes.

Makes 24 muffins.

—Mrs. W. Atkins

Wheat Germ Muffins

1 Tbsp. butter
¾ cup granulated sugar
1 egg
1 cup wheat germ
¾ cup whole wheat flour
¼ cup unbleached white
    flour
1 tsp. baking soda
1 cup buttermilk

Cream butter and sugar and add egg. Mix dry ingredients and add alternately with buttermilk to creamed mixture.

Pour into greased muffin tins and bake at 350° F for 15 to 20 minutes.

Makes 12 muffins.

—Audrey Moroso

Oatmeal Muffins

1 cup oatmeal
1 cup buttermilk
1 egg
½ cup brown sugar
½ cup oil
1 cup flour
½ tsp. salt
1 tsp. baking powder
½ tsp. soda

Soak oatmeal in buttermilk for 1 hour. Add egg, sugar and oil, and beat well. Combine dry ingredients and stir into oatmeal mixture.

Fill greased muffin tins and bake at 400° F for 15 to 20 minutes.

Makes 12 large muffins.

—Kass Bennett

Flaky Biscuits

1 cup whole wheat flour
1 cup unbleached white flour
1 Tbsp. baking powder
½ tsp. salt
½ cup butter
2 eggs, beaten
½ cup milk

Sift dry ingredients together. Cut in butter until mixture is the texture of small peas. Combine eggs and milk and add to the flour mixture, stirring until moistened.

Turn dough onto a floured board. Roll out to ½-inch thickness. Fold in thirds and roll out again. Repeat 5 times.

Cut into 2-inch rounds. Place on a lightly greased cookie sheet and bake at 400° F for 8 to 10 minutes.

Makes 12 to 15 biscuits.

—Jan Post

Scotch Soda Scones

These sweet scones are cooked on top of the stove rather than in the oven. Quickly assembled, they are especially delicious served warm with butter, fresh strawberries and whipped cream.

1½ cups flour
½ tsp. baking soda
½ tsp. cream of tartar
¼ cup granulated sugar
Salt
¼ cup lard
½ cup sour milk

Combine flour, baking soda, cream of tartar, sugar and a pinch of salt. Cut in lard until mixture resembles coarse meal. Add milk and mix with a fork until dough forms a ball.

Divide dough in half. Form each half into a ball, pat down and divide into quarters. Pat into biscuit shape.

Wipe heavy frying pan gently with lard. Fry biscuits on very low heat approximately 15 to 20 minutes per side, turning once.

Makes 8 biscuits.

—Donna Gordon

Whole Wheat Dill Biscuits

2 cups flour
1½ tsp. baking soda
1½ tsp. salt
2 tsp. chopped fresh dill
¼ cup butter
1 egg
⅓ cup light cream
Melted butter

Sift 1⅓ cups flour, baking soda and salt into a bowl. Add remaining ⅔ cup flour and dill. Cut butter into dry ingredients until it resembles coarse meal.

Lightly beat egg and add cream. Stir into flour mixture to form a smooth, soft dough.

Turn out onto a lightly floured board and knead for 30 seconds. Roll out to ½-inch thickness with 1½-inch round cutter.

Bake on lightly greased cookie sheets at 425° F for 10 to 15 minutes. Remove and brush tops with melted butter.

Makes 24 biscuits.

—Katherine Dunster

Cheese Crisps

½ cup butter, at room temperature
2 cups grated Swiss cheese
1½ cups flour
½ tsp. salt

Cream together butter and cheese. Add flour and salt and mix well. Form into 1-inch balls. Place on a cookie sheet and flatten with a floured fork.

Bake at 350° F for 12 to 15 minutes, or until pale gold around edges.

Makes 5 dozen biscuits.

—Eileen Deeley

Chapatis

This is a thin unleavened bread of Indian origin.

4 cups flour
1 tsp. salt
3 Tbsp. melted butter
1-1⅔ cups warm water

Combine flour, salt and melted butter. Add enough water to make a dough that is soft but not wet. Knead for 10 minutes, divide into 24 pieces and roll each into a thin circle. Fry in oil until lightly browned on both sides. Serve warm with curried dishes.

Makes 24 chapatis.

Sesame Cheese Strips

¼ cup sesame seeds
1 cup flour
½ tsp. salt
½ tsp. sugar
½ tsp. ginger
1 cup grated Cheddar cheese
1 egg yolk, beaten
⅓ cup melted butter
1 Tbsp. water
½ tsp. Worcestershire sauce

Toast sesame seeds at 300° F until golden, stirring often. Cool.

Sift flour, salt, sugar and ginger into bowl. Add cheese and sesame seeds and mix lightly with a fork. Combine egg yolk, butter, water and Worcestershire sauce. Add to flour mixture and stir lightly to blend. Shape dough into a ball and roll out to ⅛-inch thickness. Cut into strips.

Bake at 350° F for 10 minutes.

Makes 4 dozen strips.

Cheese Snaps

1½ cups flour
½ tsp. salt
½ tsp. cayenne
¼ lb. Cheddar cheese, grated
¼ lb. butter
1-2 Tbsp. ice water, to moisten

Combine flour, salt, cayenne and cheese. Cut in butter until mixture resembles coarse meal. Add enough water to moisten dough to rolling consistency.

Roll to a ¼-inch thickness and cut into 1-inch strips. Mark 1-inch lengths on strips.

Bake at 375° F for 10 minutes. When cool, cut into squares, following markings made before baking.

Makes 5 dozen cheese snaps.

—Stephanie James

Crusty French Bread

1 heaping Tbsp. butter
1 heaping Tbsp. salt
1 heaping Tbsp. sugar
2 cups boiling water
1 Tbsp. dry yeast
⅔ cup lukewarm water
1 tsp. sugar
6-6½ cups unbleached white
  flour
Yellow corn meal

In a large mixing bowl, combine the butter, salt, sugar and boiling water. Stir as it dissolves.

Sprinkle the yeast over the ⅔ cup lukewarm water and l tsp. sugar. Let rest 10 to 15 minutes in a warm, but turned-off, oven.

When the butter mixture is lukewarm, add yeast mixture and mix well. Start adding the flour, one cup at a time, mixing well after each addition. When 4 cups have been added, beat vigorously for about 10 minutes with a wooden spoon. Gradually add remaining flour. When it becomes too stiff to mix with the spoon, turn out onto a floured board and knead, adding flour as necessary, until it is satiny smooth and very elastic.

Form into a ball, put it in a large greased bowl, cover and let rise until doubled in size — 1½ hours. Punch it down and let rise again until doubled — about 1 hour.

Prepare the baking sheet by buttering it and sprinkling yellow corn meal lightly over the butter.

Divide the dough into 3 parts and shape into very long, very slender loaves as follows. Roll each part into a rectangle about 14 to 15 inches long and 8 to 10 inches wide. Roll up the long side of the rectangle tightly until it is a narrow, even loaf about 1½ inches wide. Seal the seam and the ends by pinching, and place on the baking sheet. Cover and let rise until double in size. Brush tops of the loaves with cold water. Bake at 375° F for about 1 hour, brushing with cold water every 15 or 20 minutes. Makes 3 loaves.

- Nicole Chartrand

The Best Cheese Bread

7-8 cups flour
⅓ cup honey
1 Tbsp. salt
2 Tbsp. yeast
2 cups water
⅔ cup milk
3 cups grated old Cheddar
  cheese

In large warm bowl, mix together 2 cups flour, honey, salt and yeast.

Combine water and milk in a saucepan and heat to 120 to 130° F.

Gradually add liquid to yeast mixture and beat for 2 minutes. Add grated cheese and ½ cup flour, beating until smooth. Gradually stir in enough of the remaining flour to make a stiff dough.

Turn onto a floured board, knead for 10 minutes and form into a ball. Place in a greased bowl and cover with wax paper and a damp tea towel. Place in an oven that has been heated by a pan of hot water and let rise for 1½ hours. Punch down and let rest for 10 minutes.

Shape dough into 3 equal-sized loaves and place in greased loaf pans, cover with wax paper and let rise for 1 hour. Bake at 375° F for 40 minutes.

Makes 3 loaves.

—Anne Millage

Health Bread

2½ cups scalded milk
½ cup oil
½ cup molasses
4 tsp. salt
1 cup rolled oats
½ cup sesame seeds
1 cup wheat germ
2 Tbsp. yeast
2 Tbsp. brown sugar
1½ cups warm water
5-7 cups unbleached white
  flour
3-5 cups whole wheat flour

Combine scalded milk, oil, molasses and salt. Mix together rolled oats, sesame seeds and wheat germ. Pour scalded milk mixture over rolled oats mixture.

Dissolve yeast and brown sugar in warm water. When milk-oats mixture has cooled to lukewarm, add yeast to it. Stir in flour and knead into a soft dough.

Let rise in a warm place for 1 hour. Punch down and place dough in 3 greased loaf pans. Let rise for 1 to 1¼ hours. Bake at 350° F for 45 to 60 minutes.

Makes 3 loaves.

—Carol Frost

Herb Loaf

2 Tbsp. sugar
2 pkgs. dry yeast
2 cups warm water
2 tsp. salt
2 Tbsp. butter
½ cup & 1 Tbsp. grated
  Parmesan cheese
4½ cups flour
1½ Tbsp. dried oregano

Dissolve sugar and yeast in warm water in a large bowl. Add salt, butter, ½ cup cheese, 3 cups flour and oregano. Beat on low speed of electric mixer until blended, then on medium speed for 2 minutes. Add balance of flour by hand until well blended.

Cover and let rise for 45 minutes. Stir down and beat for 30 seconds. Turn into greased 1½-quart casserole dish, sprinkle with 1 Tbsp. Parmesan cheese and bake at 375° F for 55 minutes.

Makes 1 loaf.

—*Shirley Hill*

Old-Fashioned Honey Wheatbread

1½ cups water
1 cup cream-style cottage
  cheese
½ cup honey
¼ cup butter
2 cups unbleached white
  flour
2 Tbsp. brown sugar
3 tsp. salt
2 pkgs. yeast
1 egg, beaten
5½-6 cups whole wheat flour

Heat water, cottage cheese, honey and butter until very warm — 120 to 130° F. Combine with white flour, sugar, salt, yeast and egg and beat for 2 minutes with electric mixer at medium speed. Stir in remaining flour by hand to make a stiff dough.

Knead well and place in a greased bowl. Cover and let rise 45 to 60 minutes — until double in size.

Punch down dough, divide into 2 pieces, shape and place in greased loaf pans. Let rise again for 45 to 60 minutes. Bake at 350° F for 40 to 50 minutes.

Makes 2 loaves.

—*Laura Poitras*

Challah

This traditional Jewish egg bread can make a beautiful gift.

1½ cups milk
¼ cup sugar
3 tsp. salt
⅓ cup butter
3 eggs
2 pkgs. dry yeast
½ cup warm water
7½ cups flour
Poppy seeds

Combine milk, sugar, salt and butter. Heat until butter melts, then cool to lukewarm.

Beat eggs and reserve 3 Tbsp. for glazing. Soften yeast in the warm water in a large bowl. Stir in the eggs and milk mixture. Beat in 4 cups of the flour until smooth. Beat in enough of the remaining flour to make a smooth dough. Turn out and knead on floured surface until smooth and elastic — 15 minutes.

Place in a bowl, cover and let rise for 1½ hours. Punch down and let rise for another 30 minutes. Punch down and turn out onto board. Divide the dough into six equal portions. Form two braids and place them on two greased cookie sheets.

Let rise for one hour. Brush with the reserved egg, to which a tablespoon of water has been added. Sprinkle with poppy seeds.

Bake at 350° F for 30 minutes.

Makes 2 braids.

—*Ruth E. Geddes*

Richard's Raisin Bread

1 cup warm water
3 Tbsp. yeast
1 tsp. sugar
4 cups sour milk
⅔ cup oil
4 eggs, beaten
2 cups sugar
2 tsp. salt
3½ cups raisins
1 cup cracked wheat
1 cup soya flour
9 cups whole wheat flour
4½ cups unbleached white
    flour

In large bowl, combine water, yeast and 1 tsp. sugar and let stand for 5 minutes. Add sour milk, oil, eggs, sugar and salt to yeast mixture and stir gently. Add raisins. Gradually add flour, beating well after each addition.

When dough is thick enough to knead, turn onto lightly floured board. Keep adding flour, kneading well after each addition, until smooth and elastic.

Place in bowl, cover and let rise in a warm place for 30 minutes or until almost doubled. Punch down, divide into 4 equal parts and place in greased loaf pans. Let rise until double — about 1 hour. Bake at 350° F for 45 to 55 minutes.

Makes 4 loaves.

—Richard Domsy

Sprouted Eight-Grain Bread

6 cups whole wheat kernels
2½ cups assorted whole
    grains (1 cup whole rye &
    ¼ cup each whole corn,
    brown rice, soy beans,
    barley, millet & rolled oats)
¼ cup honey
1½ Tbsp. baker's yeast
¼ cup gluten flour
½ cup raisins blended with
    ¼ cup water
1 tsp. salt
½ cup oil

Soak grains, except oats, overnight. Rinse and drain. Return grains to bowl, cover, and let sit for 24 hours. Rinse and drain well again. Continue this until kernels of whole wheat are just starting to sprout — about 3 days.

Grind the sprouting grains very finely. Add remaining ingredients and knead for about 10 minutes. Place in a bowl, cover and let rise until double — about 1 hour.

Divide into 4 pieces, place in greased loaf pans and let rise until doubled. Bake at 350° F for 35 to 40 minutes.

Makes 4 loaves.

—David Slabotsky

Swedish Rye Bread

½ cup water
¼ cup butter
¼ cup brown sugar
2 tsp. salt
1 Tbsp. caraway seeds
1 Tbsp. dry yeast
1 tsp. sugar
½ cup lukewarm water
1½ cups buttermilk
2 cups rye flour
4-6 cups unbleached white
    flour

Boil together ½ cup water, butter, brown sugar, salt and caraway seeds for 5 minutes. Let cool.

Combine yeast, sugar and warm water and let sit for 10 minutes. Add to boiled mixture along with buttermilk. Add rye flour and mix well. Add white flour until dough is stiff enough to be turned onto floured board.

Knead for 10 minutes, place in bowl, cover and let rise until doubled. Form into 2 round loaves on cookie sheet and let rise until doubled. Bake at 400° F for 25 minutes.

Makes 2 loaves.

—Judy Wuest

Sunflower Wheat Germ Bread

4 Tbsp. dry yeast
¾ cup warm water
4 Tbsp. honey
1¼ cups milk
4½-5 cups flour
2 tsp. salt
½ cup wheat germ
½ cup sunflower seeds

Dissolve yeast in warm water and add honey. Stir and let sit for 10 minutes. Add milk and stir. Stir in flour one cup at a time until dough can be kneaded. Work in salt.

Knead dough in bowl for 2 minutes or until smooth and elastic. Knead in wheat germ and sunflower seeds and continue to knead for 5 minutes.

Cover with a damp towel and let rise in a warm spot until double — about 1 hour. Punch down, knead for a minute and let rest for 5 to 10 minutes.

Line 2 loaf pans with foil and grease lightly. Shape dough into 2 loaves and place in pans. Let rise, uncovered, until double. Bake at 375° F for 30 to 45 minutes. Cover with foil after 10 minutes to prevent over-browning.

Makes 2 loaves.

—Cheryl Suckling

Cracked Wheat Bread

1 tsp. sugar
1 cup warm water
2 pkgs. yeast
2 cups scalded milk
¼ cup butter
¼ cup sugar
1 Tbsp. salt
2 cups cracked wheat
2 cups cold water
9-10 cups flour

Dissolve 1 tsp. sugar in warm water and add yeast. Let stand for 10 minutes.

To hot milk, add butter, ¼ cup sugar, salt, cracked wheat and cold water. Stir yeast liquid and add milk mixture to it. Add approximately 4 cups flour and beat in. Mix in additional flour until dough leaves sides of bowl — about 5 cups.

Turn dough onto floured counter and knead. Place in greased bowl, cover and let rise until doubled. Punch down, turn out onto floured counter and cut into 4 equal pieces. Round each piece, cover and let rest for 10 minutes.

Shape into 4 loaves and place in greased loaf pans. Brush with melted butter, cover and let rise until dough is higher than pan edge. Bake at 400° F for 35 to 40 minutes.

Makes 4 loaves.

—Cecilia Roy

Finnish Coffee Braid

This moist coffee bread, rich enough to serve without butter, was invented by the contributor's grandmother.

2 Tbsp. yeast
½ cup warm water
½ tsp. sugar
1 cup warm milk
1 cup warm water
1 tsp. crushed cardamom
8 cups flour
1½ cups sugar
1 tsp. salt
3 eggs
¼ cup melted butter

Combine yeast, water and ½ tsp. sugar. Let stand for 10 minutes. Stir in warm milk, warm water, cardamom and 2½ cups flour. Let stand until foamy — 2 to 2½ hours.

In another dish, combine 1½ cups sugar, salt, eggs and melted butter. Add to yeast-flour mixture and mix well. Add 5½ cups flour. Let rise until double in bulk and punch down.

Form dough into 12 round strips, 2 inches in diameter. Work into 4 braids and place in loaf pans. Let rise until double. Brush tops with a mixture of egg and milk and sprinkle with sugar.

Bake at 350° F for 35 minutes, or until golden brown.

Makes 4 loaves.

—A.E. Koivu

Orange Bread

2 tsp. yeast
¼ cup water
Grated rind of 1 orange
¾ cup orange juice
3 Tbsp. honey
½ cup cooked soy grits
½ cup tofu
2 Tbsp. oil
2 cups flour

Dissolve yeast in water. Heat together orange rind, orange juice and 1 Tbsp. honey and simmer for 5 minutes. Stir in soy grits and remove from heat.

Cream tofu and 2 Tbsp. honey until well blended. Add orange juice mixture and yeast and mix well. Stir in oil and flour. Pour into a greased loaf pan and let rise for 1 hour. Bake at 350° F for 45 to 60 minutes.

—*Sheri Nelson*

Rosemary Bread

7⅓ cups unbleached white
   flour
2 Tbsp. rosemary leaves
1 Tbsp. salt
4 tsp. dry yeast
1 Tbsp. soft butter
2½ cups hot water

Mix together 2⅓ cups flour, rosemary, salt and yeast. Add butter and hot water. Beat for 2 minutes on medium speed of electric mixer. Mix in 1 cup flour by hand, then beat with electric mixer on high speed for 2 minutes. Add 3 to 4 cups flour, mixing with a spoon. Let rise for 1 hour in bowl.

Divide dough into 6 pieces. Roll into 6 ropes of equal length and make 2 braids. Let rise for 1 hour on a greased cookie sheet. Bake at 450° F for 25 minutes.

Makes 2 braids.

—*Lynne Hawkes*

Caraway Seed Bread

1½ tsp. dry yeast
¼ cup warm water
1½ cups hot water
¼ cup brown sugar
¼ cup molasses
1 Tbsp. salt
2 Tbsp. shortening
3 Tbsp. caraway seeds
2½ cups medium rye flour
3½-4 cups unbleached white
   flour

Combine yeast and warm water and let sit for 10 minutes. In a large bowl, mix hot water, sugar, molasses, salt and shortening. Stir in yeast mixture and caraway seeds. Add flours, mix well, cover and let rest for 10 minutes.

Knead dough for 5 to 10 minutes or until elastic. Let rise in a covered bowl in a warm spot for 1½ to 2 hours. Punch down and divide into 2 balls. Flatten balls on a greased cookie sheet and let rise 1 to 1½ hours. Bake at 375° F for 30 minutes.

Makes 2 loaves.

—*Lynne Hawkes*

Yogurt Granola Bread

2 tsp. honey
2 cups warm water
2 Tbsp. yeast
¾ cup plain yogurt
¼ cup honey
¼ cup oil
1 Tbsp. salt
4½-6 cups unbleached flour
2 cups granola

Dissolve 2 tsp. honey in warm water. Sprinkle yeast into water and let stand for 10 minutes. Add yogurt, ¼ cup honey, oil, salt and 3 cups of flour and beat with an electric mixer for 2 minutes. Add granola and mix well. Gradually add the rest of the flour.

Cover and let rise for 1 hour until doubled. Punch down and divide into 2 greased loaf pans. Let rise for 45 minutes, then bake at 375° F for 45 minutes.

—*Mary Giesz*

Onion Rolls

4½ cups warm water
1 cup powdered milk
4 Tbsp. sugar
4 Tbsp. oil
2 Tbsp. mustard
2 tsp. salt
2 eggs
1 onion, finely chopped
5-8 cups flour
2 Tbsp. yeast

Combine water, powdered milk, sugar, oil, mustard, salt, eggs and onion and mix well.

In large bowl, combine 5 cups flour and yeast. Add warm water mixture and beat well with mixer until smooth. Add enough flour to make a stiff dough. Knead until smooth and elastic. Place in a greased bowl, and let rise until doubled in bulk. Punch down.

Shape into rolls, place on greased cookie sheets, cover and let rise again until double. Bake at 350° F for 20 to 30 minutes.

Makes 3 dozen rolls.

—Marion Destaunis

Millie Taylor's Whole Wheat Sunflower Bread

2 tsp. honey
½ cup lukewarm water
1 heaping Tbsp. yeast
2 cups milk
⅓ cup honey
5 tsp. salt
⅓ cup oil
2 cups cold water
2 eggs
10-16 cups whole wheat flour
1 cup sunflower seeds

Combine honey and lukewarm water and add yeast. Let sit for 15 minutes.

Scald milk and add honey, salt, oil, cold water and eggs. Let cool to lukewarm, then add yeast and stir.

Add 10 to 13 cups of flour and sunflower seeds. Stir and knead, working in 2 additional cups of flour, until dough is smooth.

Place dough in large bowl, coat with oil, cover and let rise until doubled. Punch down and divide dough into 5 equal parts. Cover with dish towel and let sit for 15 minutes.

Shape into loaves and place in greased pans. Cover and let rise until doubled. Bake at 400° F for 20 minutes, reduce heat to 350° for another 20 minutes. Turn out of pans to cool.

Makes 5 loaves.

—Paddy & Daryl Taylor

Anadama Health Bread

2 cups water
1 cup milk
1 cup corn meal
1 cup unflavoured yogurt
4 Tbsp. shortening
1 cup molasses
3 tsp. salt
2 envelopes yeast
1 cup lukewarm water
1 tsp. sugar
1 cup wheat germ
1 cup rolled oats
1 cup granola
4½ cups whole wheat flour
4½ cups unbleached white flour

Heat water and milk until boiling. Gradually add corn meal, stirring constantly. Allow to thicken slightly, remove from heat and add yogurt, shortening, molasses and salt, stirring until blended. Cool to lukewarm.

Soften yeast in lukewarm water with sugar. Allow to sit for 10 minutes.

In a large bowl, combine corn meal mixture with yeast mixture. Add wheat germ, oats and granola, beating after each addition. Add whole wheat flour and stir until blended. Add white flour gradually and turn onto floured bread board. Knead for 10 minutes then form dough into a large ball, place in a greased bowl, cover and let rise until double. Punch down and divide into 5 pieces. Shape into balls and let rise for 10 minutes.

Shape into loaves and place in greased loaf pans, brush tops with melted butter, cover and let rise again. Bake at 375° F for 45 minutes.

Makes 5 loaves.

—Sandra Lloyd

Whole Wheat Bread

3 Tbsp. yeast
1 Tbsp. honey
1½ cups warm water
7½ cups hot water
1-2 cups powdered milk
½ cup vegetable oil
½ cup molasses
1½ Tbsp. salt
3 cups rolled oats
10 cups whole wheat flour
10-12 cups unbleached white
 flour

Dissolve yeast and honey in 1½ cups water and let sit for 10 minutes.

Combine 7½ cups water and milk powder in bowl and stir to dissolve. Add oil, molasses and salt and stir to dissolve. Stir in oats, then stir mixture into yeast combination. Add whole wheat flour 3 cups at a time, stirring well after each addition. Add white flour until dough is stiff enough to turn onto a lightly floured bread board.

Knead flour into dough until it is bouncy and no longer sticky. Place in a large bowl, cover and let rise in a warm spot for 1 hour, or until doubled. Punch down, let rest 10 minutes and divide into 6 parts.

Knead each piece lightly, roll out to form an 8" x 11" rectangle and roll up like a jelly roll. Pinch seam closed. With seam-side down, tuck ends under and place in an oiled loaf pan.

Cover and let rise in a warm spot until double. Bake at 375° F for 30 minutes, or until pans sound hollow when rapped on the bottom. Remove from pans to cool.

Makes 6 loaves.

—*Susan Burke*

Sweet Dough Cinnamon Rolls

1½ cups milk
½ cup butter
1 pkg. yeast
1 tsp. sugar
3 eggs
1 cup sugar
½ cup sour cream
½ tsp. salt
4-5 cups flour
Oil
Brown sugar
Raisins
Nuts
Cinnamon

Warm milk, add butter and dissolve yeast and 1 tsp. sugar in it. Beat eggs, add remaining sugar, sour cream and yeast-milk mixture and blend well. Add salt and enough flour to make a manageable dough.

Knead well, place in a large bowl and let rise until double.

Roll out to a ¼-inch thick circle and spread with oil and desired fillings. Cut circle into pie-shaped pieces and roll up from wide end to form crescents. Place on cookie sheets and let rise. Bake at 325° F for 15 to 25 minutes.

Makes 12 rolls.

—*Irene Simonson*

Ukrainian Easter Bread

2 pkgs. yeast
2 cups milk, scalded &
 cooled to lukewarm
8 cups flour
5 egg yolks, beaten
1 cup sugar
½ cup melted butter
1 cup currants
1 Tbsp. vanilla

Dissolve yeast in milk, add 3 cups flour and let stand in a warm place overnight.

In the morning, add egg yolks, sugar, butter, currants, vanilla and enough flour to make a light dough. Let rise until doubled.

Turn onto a floured board and knead well, adding flour if necessary. Shape into 2 loaves and place in greased loaf pans. Let rise until doubled. Bake at 400° F for 10 minutes, reduce heat to 350° F and bake for 50 minutes.

Makes 2 loaves.

—*Donna Petryshyn*

Vienna Coffee Cake

¼ cup lukewarm water
1 pkg. dry yeast
½ tsp. granulated sugar
1 cup milk
½ cup white sugar
¼ cup butter
Salt
1 egg
3 cups flour
⅓ cup sugar
¼ tsp. cinnamon
¼ cup chopped walnuts

Combine water, yeast and ½ tsp. sugar and let sit for 10 minutes. Scald milk and add ½ cup sugar, butter and pinch of salt. Cool to lukewarm and add to yeast mixture. Mix well. Add egg and 1 cup flour and beat well. Add remaining flour and beat for 3 minutes. Place in a greased tube pan.

Combine ⅓ cup sugar, cinnamon and nuts and sprinkle over cake. Let rise in a warm place until doubled in bulk. Bake at 375° F for 35 minutes.

—Dorothy Hett

Pita Bread

This Middle Eastern bread forms a pocket in the centre as it bakes, which can be split open and filled for sandwiches.

2¼-2¾ cups lukewarm water
2 pkgs. dry yeast
Pinch sugar
8 cups flour
2 tsp. salt
¼ cup olive oil
1 cup corn meal or flour

Pour ¼ cup of water into a small bowl and sprinkle with yeast and sugar. Let rest 2 to 3 minutes, then stir to dissolve completely. Set bowl in warm place for 5 minutes or until mixture has doubled in volume.

Combine flour and salt, make a well in the centre and pour in the yeast mixture, oil and 2 cups of lukewarm water.

Gently stir until well combined. Add up to ½ cup more water until dough forms a ball. Knead for 20 minutes, then let rise 45 minutes or until doubled.

Punch down and divide into 8 pieces. Roll into balls and let rest for 30 minutes.

Sprinkle 2 cookie sheets with corn meal or flour. Roll balls into round, flat loaves about 8 inches in diameter and ⅛-inch thick. Arrange 2 to 3 inches apart on sheets and let rise 30 minutes longer.

Bake at 500° F for about 10 minutes until they are brown and puffy in the centre.

Makes 8.

—Nina Kenzie

Dinner Rolls

2 Tbsp. yeast
½ cup warm water
1 tsp. sugar
3 eggs
½ cup oil
2 tsp. salt
2-3 cups warm water
7½-8 cups flour

Dissolve yeast and sugar in ½ cup warm water. Mix together eggs, oil, salt and warm water, Add yeast and enough flour to make dough soft.

Allow dough to double, punch down and allow to rise again. Shape into rolls and let rise until doubled. Bake at 375° F for 15 minutes.

—Delia Schlesinger

Fresh Raspberry Cake

½ cup butter
¾ cup honey
2 eggs, well beaten
2 cups unbleached flour
¼ tsp. salt
2 tsp. baking powder
2 Tbsp. milk or cream
1 cup fresh raspberries

Cream butter and honey. Add eggs and mix until light and fluffy. Sift together dry ingredients and add to creamed mixture alternately with milk. Fold in berries.

Bake in a greased and floured 8-inch square pan at 350° F for 40 to 50 minutes. Serve with whipped cream or ice cream.

—Mary Giesz

Rhubarb Cake

2½ cups flour
¼ tsp. salt
1 tsp. baking powder
½ cup butter
1 egg
1½ cups sugar
4 cups cooked chopped
   rhubarb
½ cup melted butter
2 eggs, beaten

Combine 2 cups flour, salt and baking powder. Cut in butter until mixture is crumbly, then stir in 1 egg. Reserve 1 cup of mixture for topping and flatten remainder in greased 8-inch square pan.

Mix together remaining ½ cup flour, sugar, rhubarb, butter and beaten eggs. Pour into pan and top with reserved pastry.

Bake at 350° F for 1 hour.

—Marie Sadoway

Carrot Cake

3 cups flour
2 tsp. baking soda
1½ tsp. baking powder
2 tsp. cinnamon
1 cup honey
1 cup oil
4 eggs
2 cups grated carrot
1 cup raisins or chopped
   nuts

Measure flour, baking soda, baking powder and cinnamon into bowl. Stir and add honey, oil and eggs. Beat hard by hand for 1 minute. Add carrot and nuts or raisins and beat to mix.

Pour into greased 9" x 13" pan and bake at 350° F for 35 minutes.

—Lynn Hill

Coffee Cake

This dessert is served daily in the Bell Telephone cafeteria at the head office in Toronto. My aunt, an employee, requested the recipe, and the chef scaled it down to household proportions.

½ cup butter
1¼ cups sugar
2 eggs
1 tsp. baking soda
1 cup sour cream
1½ cups flour (half whole
   wheat)
½ tsp. salt
1½ tsp. baking powder
1 tsp. vanilla
1 Tbsp. cinnamon
2 Tbsp. chopped nuts

Cream butter. Add 1 cup sugar gradually, creaming well. Add eggs one at a time, beating until light after each. Stir baking soda into the sour cream. Sift together flour, salt and baking powder. Add sour cream and flour mixtures alternately to the creamed mixture, beating well. Stir in vanilla.

For topping, mix together the ¼ cup sugar, cinnamon and nuts. Spoon half the batter into an 8-inch square pan. Sprinkle with half the topping. Smooth on the remaining batter, then sprinkle on the rest of the topping. Bake at 350° F for 45 minutes. Serve warm.

—Merilyn Mohr

Spicy Yogurt Raisin Cake

½ cup butter
1 cup granulated sugar
3 eggs
2 cups flour
2 tsp. baking powder
1 tsp. salt
1 cup unflavoured yogurt
1 tsp. baking soda
1 tsp. vanilla
¾ cup raisins
1 tsp. cinnamon
½ tsp. nutmeg
¼ tsp. cloves
½ cup chopped walnuts

Cream butter and sugar together. Add eggs one at a time, beating well after each addition. Sift flour with baking powder and salt and add gradually to butter mixture. Combine yogurt and baking soda and add to butter a few tablespoons at a time, along with the vanilla.

Combine raisins, spices and walnuts. Pour half the batter into a 9-inch square pan. Sprinkle raisin mixture over top and pour on remaining batter.

Bake at 350° F for 40 minutes.

—Christine Ferris

Apple Spice Cake

3 cups flour
1½ cups sugar
1½ tsp. baking soda
½ tsp. salt
1 tsp. cinnamon
½ tsp. allspice
½ tsp. cloves
¾ cup shortening
1½ cups apple sauce
2 eggs
1 tsp. vanilla
1 cup raisins
½ cup chopped walnuts

Sift flour, sugar, baking soda, salt, cinnamon, allspice and cloves into a large bowl. Add shortening and apple sauce. Beat with electric mixer on medium speed for 2 minutes. Add eggs and vanilla and beat for 1 more minute. Stir in raisins and nuts and blend well.

Pour into greased and floured tube pan. Bake at 350° F for 70 minutes. Cool in pan for 10 minutes, loosen with a knife and turn onto wire rack to finish cooling.

Poppy Seed Cake

¼ cup poppy seeds
1 cup buttermilk
1 cup butter
1½ cups brown sugar
4 eggs, separated
1 tsp. vanilla
2½ cups flour
2 tsp. baking powder
1 tsp. baking soda
½ tsp. salt
4 tsp. brown sugar
3 tsp. cinnamon

Soak poppy seeds in buttermilk for 20 minutes. Cream butter and 1½ cups sugar, then mix in egg yolks and vanilla.

Sift together flour, baking powder, baking soda and salt. Add flour mixture and buttermilk mixture alternately to creamed ingredients. Fold in stiffly beaten egg whites.

Pour half of batter into greased tube pan. Combine 4 tsp. brown sugar with cinnamon and sprinkle half on batter. Repeat. Bake at 350° F for 45 to 50 minutes.

—Donna Blair

Pumpkin Spice Cake

1¾ cups ground pumpkin
    flesh
2 cups flour
6 tsp. baking powder
1½ tsp. salt
2 tsp. cinnamon
1 tsp. ginger
½ tsp. nutmeg
¼ tsp. cloves
⅔ cup shortening
1½ cups honey
4 eggs
2 tsp. vanilla

Combine pumpkin, flour, baking powder, salt, cinnamon, ginger, nutmeg and cloves and mix well.

Cream shortening, honey, eggs and vanilla. Add flour mixture and mix well.

Bake at 350° F in a 9" x 13" pan for 50 to 60 minutes.

—Wayne Gochee

Old-Fashioned Raisin Cake

1 cup brown sugar
1 cup & 3 Tbsp. water
2 cups raisins
½ tsp. salt
1 tsp. cinnamon
½ tsp. ground cloves
¼ tsp. mace
¼ tsp. nutmeg
⅓ cup shortening
2 cups flour
1 tsp. baking soda
½ tsp. baking powder

Place sugar, water, raisins, salt and spices in a pan and bring to a boil. Cool. Stir in shortening and remaining ingredients.

Pour batter into greased and floured 9-inch square pan. Bake at 325° F for 1 hour or until top springs back when touched.

—Patty Robinson

Date Oatmeal Cake

This spicy snacking cake is so rich and moist that there is no need for icing.

½ cup flour
1 tsp. baking soda
1 tsp. cinnamon
1 tsp. cloves
1 cup boiling water
2 cups rolled oats
¾ cup butter
2 cups brown sugar
2 eggs
1½ cups finely chopped dates
1 cup chopped walnuts

Sift together flour, baking soda, cinnamon and cloves into a large bowl.

Pour boiling water over oats, mix well, cool slightly and blend in remaining ingredients.

Pour oatmeal mixture into dry ingredients and mix well. Bake in an 8-inch square pan at 350° F for 45 minutes.

—*Margaret Butler*

Chocolate Buttermilk Cake

1⅔ cups flour
1 cup sugar
½ cup cocoa
1 tsp. baking soda
½ tsp. salt
1 cup buttermilk
½ cup melted shortening
1½ tsp. vanilla

Mix together flour, sugar, cocoa, baking soda and salt. Beat in buttermilk, shortening and vanilla. Stir until smooth.

Spread into a greased 9" x 13" pan and bake at 375° F for 30 minutes.

—*Ruby McDonald*

White Cake

2¼ cups flour
4 tsp. baking powder
¾ tsp. salt
1½ cups granulated sugar
½ cup shortening
1 cup milk
1 tsp. salt
3 eggs

Sift together flour, baking powder, salt and sugar. Add shortening, ¾ cup milk and salt. Beat for 1 minute, then add ¼ cup milk and eggs. Beat for 2 more minutes.

Pour into 2 greased 8-inch round pans and bake at 350° F for 35 to 40 minutes or until cake springs back when lightly touched.

—*Shirley Morrish*

Grandma's Pound Cake

2 cups flour
1 cup butter
1⅔ cups granulated sugar
5 large eggs
1 tsp. almond extract

Sift flour, measure and then sift 5 times. Cream butter until frothy and pale, then add sugar gradually and mix until fluffy. Add eggs, one at a time, beating after each addition until well blended. After last egg is added, beat for 5 minutes. Fold in flour slowly by hand. Add almond extract and pour into a well greased tube pan.

Bake at 300° F for 1½ hours.

—*Mrs. R.F. Kempf*

Princess Elizabeth Cake

1 cup boiling water
1 cup chopped dates
1 cup brown sugar
½ cup butter
1 egg
1½ cups flour
1 tsp. baking powder
1 tsp. baking soda
Salt
1 tsp. vanilla
5 Tbsp. brown sugar
1 Tbsp. butter
3 Tbsp. cream
½ cup coconut
¾ cup chopped walnuts

Pour boiling water over dates. Add 1 cup brown sugar, ½ cup butter and egg. Mix well and let cool. Add flour, baking powders baking soda, salt and vanilla. Mix well, place in greased 8-inch square pan and bake at 350° F for 5 minutes.

Meanwhile, combine remaining ingredients in a saucepan and bring to a boil. Spread topping over cake, return to oven and bake for 30 to 40 minutes.

—*Eileen Caldwell*

Wacky Cake

The simplicity of this cake is hard to beat. It is assembled in the baking pan and contains no eggs, yet produces a moist cake with a delicious chocolate flavour.

1½ cups flour
1 tsp. baking powder
1 cup granulated sugar
½ tsp. cinnamon
1 tsp. baking soda
½ tsp. salt
3 Tbsp. cocoa
1 tsp. vanilla
1 Tbsp. vinegar
5 Tbsp. melted butter
1 cup lukewarm water

Combine dry ingredients in an 8-inch square pan. Add remaining ingredients, mix well and bake at 350° F for 30 minutes.

—*Sharon Steele*

Chocolate Zucchini Cake

2½ cups flour
½ cup cocoa
2½ tsp. baking powder
1½ tsp. baking soda
1 tsp. salt
1 tsp. cinnamon
¾ cup butter
2 cups sugar
3 eggs
2½ tsp. grated orange rind
2 tsp. vanilla
2 cups grated zucchini
½ cup milk
1 cup ground nuts
¾ cup icing sugar, sifted
1 Tbsp. orange juice

Combine flour, cocoa, baking powder, baking soda, salt and cinnamon. In a large bowl, combine butter and sugars then beat in eggs. Stir in 2 tsp. orange rind, vanilla and zucchini.

Stir in dry ingredients, alternating with milk and nuts. Pour into greased bundt pan and bake at 350° F for 1 hour.

Combine icing sugar with orange juice and ½ tsp. orange rind and spread over warm cake.

—*Elizabeth Eder*

Marmorkuchen

This German marble cake makes an eye-catching dessert. For added appeal, cocoa icing, page 459, may be dribbled over the top while the cake is still warm.

1½ cups granulated sugar
1 cup unsalted butter
6 eggs, separated
1½ cups flour
1½ tsp. baking powder
Grated rind & juice of 1 lemon
¾ cup cocoa powder

Cream butter and sugar until smooth. Beat in egg yolks.

Mix flour and baking powder and add slowly to creamed mixture. Add lemon rind and juice. Beat egg whites until stiff. Fold into cake mixture until just blended.

Divide dough in half. Add cocoa to one half and leave the other half white.

In the bottom of a greased bundt pan, place blobs of some of the chocolate batter then fill in the gaps with white batter. Continue alternating chocolate and white until all the batter ls used up.

Bake at 350° F for 45 minutes.

—*Kris Brown*

Chocolate Icing

½ cup sugar
1½ Tbsp. cornstarch
2-3 Tbsp. cocoa
Dash salt
½ cup boiling water
1½ Tbsp. butter
½ tsp. vanilla

Mix sugar and cornstarch together. Add cocoa and salt. Add water and cook until thick. Remove from heat and stir in butter and vanilla. Spread while hot.

—Barbara Davis

White White Icing

The amount of icing sugar in this recipe may be varied to make a soft icing for spreading or a stiffer icing for decorating.

1 lb. shortening
½ tsp. peppermint flavouring
¼ tsp. salt
1 lb. icing sugar
7 Tbsp. milk

Cream softened shortening with electric mixer. Add flavouring and salt. Beat in sugar one cup at a time with a little milk, blending well after each addition. Beat at high speed until light and fluffy.

—Sharon Cooper

Butter Icing

½ cup soft butter
1 cup less 2 Tbsp. sifted
  icing sugar
¼ cup cold milk
¼ cup boiling water
1 tsp. vanilla

Cream butter and add sugar. Beat until thick and creamy. Add milk and blend. Gradually beat in hot water, then add vanilla.

—Catherine Rupke

Lemon Honey Frosting

½ cup butter
½ cup honey
8 oz. cream cheese
1 tsp. vanilla
2 Tbsp. lemon juice
2 cups instant milk powder

Cream the butter and add honey and cream cheese. Beat until smooth. Stir in the vanilla and lemon juice and work in the milk powder, mixing until thick and creamy.

—Cary Elizabeth Marshall

Cocoa Icing

⅓ cup cocoa
2 cups icing sugar
2 Tbsp. butter
1 tsp. vanilla
Hot water

Melt cocoa and add sugar, butter and vanilla. Blend in hot water until mixture will spread smoothly.

—Roxanne Kistler

Cream Cheese Icing

8 oz. cream cheese
4 Tbsp. butter
3½ cups icing sugar
Salt
2 tsp. vanilla

Cream cheese with a fork, blend in butter, add sugar and salt, mix until smooth and spread.

—Cary Elizabeth Marshall

Dad's Cookies

1 cup butter
1 cup granulated sugar
½ cup brown sugar
1 egg
1 cup flour
1 tsp. baking powder
1 tsp. baking soda
1 cup bran flakes
1 cup rolled oats
1 cup fine coconut

Cream butter, add sugars and then the egg. Beat until light and creamy.

Sift together flour, baking powder and baking soda. Add bran flakes, oats and coconut. Stir into creamed mixture and mix well.

Drop by teaspoonfuls onto greased cookie sheets. Press down with a fork and bake at 350° F for 10 minutes or until cookies are light brown.

Makes 6 to 8 dozen cookies.
—Christine Davidson

Oatmeal Chocolate Chip Cookies

1 cup butter
1½ cups brown sugar
2 eggs
1 tsp. vanilla
1½ cups flour
2⅓ cups rolled oats
2 tsp. baking soda
1 tsp. salt
12-oz. pkg. chocolate chips
1½ cups chopped nuts

Cream butter and sugar. Beat in eggs and vanilla. Add flour, oats, baking soda and salt. Mix well and stir in chips and nuts. Drop by spoonfuls onto greased cookie sheets and bake at 350° F for 12 to 15 minutes.

Makes 6 to 8 dozen cookies.
—Sandra Lloyd

Chocolate Chip Cookies

1 cup butter
1 cup brown sugar
1 cup granulated sugar
2 eggs
1 tsp. vanilla
2¼ cups flour
3 tsp. baking powder
1 tsp. salt
1 cup chopped walnuts
12-oz. pkg. chocolate chips

Cream butter, sugars, eggs and vanilla. Add remaining ingredients in order listed. Mix well.

Drop by spoonfuls onto greased cookie sheet with 2 inches between cookies. Bake at 375° F for 8 to 10 minutes.

Makes 6 dozen cookies.
—Shirley Morrish

Oatmeal Cookies

1 cup butter
½ cup granulated sugar
1 cup brown sugar
1 egg
1 tsp. vanilla
3 Tbsp. milk
1½ cups flour
1½ cups rolled oats
¾ cup coconut
1 tsp. baking powder
1 tsp. baking soda
⅛ tsp. salt

Cream together butter and sugar, then beat in egg, vanilla and milk. Combine dry ingredients and add to creamed mixture.

Drop by spoonfuls onto greased cookie sheets and bake at 375° F for 15 to 20 minutes or until golden brown.

Makes 5 to 6 dozen cookies.
—Andrea Stuart

Tasty Oat Cookies

1 cup sunflower oil
1½ cups honey
2 tsp. vanilla
½ tsp. salt
2½ cups flour
½ cup water
4 cups large flake rolled oats
½ cup chopped walnuts
¼ cup sunflower seeds
1½ tsp. cinnamon

Cream together oil, honey, vanilla and salt. Add flour and water gradually, stirring until well mixed. When smooth, add oats, nuts, seeds and cinnamon. Mix well.

Spoon onto greased cookie sheets and bake at 350° F for 25 minutes or until golden brown.

Makes 8 to 9 dozen cookies.
—Vickie Johnson-Munn

Hermits

2 cups flour
½ tsp. baking soda
½ tsp. salt
½ tsp. cinnamon
½ tsp. nutmeg
¾ cup shortening
1 cup brown sugar
1 egg
¼ cup cold strong coffee
½ cup raisins
½ cup chopped walnuts

Combine flour, baking soda, salt, cinnamon and nutmeg. Cream shortening and sugar and add egg. Add dry ingredients to creamed mixture alternately with coffee. Stir in raisins and nuts.

Drop by teaspoonfuls onto greased cookie sheet and bake at 400° F for 6 to 8 minutes.

Makes 3 to 4 dozen cookies.

—Audrey Moroso

School Bus Cookies

1½ cups butter
2 cups brown sugar
2 eggs
1½ cups flour
2 tsp. baking powder
¼ tsp. baking soda
1 tsp. salt
¾ cup bran
1½ cups rolled oats
½ cup dates
¾ cup wheat germ

Cream butter, sugar and eggs. Sift in flour, baking powder, baking soda and salt, then stir in bran, oats, dates and wheat germ.

Mix well and drop by small spoonfuls onto a cookie sheet. Bake at 375° F for 10 to 12 minutes.

Makes 5 to 6 dozen cookies.

—Janet Stevenson

Auntie Susie's Peanut Butter Cookies

½ cup shortening
1 cup peanut butter
½ cup white sugar
½ cup brown sugar
1 egg
1½ cups flour
1 tsp. baking soda
½ tsp. baking powder
½ tsp. vanilla

Cream shortening and peanut butter. Gradually add sugars. Add egg and beat well. Sift dry ingredients together. Gradually add to creamed mixture. Stir in vanilla.

Roll batter into small balls, place on ungreased cookie sheet and flatten with a fork. Bake at 375° F for 10 to 15 minutes. Cool on a rack.

Makes 4 dozen cookies.

—Patricia Forrest

Sugar Cookies

¾ cup butter
1 cup sugar
1 egg
1 tsp. baking soda
1 tsp. cream of tartar
2 cups flour
Salt
½ cup milk
½ tsp. vanilla

Cream butter and sugar together. Stir in egg. Combine dry ingredients and add to creamed mixture alternately with milk. Stir in vanilla.

Roll out dough and cut into shapes. Bake on greased cookie sheets at 375° F for 10 to 12 minutes.

Makes 3 to 4 dozen cookies.

—Goldie Connell

Shortbread

½ lb. butter
½ cup cornstarch
½ cup icing sugar
1 cup flour

Beat butter until light and add remaining ingredients one at a time, beating well after each addition. Roll into small balls and flatten with fork.

Bake at 300° F for 30 minutes.

Makes 3 dozen.

—Shirley Hill

Digestive Cookies

½ cup whole wheat flour
½ cup unbleached white flour
½ cup wheat germ
¼ cup sugar
¼ cup sesame seeds
½ tsp. salt
½ tsp. baking powder
1 cup rolled oats
½ cup butter
½ cup cold water
1 tsp. vanilla

Mix together dry ingredients. Cut in butter, then add water mixed with vanilla to form an easily handled dough.

Roll to ¼-inch thickness. Cut out cookies with floured glass. Place on greased cookie sheets and bake at 350° F for 10 to 12 minutes.

Makes 3 to 4 dozen cookies.

—Brigitte Wolf

Sesame Seed Cookies

2 cups flour
¼ cup wheat germ
1½ tsp. baking powder
¼ tsp. salt
⅓ cup honey
¾ cup butter
2 egg yolks
¼ cup milk
1 tsp. vanilla
Sesame seeds

Mix together flour, wheat germ, baking powder and salt. Add honey and butter. When crumbly, add egg yolks, milk and vanilla.

Knead until smooth. For each cookie, shape a rounded tablespoon of dough into an oval loaf. Roll in sesame seeds.

Bake on greased cookie sheets at 375° F for 15 to 20 minutes.

Makes 4 dozen cookies.

—Bryanna Clark

Raisin Sesame Cookies

1¼ cups flour
½ tsp. baking soda
½ tsp. salt
1 tsp. cinnamon
¾ cup raisins
½ cup oil
1 cup sugar
1 egg, beaten
1¼ cups rolled oats
1 cup sesame seeds
¼ cup milk

Sift flour with baking soda, salt and cinnamon. Stir in raisins.

Beat together oil, sugar and egg. Add rolled oats, sesame seeds and milk. Gradually beat in flour mixture and stir dough until thoroughly blended.

Drop dough by heaping teaspoonfuls onto a greased cookie sheet, allowing room for cookies to spread. Bake at 375° F for 10 to 15 minutes.

Makes 4 dozen cookies.

—Holly McNally

Butterscotch Cookies

1 cup butter
2 cups brown sugar
2 eggs
1 cup walnuts
1 tsp. vanilla
1 tsp. cream of tartar
4 cups flour

Cream butter and sugar and add eggs, walnuts and vanilla. Mix cream of tartar and flour and combine with creamed mixture.

Pack into loaf pan or wrap in rolls in wax paper and chill overnight. Remove from pan and cut into thin slices. Bake at 350° F for 10 to 15 minutes.

Makes 8 dozen cookies.

—Pat McCormack

Cardamom Cookies

2½ cups flour
2 tsp. ground cardamom
3½ tsp. cinnamon
1¼ cups butter, softened
½ cup white sugar

Combine flour, cardamom and cinnamon in a bowl. In another bowl, cream together sugar and butter. Gradually add flour and spices, mixing until texture resembles coarse sand.

Form dough into ¾-inch-diameter rolls and chill until stiff — at least 1 hour. Cut into ¾-inch-thick slices and place on lightly greased cookie sheets. Bake at 350° F for 12 to 15 minutes — until very lightly browned.

Makes 4 dozen.

—Janet Jokinen

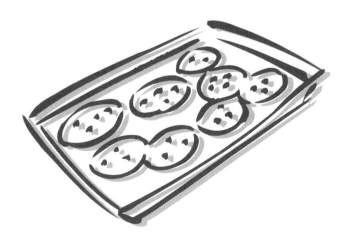

Spicy Tofu Cookies

1½ cups flour
½ cup raisins
½ cup finely chopped
  walnuts
½ cup chopped dates
½ tsp. baking soda
½ cup butter
⅔ cup honey
1 egg
8 oz. tofu
1 tsp. ginger
1 tsp. cinnamon
½ tsp. nutmeg
½ tsp. salt
1 tsp. vanilla

Mix together first 5 ingredients. Blend remaining ingredients and add to flour mixture. Combine well and drop by spoonfuls onto greased cookie sheets.

Bake at 400° F for 10 to 15 minutes.

—Renate Manthei

Cream Cheese Cookies

½ lb. butter
8-oz. pkg. cream cheese
2 cups flour
3 Tbsp. sugar
2 tsp. salt
Grape jelly

Cream butter and cheese and add flour, sugar and salt. Chill thoroughly in refrigerator. Roll out dough, using plenty of flour, and cut half into circles and half into strips. Place 1 tsp. grape jelly in centre of each circle and top with strips in the shape of an X. Press edges together.

Bake at 350° F until golden.

—Shirley Hill

Butterhorn Cookies

1 cup butter
1 egg yolk
¾ cup sour cream
2 cups flour
¾ cup sugar
1 tsp. cinnamon
¾ cup raisins

Cream the butter and yolk and add the sour cream and flour. Blend well and chill for 1 hour.

Roll out dough to ¼-inch thickness. Combine the sugar, cinnamon and raisins and sprinkle evenly over dough.

Cut dough into triangles. Roll triangles up from large end and curve to form a semi-circle. Place on ungreased cookie sheets. Bake at 375° F for 30 minutes.

Makes 2 to 3 dozen.

—Sheri Israels

Banana Date Cookies

3 ripe bananas
1 cup chopped dates
⅓ cup oil
2 cups oatmeal
½ cup sunflower seeds
1 tsp. vanilla

Mash the bananas and combine with chopped dates and oil. Add remaining ingredients and mix well.

Drop by spoonfuls onto a greased cookie sheet and flatten with a fork. Bake at 375° F for about 15 minutes.

Makes 24.

—Heather Struckett

Raisin Cookies

1 cup water
2 cups raisins
1 cup shortening
2 cups sugar
3 eggs
1 tsp. vanilla
1 cup chopped walnuts
4 cups flour
1 tsp. baking powder
1 tsp. baking soda
2 tsp. salt
1½ tsp. cinnamon
¼ tsp. nutmeg
¼ tsp. allspice

Combine water and raisins, boil for 5 minutes and cool. Cream shortening and add sugar, eggs, vanilla, cooled raisins and walnuts. Combine remaining ingredients, add to creamed mixture and blend well. Drop by teaspoonfuls onto greased cookie sheets and bake at 350° F for 12 to 15 minutes. Makes 10 dozen cookies.

—Mrs. Jack Stacey

Apple Sauce Oatmeal Cookies

½ cup shortening
1 cup sugar
1 egg
1 cup unsweetened apple
   sauce
1 tsp. baking soda
1¾ cups flour
½ tsp. salt
1 tsp. cinnamon
½ tsp. nutmeg
1 cup raisins
1 cup oatmeal

Cream together shortening, sugar and egg. Mix apple sauce and baking soda, and sift together the flour, salt and spices. Add apple sauce and dry ingredients to creamed mixture. Mix in raisins and oatmeal.

Drop by spoonfuls onto greased cookie sheet. Bake at 350° F for 10 minutes.

Makes 3 dozen.

—Audrey Moroso

Banana Oat Bars

¾ cup butter
1 cup packed brown sugar
1 egg
½ tsp. salt
1½ cups mashed ripe
   bananas (4-5 medium)
4 cups uncooked oats
½ cup coconut
1 cup chocolate chips

Cream butter and sugar until fluffy. Beat in egg, salt and bananas. Stir in remaining ingredients. Turn into greased 9" x 13" pan.

Bake at 350° F for 1 hour or until golden brown and toothpick comes clean.

Cool and cut into 2-inch bars. Store in refrigerator until needed.

—Jan Gibbs

Poppy Seed Cookies

½ cup butter
⅓ cup sugar
1 egg
1 cup flour
⅓ tsp. salt
½ tsp. vanilla
¼ tsp. grated lemon rind
2 Tbsp. poppy seeds

Cream butter and mix in sugar and egg. Combine flour and salt and add to butter along with vanilla, lemon rind and poppy seeds. Mix well.

Roll into balls and flatten on greased baking sheets. Bake at 350° F for 10 to 12 minutes.

Makes 2 dozen cookies.

—Shirley Morrish

Kislings

These are rich Christmas-time cookies.

1 cup butter
¼ cup granulated sugar
2 cups sifted flour
¼ tsp. salt
½ cup well drained, sliced
   maraschino cherries
½ cup chopped walnuts
Confectioners' sugar

Cream butter, add sugar and mix until fluffy. Add remaining ingredients and mix well. Form dough into small balls and place on ungreased cookie sheet.

Bake at 300° F for 30 to 40 minutes or until bottoms are golden.

Roll in confectioners' sugar.

Makes 3 dozen cookies.

—Bonnie Byrnes

Ginger Snaps

These cookies, accompanied with hot cocoa, have been served to overnight guests at Marshlands Inn every evening since the inn opened in 1935.

1 cup melted shortening
½ cup granulated sugar
1½ cups molasses
2 heaping tsp. baking soda
2 heaping tsp. ginger
2 heaping tsp. salt
4½ cups flour

Combine shortening, sugar and molasses. Sift baking soda, ginger and salt with flour, and stir into creamed mixture.

Shape into rectangular logs and chill overnight. Slice very thinly and bake at 350° F for 7 to 8 minutes.

Makes 10 dozen cookies.

—Marshlands Inn

Lemon Squares

1 cup butter
½ cup icing sugar
2 cups flour
4 eggs
1½ cups sugar
Pinch salt
4 Tbsp. flour
1 tsp. baking powder
8 Tbsp. lemon juice

Stir butter, icing sugar and flour together and press into a 9" x 13" pan. Bake at 350° F for 10 minutes.

Beat eggs and add remaining ingredients. Pour over cookie base and bake 25 minutes longer.

Cut into bars while hot, and sprinkle with icing sugar when cool.

—Mrs. W. Atkins

Jam Bars

½ cup shortening
½ cup sugar
½ tsp. vanilla
½ tsp. almond extract
1 egg
1½ cups flour
1 tsp. baking powder
½ tsp. cinnamon
¼ tsp. ground cloves
½ tsp. salt
Jam or marmalade

Cream together shortening, sugar, vanilla and almond extract. Stir in egg. Sift together dry ingredients, add to creamed mixture and blend well.

Spread half the dough in a greased 8-inch square pan, cover with jam or marmalade and top with remaining dough.

Bake at 400° F for 25 minutes. Cool, then cut into bars.

Makes 20 bars.

—Donna Jubb

Maple Sugar Cookies

½ cup butter
½ cup maple sugar
1 egg
½ cup milk
1 cup whole wheat flour
¾ cup unbleached white flour
½ tsp. salt
½ cup raisins

Cream together butter and maple sugar. Add egg and milk and beat. Mix in flours, salt and raisins.

Drop by teaspoonfuls onto greased cookie sheets. Bake at 325° F for 10 minutes or until browned around edges.

Makes 40 cookies.

—Andra Hughes

Soft Molasses Cookies

1 cup granulated sugar
1 cup molasses
1 cup shortening, melted
4 cups flour
2 tsp. baking soda
1 egg
1 cup cold water
1 tsp. cinnamon
½ tsp. ground cloves
1 tsp. salt

Cream together sugar, molasses and shortening. Stir in 1 cup flour, baking soda, egg and water.

Sift together remaining 3 cups flour, cinnamon, cloves and salt. Stir into creamed mixture.

Refrigerate for 1 hour, then drop by teaspoonfuls onto cookie sheet. Bake at 375° F for 12 to 15 minutes.

Makes 8 dozen cookies.

—Janice Touesnard

Date Squares

1 lb. dates
¾ cup hot water
Salt
1 tsp. vanilla
1½ cups flour
½ tsp. baking soda
1½ cups rolled oats
1½ cups brown sugar
1 cup butter

Combine dates, hot water and salt in a saucepan. Cook over medium heat until dates are soft and water is absorbed. Add vanilla and let cool.

Stir flour and baking soda together. Add oats and brown sugar and mix well. Work in butter with fork until mixture is crumbly.

Spread half the mixture in the bottom of a 9-inch square pan and pat down. Cover with date filling and pat remaining mixture on top.

Bake at 350° F for 20 to 25 minutes.

—Mrs. Fred Smith

Red Bran Muffins at Uniwat

1½ cups whole wheat flour
¼ cup soya flour
1½ cups raw bran
¼ cup wheat germ
1½ tsp. baking powder
1½ tsp. baking soda
1 tsp. salt
¼ cup brown sugar
2 eggs
½ cup oil
¼ cup molasses
1½ cups buttermilk
1 tsp. vanilla
½ cup each raisins & currants
½ cup chopped nuts or sunflower seeds

Combine flours, bran, wheat germ, baking powder, baking soda, salt and brown sugar and blend.

Beat together eggs, oil, molasses, buttermilk and vanilla. Add to dry ingredients and blend. Stir in raisins, currants and nuts or seeds.

Fill well-greased muffin tins three-quarters full. Bake at 400° F for 20 minutes.

Makes 24 large muffins.

—Jacqueline Dysart

Anna Lieb's Brownies

My grandmother, who lived with us until I was 17 years old, was an excellent cook with a pronounced Old-World style. In order to preserve her recipes, I tried following her around the kitchen making notes on quantities used and steps followed. This worked for a few uncomplicated treats, but was unsuccessful for her more intricate creations. One recipe which we have managed to duplicate is her brownies. Always moist and rich, they are my idea of what brownies should be.

1 cup butter
2 cups sugar
4 eggs
4 squares unsweetened chocolate, melted
2 cups flour
1 Tbsp. baking powder
1 tsp. salt
2 tsp. vanilla
1 cup chopped walnuts or slivered almonds

Cream together butter and sugar until light. Beat in eggs. Add melted chocolate and beat again. Mix in flour, baking powder, salt and vanilla.

Spread mixture in a greased 9" x 13" baking pan and sprinkle liberally with nuts. Bake at 350° F for 35 minutes. When cool, cut in squares.

Makes 2 dozen brownies.

—Alice O'Connell

Sesame Seed Bars

2 cups hulled, raw sesame seeds
1¼ cups honey

Brown sesame seeds lightly in a heavy preheated skillet.

Combine seeds with honey in a saucepan and cook to hard ball stage (265° F), stirring frequently with a wooden spoon.

Pour onto an oiled cookie sheet and spread to ⅛-inch thickness. Score into 1¾ x 1½ inch bars while still warm. Cool and break into pieces.

Place on cake rack for one day for crispier, less sticky bars. If storing bars, place wax paper between layers.

—N. Kariel

Lynn's Granola Bars

1 cup butter
1 cup brown sugar
2 eggs
¼ cup molasses
1 tsp. vanilla
1¾ cups flour
½ tsp. baking soda
½ tsp. salt
½ cup powdered milk
1½ cups rolled oats
¾ cup wheat germ
¾ cup coconut
¾ cup sunflower seeds
¾ cup chopped dried fruit
⅓ cup sesame seeds

Cream together butter, brown sugar, eggs, molasses and vanilla. Sift together flour, baking soda, salt and powdered milk, add to creamed mixture and blend well. Add remaining ingredients and mix well.

Spread in a 9" x 13" pan and bake at 350° F for 20 to 25 minutes or until golden.

—Judy Wuest

Banana Oat Muffins

1 cup unbleached flour
½ cup brown sugar
2½ tsp. baking powder
½ tsp. salt
¼ tsp. baking soda
¾ cup oats
1 egg, beaten
3 Tbsp. oil
½ cup milk
½ cup mashed banana
⅓ cup chopped nuts

Combine flour, sugar, baking powder, salt and baking soda. Stir well to blend. Stir in oats. Add remaining ingredients and stir with a fork until dry ingredients are just moistened.

Fill well-greased muffin tins two-thirds full. Bake at 400° F for 18 to 20 minutes.

Makes 12 muffins.

—Nan & Phil Millette

Blueberry Oat Muffins

1 cup rolled oats
1 cup buttermilk
1 cup flour
1 tsp. baking powder
½ tsp baking soda
½ tsp. salt
¼ cup brown sugar
1 egg, beaten
4 Tbsp. melted shortening
1 cup blueberries

Combine oats and buttermilk and let stand for 1 hour. Stir together flour, baking powder, baking soda, salt and sugar.

Add egg and shortening to oat mixture. Stir this into dry ingredients until just mixed. Fold in blueberries. Fill greased muffin tins two-thirds full. Bake at 400° F for 20 minutes.

Makes 12 large muffins.

—Eva Whitmore

Banana Bran Muffins

1 cup sour milk
2 Tbsp. molasses
1 egg
2 Tbsp. butter
⅔ cup raisins
½ cup walnuts
1½ cups bran
1 cup whole wheat flour
½ cup brown sugar
½ tsp. salt
½ tsp. baking soda
2 tsp. baking powder
1 cup mashed bananas

Combine milk, molasses, egg, butter, raisins, walnuts and bran in a bowl and stir to blend. Sift together dry ingredients and add to moist mixture. Add bananas and stir only enough to moisten.

Fill greased muffin tins three-quarters full and bake at 375° F for 20 to 25 minutes.

Makes 24 muffins.

—Kathy Crawley

Raspberry Bars

1 cup butter, softened
⅓ cup sugar
2 egg yolks
2 cups flour
1 cup raspberry jam
4 Tbsp. confectioners' sugar
½ cup chopped walnuts

Cream butter and sugar. Beat in egg yolks, then stir in flour, half a cup at a time. Press half the dough into a 9-inch square baking pan. Spread with jam and top with remaining dough. Sprinkle with confectioners' sugar and walnuts.

Bake at 375° F for 35 minutes. When cool, cut into bars.

Makes 27 bars.

Cranberry Oatmeal Muffins

¾ cup unbleached flour
¾ cup whole wheat flour
1 cup rolled oats
½ cup brown sugar
1 Tbsp. baking powder
1 tsp. salt
1 tsp. cinnamon
1 cup fresh or frozen cranberries
¼ cup butter
1 cup milk
1 egg

Combine dry ingredients. Toss the cranberries with 1 Tbsp. of dry ingredients and set aside. Melt butter and combine with milk and egg. Stir butter mixture into dry ingredients and then add cranberries.

Fill muffin tins two-thirds full and bake at 425° F for 15 to 20 minutes. Let stand 5 minutes before removing from pans.

Makes 12 muffins.

—Kathleen Walker

Cranberry Muffins

¾ cup halved,
    raw cranberries
½ cup icing sugar
1 egg
1 cup milk
¼ cup oil
1 cup whole wheat flour
1 cup unbleached flour
3 tsp. baking powder
½ tsp. salt
¼ cup sugar

Mix cranberries and icing sugar well and set aside.

Beat egg, milk and oil together. Add whole wheat flour, then sift together and add remaining ingredients. Stir just to blend. Fold in cranberries with as few strokes as possible.

Fill greased muffin tins two-thirds full. Bake at 350° F for 20 minutes.

Makes 18 muffins.

—Ann Fraser

Orange Raisin Muffins

½ cup shortening
1 cup brown sugar
1 egg
¾ tsp. baking soda
Rind of ½ orange, grated
1 cup sour cream
2 cups flour
1 tsp. baking powder
¼ tsp. salt
1 tsp. cinnamon
1 cup chopped raisins
½ cup chopped nuts

Cream shortening and add sugar and egg. Mix baking soda, orange rind and sour cream. Combine dry ingredients and add to creamed mixture alternately with sour cream. Add raisins and nuts, mixing to just combine.

Fill greased muffin tins two-thirds full. Bake at 350° F for 15 to 20 minutes.

Makes 24 muffins.

—Sally Ireland

Raspberry Oatmeal Muffins

1 cup flour
3 tsp. baking powder
½ tsp. salt
¾ cup rolled oats
¼ cup brown sugar
1 egg
¼ cup melted butter
⅓ cup milk
1 cup mashed, fresh or
    frozen raspberries

Measure dry ingredients into a large mixing bowl. Stir with a fork until well blended.

Whisk or beat egg, butter and milk. Stir in dry ingredients and mix briefly. Add raspberries and mix until evenly blended. Fill greased muffin tins two-thirds full. Bake at 400° F for 20 minutes, or until done.

Makes 12 large muffins.

—Linda Palaisy

Currant Corn Meal Muffins

⅓ cup shortening
1 cup sugar
2 eggs
1¼ cups corn meal
¾ cup flour
2½ tsp. baking powder
¾ tsp. salt
½ cup currants
1 cup milk

Cream together the shortening, sugar and eggs. Combine corn meal, flour, baking powder and salt, and add to creamed mixture along with currants. Add milk and stir to just mix.

Place in greased muffin tins and bake at 400° F for 25 minutes.

Makes 12 muffins.

—Linda Fickling

Apple Honey Deluxe Granola Muffins

½ cup whole wheat flour
½ cup raw bran
⅓ cup wheat germ
½ cup rolled oats
½ cup ground walnuts
¼ cup soy flour
2½ tsp. baking powder
½ tsp. cinnamon
½ cup milk
1 egg, beaten
⅓ cup honey
2 Tbsp. safflower oil
1 cup finely grated cooking apple

Mix together in a large bowl whole wheat flour, bran, wheat germ, oats, walnuts, soy flour, baking powder and cinnamon. Combine milk, egg, honey, oil and apple and stir into dry ingredients to just moisten.

Fill greased muffin tins two-thirds full and bake at 375° F for 20 minutes.

Makes 12 large muffins.

—Carolyn Cronk

Date Orange Muffins

1 orange
½ cup orange juice
½ cup chopped dates
1 egg
½ cup butter
1½ cups flour
1 tsp. baking soda
1 tsp. baking powder
⅔ cup sugar
½ tsp. salt

Cut orange into quarters and remove seeds. Place in blender and whirl with orange juice until well blended. Drop in dates, egg and butter and blend until combined.

Sift together flour, baking soda, baking powder, sugar and salt. Pour orange mixture into dry ingredients and mix to just moisten.

Fill greased muffin tins two-thirds full and bake at 400° F for 15 to 18 minutes.

Makes 18 muffins.

—Jane Lott

Lemon Muffins

2 cups flour
½ cup & 2 Tbsp. sugar
1 Tbsp. baking powder
1 tsp. salt
½ cup butter
½ cup fresh lemon juice
Rind of 1 or 2 lemons, grated
2 eggs

Combine flour, ½ cup sugar, baking powder and salt. Blend well.

Melt butter, remove from heat and stir in lemon juice, rind and eggs. Stir into dry ingredients until well moistened.

Fill greased muffin tins. Sprinkle tops with sugar. Bake at 400° F for 15 minutes.

Makes 12 large muffins.

—Linda Charron

Pumpkin Muffins

1 cup sugar
⅔ cup oil
2 eggs
1½ cups whole wheat flour
1 tsp. baking powder
1 tsp. baking soda
Cloves
1 tsp. cinnamon
¼ tsp. mace
½ tsp. nutmeg
¼ tsp. ginger
½ tsp. salt
1 cup pumpkin
1 cup raisins

Cream together sugar and oil. Add eggs and mix thoroughly. Combine dry ingredients.

Add pumpkin to moist ingredients, followed by dry mixture. Stir in raisins.

Fill greased muffin tins two-thirds full and bake at 350° F for 25 minutes.

Makes 18 muffins.

—*Karen Bowcott*

Rhubarb Muffins

1 cup brown sugar
¼ cup salad oil
1 egg
2 tsp. vanilla
1 cup buttermilk
1½ cups finely diced
  rhubarb
½ cup walnut pieces
2½ cups flour
1 tsp. baking powder
1 tsp. baking soda
½ tsp. salt

Combine brown sugar, oil, egg and vanilla. Beat until well blended. Stir in buttermilk, rhubarb and nuts.

Sift flour with baking powder, baking soda and salt. Add all at once to the rhubarb mixture and stir until just moistened.

Fill greased muffin tins two-thirds full. Bake at 400° F for 15 to 20 minutes.

Makes 24 muffins.

—*Ann Fraser*

Spicy Muffins

1 cup flour
3 tsp. baking powder
½ tsp. salt
½ cup oat flakes
½ cup wheat germ
½ cup sunflower seeds
½ cup raisins
1 tsp. cinnamon & ¼ tsp.
  cloves or 1 Tbsp. grated
  orange rind & ½ tsp.
  ground nutmeg
¾ cup milk
¼ cup oil
¼ cup honey
2 Tbsp. molasses
1 egg

In large bowl, stir flour, baking powder, salt, oat flakes, wheat germ, sunflower seeds, raisins and spices. In small bowl, mix together milk, oil, honey, molasses and egg.

Make a well in the centre of the flour mixture and blend the wet ingredients with the flour mixture until just combined.

Place in greased muffin tins and bake at 350° F for 15 minutes — until muffins are light brown.

Makes 12 muffins.

—*Leslie Reid*

Spicy Apple Wheat Germ Muffins

1½ cups flour
½ cup lightly packed brown
   sugar
1 Tbsp. baking powder
½ tsp. salt
¾ tsp. cinnamon
¼ tsp. nutmeg
½ cup wheat germ
1 cup peeled, finely chopped
   apple
½ cup raisins (optional)
2 eggs
½ cup milk
¼ cup melted butter

Mix together flour, sugar, baking powder, salt and spices. Stir well to blend. Stir in wheat germ, apple and raisins.

Beat eggs, milk and melted butter in small bowl until thoroughly combined. Add all at once to dry ingredients. Stir until all ingredients are just moistened.

Fill well-greased muffin tins two-thirds full and bake at 400° F for 20 to 25 minutes.

Makes 12 muffins.

—Sharon McKay

Date Nut Muffins

1 cup pitted, chopped dates
¾ cup boiling water
1 egg
½ cup sugar
¼ cup butter
¾ tsp. salt
1 tsp. vanilla
½ cup chopped walnuts
1¼ cups flour
¼ cup wheat germ
1 tsp. baking powder
1 tsp. cinnamon
¼ tsp. allspice
¼ tsp. nutmeg
1 tsp. baking soda

Soften dates in boiling water and allow to cool. Beat egg and gradually add sugar, butter, salt and vanilla. Add nuts.

Combine dry ingredients, except baking soda. Stir baking soda into dates and add to egg mixture. Stir in dry ingredients, mixing until just blended.

Spoon into lightly greased muffin tins. Bake at 375° F for 15 to 20 minutes.

Makes 12 muffins.

—Maxine Farr-Jones

Canadian Air Force Wheat Germ Muffins

When Princess Elizabeth visited Canada in the early 1950s, she was flown on a Canadian Air Force craft. On board, she was served these muffins, baked especially for her by the Air Force chef.

2½ cups whole wheat flour
1¼ cups wheat germ
7 tsp. baking powder
1½ cups raisins
¾ tsp. salt
¾ cup butter
¾ cup sugar
3 eggs
2 cups milk

Combine flour, wheat germ, baking powder, raisins and salt. Cream together the butter and sugar and add eggs and milk. Add the liquid ingredients to the dry, mixing as little as possible.

Bake in greased muffin tins at 375° F for 15 to 20 minutes.

Makes 24 large muffins.

—Sandra James-Mitchell

Honey Walnut Bread

1 cup milk
1 cup honey
½ cup sugar
¼ cup oil
2 egg yolks
1½ cups unbleached flour
1 tsp. salt
1 tsp. baking soda
1 cup whole wheat flour
1 cup chopped walnuts

Scald milk and stir in honey and sugar until sugar dissolves. Cool. Beat in oil and egg yolks. Sift together unbleached flour, salt and baking soda. Stir in whole wheat flour. Add nuts, then milk mixture. Stir to just blend. Spoon into 2 greased loaf pans.

Bake at 325° F for 1 hour, or until toothpick inserted in loaf comes out clean. Cool in pans for 15 minutes, then turn out onto rack.

Makes 2 loaves.

—Ingrid Birker

Fruity & Nutty Tea Loaf

⅓ cup butter
⅔ cup sugar
2 eggs
1 cup mashed bananas
1½ cups flour
2¼ tsp. baking powder
½ tsp. salt
½ cup oatmeal
½ cup blueberries
¼ cup raisins
½ cup chopped pecans

Cream butter and sugar and add eggs. Add mashed bananas. Combine flour, baking powder, salt and oatmeal. Add to creamed mixture. Stir in blueberries, raisins and nuts.

Pour into greased loaf pan and bake at 350° F for 1 hour.

—Audrey Moroso

Nuts & Seeds Bread

2 cups flour
1 tsp. baking powder
1 tsp. baking soda
½ tsp. salt
1 cup brown sugar
½ cup chopped nuts
2 Tbsp. sesame seeds
2 Tbsp. poppy seeds
1 egg, beaten
1 cup milk
¼ cup oil

Mix dry ingredients together. Combine egg, milk and oil, then add to dry mixture.

Pour batter into greased loaf pan and bake at 350° F for 45 minutes.

—Linda Purvis

Blueberry Banana Bread

1 cup blueberries
1¾ cups flour
2 tsp. baking powder
¼ tsp. baking soda
½ tsp. salt
⅓ cup butter
⅔ cup sugar
2 eggs
1 cup mashed bananas

Toss berries with 2 Tbsp. flour. Sift remaining flour, baking powder, baking soda and salt.

Cream butter and beat in sugar until light and fluffy. Beat in eggs one at a time. Add flour mixture and bananas alternately in 3 parts to butter mixture. Stir in berries.

Spoon into greased loaf pan and bake at 350° F for 50 minutes.

—Gillian Richardson

Cranban Ring

1 banana, mashed
1 cup fresh cranberries, halved
¼ cup walnuts
1¾ cups flour
2 tsp. baking powder
1 tsp. salt
½ cup sugar
1 egg, beaten
½ cup milk
¼ cup oil

Mix banana, berries and nuts. Combine flour, baking powder and salt. Add sugar, egg, milk and oil. Stir in fruit until just mixed.

Spoon into greased ring mould and bake at 400° F for 35 minutes.

—Andrea Hamilton

Peanut Butter Bread

This recipe produces a very dense, moist loaf with a pleasant peanut butter taste. It could be eaten plain or could serve as the basis for a sandwich.

¾ cup sugar
½ cup peanut butter
1 tsp. vanilla
1¾ cups milk
2¼ cups flour
4 tsp. baking powder
½ tsp. salt

Cream together sugar, peanut butter and vanilla. Add milk and mix well. Combine flour, baking powder and salt. Add to creamed mixture and beat well.

Place in greased loaf pan and bake at 350° F for 45 to 50 minutes, or until golden brown. Allow to cool for 10 minutes before removing from pan.

Carrot Nut Loaf

1½ cups unbleached flour
1 cup whole wheat flour
2½ tsp. baking powder
1 tsp. baking soda
1 tsp. salt
¾ cup brown sugar
2 eggs
1 cup & 2 Tbsp. water
2 Tbsp. melted shortening
½ cup chopped nuts
½ cup raisins
1¼ cups grated raw carrots

Sift flours, baking powder, baking soda, salt and sugar together. Combine eggs, water and shortening and add to dry ingredients. Fold in nuts, raisins and carrots.

Pour into greased loaf pan and let stand for 5 minutes. Bake at 350° F for 1 hour.

—Ruth Hughes

Lemon Sesame Bread

¼ cup oil
½ cup honey
3 eggs
Juice of 1 lemon
Rind of 2 lemons, grated
½ cup sesame seeds
¼ cup soy flour
1 cup whole wheat flour
1½ Tbsp. milk powder
½ tsp. salt
2 tsp. baking powder
TOPPING:
Juice of 1 lemon
3 Tbsp. honey

Beat oil and honey together until blended, then beat in eggs, lemon juice and rind. Stir the dry ingredients together, then stir into the liquid mixture.

Bake in greased loaf pan at 350° F for 45 minutes.

To make topping, combine lemon juice and honey, heating if necessary. Poke holes in the warm loaf with a toothpick and pour topping over it. Cool for 10 minutes before serving.

—Norah Ashmore

Coconut Orange Loaf

2½ cups flour
1 cup sugar
¼ tsp. mace
3½ tsp. baking powder
¾ tsp. salt
3 tsp. grated orange rind
½ cup orange juice
¾ cup milk
2 eggs, beaten
2 Tbsp. oil
½ cup coconut
1 cup raisins

Mix together flour, sugar, mace, baking powder, salt and orange rind. Make a well in the centre.

Combine orange juice, milk, eggs and oil and pour into well. Blend well. Add coconut and raisins.

Pour into greased loaf pan and bake at 350° F for 1 hour.

—Jacqueline Dysart

Savoury Cheddar Bread

2 cups flour
4 tsp. baking powder
1 Tbsp. sugar
½ tsp. garlic powder
½ tsp. oregano
¼ tsp. dry mustard
1¼ cups grated Cheddar
   cheese
1 egg, beaten
1 cup milk
1 Tbsp. butter, melted

Stir together the flour, baking powder, sugar, garlic powder, oregano, dry mustard and cheese. Combine egg, milk and butter and add all at once to dry ingredients, stirring until just moistened.

Spread batter in a greased loaf pan and bake at 350° F for 45 minutes. Cool 10 minutes on a wire rack before removing from pan.

—Nan & Phil Millette

Cranberry Loaf

1 cup white sugar
2 Tbsp. butter
1 egg, beaten
1 cup raw cranberries
1 cup raisins
2 cups flour
½ tsp. baking soda
1½ tsp. baking powder
½ tsp. salt
Juice of 1 orange
Water
½ cup chopped walnuts

Cream sugar and butter and add egg. Toss cranberries and raisins with ¼ cup flour and set aside. Sift together remaining dry ingredients and add to creamed mixture alternately with orange juice that is combined with enough hot water to make ¾ cup. Fold in fruit and nuts.

Place in greased loaf pan and bake at 325° F for 1 hour. Let sit, well wrapped, for one day before using.

—Mary Lou Garlick

Braided Wheat Germ Bread

1 tsp. sugar
½ cup warm water
2 Tbsp. yeast
½ cup butter
1 cup cottage cheese
1¼ cups wheat germ
1 cup raisins
⅓ cup honey
3 eggs
1 tsp. grated orange rind
1 tsp. salt
4-4½ cups flour

In large bowl, dissolve sugar in warm water. Add yeast and let stand for 10 minutes. Heat butter and cottage cheese until butter melts. Let cool slightly and add to yeast mixture. Stir in wheat germ, raisins, honey, eggs, orange rind and salt. Add 3 to 4 cups flour to make a soft dough. Turn onto floured board and knead, adding flour if it is too sticky. Place in a greased bowl, turning to grease top. Cover and let rise for 1 to 1½ hours, or until doubled in bulk.

Punch down and divide in half. Divide each half into thirds and roll into 12-inch lengths. Braid together, pinching ends. Place on greased cookie sheet, cover and let rise for 1 hour. Bake at 350° F for 30 to 35 minutes.

Makes 2 braids.

—Carolyn Howatson

Sweet & Sour Pork with Peaches, page 403

Chicken and Bell Peppers, page 319

Green Bean and Potato Salad, page 191

Dutch Cherry Cake, page 580; White Chocolate Mocha Java Bars, page 13; Kipfel, page 16; Lace Cookies, page 15

Orange Waffles, page 5

Carrot Mincemeat, page 577

Malpeque Oyster Stew, page 261

Oriental Rice Salad, page 216

Cranberry-Filled Braid

BREAD:
2 Tbsp. sugar
1 pkg. yeast
⅓ cup warm water
3-3½ cups flour
¼ cup sugar
1 tsp. salt
1 tsp. shredded orange peel
⅓ cup orange juice
⅓ cup milk
¼ cup butter
1 egg
FILLING:
⅔ cup cranberries
¼ orange, unpeeled
⅓ apple, unpeeled
⅓ cup sugar
1 Tbsp. cornstarch
ICING:
½ cup icing sugar
2 tsp. orange juice
Toasted, sliced almonds

Combine 2 Tbsp. sugar, yeast and warm water. Let sit for 10 minutes. Combine 1 cup flour, sugar, salt and orange peel. Heat together orange juice, milk and butter until warm and add to flour mixture. Add yeast mixture and stir in egg. Add remaining flour to make a soft dough. Knead for 5 to 10 minutes. Place dough in greased bowl, cover and let rise until doubled in bulk — 1 to 1½ hours.

Meanwhile, prepare the filling. Chop all fruit together until fine. Add sugar and stir until dissolved. Add cornstarch and cook until thick and bubbly. Cool.

Punch down dough and let sit for 10 minutes. On lightly floured surface, roll dough into a 9-by-12-inch rectangle. Cut into three 12-by-3-inch strips. Spread cranberry mixture down centre of each strip, bring long edges together and pinch to seal. Place strips side by side, seam down, on a greased baking sheet. Braid and secure ends. Cover and let rise until doubled.

Bake at 350° F for 20 minutes, or until golden.

To make icing, combine icing sugar and orange juice. Drizzle over warm braid and sprinkle with toasted almonds.

Makes 1 braid.

—Karen Quinney

Crescia

This is a traditional Italian Easter-bread recipe from the Marche region of Italy. It has a strong peppery flavour, and although the recipe makes a very large, round loaf, it will not last long.

3 tsp. sugar
3 Tbsp. yeast
1½ cups warm water
12 eggs
1 lb. butter, melted
12 oz. Parmesan cheese
1 tsp. salt
2 Tbsp. pepper
6-8 cups flour

Dissolve sugar and yeast in water. Cover and let sit for 10 minutes. Beat eggs well and add melted butter. Add yeast mixture, stirring well. Stir in cheese, salt and pepper. Gradually add flour, blending well, until stiff batter dough results.

Pour into a large oiled casserole dish, cover and let rise for 1½ hours, or until doubled in bulk. Bake at 325° F for 1 to 1½ hours.

Makes 1 large loaf.

—Mikell Billoki

Potica

This is a traditional recipe for Yugoslavian Christmas bread.

3½ cups flour
1 pkg. yeast
1 cup milk
2 Tbsp. sugar
2 Tbsp. butter
1 tsp. salt
1 egg
FILLING:
2 cups finely ground walnuts
1 egg, beaten
¼ cup brown sugar
2 Tbsp. honey
2 Tbsp. milk
1 Tbsp. melted butter
1 tsp. cinnamon
½ tsp. vanilla

Stir together 1½ cups flour and the yeast. Heat milk, sugar, butter and salt until just warm. Add to flour-yeast mixture. Add egg and beat with electric mixer at low setting. Scrape bowl. Beat for 3 minutes at high speed. Stir in remaining flour to make a moderately stiff dough. Turn out and knead until smooth and elastic. Place in greased bowl and let rise until doubled — about 1½ hours.

Combine filling ingredients and set aside.

Punch dough down and let sit for 10 minutes. Roll out until very thin and approximately 20 by 30 inches. Spread with nut filling and roll up along longer side. Pinch edge to seal. Place in U-shape on greased baking sheet and let rise until doubled. Bake at 350° F for 30 to 35 minutes.

—Marie Yelich

Cracked Rye Bread

4 cups hot water
1½ Tbsp. salt
¾ cup brown sugar
⅜ cup shortening
1 Tbsp. yeast
⅜ cup warm water
2 cups rye flour
2 cups cracked rye
8 cups unbleached flour

Mix together hot water, salt, sugar and shortening. Let cool to lukewarm. Combine yeast and warm water and let sit for 10 minutes. Pour into hot-water mixture. Add flours until dough cannot be mixed any longer. Knead, adding flour as required, until dough is smooth and satiny. Cover and let rise for 1½ hours.

Punch down and let sit for 10 minutes. Place in greased loaf pans and let rise for 1¼ hours. Bake at 375° F for 45 minutes.

Makes 3 to 4 loaves.

—*Lynne Hawkes*

Dark Rye Bread

3 Tbsp. yeast
1 tsp. brown sugar
1 cup warm water
½ cup dark molasses
½ cup boiling water
2 Tbsp. butter
2 Tbsp. caraway seeds
2 tsp. salt
½ cup wheat germ
2¾ cups dark rye flour
2½-2¾ cups unbleached flour

Dissolve yeast and brown sugar in warm water. In large bowl, combine molasses, boiling water, butter, caraway seeds and salt, stirring until butter melts. Cool to lukewarm. Stir in yeast mixture and wheat germ. Stir in all of rye flour and as much unbleached flour as you can mix in with a spoon. Turn onto floured board. Knead in enough of remaining flour to make a medium-stiff dough that is smooth and elastic. Place in greased bowl, turning once to grease surface. Cover and let rise until doubled — about 1½ hours.

Punch down dough and divide in half. Cover and let sit for 10 minutes. Shape into 2 loaves and place in pans. Cover and let rise again until doubled — about 1 hour. Brush tops of loaves with water. With sharp knife, gently score tops of loaves diagonally at 2-inch intervals. Bake at 350° F for 45 minutes.

Makes 2 loaves.

—*Janet Ueberschlag*

Greek Easter Bread

1 pkg. yeast
½ cup warm water
2 cups warm milk
2 cups & 1 Tbsp. sugar
6-8 cups flour
5 eggs
1 orange peel, grated
1 lemon peel, grated
½ tsp. crushed cardamom seeds
½ lb. butter, melted
1 egg white, beaten

Dissolve yeast in water. Add 1 cup warm milk, 1 Tbsp. sugar and 1½ cups flour to make a pudding-like batter. Cover and let stand in warm place for 1 hour.

Meanwhile, combine 2 cups sugar and eggs. Place 5 cups flour in large pan and add orange and lemon peel, cardamom, remaining 1 cup milk and melted butter. Stir in yeast mixture and then sugar-egg mixture. Add flour as needed to make a kneadable dough. Knead gently.

Place dough in clean, oiled pan, cover and let rise for about 8 hours. Punch down, knead lightly again and divide into 9 balls.

Shape each ball into a long strip — 18 to 24 inches — then braid 3 strips together. Place the 3 loaves on a greased cookie sheet, cover and let rise for 2 hours. Brush the top of the loaves with lightly beaten egg white and bake at 325° F for 30 minutes.

Makes 3 loaves.

—*Patrick A. Thrasher*

Old Fort Henry Brown Bread

1 pkg. yeast
3 cups lukewarm water
6 cups whole wheat flour
1 Tbsp. salt

Dissolve yeast in water. Mix in flour and then salt. Knead for 2 minutes. Let stand for 10 minutes, then form into loaves and place in loaf pans. Cover and let rise in a warm place for 45 minutes, or until doubled in bulk.

Place in 500° F oven and reduce heat to 375°. Bake for 50 minutes or until done.

Makes 2 loaves.

—*St. Lawrence Parks Commission*

Sprouted Wheat Bread

2 Tbsp. yeast
½ cup warm water
2½ cups water
1 tsp. salt
¼ cup honey
¼ cup oil
6 cups whole wheat flour
2 cups wheat sprouts

Dissolve yeast in warm water. Add water, salt, honey, oil and 4 cups flour and beat well. Cover and let stand for 1 hour. Stir in remaining flour and sprouts. Knead for 5 to 10 minutes. Place in oiled bowl, cover and let rise for 1½ hours. Punch down and knead for 1 minute.

Shape into 3 loaves and place in oiled bread pans. Let rise, then bake at 350° F for 50 minutes.

Makes 3 loaves.

Sesame Wheat Bread

This recipe results in a somewhat heavy bread, which is particularly delicious toasted and spread with honey for breakfast.

4 cups milk, scalded
½ cup packed brown sugar
½ cup honey
5 tsp. salt
¾ cup butter
4 pkgs. yeast
1¼ cups warm water
1 cup sesame seeds, lightly toasted
¾ cup wheat germ
6 cups whole wheat flour
6 cups unbleached flour

Combine scalded milk, sugar, honey, salt and butter and cool to lukewarm. Dissolve yeast in warm water and add to cooled milk mixture. Stir in sesame seeds, wheat germ and whole wheat flour. Add unbleached flour. Knead until dough is smooth and satiny. Cover and let rise until doubled — about 1 hour.

Punch down and let sit for 15 minutes. Divide into 4 loaves and place in greased loaf pans. Let rise until doubled — about 1 hour. Bake at 425° F for 45 to 55 minutes.

Makes 4 loaves.

—*Heidi Magnuson-Ford*

Onion Rye Bread

2 cups milk, scalded
¼ cup sugar
4 tsp. salt
¼ cup oil
1 pkg. yeast
1 cup warm water
6 cups unbleached flour
2 Tbsp. caraway seeds
1 cup chopped onion
2 cups dark rye flour
Cornmeal
Milk

Combine scalded milk, sugar, salt and oil and let cool to lukewarm. Soften yeast in warm water and add to cooled milk mixture. Stir in unbleached flour, caraway seeds, onion and rye flour. Knead until smooth and elastic, adding more rye flour if needed. Place in greased bowl, cover and let rise until doubled — about 1 hour.

Punch down and let rise again until doubled. Place in greased loaf pans that have been sprinkled with cornmeal. Brush tops with milk and let rise for 1 hour, or until doubled. Bake at 350° F for 1 hour.

Makes 3 loaves.

—*Lois Jaman*

Honey Whole Wheat Buns

1 tsp. honey
2 pkgs. yeast
½ cup warm water
2 eggs, beaten
½ cup melted shortening
¾ cup honey
¼ cup sugar
1 Tbsp. salt
2 cups milk, scalded & cooled
4 cups unbleached flour
3 cups whole wheat flour

Combine honey, yeast and water and let sit for 10 minutes. Mix together eggs, shortening, honey, sugar, salt, milk, 2 cups unbleached flour and whole wheat flour. Add yeast mixture. Knead dough with remaining 2 cups unbleached flour. Let rise until doubled in size — 1½ hours.

Punch down. Shape into rolls and place on greased cookie sheet. Let rise for another hour. Bake at 400° F for 10 to 15 minutes.

Makes 24 rolls.

—*Laine Roddick*

English Muffins

1 cup milk
2 Tbsp. sugar
1 tsp. salt
¼ cup butter
1 pkg. yeast
1 cup warm water
5½ cups flour
Cornmeal

Scald milk and stir in sugar, salt and butter. Cool to lukewarm. Sprinkle yeast in warm water in large bowl and stir until dissolved. Add milk mixture and 3 cups of flour and beat until smooth. Add enough flour to make soft dough. On floured board, knead 10 minutes, adding flour as necessary. Place in greased bowl, turning to grease top. Cover and let rise for 1 hour.

Punch down and divide in half. On board, roll out dough to ½-inch thickness. Cut with 4-inch round cutter. Roll in cornmeal and let stand for 30 minutes. Cook on medium-hot griddle for 15 minutes. Turn and cook for another 15 minutes.

Makes 24 muffins.

—*Reo Belhumeur*

Bread Pretzels

2 cups warm water
1 Tbsp. dry yeast
½ tsp. sugar
4½ cups whole wheat flour
1 egg yolk, beaten
Coarse salt

Dissolve yeast and sugar in warm water. Stir in the flour and knead for 8 to 10 minutes. Cover and let rise in a warm place until doubled in bulk.

Punch down and form into 12 small balls. Roll each out into a sausage shape, then form into pretzel shape. If desired, brush with beaten egg yolk and sprinkle with coarse salt. Allow to rise until not quite doubled. Bake at 475° F for about 10 minutes.

Makes 12 pretzels.

—*Mary Flegel*

Oatmeal Jumbles

1¾ cups flour
½ tsp. baking soda
½ tsp. salt
½ tsp. ginger
½ tsp. nutmeg
½ tsp. cinnamon
½ tsp. cloves
1 cup shortening
⅔ cup brown sugar
1 egg
½ cup molasses
2 cups rolled oats
½ cup raisins

Sift together flour, baking soda, salt, ginger, nutmeg, cinnamon and cloves. Cream together shortening and sugar, then stir in egg and molasses. Add dry ingredients a third at a time. Stir in oats and raisins and drop by teaspoonful onto greased cookie sheets. Flatten with fork. Bake at 350° F for 15 minutes.

Makes 3 dozen large cookies.

—*Judith Goodwin*

Stephen's Chocolate Oatmeal Cookies

½ cup shortening
½ cup white sugar
½ cup brown sugar
1 cup flour
1 tsp. baking powder
½ tsp. salt
1 egg
5 Tbsp. cocoa
2 Tbsp. melted butter
1 tsp. almond extract
1 cup oatmeal

Cream together shortening and sugars. Sift together flour, baking powder and salt and add to creamed mixture. Beat in egg, cocoa, butter and almond extract. Stir in oatmeal.

Drop by teaspoonful onto greased cookie sheets and flatten with a fork. Bake at 350° F for 8 to 10 minutes.

Makes 4 dozen cookies.

—*Valerie Arnason*

Chocolate Goodies

1 cup brown sugar
¼ cup butter
2 Tbsp. cocoa
¼ cup milk
½ tsp. vanilla
1 cup rolled oats
¼ cup wheat germ
½ cup coconut
¼ cup sesame seeds
½ cup sunflower seeds

Combine sugar, butter, cocoa and milk in a large saucepan and stir over medium heat until butter melts. Bring to a boil and cook for 2 minutes, stirring occasionally. Remove from heat and stir in remaining ingredients.

Drop by spoonfuls onto wax paper and allow to cool.

Makes 3 dozen cookies.

—*S. Pedersen*

Zucchini Oatmeal Cookies

½ cup softened butter
¾ cup honey
1 egg
2 cups whole wheat flour
1 tsp. baking soda
½ tsp. cinnamon
¼ tsp. cloves
¼ tsp. nutmeg
1 cup oats
1 cup raisins
1 cup grated zucchini

Cream butter, honey and egg in a large bowl.

Combine flour and spices in small bowl, and the oats and raisins in another bowl. Add both to moist ingredients a little at a time. Stir in zucchini gradually until well mixed.

Drop by teaspoonful onto greased cookie sheets and flatten with a fork. Bake at 375° F for 10 to 12 minutes.

Makes 5 dozen cookies.

—*Sue Summers*

Orange Chocolate Cookies

½ cup butter
½ cup sugar
1 egg
2 tsp. grated orange rind
2¼ cups flour
½ tsp. salt
1½ tsp. baking powder
Melted semisweet chocolate
Finely chopped nuts

Cream butter and add sugar, egg and orange rind. Mix flour, salt and baking powder and add to butter mixture.

Roll out on floured surface to about ⅛ inch and cut into desired shapes. Bake at 350° F for 10 minutes. Spread melted chocolate on cooled cookies and top with chopped nuts.

Makes 4 dozen cookies.

—*Barbara & Dana Leahey*

Deluxe Cookies

1 cup white sugar
1 cup brown sugar
2 eggs
1 cup peanut butter
2 tsp. vanilla
1 lb. butter
2½-3 cups flour
2 Tbsp. baking soda
3 cups rolled oats
1½ cups chocolate chips
1½ cups raisins
1½ cups chopped walnuts
1 cup sesame seeds

Cream together sugars, eggs, peanut butter, vanilla and butter until smooth. Add flour and baking soda and mix until dough does not stick to hands. Mix in remaining ingredients.

Roll into balls, place on greased cookie sheets and flatten with a fork. Bake at 350° F for 15 minutes.

Makes 8 to 9 dozen cookies.

—Karen Diemert

Peanut Butter Chocolate Chip Cookies

½ cup shortening
½ cup brown sugar
½ cup white sugar
½ cup peanut butter
1 egg, beaten
½ tsp. vanilla
1½ cups flour
½ tsp. salt
½ tsp. baking soda
⅔ cup chocolate chips
¼ cup chopped peanuts

Cream together shortening and sugars. Add peanut butter and blend. Stir in egg and vanilla.

Mix together remaining ingredients in a separate bowl, and then combine with creamed mixture.

Place by teaspoonful on greased cookie sheets and flatten with a fork. Bake at 350° F for 12 to 15 minutes.

Makes 3 to 3½ dozen cookies.

—Jane Lott

Rice Cookies

1 cup rice flour
¼ cup salt
1½ tsp. baking powder
4 Tbsp. sesame oil
¼ cup maple syrup
1 tsp. vanilla
¼ cup water
½ cup coconut
½ cup finely ground pecans

Combine flour, salt and baking powder and work oil into this mixture. Mix together maple syrup, vanilla and water. In another bowl, combine coconut and pecans. Add water and nut mixtures alternately to dry ingredients. Shape into roll, wrap well and chill until firm. Slice and place on greased cookie sheets. Bake at 350° F for 10 minutes, or until light gold.

Makes 2 dozen cookies.

—Hazel Baker

Cardamom Cinnamon Nuggets

1¼ cups butter
½ cup sugar
2 cups unbleached flour
½ cup whole wheat flour
Salt
2 tsp. cinnamon
2 tsp. cardamom
¾ cup walnuts

Cream butter and sugar and gradually add flours, pinch of salt, cinnamon, cardamom and walnuts. Divide dough into quarters. Shape into logs and chill well. Cut into ¼-inch slices, place on greased cookie sheets and bake at 375° F for 10 minutes.

Makes 4 dozen cookies.

—Gwen Miller

Wheaty Walnut Trailblazers

1 cup rolled oats
2 cups whole wheat flour
1 cup unbleached flour
½ cup skim milk powder
2 tsp. baking soda
1½ tsp. cinnamon
¼ tsp. salt
1 cup butter
1¼ cups brown sugar
2 eggs
1 Tbsp. grated orange rind
1½ cups chopped walnuts
1 cup raisins

Combine rolled oats, flours, milk powder, baking soda, cinnamon and salt. Cream together butter, sugar, eggs and orange rind. Stir dry ingredients into creamed mixture and add walnuts and raisins.

Drop by teaspoonful onto greased cookie sheets and bake at 375° F for 10 to 15 minutes.

Makes 8 to 10 dozen cookies.

—Bertha B. Bumchuckles

Italian Anise Cookies

2½ cups flour
½ cup sugar
3 tsp. baking powder
1 tsp. ground anise
⅓ cup soft butter
3 eggs

Sift together dry ingredients and cut in butter. Beat in eggs with fork until dough is smooth. Mix well with hands.

Wrap in plastic and refrigerate overnight. Roll to ¼-inch thickness and cut into circles.

Bake on greased cookie sheet at 350° F for 8 to 10 minutes, until lightly browned.

Makes 3 to 4 dozen cookies.

—Linda Townsend

German Springerle Cookies

6 eggs
3 cups sugar
6 cups flour
¾ cup whole anise seed

Beat eggs and sugar together with electric mixmaster on high until thick and creamy — about 4 minutes. Reduce speed to low and slowly add flour, scraping down and mixing thoroughly. Dough will be stiff.

Liberally flour a pastry board and scoop dough out onto it. Knead dough until it has a smooth surface, incorporating as much flour as necessary to keep it from sticking.

Clean off board and reflour. Using a regular rolling pin, roll dough into ¾-inch-thick rectangle. Flour springerle rolling pin and evenly press down design into dough. Cut cookies apart and place on greased cookie sheet that has been sprinkled with anise seed. Set aside overnight to dry.

Bake at 300° F for 10 minutes, or until bottoms are golden brown.

—Edith Cumming Coe

Grandma's Man-Sized Cookies

2 cups raisins
1 cup water
1 cup shortening
2 cups sugar
3 eggs
4 cups flour
1 Tbsp. baking soda
1 Tbsp. baking powder
1 Tbsp. salt
1½ Tbsp. cinnamon
¼ Tbsp. allspice
½ cup nuts

Boil raisins in water until almost dry, then cool. Cream shortening and sugar and add eggs. Beat well.

Combine dry ingredients and add to creamed mixture. Stir in raisins and nuts and mix well.

Form into balls, place on greased cookie sheets and flatten with a fork. Bake at 350° F for 10 minutes.

Makes 10 dozen cookies.

—Crystal Burgess

Italian Jam & Nut Cookies

4 eggs
1 cup oil
1¼ cups sugar
2 Tbsp. lemon juice
Flour
4 tsp. baking powder
Plum jam
1 cup raisins
1½ cups coarsely chopped
   walnuts

Beat together eggs, oil, sugar and lemon juice. Add enough flour to form soft dough. Add baking powder. Continue adding flour until a soft, but not sticky, dough is formed. Knead dough a little, then cut into 4 pieces.

Roll each piece of dough out ¼-inch thick. Spread jam on the dough, then sprinkle with raisins and nuts. Roll up like a jelly roll and seal the edges. Bake on a cookie sheet for 20 minutes at 350° F. Remove from oven and cut l-inch thick at an angle. Turn off oven and return cookies to it until oven has completely cooled.

Makes 4 dozen cookies.

—Mary Andrasi

Persimmon Cookies

Persimmon, an Oriental fruit, is unfamiliar to many North Americans. As in this recipe, the persimmon can be used to make a very tasty cookie. It is also delicious eaten raw. One serving method is to place the raw, ripe (very soft) fruit in a paper towel and freeze it until it is hard. Cut off the top and eat — it will resemble sherbet.

2 cups whole wheat flour
1 tsp. baking soda
¼ tsp. salt
1 tsp. cinnamon
½ tsp. nutmeg
½ tsp. cloves
½ cup butter
½ cup sugar
1 tsp. grated lemon or
   orange rind
1 egg, beaten
1 tsp. vanilla
1 cup persimmon pulp
   (approximately 2
   persimmons)
½ cup raisins

Sift together flour, baking soda, salt, cinnamon, nutmeg and cloves. Cream butter and sugar, then add rind, egg, vanilla and pulp. Blend well and add dry ingredients. Stir in raisins.

Drop by teaspoonful onto greased cookie sheets and bake at 350° F for 20 minutes.

Makes 3 dozen cookies.

—Lisa Calzonetti

Orange Currant Cookies

2¼ cups flour
1 tsp. baking soda
½ tsp. salt
½ tsp. ginger
½ tsp. cinnamon
½ cup butter, softened
⅓ cup brown sugar
1 egg
½ cup molasses
¼ cup orange juice
½ cup currants

Combine flour, baking soda, salt, ginger and cinnamon. Cream butter and sugar, then add egg. Beat in molasses and orange juice, then dry ingredients. Stir in currants.

Drop by teaspoonful onto greased cookie sheets and bake at 350° F for 10 minutes.

Makes 3 to 4 dozen cookies.

—Cheryl Lenington Suckling

Banana Cookies

2¼ cups flour
2 tsp. baking powder
½ tsp. salt
¼ tsp. baking soda
⅔ cup butter
1 cup sugar
2 eggs
1 tsp. vanilla
6 oz. chocolate chips
1 cup mashed ripe banana

Sift together flour, baking powder, salt and baking soda. Cream together butter, sugar, eggs and vanilla. Add dry ingredients and blend well. Stir in chocolate chips and banana. Drop by teaspoonful onto greased cookie sheets. Bake at 400° F for 12 to 15 minutes.

Makes 4 dozen cookies.

—Linda Charron

Almond Shortbread

These cookies are common Christmas fare in Finland, where most shortbreads contain almonds.

¾ lb. butter
2 cups sugar
1 egg
½ tsp. vanilla
¾ cup finely ground
    almonds
3 cups flour (approximate)

Cream butter and sugar. Beat in egg and vanilla and stir in almonds and flour.

Place dough in cookie press or pastry bag and squeeze into desired shape on cookie sheets. Bake at 350° F for 10 minutes, or until light gold.

Makes 4 dozen cookies.

—Eila Koivu

Eat Mores

1 cup peanut butter
1 cup honey
1 cup carob powder
½ cup raisins
½ cup coconut
1 cup sunflower seeds
1 cup sesame seeds

Melt peanut butter and honey in top of double boiler. Add carob powder and mix. Add remaining ingredients.

Press into lightly buttered 9" x 9" pan. Cover and refrigerate for 2 to 3 hours, then cut into squares.

—Dorothy McEachern

Date Pinwheel Cookies

½ cup butter
¼ cup honey
½ cup brown sugar
1 egg
2 cups flour
¼ tsp. baking soda
¼ tsp. salt
FILLING:
1½ cups chopped dates
Rind of 1 orange, grated
¼ cup honey
1 cup orange juice
Salt

To make cookie dough, cream together butter, honey and sugar. Beat in egg. Sift together flour, baking soda and salt and add to creamed ingredients. Mix to form a dough.

Meanwhile, combine dates, orange rind, honey, orange juice and salt. Cook over low heat until fairly dry. Cool.

Roll dough into an oblong shape about ¼-inch thick. Spread with date mixture and roll up like a jelly roll. Wrap in wax paper and refrigerate for a few hours, or overnight. Slice and bake at 375° F for 12 minutes.

Makes 2 dozen cookies.

—Christine Griffiths

Cranberry Cookies

This recipe results in a flavourful and colourful Christmas cookie which is not overly rich or sweet.

½ cup butter
¾ cup white sugar
¾ cup brown sugar
1 egg, beaten
¼ cup milk
3 cups flour
1 tsp. baking powder
¼ tsp. baking soda
½ tsp. salt
1 tsp. lemon juice
3 cups chopped cranberries
1 cup chopped nuts

Cream together butter and sugars. Add egg and milk. Sift together flour, baking powder, baking soda and salt and add to creamed ingredients, mixing well. Add lemon juice, cranberries and nuts.

Drop by teaspoonful onto greased cookie sheets and bake at 375° F for 15 minutes.

Makes 8 dozen cookies.

—Helen Hawkes

Banana Bars

½ cup butter
1 cup sugar
2 eggs
1 tsp. almond extract
2 cups sliced ripe bananas
2 cups flour
1 tsp. baking powder
¼ tsp. salt
¼ tsp. baking soda
½ cup chopped almonds
1 cup chopped dates
Icing sugar

Cream butter and sugar. Beat in eggs one at a time until fluffy. Add almond extract and bananas. Sift together dry ingredients and stir into batter. Add almonds and dates.

Spread in greased 9" x 13" baking pan and bake at 350° F for 30 minutes. While still warm, sprinkle lightly with icing sugar.

Makes 4 to 5 dozen bars.

—Ann Budge

Kourabiedes

This is a traditional recipe for Greek shortbread cookies.

1 lb. unsalted butter, softened
1 cup icing sugar
1 Tbsp. brandy
Juice of 1 orange
1 tsp. vanilla
1 tsp. almond extract
5-6 cups flour
½ cup ground almonds

Whip butter for 10 minutes, until light and fluffy. Gradually add ½ cup icing sugar. Combine brandy, orange juice, vanilla and almond extract. Add liquid and part of flour alternately to butter-sugar mixture, ½ cup of flour at a time, until all liquid has been added. Add ground almonds. Add remaining flour ¼ cup at a time until dough forms a ball, and sides of bowl come clean. Form into 1-inch balls, flatten on greased cookie sheet and poke with finger to form a dent.

Place in oven preheated to 350° F and immediately reduce temperature to 200° F. Bake for 1½ hours. Sift remaining icing sugar over cooled cookies.

Makes 6 to 8 dozen cookies.

—Patricia Forrest

Mom's Chocolate Shortbread

¾ cup flour
2 Tbsp. cocoa
½ cup butter
2 Tbsp. white sugar
1½ tsp. salt
2 eggs
1¼ cups brown sugar
1 Tbsp. flour
½ tsp. baking powder
½ cup coconut
¾ cup chopped nuts
1 tsp. vanilla
ICING:
1 cup icing sugar
2 Tbsp. butter
1 heaping Tbsp. cocoa
Boiling water

Combine flour, cocoa, butter, white sugar and 1 tsp. salt. Press into a greased 8-inch-square cake pan. Bake at 300° F for 20 minutes.

Cream together eggs, remaining ½ tsp. salt, brown sugar, flour and baking powder. Add coconut, nuts and vanilla and mix well. Pour over shortbread base. Raise oven temperature to 350° F and bake for 20 minutes.

To make icing, combine icing sugar, butter, cocoa and enough boiling water to make a creamy mixture. Pour over baked shortbread. Cut into squares.

Makes 2 to 3 dozen squares.

—Dianne Radcliffe

Irene Cable's Fig Bars

2 cups dried figs
1½ cups water
Sugar
2 tsp. vanilla
1 cup shortening
1 cup brown sugar
2 eggs, beaten
3 cups flour
¾ tsp. salt
1 tsp. cream of tartar
½ tsp. baking soda
1 Tbsp. hot water

Soak figs in water overnight. Chop well, cook until thick and add sugar to taste. Cool. Add 1 tsp. vanilla.

Cream shortening and sugar. Add eggs and beat until light and fluffy. Sift together flour, salt and cream of tartar. Add half of this to creamed mixture, then add remaining 1 tsp. vanilla, baking soda and hot water. Stir in remaining flour mixture. Chill dough.

Roll out to ⅛-inch thickness on floured surface and cut into 3-inch strips. Place fig mixture down centre and fold each side over the filling. Cut into 1½-inch pieces, place on floured cookie sheets and bake at 375° F for 12 to 15 minutes.

Makes 4 to 5 dozen bars.

—Karin Mayes

Nanaimo Bars

¾ cup & 1 Tbsp. butter
5 Tbsp. sugar
5 Tbsp. cocoa
1 tsp. peppermint extract
1 egg
2 cups finely crushed
   graham crackers
½ cup vanilla pudding
2 cups icing sugar
2 oz. unsweetened chocolate

Heat ½ cup butter, the sugar, cocoa and peppermint in saucepan. Beat in egg and stir until consistency of custard. Remove from heat and stir in crushed graham crackers. Press mixture into a greased 8-inch square pan.

Cream together ¼ cup of remaining butter, the pudding and icing sugar. Spread over graham cracker layer.

Melt chocolate with remaining 1 Tbsp. butter, then pour over second layer. Let sit for a few minutes, then refrigerate for an hour before cutting.

Makes 3 dozen squares.

—Margie Hancock

Chocolate Chip Bars

½ cup butter
1¼ cups brown sugar
¼ cup white sugar
2 eggs, separated
½ tsp. vanilla
1 cup flour
1 tsp. baking powder
⅛ tsp. salt
Chocolate chips
1 cup coconut

Cream together butter, ¼ cup brown sugar, white sugar and egg yolks. Add vanilla. Sift together flour, baking powder and salt and add to creamed mixture. Spread in greased 9" x 13" pan. Sprinkle with chocolate chips.

Beat egg whites and remaining 1 cup brown sugar until stiff. Fold in coconut. Spread evenly over mixture in pan. Bake at 350° F for 20 to 30 minutes. Cut into bars while still warm, then cool in pan.

Makes 3 dozen bars.

—Pauline Longmore

Chocolate Cheese Brownies

8 oz. cream cheese
⅓ cup white sugar
3 eggs
½ tsp. vanilla
2 oz. unsweetened chocolate
½ cup butter
1 cup brown sugar
¾ cup flour
¾ tsp. baking powder
¼ cup chopped nuts

Blend cream cheese, white sugar, 1 egg and vanilla until smooth. Melt chocolate and butter and cool. Cream together remaining 2 eggs and brown sugar and beat in chocolate mixture. Sift together flour and baking powder and mix into chocolate.

Pour half the batter into a greased 9-inch cake pan. Spoon cream cheese mixture on top, spread out carefully and pour remaining batter over all. Sprinkle with nuts. Bake at 350° F for 45 to 50 minutes.

Makes 1 to 2 dozen brownies.

—Linda Townsend

Scottish Currant Slices

Pastry for 2 double 9-inch
    pie shells
1½ cups currants
½ tsp. cinnamon
¼ tsp. allspice
1 Tbsp. butter
1 Tbsp. lemon juice
½ cup sugar
2 tsp. cornstarch
½ cup water
3½ cups thinly sliced apples
Milk
Sugar

Combine currants, cinnamon, allspice, butter, lemon juice and sugar in saucepan. Stir together cornstarch and water until smooth. Add to currant mixture and bring to a boil stirring constantly, then simmer for 5 minutes until very thick. Cool.

Divide pastry in half. Roll out one half and line a jelly roll pan with it, pressing the dough part way up the sides. Spread with cooled currant mixture and top with sliced apples. Roll out remaining pastry and lay on top, sealing edges so that the filling is enclosed.

Brush top with milk and sprinkle with sugar. Bake at 450° F for 10 minutes, reduce heat to 375° and continue baking for 20 minutes. Cut into squares when cool.

Makes 6 dozen squares.

—Elma MacLachlin

Orange Squares

½ cup shortening
1 cup sugar
1 egg
Juice & grated rind of 1 large
    orange
2 cups flour
1 tsp. baking soda
1 tsp. baking powder
½ tsp. salt
1 cup sour milk
1 cup raisins

Cream together shortening and sugar. Add egg and orange juice and rind. Sift flour, baking soda, baking powder and salt and add to creamed mixture alternately with sour milk. Stir in raisins. Place in greased 9" x 13" baking pan and bake at 350° F for 35 minutes. Let cool before cutting and removing from pan.

Makes 3 to 4 dozen squares.

—Orian Steele

Boterkoek

This is a well-known and much loved recipe to many Dutch-Canadians.

1 cup butter
1 cup sugar
1 egg
1 tsp. almond extract
2 cups flour
Milk
Slivered almonds

Cream together butter and sugar. Add egg, almond extract and then flour, mixing well by hand. Press evenly onto cookie sheet, making a ½-inch-thick layer. Wet the surface lightly with milk and press in almond slivers. Bake at 375° F for 30 minutes. Cut into squares while still warm.

Makes 20 squares.

—Wilma Zomer

Carrot Granola Bars

⅓ cup butter
¾ cup brown sugar
1 egg
¾ cup flour
¼ cup skim milk powder
1 tsp. baking powder
1 tsp. salt
½ tsp. cinnamon
1 cup grated carrots
1-1½ tsp. maple extract
1 tsp. vanilla extract
1½ cups granola
½ cup raisins

Cream together butter and sugar. Add egg and beat until fluffy. In separate bowl, stir together flour, milk, baking powder, salt and cinnamon. Stir into creamed mixture. Add carrots, maple and vanilla extracts, granola and raisins. Mix thoroughly. Turn batter into greased 9" x 13" pan and bake at 350° F for 30 minutes. Cut into bars while still warm, then allow to cool thoroughly before removing from pan.

Makes 4 dozen bars.

—Sue Summers

Coconut Squares

3 eggs
2 cups brown sugar
1 tsp. vanilla
2 cups coconut
½ cup chocolate chips
½ cup currants or raisins
½ cup chopped walnuts
½ cup wheat germ
½ cup flour

Beat eggs until foamy. Add remaining ingredients and mix well. Spread in greased 9" x 13" pan and bake at 350° F for 30 minutes.

Makes 4 dozen squares.

Cranberry Coffee Cake

½ cup butter
1 cup sugar
2 eggs, beaten
1 tsp. baking powder
1 tsp. baking soda
2 cups flour
½ tsp. salt
1 cup sour cream
½ Tbsp. almond extract
1 cup cooked cranberries
½ cup chopped nuts
TOPPING:
¾ cup icing sugar
½ tsp. almond extract
1 Tbsp. warm water

Cream together butter, sugar and eggs. Sift dry ingredients together, then add to creamed mixture. Add sour cream and almond extract.

Place half the batter in greased 9" x 9" cake pan. Spoon cooked cranberries evenly over this, then top with remaining batter. Sprinkle nuts on top. Bake at 350° F for 55 minutes.

To make topping, combine icing sugar, almond extract and warm water to form a thin paste. Drizzle over warm cake.

—Helen Hawkes

Plum Squares

3 cups flour
3 tsp. baking powder
1 tsp. salt
¼ cup sugar
⅓ cup butter, softened
2 eggs, beaten
6 Tbsp. milk (approximately)
½ cup plum jam
3 cups fresh or frozen plums, pitted & sliced in half

In large bowl, mix flour, baking powder, salt and sugar. Add butter and cut in finely. Add eggs and enough milk to make a dough that will cling together, but is not too sticky. Gather into a ball and cut into 2 pieces.

On floured surface, roll out one piece of dough to fit cookie sheet. Spoon jam over dough and then arrange plums with skin side down. Roll out next piece of dough to cookie-sheet size and cut into strips to make a lattice top. Bake at 350° F for about 30 minutes, or until golden.

Makes 4 dozen squares.

—Julie Herr

Shaker Plum Coffee Cake

¾ cup sugar
1 egg
¼ cup shortening
½ cup milk
1½ cups flour
2 tsp. baking powder
½ tsp. salt
8-10 plums, pitted & halved
TOPPING:
½ cup brown sugar
3 Tbsp. flour
1 tsp. cinnamon
3 tsp. melted butter
½ cup chopped nuts

Cream sugar, egg and shortening until fluffy, then stir in milk. Sift dry ingredients together and beat into creamed mixture. Spread dough in greased 9" x 9" cake pan. Top with rows of plums.

To make topping, combine remaining ingredients until crumbly. Sprinkle over plums. Bake at 375° F for 35 minutes.

—Carole Zobac

Rhubarb Sour Cream Coffee Cake

½ cup butter
1½ cups brown sugar
1 egg
1 cup whole wheat flour
1 cup unbleached flour
1 tsp. baking soda
½ tsp. salt
1 cup sour cream
1½ cups rhubarb, cut into ½-inch pieces
½ cup chopped walnuts or pecans
TOPPING:
½ cup butter
1 cup sugar
½ cup light cream
1 tsp. vanilla

Cream together butter, brown sugar and egg until light and fluffy. Combine flours, baking soda and salt. Add to creamed mixture alternately with sour cream, mixing well after each addition. Stir in rhubarb and nuts.

Spoon into well-greased 9" x 13" cake pan. Bake at 350° F for 35 to 40 minutes.

To make topping, combine butter, sugar, cream and vanilla in small saucepan. Heat until butter melts, then pour over cooled cake.

—Valerie Gillis

Apple Gingerbread

4 apples, peeled & sliced
2 cups flour
1½ tsp. baking soda
½ tsp. salt
½ cup sugar
1 tsp. ginger
1 tsp. cinnamon
½ cup butter
¾ cup molasses
1 egg
1 cup boiling water

Place apples in greased 9" x 9" cake pan. Sift together flour, baking soda, salt, sugar, ginger and cinnamon. Add butter, molasses and egg and mix well. Add boiling water and beat well. Pour mixture over apples and bake at 350° F for 30 minutes.

—Judy Wuest

Vegetable Cake

3 eggs, separated
1½ cups sugar
1 cup oil
3 Tbsp. hot water
1 cup shredded carrots
1 cup shredded beets
½ tsp. salt
1 tsp. cinnamon
2 cups flour
1 tsp. vanilla
2½ tsp. baking powder

Cream together egg yolks, sugar, oil and hot water. Add carrots, beets, salt, cinnamon, flour and vanilla. Beat egg whites with baking powder until stiff, then fold into batter. Place in greased 9" x 13" pan and bake at 350° F for 40 minutes.

—Joanne Graham

Orange Sponge Cake

3 eggs, separated
¼ tsp. cream of tartar
1 cup sugar
2 tsp. grated orange rind
⅓ cup orange juice
1¼ cups flour
1½ tsp. baking powder
¼ tsp. salt
GLAZE:
Juice of 1 orange
¼ cup sugar

Beat egg whites with cream of tartar until stiff. Add yolks one at a time, beating well after each addition. Add sugar gradually, beating well. Add rind and juice.

Sift together flour, baking powder and salt and fold into liquid ingredients. Place batter in greased tube pan and bake at 325° F for 18 to 20 minutes.

Combine orange juice and sugar to make glaze and pour over warm cake.

—Lee Robinson

Hazelnut Cake

This cake is low in flour and sugar, but high in protein. It is especially delicious served with whipped cream.

2 Tbsp. flour
2½ tsp. baking powder
4 eggs
½ cup sugar
1 cup hazelnuts

Sift together flour and baking powder. Place eggs and sugar in blender and process until smooth. Add hazelnuts gradually and continue to process until all nuts are finely ground. Add flour mixture and mix well. Pour into two 8-inch layer cake pans with greased waxpaper-lined bottoms. Bake at 350° F for 20 minutes.

—Kass Bennett

Anise Seed Cake

1½ cups flour
½ tsp. salt
½ cup butter
1 cup sugar
2 eggs, separated & beaten
½ cup milk
1 tsp. anise seeds
1 tsp. baking powder

Sift together flour and salt. Cream butter and sugar and add egg yolks. Add milk alternating with flour-salt mixture. Fold in stiffly beaten egg whites and anise seeds. Add baking powder and mix well. Pour into greased loaf pan. Bake at 350° F for 55 minutes.

—Katherine Dunster

Coconut Pound Cake

1 cup butter
2 cups sugar
5 eggs
3 cups flour
¼ tsp. salt
1 cup milk
1½ cups coconut
1 tsp. lemon juice
½ tsp. vanilla

Cream butter and sugar together until fluffy. Add eggs one at a time, beating well after each addition. Sift flour with salt and add alternately with milk to creamed mixture, beating after each addition. Add coconut, lemon juice and vanilla. Turn into greased and floured tube pan. Bake at 325° F for 90 minutes. Cool for 10 minutes, then remove from pan and cool on rack.

—Sheila Couture

Apple Blackberry Cake

¾ cup butter
¾ cup sugar
4 eggs
3 cups flour
1½ tsp. baking powder
¾ tsp. salt
1½ tsp. baking soda
1½ cups sour cream
1½ tsp. vanilla
1 tsp. cardamom
2 cups peeled, chopped apples
1 cup blackberries
½ cup firmly packed brown sugar

Cream butter and sugar until fluffy. Add eggs one at a time, beating well after each addition. Sift together flour, baking powder, salt and baking soda. Add to creamed ingredients alternately with sour cream. Stir in vanilla and cardamom, then fold in apples.

Pour half the batter into greased 9" x 13" cake pan. Cover with blackberries and sprinkle with brown sugar. Top with remaining batter. Bake at 325° F for 40 to 50 minutes.

—Grietje Waddell

Sour Cream Spice Cake

1 cup shortening
½ cup brown sugar
2 eggs, beaten
1 cup molasses
1 cup sour cream
1 tsp. salt
½ tsp. nutmeg
½ tsp. ginger
1 tsp. cloves
1 tsp. baking soda
1 tsp. cream of tartar
3 cups flour
1 cup raisins
½ cup chopped nuts

Cream together shortening and sugar. Add eggs, then molasses and sour cream. Combine salt, nutmeg, ginger, cloves, baking soda and cream of tartar with flour and add to creamed ingredients. Mix well, then stir in raisins and nuts. Place in greased 9-inch cake pan and bake at 350° F for 1 hour.

—Jan Johnson

Spiced Yogurt Pound Cake

1 cup butter, softened
2 cups sugar
3 eggs
⅔ cup plain yogurt
1 tsp. vanilla
2¼ cups flour
½ tsp. baking soda
½ tsp. salt
1 tsp. mace
½ tsp. allspice
½ tsp. cinnamon
¼ tsp. cloves
2 oz. unsweetened chocolate, grated

Cream butter until fluffy, then gradually beat in sugar. Add eggs one at a time, beating well after each addition. Stir in yogurt and vanilla.

Sift together flour, baking soda, salt, mace, allspice, cinnamon and cloves and stir into creamed mixture. Beat for 4 minutes, then fold in chocolate.

Place batter in greased and floured bundt pan. Bake at 325° F for 70 minutes. Cool in pan for 10 minutes, then turn onto rack to finish cooling.

—Elizabeth Clayton Paul

Great Aunt Bessie's Maple Cake

This recipe was developed by the contributor's Great Aunt Bessie. It became such a favourite of the young members of the family that she continued to bake it on her birthday each year, when the family gathered for a reunion.

½ cup butter
½ cup sugar
½ cup maple syrup
1 tsp. vanilla
2 eggs, well beaten
1¾ cups flour
½ tsp. salt
2½ tsp. baking powder
¼ cup milk
½ cup chopped walnuts
FROSTING:
1 cup maple syrup
2 egg whites
Salt

Cream together butter and sugar. Gradually add maple syrup and vanilla and cream well again. Add eggs and mix well. Sift together dry ingredients and add to creamed mixture alternately with milk. Stir in chopped nuts.

Pour into 2 greased and floured 8-inch cake pans. Bake at 375° F for 25 to 30 minutes.

To make frosting, cook maple syrup to soft ball stage. Beat egg whites with pinch of salt until peaks form. Add cooled syrup in fine stream, beating constantly. Frost cooled cake.

—Joyce Barton

Chestnut Cake

This traditional French cake takes a considerable amount of work, but the result — an almost fondant-fudge-like cake — is well worth it. When selecting chestnuts, pick fresh, plump, shiny nuts without insect bites. Vanilla sugar is made by placing a vanilla bean in a jar of sugar for a few days.

60 chestnuts (1½ lbs.)
1 cup skim milk
1 lb. fruit sugar
1 tsp. vanilla sugar
½ lb. unsalted butter
6 eggs, separated
Salt

To prepare chestnuts, make 2 incisions crosswise at the top of each nut and place them in a skillet. Cover with water and boil for 8 minutes. Remove from heat, but leave in water. Peel chestnuts, then place in another skillet with 3 cups water and 1 cup skim milk. Simmer for 30 rninutes. Drain and force through fine-mesh sieve a few at a time to make a purée the consistency of fine noodle threads.

Blend chestnut purée with fruit sugar and vanilla sugar. Beat in the butter until smooth. Beat in egg yolks one at a time.

Combine salt and egg white and beat until stiff peaks form. Take one-quarter of this and beat it into the chestnut paste. Fold remaining egg whites gently into batter.

Place batter in greased tube pan and bake at 375° F for 30 to 45 minutes.

—*J.A. Guy Bacon*

Banana Yogurt Cupcakes

½ cup butter
1 cup honey
2 eggs
2 ripe bananas, mashed
2 tsp. lemon juice
1 tsp. grated lemon rind
1 cup whole wheat flour
1 cup & 2 Tbsp. unbleached flour
1 tsp. baking soda
½ tsp. salt
½ cup yogurt

Cream butter, then add honey and mix. Add eggs one at a time, beating well after each addition, then bananas. Stir in lemon juice and rind.

Sift together flours, baking soda and salt and add to creamed mixture alternately with yogurt. Spoon into prepared muffin tins and bake at 350° F for 15 to 20 minutes.

Makes 24 cupcakes.

—*Linda Ewert*

Carrot Walnut Cupcakes

1 cup oil
¾ cup brown sugar
2 eggs
1 tsp. vanilla
1½ cups flour
1½ tsp. baking soda
½ tsp. salt
1 tsp. cinnamon
½ tsp. nutmeg
2 cups finely shredded carrots
1 cup finely chopped walnuts

Combine oil, sugar, eggs and vanilla in large bowl. Beat until thick. Sift together flour, baking soda, salt, cinnamon and nutmeg and add to creamed ingredients. Stir in carrots and walnuts. Place in prepared muffin tins and bake at 350° F for 20 minutes.

Makes 18 to 20 cupcakes.

—*Anne Sanderson*

Coconut Black Walnut Pound Cake

This is a delicious, moist, heavy cake, equally successful with black or regular walnuts.

2 cups sugar
1 cup oil
4 eggs, beaten
3 cups flour
½ tsp. baking soda
½ tsp. salt
½ tsp. baking powder
1 cup buttermilk
1 cup chopped black walnuts
1 cup flaked coconut
2 tsp. coconut extract

Combine sugar, oil and eggs and beat well. Mix together flour, baking soda, salt and baking powder. Add to sugar mixture alternately with buttermilk, beating well after each addition. Stir in walnuts, coconut and extract. Pour into greased and floured 10-inch bundt pan and bake at 325° F for 65 minutes.

—Dorothy Hollis

Greek Walnut Cake

The honey syrup for this cake can also be used for baklava.

CAKE:
¾ cup oil
½ cup honey
3 eggs
2 tsp. grated orange rind
1 cup flour
1½ tsp. baking powder
½ tsp. cinnamon
¼ tsp. salt
⅛ tsp. nutmeg
⅓ cup milk powder
1½ cups finely chopped
  walnuts
HONEY SYRUP:
1 lemon
1 cup sugar
2" stick cinnamon
2 whole cloves
1 cup honey
1 Tbsp. brandy

To make cake: Beat oil and honey until light — about 5 minutes. Beat in eggs, one at a time. Add orange rind. Sift together all dry ingredients except walnuts. Add to liquid mixture alternately with ¼ cup water. Stir in walnuts. Bake in a greased 9" x 9" pan at 350° F for 35 minutes, or until a toothpick inserted in the centre comes out clean.

To make honey syrup: Juice the lemon, reserving 1½ tsp. of juice. Place the lemon rind in a heavy saucepan with 1 cup water, sugar, cinnamon stick and cloves. Bring to a boil, lower heat and cook without stirring for about 25 minutes, or until 230° F is reached on a candy thermometer. Pick out rind and spices. Stir in lemon juice, honey and brandy. Cool. Makes 2 cups.

—Susan O'Neill

Ruth's Pineapple Cake

"An easy pineapple cake — it was a delicate bronze coming out of the oven. Excellent pineapple flavour," says our Vermont tester.

2 cups flour
1½ cups sugar
2 eggs
2 tsp. baking soda
½ tsp. salt
1 tsp. vanilla
2 cups crushed pineapple,
  undrained
1 cup chopped walnuts

Combine all ingredients and beat until smooth. Pour into greased jelly-roll pan and bake at 325° F for 35 minutes.

—Linda A. Petree

Nutmeg Feather Cake

This is a light-textured yellow cake that calls you back for seconds because it is not too rich.

¼ cup butter
¼ cup shortening
1½ cups sugar
3 eggs, beaten
1 tsp. vanilla
2 cups flour
salt
2 tsp. nutmeg
1 tsp. baking soda
2 tsp. baking powder
1 cup buttermilk

Cream together butter, shortening and sugar. Add eggs and vanilla. Sift together flour, salt, nutmeg, baking soda and baking powder. Add to creamed ingredients alternately with buttermilk. Pour into greased 9" x 13" pan and bake at 350° F for 35 to 40 minutes.

—Doris M. Denicola

October Celebration Cake

"Every cook has his/her trademark — this is mine. Weighing in at just under four pounds, this glorious bit of chocolate and hazelnut heaven was created three years ago to celebrate two Iowa harvests — the first 'Ioa Teritory' harvest gathered in by my great-great-grandfather, Joel Riley Hough, in the fall of 1841 and our own corn and soybean harvest more than 140 years later."

1 cup softened butter
¼ cup shortening
2 cups brown sugar
2 Tbsp. white corn syrup
3 eggs
½ cup sour cream
2 Tbsp. orange liqueur
4 oz. unsweetened
   chocolate, melted
2 oz. German sweetened
   chocolate, melted
2 tsp. baking soda
2 tsp. vanilla
½ tsp. salt
2 cups flour
½ cup plus 2 Tbsp. hot
   coffee
1 cup chopped, roasted
   hazelnuts
CHOCOLATE GLAZE:
½ cup chocolate chips
1 Tbsp. butter
1 Tbsp. milk
1 Tbsp. white corn syrup
½ tsp. vanilla
sliced almonds for garnish

In large bowl, cream together butter, shortening, sugar and corn syrup. Add eggs one at a time, beating well after each addition. Add sour cream, orange liqueur, chocolates, baking soda, vanilla and salt. Beat until well blended. Add flour and coffee alternately, beating well after each addition. Fold in hazelnuts. Pour into greased and floured bundt pan and bake at 325° F for 65 to 70 minutes, or until toothpick inserted deep into cake comes out clean. Cool in pan for 10 minutes, then turn out onto serving plate and cool completely.

Meanwhile, prepare glaze: Measure ingredients (except almonds) into small saucepan and place over medium heat. Bring to a full boil, remove from heat and spoon over cake, allowing glaze to run down the sides. Garnish with almonds.

Serves 16.

—Ellen Ross

Traditional Lithuanian Honey Cake

4 eggs
¾ cup sugar
¾ cup honey
½ cup oil
1 cup milk
3 tsp. baking powder
½ tsp. baking soda
2½ cups flour
1 Tbsp. mixed spices
   (cinnamon, cloves, ginger,
   cardamom

Beat eggs, then add sugar, honey, oil and milk. Sift together baking powder, baking soda, flour and spices, and add to liquid ingredients. Stir to blend. Pour into greased bundt pan, and bake at 350° F for 1 hour.

—Linda Barsauskas

Best Ever Banana Cake

An old favourite, this banana cake adds a broiled caramel topping for a delicious new twist.

½ cup butter
1½ cups sugar
2 eggs, well beaten
1 cup mashed bananas
1 tsp. vanilla
2 cups flour
½ tsp. baking powder
¾ tsp. baking soda
½ tsp. salt
¼ cup sour milk
CARAMEL TOPPING:
⅓ cup coconut or chopped
   nuts
3 Tbsp. butter, melted
½ cup brown sugar
1 Tbsp. cream

Cream butter and sugar together, then beat in eggs, bananas and vanilla. Sift together flour, baking powder, baking soda and salt. Add to creamed mixture alternately with milk, beating well after each addition. Bake in greased and floured 9" x 9" pan at 350° F for 50 to 60 minutes.

Meanwhile, combine topping ingredients. Spread over warm cake in pan and brown under broiler until bubbling.

—Niva Rowan

Blue Ribbon
Spice Cake

"This is my grandmother's recipe. She was the cook at the Toledo Women's Club for many years. I entered this in the Monroe County Fair and it was a first-prize winner. Do not worry about overbeating this cake — the more it is beaten, the better the texture."

1 cup butter
2¼ cups sugar
5 eggs
1 Tbsp. cloves
1 Tbsp. cinnamon
salt
1 tsp. baking soda
1 cup sour milk
3 cups flour

Cream together butter and sugar until fluffy. Add eggs, one at a time, beating well after each addition. Add cloves, cinnamon and salt and beat well. Dissolve baking soda in milk, then add to creamed mixture alternately with flour, beating well. Pour into greased and floured bundt pan and bake at 350° F for 45 to 50 minutes.

—*Evelyn Nofziger*

Russian
Poppy Seed Cake

Loaded with poppy seeds, this is an irresistible cake. All the tasters in Vermont ate more of this cake than they needed and still came back for more.

2 cups poppy seeds
2 cups milk
1 cup honey
1½ cups butter
1 cup sugar
5 eggs, separated
1 tsp. almond extract
1½ cups whole wheat flour
1½ cups white flour
2 tsp. baking powder
½ tsp. salt

Heat poppy seeds, milk and honey to boiling point, then set aside to cool.

Cream together butter and sugar, then add egg yolks and almond extract. Sift together flours, baking powder and salt. Add flour mixture and poppy seed mixture alternately to creamed mixture, beating well. Gently fold in stiffly beaten egg whites. Pour into greased and floured bundt pan. Bake at 350° F for 40 to 50 minutes.

—*Christine A. Lichatz*

Cream Cheese Pound
Cake with Cranberries

For orange rind rich with flavour, dry orange peels (preferably from Mandarin oranges), then grind them. They can be stored in a tightly capped jar or in the freezer.

1 cup butter
½ lb. cream cheese
4 eggs
2 cups brown sugar
1 tsp. vanilla
1 Tbsp. dried orange rind soaked in 1½ Tbsp. lemon juice
2¼ cups flour
1½ tsp. baking powder
1 cup cranberries with ¾ tsp. orange rind

Beat butter and cream cheese until fluffy. Add eggs one at a time, beating until fluffy after each addition. Add sugar and beat well, then add vanilla and orange rind-lemon juice mixture. Sift flour and baking powder together, then fold into creamed mixture. Drop half the batter into bundt pan that has been greased and dusted with brown sugar. Sprinkle liberally with cranberries and top with remaining batter. Bake at 350° F for 60 to 70 minutes.

—*Helen P. Slama*

Blackberry Jam Cake

"This cake is a favourite to take to picnics and cake sales. The flavours of the blackberry jam and bananas blend to produce an exceptionally moist and tasty cake."

1 cup packed brown sugar
½ cup butter
1 cup blackberry jam
1 cup mashed bananas
2 cups flour
¼ tsp. cloves
¼ tsp. cinnamon
¼ tsp. nutmeg
1 tsp. baking powder
1 tsp. baking soda
½ cup buttermilk
2 eggs, beaten
1 cup chopped walnuts

Cream together sugar and butter. Add jam and bananas and mix well. Sift flour with cloves, cinnamon, nutmeg and baking powder. Dissolve baking soda in buttermilk. Add flour mixture alternately with buttermilk to creamed mixture, beginning and ending with flour. Mix well, add eggs and mix again. Add walnuts. Pour into greased and floured 9" x 13" baking pan and bake at 350° F for 40 minutes.

—*James Mottern*

Southern Spicy Gingerbread

Served warm with freshly made applesauce or whipped cream, this gingerbread is hard to beat.

2 eggs
¾ cup brown sugar
¾ cup molasses
¾ cup melted shortening
2½ cups flour
2 tsp. baking soda
2 tsp. ginger
2 tsp. cinnamon
½ tsp. cloves
½ tsp. nutmeg
½ tsp. baking powder

Beat eggs, then add sugar, molasses and shortening. Sift together dry ingredients, then add to creamed mixture. Stir in 1 cup boiling water. Pour cake into greased 9" x 13" pan and bake at 350° F for 30 to 40 minutes.

—*Carole Creswell*

Oatmeal Cake

"This cake is the favourite at all our Hill gatherings and of our friends from out of town."

1½ cups boiling water
1 cup oats
1 cup brown sugar
1 cup white sugar
½ cup shortening
2 eggs
1½ cups flour
1 tsp. salt
1 tsp. baking powder
1 tsp. baking soda

Pour boiling water over oats and let stand for 20 minutes. Cream together sugars and shortening, then beat in eggs, one at a time. Combine dry ingredients and add alternately with oats to creamed mixture. Bake in greased bundt pan at 350° F for 35 minutes.

—*Patricia DeVelder*

Coconut Carrot Cake

2 cups flour
2½ tsp. baking soda
1½ tsp. cinnamon
2 tsp. salt
1 cup oil
2 cups sugar
3 eggs
1 cup crushed pineapple
2 cups grated carrots
1½ cups grated coconut
½ cup chopped nuts

Mix together flour, baking soda, cinnamon and salt. Beat together oil, sugar and eggs thoroughly, then add flour mixture and beat until smooth. Fold in pineapple, carrots, coconut and nuts. Pour into a greased 9" x 13" baking pan and bake at 350° F for 50 to 60 minutes. Frost with Coconut Cream Frosting (page 502).

—Paddi Caldwell

Rhubarb Cake

½ cup butter
1½ cups brown sugar
1 egg
1 tsp. baking soda
1 cup buttermilk
2 cups flour
2 cups chopped rhubarb
1 tsp. vanilla
1 tsp. cinnamon
¼ tsp. cloves
TOPPING:
½ cup sugar
1 tsp. cinnamon
1 Tbsp. butter

Cream together butter, sugar and egg. Dissolve baking soda in buttermilk. Combine flour, rhubarb, vanilla, cinnamon and cloves. Add buttermilk and flour mixture to creamed ingredients and stir until just mixed. Pour into greased 9" x 9" pan.

Combine topping ingredients and sprinkle over cake. Bake at 350° F for 40 to 45 minutes.

—Annemarie Berryman

Double Chocolate Zucchini Cake

A great way to get zucchini into zucchini haters, this cake improves in flavour if allowed to sit for a day before it is eaten.

3 cups flour
1½ tsp. baking powder
1½ tsp. cinnamon
1¼ tsp. salt
1 tsp. baking soda
⅛ tsp. cloves
1½ cups oil
2⅓ cups packed brown sugar
4 eggs
2 oz. unsweetened chocolate, melted
3 zucchini, grated
1 cup chocolate chips
1 cup chopped nuts

Combine flour, baking powder, cinnamon, salt, baking soda and cloves and set aside. Beat together oil and sugar, then add eggs, one at a time, beating well after each addition. Gradually beat in melted chocolate, then dry ingredients. Beat until smooth. Fold in zucchini, chocolate chips and nuts. Pour into greased and floured bundt pan and bake at 350° F for 1 hour 20 minutes. Frost with Chocolate Cake Glaze (page 502).

—Debra J. Eddy

Crusty Blueberry Batter Cake

"Although originally made by my grandmother, my mother deserves the credit for this cake. It was she who figured out the proper measurements from my grandmother's 'two handfuls of this and a pinch of that.' This cake has a crisp, sweet top crust, with a delicious moist cake layer and, best of all, a sweet, thickened layer of blueberries."

2 cups blueberries
juice of ½ lemon
1¾ cups sugar
3 Tbsp. butter
1 cup flour
1 tsp. baking powder
¼ tsp. salt
½ cup milk
salt
1 Tbsp. cornstarch

Grease a 9" x 13" pan and line with blueberries. Sprinkle with lemon juice. Cream together ¾ cup sugar and butter. Sift together flour, baking powder and ¼ tsp. salt. Add milk, alternating with flour, to creamed mixture. Pour evenly over berries — do not mix berries into batter. Combine remaining 1 cup sugar with salt and cornstarch and sprinkle over batter. Pour 1 cup boiling water over all.

Bake at 375° F for 1 hour. Serve cold from pan.

—J.L. Moorehouse

Tiger Cake

This cake combines with great success the flavours of chocolate and orange. It is a cake that can be made in a hurry and served simply sprinkled with confectioners' sugar.

½ cup butter
1 tsp. salt
½ tsp. vanilla
1¼ cups sugar
2 eggs
2½ tsp. baking powder
2 cups flour
⅔ cup milk
1 oz. unsweetened chocolate
  or 3 Tbsp. cocoa
2 Tbsp. grated orange rind

Cream together butter, salt, vanilla and sugar, then add eggs, one at a time, beating well. Sift together dry ingredients and add to creamed mixture alternately with milk. Divide batter in half.

Melt chocolate (or dissolve cocoa in 2 Tbsp. water) and add to half of batter. Add orange rind to other half. Pour orange batter into greased 9" x 9" pan. Pour chocolate batter on top and cut through with a knife, just enough to create a marbled effect. Bake at 350° F for 30 minutes. Frost with Orange Frosting (page 502).

—Donna Parker

Pumpkin Bundt Cake

Our Camden East tester says, "This cake will become a family favourite in our house. It mixes up fast and is a moist, lightly spiced cake."

3 cups flour
2 tsp. baking soda
2 tsp. baking powder
3 tsp. cinnamon
1 tsp. salt
4 eggs, beaten
2 cups sugar
1¼ cups oil
2 cups cooked, mashed
  pumpkin
½ cup chopped pecans
½ cup chocolate chips

Sift flour, baking soda, baking powder, cinnamon and salt together twice. Beat eggs and sugar together. Add oil and pumpkin, then blend in flour mixture. Fold in pecans and chocolate chips. Bake in greased and floured bundt pan at 350° F for 60 minutes. Let cool in pan for 10 minutes, then turn out onto cooling rack.

—Gladys Sykes

Sweet Potato Cake

½ cup shortening
1 cup sugar
2 eggs
1 cup cooked, mashed sweet
   potato
2 cups flour
½ tsp. salt
2 tsp. baking powder
¼ tsp. baking soda
¼ tsp. cloves
½ tsp. cinnamon
½ tsp. nutmeg
½ cup milk
½ cup chopped nuts

Cream together shortening and sugar, then add eggs, beating after each addition. Add sweet potato. Sift together flour, salt, baking powder, baking soda, cloves, cinnamon and nutmeg. Add to creamed mixture alternately with milk. Fold in nuts. Bake in greased bundt pan at 350° F for 45 to 50 minutes.

—*Betty Hay*

Pumpkin Yogurt Cake

"Last year I had an extraordinarily good crop of pumpkins, and every day for a week, I adapted recipes to use pumpkin. This one was a definite success."

2½ cups flour
1 tsp. baking soda
½ tsp. cinnamon
½ tsp. ginger
½ cup butter
1 cup sugar
2 eggs
1 cup yogurt
1 cup cooked, mashed
   pumpkin

Combine flour, baking soda, cinnamon and ginger. Melt butter, then stir in sugar and eggs, beating well. Add flour mixture and yogurt and pumpkin alternately. Mix well. Pour into 2 greased 9-inch cake pans and bake at 350° F for 30 to 35 minutes. Frost with Vanilla Butter Frosting (page 502).

—*Marcia D. Powers*

Sour Cream Chocolate Cake

This cake has a really good sweet-and-sour taste complemented by a dense texture.

3 oz. semisweet chocolate
2 Tbsp. butter
3 eggs, separated
1½ cups sugar
1 cup sour cream
1 cup flour minus 2 Tbsp.

Melt chocolate in double boiler, then add butter. Beat egg whites with 1 cup sugar until peaks hold their shape, then set aside. Beat yolks with remaining ½ cup sugar until thick. Fold chocolate and sour cream into yolks. Alternately, one third at a time, fold egg whites and flour into chocolate mixture, mixing only until smooth.

Line bottom of two 8"-round cake pans with waxed paper, then butter bottom and sides and flour lightly. Divide batter between pans and bake at 325° F for 25 minutes. Cool briefly in pans, then invert onto cooling rack. Frost with Chocolate Cream Frosting (page 502).

—*Bobbi Hobbs*

Lincoln's Favourite Cake

"This recipe is from my grandmother's cookbook. The story she wrote along with it is this: 'Long ago, a certain French caterer in Lexington, Kentucky, made a wonderful white cake in honour of his countryman, Lafayette, who visited the city. The snow-white cake was beautifully decorated with coloured sugar. The recipe for this famous cake originated in the household of Mary Todd, who later made the cake for Abraham Lincoln.' Whether or not the recipe's history is accurate, this is definitely the best white cake I have ever eaten."

1 cup butter
2 cups sugar
3 cups flour
3 tsp. baking powder
1 cup milk
1 tsp. vanilla
1 cup chopped blanched
 almonds, floured
6 egg whites
¼ tsp. salt

Lightly cream together butter and sugar. Sift together flour and baking powder and add to creamed mixture alternately with milk. Add vanilla and nuts. Beat egg whites with salt until stiff, then fold into batter. Pour into two 9"-round cake pans. Bake at 350° F for 35 minutes.

—Penny Fetter

Old Saratoga County House Fruit Cake

Producing a heavy, dense cake, strong with molasses flavour, this recipe came to the contributor from a former cook at the Saratoga County House, Saratoga Springs, New York.

1 cup sugar
1 cup shortening
2 eggs, lightly beaten
2¼ cups dark molasses
1 rounded Tbsp. baking soda
5 cups flour, sifted several
 times
½ tsp. salt
1 tsp. cinnamon
1 tsp. cloves
½ tsp. nutmeg
1 tsp. allspice
1 cup raisins
4 cups chopped apples

Cream together sugar and shortening. Beat in eggs and 2 cups molasses. Dissolve baking soda in remaining ¼ cup molasses, then stir into sugar mixture. Sift flour, salt, cinnamon, cloves, nutmeg and allspice together, then stir into creamed mixture. Fold in raisins and apples. Spoon into well-greased bundt pan and bake at 275° F for 1½ hours or until done.

—Kenneth P. Sherman

Chocolate Brownie Cake

"A friend, knowing my love of chocolate, created this cake for my birthday a few years ago — it's a chocolate-lover's dream come true."

6 oz. unsweetened chocolate
¾ cup butter, softened
2¼ cups sugar
4 eggs
1 tsp. vanilla
2 cups flour
1½ tsp. baking powder
¼ tsp. salt
1½ cups milk

Melt chocolate and set aside to cool. Cream together butter and sugar until light and fluffy. Beat in eggs, one at a time, then beat in chocolate and vanilla. Sift flour, baking powder and salt together, then add to creamed mixture alternately with milk. Grease and flour three 9-inch cake pans and divide batter among them. Bake at 350° F for 25 to 30 minutes.

—Bobbie Nelson

Prize Date & Orange Cake

"This was one of my favourite cakes when my mother used to make it. It is delicious and moist. I glaze the cake with ½ cup sugar dissolved in the juice of one orange."

½ cup butter
½ cup sugar
½ cup chopped walnuts
1 cup chopped dates
rind of 1 orange, grated
2 cups flour
1 tsp. baking powder
1 cup sour milk
1 tsp. baking soda, dissolved in 1 tsp. warm water

Cream together butter and sugar. Fold in nuts, dates and orange rind. Sift together flour and baking powder and add to creamed mixture alternately with milk. Stir in dissolved baking soda. Bake in greased bundt pan at 325° F for 40 minutes.

—Mrs. John R. Stanley

Applesauce Cake

"This is my grandmother's recipe — it takes me back to my visits to her house, where the kitchen was filled with the smell of cinnamon and cloves."

1 cup sugar
½ cup butter
1 egg
1 cup applesauce
1 tsp. baking soda
1 cup flour
salt
1 tsp. cinnamon
1 tsp. allspice
1 cup raisins
1 cup chopped walnuts

Cream together sugar and butter, then beat in egg. Mix together applesauce and baking soda. Sift together flour, salt, cinnamon and allspice. Add applesauce and dry ingredients alternately, in thirds, to creamed mixture. Fold in raisins and nuts. Pour into greased loaf pan and bake at 375° for 50 to 60 minutes.

—Jeanne Reitz

Cocoa Applesauce Cake

"I received this recipe from my German mother-in-law. It had been in her family for years, and I am passing it on to mine. If you can keep eager eaters away from it, this cake tastes better after ageing for three or four days."

1 cup sugar
½ cup shortening
1½ cups applesauce
2 cups flour
2 tsp. baking soda
3 Tbsp. cocoa
1 tsp. cinnamon
¼ tsp. cloves
pinch nutmeg
pinch allspice
pinch salt
1 cup chopped pecans

Cream together sugar and shortening, then stir in applesauce. Sift together flour, baking soda, cocoa, cinnamon, cloves, nutmeg, allspice and salt. Add to creamed mixture, mix well, then fold in nuts. Bake in greased bundt pan at 350° F for 50 to 60 minutes.

—Frances Slater

Upside-Down Macaroon Cake

⅓ cup butter
2 cups sugar
3 eggs, separated
1¼ cups milk
1 cup flour
1 tsp. baking powder
coconut
2 Tbsp. cornstarch
salt
1 tsp. vanilla

Cream together butter and ½ cup sugar. Add 2 egg yolks, ½ cup milk, flour and baking powder and mix well. Place in two 8-inch cake pans lined with waxed paper. Beat 3 egg whites with 1 cup sugar until stiff and glossy. Spread over cakes and sprinkle with coconut. Bake at 350° F for 20 to 30 minutes, or until golden brown.

Meanwhile, prepare filling: Combine remaining ½ cup sugar, cornstarch, salt, remaining egg yolk and vanilla in heavy pot. Add remaining milk slowly while cooking over medium heat. Cook until thickened. Spread as filling between cooled cake layers.

—Jane Matthews

Gâteau Marguerite

"This recipe originated in a Belgian convent. It is dense and rich — just dust with icing sugar to serve." Our Camden East tester says this is one of the three best cakes he has ever eaten.

1 cup butter
1¼ cups sugar
¼ tsp. salt
juice of 1 lemon
4-5 eggs, separated
3 cups flour
1 Tbsp. baking powder
8 oz. semisweet chocolate, chopped
2 cups ground hazelnuts

Beat together butter, sugar, salt, lemon juice and egg yolks until creamy. Stir in flour, baking powder, chocolate and nuts. Beat egg whites until stiff, then gently fold into batter. Pour into well-greased and floured 9½-inch springform pan. Bake at 350° F for 1 to 1½ hours, or until toothpick inserted in middle comes out clean.

—Trudi Keillor

Mama's Johnny Cake

"My grandmother lived in a grand house in Toronto and entertained a great deal. This recipe was served often, even to the likes of Mrs. Timothy Eaton Senior, who summoned my grandmother's cook for the recipe."

¼ cup butter
1 cup sugar
2 eggs, beaten
1 cup flour
3 tsp. baking powder
1 cup cornmeal
2 Tbsp. beef **or** chicken stock
1 cup milk

Cream butter then blend in sugar and eggs. In another bowl, sift together flour and baking powder, then stir in cornmeal. Add stock to milk. Mix dry ingredients and milk mixture alternately into butter-sugar mixture.

Pour into a 9" x 9" pan and bake at 375° F for 30 to 40 minutes. Serve warm as an alternative to rolls or bread.

—Mary Matear

Grandma Garvey's Swedish Meringue Cake

½ cup butter
½ cup sugar
4 eggs, separated
1 cup plus 2 Tbsp. flour
2 tsp. baking powder
⅓ cup milk
1 tsp. vanilla
¼ tsp. cream of tartar
1 cup sugar
¾ cup finely chopped walnuts
1 cup heavy cream
2 Tbsp. powdered sugar

Cream together butter and sugar. Add egg yolks, one at a time, beating well after each addition. Combine flour with baking powder, and milk with vanilla. Add alternately to creamed mixture and mix well. Spread evenly in two greased 8"-round cake pans.

Beat egg whites and cream of tartar until frothy. Add sugar very slowly, continuing to beat until meringue holds stiff peaks. Spread evenly over batter. Top one of the pans with nuts.

Bake at 300° F for 40 minutes, or until meringue starts to brown. Whip together cream and powdered sugar. Using the nut-topped cake as the bottom layer, stack the cakes, with whipped cream between the layers.

—Diane Milan

Coconut Cream Frosting

1 cup coconut
3 oz. cream cheese
¼ cup butter
3 cups icing sugar
1 Tbsp. milk
½ tsp. vanilla

Toast coconut and cool. Cream cheese with butter, then add sugar, milk and vanilla. Beat until smooth, then stir in half the coconut. Frost cake and top with remaining coconut.

Frosts a 9" x 13" cake.

—Paddi Caldwell

Chocolate Cake Glaze

1 cup icing sugar
1 Tbsp. butter, melted
salt
2 Tbsp. corn syrup
½ tsp. vanilla
1 oz. semisweet chocolate curls

Beat together sugar, butter and salt, then add corn syrup, 2 Tbsp. water and vanilla, stirring until smooth. Garnish cake with chocolate curls after spreading with glaze.

Frosts a bundt cake.

—Debra J. Eddy

Chocolate Cream Frosting

5 oz. semisweet chocolate
½ cup sugar
3 eggs
2 Tbsp. coffee liqueur
1 cup softened butter

Melt chocolate and let cool. Mix sugar and eggs in top of double boiler and cook, stirring constantly, until thickened. Remove from heat and pour into glass or metal bowl. Fold in chocolate and coffee liqueur, then beat in butter in chunks until smooth. Chill.

Frosts a 2-layer cake.

—Bobbi Hobbs

Orange Frosting

1 egg yolk, beaten
3 Tbsp. butter
2 cups icing sugar
3 Tbsp. orange juice
1 tsp. grated orange rind
salt

Combine all ingredients and beat well.

Frosts a 9" x 9" cake.

—Donna Parker

Vanilla Butter Frosting

4 Tbsp. softened butter
2 Tbsp. yogurt
1 tsp. vanilla
2 cups icing sugar

Beat butter until light and fluffy, then add remaining ingredients. Beat well.

Frosts a 2-layer cake.

—Marcia D. Powers

Bohemian Kolache

"Bohemia forms the westernmost part of Czechoslovakia. This is my grandmother's recipe. She lived in Wilson, Kansas, which is known as the Czech capital of Kansas."

1 pkg. yeast
⅓ cup plus 1 tsp. sugar
¾ cup milk, scalded
⅓ cup shortening
½ tsp. salt
½ tsp. grated lemon peel
¼ tsp. mace **or** nutmeg
3¼-3½ cups flour
2 eggs, beaten
1 lb. dried apricots **or** prunes
sugar
1 Tbsp. lemon juice

Dissolve yeast in ¼ cup warm water, then add 1 tsp. sugar. Combine milk, ⅓ cup sugar, shortening, salt, lemon peel and mace. Cool, then stir in 1 cup flour. Beat vigorously for 2 minutes, then add yeast and eggs and beat well. Add enough flour to make a soft dough. Turn out on a floured board and knead for 5 minutes, or until smooth and elastic, kneading in ⅓ to ½ cup flour.

Place dough in greased bowl, cover and let rise for 1 hour. Punch down and divide in half. Cover and let rise for 10 minutes. Shape each half into 3-inch balls. Place on cookie sheet, until doubled — about 45 minutes.

Prepare filling: Cover apricots or prunes with water and cook until soft. Drain water and grind fruit. If using apricots, add sugar to taste and lemon juice.

Make depressions in dough and place filling in each ball. Bake at 350° F for 15 to 20 minutes.

—Joan McKeegan

Mrs. Rockensuess' Brünen Spätzle

"The following is an old German recipe given to my great-grandmother and passed on to me. 'Brünen' means well or spring, and 'spätzle' means a dough ball from which small pieces are cut. The result is a slightly sweet pastry, best eaten when fresh, that truly melts in your mouth."

¼ cup evaporated milk
2 Tbsp. yeast
1 Tbsp. sugar
3 cups flour
½ cup butter
½ tsp. salt
3 eggs
1 tsp. vanilla
½ cup sugar
1 cup chopped nuts

Combine milk with ¼ cup hot water. When lukewarm, add yeast and sugar, and stir to dissolve. Using pastry blender, combine 1½ cups flour with butter and salt. Combine flour and yeast mixture and let stand 20 minutes. Beat eggs lightly and add vanilla. Add to the flour-yeast mixture. Add remaining flour and combine well. Tie dough in a cheesecloth bag, or towel sprinkled with flour, leaving enough room for expansion, and place in a bowl or pail of cool water (this is called water-proofing). Bag should rise to the top in about an hour. Drain and turn out onto a platter.

Break off pieces the size of an egg, roll into "fingers" and twist into figure 8's. Push into sugar and then into nuts. Place on greased cookie sheet, cover and let rise 15 minutes in a warm place. Bake at 375° F for 12 to 15 minutes.

—Amy Kegel

Honey Nut Bread

The cottage cheese adds an interesting dimension to this exceptionally moist and flavourful bread.

3 cups white flour
2 Tbsp. yeast
1 tsp. salt
1 cup cottage cheese
4 Tbsp. butter
½ cup honey
2 eggs
2-2½ cups whole wheat flour
½ cup rolled oats
⅔ cup chopped walnuts

In a large bowl, mix 2 cups white flour, yeast and salt. Heat 1 cup water, cottage cheese, butter and honey in a saucepan until just warm. Add to flour mixture. Beat in eggs. Stir in whole wheat flour, oats and nuts. Add remaining white flour. On a floured surface, knead dough until smooth and elastic, adding more white flour if dough is sticky. Let dough rise in a warm place until it has doubled in size — about 1 hour.

Punch down dough and divide into thirds. Shape loaves and place in greased bread pans. Let rise until doubled — about half an hour. Bake at 350° F for 45 minutes, or until the loaf sounds hollow when tapped.

Makes 3 loaves.

—Shirley Miller

Ethereal Puffs

"I have been baking these muffin-shaped rolls for 20 years. Always very light in texture, they go well with any lunch or dinner menu."

1 Tbsp. yeast
1⅓ cups sifted flour plus 1 cup flour
¼ tsp. baking soda
1 cup creamed cottage cheese
½ tsp. grated onion
1 Tbsp. butter
1 tsp. salt
2 Tbsp. sugar
1 tsp. sesame seeds
1 egg
2 Tbsp. untoasted wheat germ

Mix together yeast, sifted flour and baking soda in a large bowl. In a saucepan, heat ¼ cup water, cottage cheese, onion, butter, salt, sugar and sesame seeds. After butter has melted and cheese mixture feels warm, add egg and wheat germ. Add to yeast-flour mixture. Using electric mixer, beat 30 seconds on low, then 3 minutes on high. Stir in remaining flour with a wooden spoon.

Place in a well-greased bowl, turning over to grease top. Cover and let rise 1½ hours or until doubled in size. Beat down dough. Pour into 12 greased muffin tins. Cover and let rise for 40 minutes. Bake at 400° F for 12 to 15 minutes. Cool in muffin tins for 5 minutes before removing to a rack.

Makes 12 rolls.

—Janet E. Stanford

Raisin Pumpernickel Bread

We tested this recipe largely because it came to us beautifully hand lettered, but once we tasted the bread, it stood on its own merits.

1 tsp. honey
2 Tbsp. yeast
2 Tbsp. oil
½ cup molasses
2 tsp. salt
2 tsp. fennel seeds
3 tsp. caraway seeds
2½ cups white flour
2 cups whole wheat flour
½ cup cornmeal
1½ cups raisins
2 cups rye flour
melted butter
1 egg white

In a large bowl, dissolve honey in ½ cup warm water and add yeast. When yeast is foamy, add 2 cups warm water, oil, molasses, salt, fennel and caraway seeds, white flour and whole wheat flour. Beat for at least 5 minutes with a wooden spoon. Sprinkle cornmeal, raisins and rye flour over the dough and beat well to combine.

Turn dough out onto a floured board and knead until smooth. Extra white flour may be added but use restraint, as too much flour will make the bread dry. The stickiness disappears after the dough rises. Let rise in an oiled bowl covered with a damp cloth for 1 hour. Punch down and let rise a second time for 30 minutes. Prepare two cookie sheets by greasing and dusting with cornmeal. Punch dough down, knead a bit and cut in half. Let rise 15 minutes. Shape into 2 ovals, place on cookie sheets, slash tops diagonally and brush with melted butter. Let rise again until almost doubled.

Bake at 350° F for 40 minutes. After 30 minutes, loaves may be glazed with egg white beaten with 1 Tbsp. water.

—Michael & Dyan Walters

Graham Bread

We found this bread to be light, slightly sweet and very aromatic. It was delicious served warm and was still moist and flavourful the next day.

13-oz. can evaporated milk
¼ cup melted butter
3 Tbsp. sugar
1 Tbsp. salt
1 pkg. yeast
3 cups medium graham flour
5-6 cups white flour

Combine milk with equal amount hot water, butter, sugar and salt and let stand until lukewarm.

Dissolve yeast in ½ cup warm water and add to milk mixture. Beat in graham flour with a wooden spoon, then add enough white flour to make a smooth dough.

Turn out onto floured board and knead, adding additional flour as needed to make a smooth, elastic dough. Place in greased bowl, cover, and let rise until doubled — about 1 hour. Turn out, knead briefly, then form into 2 large loaves. Place in greased bread pans and let rise, covered, until dough reaches the top of the pans. Bake at 375° F for 1 hour.

Makes 3 loaves.

—Laurabel Miller

Grandma Beckstead's Three-Day Buns

"My grandmother's house always smelled of these buns in some degree of progress. They were covered with a gingham tea towel and served with lots of fresh butter and jam."

1 tsp. sugar
1 Tbsp. yeast
7 cups flour
¾ cup sugar
1 egg
1 tsp. salt
½ cup oil

Day 1, a.m.: In a large bowl, dissolve 1 tsp. sugar in ½ cup cold water. Sprinkle yeast over and let stand until evening. Add 1 cup of flour and 2 cups of water. Mix well and let stand overnight.

Day 2, a.m.: Mix together ¾ cup sugar, egg, salt, oil and yeast mixture. Stir in remaining flour, adding more if dough is too sticky. Knead 10 minutes on a floured board, adding flour as needed. Put in a greased bowl and let stand. In evening, punch down, shape into small balls and put in greased pans. Cover and let stand overnight. Buns will almost triple in size.

Day 3, a.m.: Brush tops with butter. Bake at 350° F for approximately 15 minutes.

Yield 4-5½ dozen buns.

—Donna Beckstead

Lemon Cheese Crown

"This is a braided bread which is beautiful to look at. I have often served it with a delicate soup such as Cream of Almond Soup (page 87). The combination of cardamom, lemon and Swiss cheese has a very pleasing 'bite' to it."

3-4 cups flour
1 Tbsp. yeast
2 tsp. lemon peel
1 tsp. ground cardamom
1 cup milk
⅓ cup sugar
¼ cup butter
½ tsp. salt
1 cup finely grated Swiss
   cheese
1 egg
1 egg yolk
1 beaten egg white
1 Tbsp. sugar
1 Tbsp. sliced almonds

In a large bowl, combine 1½ cups flour, yeast, lemon peel and cardamom. In a saucepan heat milk, sugar, butter and salt just until warm and butter melts. Add to flour mixture. Add cheese, egg and yolk. Beat very well until the mixture is stretchy. Using a spoon, stir in as much of the remaining flour as possible. Knead in enough flour to make a stiff dough. Knead for 6-8 minutes. Shape into a ball and let rise till doubled in size. Punch down.

Make two balls, one with ⅔ of the dough and one with ⅓ of the dough. Cover and let rest for 10 minutes. Divide big ball into three loose strands and roll into strips. Braid. Place on a greased sheet to form a circle. Repeat with the smaller piece of dough to form three 18-inch-long ropes. Place second braid on top of first. Seal ends together. Cover and let rise until doubled — about 1 hour. Brush with egg white, sprinkle with 1 Tbsp. sugar. Sprinkle almonds on top. Bake at 350° F for 35 to 40 minutes, or until done. Cover the loaf with foil after about 20 minutes to prevent overbrowning.

—Maureen Marcotte

Dinner Rolls

"My attempts at different recipes for rolls always produced heavy, albino hockey pucks until a friend of mine taught me how to make these buns." These rolls are light and moist and make a perfect accompaniment to any meal, especially when warm and fresh from the oven.

2⅔ cups milk
6 Tbsp. butter
8 Tbsp. sugar
2 Tbsp. yeast
7 cups bread flour
2 eggs **or** ⅓ cup plain yogurt
1 Tbsp. salt

Scald milk, add butter and sugar and cool to lukewarm. Add yeast and let stand for 20 minutes in a warm place. Add 3 cups flour and eggs or yogurt and beat well. Add salt and remaining flour. Dough should be quite elastic and only slightly sticky to the touch. Cover and let rise until doubled. Stir down and let rise for another 45 minutes.

On a well-floured surface, work ¼ of the dough at a time. Knead gently just until dough is not sticky. Roll to ¾" thickness and cut into 3" circles. Place buns on greased cookie sheet. Rework trimmings of dough into the next quarter batch. Let rise for 1 hour. Bake at 400° F for 12 to 15 minutes.

Rolls may be brushed gently with melted butter just before baking, if desired. These make great hamburger buns.

Makes 5 to 6 dozen rolls.

—Jeannette McQuaid

Special Swedish Rye Bread

This bread is about as nutritious as a bread can get, as it uses both rye flour and bran-wheat cereal, as well as carrots. It is still a light bread, however, because of the white flour.

2 Tbsp. yeast
½ tsp. sugar
¼ tsp. ginger
½ cup molasses
¼ cup brown sugar
¼ cup oil
½ cup nonfat milk powder
2 tsp. (or less) salt
½ cup finely shredded carrots
2 Tbsp. grated orange peel
3 cups rye flour
6½ cups unbleached white flour
1½ cups bran-wheat cereal

Dissolve yeast in ½ cup warm water. Add sugar and ginger and let stand 3 minutes. In a large bowl, combine 3 cups hot water with molasses, brown sugar, oil, milk powder, salt, carrots and orange peel. When cooled to lukewarm, add yeast mixture, rye flour, 3 cups white flour and cereal. Blend at low speed on mixer or by hand. Stir in remaining flour. Dough will be soft and sticky.

Turn out onto a floured board and knead about 10 minutes, incorporating another 1 to 2 cups white flour. Place dough in a greased bowl and let rise in a warm place until doubled. Punch down and divide into thirds. Shape into loaves and place in 3 greased loaf pans. Let rise until doubled. Bake at 350° F for 40 to 45 minutes.

Makes 3 loaves.

—Judy Mueller

Stout Bread

"When I first tasted muesli, a Swiss style breakfast cereal, I wanted to incorporate it into a bread recipe. This is the result — a dark flavourful bread full of texture. My husband brews his own beer and stout. This is what is used, including the rich mineral sediment in the bottom of the bottle, but commercial stouts will work too."

4 pkgs. yeast
2 Tbsp. sugar
12 oz. stout
1 cup molasses
½ cup shortening
2 tsp. salt
¼ cup dill seed
rind of 3 oranges, grated
2 eggs, beaten
4-5 cups whole wheat flour
4-5 cups white flour
2 cups muesli

Dissolve yeast and sugar in 1 cup lukewarm water. Gently heat stout, ½ cup water, molasses and shortening to 140° F. Pour into large mixing bowl with salt, dill and orange rind. Add eggs, yeast mixture and ⅓ of the flour. Mix on medium speed of electric mixer for 5 minutes.

Process muesli in blender, then add to dough. Stir in enough flour to make a smooth dough. Knead on floured surface for at least 5 minutes, adding flour as needed to make a smooth elastic dough.

Place in large, greased bowl, cover and let rise until doubled — 1 to 2 hours. Punch down and let rest for 5 minutes. With greased hands, knead again for 5 minutes.

Divide dough into thirds, form into loaves and place in greased loaf pans. Cover and let rise until doubled — 1 hour. Bake at 400° F for 10 minutes, lower heat to 350° and bake for 30 minutes longer.

Makes 3 loaves.

—Christine Amy-Peterson

Janne's Dark Rye Bread

"I got this recipe from a Danish fellow student when I was at college. It is a dense European rye bread, full of whole-grain flavour and is best sliced very thinly."

¼ cup sugar
½ cup plus 1 Tbsp. strong coffee
¼ cup softened butter
1½ cups bran
½ cup wheat germ
¼ cup molasses
2 tsp. salt
2½ tsp. sugar
2 Tbsp. yeast
3 cups rye flour
2½-3 cups unbleached white flour
½ tsp. sugar
1 egg white

Place sugar in small, heavy pot and heat, stirring constantly, over medium heat until sugar is melted and dark golden brown. Remove from heat, add ½ cup coffee and return to heat. Cook, stirring constantly, until mixture is blended. Remove from heat.

Place 1¾ cups boiling water in large bowl. Add butter and stir until melted. Add bran, wheat germ, molasses, sugar-coffee mixture and salt. Cool to lukewarm.

Dissolve 2 tsp. sugar in ½ cup warm water. Add yeast and let stand for 10 minutes. Stir into lukewarm mixture, along with rye flour. Beat well, then gradually add white flour until a ball forms.

Knead on floured surface for 10 minutes, adding flour as needed to make a firm dough. Cover and let rise until doubled — about 1½ hours. Punch down and form into 2 loaves. Cover and let rise until doubled — about 45 minutes.

Combine remaining 1 Tbsp. coffee, remaining ½ tsp. sugar and egg white. Brush over loaves. Bake at 375° F for 45 minutes, brushing twice more with glaze.

Makes 2 loaves.

—Heidi Juul

Maple Oatmeal Bread

This is a very good farmers' market bread that is easy to prepare. It also makes wonderful toast.

¼ cup butter
1½ cups old-fashioned oats
½ cup maple syrup
2 tsp. salt
1 Tbsp. yeast
1 Tbsp. brown sugar
6-8 cups unbleached white flour

In a large bowl, combine butter, oats, maple syrup and salt. Pour 2 cups of boiling water over and stir. In a small bowl, mix yeast and brown sugar with ½ cup warm water. Set small bowl on top of ingredients in large bowl — it keeps the yeast warm and prevents spills as yeast foams up. After yeast has doubled and oat mixture has cooled to warm, mix the two. Add flour, 2 cups at a time, and beat well until it is all incorporated.

Knead until dough is elastic and not sticky. Allow to rise in a warm place for 1 hour. Punch down, knead briefly and divide dough in half. Shape loaves and place in greased loaf pans. Let rise for another 30 to 45 minutes. Bake at 350° F for 30 to 45 minutes, or until golden brown.

Makes 2 loaves.

—Mary Jirik

Apple Cider Bread

"The sweetness in this bread comes from the apple cider. Allow 4 to 5 hours to complete this recipe — it's worth the wait!" It rises beautifully, although the recipe calls for only whole wheat flour.

1½ Tbsp. yeast
3¼ cups warm apple cider (85°-105° F)
7-9 cups whole wheat flour
1 Tbsp. salt
¼ cup oil **or** melted butter
1½ Tbsp. cinnamon

Dissolve yeast in warm cider. Stir in 3 to 4 cups whole wheat flour to make a thick batter. Beat well with spoon. Cover loosely, and let rise for 1 hour. Stir in salt, oil and cinnamon. Mix in additional flour until dough comes away from sides of bowl.

Knead on floured board until dough is smooth — about 15 minutes. Use more flour as needed to keep dough from sticking to the board. Cover and let rise for 50 minutes. Punch down. Cover and let rise for 40 minutes. Punch down.

Shape into two loaves and place in two greased loaf pans. Let rise for 20 minutes, or until doubled. Bake in a preheated 350° F oven for 40 minutes to 1 hour. Remove from pans and let cool, or enjoy right away.

Makes 2 loaves.

—Judy Sheppard-Segal

Black Pepper Cheese Bread

"I remember coming home from school just as my mother was taking these loaves from the oven. I would have the 'heel' of the loaf with butter and a cool mug of buttermilk. We used to put on so much butter that we were sent outside to sit on the step to prevent drips on the floor."

½ tsp. dry mustard
6-6½ cups flour
1 Tbsp. salt
3 tsp. pepper
1¾ cups warm milk
2 Tbsp. active dry yeast
2 Tbsp. sugar
2 Tbsp. vegetable oil
2 large eggs
1½ cups grated Cheddar
   cheese

Combine mustard and ½ tsp. warm water. Set aside for 10 minutes to develop flavour. Combine 3 cups flour with salt and 2 tsp. pepper. Set aside.

Place warm milk and yeast in large bowl. Let stand for 10 minutes. Stir well and add sugar, oil, eggs and mustard-water mixture. Stir. Gradually beat in the flour mixture. Beat well. Stir in cheese. Stir in enough of the remaining flour to make a stiff dough.

Turn out onto a floured board and knead until smooth and elastic (about 10 minutes), adding more flour as needed. Place in a lightly greased bowl, turning to grease the top. Cover and let rise in a warm place until doubled in bulk — about 1 hour. Punch down and form into 2 loaves. Place each in a greased 9" x 5" x 3" loaf pan and cover. Let rise until doubled. Brush the loaves with milk, sprinkle with the remaining 1 tsp. of black pepper. Bake at 375° F for about 50 minutes, or until bread is golden and sounds hollow. If loaves are browning too quickly, cover lightly with foil. Turn out on wire rack to cool.

Makes 2 loaves.

—Irene Louden

Carrot-Cornmeal Dinner Rolls

"This was one of my mother's favourite recipes. As I was raising my four children 'Grandma's rolls' were always a special treat — especially when served straight from the oven, dripping with butter and homemade blackberry jelly."

1 cup packed grated carrots
1 pkg. yeast
2 tsp. sugar
¼ cup softened butter
1 egg, beaten
1½ tsp. salt
3-3½ cups flour
¾ cup cornmeal
1 Tbsp. sugar
melted butter

Simmer carrots in 1¼ cups boiling water for 5 minutes. Set aside to cool to lukewarm.

Soften yeast and 2 tsp. sugar in ¼ cup warm water. Combine butter, egg, yeast mixture, carrots and carrot water. Add salt and 2 cups flour and beat well. Stir in cornmeal and 1 Tbsp. sugar and beat. Gradually add flour to make a soft dough. Knead on floured board for 10 minutes, adding flour as needed.

Place in greased bowl, cover and let rise until doubled — about 1 hour. Punch down, then shape into 36 balls. Place 2 balls in each greased cup of muffin pan. Brush with melted butter, cover and let rise until doubled — 30 minutes. Bake at 375° F for 15 minutes.

Makes 18 rolls.

—Frances Walker

Preserves

Chunky Mustard Pickles

1 medium cauliflower
1 qt. large cucumbers
3 sweet red peppers
3 green peppers
1 qt. small cucumbers
1 qt. onions, chopped
1 qt. pickling onions
1 cup pickling salt
3 qts. water
5 cups sugar
½ cup water
4½ cups vinegar
¼ oz. celery seed
¼ oz. mustard seed
¼ cup dry mustard
¾ cup flour
1 Tbsp. turmeric

Chop cauliflower, large cucumbers and peppers into chunks. Add small cucumbers, onions and pickling onions. Cover with a brine made of the pickling salt and 3 quarts water and leave overnight. In the morning, rinse and drain well.

Combine with sugar, ½ cup water, vinegar, celery seed and mustard seed and bring to a boil. When boiling, take some of the liquid and mix to a smooth paste with dry mustard, flour and turmeric. Stir back into pickles and cook for 5 minutes. Bottle and seal.

Makes 6 to 8 quarts.

—Beth Hopkins

Dilled Green Tomatoes

15 medium-sized green
   tomatoes
Fresh dill
5 cloves garlic
5 whole cloves
2½ tsp. cayenne pepper
1 qt. vinegar
1 qt. water
⅓ cup pickling salt

Wash tomatoes and slice if necessary. Pack into 5 quart jars. Add 3 heads dill, 1 clove garlic, 1 whole clove and ½ tsp. cayenne to each jar.

Boil vinegar, water and salt for 5 minutes. Pour over tomatoes and process for 20 minutes in a boiling water bath.

Makes 5 quarts.

—E. V. Estey

Dilled Bean Pickles

3 lbs. fresh green beans
½ cup chopped fresh dill
2 cloves garlic, peeled &
   halved
2 cups water
4 Tbsp. salt
2 cups white vinegar
4 tsp. sugar
½ tsp. cayenne pepper

Parboil beans in unsalted water until tender — 5 to 10 minutes. Pack upright in sterile jars and add dill and garlic.

Heat water, salt, vinegar, sugar and cayenne to a boil. Pour over beans. Seal jars and let stand for 6 weeks.

Makes 4 to 5 pints.

—E. Evans

Dill Pickles

4 lbs. small cucumbers
Fresh dill
8 cloves garlic
3 cups water
3 cups white vinegar
5 Tbsp. pickling salt

Scrub cucumbers and soak overnight in ice water. Drain and pack into 4 hot, sterilized quart jars. Place sprays of dill and garlic cloves on top of cucumbers.

Combine remaining ingredients and bring to a boil. Pour over cucumbers and seal jars. Store for 1 month before eating.

Makes 4 quarts.

—Sheila Couture

Dilled Zucchini

6 lbs. zucchini, trimmed &
   thinly sliced
2 cups thinly sliced celery
2 large onions, chopped
⅓ cup salt
Ice cubes
2 cups sugar
2 Tbsp. dill seeds
2 cups white vinegar
6 cloves garlic, halved

Combine zucchini, celery, onions and salt in large bowl, place a layer of ice on top, cover and let stand for 3 hours. Drain well.

Combine sugar, dill seeds and vinegar in a saucepan and bring to a boil, stirring constantly. Stir in vegetables, and heat, stirring several times, just to a full boil. Ladle into hot, sterilized jars, place 1 to 2 pieces of garlic in each and seal.

Makes 8 to 10 pints.

—Laura Poitras

Swiss Chard Pickles

4 qts. Swiss chard, cut into
   1-inch pieces
8 medium onions, sliced
Pickling salt
White vinegar
4 cups white sugar
2 Tbsp. celery seed
3 Tbsp. mustard seed
½ cup cornstarch
2 Tbsp. dry mustard
1 Tbsp. curry powder
2 tsp. turmeric

Layer Swiss chard and onions in large pickling kettle and sprinkle with salt. Let stand for 1 hour. Drain and add vinegar to cover.

Stir in sugar, celery seed and mustard seed and cook until tender. Add cornstarch, mustard, curry powder and turmeric.

Seal in sterilized jars.

Makes 12 pints.

— *Dorothy Hall*

Dilled Carrots

6 cups cold water
2 cups white vinegar
½ cup pickling salt
¼ tsp. cream of tartar
6 lbs. baby carrots
6-7 cloves garlic, slivered
6-7 large sprigs fresh dill

Combine water, vinegar, salt and cream of tartar, stirring until salt is dissolved. Scrape and trim carrots. Put a slivered clove of garlic in each of 6 or 7 pint jars. Add a dill sprig to each, then pack in carrots upright. Pour vinegar mixture over carrots to fill jars.

Process for 10 minutes in a boiling water bath and store in a cool place for 3 weeks.

Makes 6 to 7 pints.

—*Kathee Roy*

Sweet Pickles

6 qts. cucumbers
¾ cup pickling salt
Boiling water
1 plum
3 pints white vinegar
4 Tbsp. white sugar
4 Tbsp. pickling salt
4 Tbsp. mustard seed &
   ½ cup mixed pickling
   spice tied in a bag
11-12 cups white sugar

Cut cucumbers into chunks and place in a large crock with ¾ cup pickling salt. Cover with boiling water and let sit overnight. In the morning, drain and wipe each piece dry. Return to crock with plum.

Heat vinegar, 4 Tbsp. sugar, 4 Tbsp. pickling salt, mustard seed and pickling spice together and add to cucumber. Cover with a plate.

Add 1 cup sugar each day for 11 to 12 days. Mix with a wooden spoon.

After 12 days, drain cucumbers and heat syrup. Place cucumbers in jars, pour syrup over and seal.

Makes 6 quarts.

—*Hilda Jackson*

Pickled Carrots Rosemary

2 hot peppers
4 cloves garlic
1 tsp. rosemary
2 lbs. carrots, peeled & cut
   into 4-inch long strips
2 cups water
2 cups white vinegar
3 Tbsp. pickling salt
3 Tbsp. sugar

Cut peppers into quarters lengthwise. Place 2 strips pepper and 1 clove garlic into each of 4 pint jars. Add ¼ tsp. rosemary to each jar. Pack tightly with carrot sticks.

Bring water, vinegar, salt and sugar to a boil, reduce heat and simmer, uncovered, for 5 minutes. Pour over carrots, seal and process for 10 minutes in boiling water bath.

Let pickles age for 1 month before eating.

Makes 4 pints.

—*Lynn Hill*

Pickled Mushrooms

This traditional Russian recipe can be used with both domestic and wild mushrooms and is especially suited to shaggy manes and the honey mushroom.

1 cup red wine vinegar
2 whole cloves
½ cup cold water
5 whole peppercorns
1 bay leaf
2 tsp. salt
2 cloves garlic, crushed
1 lb. mushrooms
1 Tbsp. vegetable oil

Combine vinegar, cloves, water, peppercorns, bay leaf, salt and garlic in a 2-quart enamelled saucepan. Bring to a boil, add mushrooms and reduce heat. Simmer, uncovered, for 10 minutes, stirring occasionally.

Cool to room temperature. Pour into 1-quart jar and slowly pour oil on top. Secure top with plastic wrap, cover tightly and let sit for at least 1 week.

Makes 1 quart.

—*Sandra Kapral*

Piccalilli

6 green peppers
6 red peppers
8 cucumbers
8 cups chopped green
    tomatoes
6 large onions
1 cup pickling salt
5 cups vinegar
2 lbs. brown sugar
2 tsp. dry mustard
2 Tbsp. mixed pickling spice,
    tied in cheesecloth

Wash peppers, cut in half and remove seeds. Peel cucumbers, cut stem ends from tomatoes and peel onions.

Put peppers, onions and cucumbers through coarse setting of meat grinder. Score tomatoes and cut into small cubes.

Measure 8 cups of tomatoes into bowl. Put ground and chopped vegetables in layers in large pot, sprinkling each layer with salt, using 1 cup salt in all. Let stand overnight.

Strain vegetables through fine-holed colander. Remove as much liquid as possible and replace vegetables in pot. Add vinegar, brown sugar, mustard and pickling spice. Cook until sauce becomes clear — about 35 minutes — stirring occasionally.

Remove pickling spice and place piccalilli in hot, sterilized jars and seal.

Makes 8 to 10 pints.

—*Mrs. W. Atkins*

Peter Piper's Pickled Peppers

10 lbs. sweet green peppers
Pickling salt
24 ice cubes
3 cloves garlic, sliced
3 cups vinegar
5 cups sugar
½ tsp. celery seed
½ tsp. turmeric
2 Tbsp. mustard seed

Slice peppers and sprinkle lightly with pickling salt. Mix in ice cubes and garlic and chill for 3 hours.

Remove garlic and drain peppers. Combine remaining ingredients in a heavy saucepan and add peppers. Bring to a boil, then place in hot jars and seal.

Makes 6 to 8 quarts.

—*Dee Lowe*

Curry Pickle

Zucchini & onions to fill 4 or
    5 quart jars, thinly sliced
Salt brine to cover zucchini
    & onion
6 cups vinegar
6 cups sugar
2 Tbsp. celery seed
2 Tbsp. dry mustard
4 Tbsp. hot curry powder
2 Tbsp. turmeric
6 whole cloves
8-10 slices ginger root
1 tsp. Tabasco sauce

Soak zucchini and onion slices in salt brine overnight. Drain and pack in jars.

Combine remaining ingredients, bring to a boil and pour over vegetables. Seal jars and let stand a few weeks before eating.

Makes 4 to 5 quarts.

—*Brigitte Wolf*

Sauerkraut

2 lbs. cabbage
4 tsp. pickling salt

Remove loose outer leaves of cabbage. Wash and drain inner head, cut into quarters and remove core. Shred or cut into ⅛-inch strips. Mix thoroughly with 3 tsp. salt by hand.

Tightly pack cabbage into clean, hot jars. Press down with fingers and cover with a piece of clean cheesecloth. Cross 2 wooden sticks on top of the cheesecloth below the neck of the jar, place lid on loosely and set in a shallow pan to catch any overflow of brine.

Store for 2 to 3 weeks at 70° F. When fermentation has stopped, wipe jars clean and remove sticks and cheesecloth. Press cabbage down firmly to release the last of the air bubbles. Combine 1 quart water with remaining 1 tsp. salt and pour over cabbage. Place lid on jar and process for 10 minutes in boiling water bath.

Makes 1 quart.

—Mary Dzielak

Honey Pickled Beets

2 qts. beets
1½ cups white vinegar
1 cup honey
1 cup water
1 tsp. salt
1 tsp. allspice
2 cups onion rings
2 tsp. each whole cloves, mustard seed & 2 cinnamon sticks placed in a spice bag

Cook the beets and slip off the skins. Combine the vinegar, honey and water in a large saucepan and add to this the salt and allspice. Drop the spice bag in and simmer for 5 minutes.

Add the beets and onion rings and simmer gently for 20 minutes.

Pack into hot sterile jars, cover with liquid and seal.

Makes 4 pints.

—Ruth E. Geddes

Watermelon Pickle

4 qts. watermelon rind
4 Tbsp. salt
3 Tbsp. alum
11 cups sugar
2 cups white vinegar
1½ tsp. whole cloves
3 sticks cinnamon

Cut rind into 1-inch cubes, place in pot and add salt. Cover with water and add alum. Bring to a boil, reduce heat and simmer for 30 minutes. Drain and rinse.

Simmer in 4 more quarts of water (or enough to cover) until tender. Add sugar and cook until transparent. Add vinegar and cook another 25 minutes. Toss in cloves and cinnamon and cook 5 minutes. Pack in 6 jars, with syrup and spices. Seal. Let sit for 2 weeks before eating.

Makes 6 pints.

—Cary Elizabeth Marshall

Hot Tamale Sauce

This sauce is delicious with Mexican cooking and almost any bean or meat dishes.

15 large ripe tomatoes
4 large peaches
3 large tart apples
4 pears
6 medium onions
3 cups diced celery
3 Tbsp. mixed pickling spice
4 tsp. salt
1½ cups cider vinegar
1 cup honey
12 small chili peppers

Blanch, peel and slice tomatoes and peaches. Core and slice apples and pears. Peel and thinly slice onions. Cut celery into small pieces. Tie pickling spice in a cheesecloth bag.

Combine all ingredients in a large pot and cook slowly until honey is dissolved and fruit is well mixed. Boil steadily, stirring occasionally, until sauce is thickened — about 40 minutes.

Turn into hot, sterile jars and seal.

Makes 3 to 4 quarts.

—*Betty Ternier Daniels*

Horseradish

2 cups grated horseradish
1 cup white vinegar
½ tsp. salt

Place horseradish in sterilized 1-quart jar. Combine vinegar and salt and pour over horseradish. Seal jar and store in a cool place.

Makes 1 quart.

—*Shirley Morrish*

Ketchup

1½ tsp. whole cloves
1 stick cinnamon
1 tsp. celery seed
1 tsp. allspice
1 cup white vinegar
8 lbs. ripe tomatoes
2 medium onions, chopped
¼ tsp. red pepper
6 apples, cut in eighths (optional)
1 cup sugar
4 tsp. salt

Add spices to vinegar and bring to a boil. Cover, turn off heat and let stand.

Mash tomatoes in a pot, add onion, pepper and apples. Heat to a boil and cook for 15 minutes. Put through a sieve. Add sugar to tomato juice and reheat to a boil. Skim. Cook down to half the original volume.

Strain vinegar mixture and add to juice with salt. Simmer, stirring frequently, for 30 minutes.

Fill hot, sterilized jars and seal.

Makes 4 to 5 pints.

—*Kathy MacRow*

Pickled Onions

Boiling water
4 lbs. pickling onions
2½ cups pickling salt
3 qts. cold water
3 cups white vinegar
1 cup water
3 cups sugar
2 Tbsp. mixed pickling spice, tied in a bag

Pour boiling water over onions and let stand 5 minutes. Drain and plunge into ice water. Drain and peel off skins.

Dissolve pickling salt in 3 quarts cold water and pour over onions. Let stand overnight. Drain and rinse several times under cold running water.

Bring vinegar, 1 cup water, sugar and spices to a boil. Reduce heat and simmer for 15 minutes. Remove spices, add onions and bring back to a boil.

Ladle into sterilized jars and fill with vinegar syrup. Seal.

Makes 5 pints.

—*Linda Forsyth*

Chili Sauce

30 ripe tomatoes, peeled & diced
8 onions, diced
3 sweet red peppers, diced
3 green peppers, diced
2 cups diced celery
2½ cups brown sugar
3 cups vinegar
3 Tbsp. pickling salt

Combine all ingredients in a large pot and mix well. Simmer, uncovered, until thick — 4½ hours. Seal into jars while hot.

Makes 5 pints.

—*Karen Herder*

Rhubarb Relish

2 qts. rhubarb, chopped into
    1-inch lengths
1 qt. onions, thinly sliced
2 cups vinegar
2 cups sugar
1 Tbsp. salt
1 tsp. cloves
1 tsp. allspice
1 tsp. cinnamon
1 tsp. pepper

Place all ingredients in a large pot and mix well. Cook slowly until rhubarb is soft, then boil for 1 hour.

Seal in sterilized jars.

Makes 4 pints.

—Shirley Gilbert

Zucchini Relish

10 cups zucchini
4 cups onions
5 Tbsp. pickling salt
1 red pepper
1 green pepper
2¼ cups vinegar
3 cups sugar
1 tsp. nutmeg
1 tsp. dry mustard
1 tsp. turmeric
1 tsp. cornstarch
2 Tbsp. celery seed
½ tsp. pepper

Grind zucchini, onions and salt and let stand overnight. Drain and rinse twice in cold water to remove salt.

Grind red and green peppers together. Add to zucchini with remaining ingredients. Cook for 30 minutes.

Ladle while hot into sterile jars and seal.

Makes 5 to 6 pints.

—Gail Berg

Tomato Juice

12 very large ripe tomatoes,
    cut in thin wedges
1 large green pepper, diced
3 medium onions, chopped
1 celery stalk, diced
⅓ cup sugar
1 Tbsp. salt

Place all ingredients in a large heavy pot. Bring to a boil, lower heat, cover and simmer for 35 minutes, stirring occasionally.

Put mixture through a food mill, strain, return juice to pot and bring to a boil. Pour into 3 hot sterilized quart jars, leaving ¼-inch head room. Screw lids on, then process in a boiling water bath for 15 minutes.

Makes 3 quarts.

—Gwen Steinbusch

Corn Relish

6 cups corn
4 onions
½ large cabbage
2½ cups vinegar
1 Tbsp. salt
2½ cups sugar
3 Tbsp. flour
1 Tbsp. mustard
1 Tbsp. celery seed
½ tsp. turmeric

Combine corn, onions, cabbage and vinegar. Bring to a boil and simmer for 30 minutes. Add salt and sugar. Blend together flour, mustard, celery seed and turmeric. Wet, then thin, with vinegar. Add to vegetables. Cook for 15 minutes. Seal in sterilized jars.

Makes 3 to 4 quarts.

—Mrs. Fred Smith

Patty's Mint Relish

1 cup packed mint leaves
6 medium onions
2 green peppers
2 lbs. apples
3 pears
¾ lb. raisins
1 oz. mustard seed
2 Tbsp. salt
2½ lbs. white sugar
1 qt. cider vinegar

Put mint, onions, green peppers, apples, pears and raisins through a meat chopper, then place in a crock.

Boil together remaining ingredients and pour over mint mixture. Let stand 1 week, bottle in sterile jars and seal.

Makes about 4 pints.

—Mary Reid

Mom's Strawberry Jam

4 cups strawberries
1 Tbsp. vinegar
3 cups white sugar

Wash and hull the strawberries. Add vinegar and bring to a boil, cover and boil for 1 minute. Add sugar and boil 20 minutes uncovered, stirring occasionally.

Pour into a large bowl and let stand overnight. Pour into sterilized jars, cover with melted paraffin wax, cool and put lids on.

Makes about 1 quart.

—*Joan Bridgeman Hoepner*

Four Berry Jam

3 cups raspberries
1 cup strawberries
2 cups blueberries
2 cups Saskatoon berries
4 cups honey
2 pkgs. powdered pectin

In a large pot, bring the berries and the honey to a rolling boil and simmer for about 15 minutes. Add the 2 packages of pectin, bring back to a rolling boil and boil for 2 minutes.

Pour into hot sterilized jars and seal.

Makes 6 pints.

—*Cary Elizabeth Marshall*

Black Currant Jam

4 cups black currants
2 cups boiling water
6 cups granulated sugar
Butter

Wash and drain the currants. Add boiling water, bring to a boil and cook for 8 minutes.

Meanwhile, warm sugar slowly in a large pan in the oven. Add to currants, mix thoroughly and bring to a boil, stirring occasionally. Boil hard for 4 minutes. Remove from heat and add small piece of butter. Skim jam and pour into sterilized jars. Seal with melted paraffin wax.

Makes 8 jelly glasses.

—*Kathy Turner*

Red Plum Jam

2 lbs. red plums
1 cup water
6 cups sugar
1 Tbsp. butter

Pit and cut up the plums. Cook, covered with water, until soft. Remove from heat, mash, and add sugar, stirring until it is completely dissolved. Cook over medium heat stirring to prevent sticking.

Boil the mixture until candy thermometer registers 220° F. Remove from heat, skim the froth and stir in the butter. Place in jars and cap.

Makes 9 jelly jars.

—*Mary Dzielak*

Blackberry & Apple Jam

3 lbs. green apples
2 cups water
2½ lbs. blackberries
9 cups sugar
½ cup lemon juice
1 Tbsp. butter

Peel, core and slice the apples. Place in a pot with water and cook until soft — about 10 to 15 minutes. Remove from heat and mash. Add the blackberries, mix thoroughly, then add the sugar and lemon juice and stir until the sugar is completely dissolved. Boil the mixture until the candy thermometer registers 220° F.

Remove from heat and skim the froth off the top of the jam with a large metal spoon. Stir in the butter. Pour into hot, sterilized jars and cap immediately.

Makes 10 jelly jars.

—*Mary Dzielak*

Yellow Tomato Marmalade

3¼ cups peeled & chopped
    yellow tomatoes
Rind of 1 large lemon, grated
¼ cup lemon juice
6 cups sugar
1 bottle Certo

Cook tomatoes, covered, for 10 minutes without any water. Add lemon rind, lemon juice and sugar. Bring to a boil over moderate heat, stirring constantly, and boil hard for 1 minute. Turn off heat. Add Certo and stir vigorously for 5 minutes. Bottle in sterile jars.

Makes 1½ pints.

—*Mary Reid*

Paradise Jelly

6 cups washed & cubed
  quince
6 cups quartered crabapples
3 cups cranberries
Granulated sugar
Rose geranium leaves

Boil quince in just enough water to cover. When it begins to soften, add apples and then cranberries. When all are soft, place in a jelly bag and drain into a bowl. Add a scant cup of sugar to each cup of fruit juice. Boil for about 20 minutes or until mixture gels when dropped onto a plate.

Pour into glasses, put a rose geranium leaf in each glass, and seal with paraffin.

Makes 6 pints.

—*Cary Elizabeth Marshall*

Wild Rose Jelly

2 cups apple juice
3 cups tightly-packed fresh
  wild rose petals
3 cups white sugar
½ bottle Certo

Heat apple juice to the boiling point. Place washed and drained rose petals in large saucepan and pour apple juice over them. Bring to a boil and boil for 20 minutes. Strain juice into another large saucepan. Add sugar, stir, bring to a boil and stir in Certo. Boil for 1 minute. Pour into sterile jelly glasses and seal with wax.

Makes 6 jelly glasses.

—*Shirley Morrish*

Peachstone Jelly

Skins, peach stones &
  overripe peaches
1¼ cups strained lemon juice
7¼ cups sugar
1 bottle Certo

Place peaches, stones and skins in a large pot and barely cover with water. Bring to a boil and simmer, covered, for 10 minutes. Place in a strainer and squeeze out juice to make 3½ cups.

Add the lemon juice and sugar and mix well. Place over high heat and bring to a boil, stirring constantly. Stir in Certo, bring to a full rolling boil and boil hard for 1 minute, stirring constantly.

Remove from heat, skim off foam and pour into jars. Cover with hot paraffin.

Makes 5 to 6 pints.

—*Ruth Anne Laverty*

Blueberry Jam

2 cups blueberries
1 cup sugar

In a 2-quart saucepan, combine blueberries and 3 Tbsp. water. Bring to a boil and cook, uncovered, for 10 minutes. Add sugar and boil, uncovered, to jam stage — about 10 minutes. Carefully pour the jam into jars.

Makes 1½ cups.

—*Glenna Keating*

Apricot Jam Amandine

1 lb. dried apricots
6 cups water
⅓ cup lemon juice
8 cups sugar
1 Tbsp. butter
2 oz. slivered almonds

Cut up the apricots and soak in water overnight. Cook gently, covered, until tender — about 20 minutes. Remove from heat, mash and stir in lemon juice and sugar until completely dissolved.

Return to heat and boil until it reaches 220° F. Remove from heat, skim the froth, and stir in the butter and almonds. Fill and cap jars.

Makes 9 jelly jars.

—*Mary Dzielak*

Raspberry or Blackberry Jam

6 cups berries
6 cups sugar

Place berries in flat-bottomed pan and mash with potato masher as they heat. Bring to a full boil and boil for 2 minutes. Add sugar and boil for 1 minute.

Remove from heat and beat with electric mixer for 4 minutes. Pour jam into hot, clean jars and pour hot wax over to seal.

Makes about 3 pints.

—*Beth Hopkins*

Rowanberry Jelly

Rowanberry is known as Mountain Ash in central Canada. The berries should be gathered after frost and should taste tart, but not so bitter that your mouth puckers.

4 qts. ripe rowanberries
1 qt. water
8 cups sugar
1 pkg. pectin

Simmer the berries in water until soft. Mash, then strain the juice through a cloth. Bring juice to a boil and add sugar. Add pectin when sugar is dissolved and boil for 1 or 2 minutes or until it tests done. Seal with ¼ inch paraffin wax.

Makes 2 pints.

—*Cary Elizabeth Marshall*

Elderberry Jelly

3 cups elderberry juice
½ cup lemon juice
7½ cups sugar
1 bottle Certo

Boil juices and sugar, then add the Certo. Bring to a full rolling boil and cook for 1 minute. Remove from the stove, stir and skim off the foam. Pour into jars and seal.

Makes 4 to 6 jelly glasses.

—*Joanne Ramsy*

Peach Chutney

6 cups peeled, chopped peaches
4 cups peeled, chopped apples
2 cups raisins
4 cups brown sugar
1½ cups cider **or** malt vinegar
2 tsp. cinnamon
1 tsp. cloves
1 tsp. allspice
2 tsp. salt
⅛ tsp. black pepper

Combine all ingredients and cook slowly, stirring frequently, until thick — about 1 hour. Pour into hot sterilized jars and seal.

Makes 4 to 5 pints.

—*Carolyn Hills*

Tomato Chutney

4 lbs. tomatoes
1 lb. chopped apples
3 onions, finely chopped
2 cups vinegar
2 Tbsp. salt
½ tsp. allspice
2 cloves garlic
2 cups honey
1 cup raisins
1 tsp. cinnamon
1 Tbsp. dry mustard
1 tsp. cayenne
1 tsp. cloves

Chop tomatoes and add remaining ingredients. Cook until thick and clear, stirring occasionally.

Seal in hot sterilized jars.

Makes 5 pints.

—*Lisa Brownstone*

Apple Jelly

4 lbs. green apples
½ cup lemon juice
3 cups water
Sugar

Wash and cut up apples without peeling or coring. Add lemon juice and water and boil until tender.

Remove from heat, mash and strain through jelly bag. Measure the juice and add 1 cup sugar for each cup of juice. Boil until juice reaches 220° F, remove from heat and skim the froth. Place in jars and cap.

—*Mary Dzielak*

Mint Jelly

1 cup packed fresh mint leaves
½ cup vinegar
1¼ cups water
1½ lbs. sugar

Wash the mint, chop finely and bring to a boil with water and vinegar. Remove from heat and let stand for a few minutes. Add sugar and bring back to a boil. Boil for 20 minutes or until jelled.

Place in jar.

—*C. Majewski*

Pineapple Jelly

1 qt. pineapple juice
1 qt. tart apple juice
6 cups sugar

Bring combined juices to a boil, stir in sugar and boil rapidly until syrup sheets. Pour into sterile jars and seal.

Makes 4 to 6 pints.

—*Janice Touesnard*

Tomato Butter

6-qt. basket ripe tomatoes
1 Tbsp. salt
4 cups white sugar
2 cups white vinegar
2 Tbsp. mixed pickling spice,
    tied in a bag

Peel and cut up tomatoes. Sprinkle with salt and let stand overnight. In the morning, pour off the juice.

Add remaining ingredients to tomatoes, place in a large heavy pot and simmer until thick — about 2 hours.

Bottle in sterile jars.

Makes 4 to 6 quarts.

—Alice Wires

Lemon Butter

This preserve is delicious spread on toast for everyday use, or on Christmas pudding for a special treat.

8 eggs, well beaten
4 cups sugar
1 cup butter
¼ cup grated lemon rind
1 cup lemon juice

Combine eggs and sugar in a double boiler. Add butter, lemon rind and lemon juice. Cook over gently boiling water, stirring frequently, until it thickens. Bottle and cool.

Makes eight 8-ounce jelly glasses.

—Kathy Turner

Banana Chutney

2 onions, finely chopped
1 lb. very ripe bananas,
    mashed
1 lb. pitted dates
1 cup cider vinegar
¾ cup brown sugar
½ cup molasses
4 cloves garlic, crushed
1-inch slice fresh ginger,
    crushed
1 Tbsp. cinnamon
½ Tbsp. nutmeg
½ Tbsp. ground cloves
½ Tbsp. ground cardamom
½ Tbsp. ground coriander
1 tsp. fenugreek
1 tsp. cumin
1 tsp. turmeric

Combine onions, bananas, dates, vinegar, sugar and molasses in a heavy saucepan. Crush all the spices, mix together and stir into banana-date mixture.

Heat quickly to a boil and stir, while boiling, for 5 minutes. Reduce heat and simmer for 20 minutes. Let cool and pour into jars. Seal.

Makes 1 quart.

—Ingrid Birker

Colonel Grey's Chutney

Chutneys, which originated in India as accompaniments to curried dishes, are now as varied as the different cultures that have adopted them. Spicy, flavourful and exotic, they add a piquant touch to chicken, pork, lamb and curries.

1 qt. vinegar
4 lbs. demerara sugar
5 lbs. Granny Smith apples
4 oz. ginger root
2 cloves garlic
1 oz. red chilies in muslin
    bag
1 tsp. cayenne pepper
2 tsp. salt
½ lb. seedless raisins

Heat vinegar and sugar until sugar is dissolved. Peel and slice apples. Scrape and grate ginger. Peel and crush garlic.

Combine all ingredients in a heavy saucepan. Cook until thick and dark, removing chilies after 5 minutes. Place in jars and seal.

Makes 2 to 3 quarts.

—Eileen Deeley

Brandied Cherries

2 lbs. sweet cherries
2 cups sugar
2 cups water
Brandy

Place unpitted cherries in a large bowl and cover with ice cold water. Let them stand for 30 to 40 minutes. Drain.

Dissolve sugar in 2 cups water, stirring all the time, and bring to a full boil. Boil rapidly for 5 minutes. Add the cherries and bring once more to a rolling boil. Remove from heat, wait until the boiling stops and repeat operation twice more, stirring gently with a wooden spoon.

Fill sterilized jars three-quarters full with fruit and syrup, place covers loosely on jars and let stand until cool, then fill each jar with brandy. Stir with a silver or wooden spoon. Seal. Turn jars upside down overnight, then store in a cool, dark place right side up, for at least 3 months before using.

Makes 4 pints.

—Kathleen Fitzgerald

Winnifred's Apple Butter

10 lbs. apples, sliced
5 cups water
4 cups sugar
1 cup corn syrup
2 tsp. cinnamon
1 tsp. allspice

Place apple slices in Dutch oven and add water. Boil and cook down for 1 hour. Sieve or put through a blender and add sugar and syrup. Return to heat and cook down until desired thickness is reached — 2 to 3 hours. Add spices and pack into jars.

Makes about 4 quarts.

—Debbie Winder

Rhubarb Marmalade

6 large oranges
6 cups finely chopped rhubarb
1 cup water
9 cups sugar

Peel and section 4 oranges. Chop pulp into small pieces, discarding rinds. Wash the other 2 oranges and cut up coarsely. Put through fine blade of food chopper.

Combine rhubarb, orange pieces and ground orange in a kettle. Add water, cover, and bring to a boil. Uncover, add sugar and stir until sugar is dissolved. Boil hard, uncovered, until mixture thickens — 20 to 30 minutes.

Skim and ladle into sterilized jars. Top with thin layer of paraffin.

Makes about ten 8-oz. jars.

—Joanne Kellog

Scotch Orange Marmalade

6 navel oranges
10 cups water
10 cups sugar
1 cup lemon juice
1 Tbsp. butter
½ cup Scotch whiskey

Shred the oranges, discarding the tough centre fibre. Put them in a pan with the water and soak overnight. The next day, cook, covered, until tender.

Let cool, then stir in the sugar and lemon juice until dissolved. Boil until mixture reaches 220° F. Remove from heat, skim the froth and stir in the butter and whiskey. Pour into jars and seal.

Makes 12 jelly glasses.

—Mary Dzielak

Peach Marmalade

1 orange
2 lemons
1 cup water
2 lbs. ripe peaches
5 cups sugar
½ bottle liquid pectin

Grind orange and 1 lemon in blender with water. Put into a small pot and add juice from the other lemon. Boil, covered, for 20 minutes.

Peel, pit and chop peaches finely. Put in large pot with citrus mixture and sugar. Boil hard for 2 minutes. Add pectin and boil until jelly thermometer reaches 221° F. Remove from heat and stir and skim foam for about 10 minutes. Pour into sterile jars and seal.

Makes 2 pints.

—Judy Wuest

Desserts

Jersey Cream Pudding

A light and fluffy pudding, this is delicious served with most fresh fruits.

2-3 eggs, separated
3 cups milk
⅓ cup sugar
¼ tsp. salt
2 heaping Tbsp. flour
¼ cup cream
1 tsp. vanilla
Nutmeg

Beat egg whites until stiff and set aside. Scald together the milk, sugar and salt in a double boiler. Mix together flour and cream to form a thin batter. Add egg yolks and stir until smooth. Slowly add hot milk to yolk mixture and stir until smooth. Return to heat, over hot water, and continue cooking and stirring until thick, at least 5 to 10 minutes. Add vanilla, fold in egg whites, pour into a bowl and top with nutmeg.

Serves 4 to 6.

—B. Caldwell

Cathy's Trifle

2-layer sponge cake
2-3 cups custard
4 cups mixed fresh chopped fruit
1 cup sherry
2 cups whipping cream, whipped
Fresh fruit to garnish

Break cake into 1-inch cubes. Combine with custard, chopped fruit and sherry in a large bowl and mix gently.

Top with whipped cream and fresh fruit.

Serves 8 to 12.

—Cathy Byard

Chocolate Pudding

1 cup flour
2 tsp. baking powder
½ tsp. salt
¾ cup sugar
6 Tbsp. cocoa
½ cup milk
4 Tbsp. melted butter
½ tsp. vanilla
1 cup brown sugar
1¾ cups hot water

Combine flour, baking powder, salt, sugar, 2 Tbsp. cocoa, milk, butter and vanilla. Spread in greased 8-inch square pan and sprinkle with brown sugar combined with remaining cocoa. Pour hot water over this. Do not stir. Bake at 350° F for 40 to 45 minutes.

—Rae Anne Huth

Fruit Bread Pudding

6 slices bread
1 banana, sliced
½ cup raisins
¼ cup walnuts
1 apple, cored & diced
1 cup brown sugar
⅔ cup water
½ tsp. cinnamon

Toast bread at 325° F for 15 minutes. Cut into cubes and combine with fruit and nuts.

Mix sugar, water and cinnamon together and add to fruit mixture. Toss to coat evenly. Let stand 5 minutes and stir again. Turn into a greased 8-inch square casserole dish.

Bake uncovered at 325° for 30 to 35 minutes.

—Helen Potts

Orange Cake Pudding

Lemon juice and rind can be substituted for orange in this dessert for an equally delicious pudding.

¼ cup flour
1 cup sugar
¼ tsp. salt
1 Tbsp. grated orange rind
½ cup orange juice
2 eggs, separated
¾ cup milk

Sift flour, sugar and salt together. Stir in orange rind and juice, egg yolks and milk. Blend well.

Beat egg whites until stiff but not dry. Pour orange mixture over egg whites and fold gently to blend.

Pour into a greased 1-quart baking dish. Set in a pan of hot water. Bake at 350° F for 50 minutes or until a knife inserted into the cake comes out clean.

—Johanna Vanderheyden

Baba au Rhum

1 tsp. sugar
1 envelope dry yeast
½ cup lukewarm water
¼ cup soft butter
2 cups granulated sugar
3 eggs
¼ tsp. salt
½ tsp. vanilla
½ tsp. grated lemon rind
2-3 cups flour
4 Tbsp. chopped red & green
   glazed cherries
2 Tbsp. chopped light raisins
½ cup corn syrup
2½ cups apricot nectar
Grated rind of 1 orange
1½ cups light rum

Dissolve 1 tsp. sugar and yeast in water. Let stand until foamy — 10 minutes. Beat together butter, ½ cup sugar and eggs until fluffy. Add salt, vanilla, lemon rind and ½ cup flour. Beat in yeast mixture and enough flour to make a drop-type batter. Add cherries and raisins.

Half-fill 30 small greased muffin tins. Let stand until batter fills tins. Bake at 375° F for 8 to 10 minutes, until golden. Remove from tins when cool.

To make rum sauce, combine in a heavy saucepan the remaining 1½ cups sugar, corn syrup, apricot nectar and orange rind. Bring to a boil and simmer until sugar dissolves — 5 minutes. Remove from heat and stir in rum. Cool.

One hour before serving, place the baba cakes in wide-mouthed jars or deep mixing bowls. Pour the sauce over them slowly, allowing it to soak in. Serve topped with whipped cream or lemon sauce.

Makes 30 baba cakes.

—Shirley Hill

Yogurt Fruit Mould

Unflavoured gelatin is a healthful alternative to prepackaged gelatin mixes. Combined with fruit and yogurt, it provides a light and delicious ending to any meal, especially on a hot summer day.

1 can chunk pineapple (in
   juice)
1 envelope unflavoured
   gelatin
2 Tbsp. honey
1 cup apple or orange juice
1 cup plain yogurt
1 banana, sliced
2 oranges, sectioned and
   seeded

Drain pineapple chunks and place juice in a small saucepan. Sprinkle gelatin over the juice and stir constantly over low heat until gelatin is dissolved — about 5 minutes. Add honey and stir until dissolved.

Pour into a 4-cup mould and add apple or orange juice and yogurt. Stir to mix yogurt evenly.

Let sit in the refrigerator for about 20 minutes or until starting to gel. Add pineapple, banana and orange sections and stir to distribute evenly.

Return to refrigerator until set — about 1 hour. Unmould by placing in a pan of hot water for a few seconds, then inverting on a plate.

—Mikell Billoki

Maple Mousse Glacée

4 eggs, separated
1 cup pure maple syrup
½ tsp. vanilla
1½ cups whipping cream

Beat egg yolks thoroughly and add maple syrup. Beat well to blend. In a heavy saucepan cook over very low heat, stirring constantly, until the consistency of a soft custard sauce is reached. Remove from heat, add vanilla and cool thoroughly.

Whip cream and fold in. Beat egg whites until stiff but not dry and fold in. Pour into parfait glasses and freeze until very firm. Let stand a few minutes at room temperature before serving. Garnish with whipped cream and toasted almonds.

Serves 6.

—Julienne Tardif

Yogurt Popsicles

1 cup plain yogurt
1 small can frozen orange
  juice
2 tsp. vanilla

Stir together and freeze in popsicle trays.

—Kathleen Fitzgerald

Raspberry Sherbet

½ cup sugar
1 cup water
1 tsp. gelatin
2 Tbsp. water
¾ cup corn syrup
1 pint raspberries, crushed
¼ cup lemon juice
¼ cup orange juice
2 egg whites

Simmer sugar and 1 cup water for 5 minutes. Soften gelatin in 2 Tbsp. water, then dissolve in hot sugar and water. Add corn syrup and cool.

Stir berries and juices into cooled syrup and freeze until firm. Beat until light and fluffy. Beat egg whites, and fold into berry mixture. Spoon into individual serving dishes and freeze.

Serves 8.

—Elizabeth Vigneault

Gooseberry Fool

This dessert can be made equally successfully with almost any fruit.

1 lb. ripe gooseberries
3 Tbsp. water
½ cup sugar
1 cup whipping cream

Top and tail gooseberries. Combine with water and sugar and stew until tender. Press through sieve and chill the purée. Beat cream until stiff. Carefully fold in gooseberry purée. Serve in individual dishes with more whipped cream.

Serves 4.

—Sheila Bear

Raspberry Bombe

Many berry juices other than raspberry can be used in this recipe.

2 envelopes plain gelatin
3 cups raspberry juice
½ pint whipping cream

Soften gelatin in small amount of cold water. Add ¼ cup boiling water to dissolve. Add gelatin mixture to berry juice. Cool until syrupy, then whip until frothy.

Whip cream until stiff. Add one quarter of juice-gelatin mixture to whipped cream and stir, then add remaining juice.

Pour into a mould or individual serving dishes and refrigerate until set. Serve topped with whipped cream and fresh raspberries.

Serves 4.

—Signe Nickerson

Nutmeg Mousse

6 eggs
1½ cups granulated sugar
2 envelopes unflavoured
  gelatin
½ cup cold water
1 Tbsp. freshly grated
  nutmeg
1 tsp. vanilla
2 cups whipping cream

Beat eggs until frothy. Gradually beat in sugar and continue beating until satiny and light.

In a small saucepan, sprinkle gelatin over water to soften. Cook over low heat, stirring occasionally, until gelatin is dissolved. Stir into the egg mixture with nutmeg and vanilla.

Whip cream until soft peaks form, and fold into egg mixture. Pour into a 2½-quart mould and chill until firm.

Serves 8 to 10.

—Mary McEwen

Syllabub

This old English dish is a frothy chilled dessert which separates into two layers.

2 egg whites
½ cup sugar
Juice of ½ lemon
1 cup whipping cream
½ cup white wine

Whip egg whites until stiff, then carefully fold in sugar and lemon juice. Whip cream until peaks form and fold this into the egg whites along with the wine. Pour into individual glasses and chill for 2 hours before serving.

Serves 4.

—Sheila Bear

Chocolate Cheesecake

This crustless cheesecake has a light airy texture. the chocolate can be omitted and the cake topped with fresh fruit for a different taste.

3 eggs, separated
8 oz. cream cheese, mashed
1 cup sour cream
½ cup sugar
1½ Tbsp. flour
½ tsp. vanilla
1 Tbsp. lemon juice
1 cup chocolate chips

Beat egg yolks and add to cream cheese. Add sour cream, sugar, flour, vanilla and lemon juice. Mix well.

Beat egg whites until stiff peaks form, and gently but thoroughly fold into batter.

Melt chocolate chips in saucepan over low heat. Swirl through batter. Pour into a lightly greased 10-inch springform pan.

Bake at 300° F for 1 hour, turn off heat and leave cake in oven for 1 more hour. Cool cheesecake, then refrigerate until serving time.

Serves 10 to 12.

—*Melissa Eder*

Pineapple Upside-Down Cake

1⅓ cups flour
¾ cup sugar
3 tsp. baking powder
½ tsp. salt
¼ cup shortening
1 egg
¾ cup milk
3 Tbsp. butter
½ cup brown sugar
9 pineapple slices

Combine flour, sugar, baking powder and salt. Cut in shortening. Mix together egg and milk and add to flour mixture.

Meanwhile, melt butter in an 8-inch square pan in oven at 350° F. Sprinkle with brown sugar, then arrange a layer of pineapple slices close together in pan, over butter and sugar. Cover with batter.

Bake at 350° F for 30 minutes.

Turn cake upside down on plate and remove from pan while still warm. Cool before serving.

Serves 9.

—*Shirley Thomlinson*

Candy Nut Roll

1 cup sugar
½ cup milk
¼ tsp. salt
1 Tbsp. melted butter
2 cups chopped dates
1 cup walnuts
1 tsp. vanilla
1-2 cups coconut

Boil sugar, milk, salt and butter to the soft ball stage. (When a little of the mixture is placed in a cup of cold water it will form a ball which loses its shape when removed from the water.)

Add the dates and boil for 3 more minutes. Remove from heat, add walnuts and vanilla, and cool to lukewarm.

Knead on a greased cookie sheet until it is no longer sticky. Roll into a long cylinder, then coat with coconut. Wrap in wax paper and chill well. Slice when cold. Keep refrigerated.

—*Signe Nickerson*

Streusel Squares

½ cup butter
1 cup granulated sugar
2 eggs
1 tsp. vanilla
1 cup sour cream or
   buttermilk
2 cups flour
¼ tsp. salt
1 tsp. baking powder
1 tsp. baking soda
⅓ cup brown sugar
1 tsp. cinnamon
¼ cup chopped walnuts

Cream together butter and granulated sugar. Mix in eggs, one at a time. Add vanilla to sour cream or buttermilk. Sift together flour, salt, baking powder and baking soda. Add dry ingredients to butter mixture gradually, alternating with cream. Combine lightly.

Place half this mixture in 9" x 13" pan. Combine remaining ingredients and sprinkle half over the batter. Spread with remaining batter and top with sugar mixture.

Bake at 350° F for 30 minutes. Cool in pan.

—Nel vanGeest

Mincemeat Squares

1½ cups brown sugar
2 eggs
2 Tbsp. molasses
1 Tbsp. butter
1 tsp. vanilla
2 cups flour
½ tsp. salt
½ tsp. baking soda
1 tsp. cinnamon
1 tsp. cloves
3 Tbsp. hot water
½ cup chopped walnuts
¼ cup raisins
1½ cups mincemeat
1½ cups icing sugar
3 Tbsp. hot milk
½ tsp. vanilla
½ tsp. almond extract

Mix thoroughly brown sugar, eggs, molasses, butter and 1 tsp. vanilla. Add flour, salt, baking soda, cinnamon, cloves, hot water, walnuts, raisins and mincemeat and mix well.

Spread smoothly in 2 well-greased 9" x 13" pans. Bake at 400° F for 12 to 15 minutes.

Combine remaining ingredients and spread over squares while they are still warm.

—Dawn Livingstone

Kiffle

These filled crescents have a rich, sour cream dough.

1 envelope dry yeast
1 Tbsp. water
2 cups flour
½ cup butter
2 eggs, separated
½ cup sour cream
Icing sugar
1 cup finely chopped walnuts
½ cup sugar
1 tsp. vanilla

Dissolve yeast in water and let stand for 10 minutes.

Cut butter into flour until crumbly. Combine egg yolks and sour cream and add dissolved yeast. Pour over flour and butter. Mix in and knead for 5 minutes. Form into a ball, place in a greased bowl, cover with wax paper and then a tea towel. Chill for 1 hour.

Divide dough into 3 equal parts. Sprinkle icing sugar onto board, roll each part into a 10-inch circle and cut into 8 wedges.

Combine walnuts, sugar, stiffly beaten egg whites and vanilla. Place some of this filling on each piece of dough and roll up from the wide end in.

Place well apart on greased cookie sheets and bake at 375° F for 25 minutes or until golden brown.

Makes 24.

—Mrs. Ed Stephens

Lithuanian Napoleon Torte

This delicious torte takes some time to assemble, but it is well worth the effort. For variety, melted chocolate, chopped nuts or chopped fruit may be added to the fillings.

PASTRY:
1 lb. butter, softened
4 cups flour
2 cups sour cream
FILLING #1:
¾ cup granulated sugar
5 Tbsp. flour
¼ tsp. salt
2 cups milk, scalded
4 egg yolks, beaten
1 tsp. vanilla
FILLING #2:
2 14-oz. cans sweetened
    condensed milk
6 egg yolks, beaten
2 tsp. vanilla
½ lb. butter, softened

To make pastry, cut butter into flour until crumbly and blend in sour cream. Form dough into 10 balls. Cover each with wax paper and refrigerate overnight.

Allow dough to stand at room temperature for 15 minutes, then roll each ball into a wafer thin circle on a lightly floured board. Prick all over and bake at 350° F for 7 to 10 minutes. Cool.

To make filling #1, mix together sugar, flour and salt in top of double boiler. Gradually add hot milk, stirring constantly. Cook and stir until mixture thickens. Pour a small amount over egg yolks, mix thoroughly and pour back into hot mixture. Cook for 2 minutes. Cool, then add vanilla.

To make filling #2, pour milk into top of double boiler and cook, stirring frequently, until thickened — about 30 minutes. Add egg yolks slowly in a thin stream, stirring constantly. Add vanilla. Cook and stir for 10 minutes. Chill. Beat butter until fluffy, then slowly beat in chilled milk mixture.

To assemble torte, place one layer of pastry on a platter and spread with either filling. Continue stacking, alternating fillings, until 1 layer of pastry remains. Frost top and sides with remaining filling. Crush remaining pastry layer and cover torte with crumbs. Refrigerate for several hours.

Serves 30.

—Diane Cancilla

Apple-Oat Squares

⅓ cup butter
½ cup brown sugar
1 cup flour
½ tsp. baking soda
½ tsp. salt
1 cup rolled oats
2½ cups peeled, sliced tart
    apples
2 Tbsp. butter
¼-⅓ cup sugar

Cream butter and mix sugar in gradually. Sift flour, add baking soda and salt, and combine with creamed mixture until crumbly. Stir in rolled oats. Spread half the mixture into a greased 8-inch square cake pan. Cover with sliced apples. Dot with butter and sprinkle with sugar (and cinnamon if desired). Spread remainder of crumb mixture on top.

Bake at 350° F for 40 to 45 minutes.

—Johanna Vanderheyden

Baklava

¾ lb. butter, cut into ¼-inch
    pieces
½ cup vegetable oil
40 sheets filo pastry
4 cups walnuts, crushed
¾ cup honey
1 Tbsp. lemon juice

Melt butter over low heat, removing foam as it rises to the surface. Remove from heat, let rest 2 to 3 minutes and spoon off clear butter. Discard milky solids.

Stir oil into butter and coat 9" x 13" baking dish with 1 Tbsp. of mixture, using a pastry brush. Lay a sheet of pastry in baking dish, brush with butter, lay down another sheet and brush with butter. Sprinkle with 3 Tbsp. of walnuts. Repeat this pattern to make 19 layers. Top with 2 remaining sheets of filo and brush with remaining butter.

Score top of pastry with diagonal lines ½-inch deep, 2 inches apart, to form diamond shapes.

Bake at 350° F for 30 minutes, reduce heat to 300° and bake 15 minutes longer, or until top is golden brown.

Remove from oven. Combine honey and lemon juice and pour slowly over baklava. Slice when cool.

—Carol Gasken

Rhubarb Squares

This recipe originated with the author's grandmother, who owned a bakery in Toronto in the 1940s. It has been adapted to make use of whole grains and natural sweeteners.

3 cups chopped rhubarb
¾ cup water
Honey
3 Tbsp. cornstarch
1 cup whole wheat flour
1 cup rolled oats
½ tsp. baking powder
¼ tsp. salt
¼ tsp. nutmeg
½ tsp. cinnamon
2 Tbsp. demerara sugar
½ cup melted butter

Cook rhubarb in ½ cup water, with honey to taste. Mix cornstarch in ¼ cup water and add to stewed rhubarb. Cook, stirring, until thickened, and set aside.

Mix remaining ingredients together. Put half the oat mixture on the bottom of an 8-inch square baking dish. Pat down and fill with rhubarb. Sprinkle remaining oat mixture on top.

Bake 35 minutes at 350° F. Allow to cool for 30 minutes before cutting into squares.

—*Sandra James-Mitchell*

Scotch Apple pudding

2 cups sliced apples
½ cup granulated sugar
¼ tsp. cinnamon
1 egg
½ cup milk
¼ tsp. salt
½ cup brown sugar
½ cup rolled oats
½ cup flour
2 tsp. baking powder
½ tsp. vanilla
⅓ cup butter

Arrange apples in bottom of buttered baking dish. Sprinkle with sugar and cinnamon.

Mix remaining ingredients and pour over apples. Bake at 350° F for 1 hour or until apples are tender.

—*Barb Curtis*

Peach Crumble

6 medium-sized peaches, peeled, pitted & thinly sliced
½ cup brown sugar, firmly packed
Dash mace
1 cup flour
½ tsp. salt
4 Tbsp. butter

Toss peach slices with ¼ cup of the brown sugar and the mace in a buttered 6-cup baking dish.

Mix flour, remaining sugar and salt in a bowl. Cut in butter. Spread over the peaches and pat down lightly. Bake at 350° F for 45 minutes or until golden. Serve warm with cream.

—*Erika Johnston*

Apple Brown Betty

1½ cups brown sugar
1¼ cups flour
⅔ cup butter
2 cups thinly sliced apples, pared & cored
Cream or milk

Rub flour, sugar and butter together to form a corn meal texture. Press half of mixture into bottom of a 10-inch square pan. Spread apples evenly on top. Cover with rest of flour mixture and pat flat with hand or fork.

Bake 15 to 20 minutes at 350° F until lightly browned and apples are tender. Serve warm with milk or cream.

—*Deborah Exner*

Blueberry Crisp

4 cups blueberries
2 Tbsp. tapioca
⅓ cup sugar
1 Tbsp. lemon juice
½ tsp. lemon peel
⅔ cup brown sugar
¾ cup rolled oats
½ cup flour
½ tsp. cinnamon
⅛ tsp. salt
6 Tbsp. butter

Combine blueberries, tapioca, sugar, lemon juice and lemon peel and mix well. Pour into greased 9-inch square baking pan.

Mix together remaining ingredients and place on top of berries.

Bake at 375° F for 40 minutes.

—*Ken Parejko*

Blueberry Buckle

¼ cup butter
¼ cup honey
1 egg
Salt
1 cup flour
1 tsp. baking soda
⅓ cup buttermilk or yogurt
2 cups blueberries
¼ cup butter
2 Tbsp. honey
⅓ cup flour
½ tsp. cinnamon

Cream together ¼ cup butter, ¼ cup honey, egg and salt. Add 1 cup flour, baking soda, buttermilk or yogurt and mix well. Spread in a greased 8-inch square cake pan. Cover with blueberries.

Combine remaining ingredients and spread over blueberries.

Bake at 350° F for 40 minutes.

—Water Street Co-op

Fresh Apple Fritters

⅝ cup flour
½ tsp. baking powder
½ tsp. salt
1 egg, separated
3 Tbsp. milk
1 cup chopped apples
Oil for deep frying
Powdered sugar

Combine flour, baking powder and salt and mix well. Beat egg yolk and milk together and stir into dry ingredients. Add apples. Beat egg white until stiff and fold into batter.

Drop by spoonfuls into oil heated to 350° F. Fry until golden brown, drain well and roll in powdered sugar. Serve with maple syrup or honey.

Serves 4 to 6.

—Janis Huisman

Strawberry Shortcake

This shortcake has a muffin-like texture and a rough exterior— all the better to trap the whipped cream and strawberries.

½ tsp. salt
3 cups flour
1 Tbsp. baking powder
4 Tbsp. granulated sugar
1 cup soft shortening
1 egg, slightly beaten with enough milk to make 1 cup of liquid
½ tsp. vanilla
1 qt. strawberries, cleaned & hulled
2 cups whipping cream, whipped

Sift together salt, flour, baking powder and sugar. Cut in shortening with pastry blender. When well blended, add egg-milk mixture and vanilla. Mix only until flour is moistened. Spoon into a greased 8-inch square pan, leaving dough in clumps. Bake at 350° F for 30 to 40 minutes. Cool. To serve, cut cake into 9 pieces, split each piece open and top with whipped cream and strawberries.

Serves 9.

Peach Kuchen

1½ cups flour
½ tsp. salt
¼ tsp. baking powder
2 Tbsp. sugar
⅓ cup butter
4-6 peaches, peeled, pitted & halved
¼ cup sugar
1 tsp. cinnamon
1 egg, beaten
1 cup whipping cream or yogurt

Combine flour, salt, baking powder and sugar. Cut in butter. Pat dough over bottom and sides of 9-inch square pan.

Arrange peaches over pastry and sprinkle with sugar and cinnamon. Bake at 400° F for 15 minutes.

Combine egg and cream or yogurt and pour over peaches. Bake 30 minutes longer. Serve warm or cold.

Serves 9.

—Adele Dueck

50/50 Pastry

1 cup whole wheat flour
1 cup pastry flour
1 tsp. salt
¾ cup shortening
2 Tbsp. water

Combine flours and salt, and cut in shortening until crumbly. Stir in water to make pastry form a ball.

Store in refrigerator or freezer until needed. Makes enough pastry for 1 double-crust pie.

—Jeannette McQuaid

Pastry

5¼ cups flour
1 Tbsp. salt
1 Tbsp. sugar
1 lb. shortening
1 large egg

Sift dry ingredients into a large bowl. Cut in the shortening.

Beat egg and add water to make 1 cup. Pour slowly into flour mixture, stopping to mix with a fork. Add only enough liquid to make pastry form a ball.

Turn out onto a floured board and knead until mixture is smooth. Divide into 4 portions, wrap well and refrigerate or freeze.

Makes enough pastry for 4 double-crust pies.

—Carolyn Hills

Sautéed Bananas

½ cup softened butter
½ cup firmly packed brown sugar
½ tsp. cinnamon
½ tsp. nutmeg
¼ tsp. cloves
Salt
4-6 bananas

Combine all ingredients except bananas and mix well.

Peel and slice the bananas in half lengthwise. To cook each banana, melt 2 Tbsp. butter-sugar mixture and sauté banana over high heat.

Serve with vanilla ice cream.

Serves 4 to 6.

—Jill den Hertog

Cumberland Sauce

This traditional sauce to accompany hot or cold roast meats is also delicious over cheesecake or ice cream.

2 oranges
1 lemon
4 Tbsp. red currant jelly
4 Tbsp. port

Grate rind from fruit, then squeeze for juices. Put rind and juices into heavy saucepan and heat gently until simmering. Add red currant jelly and stir until dissolved. Add port.

Serve warm with hot meats, chill to use with cold meats or desserts.

Makes 1 cup.

—Sheila Bear

Apple Pan Cake

2 Tbsp. butter
2 apples, quartered & thinly sliced
¼ cup firmly packed brown sugar
¼ tsp. cinnamon
3 eggs
½ cup milk
½ cup flour
¼ tsp. salt
1 Tbsp. brown sugar

Melt butter in a 9-inch round cake pan. Add apples and coat with butter. Sprinkle with ¼ cup brown sugar and cinnamon. Place in 400° F oven while preparing batter.

Mix eggs, milk, flour and salt together. Pour over the apples, sprinkle with 1 Tbsp. brown sugar, dot with butter and bake 15 to 20 minutes.

Serves 2.

—Lisa Fainstein

Fresh Raspberry Pie

Pastry for 9-inch double-crust pie
4 cups raspberries
⅔ cup sugar
2 Tbsp. quick-cooking tapioca
1 Tbsp. lemon juice
2 Tbsp. butter

Toss berries lightly with sugar and tapioca. Line a pie dish with pastry and fill with berries. Sprinkle with lemon juice and dot with butter.

Cover with top crust. Slash crust. Bake at 425° F for 20 minutes, then reduce heat to 350° and bake until filling has thickened and pastry is golden, about 40 minutes. Cool before cutting.

—Joan Airey

Raspberry Sour Cream Pie

Pastry for 9-inch pie shell
2 eggs
1⅓ cups sour cream
1 tsp. vanilla
1 cup sugar
⅓ cup flour
Salt
3 cups fresh raspberries
½ cup loosely packed brown
    sugar
½ cup flour
½ cup chopped walnuts or
    pecans
¼ cup chilled butter

Line pie plate with pastry.

Beat eggs and whisk in sour cream and vanilla. Mix sugar, flour and salt and add to egg mixture. Gently stir in raspberries. Pour into pie shell and bake at 400° F for 30 to 35 minutes or until centre is almost set.

Mix brown sugar, flour and nuts. Cut in butter until mixture is crumbly. Sprinkle over pie and return to oven for another 10 to 15 minutes.

—Carol Parry

Raspberry Flan

This recipe is fast and easy to make and there is no pastry to roll. It makes a wonderful dessert in the winter with frozen berries.

1 cup flour
Salt
2 Tbsp. sugar
½ cup butter
1 Tbsp. vinegar
1 cup sugar
2 Tbsp. flour
3 cups raspberries

Combine 1 cup flour, salt and 2 Tbsp. sugar. Add butter and vinegar and mix well with hands. Press gently into 9-inch pie plate.

Mix together gently 1 cup sugar, 2 Tbsp. flour and 2 cups raspberries. Place in pie plate. Bake at 400° F for 50 to 60 minutes. Sprinkle with remaining berries after removing from oven.

—Donna Gordon

Fresh Strawberry Pie

Baked 8-inch pie shell
1 qt. strawberries, cleaned &
    hulled
1 cup sugar
⅓ cup cornstarch
1 Tbsp. lemon juice
Whipped cream to garnish

Mix strawberries with sugar and let sit overnight. In morning, drain off juice and add water to make 1¾ cups of liquid.

Blend cornstarch to a paste with ¼ cup liquid in double boiler. Add remaining liquid and cook over direct heat, stirring constantly, until sauce boils and is clear. Place in double boiler, cover and cook another 15 minutes. Remove from heat, add lemon juice and fold in berries.

Cool to lukewarm, then pour into pie shell. Garnish with whipped cream.

—Cindy McMillan

Blueberry Chantilly Pie

Baked 9-inch pie shell
4 cups blueberries
½ cup honey
½ cup water
2 Tbsp. cornstarch
1 Tbsp. butter
2 Tbsp. Cointreau or Grand
  Marnier
1 cup whipping cream
2 Tbsp. honey
¼ tsp. almond extract
½ cup sliced almonds

Blend together 1 cup blueberries, honey and water. Add cornstarch and cook until thick. Stir in butter and Cointreau or Grand Marnier. Cool.

Fold in remaining 3 cups of blueberries and pour into baked pie shell.

Whip cream with honey and almond extract. Spoon on top of pie and sprinkle with almonds.

—David Slabotsky

Strawberry Cheese Pie

1½ cups graham cracker
  crumbs
6 Tbsp. soft butter
½ cup confectioners' sugar
8 oz. cream cheese
1 cup sugar
4 eggs
⅔ pint sour cream
1 tsp. lemon juice
1 pint strawberries
2 Tbsp. cornstarch

Mix together cracker crumbs, butter and confectioners' sugar. Press into a 9-inch pie plate. Chill.

Combine cheese, sugar, eggs, sour cream and lemon juice, and mix well with electric mixer. Pour into pie shell and bake at 350° F for 1 hour.

If using fresh berries, crush, drain and reserve juice. If using frozen berries, drain and reserve juice. Sweeten juice to taste, add cornstarch and cook until thick, for at least 10 minutes. Cool. Add berries and spread over pie.

—Ken Parejko

Fresh Blueberry Tart

This recipe provides a change from the traditional two-crust fruit pie. The crust is crispy and slightly sweet, and the whole uncooked berries make the pie taste very fresh.

1½ cups plus 2 Tbsp. flour
Salt
2½ Tbsp. sugar
½ cup unsalted butter
1 egg yolk
2-3 Tbsp. ice water
5 cups blueberries, rinsed
⅓ cup water
½ cup sugar
½-⅔ cup sour cream

Mix flour, salt and 2½ Tbsp. sugar with the butter until crumbly. Stir together the egg yolk and 2 Tbsp. of the ice water. Blend into the flour mixture until dough forms a ball, adding a little more water if necessary. Wrap pastry and chill for at least 1 hour.

Roll out pastry and line a pie plate. Chill for 30 minutes. Weight the pastry with dried peas to keep it from bubbling and bake at 400° F for 6 to 8 minutes. Remove peas, prick pastry lightly and return to oven. Bake another 10 to 15 minutes or until golden. Cool.

Combine 3 cups of blueberries with ⅓ cup water and ½ cup sugar in a heavy saucepan. Bring to a boil over medium heat, stirring constantly. Simmer, still stirring, until mixture thickens to a jam-like consistency — about 15 minutes. Cool.

Spread sour cream in the pie shell. Combine remaining 2 cups of berries with the berry jam. Spread over the cream. Serve at room temperature.

—Virginia Jamieson

Sour Cream Raisin Pie

Baked 9-inch pie shell
1½ cups sour cream
3 egg yolks, well beaten
1 cup sugar
1 tsp. cinnamon
¼ tsp. ground cloves
½ cup raisins
½ cup chopped walnuts
2½ Tbsp. flour

Combine sour cream and egg yolks. Combine remaining ingredients, add to cream-egg mixture and place in a double boiler.

Cook, stirring constantly, until mixture is consistency of heavy cream filling and has turned brown in colour.

Pour into pie shell. Chill before serving.

—Freda Creber

Crabapple Pie

Pastry for 9-inch
   double-crust pie
4 cups sliced crabapples
¾ cup sugar
1 tsp. cinnamon
1 tsp. nutmeg
1 Tbsp. butter

Line pie plate with pastry and fill with sliced crabapples. Combine sugar and spices and sprinkle over the crabapples. Dot with butter and top with pastry. Crimp edges and slash top.

Bake at 425° F for 15 minutes, reduce heat to 350° and bake 45 minutes longer.

—Sandra Lloyd

Old-Fashioned Saskatoon Pie

Pastry for 9-inch
   double-crust pie
4 cups Saskatoon berries,
   washed
2 Tbsp. water
2 Tbsp. lemon juice
¾ cup sugar
1½ Tbsp. quick-cooking
   tapioca
1 Tbsp. butter

Simmer together berries, water and lemon juice, covered, over low heat, for 3 to 4 minutes. Remove from heat and stir in sugar, tapioca and butter. Cool.

Line pie plate with pastry and fill with cooled berry mixture. Cover with top crust, trim and seal edges. Prick top, brush with milk and sprinkle with sugar.

Bake at 450° F for 15 minutes, reduce heat to 350° and bake 30 to 35 minutes longer.

—Joan Airey

Sour Cream Peach Pie

Pastry for 9-inch pie shell
1 Tbsp. flour
¾ cup sour cream
½ cup granulated sugar
⅓ cup flour
¼ tsp. almond extract
4 cups peeled, sliced
   peaches
¼ cup brown sugar

Sprinkle pie crust with 1 Tbsp. flour.

Combine sour cream, sugar, ⅓ cup flour and almond extract and stir until smooth. In pie shell, alternate layers of peaches with cream mixture, ending with cream.

Bake at 425° F for 20 minutes, reduce heat to 350° and bake another 35 minutes. Sprinkle with brown sugar and broil until golden.

Cool before serving.

—Shirley Thomlinson

Sour Cream Apple Pie

Pastry for 9-inch pie shell
2 Tbsp. flour
⅛ tsp. salt
¾ cup brown sugar
1 egg
1 cup sour cream
1 tsp. vanilla
½ tsp. nutmeg
2 cups diced tart apples
⅓ cup sugar
⅓ cup flour
1 tsp. cinnamon
¼ cup butter

Sift flour, salt and sugar together. Add egg, sour cream, vanilla and nutmeg. Beat to form a smooth batter. Add apples and pour into pie crust. Bake at 400° F for 15 minutes, reduce heat to 350° and bake another 30 minutes.

Meanwhile, combine remaining ingredients to make topping. Remove pie from oven, sprinkle on topping and return to oven. Bake for 10 minutes at 400°.

—Leah Patton

Apple Pie

Pastry for 9-inch
    double-crust pie
8 cups pared, cored & thinly
    sliced cooking apples
⅓ cup firmly packed brown
    sugar
⅓ cup granulated sugar
1 Tbsp. cornstarch or 2
    Tbsp. flour
1 tsp. cinnamon
¼ tsp. nutmeg
¼ tsp. salt
2 Tbsp. butter
Water or milk
Sugar to sprinkle on top

Place sliced apples in a large bowl. Mix sugars, cornstarch or flour, cinnamon, nutmeg and salt in a small bowl and sprinkle over the apples. Let stand for 10 minutes, until a little juice forms.

Line pie plate with pastry and pile apple mixture into it. Dot with butter and top with pastry. Seal.

Brush top of pastry with a little milk or water and sprinkle lightly with sugar. Slash top.

Bake at 375° F for 40 to 50 minutes or until juice bubbles through slashes and apples are tender.

—Marva Blackmore

Rhubarb Strawberry Crumb Pie

Pastry for 9-inch pie shell
3 cups chopped rhubarb
2 cups strawberries, sliced
1½ cups sugar
⅓ cup flour
1 cup sour cream
½ cup flour
½ cup brown sugar
¼ cup soft butter

Arrange rhubarb and strawberries in unbaked pie shell. Mix sugar and ⅓ cup flour with sour cream and pour evenly over fruit.

Combine ½ cup flour, brown sugar and butter until crumbly and sprinkle over top.

Bake at 450° F for 15 minutes, reduce heat to 350° and bake another 30 minutes, until fruit is tender.

Chill before serving.

—Margaret Silverthorn

Pecan Pie

9-inch pie shell, baked for 5
    minutes
½ cup granulated sugar
3 Tbsp. butter
1 cup corn syrup
3 eggs
1 cup pecan halves
1 tsp. vanilla

Boil together sugar, butter and corn syrup for 2 minutes. Beat eggs and mix with pecans. Pour sugar mixture over eggs and nuts. Add vanilla. Pour mixture into partially baked pie shell and bake at 350° F for 35 to 40 minutes.

—Shirley Hill

Frozen Yogurt Pie

¾ cup ground walnuts
½ cup flour
2 Tbsp. oil
1 cup tofu
¾ cup plain yogurt
¼ cup powdered milk
½ cup honey
Almond extract

Combine walnuts, flour and oil. Press into 9-inch pie plate. Bake at 450° F for 10 to 15 minutes, being careful not to burn. Cool.

Thoroughly drain the tofu and combine with yogurt. Stir with a whisk until smooth. Add milk powder 1 Tbsp. at a time. Add honey and almond extract to taste. Mix well.

Pour into pie crust and freeze overnight. Allow to stand at room temperature for 15 minutes before serving.

—Janet Flewelling

French Silk Pie

Graham cracker crust for
   9-inch pie
2 oz. unsweetened chocolate
2 Tbsp. brandy
2 Tbsp. instant coffee
1 cup butter
1 cup sugar
2 eggs
½ cup ground almonds
½ cup ground hazelnuts

Line pie plate with graham cracker crust; refrigerate.

In double boiler, melt chocolate, then stir in brandy and coffee. Cream butter and sugar together. Beat in eggs one at a time. Stir in chocolate mixture and nuts. Pour filling into shell and chill. Serve cold.

—Michael Bruce-Lockhart

Pumpkin Pie

Pastry for 9-inch pie shell
2 eggs, lightly beaten
2¾ cups cooked mashed
   pumpkin
¾ cup brown sugar
½ tsp. salt
1 tsp. cinnamon
½ tsp. ginger
¼ tsp. cloves
1⅔ cups light cream
Whipped cream to garnish

Combine all ingredients except pastry in order given. Pour into pie shell. Bake at 350° F for 45 minutes or until knife inserted in filling comes out clean. Cool. Top with whipped cream.

—Shirley Morrish

Custard Pie

Pastry for 9-inch pie shell
1¾ cups milk
3 eggs
⅓ cup honey
½ tsp. salt
⅛ tsp. nutmeg
½ tsp. vanilla

Heat milk until lukewarm. Beat eggs, then add honey, salt, nutmeg, vanilla and milk.. Blend thoroughly and pour into pie shell.

Bake at 450° F for 10 minutes. Reduce heat to 325° and bake until custard is set 30 to 40 minutes.

—Winona Heasman

Butter Tarts

Pastry for 14-16 tart shells
1½ cups brown sugar
2 eggs
1-2 tsp. butter, softened
1 tsp. vanilla
1 tsp. vinegar
½ cup raisins
4 Tbsp. milk
½ cup chopped walnuts

Combine all ingredients except pastry and mix until just blended.

Line tart shells with pastry and fill two-thirds full with mixture. Bake at 350° F for 15 minutes, until filling is firm.

Makes 14 to 16 tarts.

—Mary McEwen

Rhubarb Custard Pie

Pastry for double-crust
   9-inch pie
2 eggs
1 cup granulated sugar
1 Tbsp. melted butter
2 Tbsp. flour
2½ cups rhubarb

Beat together eggs, sugar, flour and butter. Mix in rhubarb and pour into pie shell. Top with upper crust. Bake at 400° F for 15 minutes, reduce heat to 350° and cook for another 15 minutes.

—Sharron Jansen

Walnut Cranberry Pie

Tangy, tart and attractive, this pie, with its garnish of orange slices and whole berries will be a festive addition to the Christmas menu.

Pastry for 9-inch pie shell
3½ cups fresh cranberries
½ cup seedless raisins
1½ cups sugar
2 Tbsp. flour
¼ cup corn syrup
1 tsp. grated orange rind
¼ tsp. salt
1 Tbsp. soft butter
¾ cup walnuts, coarsely chopped
Orange slices & whole cranberries to garnish

Grind cranberries and raisins together. Add sugar, flour, corn syrup, orange rind, salt and butter and mix well. Stir in nuts and turn into pie shell.

Bake at 375° F for 40 to 45 minutes. Cool.

Garnish with orange slices and whole cranberries and serve with ice cream.

—*Nina Kenzie*

Pumpkin Cheesecake

1½ cups zwieback crumbs
3 Tbsp. sugar
3 Tbsp. melted butter
16 oz. cream cheese, softened
1 cup light cream
1 cup cooked pumpkin
¾ cup sugar
4 eggs, separated
3 Tbsp. flour
1 tsp. vanilla
1 tsp. ground cinnamon
½ tsp. ground ginger
½ tsp. ground nutmeg
¼ tsp. salt
1 cup sour cream
2 Tbsp. sugar
½ tsp. vanilla

Combine crumbs, 3 Tbsp. sugar and melted butter. Press into bottom and 2 inches up the sides of a 9-inch spring pan. Bake for 5 minutes at 325° F.

Combine cream cheese, cream, pumpkin, ¾ cup sugar, egg yolks, flour, vanilla, spices and salt. Fold in stiffly beaten egg whites and turn into crust. Bake at 325° F for 1 hour.

Combine sour cream, 2 Tbsp. sugar and vanilla. Spread over cheesecake and return to oven for 5 more minutes. Chill before serving.

—*Elizabeth Clayton*

Tofu Sour Cream Cheesecake

1½ cups ground granola, without fruit
½ cup wheat germ
½ cup flour
¼ cup demerara sugar
⅔ cup melted butter
5 cakes tofu
3 cups cottage cheese (small curd)
4 cups sour cream
6 eggs
2 Tbsp. lemon juice
¼ cup maple syrup
¼ cup honey
½ tsp. sea salt
¼ tsp. ground nutmeg
¼ tsp. ground cloves
¼ tsp. ground coriander
½ Tbsp. cinnamon
1 Tbsp. ground ginger
2 tsp. vanilla
2 Tbsp. honey

Combine thoroughly granola, wheat germ, flour, sugar and butter. Press into the bottoms of two 10-inch spring pans. Chill.

Drain tofu. Blend together tofu, cottage cheese, 2 cups sour cream, eggs, lemon juice, maple syrup, ¼ cup honey, salt and spices. Pour over crusts in pans and bake for 40 minutes at 375° F. Allow to cool.

Combine 2 cups sour cream, vanilla and 2 Tbsp. honey, and pour over cooled cheesecakes. Bake for 10 minutes at 425° F. Chill before serving.

Makes 2 large cheesecakes.

—*Sunflower Restaurant*

Lemon Meringue Pie

Lemon meringue pie is a particularly fascinating dessert as it can turn out wretchedly — gelatinous and oversweet (as it is served in most restaurants) — or, if made properly, can be a creamy ambrosia of lemony custard, delicate crust and fluffy meringue. This recipe will produce the gourmet result. It takes more time than opening a package of lemon filling, but the result is incomparable.

Baked 9-inch pie shell
1 cup sugar
6 Tbsp. cornstarch
¼ tsp. salt
2 cups milk
3 eggs, separated
3 Tbsp. butter
⅓ cup lemon juice
1 Tbsp. grated lemon rind
¼ tsp. cream of tartar
3 Tbsp. sugar
½ tsp. vanilla

Combine the sugar, cornstarch and salt in the top of a double boiler. Slowly add the milk, stirring constantly. Cook and stir these ingredients over hot water until the mixture thickens — about 15 minutes. Cover the pan and allow to cook 10 minutes longer. Stir occasionally. Remove from heat. Beat the egg yolks in a separate bowl and add about ½ cup of the thickened milk. Then stir this mixture back into the double boiler. Cook and stir over boiling water for 5 to 6 minutes. Remove from heat and stir in butter, lemon juice and lemon rind. Cool this custard, stirring gently every 10 minutes or so. When cool, pour into pie shell.

For the meringue, beat egg whites with cream of tartar until they are stiff but not dry. Beat in sugar, ½ tsp. at a time, followed by vanilla. Heap onto pie and spread with spatula so that meringue goes all the way out to the crust, around the whole pie. Use a light back-and-forth motion of the spatula to make decorative waves in the meringue. Bake at 350° F for 12 to 15 minutes until the meringue is delicately browned on top.

Serves 6.

—*Alice O'Connell*

Rhubarb Cheese Pie

1¾ cups graham cracker
    crumbs
¼ cup brown sugar
⅓ cup melted butter
¼ tsp. cinnamon
¼ tsp. nutmeg
3 cups diced rhubarb
1 cup honey
2 envelopes gelatin
1 cup cold orange juice
½ lb. cottage cheese
Grated rind of 1 lemon
¼ cup raisins
2 bananas, sliced

Combine cracker crumbs, brown sugar, butter, cinnamon and nutmeg and press into 2 7-inch pie plates. Chill.

Stew together rhubarb and honey until rhubarb is just tender but not mushy. Soften gelatin in ½ cup orange juice, then add to hot rhubarb, stirring gently until dissolved.

Stir remaining ½ cup of orange juice into cottage cheese, a little at a time. Then add to rhubarb mixture along with lemon rind and raisins. Place in freezer until mixture begins to thicken — 10 to 15 minutes — then pour into pie shells and garnish with banana slices.

—*Rosande Bellaar Spruyt*

Dobosh Torte

CAKE:
2 cups flour
1 tsp. baking powder
1 tsp. nutmeg
½ tsp. salt
5 eggs
1 cup butter
1 cup sugar
2 tsp. grated lemon rind
1 tsp. vanilla
ICING:
6 oz. chocolate chips
¼ cup hot, strong coffee
¼ cup icing sugar
½ cup soft butter
4 egg yolks
2 Tbsp. rum

Sift together flour, baking powder, nutmeg and salt. Beat eggs until very thick and lemon coloured — 8 to 10 minutes. Cream butter until light, then gradually add sugar. Add eggs, lemon rind and vanilla and mix thoroughly. Add dry ingredients and mix well.

Pour into buttered loaf pan lined with wax paper and bake at 300° F for 1½ hours. Cool thoroughly.

Meanwhile, make icing. Place chocolate in blender at high speed for 6 seconds. Add coffee and blend for another 6 seconds. Add sugar, butter, egg yolks and rum and blend for a final 15 seconds.

Carefully slice cooled cake horizontally into 4 layers. Spread each layer with icing and reassemble. Top with icing.

Serves 10.

—*Kitty Pope*

Alsatian Torte
with Berry Filling

BASE:
1½ cups flour
¼ cup sugar
½ cup butter
1½ tsp. baking powder
1 egg
1 tsp. vanilla
FILLING:
3-4 cups blueberries or
    strawberries
Grated rind of 1 lemon or
    lime
2 Tbsp. sugar
CUSTARD:
2 cups sour cream
2 egg yolks
¼ cup sugar
2 Tbsp. lemon or lime juice

Combine the ingredients for base in a bowl. Combine well, mixing by hand, and pat evenly in the bottom of a greased, 12-inch springform pan. Lightly mix berries, rind and sugar and sprinkle evenly over dough. Whisk together custard ingredients and pour evenly over berries. Bake at 350° F for 1 hour or until firm and golden brown on top. Cool before serving .

Serves 8 to 10.

—*Janice Graham*

Frozen Blueberry
Ripple Cheesecake

1 cup sugar
⅓ cup water
⅛ tsp. cream of tartar
3 egg whites
16 oz. cream cheese
½ cup sour cream
2 tsp. vanilla
1 Tbsp. grated lemon rind
½-1 cup blueberry preserves
    or blueberry jam
Whipped cream
Blueberries

Combine sugar, water and cream of tartar in a small saucepan and bring to a boil. Boil rapidly until syrup registers 236° F on a candy thermometer — 5 to 9 minutes.

Meanwhile in large bowl of electric mixer, beat egg whites until stiff. Pour hot syrup in a thin stream over egg whites while beating constantly. Continue beating until very stiff peaks form and mixture cools — 10 to 15 minutes.

Beat cream cheese, sour cream, vanilla and rind until light and fluffy. Gently fold meringue into cheese mixture until well blended.

Spoon one-quarter of blended mixture into a decorative serving dish or bowl and drizzle blueberry preserves over this. Continue to layer in this manner, then run knife through completed layering to give a swirl effect. Freeze overnight or until firm. Decorate with whipped cream and berries and serve.

Serves 12.

—*Joann Alho*

Chocolate Amaretto
Cheesecake

Already a rich dessert, this cheesecake is made even more delicious by the addition of chocolate and amaretto. As cheesecakes are egg-based, it is very important to cook at a low temperature and to store in the refrigerator.

CRUST:
1¼ cups chocolate wafer
    crumbs or 1 cup graham
    wafer crumbs & ¼ cup
    cocoa
2 Tbsp. sugar
¼ cup melted butter
FILLING:
16 oz. cream cheese
½ cup sugar
2 large eggs
6 oz. semisweet chocolate,
    melted & cooled
½ tsp. almond extract
1 tsp. vanilla
⅓ cup amaretto
⅔ cup sour cream
TOPPING:
2 oz. semisweet chocolate
1 tsp. shortening

Combine crumbs, sugar and melted butter and press into bottom and halfway up sides of greased 8-inch springform pan. Chill while making filling.

Beat cream cheese until smooth. Beat in sugar gradually. Beat in eggs one at a time at low speed. Add cooled chocolate, flavourings, amaretto and sour cream. Beat at low speed until thoroughly blended then pour into prepared pan.

Bake at 300° F for 1 hour. Turn off heat and leave cake in oven for 1 hour longer. Cool in pan at room temperature, then chill for at least 24 hours in refrigerator.

For topping, melt chocolate with shortening and spread over top of cake.

Serves 8.

—*Vanessa Lewington*

Chocolate Mousse Torte

This dessert is so rich that it will easily serve 12 chocolate-loving people.

Butter
Fine bread crumbs
6 oz. unsweetened chocolate
2 oz. semisweet chocolate
1 Tbsp. dry instant coffee
¼ cup boiling water
8 eggs, separated
⅔ cup sugar
1 tsp. vanilla
⅛ tsp. salt
1 cup whipping cream, whipped

Butter a 9-inch pie plate and dust with bread crumbs. Place chocolate in top of double boiler over hot water. Dissolve coffee in boiling water and stir into chocolate. Cover and melt over low heat, stirring occasionally. Cool slightly.

Beat egg yolks for 5 minutes or until pale and thickened. Gradually add sugar, beating on high for another 5 minutes. Add vanilla and chocolate mixture. Beat slowly until smooth.

Add salt to egg whites and whip until whites hold shape but are not stiff. Fold half the egg whites into chocolate mixture in three additions, then fold chocolate into remaining whites. Remove 3½ cups of mousse, cover and refrigerate.

Line pie plate with remaining mousse and bake at 350° F for 25 minutes. Turn oven off, but leave torte there for 5 more minutes. Remove and cool completely. Place chilled mousse in baked shell and refrigerate for at least 2 to 3 hours. Top with whipped cream and serve.

Serves 12.

—Brenda Kennedy

Bakewell Tart

Pastry for 9-inch pie shell
2 Tbsp. jam
⅓ cup butter
½ cup sugar
½ cup rice flour
¼ cup ground almonds
1 egg, beaten
Almond extract
Blanched almonds

Line pie plate with pastry and spread with jam. Cream butter and sugar. Add rice flour and ground almonds alternately with beaten egg. Add a few drops of almond extract.

Spread mixture over jam and decorate with a lattice of pastry strips and blanched almonds. Bake at 375° F for 40 to 45 minutes.

—Sue Davies

Raspberry Blueberry Pie

Pastry for double 9-inch pie shell
1½ cups raspberries
2 cups blueberries
⅔ cup sugar
2 Tbsp. instant tapioca
½ tsp. grated lemon rind
2 Tbsp. lemon juice
2 Tbsp. butter

Lightly toss together berries, sugar, tapioca, lemon rind and lemon juice. Place in pastry-lined pie shell and dot with butter. Cover with top crust, flute edges and cut vents. Bake at 425° F for 15 minutes, reduce heat to 350° and bake for 30 more minutes .

—Valerie Gillis

Raspberry Yogurt Custard Tart

SHELL:
¾ cup unbleached flour
¾ cup whole wheat flour
¾ cup butter
2 Tbsp. sugar
1 Tbsp. vinegar
FILLING:
1 cup sugar
½ cup flour
3 eggs
2 cups yogurt
3½ cups raspberries

Combine shell ingredients until crumbly. Press onto bottom and sides of 10-inch springform pan.

For filling, mix sugar and flour. Stir in eggs and yogurt until well blended. Fold in 3 cups raspberries until blended. Pour into shell and bake at 375° F for 50 minutes. Cool completely and remove from pan. Top with remaining ½ cup raspberries.

—Billie Sheffield

Almond Lemon Tart

BASE:
3 eggs, separated
¾ cup sugar
Grated peel of 1 lemon
1 cup finely ground almonds
1 Tbsp. flour
Salt
TOPPING:
3 lemons
2 egg whites
¼ cup sugar
¾ cup finely ground almonds

To make base, beat egg yolks until pale yellow. Beat in sugar, then stir in lemon peel, almonds, flour and salt. Beat egg whites until stiff and fold into batter. Butter a 10-inch springform pan, pour in batter and bake at 350° F for 30 minutes, or until light brown and pulling away from sides of pan.

Meanwhile, make topping. Peel lemons and separate them into segments, removing pith. Beat egg whites, adding sugar 1 Tbsp. at a time. Fold in ground almonds.

Cover base of cake with lemon segments and spread almond mixture over top. Return to oven for another 15 minutes to brown.

—Lucetta Grace

Grasshopper Pie

CRUST:
1¼ cups finely crushed
   chocolate wafers
¼ cup sugar
3 Tbsp. melted butter
FILLING:
1½ tsp. gelatin
6 Tbsp. cold water
¼ cup sugar
1 egg yolk, slightly beaten
⅓ cup crème de menthe
¼ cup white crème de cacao
1 cup whipping cream
TOPPING:
1 cup whipping cream
2 Tbsp. sugar
1 square semisweet
   chocolate, shaved

Combine crust ingredients and press into bottom and sides of well-buttered 9-inch pie plate. Bake at 450° F for 2 to 3 minutes and cool.

To make filling, sprinkle gelatin over cold water in small saucepan. Place over low heat and stir until dissolved. Combine sugar and egg yolk in a bowl and add gelatin and liqueurs. Chill until the consistency of unbeaten egg whites. Whip cream and fold into gelatin mix. Pour into crust and chill for 3 to 4 hours.

For topping, whip cream and sugar. Spoon onto pie and top with shaved chocolate.

—Kirsten McDougall

Creamy Chocolate Rum Pie

Pastry for 9-inch pie shell
1 oz. unsweetened chocolate
1 Tbsp. butter
2 eggs
1 cup sugar
½ cup maple syrup
½ tsp. vanilla
½ cup pecan halves
3 egg yolks
½ cup cold water
1 Tbsp. gelatin
⅓ cup dark rum
1½ cups whipping cream
Chocolate curls

Combine chocolate and butter in a small saucepan and set over low heat until melted.

Beat eggs, ⅓ cup sugar, syrup, chocolate mixture and vanilla together until blended. Stir in pecans and pour into pastry-lined pie plate. Bake at 375° F until filling is set and pastry browned — 15 to 20 minutes. Cool.

Beat egg yolks until foamy. Gradually beat in remaining ⅔ cup sugar. Combine cold water and gelatin in a saucepan. Let stand for 5 minutes, then heat, stirring, just to boiling point. Gradually beat into egg yolk mixture and stir in rum. Set bowl aside in ice water to cool, then chill until it begins to hold its shape when dropped from a spoon. Whip cream until stiff and fold into gelatin mixture. Place in ice water and chill until mixture holds peaks. Spoon over cooled chocolate mixture in pie shell. Garnish with chocolate curls and chill until shortly before serving time.

—Marian da Costa

Black Bottom Eggnog Pie

Pastry for 9-inch pie shell
1 Tbsp. gelatin
$\frac{1}{3}$ cup cold water
4 tsp. cornstarch
$1\frac{1}{3}$ cups light cream
4 egg yolks, beaten
$\frac{1}{4}$ cup honey
$\frac{3}{4}$ Tbsp. dark rum
$\frac{1}{4}$ cup carob powder
2 Tbsp. oil
1 tsp. vanilla
3 egg whites
Salt
1 Tbsp. liquid honey
1 cup whipping cream, whipped

Line pie plate with pastry and bake at 325° F for 20 minutes or until golden. Cool.

Sprinkle gelatin over cold water to soften. In top of double boiler, dissolve cornstarch in light cream. Add beaten egg yolks and $\frac{1}{4}$ cup honey. Cook over boiling water, stirring constantly, until custard begins to thicken. Remove from heat, remove 1 cup custard and set aside.

Stir gelatin into remaining hot custard to dissolve completely. Add rum and set aside to cool, then refrigerate until nearly set.

Combine carob and oil and dissolve in reserved 1 cup custard. Add vanilla and pour into pie shell.

Beat egg whites and salt, adding honey gradually to make a stiff meringue. Fold meringue carefully into chilled custard. Pile on top of carob mixture, refrigerate for 1 hour, then top with whipped cream.

—Anne-Marie Dupuis

Gerri's Banana Cream Pie

Pastry for 10-inch pie shell
$\frac{3}{4}$ cup sugar
$\frac{1}{4}$ cup cornstarch
$\frac{1}{2}$ tsp. salt
1 Tbsp. gelatin
4 egg yolks
3 cups milk
2 Tbsp. butter
1 tsp. vanilla
1 cup whipping cream
4 medium bananas, thinly sliced
Lemon juice

Line pie plate with pastry and bake at 325° F for 20 minutes, or until done. Combine sugar, cornstarch, salt and gelatin. Beat in egg yolks and milk until very smooth. Cook mixture over low heat until thickened — 15 minutes — stirring constantly. Stir in butter and vanilla. Cover and chill.

Whip cream. Reserving some banana for garnish, fold cream and bananas into custard and spoon into pie crust. Chill.

Dip remaining banana slices into lemon juice and garnish top of pie.

—Eila Koivu

Orange Chiffon Pie

Pastry for 9-inch pie shell
3 Tbsp. flour
$\frac{1}{3}$ cup sugar
Salt
3 eggs, separated
2 Tbsp. lemon juice
1 cup orange juice
$\frac{1}{2}$ tsp. vanilla
1 Tbsp. butter
3 Tbsp. cream
Sesame seeds

Line pie plate with pastry and bake at 325° F for 20 minutes, or until golden. In top of double boiler, combine flour, sugar, salt, egg yolks, lemon juice and orange juice. Cook, stirring, over boiling water until very thick. Remove from heat and stir in vanilla, butter and cream. Cover pan and set in cold water. Beat egg whites until stiff and fold into orange mixture. Pour into pie shell and garnish with sesame seeds. Bake at 400° F for 10 minutes. Cool before serving.

—Lisa Calzonetti

Danish Rice Dish

This dish is traditionally served as part of a Danish Christmas dinner.

¾ cup brown rice
4 cups milk
2 tsp. vanilla
2 tsp. almond extract
1½ Tbsp. sugar
1 cup whipping cream
1 cup ground almonds
2 cups raspberries

Cook rice in milk over low heat until tender — this will take a long time. Cool. Add vanilla, almond extract and sugar. Blend well. Whip cream and fold into mixture along with almonds. Refrigerate.

When ready to serve, warm raspberries and serve on top of pudding.

Serves 8.

— *G.L. Jackson*

Maple Syrup Baba

1 tsp. sugar
½ cup warm water
1 Tbsp. yeast
1½ cups flour
½ cup butter
¼ cup sugar
4 eggs, beaten
½ tsp. salt
1½ cups maple syrup
⅓ cup water
1 Tbsp. rum
Whipped cream

Dissolve sugar in warm water, sprinkle with yeast and let stand for 10 minutes. Stir well. Beat in ½ cup flour. Cover and let rise until double in bulk — about 30 minutes.

Cream butter and sugar. Beat in eggs alternately with remaining flour and salt until batter is smooth. Beat in yeast mixture. Turn into greased 8-inch tube pan. Cover and let rise until doubled in bulk — ½ to 1 hour.

Bake at 350° F until nicely browned. Cool in pan, then turn onto plate. Bring syrup, water and rum just to a boil. Prick baba all over with skewer and pour syrup over. Continue basting until baba is well soaked. Serve with whipped cream.

Serves 10.

— *Renée Porter*

Mai Tai Pie

This dish is so named because it contains many of the same ingredients as the Mai Tai drink — pineapple juice, rum and orange liqueur. Curaçao, the generic name for orange liqueurs, has been produced by the Dutch since the 16th century using the dried peel of green oranges from the West Indian island of Curaçao. It is now made in a number of different ways and marketed under several names — Grand Marnier, Triple Sec and Cointreau to name a few.

CRUST:
1 cup coconut
6 Tbsp. butter, melted
FILLING:
1 envelope gelatin
½ cup sugar
4 eggs, separated
¾ cup pineapple juice
¼ cup lime juice
⅓ cup light rum
2 Tbsp. orange liqueur
½ cup whipped cream

Combine coconut and butter and press into 9-inch pie plate. Bake at 300° F for 25 minutes.

Blend gelatin with ¼ cup sugar, then beat in egg yolks until well blended. Gradually blend in pineapple juice. Cook until slightly thickened, remove from heat and stir in lime juice, rum and liqueur. Chill, stirring often, until thickened.

Beat egg whites, slowly adding remaining ¼ cup sugar. Fold into gelatin mixture along with whipped cream, then spoon into cooled pie shell. Chill for at least 3 hours.

— *Anna J. Lee*

Orange Blossom Pudding

2 Tbsp. gelatin
2 cups sugar
¼ tsp. salt
2½ cups orange juice
4 egg yolks, beaten
1 Tbsp. grated orange peel
3 Tbsp. lemon juice
1 cup orange sections
2 cups whipping cream

Combine gelatin, sugar and salt. Stir 1 cup orange juice into egg yolks and then stir into gelatin mixture.

Bring to a boil over medium heat, stirring constantly. Remove from heat and stir in orange peel, remaining orange juice and lemon juice.

Chill, stirring occasionally, until mixture falls from spoon in lumps. Stir in orange sections. Whip cream until stiff and fold in.

Pour into 1-quart mould and chill until set.

Serves 10.

—Beth Killing

Rich Ricotta Custard

1 cup ricotta cheese
3 egg yolks
1 cup milk
⅓ cup sugar
1 Tbsp. rum
Grating of orange rind

Beat together cheese, egg yolks, milk and sugar. Add rum and orange rind to flavour. Bake at 325° F until set — about 45 minutes. Serves 4 to 6.

—Elizabeth Templeman

Burnt Almond Sponge

This is definitely a dessert for a special occasion. The wonderful taste makes the work worthwhile.

½-¾ cup chopped almonds
1 Tbsp. gelatin
1¼ cups milk
1¼ cups sugar
½ tsp. salt
1 cup whipping cream
1 tsp. vanilla
1 Tbsp. sherry (optional)

Toast almonds and set aside 1 Tbsp. for garnish. Sprinkle gelatin in ¼ cup cold water, then warm to dissolve.

Scald milk. Caramelize sugar in heavy saucepan, being careful not to burn it. Remove pan from heat when all the sugar is liquid.

Add milk to caramelized sugar a little at a time. The mixture will boil up each time. Stir constantly as milk is being added. Add salt and gelatin.

Refrigerate mixture and chill until partially set — the consistency of egg whites. Beat until spongy. Without washing beaters, whip cream until stiff, adding vanilla and sherry. Fold into spongy mixture along with almonds. Spoon into serving bowl and sprinkle with reserved almonds. Chill until set.

Serves 6 to 8.

—Megan Sproule

Mandarin Mousse

2 10-oz. cans mandarin orange sections, well drained
2 Tbsp. lemon juice
2 Tbsp. orange liqueur
1 tsp. vanilla
¼ cup cold water
1 envelope gelatin
½ cup sugar
2 cups whipping cream

Purée mandarins until smooth. Turn into large bowl and add the lemon juice, liqueur and vanilla. Pour water into measuring cup and add gelatin to soften. Turn into saucepan and heat, stirring constantly, over medium heat until mixture becomes almost clear — approximately 2 minutes. Add sugar and stir until dissolved.

Stir into fruit mixture and cool to room temperature. Whip cream until it will hold soft peaks. Stir in quarter of mixture, then fold in remaining cream. Turn into dessert dishes and chill until set, approximately 2 hours.

Serves 6.

—Judy Black

Danish Rum Soufflé

3 eggs, separated
1 egg yolk
1 cup sugar
¼ cup rum
1 envelope gelatin
¼ cup cold water
1 cup whipping cream
Unsweetened chocolate

Beat egg yolks and ½ cup sugar until light lemon colour. Add rum. Dissolve gelatin in water and heat over boiling water. Stir into yolk mixture. Beat cream until stiff.

In another bowl, beat egg whites until stiff but still moist. Add remaining ½ cup sugar gradually. Fold cream into yolk mixture then fold in whites. Pour into serving dish and chill for 4 to 6 hours. Serve with curls of unsweetened chocolate sprinkled on top.

Serves 4 to 6.

—*Ruth Burnham*

Blintz Soufflé

BATTER:
½ cup butter
1 cup sugar
6 eggs
1½ cups sour cream
½ cup orange juice
1¼ cups flour
2 tsp. baking powder
½ tsp. baking soda
FILLING:
8 oz. cream cheese, softened
16 oz. small curd cottage cheese
2 egg yolks
1 Tbsp. sugar
1 tsp. vanilla

Cream butter and sugar together. Add remaining batter ingredients and mix well. Pour half of the batter into a greased 9" x 13" pan.

Combine filling ingredients and mix well. Pour over batter and spread. Pour remaining half of batter on top. Bake at 350° F for 50 to 60 minutes.

Serves 8.

—*Nancy Chesworth Weir*

Lemon Snow Pudding with Custard Sauce

4 Tbsp. cornstarch
1 cup sugar
Salt
½ cup cold water
1¾ cups hot water
4 Tbsp. lemon juice
2 tsp. grated lemon peel
2 egg whites
CUSTARD SAUCE:
2 egg yolks
1 tsp. cornstarch
2 Tbsp. sugar
Salt
¾ cup milk

Mix cornstarch, sugar and salt in saucepan. Add cold water, mix until smooth and then add hot water. Stir over medium heat until thickened.

Remove from heat and add lemon juice and peel. Fold into stiffly beaten egg whites and chill.

To make custard sauce, combine all ingredients and heat slowly, until mixture coats spoon. Chill. Serve over pudding.

Serves 6 to 8.

—*Patricia E. Wilson*

Grand Marnier Mousse

1 cup sugar
1 envelope gelatin
6-oz. can orange juice
    concentrate, thawed
5 egg yolks
3 Tbsp. Grand Marnier
8 egg whites
1 cup whipping cream

Mix ½ cup sugar with gelatin in heavy pot. Add orange juice concentrate and heat over medium-low heat until warm, stirring often.

Beat yolks until blended and stir in about ¼ cup hot orange mixture. Slowly add this mixture to pot, stirring constantly. Continue to cook and stir over medium-low heat until thickened — 5 to 10 minutes. Add Grand Marnier. Remove from heat and cover with wax paper. Let cool at room temperature.

Beat egg whites in large bowl. Gradually add remaining ½ cup sugar and continue beating until it will hold soft peaks. Whip cream until it will hold soft peaks. Fold orange mixture into whipping cream, then into egg whites. Refrigerate until firm or freeze for 2 hours, then store in refrigerator.

Serves 6 to 8.

—Heather Petrie

Pavlova and Yogurt Chantilly

2 egg whites
1 tsp. white wine vinegar
3 Tbsp. hot water
1 cup sugar
1 tsp. cornstarch
1 tsp. vanilla
⅔ cup whipping cream
⅔ cup unflavoured yogurt
2 Tbsp. confectioners' sugar
2 kiwi fruit, peeled and sliced

Combine egg whites, vinegar, water, sugar, cornstarch and ½ tsp. vanilla in large bowl and beat until mixture holds a firm peak. Mark an 8-inch circle on a piece of foil on a cookie sheet. Heap the meringue onto the foil and spread it evenly within the circle. Bake at 250° F for 1½ hours. When cool, transfer to a serving plate.

Whip the cream until stiff. Fold in yogurt, sugar and remaining ½ tsp. vanilla. Chill well. Just before serving, pile the whipped cream mixture onto the meringue and top with sliced fruit.

Serves 6 to 8.

—Sylvia Petz

Piña Colada Custard

If available, 2 cups fresh pineapple could be substituted for the canned pineapple indicated in the recipe.

3 eggs
¼ cup honey
Salt
2 cups scalded milk
½ cup grated coconut
1 tsp. vanilla extract or 1
    Tbsp. rum
14-oz. can unsweetened
    pineapple
Toasted pecans

Place eggs in heavy pot and whisk to just blend. Add honey and a pinch of salt and slowly pour in the hot milk, stirring constantly. Add coconut and cook over medium heat until thickened — about 10 minutes. Stir in vanilla or rum.

To serve, place pineapple in bottoms of bowls and ladle on custard. Sprinkle with pecans.

Serves 4.

—Bertha B. Bumchuckles

Creamy Ambrosia

This recipe results in a rich, creamy ice cream that, once tasted, will destroy the appeal of all commercial products. The flavouring can be varied to include other liqueurs and/or fruits. Some particularly tasty combinations are raspberry liqueur and raspberries, Tia Maria and peach, amaretto and slivered almonds — anything that appeals. The ice cream can be removed from the mould and garnished with fruit if desired.

¾ **cup sugar**
3 **eggs**
3 **egg yolks**
2 **Tbsp. amaretto liqueur**
2 **cups whipping cream**

Combine sugar, eggs and yolks in top of double boiler. Heat slowly over hot water until just warm, stirring constantly — about 10 minutes.

Place in large bowl and beat on high speed until thickened and somewhat stiff — 15 minutes. Beat in liqueur. (If using fruit, add most at this point, saving a few pieces to stir in by hand at the end.)

Whip cream until soft peaks form. Fold gently but thoroughly into egg mixture. Place in freezer container and freeze for at least 6 hours.

Serves 6.

Melissa's Orange Sherbet

½ **envelope gelatin**
¼ **cup orange juice**
⅓ **cup honey**
1 **cup whipping cream**
¾ **cup & 2 Tbsp. orange juice**

Heat gelatin and orange juice over low heat until gelatin dissolves — about 5 minutes — stirring constantly.

Mix remaining ingredients and add to gelatin mixture. Freeze in pie plate until firm. Beat with mixer or in blender until smooth, then refreeze in covered container.

Serves 4.

—Linda Townsend

Strawberry Sorbet

½ **cup water**
½ **cup honey**
4 **cups strawberry purée**
1 **Tbsp. lemon juice**

Heat together water and honey until just mixed. Let cool. Add remaining ingredients and mix well.

Freeze in large pan until edges are solid but middle is still mushy. Cut up and blend until smooth and opaque.

Pour into serving bowl and freeze until firm. Remove from freezer and let sit for 10 minutes before serving.

Serves 4 to 6.

—Linda Townsend

Marble Gelatin

This light, nutritious dessert may also be served as a refreshing summer snack if poured into popsicle moulds and frozen.

3 **Tbsp. gelatin**
1 **cup cold apple juice**
2 **cups hot puréed zucchini**
½ **cup maple syrup**
Salt
½ **cup mashed strawberries**
Whipped cream

Soften gelatin in cold fruit juice, then add hot puréed zucchini, maple syrup and salt. Stir until dissolved, then add mashed strawberries in a swirl for desired marble effect. Refrigerate until firm. Dot with whipped cream and serve.

Serves 6 to 8.

—Anne-Marie Dupuis

Primavera Sherbet

2 **bananas**
2 **eggs, separated**
2 **cups sugar**
¾ **cup orange juice**
¼ **cup lemon juice**
1 **cup unsweetened pineapple juice**
1 **cup unsweetened grapefruit juice**

Mash bananas, then add egg yolks and sugar and mix thoroughly. Beat egg whites until stiff and mix gently into banana mixture. Add fruit juices and combine. Pour into refrigerator trays and freeze until beginning to set. Put mixture back into bowl and beat again. Return to trays and freeze until set.

Serves 8 to 10.

—Elma MacLachlan

Frozen Tortonies

1 egg white
4 Tbsp. sugar
1 cup whipping cream
2 tsp. vanilla
½ cup semisweet chocolate
  chips
1 tsp. shortening
¼ cup chopped nuts

Beat egg white until stiff. Gradually add 2 Tbsp. sugar and beat until satiny. Whip cream, add remaining 2 Tbsp. sugar and vanilla. Fold cream mixture into egg white mixture, pour into freezing tray and chill well.

Melt chips and shortening in double boiler over hot water and fold in nuts. Drizzle chocolate mixture over cream mixture. Fold gently and freeze. Allow to soften slightly before serving.

Serves 4.

—André-Gilles Chartrand

Frozen Orange Soufflé

This dessert will look beautiful if orange shells are used as the serving dishes. Cut off the top quarter of each orange, remove fruit, dry well and fill.

3 egg yolks
¾ cup icing sugar
2 tsp. grated orange peel
¼ cup fresh orange juice
¾ tsp. orange liqueur
1 cup whipping cream,
  whipped

Beat egg yolks and sugar until smooth — about 1 minute. Stir in orange peel, juice and liqueur. Fold in whipped cream. Pour about ¾ cup of the soufflé mixture into each serving dish. Freeze until firm — 4 to 6 hours.

Serves 6.

—Pam Collacott

Apfelstrudel

1 Tbsp. oil
1 egg
⅓ cup warm water
¼ tsp. salt
1½ cups flour
⅓ cup melted butter
6 Tbsp. fine dry bread
  crumbs
8 cups thinly sliced, peeled
  apples
3 Tbsp. sugar
½ tsp. cinnamon
2 Tbsp. dark rum
½ tsp. nutmeg
½ cup seedless raisins
Icing sugar
Whipped cream

Beat together oil, egg, water and salt. Add flour while beating, until a firm dough is formed which pulls away from the bowl. Knead until smooth and elastic. Cover and allow to rest for 30 minutes, then cut into 2 equal portions. Roll out each piece on a floured surface to 12" x 18" rectangle. Brush each with melted butter and sprinkle bread crumbs evenly over the surface. Spread apples down centre of each portion lengthwise. Mix sugar, cinnamon, rum, nutmeg and raisins together, divide in half and sprinkle each portion with the mixture. Fold the dough over the filling, first one side, then the other. Slide rolls onto greased baking sheet and brush each with melted butter. Bake at 400° F for 45 minutes. Slice rolls when warm and serve warm or cold, sprinkled with icing sugar and topped with whipped cream.

Serves 8.

*—Margaret & Christopher
Babcock*

Kiwi Sherbet

Invented at Christmastime, when kiwi are very cheap, this is a light, fruity dessert, the perfect end to a heavy meal.

1 envelope gelatin
½ cup cold water
½ cup boiling water
Juice of 1 lemon
1 cup milk
1 cup sugar
7 kiwi fruit
¼ cup white rum

Soften gelatin in cold water. After 20 minutes, add boiling water and whisk to dissolve. Add lemon juice, milk and sugar. Mash 3 peeled kiwi and add to mixture. Add about ¼ cup white rum and place sherbet in freezer in a shallow pan or metal bowl.

Rewhisk when it forms crystals — at least twice. Do not let it freeze hard — keep breaking up the crystals. Allow about 4 hours for freezing. Just before serving, slice 1 kiwi into each of 4 individual serving dishes, placing slices in bottom and up sides. Add sherbet and top with a kiwi slice.

Serves 4.

—Randi Kennedy

Peach Soufflé

3 eggs, well beaten
½ cup milk
½ cup whole wheat pastry
  flour
½ tsp. salt
2 Tbsp. butter, melted
1 Tbsp. lemon juice
2 cups peaches, peeled &
  sliced
3 Tbsp. sugar
Sour cream
Cinnamon

Beat eggs, milk, flour and salt until smooth. Melt butter in 9-inch pie plate and pour in batter. Bake at 450° F on lower shelf of oven for 15 minutes, pricking several times to collapse some of the puffiness. Reduce to 350° and continue baking for another 10 minutes or until golden brown on top.

Remove from pan and drizzle with lemon juice. Spoon sweetened fruit over the top and garnish with sour cream and cinnamon.

—Lisa Calzonetti

Peach Cream Kuchen

2 cups flour
¾ cup sugar
¼ tsp. baking powder
1 tsp. salt
½ cup butter
6 large peaches, peeled &
  thinly sliced
1 tsp. cinnamon
2 egg yolks, beaten
1 cup sour cream

Sift together flour, ¼ cup sugar, baking powder and salt. Cut in butter until mixture resembles fine crumbs.

Press firmly against bottom and sides of greased, 9-inch springform pan. Arrange peaches evenly over crumbs. Combine remaining sugar and cinnamon and sprinkle over peaches.

Bake at 400° F for 15 minutes. Blend egg yolks and sour cream and spoon over peaches. Bake for another 20 minutes or until golden.

Serves 8.

—Midge Denault

Mongo's Pumpkin Roll

¾ cup flour
2 tsp. cinnamon
1 tsp. baking powder
1 tsp. ginger
½ tsp. salt
½ tsp. nutmeg
3 eggs
1 cup sugar
⅔ cup cooked, mashed
  pumpkin
Icing sugar
4 cups vanilla ice cream,
  softened

Mix together flour, cinnamon, baking powder, ginger, salt and nutmeg and set aside. Beat eggs until thick, about 5 minutes, then gradually beat in sugar. Mix in pumpkin and flour mixture.

Line a 10" x 15" jelly roll pan with greased wax paper. Spread batter in pan and bake at 375° F for 15 minutes, or until top springs back when touched. Turn cake onto towel sprinkled with icing sugar. Remove paper and roll cake end to end. Cool.

Unroll cake, spread with ice cream and reroll. Wrap and freeze. Let stand at room temperature for 10 to 15 minutes before serving.

Serves 8.

—Kathy Major

Icelandic Vinarterta

This is a traditional Icelandic recipe. The cookielike layers of cake are stacked with a prune filling spread between them.

CAKE:
3½ cups flour
1 tsp. cardamom
2¼ tsp. baking powder
1 cup unsalted butter
1 cup sugar
1 tsp. vanilla
3 eggs
FILLING:
2 lbs. extra large prunes
1 tsp. cinnamon
1 tsp. almond extract

Combine and sift flour, cardamom and baking powder. Cream butter and sugar until light. Add vanilla, then eggs one at a time, beating well after each addition. Add dry ingredients, half a cup at a time, to make a medium stiff dough.

Divide dough into 5 equal parts. Form each into a round ball, flatten evenly on a floured board and carefully roll into a circle. Place each in a greased, 9-inch cake pan. Bake two at a time at 375° F on separate racks for 6 minutes. Cool.

For filling, cook prunes until tender. Remove pits and add cinnamon and almond extract. Mix well and chill. Spread between layers of cake, building evenly, and refrigerate overnight.

Serves 6 to 8.

—Mrs. N.E. Udy

Plum Kuchen

5 large or 10 small plums
½ cup sugar
¼ cup butter
2 eggs
1 cup flour
1½ tsp. baking powder
½ tsp. salt
¼ cup milk
3 Tbsp. butter
1 tsp. cinnamon
¼ tsp. nutmeg
Apricot **or** currant jelly

Cut plums into halves or quarters, depending on size. Place ¼ cup sugar, butter, eggs, flour, baking powder, salt and milk in large bowl. Beat at low speed until mixture leaves sides of bowl, scraping bowl constantly. Spread dough in lightly greased, 9" x 13" baking pan. Arrange plums, skin side up and overlapping, on top of crust.

Melt butter, stir in remaining ¼ cup sugar, cinnamon and nutmeg and spoon over plums. Bake at 375° F for 30 to 35 minutes. While still hot, brush with melted jelly.

Serves 8.

—Elsie Marshall

Hot Fudge Cake

1 cup flour
2 tsp. baking powder
¼ tsp. salt
¾ cup sugar
5 Tbsp. cocoa
½ cup milk
2 Tbsp. melted butter
1 cup brown sugar
2 cups boiling water

Sift together flour, baking powder, salt, sugar and 1 Tbsp. cocoa. Stir in the milk and melted butter. Place in an ungreased, square cake pan. Combine the brown sugar and 4 Tbsp. cocoa. Spread over the mixture in the pan. Pour the boiling water over the whole mixture just before putting it into the oven. Do not stir.

Bake at 350° F for 45 to 55 minutes.

Serves 4 to 6.

—Catherine Gardner

Apple Gingerbread Cobbler

4 medium apples, peeled,
   cored & sliced
½ cup brown sugar
1 cup water
1 Tbsp. lemon juice
¼ tsp. cinnamon
¼ cup sugar
1 egg
½ cup buttermilk
¼ cup molasses
2 Tbsp. oil
1 cup flour
½ tsp. baking soda
½ tsp. baking powder
½ tsp. ginger
¼ tsp. nutmeg
¼ tsp. salt
2 tsp. cornstarch

Combine apples, brown sugar, water, lemon juice and cinnamon. Cover and cook until apples are tender.

Beat together sugar, egg, buttermilk, molasses and oil. Stir together flour, baking soda, baking powder, spices and salt. Add to egg mixture and beat until smooth.

Combine cornstarch and 1 Tbsp. cold water and stir into apple mixture. Pour into 1½-quart casserole dish. Spoon gingerbread mixture on top.

Bake at 350° F for 30 minutes.

—Carole Creswell

Fresh Orange Cake

4 medium oranges
1½ cups sugar
¼ cup shortening
2¼ cups flour
2 tsp. baking powder
¼ tsp. baking soda
1 tsp. salt
2 egg whites
ICING:
½ cup butter, softened
2 egg yolks
⅛ tsp. salt
¼ cup orange-sugar mixture
1 tsp. grated orange rind
¼ tsp. grated lemon rind
3½ cups icing sugar

Grate rind from 2 oranges. Peel and section 3 oranges, then cut into tiny pieces. Squeeze remaining orange and add juice to cut up oranges. To 1¼ cups of this add ½ cup sugar and stir well. Set aside ¼ cup for the icing.

Cream shortening and remaining 1 cup sugar well. Sift dry ingredients, then add to creamed mixture alternately with orange juice mixture. Add 1 Tbsp. grated orange rind.

Beat egg whites until stiff and fold into mixture. Pour into 2 greased and floured 8-inch round cake pans and bake at 350° F for 25 minutes.

For icing, mix together all ingredients and fill and frost cooled cake.

Serves 8 to 10.

—Jane Hess

Rhubarb Apple Compote

This rhubarb-apple sauce is delicious served with warm custard for dessert, or served over pancakes for Sunday brunch.

5 rhubarb stalks, chopped
½ cup water
5 apples, diced
½ tsp. cinnamon
⅛ tsp. coriander
¼ cup honey

Cook rhubarb in water for 10 minutes. Add diced apples and spices. Cook for 20 more minutes, then add honey.

Serves 6.

—Louise Carmel

Honey Cake

3 eggs
1 cup sugar
¾ cup oil
½ cup honey
¼ cup maple syrup
3 cups flour
2 tsp. baking powder
1 tsp. cinnamon
1 cup warm coffee or tea
1 tsp. baking soda
1 tsp. vanilla

Combine eggs and sugar on high speed of mixmaster. Add oil, honey and maple syrup on low speed. Sift together flour, baking powder and cinnamon. Combine coffee or tea and baking soda and let cool. Add to creamed mixture alternately with dry ingredients. Add vanilla.

Bake in greased tube pan lined with wax paper at 350° F for 1¼ hours. Let cool for at least 1 hour before removing from pan.

Serves 10 to 12.

—Kathryn MacDonald

Baked Pears

4 pears
½ cup sugar
1 cup water
Grated peel of ½ lemon
Ginger
WHIPPED CREAM SAUCE:
½ cup sugar
¼ cup Grand Marnier
½ cup whipping cream
2 egg yolks

Cut pears in half and core. Combine sugar, water, lemon peel and ginger and heat to dissolve sugar. Pour over pears and bake at 350° F for 20 minutes. Drain and cool.

Prepare cream sauce by combining all ingredients and whipping until stiff peaks form. Spoon over pears.

Serves 4.

—Jill Harvey-Sellwood

Cantaloupe Alaska

3 ripe cantaloupes, chilled
4 egg whites
Salt
½ cup sugar
2 cups firm vanilla ice cream
2 Tbsp. halved, blanched
   almonds

Cut cantaloupes in half, remove seeds and level base. Beat egg whites and salt until stiff and gradually beat in sugar until meringue is very glossy.

Place melons on cookie sheet, put 1 scoop of ice cream in each half and spread meringue over ice cream and top edge of melon. Sprinkle with almonds. Bake at 500° F for 2 minutes, or until meringue is golden. Serve immediately.

Serves 6.

—Pam Collacott

Blueberry Cobbler

3 cups blueberries, fresh or
   frozen
½ cup water
½ cup sugar
1 tsp. lemon juice
½ tsp. cinnamon
1½ cups flour
2 Tbsp. butter
2 tsp. baking powder
¼ tsp. salt
2 Tbsp. sugar
⅓-½ cup milk

Wash blueberries and mix with the water, sugar and lemon juice in bottom of 8-inch pan. Sprinkle with cinnamon.

Stir together flour, butter, baking powder, salt and sugar with a fork until mixture is consistency of corn meal. Stir in milk. Roll dough on floured board, cut into serving-sized squares to fit pan and place over berries. Sprinkle with a little sugar and brush with some melted butter.

Bake uncovered at 400° F for 25 minutes.

Serves 6.

—Janet Ueberschlag

Baked Apricots

6 apricots
1 cup brown sugar
1 cup sour cream

Halve apricots and place in shallow baking dish. Sprinkle with brown sugar and top with sour cream. Cook at 325° F for 15 to 20 minutes or until apricots are soft but not mushy.

Serves 6.

—Dee Clarke

Maple Baked Apples

6 apples
⅔ cup chopped walnuts
½ cup maple syrup
¼ cup raisins
3 Tbsp. butter, melted
Nutmeg
½ cup apple cider
Whipping cream

Trim a slice from bottom of each apple so it will stand upright in pan. Core apples to within ½ inch of bottom and make a shallow cut around the middle of each to allow for expansion during cooking. Fill centres with equal amounts of nuts and raisins and set apples in a shallow pan so that they do not touch one another.

Pour some syrup into each apple, then a bit of the melted butter. Sprinkle nutmeg over top and bake at 375° F for 30 to 40 minutes, basting frequently with apple cider while cooking.

Serve hot with cream.

Serves 6.

—Lynn Tobin

Chocolate Dipped Strawberries

Nuts and other fruits can also be used with this recipe. A simple but elegant dessert is to fill a fondue pot with chocolate, melt it at the table and supply guests with bowls of assorted fruit for dipping.

1 quart large, well-shaped & firm strawberries
12 oz. semisweet chocolate chips

Leave stems on berries and make certain that they are completely dry. Melt chocolate in top of double boiler over hot, not boiling, water.

One at a time, dip pointed end of berries halfway into chocolate. Place on cookie sheet lined with wax paper and place in freezer for a few minutes, then refrigerate until set. Serve within a few hours.

—*Louise McDonald*

Royal Cheddar Cheesecake

This is a very rich, creamy cheesecake with a tang of lemon and a hint of cheddar.

CRUST:
1½ cups graham cracker crumbs
3 Tbsp. sugar
1 tsp. grated lemon rind
6 Tbsp. butter, melted
FILLING:
4 8-oz. pkgs. cream cheese
1 cup finely grated Cheddar cheese
1¾ cups sugar
5 eggs
½ cup heavy cream
½ tsp. vanilla
1 tsp. lemon rind

To make crust: Mix crumbs, 3 Tbsp. sugar, 1 tsp. lemon rind and butter. Press evenly in the bottom and up the sides of a 9" springform pan. Chill.

To make filling: In a food processor or with an electric mixer, beat cream cheese and Cheddar cheese together thoroughly. Mix in 1¾ cups sugar until creamy smooth. Beat in eggs, one at a time, then cream, vanilla and 1 tsp. lemon rind. Pour into prepared crust. Bake in very hot oven (500° F) for 12 minutes; reduce heat to 300° and bake for 2 hours, or until firm in the centre. Cool cake completely in pan on wire rack. Chill.

To serve, loosen cake around edges with a knife and remove springform. May be covered with any sliced fresh fruit.

—*Kristine Mattila*

Elegant Grapes

2 cups seedless grapes
1 cup sour cream
½ cup brown sugar
Grated orange rind
Tia Maria

Combine grapes and sour cream, and sprinkle with brown sugar. Chill for at least 2 hours. Add Tia Maria to taste, sprinkle with orange rind and serve

Serves 4.

—*Elsie Marshall*

Fruit Fritters

2 eggs, separated
½ cup milk
1 cup flour
½ tsp. salt
2 tsp. sugar
2 Tbsp. melted butter
Oil
2 bananas, sliced
2 apples, peeled, cored & quartered
2 pears, peeled, cored & quartered
2 peaches, peeled, pitted & quartered
Sugar
Custard

Beat egg yolks until light, then add milk. Sift together flour, salt and sugar and add to milk-egg mixture. Add butter. Beat egg whites until stiff and fold into batter.

Heat oil. Dip fruit in batter and fry in hot oil a few at a time. Cook until golden brown. Remove and drain on paper towels. Roll in sugar, then keep warm while making remaining fritters. Serve with custard if desired.

Serves 4.

—*Patricia E. Wilson*

Maple Cheesecake

Truly a cheesecake for maple-syrup lovers, this one is rich, creamy and smooth.

CRUST:
1¾ cups graham wafer
   crumbs
¼ cup butter, melted
3 Tbsp. brown sugar
FILLING:
½ cup flour
¼ tsp. baking soda
¼ tsp. salt
3 eggs
¾ cup sugar
8 oz. cream cheese
1¼ cups heavy cream
1 cup maple syrup
1 tsp. vanilla
TOPPING:
1 cup heavy cream
½ cup maple syrup
pecans for garnish

For crust: Mix together crust ingredients and press into springform pan. Bake at 350° F for 10 minutes.

For filling: Sift together flour, baking soda and salt. Beat eggs thoroughly. Add sugar and blend well. Cream the cream cheese until fluffy. Add cream slowly and beat until smooth. Blend in 1 cup maple syrup, egg mixture and flour mixture. Add vanilla and mix well.

Pour filling into crust. Bake at 350° F for 1½ hours, or until centre has set. Turn off oven and let sit for 15 minutes. Chill.

Just before serving, whip cream and ½ cup maple syrup together and spread over cheesecake. Garnish with pecans.

—Jane Durward

Ginger Cheesecake

A refreshingly different cheesecake, this one blends fresh gingerroot and crystallized ginger.

CRUST:
1½ cups graham cracker
   crumbs
6 Tbsp. butter, melted
2 Tbsp. sugar
FILLING:
16 oz. cream cheese
½ cup (or less) sugar
2 eggs
3 tsp. lemon juice
2 Tbsp. freshly ground or
   grated gingerroot
TOPPING:
1½ cups sour cream
5 Tbsp. sugar
3 Tbsp. (or more) chopped
   crystallized ginger

Make crust by combining crumbs, butter and sugar. Press into springform pan. Bake at 350° F for 8 minutes.

Beat filling ingredients together until smooth. Pour into crust. Bake at 350° F for 20 to 25 minutes.

Mix topping ingredients together. Spread over cheesecake while it is still hot from the oven. Turn oven off and place cheesecake back in oven for a few minutes. Remove and chill well before serving.

Serves 8.

—Marian da Costa

Honey Cheesecake

CRUST:
1½ cups graham cracker
   crumbs
½ cup butter, melted
2 Tbsp. sugar
FILLING:
16 oz. cream cheese
⅓ cup honey
2 tsp. cinnamon
2 eggs
2 heaping Tbsp. sour cream
1 tsp. vanilla
TOPPING:
½ pint plus 2 Tbsp. sour
   cream
1 tsp. vanilla
2 Tbsp. honey
juice of ⅓ lemon
SAUCE:
1½ cups sliced strawberries
½ cup brandy

Combine crust ingredients and press into large springform pan. Bake at 350° F for 10 minutes, then cool for 5 minutes.

Mix all filling ingredients together and spoon into cooled crust. Bake at 325° F for 30 minutes. Turn heat off and leave pie in oven for 10 more minutes.

Combine topping ingredients and pour over filling. Bake for 8 minutes at 400° F. or until set. Combine berries and brandy, and spoon over cake.

—Lisa Reith

Rhubarb Dessert Torte

The rich shortbread-like base of this recipe is topped with a rhubarb custard and meringue, producing a mouthwatering dessert with very little effort.

BASE:
1 cup butter
2 cups flour
2 Tbsp. sugar
CUSTARD:
5 cups finely chopped rhubarb
2 cups sugar
1 cup cream
6 egg yolks
4 Tbsp. flour
¼ tsp. salt
juice & rind of 2 oranges
MERINGUE:
6 egg whites
¾ cup sugar
2 tsp. vanilla
coconut

Combine ingredients for base and blend well. Press into 9" x 13" pan and bake at 350° F for 10 minutes.

Combine custard ingredients and pour into baked crust. Bake at 350° F for 45 minutes.

Beat egg whites until peaks form, adding sugar 2 Tbsp. at a time. Add vanilla and spread on baked custard. Top with coconut and bake at 400° F until browned — 10 minutes.

Serves 10.

—Dave & Essie Bergen

Apple Bavarian Torte

CRUST:
⅓ cup softened butter
⅓ cup sugar
½ tsp. salt
1 cup flour
FILLING:
1 cup cottage cheese
⅓ cup sugar
½ tsp. vanilla
1 egg
TOPPING:
4 cups sliced apples
sugar to taste
1 tsp. cinnamon
CRUMBLE:
3 Tbsp. butter
⅓ cup flour
⅓ cup sugar
¼ cup sliced almonds for garnish

Make crust by mixing ingredients together and pressing into bottom of an 8" x 8" pan

Mash cottage cheese, then stir in sugar, vanilla and egg until well blended. Spread on top of crust. Place ingredients for topping with 3 Tbsp. water in saucepan and cook over low heat until apples are just slightly tender. Spread carefully over filling.

Combine ingredients for crumble and sprinkle over topping. Arrange almonds on top. Bake at 425° F for 20 minutes, lower heat to 375° and bake for 40 minutes more, or until golden brown. Garnish with sliced almonds. Torte must be cut in pan.

Serves 6 to 8.

—Juanita Bryant

Chocolate Cream Pie

"Put on a pot of coffee, light a fire and put the kids to bed. This pie is the perfect accompaniment — creamy, rich, chocolatey and delicious."

PASTRY:
1½ cups flour
½ tsp. salt
½ cup very cold butter
1 egg yolk
FILLING:
1 cup plus 2 Tbsp. sugar
½ tsp. salt
1 Tbsp. flour
4 Tbsp. cornstarch
3⅔ cups whole milk
6 Tbsp. cocoa
2 Tbsp. oil
2 eggs, beaten
2 Tbsp. butter
1 tsp. vanilla
whipped cream

To make pastry: Combine flour and salt. Cut in butter until crumbly. Add egg yolk and ¼ cup, or more, cold water and toss until dough forms a ball. Put into a plastic bag and knead a few seconds. Chill for at least 1 hour. Roll out on lightly floured board and place in 10-inch pie plate. Crimp edges and prick all over with a fork. Bake at 350° F for 20 minutes, remove from oven and prick again if crust has puffed up. Bake for 20 minutes more.

To make filling: Combine sugar, salt, flour, cornstarch, milk, cocoa and oil. Heat to boiling, stirring constantly until mixture thickens. Remove from heat. Stir about half of chocolate mixture into eggs until completely blended. Pour mixture back into saucepan and continue cooking, stirring constantly until mixture boils again. Remove from heat and blend in butter and vanilla. Pour into crust and chill. Serve with whipped cream.

—Julia Dement

Apple Meringue Pie with Hazelnut Pastry

Multilayered flavours make this pie exceptional.

PASTRY:
¾ cup plus 2 Tbsp. flour
1 tsp. baking powder
½ cup plus 1 Tbsp. sugar
½ tsp. vanilla
¼ tsp. almond extract
⅛ tsp. cloves
1 tsp. cinnamon
1 egg white and ½ yolk
  (reserve other half)
½ cup plus 2 Tbsp. unsalted
  butter, cut up
½ cup plus 2 Tbsp. ground
  hazelnuts
1 Tbsp. milk
FILLING:
10 tart green apples
juice of 1 lemon
⅔ cup sugar, plus more as
  needed
¼ tsp. cinnamon
4 Tbsp. butter
2 Tbsp. flour
MERINGUE:
4 Tbsp. Frangelico (hazelnut)
  liqueur
2 Tbsp. cornstarch
6 large egg whites
¾ cup sugar
salt
1 tsp. vanilla
2 Tbsp. raspberry jam

To make crust: In large bowl, sift together flour and baking powder. Add sugar, vanilla, almond extract, spices and egg and mix together well. Add butter and hazelnuts and knead quickly with fingers to blend. Divide dough in half, reserving one half in freezer. Press other half evenly over bottom and sides of a 9-inch pie plate. Mix reserved ½ egg yolk with 1 Tbsp. milk and brush crust all over. Repeat process with other half. Bake at 350° F for 25 to 30 minutes.

To make filling: Pare and core apples and cut into ¼-inch slices. Mix with lemon, sugar and cinnamon. In large frying pan with lid, melt butter, add flour and cook for 1 minute. Add apple mixture and stir to coat evenly. Cover and cook until just tender, stirring occasionally. Taste for sweetness and add more sugar to taste.

To make meringue: In small saucepan, mix Frangelico and cornstarch until smooth, then add 1 cup boiling water. Put over high heat, stirring briskly until just clear. Chill completely, in freezer. In large bowl, beat egg whites until just foamy. Continue beating while adding sugar until mixture is stiff but not dry. Beat in cornstarch mixture in thirds. When smooth, add salt and vanilla.

To assemble: Brush raspberry jam evenly over crusts. Spoon apple mixture into crusts. Mound meringue on top, making decorative peaks with the back of a spoon. Bake at 350° F for 10 minutes, or until browned.

Makes 2 pies.

—Sandra Lance

Burgundy Berry Pie

2 cups cranberries
2 cups blueberries
½ cup honey
3 Tbsp. cornstarch
⅛ tsp. salt
⅛ tsp. nutmeg
pastry for 9-inch pie shell

Thaw and drain cranberries and blueberries if frozen. Mix honey, cornstarch, salt and nutmeg. Add berries and pour into pie shell. Bake at 425° F for 15 minutes, lower oven temperature to 375° and bake for 35 to 50 minutes longer.

—Judy Mueller

Amaretto Yogurt Cream Cheese Pie

This is a very rich Amaretto-laden dessert that is quick and easy to prepare. Be sure to allow it to set overnight.

CRUST:
2 cups crushed ladyfingers
⅓ cup finely chopped lightly
  toasted almonds
¼ cup Amaretto
3 Tbsp. butter, melted
FILLING:
8 oz. cream cheese, softened
½ cup yogurt
½ tsp. vanilla
¼ cup honey
⅓ cup Amaretto
¼ cup finely chopped lightly
  toasted almonds

Combine crust ingredients and mix well. Press firmly into bottom and sides of 8-inch pie pan. Bake at 325° F for 10 minutes. Cool.

To make filling: Combine all ingredients and beat until completely smooth. Spread in pan. Chill overnight and top with ¼ cup almonds before serving.

—Nancy Scott

Rhubarb Cream Pie

Developed by the contributor's Pennsylvanian mother-in-law for farmhands during haying, this rhubarb pie is for cinnamon lovers.

pastry for 9-inch pie shell
2 lbs. rhubarb, cut into ½" pieces
1½ cups brown sugar
3 Tbsp. quick-cooking tapioca
2 eggs
¼ cup heavy cream
2 Tbsp. cinnamon
2 Tbsp. butter

Line pie plate with pastry. Combine rhubarb, sugar, tapioca, eggs, cream and cinnamon. Toss gently to coat rhubarb. Place in pastry and dot with butter. Bake at 425° F for 10 minutes, reduce heat to 350° and bake for another 20 to 30 minutes.

—Patricia P. Marzke

Dakota Prairie Pumpkin Pie

"This recipe has been handed down with pride through six generations since Charles and Ann Ashton settled in South Dakota in 1881. No family gathering would be complete without it."

4 cups pumpkin purée
4 cups sugar
1 tsp. salt
2 tsp. cinnamon
1 tsp. nutmeg
6 eggs, lightly beaten
4 cups milk
1 cup light cream
1 Tbsp. vanilla
pastry for 3 9-inch pie shells
whipped cream & chopped walnuts for garnish

Combine pumpkin, sugar, salt, cinnamon and nutmeg. Blend in eggs, milk, cream and vanilla. Pour into pie shells and bake at 400° F for 50 minutes, or until firm. Cool on a rack. Garnish with whipped cream and chopped walnuts.

Makes 3 pies.

—Mrs. Charles Weinberger

The Best of All Buttermilk Pie

"My daughter and I tried many buttermilk pie recipes through the years and finally found the right combination: neither too sweet nor too sour."

3 cups sugar
½ cup flour
6 eggs
1 cup buttermilk
¾ cup butter, melted
1 Tbsp. vanilla
pastry for 9-inch pie shells

Mix sugar and flour and set aside. Whisk eggs, add buttermilk, butter and vanilla. Mix well. Slowly add flour-sugar mixture and beat thoroughly. Pour into unbaked pie shells. Bake at 325° F for 1 hour.

Makes 2 pies.

—Peggy Peabody

Sweet Potato Pecan Pie

"This pie holds a special place in my childhood memories."

¼ cup butter
½ cup sugar
1 cup cooked, mashed sweet potato
3 eggs
⅓ cup milk
½ tsp. salt
1 tsp. vanilla
1 cup chopped pecans
pastry for 9-inch pie shell

Cream butter and sugar until smooth. Add sweet potato and eggs and blend well. Mix in milk, salt, vanilla and pecans. Pour into pastry shell and bake at 425° F for 10 minutes. Reduce oven temperature to 325° and bake for another 45 minutes.

—Christine Taylor

Almond Orange Pie with Grand Marnier Cream

"A melt-in-your-mouth indulgence for after that trip through Customs with your coveted bottle of Grand Marnier. While not an instant recipe, it is well worth the effort."

SHELL:
1½ cups pastry flour
½ tsp. ginger
½ tsp. nutmeg
⅛ tsp. salt
⅔ cup butter
⅔ cup sugar
½ cup ground almonds
1 large egg yolk
FILLING:
2 navel oranges, rind grated & reserved
1 cup plus 3 Tbsp. sugar
2 Tbsp. fresh lemon juice
3 Tbsp. softened butter
1 tsp. vanilla
½ tsp. almond extract
2 Tbsp. flour
2 eggs plus 2 egg whites
2 Tbsp. Grand Marnier
GLAZE:
1 large egg yolk beaten with 1 tsp. heavy cream
⅓ cup sliced almonds

To make shell: Blend flour, spices and salt with butter until mixture resembles coarse meal. Blend in sugar, ground almonds and egg yolk plus 1 to 2 tsp. cold water to form a soft dough. Form into 2 balls and chill for 30 minutes. Roll half the dough between sheets of waxed paper to ⅛-inch thickness and fit into 9-inch pie plate, leaving ½-inch overhang. Roll the other half to ⅛-inch thickness, and chill for 30 minutes.

To make filling: Section oranges, removing pith and membranes. In stainless-steel or enamel pot, combine sections with orange rind, 3 Tbsp. sugar, lemon juice and ½ cup water.

Bring to a boil and reduce to ¾ cup. Cool. Cream butter and remaining 1 cup sugar. Add vanilla, almond extract, flour, eggs and egg whites. Mix well. Add orange mixture and Grand Marnier and pour into shell.

Cut remaining dough into strips and lay across pie in a lattice pattern. Fold in overhang and crimp edges. Pour glaze over pie. Sprinkle with sliced almonds.

Bake at 350° F for 45 minutes, or until almonds are golden and filling puffs up through lattice. May be served with a topping of 1½ cups heavy cream whipped with 3 Tbsp. confectioners' sugar and 2 Tbsp. Grand Marnier if desired.

—Anne Creighton

Baked Maple Pudding

SAUCE:
1 cup maple syrup
2 tsp. butter
PUDDING:
1 cup flour
1½ tsp. baking powder
⅓ cup demerara sugar
1 Tbsp. shortening
1 egg
⅓ cup milk
½ cup unsweetened coconut

Bring maple syrup and 1 cup water to a boil, then remove from heat. Add butter and set aside.

Sift together flour and baking powder. Cream sugar and shortening together. Beat in egg. Add dry ingredients alternately with milk to creamed mixture. Beat until smooth. Spread cake batter into greased 8" x 8" pan. Pour sauce over and sprinkle coconut evenly over top. Bake at 350° F for 35 minutes. Serve warm.

Serves 6 to 8.

—Shelley Bishop

Fruit Platz

"This is a recipe given to us by an elderly gentleman who recalled it from his youth on the Prairies, stating they often used wild berries in summer and dried apples in winter."

CRUST:
1¾ cups flour
1 tsp. baking powder
½ tsp. salt
⅓ cup butter
1 egg, beaten
FILLING:
2½ cups sliced fruit
TOPPING:
½ cup sugar
1 Tbsp. softened butter

To assemble: Make crust by combining dry ingredients and cutting in butter. Add ½ beaten egg and ¼ cup cold water to make a soft dough. Press dough into greased 8" x 8" pan, pressing mixture about 1 inch up the sides. Add fruit, spreading evenly over crust. Combine topping ingredients and spread over fruit. Bake at 350° F for 50 to 60 minutes.

Serves 6 to 8.

—Judith Almond-Best

Patchberry Pie

A variation of the standard rhubarb pie that is delicious served warm with ice cream. Frozen rhubarb or currants can be used for a midwinter treat.

FILLING:
2 eggs
$\frac{5}{8}$ cup flour
$\frac{1}{2}$ tsp. salt
2 Tbsp. butter, melted
2$\frac{1}{2}$ cups sugar
2 cups red currants
7 cups chopped rhubarb, cut into 1" pieces
pastry for three 9-inch pie shells
CRUMB TOPPING:
$\frac{2}{3}$ cup flour
1 cup brown sugar
1 tsp. salt
$\frac{2}{3}$ cup butter, melted
2 cups rolled oats

Beat eggs lightly, then combine with flour, salt, 2 Tbsp. butter and sugar. Add currants and rhubarb and fill crusts. Combine crumb topping ingredients and sprinkle on top. Bake at 425° F for 10 minutes, then at 350° for 40 to 50 minutes.

Makes 3 pies.

—*Kim Allerton*

Maple Custard

$\frac{1}{2}$ cup maple syrup
3 eggs, beaten
2 cups milk
salt
mace

Add syrup to eggs and beat well. Beat in milk and salt. Spoon into 4 custard cups and sprinkle with mace. Place cups in pan with 1 inch water. Bake at 350° F for 40 minutes.

Serves 4.

—*Mrs. L.M. Cyre*

Lemon Custard Pudding

$\frac{3}{4}$ cup sugar
1 Tbsp. butter
2 eggs, separated
2 Tbsp. flour
1 cup milk
juice of 1 lemon

Cream sugar and butter together. Beat egg yolks and add to sugar-butter mixture. Mix in flour, milk and lemon juice. Beat egg whites until stiff and fold into batter. Pour into small, buttered ovenproof dish. Place dish in pan containing $\frac{1}{2}$ inch water. Bake at 325° F for about 50 minutes.

Serves 2 to 3.

—*Ruth Henly*

Pumpkin Pecan Tarts

Make these tarts with frozen pumpkin purée for a midwinter flavour pick-up. To freeze pumpkin, bake at 300° F until soft (baking time will depend on size of pumpkin), remove filling from shells, discard seeds, purée, then freeze.

FILLING:
$\frac{1}{2}$ cup milk
$\frac{1}{2}$ cup light cream
2 eggs
1$\frac{1}{2}$ cups puréed pumpkin
$\frac{2}{3}$ cup brown sugar
1 tsp. cinnamon
$\frac{1}{2}$ tsp. salt
$\frac{1}{2}$ tsp. ginger
$\frac{1}{2}$ tsp. cloves
$\frac{1}{2}$ tsp. allspice
1 tsp. vanilla
24 unbaked tart shells
TOPPING:
1 cup chopped pecans
$\frac{2}{3}$ cup brown sugar
3 Tbsp. butter, melted
whipped cream for garnish
pecan halves for garnish

Place all filling ingredients in blender or food processor and blend for 2 minutes. Pour into tart shells and bake at 425° F for 15 minutes. Reduce heat to 275° and bake for 30 minutes more, or until a toothpick inserted in the centre comes out clean. Let tarts cool.

For topping: Mix nuts and sugar. Stir in butter until mixture is uniformly moist. Sprinkle over tarts. Broil about 5 inches from heat for 1 to 2 minutes. Serve with whipped cream and pecan halves.

Makes 24 tarts.

—*J. W. Houston*

Figs & Pears in Rum Custard Sauce

½ cup sugar
1 cup water
½ tsp. vanilla
1 tsp. grated orange rind
1 tsp. grated lemon rind
24 fresh figs or dried figs
  that have been soaked
8 fresh pears, peeled &
  halved
½ cup dark rum
RUM CUSTARD SAUCE:
1 Tbsp. cornstarch
1½ cups milk
4 egg yolks
¼ cup sugar
⅛ tsp. salt
½ cup juice from marinade
2 tsp. dark rum
2 cups heavy cream, whipped

Combine sugar, water, vanilla and grated rind in saucepan. Stir over low heat until mixture comes to a boil. Cut 12 figs in half and leave remainder whole. Add fruit to saucepan, reduce heat and simmer 3 to 4 minutes if the figs are fresh, 10 minutes if dried. Add rum. Marinate fruit in this syrup for 1 to 2 hours in a cool place.

Prepare custard by dissolving cornstarch in ¼ cup cold milk. Add egg yolks and beat lightly. Add remaining 1¼ cups milk, sugar and salt and bring to a simmer, stirring, in a double boiler. Add ½ cup juice from marinade and cook until thickened. Cool. Add rum and chill.

To serve: Place fruit in a large serving bowl. Pour the sauce over and top with whipped cream .

Serves 6 to 8.

—*Ingrid Birker*

Steamed Cranberry Pudding

"This recipe was given to me by a good friend whose family serves it at every Christmas dinner. It has since become a holiday favourite for our family too." The pudding has a tart cranberry taste, well complemented by the sweetness of the sauce.

PUDDING:
2 cups cranberries
½ cup molasses
2 tsp. baking soda
1½ cups flour
HOT BUTTER SAUCE:
½ cup butter
1 cup sugar
½ cup light cream
1 tsp. vanilla

Cut cranberries in half and pour molasses over them. Dissolve baking soda in ½ cup boiling water, then add to cranberries. Stir in flour. Place in well-greased 1-lb. can, and cover with foil. Place in covered kettle with boiling water and steam for 1½ hours.

Meanwhile, prepare sauce: Cream butter and sugar together. Add cream, then place in double boiler and cook until sugar is dissolved. Do not boil. Stir in vanilla. Spoon over pudding while hot.

Serves 8 to 10.

—*Susan Holec*

Baked Orange Pudding

"This recipe has been in my family for well over 50 years and is still going strong. Easy to make, it is simply scrumptious with whipped cream."

SAUCE:
1 cup sugar
1 Tbsp. flour
1 Tbsp. butter
juice & rind of 1 or more
  oranges
BATTER:
½ cup sugar
1 cup flour
1 tsp. baking powder
1 tsp. butter
½ cup milk
⅛ tsp. salt

Make sauce by mixing sugar and flour in saucepan. Melt butter in 2 cups hot water. Add to saucepan with orange juice and rind. Bring to a boil and pour into greased 9" x 9" baking dish.

Mix batter ingredients together and spoon over sauce. Bake, uncovered, at 350° F for 40 to 50 minutes, or until golden brown. Serve warm.

Serves 4.

—*H. Jean Brown*

Berries in Lemon Mousse

4 cups blueberries,
   raspberries or strawberries
1 cup sugar
5 eggs, separated
juice of 2 large lemons
1 cup heavy cream, whipped
2 Tbsp. grated lemon rind

Wash berries, remove stems and drain well. Pour into glass serving bowl and sprinkle with ¼ cup sugar. In top of double boiler, beat egg yolks with remaining ¾ cup sugar until light yellow in colour. Add lemon juice and continue to cook over simmering water, whisking constantly, until mixture is thick enough to heavily coat a spoon. Remove from heat and allow to cool. Beat egg whites until stiff but not dry. Fold gently into cooled lemon mixture. Fold in whipped cream and lemon rind. Be sure everything is well incorporated and the mousse is very smooth. Chill well. Immediately before serving, cover berries with mousse.

Serves 4 to 6.

—Holly Andrews

Frozen Soufflé with Hot Strawberry Sauce

Our Vermont tester says, "Deliciously different and very easy to prepare, this was gone as soon as I put it out for testing."

½ gallon vanilla ice cream
12 almond macaroons,
   crumbled
5 Tbsp. Grand Marnier or
   orange liqueur
2 cups heavy cream
½ cup chopped, toasted
   almonds
icing sugar
SAUCE:
2 quarts strawberries, halved
½ cup sugar
6 Tbsp. Grand Marnier or
   orange liqueur

Soften ice cream slightly, then stir in macaroons and liqueur. Whip cream until thick, then fold into ice cream. Spoon into angel-food pan and sprinkle surface with almonds and icing sugar. Cover with plastic wrap and freeze until firm — at least 5 hours, but preferably overnight.

Prepare sauce just before serving. Place berries in saucepan with sugar and simmer until just soft. Remove from heat and stir in liqueur.

Unmould soufflé and top with sauce.

Serves 12 to 16.

—Sherry Mowat Spruit

Blueberry Crisp

4 cups blueberries, fresh or
   frozen
¾ cup sugar
1 tsp. nutmeg
⅓ cup butter
⅓ cup brown sugar
6 Tbsp. flour
¾ cup oatmeal
1 tsp. cinnamon

Place berries in greased 9-inch casserole dish. Mix sugar and nutmeg and pour over berries. Cream butter and brown sugar. Add flour, oatmeal and cinnamon. Crumble over berries. Bake at 350° F for 30 minutes. Good warm or cold, topped with ice cream or yogurt.

Serves 4 to 5.

—Valerie L. Arnason

Oranges Glacées

6 oranges
2 Tbsp. orange liqueur
1½ cups sugar

Remove a thin layer of peel from 2 oranges. Cut into strips and soak in liqueur. Peel oranges. Slice as thinly as possible, removing seeds. Arrange on shallow heatproof serving dish. Boil sugar and ½ cup water together, stirring constantly until golden. Pour carefully over oranges. Garnish with liqueur-soaked peel. Refrigerate for at least 8 hours.

Serves 6.

—Patricia Daine

Flaming
Apple Brandy Crêpes

"I invented this easy yet elegant dish so New Year's Eve guests could ring in 1987 with delicious (but inexpensive) style. Serve with cream."

CRÊPES:
2 Tbsp. butter, melted
1½ cups milk
⅔ cup flour
½ tsp. salt
3 eggs
oil for frying
FILLING:
4 large tart cooking apples
1 Tbsp. flour
1 Tbsp. butter
½ cup brown sugar
1 tsp. cinnamon
⅛ tsp. nutmeg
4 oz. brandy

In medium bowl, with wire whisk, beat all crêpe ingredients together, except oil, until smooth. Cover and refrigerate batter for at least 2 hours.

Heat and swirl a scant teaspoon of oil in 10-inch skillet. Pour a scant ¼ cup batter into pan and swirl to coat. Cook for about 2 minutes over medium heat, or until top is just set and bottom is browned. With metal spatula, loosen crêpe all around and turn over. Cook other side until just browned — about 30 seconds. Slide cooked crêpe onto a plate. Repeat with remaining batter, stacking crêpes as they are cooked.

Prepare filling: Pare and slice apples as if for pie. Toss with flour to coat, then set aside. In saucepan, melt butter, then add sugar and spices. Add apples and stir to coat. Add half the brandy. Over low heat, simmer and stir often until apples are tender — about 15 minutes. If mixture becomes a little dry, add a bit of water or more brandy.

To serve: Fill and roll 4 crêpes. Transfer each crêpe to a serving plate. Gently heat remaining 2 oz. of brandy. Divide among crêpes, and set alight. Pass pitcher of cream for drizzling over each serving.

Serves 4.

—Sandy Robertson

Crème Brûlée

Serve this very rich pudding with fresh fruit for a tasty and colourful dessert.

4 egg yolks
1 Tbsp. castor sugar
2 cups heavy cream
1 vanilla bean, split
handful unblanched almonds
sugar

Mix egg yolks and castor sugar well. Place cream and vanilla bean in top of double boiler. Cover and bring to scalding point, remove vanilla bean and pour cream onto egg yolks, whisking well. Return to pan and cook until thickened, stirring constantly. Do not allow to boil. Pour into serving bowl and let stand overnight.

Prepare praline: Place almonds in heavy saucepan. Heat until nuts begin spitting. Add sugar to cover nuts and bottom of pan. Cook without stirring over medium heat until sugar has turned dark caramel in colour. Pour onto well-oiled plate and cool. When cold, pound in mortar and pestle until praline is in small pieces. Two hours before serving, place pralines on pudding.

Serves 6.

—Crissie Hunt

Pears in Chocolate

This very elegant dessert is much easier to prepare than the final product would lead you to believe.

6 ripe but firm pears
   (Bartlett or Anjou), with
   stems intact
1 cup sugar
2 4" cinnamon sticks
4 cloves
juice of 1 small lemon
2 Tbsp. crème de menthe
4 oz. semisweet chocolate
¼ cup butter

Carefully peel pears and cut bottoms flat so they will stand upright. In heavy pan, heat sugar, 4 cups water, spices, lemon juice and crème de menthe. Simmer for 15 minutes. Add pears and stew in syrup, turning frequently, for about 30 minutes, or until tender. Chill overnight in syrup.

Melt chocolate and butter in double boiler over hot water. Drain pears and pat dry. Dip pears in chocolate sauce, coating evenly. Place on waxed paper and chill. Allow to return to room temperature before serving.

Serves 6.

—Kathryn MacDonald

Poppy Seed Fruit Salad Dressing

3 Tbsp. onion juice
1 cup honey
1 Tbsp. dry mustard
2 tsp. salt
⅔ cup cider vinegar
2 cups oil
3 Tbsp. poppy seeds

Make onion juice by grinding a large onion in a blender or food processor, then scraping pulp into a strainer over a bowl. Press pulp with a spoon to remove juice. Set aside.

Mix honey, mustard, salt and vinegar in blender on slow speed. Add onion juice and continue blending. Add oil to blender a few drops at a time, still on slow speed, then in a thin stream, until dressing is thick. At the very last, add poppy seeds, blending just to incorporate. Store in refrigerator. Serve on fruit such as melons, green grapes, pineapple, pears or as a dressing for fruit salad.

—*Kristine Marie Halls Reid*

Strawberry Ambrosia

"While cross-country skiing in the American Berkebeiner in 1977, I was billeted at a home in Hayward, Wisconsin, where I was treated to superb meals each day. The one dessert which so impressed me that I sat down and wrote out the recipe from the woman's cards was this one. It was a real treat to try broiled fruit, and the contrast with the ice cream was not only delightful to the taste buds but visually appealing as well. It was hot, cold and crunchy."

2 ripe bananas, sliced
1 cup halved or quartered strawberries
2 oranges, peeled & cut into bite-sized pieces
1 Tbsp. lemon juice
1 cup brown sugar
6 Tbsp. butter, melted
⅔ cup sliced almonds
French vanilla ice cream

Toss together bananas, strawberries, oranges and lemon juice. Place in a 10-inch pie plate. Stir together sugar, butter and almonds. Sprinkle over fruit. Broil 6 to 8 inches from heat until sugar melts and almonds are lightly toasted. Cool for a few minutes. Spoon over ice cream in individual dishes.

Serves 4.

—*Lorne A. Davis*

Golden Dressing for Fruit

"This is a sweet but tangy cooked dressing that is delicious served over fruit salad for brunch or over fruit for dessert."

¼ cup orange juice
¼ cup lemon juice
¼ cup pineapple juice
2 eggs, beaten
½ cup sugar
½ cup heavy cream, whipped

Heat juices and add eggs and sugar, stirring. Cook until spoon is coated. Set pan in cold water and stir until cool. When cool, add whipped cream.

—*Mary-Eileen McClear*

Lemon Ice Cream

This recipe will last for months in the freezer—but is not likely to if ice-cream lovers know where it is.

2 lemons
3 eggs, separated
¾ cup sugar
1 cup heavy cream

Squeeze juice from lemons to make 5 Tbsp. Finely grate peel from 1 lemon. Place egg whites in large bowl and beat until stiff peaks form. Gradually add ¼ cup sugar, continuing to beat. Sprinkle with lemon peel. Place yolks in another bowl and whisk with remaining ½ cup sugar and lemon juice. Fold into egg whites until just blended.

In another bowl, whip cream until soft peaks form. Fold into egg mixture, gently but thoroughly. Place in freezer container and freeze for several hours.

Serves 6 to 8.

—*Laurabel Miller*

Ruth's Pecan Ice Cream

"I developed this recipe when I was a teenager, somehow managing to convince my mother that just one more test was needed to make sure I had it right! One day I ran out of ice for the ice-cream machine in the midst of the procedure, which would have been disastrous except that, just then, it began to hail. I was able to finish cranking using hailstones instead of ice, and the ice cream turned out just fine."
Make vanilla sugar by placing a vanilla bean in a jar of white sugar and letting it sit for several weeks.

4 cups milk
2 cups heavy cream
1 small vanilla bean
2 egg yolks
4 eggs
2 cups vanilla sugar
1 Tbsp. cornstarch
½ tsp. salt
¼ cup sugar
¼ lb. pecans

Scald milk and cream with vanilla bean. Discard bean (or rinse well and keep for re-use).

Blend together yolks, eggs, vanilla sugar, cornstarch and salt. Cook in top of double boiler, stirring constantly. When warm, slowly stir in milk-cream mixture. Continue heating until thick enough to coat the back of a spoon. Chill.

Place sugar and pecans in heavy skillet and cook over low heat until sugar has melted and is light brown. Cool, then crush.

When custard is very cold, freeze in ice-cream machine, following manufacturer's instructions. Mix in pecans when done.

Makes approximately 3 quarts.
—*Ruth Ellis Haworth*

Cantaloupe Sherbet

"When the eight cantaloupe plants in our first Georgia garden yielded more than 40 luscious cantaloupes in three weeks, we developed this recipe. Since frozen melon purée works just as well as fresh, we can now remember midsummer during the dark and dreary days of winter; the beautiful green-flecked orange sherbet tastes just like fresh, ripe cantaloupes."

2 cups heavy cream
1 cup sugar
2 medium cantaloupes
  (7 cups purée)
½ cup lemon juice
¼ cup lime juice
finely grated rind of 1 lime
2 Tbsp. Cointreau **or**
  Triple Sec

Heat cream to scalding. Stir in sugar until dissolved. Chill. Seed, peel and purée cantaloupe in food processor. Add lemon and lime juices and grated rind to purée. Chill thoroughly. Mix in chilled cream and liqueur. Freeze in ice-cream maker according to its directions.

Makes ½ gallon.

NOTE: To enjoy cantaloupe sherbet all year, add lemon and lime juices to fresh purée and freeze in glass jars with lids. Leave 1-inch headspace for expansion.

—*Susan Hodges & Tim Denny*

Best Vanilla Ice Cream

Topped with rhubarb sauce, this ice cream makes a very special early-summer treat. Simply cook sliced rhubarb until tender, then add sugar and cinnamon to taste. The use of buttermilk makes this recipe very unusual — the result is less rich and the taste is lovely.

1½ cups sugar
1 Tbsp. flour
¼ tsp. salt
4-5 eggs, beaten
3 cups milk
2 cups cold buttermilk
3 cups heavy cream
3 tsp. vanilla

Combine sugar, flour and salt, then add to beaten eggs. Heat milk to scalding and slowly add egg mixture. Cook over low heat, stirring constantly, until thick enough to coat a spoon. Set pot in ice water and stir until cooled to room temperature.

Add buttermilk, cream and vanilla, then churn in ice-cream maker, following instructions on machine.

Makes approximately 1 gallon.
—*Susan Hodges & Tim Denny*

Beverages

Vegetable-Fruit Juice I

1 large carrot, cleaned & cut
   in chunks
1 small apple, cored & cut in
   chunks
1 small orange, peeled,
   seeded & cut in chunks
Apple juice

Using an electric blender
liquify orange, apple and carrot
with 2 cups apple juice until
fruit particles are as small as
possible. Fill the blender with
more apple juice and blend for a
few more seconds.

Makes 4 glasses.

—Maria Gosse

Vegetable-Fruit Juice II

1 small raw beet, peeled &
   cut in chunks
1 small apple, cored & cut in
   chunks
1½ cups orange juice
Apple juice

Using an electric blender,
liquify beet, apple and orange
juice until fruit particles are as
small as possible. Fill the
blender with apple juice and
blend again for a few seconds.

Makes 4 glasses.

—Maria Gosse

Papaya Cooler

6 oz. papaya juice
3 oz. strawberries
⅓ banana
1 Tbsp. raw sugar or honey

Mix all ingredients in a blender
with 1 cup of crushed ice. Serve
in tall frosted glass.

—Kattie Murphy

Tomato-Vegetable Cocktail

*This easily made tomato drink
is far more flavourful and less
expensive than similar
commercial beverages. It can be
cooked for a longer or shorter
time than that suggested,
depending upon the thickness
desired.*

16 large ripe tomatoes
½ cup carrots, chopped
½ cup celery, chopped
½ cup onion, chopped
2 tsp. salt
2 Tbsp. lemon juice
1 tsp. Worcestershire sauce
Dash Tabasco sauce

Wash, core and chop
tomatoes. Combine with
remaining ingredients in a heavy
saucepan. Bring to a boil, lower
heat slightly and cook rapidly
until vegetables are tender. Press
through a strainer or food mill.

To store, ladle into quart jars
leaving ¼-inch headroom. Seal
and process 15 minutes in water
bath.

Shake well before using.

Makes 2 quarts.

—Debbie Walker

Ginger Tea

2½ cups water
2 inches fresh green ginger,
   coarsely grated
4 tsp. honey or brown sugar
½ lemon, sliced

Combine ingredients and boil,
uncovered, for 10 to 15 minutes.
Strain and serve in mugs.

Serves 2.

—Cary Elizabeth Marshall

Rhubarb Punch

3 lbs. fresh rhubarb
16 cups water
6 cloves
1½ cups honey
Juice & pulp of 3 oranges &
   1½ lemons

Combine rhubarb, water and
cloves and simmer for 10
minutes. Strain. Add honey,
oranges and lemons. Serve
chilled.

Serves 20.

—David Slabotsky

Fruit Smoothy

1 orange
1 banana
2 apples
2 cups milk
½ cup sesame seeds
1 tsp. cinnamon

Combine all ingredients in a blender and mix until smooth. This can be served as a drink, or frozen for a cool dessert.

Serves 2 to 4.

—Sheri Nelson

Cranberry Tea

This may be served either hot or cold, but is especially delicious in the winter, served as a hot appetizer.

1 qt. cranberries
1 qt. water
2 sticks cinnamon
6 oranges
3 lemons
2 cups sugar

Cook together the cranberries, water and cinnamon. Mash and put through a sieve. Add sugar and the juice from the oranges and lemons. To increase quantity, 1 large can frozen orange juice and 1 small can frozen lemonade may be added, with additional water to taste.

Basic recipe serves 6.

—Anne Erb

Lemonade Concentrate

2 Tbsp. grated lemon rind
¾ cup fresh lemon juice
1 oz. citric acid
3 cups granulated sugar
2 cups boiling water

Combine all ingredients and stir until completely dissolved. Store in refrigerator and mix with water to make desired strength.

—Jane Cuthbert

Carob-Banana Milkshake

1 medium banana
1 egg
1½ Tbsp. honey
½ tsp. vanilla extract
2 Tbsp. carob powder
3½ cups whole milk

Blend all ingredients using an electric blender.

Makes 4 glasses.

—Maria Gosse

Vanilla Milkshake

This recipe and the eight that follow, sent in by Maria Gosse of Botwood, Nfld., can be made into popsicles by freezing in ice cube or popsicle trays.

1 egg
2½ Tbsp. honey
½ tsp. vanilla extract
½ cup milk powder
3½ cups whole milk

Blend all ingredients using an electric blender.

Makes 4 glasses.

Apple Milkshake

1 large apple, peeled, cored & quartered
1 egg
2 Tbsp. honey
½ tsp. cinnamon
½ cup milk
3 cups plain yogurt

Liquify in an electric blender first 5 ingredients. Then buzz blender again for a second to blend in the yogurt.

Makes 4 glasses.

Peach or Apricot Milkshake

4 peaches or apricots, fresh or frozen, peeled
1 egg
2 Tbsp. honey
A few drops almond extract
½ cup milk
1½ cups plain yogurt

Liquify together in an electric blender first 5 ingredients. Then buzz blender again for just a second to blend in the yogurt.

Makes 4 glasses.

Orange-Banana Milkshake

1 medium-sized banana
3 Tbsp. frozen undiluted orange juice
2 Tbsp. honey
1 egg
½ tsp. vanilla extract
½ cup milk
2 cups plain yogurt

Liquify together in an electric blender first 6 ingredients. Then buzz blender again for just a second to blend in the yogurt.

Makes 4 glasses.

Grape Milkshake

6 oz. frozen undiluted grape
  juice
1 egg
1½ Tbsp. honey
3 cups plain yogurt

In an electric blender, liquify
first 3 ingredients. Then buzz
blender again for a second to
blend in the yogurt, until
milkshake is thoroughly mixed.

Makes 4 glasses.

Banana Milkshake

2 medium bananas
1 egg
2 Tbsp. honey
½ tsp. vanilla
½ cup milk
1½ cups plain yogurt

Liquify together first 5
ingredients using electric
blender. Then buzz blender
again for just a second to blend
in the yogurt.

Makes 4 glasses.

Pineapple Milkshake

1 14-oz. can pineapple chunks
1 Tbsp. honey
1 egg
2 cups plain yogurt

Liquify together first 3
ingredients and ½ cup of the
yogurt in an electric blender.
Then buzz blender again for just
a second to add remaining 1½
cups yogurt.

Makes 4 glasses.

Peanut Butter Milkshake

4 Tbsp. peanut butter
1 egg
½ tsp. vanilla extract
2 Tbsp. honey
½ cup milk
2½ cups plain yogurt

Liquify together in electric
blender first 5 ingredients. Then
buzz blender again for just a
second, to blend in the yogurt.

Makes 4 glasses.

Strawberry Milkshake

1 cup fresh or frozen
  strawberries (do not thaw if
  frozen)
1 egg
2 Tbsp. honey
½ cup milk
Few drops almond extract
1½ cups plain yogurt

Liquify together first 5
ingredients using electric
blender. Then buzz in blender
again for just a second to blend
in the yogurt.

Makes 4 glasses.

Hot Cider

3 qts. apple cider
⅔ cup brown sugar
¼ tsp. salt
1 tsp. whole allspice
1 tsp. whole cloves
4 cinnamon sticks
¼ tsp. nutmeg

Heat 2 cups cider with sugar
and salt, stirring until sugar
dissolves. Pour into slow cooker
with remaining cider. Tie spices
in cloth bag and drop into cider.
Cover and simmer for 2 to 3
hours. Remove spices at serving
time.

—*Mary Lou Ross*

Mulled Cider

1 orange
1 lemon
1 lime
1 cup sugar
1 egg, beaten until frothy
72-oz. can apple cider
½ tsp. allspice
3-4 cinnamon sticks
3-4 whole cloves

Combine juices of orange,
lemon and lime. Simmer
together with sugar and egg. Add
remaining ingredients, simmer
15 minutes longer and serve hot.

—*Pat McCormack*

Summer Spritzer

2 cups sugar
7 cups water
12 oz. frozen orange juice
12 oz. frozen lemonade
2 cups vodka, rum or gin

Boil together sugar and water until sugar is dissolved. Chill. Add remaining ingredients, mix well and freeze.

To serve, put 1 scoop in tall glass and fill with mineral water.

—Eileen Deeley

Coffee Liqueur

2 cups granulated sugar
1½ cups water
2 Tbsp. coffee
1 Tbsp. vanilla
26-oz. bottle alcool

Combine all ingredients except alcohol in heavy sauce pan. Bring to a rolling boil. Let cool and strain. Add alcohol, and bottle.

—L. Howson

Sangria

This cool summer punch of Spanish origin is easily expanded to serve a crowd. Wine may simply be poured into the pitcher or punch bowl as it is needed, and additional soda, ice and fruit slices stirred in.

2 bottles red wine
1 bottle club soda
1 cup brandy
2 cups orange juice
Lemon, orange & lime slices
Ice cubes

Mix red wine, club soda, brandy and orange juice. Add enough ice cubes to chill thoroughly. Top with lemon, orange and lime slices.

Serves 8.

Rumple

Created as a hot pick-me-up after a long winter's day of outdoor activity, rumple can be made to serve two or 20.

5 cups apple juice
6 oz. maple syrup or honey
6 oz. rum
6 cinnamon sticks

Heat apple juice until steaming and add sweetener. Pour into 6 mugs with rum. Add cinnamon stick and serve immediately.

Serves 6.

—Christine Campbell

Mulled Wine

½ cup water
¼ cup orange juice
¼ cup sugar
1 cinnamon stick
2 cloves
½ lemon, thinly sliced
1½ cups wine
2 oz. brandy

Boil water, orange juice, sugar, cinnamon and cloves for 5 minutes. Add lemon slices and let stand for 10 minutes. Add wine and heat gradually, but do not boil. Add brandy at serving time.

Serves 2.

—Cheryl Suckling

Hot Cranberry Wine Cup

4 cups cranberry juice
2 cups water
½ cup honey
1 cinnamon stick
12 cloves
1 lemon, sliced
2 bottles Burgundy wine
1¼ cup lemon juice
Nutmeg

Combine in a large non-aluminum pot, the cranberry juice, water, honey, cinnamon, cloves and lemon. Bring to a boil, stirring, and continue cooking until honey is dissolved. Add wine and lemon juice. Heat gently and serve in preheated mugs, sprinkled with nutmeg.

—Bryanna Clark

Lemon Beer

2 lemons
1 lb. brown sugar
1 lb. granulated sugar
½ cup thick syrup
8 quarts water
¼ tsp. dry yeast
Handful raisins

Grate rind from lemon and set aside. Cut lemons into ¼-inch slices.

Combine sugars, syrup and lemon rind in a pail. Boil 2 quarts water and pour over sugar mixture. Add remaining cold water and lemon slices. Add yeast, cover and let sit overnight.

Strain through cheesecloth and pour into bottles. Add ¼ tsp. sugar and a few raisins to each bottle. Cap tightly and store in a cool place for at least 7 days before using.

Makes about 8 quarts.

—Iris White

Raspberry Punch

16 oz. raspberry cordial
6 oz. frozen lemonade
    concentrate
6 oz. frozen orange juice
    concentrate
20 oz. pineapple juice
2 qts. water
26 oz. sparkling mineral
    water
1 bottle white rum

Combine all ingredients in a punch bowl. Add ice cubes just before serving.

—Cheryl Suckling

Irish Coffee

2 jiggers Irish whiskey
2 tsp. demerara sugar
Fresh hot coffee

Warm whiskey and sugar together and pour into 2 coffee cups. Fill cups about three quarters full with coffee and top with whipped cream.

Serves 2.

—Mary Patton

May Bowl

Sweet woodruff sprigs
1¼ cups icing sugar
4 bottles Moselle wine
1 cup brandy
1 qt. soda water or
    champagne
Orange slices
Fresh pineapple sticks
Strawberries

Combine 12 sprigs woodruff, sugar, 1 bottle Moselle and brandy. Cover and let sit for 30 minutes. Remove woodruff. Stir and pour over a block of ice in a punch bowl. Add remaining ingredients.

—Cary Elizabeth Marshall

Café Brûlot

For those with a flair for the dramatic (and some skill), this can be prepared at the table in a chafing dish, adding a flaming spoonful of brandy before stirring in the coffee.

1 tsp. whole allspice
3 sticks cinnamon, broken
Grated rind of 2 oranges & 1
    lemon
5 Tbsp. sugar
1 cup brandy or cognac
5 cups strong, fresh, hot
    coffee

Warm together spices, orange and lemon rind, sugar and brandy, but do not boil. Stir to dissolve sugar. Add coffee. Strain into cups and serve.

Serves 6.

—Cary Elizabeth Marshall

Cranberry Punch

2 cups sugar
1 cup water
2 bottles gin
2 48-oz. tins grapefruit juice
1 bottle cranberry juice
2 cups cold tea

Boil sugar and water together and cool. Combine in punch bowl with remaining ingredients. Add ice cubes just before serving.

Brunch Punch

This is a variation of a traditional wedding breakfast punch in which champagne is used in place of white wine.

4 bottles dry white wine
2 qts. orange juice
1 bottle club soda
Orange slices

Combine all ingredients in a punch bowl and add ice cubes just before serving.

Elderflower Crush

This is a cooling summer drink which is especially good during haying. The elderflower bushes bloom in June, and the florets should all be open when the head is picked.

4 lbs. sugar
2½ oz. citric acid
20 elderflower heads
2 lemons, sliced
5 cups boiling water

Place sugar in bottom of bucket, with citric acid on top. Add elderflower heads and lemons. Pour boiling water over top, then stir with wooden spoon until sugar is completely dissolved. Cover pail with a cloth and keep in a cool place. Stir once or twice a day for 5 days.

—Meg Weber-Crockford

Tiger's Milk

1 large banana
½ cup yogurt
3 Tbsp. honey
1½ cups milk
½ tsp. cinnamon

Blend all ingredients together and serve.

Serves 2.

—Sandra Cameron

Mint Lemonade

4 cups sugar
5 cups water
Juice of 12 lemons
Juice of 4 oranges
Grated rind of 2 oranges
2 cups crushed mint leaves

Simmer sugar and water for 5 minutes, then cool. Add lemon and orange juices. Pour mixture over orange rind and mint leaves. Strain into jar and store in refrigerator. To serve, mix with equal amounts of water and add ice.

Makes 20 to 24 servings.

—Cheryl Lenington Suckling

Banana Cow

1 banana
½ cup milk
1 Tbsp. honey
⅛ tsp. vanilla
1 cup crushed ice

Place all ingredients in blender and blend until smooth.

—S. Pedersen

Pineapple Punch

The appearance of this fruit punch is enhanced if an ice ring is placed in the punch bowl. Into a tube cake pan, pour 1 inch of any fruit juice and freeze. Arrange fruit slices on frozen juice and cover with another inch of juice. Freeze thoroughly. Place in punch bowl at serving time.

8 cups lemon juice
5 cups lime juice
4 cups sugar
24 cups unsweetened
   pineapple juice
10 cups orange juice
2 cups chopped mint leaves
45 cups ginger ale
16 cups club soda
6 cups quartered
   strawberries

Heat lemon and lime juices with sugar until sugar is completely dissolved. Combine with pineapple and orange juices. Add mint leaves and chill thoroughly. Add ginger ale, club soda and strawberries just before serving. Place in punch bowls with ice ring.

Makes 28 quarts.

—Donna Petryshyn

Pink Banana Whip

2 cups chilled
   cranberry-apple juice
2 cups fresh orange juice
1 ripe banana
6 ice cubes, crushed

Buzz all ingredients in blender and serve immediately.

Serves 3.

—Kathleen Walker

Swedish Ginger Cookies, page 15; Chocolate Peanut Butter Squares, page 13; Orange Pecan Muffins, page 3

Landlubber's Gumbo, page 102

Flaming Apple Brandy Crêpes, page 561

Vita Quencher, page 575

Lemon Cheese Crown, page 505

Curried Pasta Salad, page 432

Eggs in Nests, page 56

Steamed Sole with Tomato Coulis, page 260

Tom's Special Summer Delight

1 large bag frozen
  strawberries
40 oz. white rum
Ice cubes
Ginger ale or club soda

Place strawberries in 64-oz. plastic container. Pour rum over top, cover tightly and refrigerate for at least 3 months.

To serve, fill tall glasses one-third full with strawberry-rum mixture, add 2 ice cubes and fill with ginger ale or club soda.

Makes 32 servings.

—Kirsten McDougall

Cranberry Spritzers

2 cups cranberry juice
1 cup white wine, chilled
Ice cubes
Soda water or mineral water,
  chilled
Mint leaves & lemon slices

Mix juice and wine. Pour into glasses with ice until two-thirds full. Top with chilled soda or mineral water. Garnish with lemon slices and mint leaves.

Serves 6.

—Louise McDonald

Castilian Hot Chocolate

½ cup unsweetened cocoa
2 Tbsp. & 1 tsp. cornstarch
½ cup water
¾ cup honey, melted
1 quart milk

Combine cocoa, cornstarch and water in blender. Gradually add honey and blend. Whisk this mixture with milk in saucepan, continuing to stir as you bring it to a simmer.

Simmer, stirring often, for about 10 minutes. It will be glossy, smooth and almost as thick as pudding. Serve hot.

Serves 6.

—Lorna Wollner

Energy Drink

2 cups fresh-squeezed
  orange juice
1 banana
1-2 slices fresh pineapple
1 tsp. honey
⅔ cup crushed ice

Mix orange juice, banana, pineapple and honey in blender. Add ice and blend again.

Serves 2.

—Irma Leming

Blueberry Drink

This hot fruit drink is particularly tasty after a day of outdoor winter activity.

2 cups blueberries
3 cups water
1 cup sugar
2 Tbsp. cornstarch

Combine all ingredients and blend well. Heat to boiling and serve.

Makes 6 cups.

—Devon Anderson

Sierra Sunrise

This makes a pleasant Sunday brunch drink.

6-oz. can frozen orange juice
  concentrate
1 cup cream
¾ cup sherry
1 egg
Salt
4 ice cubes, crushed

Place all ingredients in blender and mix at high speed until frothy and well blended.

Serves 2.

—Louise Oglaend

Rich & Creamy Eggnog

½ cup sugar
¼ tsp. cinnamon
Nutmeg
3 eggs, separated
2 cups whole milk
1 cup light cream
Rum

Combine sugar, cinnamon and dash of nutmeg. Beat egg whites to soft peak stage, then gradually beat in half the sugar mixture until stiff peaks form.

Beat egg yolks until lemon coloured, then add remaining sugar mixture and beat until thick and smooth. Fold gently but thoroughly into beaten egg whites. Stir in milk and cream and mix well.

To serve, place 1 oz. rum in each glass, and fill with eggnog.

Serves 4.

—Linda Plant

Yogurt Sip

1 cup frozen peaches, thawed slightly
2 bananas, very ripe
2 cups plain yogurt
¼ cup peach brandy
¼ cup light rum
2 Tbsp. honey
Nutmeg

Blend together fruit and yogurt. When smooth, add remaining ingredients. Blend for a few more seconds and serve cool.

Serves 4.

—Charlene Skidmore

Banana Punch

48 oz. orange juice
4 eggs
5 bananas
26 oz. club soda
13 oz. vodka
Ice cubes

Mix orange juice, eggs and bananas in blender until smooth. Just before serving, add club soda, vodka and ice cubes.

Makes 36 cups.

—Sonja Machholz

Mulled Ale

1 orange peel spiral
Whole cloves
6 small, red apples
3 12-oz. bottles ale
3 cups dark rum
⅔ cup sugar
⅛ tsp. ginger

Stud orange spiral with cloves ½-inch apart. Place in shallow pan along with apples and bake, uncovered, for 20 minutes.

In large, heavy saucepan, combine ale, rum, sugar and ginger and bring to a boil, stirring until sugar is dissolved. Place hot orange spiral and roasted apples into ale mixture and keep at low heat. Serve.

Makes six 10-ounce servings.

—Susan Shaw

La Ponce de Gin de Grand-père

In the 18th century, Frederic Tolfrey, originally from France, was offered this drink in Canada and wrote down the recipe in his diary. Ever since, the recipe has been passed on from generation to generation not only as a tonic against the harshness of Canadian winters, but also as a cold and flu remedy.

¼ cup gin
3 Tbsp. lemon juice
1 tsp. honey
1 whole clove
⅔ cup boiling water

Combine all ingredients and let steep for a few minutes before drinking.

Serves 1.

—Nicole Morin

Almond Liqueur

3 oz. chopped raw almonds
Cinnamon
1½ cups vodka
½ cup sugar syrup

Place almonds, pinch of cinnamon and vodka in sterilized glass jar. Shake well to combine ingredients, then cover and steep for 2 weeks. Strain, then sweeten with sugar syrup. Replace in jar and let sit for a few weeks more.

Makes 16 ounces.

—Rosy Hale

Maple Syrup Liqueur

4 oz. maple syrup
8 oz. rye whiskey

Combine ingredients in jar with tight-fitting lid. Shake for 2 minutes. For the next 2½ to 3 weeks, shake the container daily for 1 minute.

Serve as a liqueur or an aperitif poured over crushed ice.

Makes 12 ounces.

—Don Smillie

Glogg

1½ cups gin
2 cinnamon sticks
3 Tbsp. cardamom seeds
10 cloves
Almonds
Raisins
Fruit peel
1½ cups port
1 cup sugar
1 cup water
Juice of ½ lemon
15 cups red wine

Combine gin, cinnamon sticks, cardamom seeds and cloves and soak for at least 3 days. Soak almonds, raisins and fruit peel to taste in port for 1 day.

Make syrup by boiling together sugar, water and lemon juice until sugar is dissolved.

Place wine in large, heavy pot, add strained gin (discard spices), port and fruit and heat slowly, adding syrup. Heat until very hot, but do not boil.

Serves 20.

—Ulrika Schmidt

Irish Cream Liqueur

3 eggs
1 cup whipping cream
1 cup condensed milk
3 Tbsp. chocolate
¼ tsp. almond extract
12 oz. rye

Place all ingredients in blender and blend. Bottle and store in the refrigerator. This will keep for up to 3 weeks.

Makes 32 ounces.

—Anne Nuttall

Holiday

Cranberry Brandy

"Here in Alaska, wild berries of all kinds are plentiful — this recipe also works well with raspberries or blueberries. Serve this brandy over vanilla ice cream, or just sip it plain. It also makes a wonderful gift."

3 quarts cranberries
32 oz. brandy
4 cups sugar
3 cups water

Mash berries in large bowl, then add brandy. Cover and let stand for 24 hours, stirring twice. Separate juice from pulp, using jelly strainer or coffee filter, and discard pulp.

Cook sugar in water, stirring, until mixture becomes clear. Cool. Mix sugar syrup with brandy and stir well. Pour into clean bottles and cap.

Makes approximately 80 oz.

—*Chris Thorsrud*

Vita Quencher

1 qt. raspberries or
    blackberries
1 cup white vinegar
sugar

Place berries in stainless steel or glass bowl. Mix vinegar with 1 cup water and pour over berries. Let stand, covered, for 24 to 48 hours, then squeeze through strainer.

Measure juice, pour into stainless steel pot and add an equal amount of sugar (approximately 3 cups). Boil, stirring occasionally, for 20 minutes. Cool, then refrigerate for up to several weeks or freeze.

To serve, use 3 Tbsp. concentrate mixed with water to make one 8-oz. glass.

Makes 1 quart concentrate.

—*Anita L. Weidemoyer*

Mary's Wassail

"I serve this drink every year at my open house. It is very warming but not so alcoholic that I worry about my guests driving afterwards. In fact, the wine can be left out altogether. In that case, increase the amount of sugar to 1 cup."

1 gallon apple cider
⅓ cup brown sugar
6-oz. can frozen lemonade
6-oz. can frozen orange juice
12 cloves
6 whole allspice
1 tsp. nutmeg
4" stick cinnamon
1 bottle port wine
½ tsp. Angostura bitters

Combine cider, sugar, lemonade and orange juice in large kettle. Tie cloves and allspice in a small piece of cloth (or place in a tea ball) and add to juices. Add nutmeg and cinnamon stick and simmer gently for 20 minutes. Add wine and heat to steaming, but do not boil. Remove spice bag.

Serves approximately 20.

—*Mary Irwin-Gibson*

Eggnog Supreme

"This is my mother's recipe and is, quite simply, the best eggnog I have ever tasted."

12 eggs, separated
1 cup sugar
13 oz. brandy
26 oz. rye or rum
2 cups light cream
3 cups heavy cream
nutmeg

Combine egg yolks and sugar in large punch bowl. Beat until thick and lemon-coloured, then slowly add brandy, rye or rum and light cream. Beat to blend well, then chill for at least 1 hour.

Beat egg whites until stiff. Whip heavy cream till stiff in large bowl, then fold in egg whites. Add gently to alcohol mixture. Sprinkle with nutmeg.

Serves 12 to 16.

—*Lynne Collier*

Holiday Stuffing

3 cups chopped tart apples
¼ cup brandy
1¼ cups chopped onions
1-2 cloves garlic, minced
½ cup chopped celery
¾ cup chopped celery leaves
½ cup butter
1½ tsp. salt
¾ tsp. thyme
½ tsp. sage
1½ tsp. white pepper
1 bay leaf
10 cups dry bread cubes

Marinate apples in brandy for 15 minutes. Sauté onions, garlic, celery and celery leaves in butter for 3 to 5 minutes. Mix seasonings and toss with bread. Add all other ingredients to bread and mix well. Stuff turkey and roast according to personal preference.

Makes enough to stuff a 20-lb. turkey.

—*Julie Hustvet*

Mabel's Cranberry Salad

"Made originally by my grandmother, this cool, sweet-tart salad is as much a part of my holiday as the turkey."

4 cups fresh cranberries
2 cups sugar
2 cups halved seedless red grapes
½ cup chopped nuts
1 cup heavy cream, whipped

Mince cranberries in a grinder or food processor. Mix in sugar. Place in a colander and set colander in a bowl deep enough to allow cranberries to drain. Cover with foil and let drain in refrigerator overnight. Don't shortcut this step. Mix drained cranberries with remaining ingredients and chill. It can be kept for several days in the refrigerator.

Makes 6 servings.

—*Margo Hamilton*

Norwegian Fruit Soup

"Served as a dessert every Christmas Eve in our home, this recipe for 'Sot Suppe' came from Norway in 1913 and makes a tasty sauce over sponge cake or ice cream."

1 lb. dark raisins
1 lb. pitted prunes
2 cinnamon sticks, broken
10 whole cloves
6 cups water or
3 cups water & 3 cups red wine
3 Tbsp. minute tapioca
½ cup sugar
1 orange, quartered & thinly sliced
1 apple, unpeeled, cored & quartered
1 cup orange juice

Slowly bring raisins, prunes, cinnamon sticks, cloves and water to a boil. Add tapioca and sugar. Cook until tapioca is transparent. Add orange and apple. Cook for 2 to 3 minutes. Add orange juice. Serve warm or cold, with cream if desired.

Serves 8.

—*Mary Linstad*

Tortière

Rated "the best" by the Camden East test kitchen, this recipe originated in a high-school home-economics class. Both the tortière and the herb sauce freeze well.

SPECIAL DOUGH FOR CRUST:
2¼-2½ cups flour
2 tsp. baking powder
1 tsp. salt
½ lb. shortening
½ cup hot water
2 tsp. lemon juice
1 egg, well beaten
FILLING:
1 lb. lean ground pork
1 onion, finely chopped
½ tsp. salt
¼ tsp. pepper
½ tsp. thyme
½ tsp. sage
½ tsp. dry mustard
½ tsp. cloves
1 potato, boiled & mashed
HERB SAUCE:
1 stalk celery with leaves, minced
2½ cups consommé
½ tsp. sage
½ tsp. thyme
¼ cup butter
¼-½ cup flour
1 Tbsp. parsley
1 cup chopped mushrooms

For crust: Combine flour, baking powder and salt in large mixing bowl. Measure ⅔ cup cold shortening and cut into flour until mealy. Completely dissolve remaining ½ cup shortening in hot water (heat as necessary to dissolve). Cool. Add lemon juice and egg to water-shortening mixture. Mix liquid into flour mixture until dough leaves sides of bowl. Turn onto lightly floured board and knead for about 1 minute, or until all flour is blended. Wrap in waxed paper, refrigerate for 1 to 12 hours. Roll out ⅔ of the dough and line a casserole dish. Reserve ⅓ for top crust.

For filling: Simmer meat and ½ cup water for 45 minutes. Add onion and seasonings and simmer for 15 minutes. Mix in mashed potato and cool. Place in bottom crust, top with remaining dough and slit crust. Bake at 400° F for 30 minutes.

For sauce: Simmer all ingredients except flour, parsley and mushrooms for 1 hour. Mix flour with 1 cup cold water. Add to sauce and stir until thickened, then add parsley and mushrooms. Simmer for 10 minutes. Serve with tortière.

Serves 8 to 10.

—Kim Allerton

Carrot Mincemeat

2 cups grated carrots
2 cups raisins
1 whole lemon
5 cups chopped apples
1 cup mixed fruit peels
2 cups sugar
1 tsp. salt (optional)
2 tsp. cinnamon
1 tsp. cloves
½ cup molasses
½ cup cider or apple juice

Grind together carrots, raisins and lemon. Add apples, fruit peels, sugar, salt, cinnamon and cloves. When thoroughly mixed, add molasses and cider or juice. Cook over low heat until carrots and apples are tender. Can be sealed in jars while hot or packed in containers for freezing. Use for pies or tarts.

Makes about 2½ quarts.

—Mrs. V.T. Stone

Hot Cross Buns

"This is my mother's recipe and has been in our family for many years."

1 Tbsp. yeast
1 tsp. sugar
2 cups milk
½ cup sugar
1½ tsp. salt
1 egg, beaten
⅓ cup butter, melted
5-6 cups flour
¾ tsp. cinnamon
¾ cup raisins
ICING:
1 cup icing sugar
milk

Add yeast and 1 tsp. sugar to ½ cup warm water. Let sit for 10 minutes. Warm milk in saucepan, add ½ cup sugar, salt, egg and butter. Pour into large bowl, add yeast mixture and stir. Add 5 cups flour, cinnamon and raisins. Mix well. If dough is very sticky, add 1 more cup flour. Knead as for bread dough until smooth. Cover and let rise until doubled. Punch down, knead briefly and cut into buns. Place buns on a 9" x 13" cookie sheet and cut a cross in the top of each. Let rise until doubled in size. Bake at 325° F for 25 minutes, or until golden brown. After they have cooled a bit, put icing in each cross. Icing sugar blended with enough milk to form a paste works well.

Makes 24 buns.

—Sharon McKay

Hungarian Filled Pastries

Although time-consuming to prepare, these festive pastries are well worth the effort. The pastry is rich and flaky.

PASTRY:
5 cups flour
½ tsp. salt
2 cups shortening or lard or butter
5 egg yolks
½ cup red wine
1 pint sour cream
1 tsp. baking powder
FILLING:
4 egg whites
2 cups crushed walnuts
1 cup sugar
2 tsp. vanilla

Mix pastry ingredients with pastry cutter until chunky. Refrigerate for 1 hour.

Meanwhile, prepare filling: Beat egg whites until soft peaks form. Fold in nuts, sugar and vanilla.

Divide dough into quarters. On surface well dusted with confectioners' sugar, roll one quarter at a time into 10-inch squares. Cut each into sixteen 2½-inch squares. Place ¼ to ½ tsp. filling in centre of each. Fold corners into centre. Bake on ungreased cookie sheets at 375° F for 12 to 15 minutes, or until edges turn golden.

Makes approximately 60 pastries.

—Dianne Baker

Cardamom Bread

"My dad made this bread every Christmas for years, and I have carried on the tradition, with my own recipe evolving over time."

6 cups milk
½ cup butter
¾ cup honey
1½ tsp. ground cardamom
1 Tbsp. yeast
4 eggs, lightly beaten
6 cups whole wheat flour
12-15 cups unbleached white flour
2 Tbsp. salt
EGG WASH:
1 egg
3 Tbsp. water
GLAZE:
½ cup icing sugar
2 tsp. hot milk
¼ tsp. vanilla
almond halves

Scald milk. Combine with butter, honey and cardamom. Let cool to lukewarm in large bowl. Meanwhile, proof yeast by combining yeast and 1⅓ cups warm water. Let sit until it doubles in volume — approximately 10 minutes. When milk mixture is cool, add yeast mixture, eggs, whole wheat flour and 3 cups white flour. Beat with wooden spoon at least 100 strokes, or until dough becomes elastic. Cover and let sit in a warm place for about 1 hour.

Stir down sponge and stir in salt and 9 to 12 cups flour, 2 cups at a time. Turn out onto a board and knead dough until smooth and elastic — about 10 minutes. Put in greased bowl, cover with a damp cloth and put in a warm place until doubled. Punch down and let rise again. Punch down and turn out onto a lightly floured board.

Cut dough into 8 sections. Cut each section into 3 pieces. With your hands, roll each piece into a rope 15 to 18 inches long. Braid 3 pieces together, pinch ends and tuck underneath. Repeat for remaining dough. Place 2 braids side by side on foil-lined cookie sheets. Cover and let rise until doubled.

Mix egg and water together (egg wash) and brush each loaf. Bake at 350° F for 20 to 25 minutes. Let cool. Mix glaze and drizzle over loaves, pressing almond halves into glaze for decoration.

Makes 8 large braids.

—Leslie Pierpont

Festive Wild Rice

Wild rice is actually a grass, not a rice, and nutritionally is closer to wheat than to rice. Its nutty taste is incomparable, but for economy, a blend of wild and brown or basmati rice could be substituted. To prepare, wash well several times, then cook, without stirring, in boiling water (4 cups water to 1 cup rice) for 40 minutes. One cup dry rice makes 3 cups cooked rice.

2 Tbsp. oil
2 green peppers, chopped
2 onions, chopped
1 clove garlic, minced
2 cups canned tomatoes
½ cup raisins
½ cup blanched almonds
1 tsp. curry
1 tsp. thyme
salt & pepper
2 cups cooked wild rice

Heat oil and sauté green peppers, onions and garlic. Add tomatoes, ¼ cup raisins, ¼ cup almonds, curry, thyme and salt and pepper. Simmer for 10 minutes. Put rice in greased casserole dish and cover with sauce. Sprinkle with remaining raisins and nuts. Cover and bake at 400° F for 45 minutes.

Serves 6 to 8.

—Rachel Grapentine

Flaky Swedish Buns

"These buns are my mom's recipe. She learned to make them by watching my grandmother, and the recipe was never written down until my sister and I wanted it. We watched Mom and never let her add a thing until we knew what it was and how much! They are a little time-consuming to make, but well worth the effort."

3 pkgs. yeast
2 Tbsp. plus 1 cup sugar
1½ tsp. salt
4 tsp. ground cardamom
5 cups scalded milk
4 eggs, beaten
10-10½ cups flour
⅔ cup butter, softened
ALMOND ICING:
¼ cup soft butter
2 cups icing sugar
1 tsp. almond extract
few drops of milk
crushed walnuts

Dissolve yeast in ½ cup warm water with 2 Tbsp. sugar and let sit for 10 minutes. In large bowl, combine 1 cup sugar, salt and cardamom. Pour in scalded milk and mix. Add eggs and beat in well. Cool to lukewarm. Add yeast and mix well. Add 4 cups flour and beat in. Knead in another 6 to 6½ cups flour. Butter counter before rolling out. Roll out half the dough and spread with butter. Cut dough into quarters and pile pieces on top of each other. Roll out and butter again, continuing until half the butter is used up. Place dough in freezer.

Roll out second half of dough in the same manner. Put second piece of dough in freezer and take out first. Roll out dough. Cut into strips 5 inches by ½ inch, twist tightly and tie in a knot. Repeat with second half of dough. Place on cookie sheets, cover and let rise for 2 to 2½ hours. Bake at 350 to 375° F for 15 to 20 minutes (until brown). Cool and ice with almond icing, and roll in crushed walnuts.

For icing: Cream butter, gradually adding the icing sugar. Add the almond extract and mix well. If too stiff to spread, add a few drops of milk.

Makes approximately 4 dozen buns.

—Lynne Collier

Fresh Cranberry Nut Bread

The slightly tart cranberries are especially appreciated by those who dislike the usual rich holiday fare.

2 cups cranberries, chopped
2½ cups sugar
2 eggs, lightly beaten
⅓ cup butter
2 cups milk
5 cups flour
7 tsp. baking powder
1 tsp. salt
1 cup chopped walnuts

Mix cranberries with ½ cup sugar and set aside. Cream remaining 2 cups sugar and eggs. Cream in butter and add milk. Sift flour, baking powder and salt, then add dry ingredients to the creamed mixture. Stir in cranberries and walnuts. Turn into 2 greased 9" x 5" loaf pans. Bake at 350° F for 1 hour.

Makes 2 loaves.

—Kathryn MacDonald

Russian Wafers

"My daughter brought this recipe home in a collection of recipes showing how Christmas is celebrated around the world."

1 cup butter
1 cup sugar
2 eggs, well beaten
2 tsp. vanilla
2 cups flour
3 tsp. baking powder
½ tsp. salt
nutmeg

Cream butter and sugar together. Beat in eggs and vanilla. Add dry ingredients, mixing until very smooth. Chill dough overnight.

Roll dough out on a cookie sheet and cut into wafer-sized rectangles with sharp knife. (Cookies will break apart like crackers when cooked and cooled.) Sprinkle with sugar and nutmeg. Bake at 400° F for about 8 minutes.

—Linda Palaisy

Chocolate Rum Balls

"These are a Christmas tradition in our home, but they also make a lovely gift any time of the year."

1½ cups graham cracker
   crumbs
1 cup icing sugar
1 cup ground almonds
2-3 Tbsp. cocoa
¼ cup honey
3 Tbsp. dark rum
semisweet chocolate, melted

Mix together graham cracker crumbs, sugar, almonds and cocoa. Gently warm honey and stir in rum. Mix into dry ingredients. Form into 1-inch balls and roll in melted chocolate.

Makes approximately 2½ dozen.

—Susan O'Neill

Pulla—Finnish Coffee Bread

Pulla is an age-old bread that can be enjoyed year-round, although I often give it as Easter or Christmas gifts. It is best enjoyed with a fresh cup of coffee after an invigorating, steamy sauna."

2 cups milk
14-18 cardamom pods
1 pkg. yeast
1 cup sugar
4 eggs, lightly beaten
8-9 cups white flour
¼ cup butter, melted

Scald milk and let cool to lukewarm. Remove cardamom seeds from pods and crush.

Dissolve yeast in ½ cup warm water. Add cardamom, yeast mixture, sugar and all but 1 Tbsp. eggs to milk. Pour into large bowl. Add 4 cups flour, then melted butter. Mix well. Continue adding flour, one cup at a time, until dough is firm enough to knead. Knead for 10 minutes on a floured board, incorporating the remaining flour. Cover and let rise in a greased bowl — 1½ to 2 hours.

Punch down, divide dough in half and knead for a few minutes. Let rest for 15 minutes.

Divide each portion into 3 pieces, shape each piece into a rope about 1 foot long and braid together. Brush with remaining 1 Tbsp. egg. Let rise, covered, for 30 minutes. Bake at 350° F for about 30 minutes, or until golden.

Makes 2 loaves.

—Shari Suter

Dutch Cherry Cake

"This is a good dessert that is not overly sweet. We often had this on Valentine's Day when I was a child."

CRUST:
1¼ cups flour, sifted
½ tsp. baking powder
¼ tsp. salt
1 Tbsp. sugar
½ cup cold butter
1 egg
FILLING:
3 cups frozen red sour
  cherries or 3 cans sour
  cherries, drained
½ cup sugar
1 Tbsp. flour
¼ tsp. cinnamon
2 Tbsp. butter
TOPPING:
1 cup sour cream
1 egg

To make crust: Combine flour, baking powder, salt and sugar, mixing well. Cut in butter until mixture resembles coarse crumbs. Add egg and mix with a fork; then, using hands, work into a stiff dough. Press mixture into 9" x 9" pan. Crust should come up about 1 inch on the sides.

Scatter cherries evenly over crust. Combine sugar, flour and cinnamon. Cut in butter to make a crumb mixture; sprinkle over cherries. Bake at 350° F for 55 minutes. If a topping is desired, beat sour cream and egg together and spoon over top. Return cake to oven, turn oven off and let sit for 5 to 10 minutes. Serve warm or cold.

Serves 6.

—Nancy R. Franklin

Christmas Cake

Editor's note: This is my mother's Christmas cake recipe. She has been making it for as long as I can remember and now I make it too. It has been used for each child's wedding cake and is given away as gifts every Christmas. Traditional fruitcake pans are three pans, round or square, of 6-, 4- and 2-pound size. Put the cakes in the oven, largest first, so that all will be done at the same time.

½ lb. currants
1 lb. raisins
½ lb. candied cherries
4 oz. preserved citron
4 oz. mixed fruit peel
1½ candied pineapple rings
¼ lb. dates
½ lb. almonds
2 cups flour
½ lb. sugar
½ lb. butter
¼ cup molasses
5 eggs
1 tsp. cinnamon
½ tsp. each: cloves, nutmeg,
  allspice, baking soda, salt
½ cup grape juice
½ cup orange juice
½ cup lemon juice

Wash currants and raisins. Halve cherries. Chop citron, peel, pineapple and dates. Combine all fruit with almonds. Dredge in ¼ cup flour. Allow to stand for 8 hours.

Cream sugar and butter, add molasses and eggs and beat well. Sift remaining flour with dry ingredients. Add to sugar-butter mixture alternately with juices. Beat thoroughly. Pour over fruit and blend well.

Prepare Christmas cake pans by greasing thoroughly and lining with 2 layers of foil. Bake cakes at 250° F for 30 to 45 minutes.

Makes 12 lbs. of cake.

—Flora Cross

Pannetone—Italian Christmas Bread

"When an Italian visiting Canada tasted this, he declared it to be as good as those sold in fancy blue boxes in Italy. It has become our traditional Christmas breakfast accompanied by champagne cocktails and coffee."

1 Tbsp. yeast
5-6 cups flour
1 tsp. anise extract or fennel
 seed
½ tsp. salt
¾ cup butter, melted
2 whole eggs, plus 4 yolks
1 cup sugar
½ cup seedless raisins
½ cup white raisins
½ cup finely chopped citron
2 Tbsp. butter, melted

Sprinkle yeast over ¼ cup warm water. When yeast is soft, add ½ cup flour and mix to form a small ball. Cover and let rise 1½ to 2 hours.

Put 2 cups flour in a large bowl, add dough and ½ cup warm water. Knead in the bowl to make a ball. Cover and let rise 2 hours.

To dough, add 1½ cups flour, anise or fennel, salt and ¾ cup butter. Beat eggs plus yolks, sugar and ½ cup warm water together and add to dough. Knead in the bowl and add fruits. Turn out onto a floured board and knead, incorporating remaining flour. Cover and let rise 2 to 4 hours. Punch down and leave in refrigerator overnight.

The next day, grease two 8-inch flat-bottomed casserole dishes. Punch down bread and divide in half. Press dough evenly into dishes, cover and let rise 2 to 4 hours in a warm place. Mark a cross in the top of each loaf. Bake at 400° F for 5 minutes, then pour 1 Tbsp.

melted butter in each cross. Bake 15 minutes longer. Lower heat to 375° and bake for 40 minutes. Loaves will be mushroom-shaped.

Makes 2 loaves.

—*Hazel R. Baker*

Calsengel

"My grandparents came to America from northern Italy in 1910, and we still enjoy many of the recipes my grandmother cooked. This rich, filled cookie was always anxiously anticipated at Christmastime." The filling improves if it is made one to two days in advance.

FILLING:
1 lb. raisins
½ lb. almonds, ground
grated rind of 1 orange
½ tsp. cinnamon
1 cup sugar
½ cup honey
PASTRY:
6 cups flour
3 tsp. salt
3 tsp. baking powder
1 cup shortening
oil for deep frying
egg wash (1 egg beaten with 2
 Tbsp. water)
2 cups honey

For filling: Wash raisins and mix with almonds, orange rind, cinnamon and sugar in saucepan. Cover with water and cook for 15 to 20 minutes, stirring often. Mix in ½ cup honey, cool and refrigerate.

For pastry: Mix flour, salt, baking powder and shortening until mixture resembles coarse meal. Add 1½ cups cold water until dough sticks together. Knead a few minutes. Roll dough out to ⅛-inch thickness on a floured surface. Cut into 2-by-3-inch rectangles with a pastry cutter. Place about 2

Tbsp. of filling on each rectangle. Brush edges with egg wash. Cover with another rectangle and crimp edges with a fork to seal. Deep-fry each cookie until lightly browned and crisp. Drain on paper towelling.

Heat about 2 cups honey in saucepan. Using a slotted spoon, dip each cookie in hot honey to coat. Cool. May be stored in a cool, dry place.

Makes 3 to 4 dozen.

—*Michelle Sollohub*

Kentucky Jam Cake

"In Kentucky, Jam Cake is a holiday tradition along with turkey, country ham and Christmas cookies."

1 cup butter
2 cups sugar
3 eggs
1 cup jam, preferably
 blackberry
3 cups white flour
1 tsp. baking soda
1 tsp. nutmeg
1 tsp. ground cloves
1 cup buttermilk
½ cup orange juice

Cream butter and sugar together. Mix in eggs and jam. Mix together flour, baking soda, nutmeg and cloves. Add butter mixture to dry ingredients alternately with buttermilk and orange juice. Beat well. Pour into a greased tube pan. Bake at 325° F for 45 to 60 minutes.

—*Sharon Fuller*

Pebernødder

Pebernødder directly translates to "pepper nuts." they are a traditional Christmas cookie in Denmark, where they are placed in woven heart "baskets" and hung on the Christmas tree.

½ cup plus 3 Tbsp. butter
1⅔ cups flour
⅔ cup sugar
½ tsp. vanilla
½-¾ tsp. white pepper
2 Tbsp. cream

Cut butter into flour. Add remaining ingredients, mixing well. Roll dough into long, thin ropes about the size of your little finger. Cut into ½-inch sections. Place on cookie sheet and bake at 350° F for about 10 minutes.

—Kristine Marie Halls Reid

Filbert Confection Creams

1 cup filberts
½ cup butter
1 egg
¼ cup sugar
2 Tbsp. cocoa
2 tsp. vanilla
¼ tsp. salt (optional)
1¾ cups vanilla wafer crumbs
½ cup flaked coconut
ICING & GLAZE:
⅓ cup butter
1 egg
½ tsp. vanilla or peppermint extract
2 cups sifted powdered sugar
4 squares semisweet chocolate

Chop filberts but do not grind too finely. Spread them in a shallow pan, toast at 350° F for 5 to 10 minutes, stirring occasionally, until lightly browned.

In saucepan, combine butter, egg, sugar, cocoa, vanilla and salt. Cook over low heat until mixture thickens and becomes glossy. Combine filberts, crumbs and coconut in large bowl. Add cocoa mixture to this, blending well. Pack evenly into a greased 9" x 9" pan. Set aside.

To make icing and glaze: Cream butter and add egg and extract. Beat well. Beat in sugar until smooth and creamy. Spread over cocoa base. Chill in freezer for a few minutes to firm it. Melt chocolate squares over hot water and spread over icing. When partially set, cut into ½-inch squares. Refrigerate until ready to serve.

Makes 36 squares

—Sybil D. Hendricks

Steamed Carrot Pudding

"This pudding was traditionally served at Christmas in my family. Coins were always stuck into the pudding before cooking, and anyone finding a coin was guaranteed good luck."

2 Tbsp. sour milk
½ tsp. baking soda
1 tsp. salt
1 tsp. cinnamon
½ tsp. allspice
⅛ tsp. nutmeg
½ cup flour
1 cup grated carrot
1 cup grated potato
1¼ cups soft bread crumbs
1 cup raisins (mix light & dark)
1 cup currants
1 cup packed brown sugar
¾ cup suet or ½ cup shortening
SPICED RUM SAUCE:
1 cup packed brown sugar
2 Tbsp. cornstarch
¼ cup dark rum
¼ tsp. nutmeg
2 Tbsp. butter

Combine milk and baking soda. Mix salt, cinnamon, allspice and nutmeg with flour. Add milk mixture and remaining pudding ingredients and place in well-greased ceramic pudding mould, bowl or canning jar. Make sure you leave space for expansion during steaming. If using mould or bowl, wrap in a cloth. Steam for 3 hours.

For sauce: In heavy saucepan, mix together brown sugar and cornstarch. Stir in 1½ cups water. Bring to a boil, stirring constantly. Reduce heat, add rum, nutmeg and butter and simmer for 2 minutes. Makes 2 cups.

Serves 8.

—Mary Lou Garlick

Suggested Menus

Summer Solstice

Artichoke Heart Sauce (p.420)
Buttered Fettuccine

Phil's Lamb (p.388)
Garden Rice (p.202)
Dill & Creamed Spinach (p.160)
Cauliflower Pecan Salad (p.139)

Raspberry Flan (p.531)
Strawberry Shortcake (p.529)

Barbecue for Eight

Shrimp & Artichoke Tarts (p.252)

Barbecued Arctic Char (p.245)
Hot German Potato Salad (p.159)
September Garden Zucchini (p.121)
Spinach Orange & Mango Salad (p.140)

Creamy Ambrosia with Fresh Fruit (p.546)

Picnic To Travel

Devilled Eggs (p.48)

Cold Ham Pie (p.387)
Cold Barbecued Chicken (p.277)
Shrimp Cooked in Beer (p.250)
Nancy's Dill Dip (p.146)
Assorted Raw Vegetables

Fresh Fruit
Raspberry Bars (p.467)
Peanut Butter Chocolate Chip Cookies (p.480)

Candlelight Dinner for Two

Coquilles St. Jacques (p.237)

Pheasant with Rice Stuffing (p.312)
Caesar Salad (p.128)
California Corn (p.152)

Burnt Almond Sponge (p.543)

Harvest Dinner

Dilled Tomato Soup (p.88)

Cornish Game Hens Indienne (p.311)
Broccoli with Wild Rice (p.150)
Tossed Salad with Chili French Dressing (p.144)
Baked Corn (p.152)

Pumpkin Pie (p.535)
Yogurt Fruit Mould (p.523)

Party Menu for Twenty

Rumaki (p.386)
Almond Mushroom Paté (p.147)
Herbed Cheese Dip (p.38)
Crudités
Cheese Stuffed Meatballs (p.352)
Rabbit Paté Camille (p.283)
Olive Ball Snacks (p.50)
Angels on Horseback (p.254)

Herbed Leg of Lamb (p.362)
Paella (p.215)
Scalloped Potatoes (p.118)
Three Bean Salad (p.127)
Salpicon (p.137)

Family Christmas Dinner

Rich & Creamy Eggnog (p.572)
Crab Delight (p.235)
Raw Vegetables & Crackers

Roast Turkey with Russian Dressing (p.280)
Cranberry Sauce
Potato Casserole (p.157)
Crunchy Broccoli (p.149)
Tossed Salad with Creamy Garlic Dressing (p.144)

Pavlova & Yogurt Chantilly (p.545)
Chocolate Cheesecake (p.525)

Buffet Brunch

Piraeus Shrimp (p.248)
French Bread

Tomato Basil Tart (p.24)
Vegetable Cheese Pie (p.41)
Terrine of Pork (p.358)

Artichoke Salad (p.136)
Turkish Yogurt & Cucumber Salad (p.138)
Tossed Salad with Olga's Dressing (p.133)

Orange Blosssom Pudding (p.543)
Sesame Seed Cookies (p.462)

New Year's Eve Buffet

Cape House Inn Iced Buttermilk with Shrimp Soup (p.92)

Beef Wellington (p.342)
Stuffed Snapper with Orange & Lime (p.244)
Potatoes Moussaka (p.159)
Marinated Mushrooms (pp.131, 192)
Cauliflower Spinach Toss (p.139)

Lithuanian Napoleon Torte (p.527)

Post Cross-Country Skiing Dinner

Mulled Ale (p.572)
Chicken Liver Paté Casanova (p.282)
Crackers

Canadian Ski Marathon Sauce (p.377)
Buttered Noodles
Tossed Salad with Celery Seed Dressing (p.134)

Assorted Cheeses

After Theatre Supper

Tiopetes (p.50)

Mulligatawny Soup (p.78)
Flaky Biscuits (p.445)
Ruth's Fall Vegetable Vinaigrette (p.137)

Chocolate Dipped Strawberries (p.552)

Dinner for Two

Parsley Soup (p.80)

Scallops in Wine (p.252)
Donna's Rice Pilaf (p.203)
Green Bean Timbales (p.149)

Syllabub (p.524)

Index